The Sensible and Intelligible Worlds

New Essays on Kant's Metaphysics and Epistemology

Edited by

KARL SCHAFER AND NICHOLAS F. STANG

OXFORD
UNIVERSITY PRESS

Great Clarendon Street, Oxford, OX2 6DP,
United Kingdom

Oxford University Press is a department of the University of Oxford. It furthers the University's objective of excellence in research, scholarship, and education by publishing worldwide. Oxford is a registered trade mark of Oxford University Press in the UK and in certain other countries

First Edition published in 2022

Published in the United States of America by Oxford University Press
198 Madison Avenue, New York, NY 10016, United States of America

British Library Cataloguing in Publication Data
Data available

Library of Congress Control Number: 2022935259

ISBN 978–0–19–968826–5

DOI: 10.1093/oso/9780199688265.001.0001

Printed and bound by
CPI Group (UK) Ltd, Croydon, CR0 4YY

Contents

List of Contributors

Uygar Abaci is Associate Professor of Philosophy at Penn State University.

Lucy Allais is Professor of Philosophy at Johns Hopkins University.

Ralf M. Bader is Professor of Philosophy at the University of Fribourg.

Andrew Chignell is Laurence S. Rockefeller Professor in Religion, Philosophy, and the Center for Human Values at Princeton University.

Dina Emundts is Professor of History of Philosophy at Freie Universität Berlin.

Stefanie Grüne is Wissenschaftliche Mitarbeiterin at Freie Universität Berlin.

Desmond Hogan is Professor of Philosophy at Princeton University.

Anja Jauernig is Professor of Philosophy at New York University.

Jessica Leech is Senior Lecturer in Philosophy at King's College, London.

Colin Marshall is Associate Professor of Philosophy at the University of Washington, Seattle.

Tobias Rosefeldt is Professor of Classical German Philosophy at Humboldt-Universität zu Berlin.

Timothy Rosenkoetter is Associate Professor of Philosophy at Dartmouth College.

Karl Schafer is Professor of Philosophy at the University of Texas at Austin.

Nicholas F. Stang is Associate Professor of Philosophy and Canada Research Chair at the University of Toronto.

Clinton Tolley is Professor of Philosophy at the University of California, San Diego.

List of Abbreviations

Titles of works of Kant are abbreviated according to their German titles and in the style recommended by *Kant-Studien*. Except as noted otherwise, citations are to volume and page of the *Akademie Ausgabe* (AA):

Immanuel Kant, *Gesammelte Schriften*, ed.: Vols. 1–22 Preussische Akademie der Wissenschaften, Vol. 23 Deutsche Akademie der Wissenschaften zu Berlin, from Vol. 24 Akademie der Wissenschaften zu Göttingen. Berlin: Reimer then De Gruyter, 1900–.

Unless noted otherwise by individual authors, Kant is quoted according to the Cambridge translations of the works of Kant specified below. Where no translation is listed, the Cambridge series does not include one.

A/B	*Kritik der reinen Vernunft*, A edition (AA 4), B edition (AA 3). *Critique of Pure Reason*. Trans. & Ed. Paul Guyer & Allen Wood. Cambridge: Cambridge University Press, 1998.
Anth	*Anthropologie in pragmatischer Hinsicht* (AA 7). *Anthropology from a Pragmatic Point of View*. Trans. R. Louden. In *Anthropology, History, and Education*. Ed. G. Zöller & R. Louden. Cambridge: Cambridge University Press, 2007.
BDG	*Der einzig mögliche Beweisgrund zu einer Demonstration des Daseins Gottes* (AA 02). *The Only Possible Argument in Support of a Demonstration of the Existence of God*. In *Theoretical Philosophy, 1755–1770*. Trans. & Ed. D. Walford & R. Meerbote. Cambridge: Cambridge University Press, 1992.
Br	*Briefwechsel* (AA 10–13). *Correspondence*. Trans. & Ed. A. Zweig. Cambridge: Cambridge University Press, 1999.
EEKU	*Erste Einleitung in die Kritik der Urteilskraft* (AA 20). *First Introduction to the Critique of the Power of Judgment*. In *Critique of the Power of Judgment*. Trans. & Ed. P. Guyer & E. Matthews. Cambridge: Cambridge University Press, 2000.
FM	*Welches sind die wirklichen Fortschritte, die die Metaphysik seit Leibnitzens und Wolf's Zeiten in Deutschland gemacht hat?* *What Real Progress Has Metaphysics Made in Germany since the Time of Leibniz and Wolff?* In *Theoretical Philosophy after 1781*. Trans. & Ed. H. Allison & P. Heath. Cambridge: Cambridge University Press, 2002.
GMS	*Grundlegung zur Metaphysik der Sitten* (AA 4). *Groundwork of the Metaphysics of Morals*. In *Practical Philosophy*. Trans. & Ed. M. J. Gregor. Cambridge: Cambridge University Press, 1996.
HN	*Handschriftlicher Nachlass* (AA 14–23).

IaG *Idee zu einer allgemeinen Geschichte in weltbürgerlicher Absicht* (AA 8).
Idea for a Universal History with a Cosmopolitan Aim. In *Anthropology, History, and Education*.

KpV *Kritik der praktischen Vernunft* (AA 5).
Critique of Practical Reason. In *Practical Philosophy*.

KrV *Kritik der reinen Vernunft* (AA 3–4).
Critique of Pure Reason.

KU *Kritik der Urteilskraft* (AA 5).
Critique of the Power of Judgment. Trans. & Ed. P. Guyer & E. Matthews. Cambridge: Cambridge University Press, 2000.

Log *Jäsche Logik* (AA 9).
Jäsche Logic. In *Lectures on Logic*. Trans. & Ed. J. M. Young. Cambridge: Cambridge University Press, 1992.

MAN *Metaphysische Anfangsgründe der Naturwissenschaften* (AA 4).
Metaphysical Foundations of Natural Science. In *Theoretical Philosophy after 1781*.

MonPh *Metaphysicae cum geometria iunctae usus in philosophia naturali, cuius specimen I. continet monadologiam physicam* (AA 1).
The Employment in Natural Philosophy of Metaphysics Combined with Geometry, of Which Sample 1 Contains the Physical Monadology. In *Theoretical Philosophy*, 1755–1770.

MS *Die Metaphysik der Sitten* (AA 6).
The Metaphysics of Morals. In *Practical Philosophy*.

MSI *De mundi sensibilis atque intelligibilis forma et principiis* (AA 2).
On the Form and Principles of the Sensible and Intelligible World ('Inaugural Dissertation'). In *Theoretical Philosophy*, 1755–1770.

NEV *M. Immanuel Kants Nachricht von der Einrichtung seiner Vorlesungen in dem Winterhalbenjahre von 1765–1766* (AA 2).
M. Immanuel Kant's Announcement of the Program of His Lectures for the Winter Semester 1765–1766. In *Theoretical Philosophy, 1755–1770*.

NG *Versuch, den Begriff der negativen Größen in die Weltweisheit einzuführen* (AA 2).
Attempt to Introduce the Concept of Negative Magnitudes into Philosophy (AA 2). In *Theoretical Philosophy, 1755–1770*.

OP *Opus Postumum* (AA 21–22).
Opus Postumum. Trans. & Ed. E. Förster & M. Rosen. Cambridge: Cambridge University Press, 1993.

Prol *Prolegomena zu einer jeden künftigen Metaphysik* (AA 4).
Prolegomena to Any Future Metaphysics. In *Theoretical Philosophy after 1781*.

Refl *Reflexionen* (AA 14–19).
Selections in *Notes and Fragments*. Trans. and Ed. P. Guyer & C. Bowman & F. Rauscher. Cambridge: Cambridge University Press, 2005.

RezSchulz	Recension von Schulz's Versuch einer Anleitung zur Sittenlehre für alle Menschen (AA 8). Review of Schulz's *Attempt at an Introduction to a Doctrine of Morals for All Human Beings*. In *Practical Philosophy.*
RGV	*Die Religion innerhalb der Grenzen der bloßen Vernunft* (AA 6). *Religion within the Boundaries of Mere Reason.* In *Religion and Rational Theology*. Trans. & Ed. A. Wood & G. di Giovanni. Cambridge: Cambridge University Press, 1996.
SF	*Der Streit der Fakultäten* (AA 07). *The Conflict of the Faculties.* In *Practical Philosophy.*
TG	*Träume eines Geistersehers, erläutert durch die Träume der Metaphysik* (AA 2). *Dreams of a Spirit-Seer Elucidated by Dreams of Metaphysics.* In *Theoretical Philosophy 1755–1770.*
UD	*Untersuchung über die Deutlichkeit der Grundsätze der natürlichen Theologie und der Moral* (AA 2). *Inquiry Concerning the Distinctness of the Principles of Natural Theology and Morality*. In *Theoretical Philosophy 1775–1770.*
ÜE	*Über eine Entdeckung, nach der alle neue Kritik der reinen Vernunft durch eine ältere entbehrlich gemacht werden soll* (AA 8). *On a Discovery Whereby Any New Critique of Pure Reason Is to Be Made Superfluous by an Older One*. In *Theoretical Philosophy after 1781.*
V-Anth/Collins	Vorlesungen Wintersemester 1772/1773 Collins (AA 25). Translation in *Lectures on Anthropology*. Trans. & Ed. A. Wood & R. Louden. Cambridge: Cambridge University Press, 2012.
V-Lo/Blomberg	Logik Blomberg (AA 24). Translation in *Lectures on Logic.*
V-Lo/Busolt	Logik Busolt (AA 24).
V-Lo/Dohna	Logik Dohna-Wundlacken. Translation in *Lectures on Logic.*
V-Lo/Philippi	Logik Philippi.
V-Lo/Pölitz	Logik Pölitz.
V-Lo/Wiener	Wiener Logik. Translation in *Lectures on Logic.*
V-Met/Dohna	Metaphysik Dohna (AA 28). Selections translated in *Lectures on Metaphysics*. Trans. & Ed. K. Ameriks & S. Naragon. Cambridge: Cambridge University Press, 1997.
V-Met/Herder	Metaphysik Herder (AA 28). Selections translated in *Lectures on Metaphysics.*
V-Met-K_2/Heinze	Metaphysik K_2 (Heinze, Schlapp) (AA 28). Selections translated in *Lectures on Metaphysics.*
V-Met-K_3/Arnoldt	Metaphysik K_3 (Arnoldt, Schlapp) (AA 28).
V-Met-K_3E/Arnoldt	Ergänzungen Kant Metaphysik K_3 (Arnoldt) (AA 29)
V-Met-L_1/Pölitz	Metaphysik L_1 (Pölitz) (AA 28). Selections translated in *Lectures on Metaphysics.*

V-Met-L_2/Pölitz	Metaphysik L_2 (Pölitz, Original) (AA 28). Translation in *Lectures on Metaphysics*.
V-Met/Mron	Metaphysik Mrongovius (AA 29). Translation in *Lectures on Metaphysics*.
V-Met/Schön	Metaphysik von Schön, Ontologie. (AA 28).
V-Met/Volckmann	Metaphysik Volckmann (AA 28). Selections translated in *Lectures on Metaphysics*.
V-MS/Vigil	Metaphysik der Sitten Vigilantius (AA 27). Translated in *Lectures on Ethics*. Trans. & Ed. P. Heath & J. Schneewind. Cambridge: Cambridge University Press.
V-Phil-Th/Pölitz	Philosophische Religionslehre nach Pölitz (AA 28). Lectures on Philosophical Doctrine of Religion. In *Religion and Rational Theology*.
V-Th/Baumbach	Danziger Rationaltheologie nach Baumbach (AA 28).
V-Th/Volckmann	Natürliche Theologie Volckmann nach Baumbach (AA 28).
ZeF	*Zum ewigen Frieden* (AA 8). *Towards Perpetual Peace*. In *Practical Philosophy*.

Introduction

Karl Schafer and Nicholas F. Stang

1. Kant in the Twenty-First Century

It is an exciting time to be working on Kant. Judging by the number of articles, books, conferences, journals, and academic societies now dedicated to Kant's philosophy, we are living through an explosion of interest in the sage of Königsberg comparable to the "return to Kant" movement at the end of the nineteenth century.[1] This era of Kant research is distinguished not only quantitatively by the amount of work being done, but qualitatively by its breadth and reach. Long gone are the days when Kant was known solely as the author of his three *Critiques*, or conceived as a lone genius in splendid isolation. Scholarship on Kant's theory of history, his social theory, his geography, anthropology, teleology, his views on race, his work before 1781 and his writings after 1800, as well as his writings on natural science, has grown exponentially at the same time as scholars have turned increasingly to Kant's historical and cultural context, moving outwards from Königsberg to Prussia to the rest of the German states to Europe and the larger world of the eighteenth century and what Kant called the "age of Enlightenment." Likewise, scholars have examined Kant's relations to his contemporaries (Blumenbach, Euler, Feder, Garve, Green, Hamann, Herder, Mendelssohn, Lambert, Plattner, Schultz, Tetens, von Herbart), immediate forebears (Baumeister, Baumgarten, Bilfinger, Budde, Crusius, Gottsched, Knutzen, Lange, Meier, Sulzer, Wolff, etc.), and of course his successors in "post-Kantian" Idealism and Romanticism (not only Fichte, Schelling, and Hegel, but also Bardili, Goethe, Jacobi, Maimon, Niethammer, Reinhold, Schiller, the Schlegels, Schulze, de Stäel, and many others).[2] There is hardly an area of Kant's writings, or his relation to European or world philosophy of his day, that is not the subject of a sizable, and growing, scholarly literature.

At the same time as this massive expansion of the quantity and the qualitative reach of Kant scholarship, we are also living through a great internationalization of Kant research: the most recent Kant Congress, held in Oslo in August 2019, welcomed over two hundred scholars representing more than a dozen countries across five continents. In addition to the Kant-Gesellschaft (which organizes the Kant Congress every four years) there are Kant societies in dozens of countries and, by our count, twelve journals specializing in Kant, publishing in nine languages (English,

[1] For an overview of Neo-Kantianism in this sense, see Beiser (2014).

[2] For recent overviews of Kant in a historical context, see Watkins (2005), Beiser (2009), and Förster (2012), as well as Kuehn (2001).

Karl Schafer and Nicholas F. Stang, *Introduction* In: *The Sensible and Intelligible Worlds: New Essays on Kant's Metaphysics and Epistemology.* Edited by: Karl Schafer and Nicholas F. Stang, Oxford University Press. © Karl Schafer and Nicholas F. Stang 2022.
DOI: 10.1093/oso/9780199688265.003.0001

French, German, Italian, Japanese, Korean, Portuguese, Russian, and Spanish). Several of the contributors to this volume were honored to be present at the inaugural meeting of the Chinese Kant Society in May 2019 at Peking University, Beijing. There is now a large, and growing, body of scholarship on the relation of Kant's philosophy to classical Chinese (especially Confucian) philosophy, as well as Indian, African, and Indigenous philosophy in the Americas. It is very much to be hoped that this trend will continue and that scholarship will become genuinely cosmopolitan in the Kantian sense.[3]

No single collection of essays could possibly do justice to the full extent of the world of Kant scholarship, and this volume is no exception. The chapters in this volume represent a relatively limited example of the kind of research now being done, geographically, generationally, and thematically, on Kant. Geographically, our authors did their graduate work in Germany, Switzerland, the UK, or North America, and all still reside there. Thematically, these essays concern what Kant would call "theoretical philosophy," but which, bowing to contemporary usage, we have dubbed "metaphysics and epistemology" in the subtitle to this volume. Generationally, our authors are what is conventionally dubbed "mid-career"—tenured (or its equivalent in the UK and European systems) within roughly the last ten years.

One of the most notable features of Kant scholarship among this generation of scholars is the resurgence of what has become known as the "metaphysical" reading of Kant. (This is sometimes, less accurately, called the "Leibnizian" reading. But, as we discuss below, this terminology tends to conflate two issues that are best kept separate: "how metaphysical" Kant's ambitions are and how continuous his philosophy is with that of Leibniz.) While this reading is not shared by all of the authors in this volume, and there is significant disagreement even among those who do, it was the original inspiration for this volume, so we want to devote the rest of this Introduction to briefly commenting on this turn in Kant scholarship.

This "metaphysical turn" in Kant scholarship draws inspiration from the work of scholars like Karl Ameriks, Robert Adams, Eric Watkins, and Rae Langton—but has been expanded in many directions.[4] The core issue here is how to read the various claims Kant makes about "things in themselves" and "noumena." We will refer to these claims as Kant's "noumenal discourse." In various places, Kant says that things in themselves (or noumena; for the purposes of this Introduction we will not carefully separate them, though we think the terms differ both in intension and extension) cause appearances,[5] ground the sensible world,[6] that they are substances,[7] that

[3] *IaG*, 8:28.

[4] See, for example, Adams (1997), Ameriks (2000, 2003, 2012), Langton (1998), and Watkins (2005). Going back further, the metaphysical turn also draws inspiration from an older tradition in German Kant scholarship, e.g. the work of Erich Adickes, Heinz Heimsoeth, Hans Vaihinger, and Max Wundt.

[5] A190/B235, A387, A494/B522; *Prol*, 4:289, 4:314, 4:318; *GMS*, 4:451; and *ÜE*, 8:215.

[6] *Prol* §59, 4:360.

[7] *KU*, 5:196; *ÜE*, 8:207, where things in themselves are described as the "supersensible substrate" of appearances. At A358 he entertains the possibility that thinking substances underlie outer as well as inner appearances.

they possess reality,[8] that they are one and many,[9] and that they exist.[10] This noumenal discourse appears to involve many, if not all, of the pure concepts of the understanding: cause, substance, reality, unity, plurality, existence, etc.

The status of noumenal discourse, and Kant's tendency to use categories in noumenal discourse while simultaneously denying that categories have any "use" or "application" or "sense" in such contexts, has of course been controversial since the publication of the A edition of the first *Critique* in 1781. Within Kant scholarship of the twentieth and twenty-first centuries, the "methodological" or "deflationary" reading of noumenal discourse pioneered by Henry Allison, Graham Bird, Arthur Collins, and Gerold Prauss long held sway.[11] One of the main developments in Kant scholarship of the past decades has been the decline of that deflationary reading in favor of a more metaphysically committal reading of noumenal discourse (although the deflationary reading still has its defenders).

There are various axes along which "noumenal discourse" can be read as more "deflationary" or more "inflationary." Among them are:

1. *Semantic*. One axis on which readings of noumenal discourse can vary is how they understand the semantic function or role of such discourse. On the more deflationary end, one can understand the role of noumenal discourse in completely non-descriptive terms—for example, as expressing our epistemic limits or reminding us of the dependence of our cognition on intuition. Somewhat more inflationary is the view, defended in some places by Henry Allison, that the role of noumenal discourse is descriptive, but all it does is abstract from our specifically spatiotemporal cognition and its specifically spatiotemporal objects.[12] So noumenal discourse is no less descriptive than discourse about "the average American household" but neither is it about some distinct "average" object, above and beyond individual households and their constituents. More inflationary yet are readings on which the status of (at least some) noumenal discourse within theoretical philosophy is straightforwardly descriptive of objects and their properties, insofar as those objects and their properties do not depend on our experience of them. When we talk about the revival of "metaphysical" readings of Kant we are talking about readings that are semantically inflationary in this sense. They take Kant's claims about noumena at "face value" as *descriptions* of how objects are constituted "in themselves."
2. *Doxastic*. Another axis along which readings of noumenal discourse might vary is to what extent they take Kant's claims about noumena to report his own views, rather than views one might hold or that it would be tempting to hold or that were common in eighteenth-century German rationalism. On the extreme end would be the readings on which the very concept of things in themselves is

[8] *ÜE*, 8:154, a text rightly emphasized by Adickes (1924, p. 40).

[9] *ÜE*, 8:209n, where Kant denies that the "supersensible substrate of matter" is divided the way matter is. We are taking it as prima facie plausible that if something can be said to be divided, or not divided, then it can be said to be one (e.g. an indivisible unity, or a unity divisible into its parts) or many (a plurality of parts).

[10] *Prol* §32, 4:314; A358; A536/B564; A538/B566.

[11] Bird (1962), Prauss (1974), Allison (1983, 2004), and Collins (1999).

[12] Allison (2004).

incomprehensible to us and the point of the *Critique* is to educate the reader to the standpoint where she will see this.[13] On the other end would be the view of Erich Adickes, according to which Kant's view that we are affected by a multiplicity of substantial loci of force was part of his basic experience of the world that he never gave up even after making the Copernican turn.[14] On Adickes's reading, Kant is committed to noumenal discourse at a level of conviction untouchable by philosophical arguments. Likewise, the old "patchwork" hypothesis held that the *Critique* contains passages that no longer represent Kant's considered views in 1781, but are mere holdovers from his pre-Critical theory.[15] Intermediate readings are, of course, possible: some noumenal discourse represents Kant's real commitments about things in themselves, while some merely describes noumena as represented under various "transcendental illusions."

3. *Epistemic*. The final axis on which readings of noumenal discourse might vary is the epistemic status they assign to it. At one extreme, noumenal discourse might represent mere private opinions held by Immanuel Kant. At the other extreme, it would be taken to be something Kant takes himself to know, which would at least sit uneasily with Kant's repeated claims that we know nothing of things in themselves. The more plausible intermediate position would be that noumenal discourse has some epistemic status higher than mere opinion, but short of knowledge or cognition; perhaps what Kant calls "belief" or a form of knowledge that falls short of *Wissen* in his demanding technical sense.[16] Of course, different kinds of noumenal claims within theoretical philosophy might have different epistemic statuses (e.g. we might know that something "in itself" affects us while merely thinking of "it" as a plurality of things), just as theoretical noumenal discourse has a different epistemic status than practical noumenal discourse.

These three axes are, to some extent, independent of one another. For instance, one can hold fixed the semantic status while varying its epistemic credentials; for instance, one can hold that noumenal discourse is intended to be straightforwardly descriptive while taking it to report a mere opinion, a belief, or full-fledged knowledge. Likewise, Kant could in principle be fully committed to noumenal discourse, while regarding this either as a matter of personal opinion, rational belief, or full-fledged knowledge. But the mutual independence is not total. If noumenal discourse merely expresses our epistemic limitations, or an abstraction from specifically spatiotemporal cognition, it is hard to see how this might merely be a matter of opinion. And, at least on some readings of what Kant means by "cognition," the question of whether some representation counts as a cognition of an object in Kant's sense

[13] E.g. Melnick (1973, p. 152).

[14] Adickes (1924, pp. 14, 19).

[15] For classical articulations of the "patchwork reading," see Vaihinger (1881–92) and Kemp Smith (1918).

[16] For an important recent discussion of these distinctions, see Chignell (2007a, 2007b), and especially the distinctions among Hardline, Moderate, and Liberal readings of Kant's commitment to things in themselves at the end of that paper.

involves elements that cut across the semantic-epistemic divide as it is generally understood today.[17]

When we talk about the metaphysical reading of Kant we mean a reading on which noumenal discourse is (semantically) descriptive discourse that reports claims to which (doxastically) Kant is positively committed. We will not stipulatively build into our conception of the metaphysical reading any particular position along the epistemic axis: readings on which noumenal discourse represents Kant's private opinion will count as "metaphysical" just as much as readings on which it represents knowledge. So when we say that the "metaphysical reading" has become more prominent in this generation of Kant scholars, we mean that this generation is more willing to attribute to Kant positive descriptive claims about the constitution and nature of things in themselves than previous scholars and to directly inquire into Kant's views about the nature of "noumenal reality."[18]

The increasing interest in Kant's "metaphysics" is not limited to his noumenal metaphysics, even if that is the clearest demarcation between older readings and newer work. Along with this greater interest in Kant's metaphysics of noumena has come a tendency to focus on the specifically metaphysical aspects of Kant's theory of experience and its objects. One motivating factor here is the increasing recognition of the distinction between *Wissen* and *Erkenntnis*, and the conviction that the Transcendental Analytic constitutes a theory of *Erkenntnis* but not a theory of how we know, how we have *Wissen*, of objects in space and time.[19] This means that there has been a tendency, not to neglect specifically "epistemological" issues, but to see them as only directly addressed elsewhere in the *Critique*, and to focus on the Analytic as a theory of how cognition is possible and as a metaphysics of spatiotemporal objects and the grounds of their real possibility.

This increasing comfort with, and interest in, the metaphysics in Kant's philosophy goes hand in glove with an increased knowledge and interest in Kant's metaphysical background in eighteenth-century German rationalism. A number of authors in this volume have written extensively about Kant's pre-Critical metaphysics, as well as his relation to other figures, like Wolff, Baumgarten, Crusius, and his own teacher, Martin Knutzen. Reading Kant in this light naturally emphasizes the rationalist metaphysical aspects of his philosophy. This is also influenced, we think, by the return of many traditional rationalist topics in metaphysics in recent analytic philosophy. Since the revival of metaphysics in analytic philosophy (by Lewis, Kripke, Plantinga, and others) in recent decades there has been increasing attention to traditional metaphysical topics and doctrines, like the Principle of Sufficient Reason, modes of existence, monism, and, most famously of all, grounding. Several authors in this volume have explicitly connected topics in Kant's metaphysics to metaphysical

[17] Several of the chapters in this volume tackle this theme. For other important work on it, see Smit (2000, 2009), Watkins & Willaschek (2017), and Tolley (2020). For a reading of transcendental psychology in Kant which focuses on the nature of cognition, see Hatfield (1990).

[18] In this respect, the seminal work of Karl Ameriks (see especially the Introduction to Ameriks, 2000, and the papers collected therein) is the dominant influence in the metaphysical turn within Kant scholarship.

[19] Again several of the chapters below discuss this issue. Compare Smit (2000, 2009), Tolley (2020), Watkins & Willaschek (2017).

debates currently being conducted in contemporary philosophy: causation, the nature of possible worlds, modality, and grounding. So, as analytic philosophers have put many of the traditional topics of metaphysics back "on the menu," Kant scholarship, as represented by the authors in this volume, has increasingly turned to these issues in Kant and his predecessors and contemporaries in eighteenth-century German philosophy.

It is also worth noting that describing this new turn in Kant scholarship as the "Leibnizian" reading is at least misleading. After all, as many of the authors in this volume have emphasized, not only are the differences between Leibniz and the "Leibnizians" (e.g. Wolff and Baumgarten) substantial, but there are deep differences between Kant and his Leibnizian predecessors, even at the level of pure metaphysics. For instance, it has been a main theme of Desmond Hogan's work for over a decade that Kant's philosophical work is motivated by the defense of a non-Leibnizian libertarian view of free will that puts in principle limits on the rational intelligibility of reality.[20] And Nicholas Stang's 2016 book puts at its very center the difference between Kant's (Critical and pre-Critical) metaphysical theory of modality and what he calls the "logicist" view of Leibniz, Wolff, and Baumgarten.[21] Anja Jauernig, in her forthcoming works, argues that, properly read, Leibniz is closer to Kant than has previously been appreciated, but Jauernig has done more than probably anyone to distinguish Leibniz so interpreted from the "Leibnizians."[22] It is thus more helpful to refer to this as the "metaphysical" as opposed to the "Leibnizian" or "rationalist" reading of Kant.

While by no means all of the contributors to this volume share the "metaphysical" reading of Kant we hope that this is a helpful lens through which to think of this volume and the many themes that are treated in its pages.

2. Summary of Chapters

The chapters in this volume are organized thematically, following, very roughly, the order of discussion of the first *Critique* itself: we begin with affection and sensibility, move to discussing the cognitive subject and its capacities, then we consider the "labyrinth of the continuum" and the nature of transcendental idealism, and we end by considering the transition from theoretical to practical philosophy.

In "Being Realistic about Kant's Idealism," Tobias Rosefeldt confronts one of the oldest problems for transcendental idealism, the problem of affection. Given that appearances non-causally depend upon the content of experience, can they also be among the causes of the matter of that experience? And is this "empirical affection" compatible with "noumenal affection," that is, with things in themselves causally affecting our sensibility as well? Rosefeldt argues that phenomenalist interpretations cannot account for empirical affection. Drawing on contemporary work in the metaphysics of perception, he develops a sophisticated non-phenomenalist reading of idealism, according to which the distinction is between response-dependent properties (properties of how objects appear to us) and response-independent properties (properties

[20] Hogan (2009a, 2009b). [21] Stang (2016).
[22] For a preview of this work, see Jauernig (2008).

objects have *an sich*). He then explains how this model of transcendental idealism can account for both causal relations.

Desmond Hogan, in "Schopenhauer's Transcendental Aesthetic," also discusses a classic problem in the foundations of Kant's theory of sensibility, the "neglected alternative" objection to his theory of space and time. According to this famous objection, Kant's argument from the a priori unknowability of things in themselves to their non-spatiotemporality overlooks the possibility that space and time are both subjective forms of our intuition (hence knowable a priori) and objective (albeit unknowable) forms of things in themselves. Hogan notes that one of Kant's most admiring and insightful nineteenth-century readers, Arthur Schopenhauer, thought the argument of the Transcendental Aesthetic established its conclusion with absolute certainty, and he proposes that we might learn why Kant thought his argument was valid by examining Schopenhauer's reasons for judging it so. Schopenhauer took the Aesthetic proof of the subjectivity of space and time to depend on two metaphysical premises: that being spatiotemporal entails being subject to a form of the Principle of Sufficient Reason (PSR), and the thing in itself (the will, according to Schopenhauer) is not bound by the PSR. It follows, of course, that the thing in itself is not in space and time. Hogan then returns to the Aesthetic and argues that a reading along broadly Schopenhauerian lines not only renders the argument valid, but coheres with many of Kant's other philosophical commitments in the Critical period. The core idea is that the a priori unknowability premise in the Aesthetic expresses a metaphysical claim in epistemic dress: things in themselves (in particular, the will) cannot be known a priori because they lack real a priori, that is, metaphysically determining, grounds. Schopenhauer was thus right, Hogan argues, to claim both that the Aesthetic argument is valid and that it depends implicitly on a restriction of the PSR.

In "Relation to an Object: The Role of the Categories", Lucy Allais builds upon her important discussion of transcendental idealism in *Manifest Reality* by developing her reading there of the Transcendental Deduction and Kant's account of the necessary role of the categories in empirical cognition. On Allais's account, the categories are crucial here because synthesizing and unifying the properties of objects under them is a necessary condition on possession of a determinate object of thought for empirical concept application. Crucially, as Allais understands these claims, this does not require Kant to introduce a further layer of "conceptual idealism" on top of the idealism he has already established in the Transcendental Aesthetic. Thus, Allais's account here helps to close off one common objection to her more general account of Kant's transcendental idealism.

In "Kant on Concepts, Intuitions, and Sensible Synthesis," Stefanie Grüne build upon her previous work on the relationship between concepts and intuitions in Kant to chart a middle path between two positions that have generally dominated the debate about this issue: first, strong forms of "conceptualism," on which intuitions are always the product of a concept-involving synthesis, and so have conceptual content for Kant; and second, "non-conceptualist" readings, on which concept-involving synthesis is not required for the formation of intuitions, but only for the use of such intuitions for the cognition of objects. Against the second of these, Grüne argues that traditional forms of conceptualism are right to insist that intuition always presupposes some sort of concept-involving synthesis for Kant. But, against strong forms of conceptualism, she argues that this is perfectly compatible with intuitions having "non-conceptual content," at least if we use those terms in anything like the contemporary sense of them. To do so, she draws on Kant's distinction between different kinds of concepts (obscure, clear, indistinct, and distinct) to argue, first, that the synthesis involved in intuition only presupposes "obscure concepts" for Kant, and second, that such "obscure concepts" do not count as concepts at all with respect to contemporary definitions of that term. The result is a compelling account of precisely the senses in which Kant is, and is not, a conceptualist about the content of intuition.

Jessica Leech, in "A Transcendental Argument for the Principle of Possibility," turns to the topic of modality. She observes that there are fairly familiar "transcendental arguments" (arguments from the possibility of experience) for the first three sets of Principles of Experience (Axioms of Intuition, Anticipations of Perception, Analogies of Experience) but that it is significantly less clear what the argument for the Postulates of Empirical Thinking in General is, the principles that govern the modal categories of possibility, actuality, and necessity. Focusing specifically on the principle of possibility, she reconstructs Kant's transcendental argument for this principle and then considers the role that this principle plays in the rest of the *KrV*. The fundamental role of the principle of possibility, Leech argues, is to restrict the applicability of concepts, especially pure concepts, to "possible" objects, which, according to the principle, are those that agree with the formal conditions of experience. She concludes by connecting this back to the idea that the principle of possibility is a "postulate," and Kant's analogy between the role a geometrical postulate plays in making its object possible (e.g. a circle) and the role the principle plays in making the very concept of (real) possibility itself possible, that is, applicable to concepts of objects.

In "Kant on the Epistemology of the Obvious," Timothy Rosenkoetter takes up Kant's striking claim that all and only mathematical cognition is "evident," arguing that "evident" propositions are a proper subset of "obvious" propositions, namely, those grounded in a priori intuition. The heart of the chapter develops a systematic account of when and why Kant conceives of this or that proposition as "obvious." The core idea is that certainty regarding an obvious truth is accessible to any subject who possesses "common human understanding." The fact that there are two modes of access available to the subject who currently lacks that certainty (or is outright mistaken)—one through rule-based instruction, the other through measures that regain the healthy use of the capacities that we already possess—partitions the obvious into two classes, including most of mathematics in the former class and truths such as the causal principle and the Formula of Universal Law (FUL) in the latter. Overall, Rosenkoetter argues that Kant's theory of the obvious plays a previously unrecognized role in rationalizing and tying together disparate Kantian positions that might otherwise seem unimportant or idiosyncratic.

In "How Does Kant Conceive of Self-Consciousness?," Dina Emundts tackles the vexed question of how to best understand Kant's conception of self-consciousness. In her discussion, Emundts argues that Kant's conception of self-consciousness must be understood in more robust terms than many interpreters have been comfortable with. More precisely, Emundts argues that self-consciousness must be understood to involve a consciousness of *a real, existing thing* as opposed to (say) a consciousness of a merely intentional object or "thought-thing." As such, while Emundts acknowledges that our self-consciousness does not meet the requirements that Kant places on genuine "cognition" (*Erkenntnis*) or "knowledge" (*Wissen*) in Kant's sense of these terms, she argues that it does provide us with what we today would be inclined to call "knowledge" of a real and persisting self.

Anja Jauernig directly addresses the theme of this volume, in "The Labyrinth of the Continuum: Leibniz, the Wolffians, and Kant on Matter and Monads," by arguing that a standard narrative, on which Kant rejected his early Leibniz-Wolffianism in the Critical period, is wrong on two counts. First, there is no such thing as Leibniz-Wolffian metaphysics because Leibniz and the Wolffians differed significantly on core doctrines. Second, in the Critical period, Kant's transcendental idealism retains deep similarities to Leibniz's metaphysics, as Kant became increasingly aware after 1781. In this chapter, she focuses on the compositional structure of space and matter, a key point of difference between Leibniz and the Wolffians. She reconstructs the outlines of Leibniz's theory of space and the structure of matter, both early and late, as well as the corresponding Wolffian doctrines and shows how different they were: Leibniz denied, while Wolff maintained, that bodies are composed of finitely many simple elements. After an early theory in the *Physical Monadology*, which, while ingeniously solving problems internal to the Wolffian theory of how bodies occupy space, remains within essentially Wolffian parameters, in the *KrV* Kant defends a view that is more similar to Leibniz's mature doctrine: both space and bodies are ideal, continuous, and infinitely divisible. Things in themselves may be finitely divisible into simples, and if we are guided by pure reason alone, that is how we must think of them. Kant's claim in 1790 that the *KrV* is the "true apology of Leibniz," Jauernig argues, is thus vindicated, at least on this important issue.

In "Kant's Appearances as Object-Dependent Senses," Clinton Tolley intervenes in the debate between "two world" and "one world" interpretations of transcendental idealism by arguing that neither side has adequately taken account of the character of appearances (immediate objects of intuition) as *representations* in their own right. Against the widespread tendency either to read Kant's repeated characterizations of appearances as representations as phenomenalist (identifying them with states of our minds), or to dismiss such passages as confusions on Kant's part, Tolley develops a sophisticated tripartite account of Kant's metaphysics of appearance, modeled on Frege's tripartite distinction of act, content (sense), and object (referent): there is the act of intuition, the immediate content of that intuition (appearance, sense), and the real thing thereby presented by that content (object = *x*, thing in itself). A key innovation in Tolley's "Fregean" reading of Kant is that the appearance (the immediate object of intuition) represents the thing that causes the act of which it is the object, analogous to the way in which a Fregean sense is a "way of being-given" (*Art des Gegebenseins*) of an object (referent).

In "Kant's Conception of Cognition and Our Knowledge of Things in Themselves," Karl Schafer picks up on some important ideas of Houston Smit to present an interpretation of what Kant means by "cognition" (*Erkenntnis*). In doing so, Schafer argues that we should distinguish cognition in this sense from the sort of knowledge that is the focus of much of contemporary epistemology. Crucial to Schafer's reading is the idea that in cognizing an object, we must be (at least implicitly) conscious of that object as something that places real, objective correctness conditions on our representation of it. Schafer then shows how the various other constraints that Kant places on cognition follow from this basic idea, and explains how the resulting conception of cognition allows us to reconcile Kant's insistence that things in themselves exist and have certain general features with his denial that we can have theoretical cognition of them.

Debates about Kant's transcendental idealism, as Ralf Bader points out in "Noumena as Grounds of Phenomena," are carried out on both exegetical and systematic grounds. Bader's chapter is a sophisticated systematic articulation and defense of a "two world" (more precisely, "two domain") interpretation of that idealism. Bader's model of transcendental idealism has two core ideas. First, a "multiple domain" supervenience relation between the phenomena and the noumenal allows phenomenal properties to supervene on noumenal properties, without assuming that noumena are numerically identical to phenomena. Second, "coordination relations" between the two domains allow us to make precise the idea that phenomenal properties may supervene on particular distributions of noumenal properties, rather than always doing so holistically. Bader shows that this purely systematic reconstruction also has several exegetically appealing features: it allows for some phenomena to depend specifically on some noumena (e.g. my empirical character on my intelligible character), without assuming that all do so; it distinguishes between transcendental properties (which are relevant to the grounding of phenomena) from transcendent properties (which are not); it does not violate noumenal ignorance, for we know only the "outputs" of the supervenience relation, and cannot infer back to non-trivial knowledge of the subvening noumenal domain; and it shows that, while spatiotemporal properties and relations supervene on noumenal properties and relations, space and time are not themselves noumenal.

In "Thing and Object," Nicholas Stang considers a question that has driven much scholarship on transcendental idealism: are appearances numerically identical to the things in themselves that appear, or numerically distinct? He points out that much of the debate on this question has assumed that this is equivalent to the question of whether they are the same *objects*, but provides textual, historical, and philosophical evidence that "object" (*Gegenstand*) and "thing" (*Ding*) have different meanings for Kant. A thing is a locus of intensively gradable causal force, reality. He argues that appearances and things in themselves are not identical as objects, because the very concept of object-identity is tied, for Kant, to the concept of an intellect that would cognize the numerical identity of the objects in question. Because no intellect can be both discursive and intellectual, no intellect could cognize the numerical identity of objects across the phenomenal-noumenal divide, and thus the claim that they are identical has no content. However, the very same things, the same reality, can be given to our sensible intellects, and to divine intuitive intellect, as two non-overlapping domains of objects. Identity readings are thus shown to be right about the *same thing* relation, while non-identity readings are vindicated on the numerical identity of *objects*.

In his "Kant's One-World Phenomenalism: How the Moral Features Appear," Andrew Chignell makes new headway in the long-standing debate about the proper interpretation of Kant's transcendental idealism, by considering this question from the perspective of Kant's practical philosophy. More precisely, Chignell argues that Kant's practical philosophy requires a particular interpretation of transcendental idealism, which Chignell labels "One World Phenomenalism." On this view, Kant's distinction between things in themselves and appearances is to be understood in terms of a distinction between the features things really have and the features they appear (in our experience) to have. This sort of "metaphysical two-aspect" view has become popular in recent years, but Chignell's view is distinctive, both because of his emphasis on the existence of features that "straddle" the dividing line between things in themselves and appearances and because of his emphasis on the practical, and indeed moral, considerations that commit Kant to this view.

In "Kant's Enigmatic Transition: Practical Cognition of the Supersensible," Uygar Abaci takes up the vexed question of how (and to what degree) the additional resources provided by practical reason extend our cognitive grasp of things in themselves for Kant. Drawing on the recent wave of work on Kant's conception of cognition, Abaci argues that "practical cognition" should be understood to be a legitimate form of cognition in Kant's most fundamental sense of this term, which Abaci takes to involve a conscious and determinate representation of really possible objective contents. On this basis, Abaci goes on to argue that for Kant this sort of practical cognition allows us to achieve genuine cognition of the supersensible, even though we lack any intuitions of such supersensible objects.

In "Kant's Derivation of the Moral 'Ought' from a Metaphysical 'Is,'" Colin Marshall argues for a novel, more metaphysically robust reinterpretation of the foundations of Kant's metaethics. At the core of Marshall's account is the idea, which will be shocking to some Kantians, that Kant's views represent an attempt to develop an *analytical reduction* of practical normative facts to metaphysical facts about the nature of our faculties. Thus, on Marshall's reading, far from being an opponent of such reductive accounts in metaethics, Kant is actually a pioneer with respect to them. More precisely, for Marshall, Kant develops a reductive explanation of normative facts to facts about the faculty of reason, as this is realized in imperfectly rational creatures like us. The result is a reading of Kant that has the potential to reshape our understanding of Kant's place within the history of metaethics.

3. Whither Kant?

Some readers will notice that many central themes, even of Kant's theoretical philosophy, are absent from this volume. We of course agree, and we do not mean to suggest that these topics are unimportant or to deny that much excellent work is being done on them by both established scholars and younger researchers. But we also want to take the occasion of this Introduction to indicate where we hope to see more work done in the coming years and decades.

Perhaps ironically in a volume that so heavily features the "metaphysical" reading, the first such area is the need for further defense and elaboration of the "deflationary" (sometimes called "methodological" or "epistemic") reading made most famous in English by the pioneering work of Henry Allison. While neither of the editors subscribes to this reading, we think the time is ripe for a new formulation and defense of it. Not only would this curb the excesses of the "metaphysical" reading and spur metaphysical readers to sharpen their arguments and defenses, it would also help us all do justice to the textual grounds that have inspired so many philosophers to read Kant in a "deflationary" fashion. The need for such a defense is especially striking, insofar as there is a clear gap between specialists in Kant's theoretical philosophy—who, as noted above, tend today to read Kant in a more metaphysically-committal fashion—and non-specialists—who continue to be very attracted to "more deflationary" interpretations of Kant. This seems to us to be a sign to specialists like ourselves that we may be underestimating the power of more deflationary readings.[23] So we hope that, somewhere out there among the next generation of Kant scholars, someone is taking up the "deflationary" cause in this way.

In a similar vein, we also hope that metaphysical readers will do more, not merely to argue that Kant is positively committed to certain claims in "noumenal discourse," but to explain why he is entitled to these claims. In line with the distinctions we drew earlier, such an explanation would have at least two parts: an explanation of the precise epistemic status of noumenal discourse within Kant's philosophy (both theoretical and practical), as well as an explanation of its "semantic status" and why Kant is licensed in attributing that status to it. Further work on this area may alleviate the suspicion, felt acutely in some quarters, that the metaphysical reading oversteps Kant's own restriction of the "sense" and "significance" of the categories to phenomena.[24]

Since this problem about the categories—Kant seems both to require and to deny the possibility of applying categories to things in themselves—was a main motivation for early post-Kantian idealism, it is also to be hoped that this new "metaphysical" trend in Kant scholarship will increasingly engage with German Idealism. One of the authors in this volume (Dina Emundts) is a Hegel scholar of international renown, and several others have substantial research interests in German Idealism, so it is not as though this area has been completely neglected here. But it is our hope that the level of detail with which "metaphysical readers" have engaged with Kant's predecessors in German rationalism will be mirrored by a similar level of engagement with Kant's successors, not just the "big three" (Fichte, Schelling, and Hegel), but less-often studied figures like Reinhold, Maimon, and Schulze.[25]

Likewise, while the increasing attention to Kant's rationalist inheritance has been a source of great insight, we also worry that his debt to empiricism has been comparatively neglected in recent scholarship. In particular, Kant's response to Hume, once one of the mainstays of Kant scholarship, has been downplayed in much recent

[23] Associated with this worry is the concern that specialists, in their interpretative work, may have come to overemphasize non-canonical sources—such as lecture notes and *Reflexionen*—over the texts that Kant chose to publish in his own name during his lifetime.

[24] For example, see Kohl (2015) for an argument that "noumenal discourse" can at most make analogical use of the categories.

[25] That level of engagement, of course, is now standard in the scholarship on post-Kantian German Idealism; see, for instance, the works of Dieter Henrich, Eckart Förster, Paul Franks, Frederick Beiser, and Karl Ameriks. Our hope is that this "metaphysical turn" in Kant scholarship will increasingly engage with that scholarship as well.

work.[26] It is our belief that a renewed engagement with Hume would only strengthen the metaphysical reading developed by many of the authors in this volume.[27]

Finally, while this is a volume specifically about Kant's theoretical philosophy, we also find regrettable the increasing scholarly split between those who work on Kant's theoretical philosophy and his practical philosophy. While several of the chapters in this volume touch on practical issues, and many of the authors here represented have written about practical topics like freedom, and some have even written about Kant's aesthetics, none has attempted the kind of comprehensive scholarship on all of Kant's writings practiced in English by Paul Guyer, Henry Allison, or Karl Ameriks, and in German by Gerold Prauss, Manfred Baum, or Marcus Willaschek. It is our hope that Kant scholars who work on the details of his metaphysics will increasingly also work on the classic problems of his moral philosophy (e.g. the various formulations of the categorical imperative, the problem of lying to the murderer at the door, etc.) as well as other topics in Kant's system.

Let us conclude by emphasizing the limited range of these remarks. We are fully aware that all of the topics we have mentioned (the epistemic reading, the possibility of the noumenal use of the categories, German Idealism, Hume, the full gamut of Kant's writings) have been extensively researched by the great scholars of prior generations, and are currently being researched by younger scholars. Our remarks are directed at a small swath of Kant scholars geographically, generationally, and thematically, the mid-career and younger scholars among whom the "metaphysical reading" has been one main trend in Kant scholarship for the last decade or so. These remarks express the editors' hopes about how this small part of the larger universe of Kant studies will develop in the coming years.

4. Note on This Volume

First, the original plan for this volume was to be a collection of essays by the "younger" generation of metaphysically inclined readers of Kant. However, the inevitable happened and we all got older, the publication of the volume was delayed (solely the fault of the editors), and now it is not clear how young any of us is anymore. So even if we are not the *enfants terribles* we once thought we were, we hope these chapters find a receptive audience.

Second, the title of this volume is a reference to the title of Kant's 1770 Inaugural Dissertation, *De mundi sensibilis atque intelligibilis forma et principiis*. It is not intended to commit us, the editors, much less our authors, to the controversial claim that sensible and intelligible objects constitute a world, much less that they constitute

[26] For some recent attempts to argue that the metaphysical reading is compatible with an emphasis on Hume's influence on Kant, see Thielke (2003), Guyer (2008), and Schafer (2022).

[27] This is yet another reason not to refer to the "metaphysical" reading as "Leibnizian." For this will only intensify the comparative neglect in the contemporary literature of non-rationalist influences on Kant, such as Locke, Hume, and Tetens. Similarly, this way of framing things tends to draw our attention away from Kant's connections with the many forms of post-Kantian philosophy—ranging from German Idealism to phenomenology to critical theory and existentialism—many of which are themselves deeply metaphysical, if not always "metaphysical" in the sense one would associate with Leibniz or Spinoza.

two distinct worlds. (On our reading, there is no sensible world, but there is an intelligible world, so no question of the "identity" of worlds can arise.) It merely sounded like a good title.

Finally, we would like to dedicate this volume to Béatrice Longuenesse, who was *Doktormutter* to several people in this volume, and was a key mentor to many others. Since coming to the US, first at Princeton and then at NYU, Béatrice has been one of the leading lights of Kant scholarship, both in North America and internationally. She has exercised a major influence over our generation through her agenda-setting *Kant and the Capacity to Judge* (Princeton, 1997; a translation and revision of *Kant et le pouvoir de juger*, Vrin, 1993), as well as *Kant and the Human Standpoint* (Cambridge, 2005), *Hegel's Critique of Metaphysics* (Cambridge, 2007; a translation and revision of *Hegel et la critique de la métaphysique*, Vrin, 1981) and *I, Me, Mine: Back to Kant and Back Again* (Oxford, 2016). In addition to her scholarly work, Béatrice has also had an enormous impact on the field through her mentorship and training of young scholars, and of course by her radiant personality. Béatrice is by no means a "card-carrying" metaphysical reader of Kant (quite the contrary), but she has been a key influence and mentor for many of us who are. We dedicate this volume to her, in gratitude, admiration, and friendship.

References

Adams, R. M. (1997). Things in themselves. *Philosophy and Phenomenological Research*, *57*(4): 801–25.

Adickes, E. (1924). *Kant und das Ding an Sich*. Pan Verlag.

Allison, H. (1983). *Kant's transcendental idealism*. Yale University Press.

Allison, H. (2004). *Kant's transcendental idealism* (2nd edition). Yale University Press.

Ameriks, K. (2000). *Kant's theory of mind: An analysis of the Paralogisms of Pure Reason*. (New Edition). Oxford University Press.

Ameriks, K. (2003). *Interpreting Kant's Critiques*. Oxford University Press.

Ameriks, K. (2012). *Kant's elliptical path*. Oxford University Press.

Beiser, F. (2009). *German Idealism: The struggle against subjectivism, 1781–1800*. Harvard University Press.

Beiser, F. (2014). *The genesis of neo-Kantianism, 1796–1880*. Oxford University Press.

Bird, G. (1962). *Kant's theory of knowledge*. Routledge & Kegan Paul.

Chignell, A. (2007a). Kant's concepts of justification. *Noûs*, *41*(1): 33–63.

Chignell, A. (2007b). Belief in Kant. *Philosophical Review*, *116*(3): 323–60.

Collins, A. (1999). *Possible experience*. University of California Press.

Förster, E. (2012). *The twenty-five years of philosophy: A systematic reconstruction*. Harvard University Press.

Guyer, P. (2008). *Knowledge, reason, and taste: Kant's response to Hume*. Princeton University Press.

Hatfield, G. (1990). *The natural and the normative: Theories of spatial perception from Kant to Helmholtz*. MIT Press.

Hogan, D. (2009a). How to know unknowable things in themselves. *Noûs*, *43*(1): 49–63.

Hogan, D. (2009b). Three kinds of rationalism and the non-spatiality of things in themselves. *Journal of the History of Philosophy*, *47*(3): 355–82.

Jauernig, A. (2008). Kant's critique of the Leibnizian philosophy: Contra the Leibnizians, but pro Leibniz. In Daniel Garber & Béatrice Longuenesse (Eds.), *Kant and the early moderns* (pp. 41–63, 214–23). Princeton University Press.

Kemp Smith, N. (1918). *A commentary to Kant's* Critique of pure reason. Macmillan.

Kohl, M. (2015). Kant on the inapplicability of the categories to things in themselves. *British Journal for the History of Philosophy*, *23*(1): 90–114.

Kuehn, M. (2001). *Kant: A biography*. Cambridge University Press.

Langton, R. (1998). *Kantian humility: Our ignorance of things in themselves*. Oxford University Press.

Melnick, A. (1973). *Kant's Analogies of Experience*. University of Chicago Press.

Prauss, G. (1974). *Kant und das Problem der Dinge an Sich*. Bouvier.

Schafer, K. (2022). The beach of skepticism: Kant and Hume on the practice of philosophy and the proper bounds of skepticism. In P. Thielke (Ed.), *Cambridge Critical Guide to Kant's Prolegomena* (pp. 111–32). Cambridge University Press.

Smit, H. (2000). Kant on marks and the immediacy of intuition. *Philosophical Review*, *109*(2): 235–66.

Smit, H. (2009). Kant on apriority and the spontaneity of cognition. In S. Newlands & L. M. Jorgensen (Eds.), *Metaphysics and the good: Themes from the philosophy of Robert Merrihew Adams* (pp. 188–251). Oxford University Press.

Stang, N. (2016). *Kant's modal metaphysics*. Oxford University Press.

Thielke, P. (2003). Hume, Kant and the sea of illusion. *Hume Studies*, *29*(1): 63–88.

Tolley, C. (2020). Kant on the place of cognition in the progression of our representations. *Synthèse*, *197*(8): 3215–44.

Vaihinger, H. (1881–92). *Commentar zu Kants Kritik der reinen Vernunft*. 2 vols. Spemann.

Watkins, E. (2005). *Kant and the metaphysics of causality*. Cambridge University Press.

Watkins, E. & Willaschek, M. (2017). Kant's account of cognition. *Journal of the History of Philosophy*, *55*(1): 83–112.

1

Being Realistic about Kant's Idealism

Tobias Rosefeldt

1. Explaining the Content of Experience

Assume that I perceive a red cube in front of me. If I do so, I am in a representational mental state with a specific content. The content is specific in that it is different from that of a state in which I would be if I were to see a blue ball, for example. A legitimate question about this scenario seems to be the following: Why does my representational mental state have the content it actually has? Now, if I really perceive the cube rather than hallucinating or dreaming about it, a plausible answer to this question seems to be this: My representational mental state has the content it actually has partly because the perceived object has the properties it actually has. Of course, we might wonder how much about the content of my mental state can be explained by the properties of the perceived object. For example, one might argue that the fact that I represent the cube as being red not only depends on the properties of the cube but rather also on the properties of my visual sensual system. However, it is very hard to deny that the perceived object should play *some* role in explaining why my state is as it is when I perceive it. At least this assumption seems to be deeply entrenched in our normal self-understanding as cognizing beings: When we perceive an object then this object is at least partly responsible for what it going on in our minds, and it is this connection between the objects of experience and the content of our perceptual mental states that makes experience such a valuable means by which to find something out about the world around us.

In this chapter, I do not want to discuss whether this realist assumption of a dependence of the content of experience on the objects of experience is correct but rather whether it could have a place in Kant's system of transcendental idealism.[1] It seems clear from the outset that, if Kant is right, we have to give up many of our everyday beliefs about which features of our mental content depend on the objects we perceive. For example, while we normally think that we experience the cube in front of us as being extended in space and time partly because it is itself extended in space and time, Kant thinks that this feature of our perceptual content is entirely due

[1] Authors such as Lucy Allais and Colin McLear have recently argued that Kantian intuitions do not have representational content at all and that Kant rather favored a relationalist, or naïve realist, account of perception (Allais, 2015; McLear, 2016). Although this interpretation might be able to avoid the main challenge that I will discuss in the following, there is the suspicion that it can do so only by presupposing a conception of the perceived objects and properties that is too realistic in order to be compatible with any form of transcendental idealism. Stephenson (2016) has argued, for example, that Allais's relationalism about perception is incompatible with her relationalist account of appearance properties.

Tobias Rosefeldt, *Being Realistic about Kant's Idealism* In: *The Sensible and Intelligible Worlds: New Essays on Kant's Metaphysics and Epistemology.* Edited by: Karl Schafer and Nicholas F. Stang, Oxford University Press.
DOI: 10.1093/oso/9780199688265.003.0002

to the fact that space and time are our forms of intuition. However, that does not mean that Kant could not allow for other features of our perceptual content to depend on the object of experience. For example, even if it is due to the a priori forms of intuition that I represent the cube in front of me as having *some* spatial and temporal extension, those forms do not determine that I represent the object in front of me as being cubical rather than spherical, or as being smaller than the big white ball behind it rather than being bigger. These a posteriori aspects of my representation, it seems, should still depend on the perceived object.[2] The case is analogous to that of perceiving colors: Even if the constitution of my visual system should be responsible for the fact that I represent objects as colored, it is not due to the constitution of my visual system that I represent the cube in front of me as red rather than green. Again, if I am not hallucinating or dreaming, it still seems very natural to assume that it is the cube that is responsible for this fact.

So, let us assume for a moment that Kant takes the content of our experience to be partly determined by the objects we are confronted with when perceiving the world. This assumption still leaves open a crucial question about the kind of explanation of mental content which Kant assumes. For, as is well known, by "objects we are confronted with when perceiving the world" Kant could mean two things: He could mean the empirical objects, which he calls "appearances" or *phaenomena*:[3] spatially extended substances that persist in time and stand in causal relations to one another. Or he could mean the objects that are the noumenal grounds of these empirical objects and of our experience of them, which he refers to as the things as they are in themselves and which he takes to be outside space and time. Accordingly, we can distinguish between the following two kinds of explanation of mental content:

(i) *empirical explanation of the content of experience*, which assumes that a subject *A*'s perceptual mental states have the content they actually have partly because the objects of *A*'s sensible experience—i.e., certain *phaenomena*—have the properties they actually have.

(ii) *noumenal explanation of the content of experience*, which assumes that a subject *A*'s perceptual mental states have the content they actually have partly because the objects that are the noumenal grounds of *A*'s sensible experience—i.e. certain things as they are in themselves—have the properties they actually have.

We will see that that there is pretty good textual evidence that Kant took both of these explanations to be correct. What I want for in this chapter is that he was justified in doing so. This is necessary because there are certain reasons to think that both kinds of explanations are in conflict with essential feature of Kant's transcendental

[2] It is important not to misinterpret Kant's claim here that "the matter of all appearance is given to us only *a posteriori*, but its form must all lie ready for it in the mind *a priori*" (A20/B34). What Kant want to say here is that the general features of space and time result from our forms of intuition and maybe also that specific forms "lie in our mind" insofar as our forms of intuition determine which determinate spatiotemporal properties empirical objects *could* have. However, whether a certain empirical object actually has this particular determinate spatiotemporal property rather than another is obviously not something that is already determined by our forms of intuition.

[3] I will comment on a possible difference between the meanings of these two terms below.

idealism. As we will see, the force of these reasons will depend on how exactly we interpret Kant's transcendental idealism, especially his distinction between appearances and things in themselves. So, the aim of this chapter could also be described as presenting an exegetically feasible reading of Kant's transcendental idealism that is able to accommodate both of the mentioned kinds of explanation.

I will precede as follows: In the next section, I will discuss considerations that originate in the early reception of Kant's transcendental idealism and that are meant to show that Kant could accept neither empirical nor noumenal explanation of the a posteriori contents of experience without falling foul of some of his most fundamental philosophical assumptions. I will argue that these considerations at least show that there is a deep conflict between empirical explanations of mental content and a phenomenalist interpretation of Kant's idealism according to which Kantian *phaenomena* are purely intentional objects that are numerically distinct from any extra-mental object. The rest of the chapter will then be dedicated to the project of making sense of the explanation of a posteriori mental content within the framework of a more realist interpretation of Kant's idealism. In section 3, I will present a number of passages in which Kant characterizes what he means by an object of experience. I will argue that these passages imply that, when we explain the content of perceptions by means of a Kantian object of experience, we commit ourselves to an empirical as well as to a noumenal explanation. The reason is that the passages strongly suggest that Kant took the object of sensible experience and the noumenal ground of perceptions to be one and the same object. Section 4 offers the sketch of an interpretation of Kant's distinction between appearances and things in themselves that helps to make sense of this assumption. I will propose that the distinction is one between two kinds of properties that belong to one and the same extra-mental objects: properties that depend on the mental response that humans show when confronted with these objects, and properties that pertain to these objects independently of how the human mind responds to them. Section 5 then makes a more detailed suggestion as to how we should characterize our representational mental responses to objects given Kant's idealistic account of experience. In section 6, I will argue that interpreting appearance properties as response-dependent properties in the suggested sense allows Kant to explain the content of our minds by means of these properties without falling foul of the criticism from section 2. I will also try to show that my interpretation makes intelligible why Kant thought that an empirical explanation of perceptual content always implies some kind of noumenal explanation, and that it can thereby disclose the kernel of truth in Adickes's famous talk about "Kant's theory of double affection"[4] that many interpreters have found so hard to accept.

2. The Challenge

When Kant starts his project of delineating the scope and limits of human cognition, he seems to start out with an empirical explanation of the a posteriori aspects of the

[4] See Adickes (1929).

content of our experience. In the first two paragraphs of the Transcendental Aesthetic, he claims that in order for us to have experience of objects at all, these objects have to be "given to us in intuition"[5] and that the objects can only be given to us by "affecting our mind in a certain way," where the effect of the objects on the mind are "sensations." He calls intuitions that relate to an object by means of sensations "empirical intuitions" and the objects of these empirical intuitions, as far as they are not determined any further, "appearances." He also claims that the objects that are given to us through their effects on our mind "are thought through the understanding." If we take these claims at face value, we get the following picture of the role of objects for our experience: Objects have certain causal effects on our mind, namely sensations. Partly through having these effects, the objects are "given" to us, i.e., they become objects of our empirical intuition, or appearances. If these appearances are further determined by applying concepts to them in our thinking, they can become objects of our empirical knowledge. There is no evidence in the text that Kant used the term "object" ambiguously in the two paragraphs from which these quotes are taken, and that he assumed that the objects that we think through our concepts are empirical objects whereas the objects that affect our senses are "things in themselves." So it seems as if he found an empirical explanation of the a posteriori aspects of the content of our experience, and the realism that is involved in it, unproblematic and treated it as something that he could more or less presuppose before he then continued with an explanation of those aspects of the content of our experience that he found much more puzzling because they do not result from causal affection by outer objects but are given to us a priori.

Form the earliest reception of Kant's first *Critique* onward, readers have recognized the realist commitments in Kant's talk about affection in the Transcendental Aesthetic, but many of them found them wanting. The unease they had is nicely summarized in Jacobi's famous quip that without the presupposition of the thing in itself, which he took to be an implication of Kant's account of affection, he was "unable to enter Kant's system" but with it he was "unable to stay within it" (Jacobi, 2004, p. 109). Some ten years later, in his *Versuch einer neuen Darstellung der Wissenschaftslehre* from 1797/1798, Fichte claimed that, since Kant's critical philosophy so obviously did not allow for any substantial assumptions about things in themselves, we should conclude that Kant himself never actually assumed any explanation of sensations by affecting objects at all. It is true that, when we have sensations, we experience them as being accompanied by a feeling of passivity. However, Fichte adds, "the attempt to explain this original feeling further through the efficacy of a *something* is the dogmatism of the Kantians [...] which they also want to impose on Kant. This something is of course the notorious thing in itself" (1970, p. 243).

Jacobi and Fichte both seem to have thought that it would be blatantly inconsistent for Kant to assume either a noumenal or an empirical explanation of the a posteriori aspects of the content of our experience. Their reasons for refusing noumenal explanation are well known: they think that it is incompatible with Kant's assumption of noumenal ignorance, i.e., with his claim that we cannot use categories such as

[5] For this and the following quotations see *KpV* A19–20/B33–34.

that of cause and effect in order to cognize things as they are in themselves. It is less obvious why they both also seem to have taken it for granted that the affecting objects that explain why our experience has its specific contents could not be empirical objects. I think we can understand this attitude if we take into account that Jacobi and Fichte had an understanding of Kant's transcendental idealism, and of his account of the nature of appearances, that one would nowadays call a "phenomenalist interpretation."[6] According to such an interpretation, empirical objects are not real objects outside of our minds but merely intentional entities, i.e., internal objects of representations that need for their existence nothing more than these representations themselves and whose properties are completely determined by them. Uncontroversial examples for such merely intentional objects would be the objects of hallucinations and dreams.

It is easy to see why such a phenomenalist understanding of Kant's idealism cannot allow to explain the fact that we are perceiving a red cube as red and cubical by means of the properties of the red cube, i.e., of the perceived empirical object.[7] For if this cube is a merely intentional object whose existence and properties are fully grounded in our own representations, then this explanation is not available any longer. According to phenomenalism, the perceived cube exists and has the properties it actually has because our representations of it exist and have the properties they actually have, and not the other way round. The fact that explanation is an asymmetrical relation precludes the assumption that intentional objects and representations mutually explain one another. One can also see this point by looking to objects we hallucinate or imagine in dreams. To say that the unicorn I dreamed of last night was red because I represented it in my dream as being red seems fine. But to say that I represented the unicorn in my dream as being red because the unicorn I dreamed of was red seems wrong given the nature of merely intentional objects such as dreamed-of unicorns.[8]

[6] Contemporary phenomenalist interpretations of Kant's idealism are suggested by Guyer (1987), Van Cleve (1999), Oberst (2015), Stang (2015), and Jauernig (2021) to name just a few. In Jacobi's (2004 [1785]) short text "Ueber den transscendentalen Idealismus," which heavily influenced the whole post-Kantian interpretation of Kant's philosophy, the phenomenalist reading is primarily based on Kant's characterization of transcendental idealism in Fourth Paralogism in the first edition of the *Critique*. In this chapter, Kant uses his distinction between appearances and things in themselves in order to give a rather blunt argument against skepticism about the outer world, which relies on the claim that bodies are "nothing but a kind of my own representations" (A370) and hence that we can certain about the existence of bodies without having to "go beyond our own self-consciousness" (A370).

[7] For the following cf. Van Cleve (1999, pp. 165–71) and Stang (2015, pp. 5–8).

[8] Nicholas Stang (2015) has recently offered a phenomenalist interpretation of Kant's transcendental idealism that is meant to make room for empirical explanations of mental content. Stang (2015, pp. 8ff.) suggests refining the phenomenalist picture in two ways. First, he assumes that the appearances I perceive are not grounded in my individual mental states but rather in what he calls "universal experience," which in turn is grounded not only in my present mental states but rather also in future ones and those of other subjects and in the a priori forms of intuition and thinking. As Stang acknowledges, this alone would still not solve the problem of empirical affection since even if facts about my mental states only partially ground universal experience, which in turn grounds all facts about appearances, those states could still not be the causal result of appearances for nothing can be the effect of something that it even only partially grounds. So, Stang's second maneuver is to distinguish between those facts about my own mental states that ground universal experience, and those facts about them that are causally explained by outer appearances. He takes the first kind of facts to be facts about how our own mental states *seem* to us, whereas the second kind of facts, those that receive an empirical explanation, are facts about the real properties of

I think that the key to answering Jacobi's and Fichte's worries lies in a non-phenomenalist interpretation of Kant's notion of an object of experience. In the following, I will try to show that such a more realist interpretation is possible and well supported by the Kantian text. My interpretation will also reveal that, for Kant, any commitment to an empirical explanation of mental content entails an implicit commitment to a noumenal explanation of this content, and that this connection does not lead to a violation of Kant's claim of noumenal ignorance, about which Jacobi and Fichte were so worried.

3. Kant's Notion of a (Transcendental) Object of Experience

In order to see whether Kant's talk about empirical objects as the sources of affection in the *Transcendental Aesthetic* is compatible with his transcendental idealism, we have to look closer at those passages where Kant defines what one should mean by the term "object of experience" within his critical system. I will confine myself here to passages from the A edition because I think that the strongest textual support for a phenomenalist reading comes from this edition and it is hence especially interesting if the reading I will propose even works for this edition.[9]

In A104, Kant writes:

> What does it mean if one speaks of an object corresponding to and therefore also distinct from the cognition? It is easy to see that this object must be thought of only as something in general = X [...] which is opposed to our cognitions being determined at pleasure or arbitrarily [...], since insofar as they are to relate to an object our cognitions must also necessarily agree with each other in relation to it, i.e., they must have that unity that constitutes the concept of an object.

these mental states. Although I see the attraction of Stang's proposal, I find the distinction between facts about how our mental states seem to us and facts about how these states really are a bit forced and alien to Kant's system. Moreover, if we accept such a distinction, it seems plausible to assume that there should also be an explanation of facts about how our mental states seem to us, but it is not clear that Stang can accept this without ending up with exactly the kind of explanatory circle that the distinction is meant to avoid. To see this let us assume that facts about universal experience ground facts about a particular empirical object, which in turn is partially causally responsible for how my mental states are, e.g. that they have a certain content when I perceive the object. Now, if we assume that there also is a way in which this mental state seems to me, then it seems very plausible to assume that this way is also partially causally determined by the empirical object. The object is not only responsible for my perceptual state to have the content it does, for example, but also, at least partly, for it to *seem* to have the content it does. But then facts about how my own mental states seem to me cannot partially ground facts about universal experience, for otherwise the problem that nothing can be the effect of something that it partially grounds would reemerge.

[9] For an analogous interpretation that is primarily based on passages from the B edition, see Rosefeldt (2007, 2013). It is certainly an asset of any interpretation of Kant's transcendental idealism if it does not have to assume that Kant changed his views about it entirely between the two editions; see the criticism of my (Rosefeldt, 2013) interpretation by De Boer (2014). Although I admit that the Fourth Paralogism in the A edition does at least sound as if it suggests a more phenomenalistic reading of transcendental idealism than the one I prefer, I do not think that this chapter represents Kant's considered view even in 1781; for a very subtle more realist reading of the Fourth Paralogism, see Karampatsou (2022, ch. 4).

A little later he uses the terms "transcendental object" and "transcendental object = x" in order to speak about objects that, according to the quotation, are distinct from our representations (cf. A109).

The general consideration that Kant is making in the quoted passage seems clear: If we want to find out whether our representations represent an object that is distinct from these representations, we cannot compare them to this object directly, for objects are only given to us through representations (cf. also A108–109). Apart from what we know through our representations we know of the object nothing than that it is "something in general = X." However, the object poses *some* constraint on the representations we have of it that is epistemically useful for us: Any representation that represents the object has to be coherent with any other representation that represents the object. So, a meaningful criterion for when an intentional object *o* of a representation *R* is an object distinct from *R* would be that *R* is in the right kind of coherence with all other representations of *o*.

It is important to note that none of these assumptions amounts to the claim that there are no objects that are distinct from our representations and that, as responsible epistemologists, we should stop talking about them. The whole point of the passage is to get a reasonable notion of an "object corresponding to and distinct from" our representations, and when Kant says that "insofar as [our representations] are to relate to an object our cognitions must also necessarily agree with each other in relation to it" it is clear that he tries to point to a connection between coherence and correspondence rather than trying to reduce the latter to the former.[10] However, this still leaves us with two very different conceptions of what an object distinct from our representations is and of how such an object differs from objects of representations that are not in the relevant sense distinct from the representations we have of them—such as the objects of hallucinations and dreams. According to a phenomenalist reading, these objects would still be merely intentional objects, and they would be different from objects of hallucination only in that the latter are grounded only in the very representation that the hallucinating subject presently has of them, whereas objects that are distinct form their representations are fully grounded in a set of representations that also includes future representations and that of other subjects.[11] According to a more realist reading, the objects that Kant takes to be distinct from our representations would be objects whose existence and properties are not fully grounded in anyone's representations of them but that also exist and have some of their properties in themselves.

In order to decide between these two interpretations, it is useful to look at later passages in the *Critique* in which the talk about a transcendental object of experience reappears and is now connected to certain assumptions about things in themselves. The first of these passages that I want to quote is the following:

[10] I agree with Busse (n.d.) on this point. Busse defends the interesting idea that the mentioned passages from the A-deduction should be interpreted as part of a meta-semantic theory: They do not contain a revised understanding of what an object is, but rather introduce necessary conditions for our reference to objects.

[11] Cf. Stang's (2015, §2) helpful notion of "universal experience" here.

> All our representations are in fact related to some object through the understanding, and, since appearances are nothing but representations, the understanding thus relates them to a something, as the object of sensible intuition: but this something is to this extent only the transcendental object. This signifies, however, a something = X, of which we know nothing at all nor can know anything in general […], but is rather something that can serve only as a correlate of the unity of apperception for the unity of the manifold in sensible intuition, by means of which the understanding unifies that in the concept of an object. This transcendental object cannot even be separated from the sensible data, for then nothing would remain through which it is thought. (A250–51)

This passage is important for two reasons. First, it shows that when Kant uses the term "transcendental object" in the chapter on the distinction between *phaenomena* and *noumena* he uses it in exactly the sense in which he has used it in the Transcendental Deduction: Apart from what we know through our sensible representations about it, the transcendental object is nothing but "a something = x." This something serves as "a correlate of the unity of apperception for the unity of the manifold in sensible intuition" in that the only epistemologically significant use we can make of the claim that our representations relate to it is that these representations are in agreement with other representations of it. Secondly, the passage makes indubitably clear that Kant does not want to claim that we do not have any knowledge of the transcendental object at all. He calls it "the object of sensible intuition" and he says that "it cannot […] be separated from the sensible data, for then nothing would remain through which it is thought," which strongly suggests that it *is* thought through the sensible data we are given. Hence, the claim that it is something "of which we know nothing at all nor can know" can only mean that we do not know anything about it *except* what we can know about it through the sensible data we get from it. We could also say: we know nothing of it but the way it appears to us in sensible intuition.

Now, a little bit later Kant claims that no object could appear to us without existing in some sense independently from our epistemic relation to it. He writes:

> It follows naturally from the concept of appearance in general that something must correspond to it which is not in itself appearance, for appearance can be nothing for itself and outside of our kind of representation; thus, if there is not to be a constant circle, the word "appearance" must already indicate a relation to something the immediate representation of which is, to be sure sensible, but which in itself, without this constitution of our sensibility (on which the form of our intuition is grounded), must be something, i.e., an object independent of sensibility.
>
> (A251–52)

The claim here seems to be that an object can only appear to us if it is something beyond our representations of it, i.e., more than a merely intentional object. If we take the relation of appearing to a subject to involve the causing of sensations in that subject, this would mean that sensations, which constitute the matter of perceptions, have to be the effects of objects that are mind-transcendent things in themselves.

That seems to imply that Kant takes noumenal explanation of the contents of our perception to be unavoidable.

Now, the question is whether the transcendental object which is described in the first passage as the object of sensible intuition that is thought through sensible data is identical to the object that appears to the subject and, in order to do so, has to have some mind-independent existence. A positive answer to this question is strongly suggested by the fourth passage I want to quote here:

> We can call the mere intelligible cause of appearances in general the transcendental object, merely so that we have something corresponding to sensibility as a receptivity. To this transcendental object we may ascribe the whole extent and connection of our possible perceptions, and say that it is given in itself prior to all experience. But appearances are, in accordance with it, given not in themselves but only in this experience, because they are mere representations, which signify a real object only as perceptions, namely when this perception connects up with all others in accordance with the rules of the unity of experience. (A494/B522–23)[12]

Here the transcendental object is explicitly described as (a) the object to which "the whole extent and connection of our possible experience" is ascribed and as (b) the intelligible cause of appearances, i.e., as the mind-independent thing in itself which affects the mind so that it gets sensations.

So, far from abandoning the picture drawn at the beginning of the Transcendental Aesthetic, the passages about the transcendental object of experience rather confirm it: When we perceive an object then this very object has to affect us in order to produce sensations in us. The passages from the Transcendental Logic add two main lines of thought to this picture: First, the transcendental object, i.e., the very object that we perceive and by which we are affected, has to have some mind-independent existence in order to appear to us: It has to have some properties in itself, which then can be causally responsible for how the object is represented by us. Second, the fact that a representation represents a transcendental object that is distinct from us, in the sense that it has some mind-independent existence, "shows up" in an epistemologically useful way only by means of the fact that the representation stands in some kind of coherence-relation to other representations.

This general picture is also confirmed by a parallel passage from the chapter on *Phaenomena and Noumena* in the B edition where Kant writes:

> [...] if we call certain objects, as appearances, beings of sense (*phaenomena*), because we distinguish the way we intuit them from their constitution in themselves, then it already follows from our concept that we contrast them with these very same objects ["eben dieselbe"] as having this latter constitution, although we do not intuit them as such [...]. (B306)[13]

[12] An analogous claim is made in the *Prolegomena* (4:314–15; see also 4:298); strong textual support for a two-aspect interpretation, according to which one and the same objects appear to us and have properties in themselves, can also be found in the B edition, e.g. Bxxvi–xxvii and B69–70.

[13] I depart from the Guyer-Wood translation here, which surprisingly translates *eben dieselbe* as "other objects."

Kant is as explicit as one could possibly want him to be here: By characterizing empirical objects as *phaenomena* we conceptually commit to assuming that these very objects are also somehow constituted in themselves.

What we now need is an interpretation of Kant's distinction between appearances and things in themselves, and of his thesis that we can have knowledge about the former but not about the latter, that allows us to make sense of all of these claims and to explain how one and the same object can figure in an empirical as well as in a noumenal explanation of mental content.

4. Empirical Objects and Their Response-Dependent Properties

The reading which I think is best suited to account for Kant's claims about the explanation of the content of our experience is a variant of the so-called ontological two-aspect interpretation of Kant's transcendental idealism.[14] The basic idea of this interpretation is that Kant's distinction between appearances and things in themselves amounts to a distinction between two kinds of properties that both belong to the same objects: mind-dependent properties, which have to do with the way things appear to us, on the one hand, and mind-independent properties, which have to do with how the things are independently of how they appear to us, on the other. The claim that spatiotemporal properties are not properties of things in themselves but rather only of appearance is then taken to mean that these properties are in some sense dependent on our mind: empirical objects would not have them if we had different forms of intuition. That does not mean, however, that spatiotemporal properties are properties of merely intentional objects. They "can be attributed to the object itself, in relation to our sense," as Kant writes in a footnote on B69.

This claim is not only compatible with the assumption that appearance properties are properties of objects that exist independently of our minds; it rather even implies that such properties can only be had by things that have some other properties independently of us. As Kant puts it at B69: Empirical objects as well as the "qualities that we attribute to them, are always regarded as something really given, only that–insofar as this quality depends only on the kind of intuition of the subject in the relation of the given object to it this object as appearance is to be distinguished from itself as object in itself." The claim that the very objects that have spatiotemporal properties in relation to us also have to have some mind-independent properties does not mean that we have any knowledge of these things as they are in themselves, because we do not know *which* mind-independent properties these are. This fits nicely the passages from the A edition of the Transcendental Analytic we have discussed in the previous section: Transcendental objects are the "objects of our sensible intuition" and things

[14] Ontological two-aspect interpretations have been favored by a number of authors: see Dryer (1966), Langton (1998), Collins (1999), Allais (2007, 2015), Rosefeldt (2007), and, arguably, Adickes (1924). Methodological two-aspect interpretations like that of Prauss (1974, pp. 192–227) and Allison (1994, pp. 247–54; 2004, pp. 64–73) can also allow for empirical as well as noumenal affection because they take talk about the latter just to be about the same relation considered in a way in which we abstract from our forms of intuition. However, it is doubtful that such a thin notion of noumenal affection can play the systematic role that Kant wants to assign to it; for this criticism see Willaschek (2001a) and Stang (2015, p. 3 n. 14).

which we represent "through sensible data," in the sense that through perception we know of their mind-dependent appearance properties. And the very same transcendental objects are also the "intelligible cause" of appearances in that they have mind-independent properties that are causally responsible for how they appear to us.

In order to see whether the interpretation can also help to solve the problems with an explanation of the contingent aspect of the content of our intuition, we have to look more closely into the nature of mind-dependent appearance properties. We have already seen that Kant says a lot about the process that leads to an object appearing to us: Objects appear to us by causally affecting our mind and bringing about certain representational effects in us such as sensations. The claim that we only know how objects appear to us is hence often identified by Kant with the claim that we only know how they affect us:

> [...] intuition of outer objects as well as self-intuition of the mind represents both of these things *as each affects our senses, i.e. as it appears* [...]. (B69; emphasis mine)
>
> The representation of a body in intuition contains nothing at all that could pertain to an object in itself, but merely *the appearance of something and the way we are affected by it* [...]. (A44/B61; emphasis mine)
>
> [...] if we regard the objects of our senses as mere appearances then, by doing so, we admit that there is a thing in itself that grounds them, although we do not know this thing as it is in itself but rather only *its appearance, i.e. the way our senses are affected by this unknown something.* (*Prolegomena*, 4:314–15; emphasis mine)

What we know, according to the quotations, are *the ways objects affect us.*[15] I think that ways in which objects affect human subjects can be characterized by means of the kinds of representational effects which these objects have on human minds. The immediate mental effect of the affection by an object is a sensation which Kant calls the "matter" of an empirical intuition. Let us call this the *material effect of the affection.* Sensations are then given a spatiotemporal order by the mind according to its "forms" of intuition, space and time. Besides the general spatiotemporal structure of the content of empirical intuition, which is due solely to the constitution of our sensibility, there are also more specific formal aspects of it, namely the particular forms according to which certain given sensations are ordered. According to Kant's theory of cognition, this ordering cannot be understood as a merely passive reaction, but involves an activity of the subject that Kant calls "synthesis speciosa" and ascribes to the faculty of imagination (B151, B162; see also A100–101). That the

[15] I think that this way of formulating the limits of our cognition poses a problem for Karin de Boer's (2014) recent attempt to solve the challenge of empirical and noumenal affection. De Boer argues that Kant's talk about objects affecting our senses belongs to the realm of empirical scientific discourse whereas his claims about the transcendental object or the thing in itself belong to his transcendental philosophy, and she thinks that the questions whether transcendental objects or things in themselves affect us is misplaced because it confuses these two realms of inquiry. However, Kant's notion of appearance certainly belongs to his transcendental philosophy, and the fact that he so often characterizes the way objects appear to us as the way these objects affect our senses makes it very hard to believe that the theory of affection is not also a part of the latter.

imagination is active does not mean that it completely autonomously "makes up" the specific spatiotemporal orderings of sensations that result in a certain empirical cognition. Whether we perceive a given object as rectangular or as round is partially causally determined by the affecting object. So, I will call an ordering of given sensations by the imagination according to a specific spatiotemporal form the *formal effect of the affection*.

Kant's claim that all we know about given objects is the way these objects appear to us, or affect us, can then be understood as the claim that all we know of the extra-mental objects that we encounter in experience is that these objects are such that they have a certain material and formal effect on us. It is important not to identify this last claim with the assumption that the only objects of our empirical knowledge *are* the material and formal effects that result from the affection by extra-mental objects. The property of being such that this has certain effects on us is a property of the objects that have these effects on us—not of ourselves or of our own mental states.

It is a very natural thought to interpret the status that Kant assigns to appearance-properties as that of what people nowadays would call *response-dependent properties*.[16] A response-dependent property is a property of an object that has essentially to do with the kinds of responses, or effects, that object has on certain things, typically on human beings. It can be understood as the disposition of the object to elicit these effects. A typical response-dependent property within the empirical world is that of being poisonous, for example. We call things poisonous if they have the disposition to elicit certain symptoms of intoxication in us under certain circumstances. These symptoms are brought about by certain non-dispositional, chemical properties of the object, properties one usually calls the categorical base of the disposition. For example, fly agarics are poisonous because they contain muscimol, which causes symptoms of intoxication when ingested. Saying of an object that it is poisonous does not mean to ascribe to it some particular categorical property that causes intoxication. It rather means to say of an object that it has *some* property that has this effect on us. For that reason, response-dependent dispositions can be characterized as higher-order properties, properties of the form "having some first-order property with such-and-such causal role."[17] In this spirit, we can understand the claim that being poisonous for humans is an essentially response-dependent property in the following way:

> $\Box_{\text{being poisonous for humans}}\ \forall x(x$ is poisonous for humans $\leftrightarrow x$ has some property P such that x's having P causes symptoms of intoxication in humans)

Terms of the form "$\Box_{\text{being } F}$ S" are to be read as "it is true in virtue of the essence of the property of *being F* that S," and claims of this form will be called *real definitions* of the

[16] For an overview of different notions of response-dependence see Haukioja (2013). In the contemporary literature, response-dependence is treated both as a feature of concepts (see Johnston, 1989; Pettit, 1991, 1998) as well as of properties (see Johnston, 1998). I treat response-dependence exclusively as a feature of properties here.

[17] See Prior et al. (1982).

properties in question—both in allusion to Kit Fine's theory of essence.[18] Using the idea of the essence of properties and their real definitions allows us to strengthen the mere material biconditional that relates the property to a typical response without committing ourselves to the assumption that this biconditional is an analytical or conceptual truth, which is usually made in the debate about response-dependence.[19] Although this analyticity assumption is certainly plausible in the case of the property of being poisonous, we will see below that it should be avoided in the case of the properties to which Kant wants to apply his theory. I would also like to note that expressions of the form "*x*'s having *P* causes such-and-such effects in such-and-such being" are meant as generic predications here and in the following. Their truth does not require that all instantiations of *P* always cause the effects in all beings of the respective kind, but rather only that the right subclass of their exemplifications do so for the right subclass of beings in the right actual and counterfactual situations.[20]

Given a real definition like that in (1), it is not hard to see that response-dependent properties such as being poisonous have exactly the features that Kant ascribes to spatiotemporal appearance properties. Firstly, they pertain to objects only in relation to us and are dependent on our own constitution. (Fly agarics are not poisonous in themselves but rather only for certain beings: If human beings reacted differently to muscimol, fly agarics would not lose the property whose instantiation causes intoxication in the actual world; but they would no longer have the higher-order property of having some property whose instantiation causes intoxication.) Secondly, as higher-order properties they can only be had by objects that also have some first-order, response-independent properties—properties that the objects have in themselves, i.e., independently of how we react to them. (Fly agarics could not be poisonous for humans unless they had some response-independent chemical property that is causally responsible for the intoxication of humans who eat them.) And, finally, knowing that things have a certain response-dependent property does not imply any knowledge about *which* response-independent property it is that elicits the response and not even knowledge that it is always the same response-independent property that plays this role. (People knew that fly agarics are poisonous before they knew that it contains muscimol, and different kinds of things can be poisonous because of very different chemical properties.)

Given this similarity, it seems promising to interpret Kant's claim that spatiotemporal appearance properties are nothing but ways in which objects affect us as saying that these properties are essentially response-dependent. The relevant responses are not certain biological reactions in this case but rather the emergence of certain mental states in certain cognitive subjects. Let "*F*" stand for some spatiotemporal

[18] See Fine (1994). The idea of real definitions, which explicate the essence of a property, in opposition to nominal definitions, by which we define concepts, is certainly not alien to Kant's philosophy and the philosophical tradition in which it stands.

[19] See Johnston (1989, 1998) and Pettit (1991, 1998).

[20] As the literature on generics shows, it is by no means easy to make explicit what "right kind" means in each case; see Leslie & Lerner (2016). However, it seems to me legitimate to build on our implicit understanding of generic claims in my reconstructions, especially because Kant himself often uses generic idioms when stating his theory.

predicate such as "extended," "cubical," or "red." Then the general scheme for interpreting the property of being *F* as a response-dependent property is the following:

Schema for real definition of a response-dependent property

$\Box_{\text{being } F}$ $\forall x$(*x is F* $\leftrightarrow$ *x* has some property *P*[21] such that *x*'s having *P* causes *such-and-such* mental effects in us[22])

The task to fill out the dummy expression "such-and-such" is by no means trivial. We know from the literature on dispositionalist conceptions of color that, if we understand a color such as red as a disposition to produce a particular kind of visual sensory state in us, then this state must not be characterized as that of visually representing something as red, for that would make the characterization circular in a vicious way.[23] A solution that dispositionalists about color have presented is to characterize the mental state intrinsically, i.e., in non-representational terms,[24] for example as a "reddish sensation." Red can then be understood as the disposition to produce reddish sensations without the threat of circularity.

This strategy might help us for a reconstruction of Kant's talk about appearances as far as we can understand appearance properties as dispositions to produce certain *sensations* in us. Kant calls such properties "realities" and characterizes them as "that which corresponds to sensation" (A143/B182, A168/B209). Sensations are indeed characterized by Kant as "non-objective" mental states that "relate to a subject merely as the modification of its state" (A320/B376), which seems to imply that one could in principle characterize them in non-representational terms. However, the strategy would hardly help us with *all* properties that are understood as response-dependent within Kant's transcendental idealism. Some of these properties have to do with specific shapes of objects (such as that of being cubical), others with specific spatial or temporal magnitudes (such as that of being one meter long or lasting two hours), and again others with the relation in which objects stand to other objects (such as

[21] This property may well be disjunctive if many response-independent properties play the same role in bringing about the responses.

[22] Kant mostly uses pronouns like "us" and "me" in order to refer to the beings to which spatiotemporal properties are relativized. He also sometimes uses "human beings" (for example in A26/B42). What is important is that we understand these being as beings who actually have our forms of intuition. As for colors, Kant seems to think that the semantics of our talk of colors does not rest on the assumption that we react with similar color sensations to the same objects (see *Prol*, 4:451; *Anthr*, 7:168; and B45). So, while being cubical is a property that objects have in relation to all beings that actually have the forms of intuition that humans have, being red is a property that every individual human being should ascribe to objects only in relation to herself. I will ignore this difference in the following.

[23] See Boghossian & Velleman (1989, pp. 88–91). The problem with the proposal is not only that the *analysans* appears in the *analysandum*, but moreover that it does not succeed in describing the disposition as a determinate property. For if red is the disposition to be visually represented as red, then it is the disposition to be visually represented to have this very disposition. Hence, "which disposition it is depends on which disposition it disposes objects to be represented as having – which depends, in turn, on which disposition it is" (Velleman, 2009, p. 525). The circularity-problem also speaks against a proposal that Nick Stang has made me in order to align my interpretation to his own and according to which we could understand any given empirical property *P* as the (response-dependent) property of having some (response-independent) property that causes cognitive subjects to have Universal Experience in which the object is represented as having *P*.

[24] See Peacocke (1984).

that of causing some other object's state). For none of these properties are there specific sensations that would allow us to define the former by means of the latter. The mental responses that are essential for them have to do with the ordering, or "synthesizing" of sensations according to the a priori forms of space and time. This ordering is what I have called above a *formal* effect of the affection by an object, not a material one, and it seems hopeless to try to describe these effects in non-representational terms. The move to piggyback on our physical vocabulary when trying to characterize mental responses intrinsically seems philosophically dubious enough when we make it to characterize sensations as "reddish" or "blueish." But it would seem entirely silly if we extended it to describing acts of the imagination as "cubical-ish" or "lasting-two-hours-ish."

I think that a more radical response is necessary if we want to reconstruct Kant's transcendental idealism as a theory of response-dependent properties, and I also think that this response is perfectly legitimate within the Kantian setting. The general idea of this response is this: Instead of presupposing that the vocabulary by which we describe spatiotemporal features is primarily made to describe the properties of mind-independent objects and only secondarily to characterize our mental responses to these objects, we should acknowledge that, within Kant's theory, this vocabulary is primarily made to express our mental representational responses to objects and only in a second step serves to characterize properties of these objects. A satisfying exploration of this response would require a much deeper involvement with Kant's account of experience in the Transcendental Analytic than I can offer here, but I will at least present a rough sketch in the next section.

5. The Language of Appearance

Let us assume that a human subject is affected by a certain extra-mental object and reacts to it by having certain sensations and synthesizing them according to the a priori forms of space and time in a certain way. Then this material and formal response fully grounds a certain sensible and representational mental content. That means the content is what it is independently of the causal source of the affection, unlike a causal theory of mental content would have it for example. Hence, the content is not representational in the sense that, all by itself, it represents a property of the affecting extra-mental object. However, it is representational in that, by grasping it, the subject represents a certain spatiotemporal manifold. We can call this sensible content an "appearance" in the sense in which Kant uses this term in A20/B34 where he defines it as the "undetermined object of an empirical intuition." The content is undetermined in that it is not yet taken by the subject to determine properties of extra-mental objects. But it is not undetermined in the sense that it is not distinct from other contents (i.e., contents in which other sensations are synthesized in other ways). It is also not undetermined in the sense that the subject could not distinguish it from other contents. Kant takes the process of synthesis by the imagination that is involved at this stage of the genesis of cognition to have the function of making the subject aware of the represented manifold as such, and this awareness involves the ability to sensibly distinguish the different parts of the manifold from one another and to reidentify a certain manifold and distinguishing it from others.[25]

Note that when we call these sensible mental contents "appearances" then this notion of an appearance must not be confused with the notion of an appearance as an empirical object. It has often been noted in the literature that Kant's use of the term "appearance" (*Erscheinung*) wavers between two meanings,[26] and that Kant sometimes uses the term *phaenomenon* in order to refer to empirical objects and the term *apparentia* in order to speak about sensible mental contents that have not yet been determined by the subject as relating to such empirical objects.[27] In the following, I will reserve the term "appearances" for sensible mental contents, and the term "*phaenomena*" for extra-mental empirical objects.

Once we accept that a subject can grasp different sensible contents and can be aware of them and distinguish them from one another, it seems plausible to assume that the subject can express these contents by means of a vocabulary that is not *primarily* a vocabulary by which extra-mental objects and their properties are characterized. Our vocabulary would primarily be a vocabulary for appearances and only in a second step a vocabulary for characterizing phenomena. Kant's clearest commitment to this assumption can be found in his distinction between "judgments of perception" and "judgments of experience" in the *Prolegomena* where he writes:

> [...] if I say 'The air is elastic', then this judgment is to begin with only a judgment of perception; I relate two sensations in my senses to one another. If I want it to be called a judgment of experience, I then require that this connection be subject to a condition that makes it universally valid. I want therefore that I, at every time, and also everyone else, would necessarily have to connect the same perceptions under the same circumstances. (4:299)

Kant's distinction between judgments of perception and judgments of experience needs to be taken with a lot of exegetical care, of course, and it is not clear that the combination of representations that Kant calls a "judgment of perception" in the *Prolegomena* would deserve the status of a "judgment" as Kant defines this term in the B edition of the *Critique of Pure Reason*. What seems to be clear, however, is that Kant was happy to allow uses of language by which we express mental contents and their combination in our minds without at the same time claiming their full objectivity.[28] In Kant's example above, I can use the sentence "The air is elastic" in order to characterize how I "relate two sensations in my senses to one another." A bit

[25] Cf. Grüne (2009, ch. 3).

[26] Prauss (1971, pp. 13ff.), Longuenesse (1998, p. 25), and Willaschek (2001b, pp. 682–83).

[27] Cf. *MSI* (2:394) and *FM* (20:269).

[28] It is plausible to combine this idea with a non-disjunctivist account of the content of perceptual experience according to which there is no fundamental difference between the content of veridical intuitions on the one hand and hallucinations and dreams on the other. Disjunctivist interpretations of Kant's account of perceptual experience have been defended by Willaschek (1997), Allais (2015), and McLear (2016), who all think that Kant takes intuitions to be object-dependent, and criticized by Stephenson (2015) and Grüne (2017). I side here with the latter and with the following quote from the *Prolegomena*: "The difference between truth and dream, however, is not decided through the quality of the representations that are referred to objects, for they are the same in both, but through their connection according to

earlier he writes that a judgment of perception expresses "only the logical connection of perceptions in a thinking subject" (4:298), which suggests that it is not only sensations but "perceptions" in general, i.e., conscious representations, that are connected in such judgments. Both passages make it clear that for Kant the linguistic expression of our mental contents is prior to that of the properties of extra-mental objects. This view is also explicitly expressed in the following passage:

> All of our judgments are first mere judgments of perception; they hold only for us, i.e., for our subject, and only afterwards do we give them a new relation, namely to an object, and intend that the judgment should also be valid at all times for us and for everybody else; for if a judgment agrees with an object, then all judgments of the same object must also agree with one another, and hence the objective validity of a judgment of experience signifies nothing other than its necessary universal validity. But also conversely, if we find cause to deem a judgment necessarily, universally valid [...], we must then also deem it objective, i.e., as expressing not merely a relation of a perception in a subject, but a property of an object; for there would be no reason why other judgments necessarily would have to agree with mine, if there were not the unity of the object – an object to which they all refer, with which they agree, and, for that reason, also must all harmonize among themselves. (4:298)

Let us apply what Kant says here to his case of a sentence by which we characterize something as elastic. At a first stage, this sentence is used to express a judgment of perception. At this stage, the predicate "elastic" expresses a conscious mental content which a subject can grasp and distinguish from others. This mental content can be characterized as an appearance in the sense defined above: it is fully grounded in the material and formal response of a subject to a given affecting object. In the case of the state expressed by "elastic," we might understand this response as a typical synthesized sequence of sensations of pressure, or as a typical synthesized sequence of intuited movements (e.g. movements as of a piston by which the air in a barrel is compressed[29]). The copula "is" in a judgment of perception expresses what Kant calls "mere subjective validity" (4:298): it states that something appears to me at a particular situation in a particular way, i.e., that I react to it by the mental state that I associate with the term "elastic" at this occasion. We can express this use of the copula in the following way:

(1_{JP}) x is_s elastic.
(1_{JP}*) x appears-elastic to me now.

Note that the notion of *appearing-elastic* is primitive in the sense explained above: It is not based on any prior introduction of a notion of elasticity as a property of extra-mental objects, i.e., we do not first grasp what elasticity is and then define a notion of appearing to be elastic on this basis. We know what "appearing-elastic" means by

the rules that determine the combination of representations in the concept of an object, and how far they can or cannot stand together in one experience" (4:290).

[29] Cf. Kant's remark on the elasticity of air in *MAN* (4:500).

associating it with a mental content with which we are acquainted in a first-personal way.[30]

The notion of objectively being elastic, which is expressed by making a judgment of experience, is then introduced on the basis of this primitive notion of appearing-elastic. We can also say: By making such a judgment, we determine an empirical object, i.e., a *phaenomenon*, on the basis of a mental content, i.e., of an appearance. As Kant makes clear, this is done by understanding the predication "x is elastic" as part of a judgment of experience, and that means by associating another meaning with the copula "is," one that expresses "objective validity" (4:298). In the quote above, Kant defines objective validity by means of two features. The first is universal validity: Objectively being elastic means not only to appear elastic to me at that particular situation, but to appear elastic to all human beings, or maybe rather to all subjects with a sensibility that has space and time as its a priori forms, who are confronted with the thing to which we ascribe elasticity. This feature of objectively valid predication can be expressed as follows:

(1_{JE}) x is_o elastic.
(1_{JE}#) x appears-elastic to all humans at all relevant occasions.

However, universality is not all there is to objective validity. The quotes from the *Prolegomena* reassure us of what we have already seen in section 3: Kant is not committed to a *reduction* of objectivity to universal coherence, but rather wants to say that in the case of a true judgment of experience, the universal coherence among the mental reactions of different subjects at different occasions points to, and is *explained* by, the fact that there is one common object that corresponds to all of these mental reactions as their common source. It is the object *x* of which we say that it is such that it appears similarly to all of us at all occasions and which we claim to be responsible for this harmony of appearances.

This brings us back to our attempt to understand Kantian appearance properties as response-dependent properties. For given the way in which we have introduced the notion of appearing, it is clear that this notion is a causal notion and that the formulation "x *is such that it appears*..." can be spelled out in causal terms in a way that brings out the interplay between response-independent properties (properties that the thing has in itself), and response-dependent properties (properties that have to do with the way the thing appears to subjects with a mental constitution similar to ours). I would like to suggest the following final reconstruction of the objective predication of elasticity:

(1_{JE}*) *x* has the (response-dependent) property of having some (response-independent) property that causes mental states with the content *appearing-elastic* in human beings at all relevant occasions.

[30] A347/B405, A353, and A354 offer textual evidence for the assumption that Kant took mental states such as the sensations and the process of ordering sensations, in which the mental content *appearing-elastic* is grounded, to be accessible only from a first-person point of view.

This reconstruction of judgments of experience, which could easily be expanded to our previous cases of being cubical or being red, nicely corresponds to our interpretation of Kant's use of the term "transcendental object" in the A edition of the First Critique above. The objects that enter the truth-conditions of judgments of experience play two theoretical roles in Kant's theory of cognition: First, they have the function to guarantee that all true judgments of experience cohere and that there is something like a universally intersubjectively shared way that the world appears to us. Second, they play the role of being the causal source of the appearing. This role is responsible for what is realistic about Kant's idealism. For it explains why it is not entirely up to us how exactly the world appears to us.[31]

Given the proposed reconstruction of judgments of experience, we can formulate the following general scheme for real definitions of properties of the form *objectively being F*, where "F" is an appearance-predicate:

> *Schema for real definition of being$_o$ F, where "F" is an appearance-predicate:*
>
> $\Box_{\text{objectively being F}}$ $\forall x$(x is$_o$ F $\leftrightarrow$ x has some property P such that x's having P causes mental states with the content appearing-F in humans).

The scheme reveals that in real definitions of appearance properties, it is not so much the sensible spatiotemporal content associated with the appearance-predicate "*F*" that is responsible for the response-dependence of the property, but rather what is expressed by the copula "is" when it is used in an objective predication that involves such an appearance-predicate.[32] This is important in order to meet an objection similar to the one that people have raised against dispositionalist conceptions of colors namely that colors "do not look dispositional."[33] Kant can agree that being cubical "does not look dispositional" in the sense that the sensible mental content that we associate with the predicate "cubical" presents us with a certain spatiotemporal manifold and not with the disposition to appear to us as this manifold. However, as the scheme shows, this is compatible with holding that objectively being cubical is a response-dependent property. Moreover, Kant can also accept that the biconditionals in the real definitions of appearance properties are not conceptual truths. This explains why he could use neither a Husserlian eidetic contemplation of spatiotemporal mental contents nor conceptual analysis in order to argue against the transcendental

[31] My interpretation bears a certain similarity, but also a strong contrast, to that of Oberst (2015). Oberst and I agree that there is a notion of appearance understood as mental content and a notion of an appearing object which also exists and has properties in itself. We disagree in that I identify the appearing object with the empirical object, or *phaenomenon*, whereas Oberst favors a phaenomenalist interpretation of *phaenomena* as purely mental items. It would go beyond the scope of this chapter to discuss Oberst's objections against identifying *phaenomena* with appearing objects, but I at least hope to have made a strong positive textual case in favor of doing so. It should also be noted that Oberst's concession to two-aspects readings does not help him with making room for empirical explanations of mental content. Although he could accept a similar definition to the one given in (1_{JE}*) for what he calls "appearing object," this "appearing object" is not the empirical object of which we have sensible cognition.

[32] This means that we can also understand the scheme as a real definition of *objective being* in the realm of appearances. I think that Kant's famous remark about the nature of judgment in §19 of the B-Deduction can be understood as a real definition in this sense (cf. B141–42).

[33] See Boghossian & Velleman (1989), Johnston (1992).

realist who takes spatiotemporal properties to be response-independent, but rather the intricate philosophical arguments that he provides for transcendental idealism.

Let us now come back to the central question of this chapter. In its final section I want to explore whether interpreting Kant's transcendental idealism as a claim about the distinction between response-dependent and response-independent properties allows us to make it compatible with an empirical as well as a noumenal explanation of the content of experience.

6. Explaining the Content of Experience by Means of the Objects of Experience

In section 1, I have said that an empirical explanation of the contents of experience explains these contents by means of the properties of empirical objects, whereas a noumenal explanation does the same by means of the properties of the noumenal sources of the experience. Given the results of sections 3, 4, and 5, we now see that these two kinds of explanation are much closer intertwined with one another than we might have originally thought. For, on the one hand, the empirical object of a certain episode of experience—i.e., the transcendental object as far as it is represented and determined by sensible representations if these have a certain coherence and order—*just is* the noumenal source of this episode—i.e., the transcendental object as far as it exists in itself. On the other hand, if our interpretation of appearance properties as response-dependent properties is correct, then ascribing an appearance property to an extra-mental object *just is* assuming of this object that there is a way it exists in itself (i.e., a response-independent property) that is partially causally responsible for the sensible representations we have of it, a result that fits very nicely what Kant explicitly says about the conceptual connection between the concept of an appearance and that of a thing in itself.[34] Hence, for Kant, an empirical explanation of the contents of experience is one that explains these contents by means of the response-dependent properties of objects, whereas a noumenal explanation accounts for them by means of the response-independent properties of the very same objects. And, given our proposal, it is easy to see that one cannot give the first kind of explanation without the second.

This still leaves us with the questions whether these two kinds of explanation are legitimate within Kant's transcendental idealism and whether they can meet the challenge that was set up in section 2. Before I try to provide an answer, I want to introduce a bit of terminology. First, let us call a causal explanation of some state *S* *specific* if it specifies a determinate state or property as the cause of *S*, and let us call it *unspecific* if it just says that there is some cause of *S* that belongs to some general kind. (A specific explanation of the movement of a billiard ball, for example, would involve a detailed description of the kinetic state of some other billiard ball that hit

[34] Cf. the quotes from A251–52 and B306 above. In the *Groundwork* Kant claims that even common sense, although maybe in an obscure way, grasps the insight that by our passive senses we only have access to the way things appear to us, and he then adds that it follows from this immediately (*von selbst*) that we have to assume that there are things in themselves beyond their appearance (4:450–51).

the first one, while an unspecific explanation would just say that the first ball moves the way it does because *some* other ball, or *some* other physical object, exerted *some* kinetic force on it.) Second, let us call an explanation *conceptually independent* if it characterizes the *explanans* completely independently of its role in the explanation. (A drastic case of an explanation that does not fulfill this criterion would be the claim that the billiard ball moves because the event that causes this movement has occurred. Although this claim is true and refers to one particular event as the *explanans*, we are not told anything about this event beyond the fact that it the cause of what we want to explain.) Finally, let us say that an explanation is *completely satisfactory* only if it is specific and conceptually independent.

We will see that what Kant can offer as an empirical as well as a noumenal explanation of mental content is not completely satisfactory in this sense. The standard examples of empirical explanations of mental content fail to be conceptually independent, although they are specific, and the kind of noumenal explanation that Kant assumes will turn out to be not even specific. However, we will see that these limitations on explanatory success are not an objection to Kant's theory. They still allow him to say everything about the external source of our knowledge that is reasonable for a transcendental idealist to say, and they provide him with a reply to the objection that claims about this external source contradict his own restrictions of the scope of our cognitive faculties. Or so I will argue in the following.

Let us start with empirical explanation. Assume again that a certain human being *A* perceives a cubical object in front of her. An ordinary empirical explanation of the content of *A*'s perception would read as follows: *A* perceives the object in front of her as cubical because this object is cubical. Within the framework of Kant's theory of cognition, the content of *A*'s perception can be expressed by means of the primitive notion of *appearing-cubical*, and objectively being cubical should be identified with the response-dependent property of being such as to bring about mental states with the content appearing-cubical in humans. Hence, within a Kantian framework, the empirical explanation of *A*'s mental content would have to be analyzed as follows:

(2) *A* is in a perceptual state with the content *appearing-cubical* because the object in front of *A* has the (response-dependent) property of having some (response-independent) property that causes mental states with the content *appearing-cubical* in humans.

Is Kant allowed to make a claim like this given his views about transcendental idealism?

The main obstacle for an empirical explanation of mental content within a phenomenalist interpretation was that we cannot explain contingent properties of mental states by contingent properties of merely intentional objects. This obstacle has disappeared. The fact that *A*'s mental state has the content it actually has is explained by the fact that a certain extra-mental object has a certain property, and it is true that if this object did not have this property (the property of being such that this elicits such-and-such mental effects in humans) then *A* would not have perceived what she actually perceives. We should also note that although the explaining extra-mental property is response-dependent, it is not entirely determined by *A*'s mental state (or by that of other subjects), but rather also by how the extra-mental object is constituted independently of any reaction to it. For as (2) makes evident, if the object had other response-independent properties than it actually has, then this might well result in the object no longer having the response-dependent properties mentioned in (2).

However, this last remark might give rise to the suspicion that it is not the response-dependent property that explains our mental reaction to the object but rather only the response-independent property that is mentioned in its definiens. For how can a property of an object that is defined by means of the response the object provokes in somebody feature in a causal explanation of that very response?[35] In the terminology introduced above: How can an explanation that lacks the feature of conceptual independence be legitimate at all? Is such an explanation not completely trivial, as trivial as the one from Molière's *The Imaginary Invalid* that opium induces sleep because it has a dormitive virtue?

No, it is not. To understand why, we have to see that there is an important distinction between the (a)- and (b)-parts of the following two pairs of explanations:

(3.a) Opium induces sleep because it has a sleep-inducing power.
(3.b) *A* falls asleep because she ate something with a sleep-inducing power.
(4.a) Fly agarics are poisonous for humans because they have some property that causes symptoms of intoxication in humans.
(4.b) *A* showed symptoms of intoxication because she ate something poisonous, i.e., something with a property that causes symptoms of intoxication in humans.

It is true that (3.a) and (4.a) are not causal explanations. The relation between their *explanandum* and their *explanans* is purely conceptual and the *explanans* seems not exclude any possibility that is not already ruled out by the truth of the *explanandum.* However, although (3.b) and (4.b) are also not conceptually independent, their *explanans does* rule out some such possibilities. The first thing we learn by these claims is that the causal source of a certain given reaction in *A* lies in a certain object that *A* has eaten (rather than in *A* herself, for example). The second thing we learn is that the causal source is a property that would bring about effects of the same kind in other humans in similar situations. Both claims go substantially beyond what we know when we know that someone falls asleep or shows symptoms of intoxication. Of course, (3.b) and (4.b) are not what I have called "completely satisfactory." We would be better off if we could refer to the cause of the human reaction by means of a conceptually independent (e.g. chemical) characterization. But as long as we do not have such a characterization, (3.b) and (4.b) are perfectly legitimate.

Now, the explanation given in (2) is like the ones given in (3.b) and (4.b) rather than those in (3.a) and (4.a). Although it is not completely conceptually independent, we learn something substantial by it. When we are told that *A* is in a perceptual state with the content *appearing-cubical* because the object she is confronted with has the (response-dependent) disposition to cause perceptual states with that content in humans, we learn that the causal source of *A*'s mental state is placed in an extra-mental object. And we learn that this extra-mental object would have similar mental

[35] This worry corresponds to Johnston's famous "missing explanation argument" against response-dependent account of manifest properties; see Johnston (1989, 1991) and the next footnote.

effects on other human beings so that the response-dependent properties mentioned in (2) are intersubjectively accessible. I think it is exactly these two features that allow empirical explanation of mental content to play the philosophical role Kant wants it to play within his theory of transcendental idealism. It allows him to make this form of idealism compatible with the realistic intuition by which I started this chapter: When we perceive things, our representational mental states have the contents they actually have partly because the perceived objects have the properties they actually have. And it allows him to conceive of the properties of empirical objects as intersubjectively accessible although they depend on our subjective responses to them. Of course, empirical explanations such as the one provided by (2) are not completely satisfactory. It would be more satisfying if we knew which response-independent properties of the object are causally responsible for our mental reaction to it. But given Kant's view that we cannot know how things are in themselves, i.e., we can never know any of their response-independent properties, these explanations are beyond our reach.[36]

The fact that explanations such as (2) are not completely satisfactory raises the question of whether the response-dependent properties mentioned in these claims can be understood as the *causes* of the mental effects by which they are defined. Until now, I was careful only to claim that these properties can feature in legitimate *causal explanations*, and it is a controversial matter whether everything that features as the *explanans* in a causal explanation is a *cause*. Helen Beebee, for one, argues that there are correct causal explanations where the *explanans* is not a cause. One of her examples is "Kennedy died because somebody shot him": although it is true that Kennedy would not have died if nobody had shot him, Kennedy's instantiation of the property "being shot by somebody" is not a cause because it is not a particular event at all. It is only *Oswald's* shooting of Kennedy that is a cause.[37]

One might want to take a similar stance towards the explanation given in (2). Although it seems true, for example, that *A* would not be in the mental state with the content *appearing-cubical* if the object in front of her did not have the (higher-order, response-dependent) property of having some (first-order, response-independent) property that causes mental states with this content in humans, one might have doubts that this counterfactual dependence makes the higher-order property itself a cause of *A*'s mental state and insist that only the first-order, response-independent

[36] My answer to the triviality objection is similar to Menzies and Pettit's response to Johnston's "missing explanation argument." Johnston (1989, 1991) argues that in order for redness to be response-dependent, the judgment "x is red iff x appears red to humans" would have to be a priori, and he thinks that this assumption is incompatible with the correctness of the causal explanation "Things appear red to standard subjects because they are red." Menzies & Pettit (1993) object that "x appears red to standard subjects" is ambiguous between a claim about the possession of a disposition and one about the manifestation of that disposition. The first reading is the one relevant for the biconditional in the definition of redness as response-dependent, whereas the second is relevant for the causal explanation, which can be understood as the unproblematic claim that, in the relevant cases, the manifestation occurs, i.e., standard subjects show a certain mental response, because the objects have the disposition to elicit this response. Johnston (1998) has offered a revised version of his missing explanation argument, which is built on problems of specifying in a non-trivial way who the standard subjects are. However, since this argument only works if we assume that the biconditional in the definition of the response-dependent property is a conceptual truth, it need not worry us here, because, as we have seen above, Kant would not share this assumption.

[37] Beebee (2004, pp. 302–303).

property could legitimately be called a cause of it. It is not easy to decide this issue. In the contemporary literature about dispositions there is an extensive debate about whether dispositions can and should be understood as the causes of their manifestations and what account of dispositions and of causal efficacy would imply or exclude this.[38] It is also not clear whether Kant's notion of a cause would allow for the dispositional property mentioned in (2) to be a cause. In his *Lectures on Metaphysics*, he distinguishes between two kinds of causes: the *causa efficiens*, which is "a cause by means of an efficacious force," and the *conditio sine qua non*, which is the real ground of the actuality of something although it lacks this efficacious force (28:571; see also *Reflexion* 3612, 17:96). The term used for the latter kind of cause suggests that counterfactual dependence might be sufficient for it and hence dispositions would be causes of their manifestations in the sense of a *conditio sine qua non*. However, Kant's own example for this kind of cause is of a rather different kind,[39] and it is not clear that he would be willing to apply his distinction in order to account for the different senses in which higher-order dispositions and their first-order categorical bases are causes. However, even if we are cautious here, this would still not speak against the proposed interpretation. Our aim was to account for the fact that we can *explain* the contents of our mental states by means of outer objects and their phenomenal properties. What is relevant for this task is the truth of (2), no matter whether we deny the *explanans* of (2) the status of a cause of its *explanandum* or not.[40]

Let us finally come to noumenal explanation of mental content. We have already seen that there is a conceptual connection between empirical and noumenal explanation because there is a conceptual connection between appearance properties of objects and properties that these objects have in themselves. To have a response-dependent appearance property just is to have some response-independent property that is characterized by its mental effect. Hence, explaining mental content by an appearance property implies that it is the causal result of some response-independent property. Paying attention to this conceptual connection between empirical and noumenal explanation of mental content allows us to understand why Kant refers to

[38] For a good overview see McKitrick (2005), who concludes that there is at least no compulsive reason to exclude that dispositions could be causes.

[39] His example is that of the firing of a cannon where the gunpowder is the *conditio sine qua non* and the soldier who lights the fuse is the *causa efficiens* (*V-Met-L_2/Pölitz*, 28:571).

[40] It should also be noted that the philosophical, "arm-chair" explanation (1) is not the only possible empirical explanation of mental content, but Kant's theory is at least in principle open for more informative, scientific empirical explanation of mental content. Such explanations could be given if we were able to identify a phenomenal property of an empirical object that is causally responsible for a certain mental reaction but which is not characterized by this very reaction. Now, there are passages in which Kant speaks of "the light" as the means by which we are affected and which is the cause of our sensations (cf. A28, A213/B260, and *OP*, 21:79; cf. *OP*, 22:434). These passages point in the direction of a psycho-physical explanation in which we explain the occurrence of particular sensations by the occurrence of particular physical properties as their causes, e.g. the occurrence of red-ish sensations as the effect of light with a particular wave-length (cf. also A226/B273; *OP*, 21:583, 22:551). It is not clear to me whether Kant himself thought that such psycho-physical explanations are ultimately possible. (Andrew Stephenson has pointed out to me that at least in the *Anthropology* (7:153–60), Kant pretty clearly aligns outer sense to a bodily faculty.) But if they were possible they would certainly be more informative than the one given in (1). The reason is that although for Kant a physical property such as wave-length would also be a response-dependent property, its connection with the occurrence of a particular color-sensation would not be conceptual in the sense in which the connection between a disposition and its manifestation is conceptual.

empirical objects as well as to things in themselves as the objects that affect our senses and to assume that this is much less mysterious than Adickes's talk about "Kant's doctrine of double affection" suggests.

The proposed interpretation also allows us to make Kant's assumptions about affection through things in themselves compatible with his claim of noumenal ignorance. For Kant took the conceptual connection between empirical and noumenal explanation of mental content to be the only means by which we have epistemic access to noumenal explanation and to the response-independent properties on which it is based. Unlike in the case of our analogy with fly agarics and opium where we can also inquire into the nature of the chemical properties that make them poisonous and soporific, the response-independent grounds of spatiotemporal appearance properties are in principle inaccessible for us—for the well-known reasons Kant gives in the *Critique*. That means that noumenal explanation of mental content is essentially unspecific in the sense explained above. We can know that objects have *some* response-independent properties that make it possible for them to appear to us, but we can never know *which* properties these are.

I think that this lack of specificity is the kernel of Kant's claim that we can never cognize things in themselves but rather only their appearances. Whereas we have access to specific response-dependent properties of objects—i.e., can reidentify and track them by means of the mental effects they have on us, can introduce concepts for them, can find out something about their relations to other response-dependent properties, etc.—we will never be able to cognize a single response-independent property and say anything determinate about it. Not only do we not know anything about the general nature of such properties, because we have no idea what properties that cannot be constructed in space and time are like; we cannot even know anything about their identity conditions under some very general description because for all we know the same reidentifiable response-dependent appearance property could be grounded in completely different response-independent properties.[41] To put it in Kantian terms: We only cognize the way that things appear to us, but do not cognize the way they are in themselves. And that is perfectly compatible with the fact that we do know that there is some way they are in themselves.

This last remark is the key to an answer to Jacobi's and Fichte's worries about noumenal affection. For it makes clear that Kant can make certain claims about the causal role of the way that things are in themselves while at the same time assuming that we do not have any knowledge of how things are in themselves. The assumption of unspecific noumenal explanation of mental content simply does not contradict noumenal ignorance.[42] Of course, there are ways to interpret Kant's claims about

[41] My explanation of noumenal ignorance nicely aligns with the one that Karl Schafer gives at the end of his contribution to this volume. Schafer points out that Kant does not want to exclude that we have some knowledge about things in themselves, but rather only that we have cognition of them, the conditions on which are more demanding than those on the former and include capacities of discrimination and reidentification. From what I have said it follows that we lack these capacities with respect to the first-order properties of things in themselves and hence lack cognition of them, or—in "two-aspect" parlance—do not cognize them as they are in themselves.

[42] In this respect the proposed interpretation seems to me to have an advantage over Allais's version of a realist interpretation of Kant's idealism. Allais (2015, p. 255) conceives of appearance properties as essentially relational properties and she thinks that Kant's commitment to things in themselves is based on

noumenal ignorance in a stronger way, a way that *would* bring them into conflict even with unspecific noumenal explanation. One can interpret Kant's claims about the legitimate use of the categories as implying that they must not be used in *any* statement about the way that things are in themselves, not even in the unspecific one that there is some such way and that this way makes a causal difference. And one can interpret Kant's overall philosophical project as one that is meant to rule out any kind of possible skepticism, also one about the existence of an extra-mental world,[43] and conclude from this that he could not have allowed placing the source of the contingent aspects of our mental contents in some extra-mental object but would rather have confined himself to claims about our mental life itself and the feeling of passivity by which it is sometimes accompanied.

Given the substantial textual evidence that not only "the Kantians" but also Kant himself believed in noumenal explanation of mental content, I do not think that these readings are a real exegetical option. It is much more compelling to interpret the passages on which these readings are based in a way that makes them compatible with noumenal explanation.[44] This noumenal explanation is just as intimately intertwined with the empirical explanation of mental content as is Kant's notion of an object that appears to us with the notion of this very object as it is in itself. And it is this strong connection that gives Kant's notion of an object of experience the realistic bite that the reader senses in the beginning paragraphs of the Transcendental Aesthetic. As interpreters we should not be worried that this realism makes refuting skepticism about the external world more difficult than Fichte might have hoped. After all, transcendental idealism was not introduced by Kant in order to refute skepticism about *every* kind of knowledge about objects of experience. It was rather

the assumption that "there cannot be relations all the way down; there must ultimately be intrinsic natures which ground powers." Jim Kreines (2016) has objected against this argument for the existence of things in themselves that it violates Kant's own denial of the validity of inference from the conditioned to the unconditioned—e.g. inferences from the existence of relational properties to that of absolutely intrinsic ones, or from dispositions to something absolutely categorical—at the beginning of the Transcendental Dialectic. Kreines's criticism seems to me perfectly legitimate as far as Allais's account is concerned, but it does not affect the interpretation proposed here. According to this interpretation, the assumption of things in themselves is not based on the principle of pure reason "If the conditioned is given, then so is the whole series of conditions [...], which is itself unconditioned," which Kant criticizes as unjustified because it is synthetic (A307–308/B364–65). It is rather based on an analytic entailment between the concept of an appearing object and the concept of this object as it is in itself (cf. A251–52 and B306), which we have interpreted as the relation between response-dependent properties and the response-independent properties whose existence is assumed in the real definition of the former. Now, it is important to stress that we need not understand these response-independent properties as something "absolutely intrinsic" or "absolutely non-dispositional." It is a conceptual truth that follows from the concept of causation as a synthetic relation that the response-independent properties over which we quantify in the real definition of the response-dependent properties have to be *independent of the response in question*. However, this does not imply that they have to be *response-independent in all respects*. To take again the analogy of being poisonous: That x is poisonous implies that x has some properties that cause intoxication, which, as causes, are response-independent in the sense that x could have them even if they did not cause such intoxication. However, it does not imply that these properties—chemical properties in this case—could not be dispositional or response-dependent in some other respect. Hence, according to my account, Kant's claim that things have to be somehow in themselves if there is a way they appear to us is perfectly compatible with assuming that in the world of things in themselves we have "turtles all the way down" (Kreines 2016, p. 255).

[43] See note 6 above.

[44] For a more detailed criticism and response to the Jacobi-Fichte understanding of noumenal ignorance see Rosefeldt (2013).

introduced in order to explain how we can know certain things about these objects a priori. What I hope to have shown in this chapter is that the explanation that Kant gives is compatible with the idea that we are confronted with a world that is independent of us and in many respects determines the way we experience it.[45]

References

Adickes, E. (1924). *Kant und das Ding an Sich*. Pan Verlag Rolf Heisse.

Adickes, E. (1929). *Kants Lehre von der doppelten Affektion unseres Ichs als Schlüssel zu seiner Erkenntnistheorie*. J. C. B. Mohr.

Allais, L. (2007). Kant's idealism and the secondary quality analogy. *Journal of the History of Philosophy*, *45*(3): 459–84.

Allais, L. (2015). *Manifest reality: Kant's idealism and his realism*. Oxford University Press.

Allison, H. (1994). *Kant's transcendental idealism*. Yale University Press.

Allison, H. (2004). *Kant's transcendental idealism* (Revised and enlarged edition). Yale University Press.

Beebee, H. (2004). Causing and nothingness. In J. Collins, N. Hall, & L. Paul (Eds.), *Causation and counterfactuals* (pp. 291–308). MIT Press.

Boghossian, P. & Velleman, D. (1989). Color as a secondary quality. *Mind*, *98*(389): 81–103.

Busse, R. (n.d.). *Transzendentalphilosophie als Metasemantik: Kants Transzendentaler Analytik ist eine Theorie der Konstitution der denkenden Bezugnahme auf reale Gegenstände*. Manuscript.

Collins, A. (1999). *Possible experience: Understanding Kant's Critique of Pure Reason*. University of California Press.

De Boer, K. (2014). Kant's multi-layered conception of things in themselves, transcendental objects, and monads. *Kant-Studien*, *105*(2): 221–60.

Dryer, D. P. (1966). *Kant's solution for verification in metaphysics*. Allen & Unwin.

Fichte, J. G. (1970). *Versuch einer neuen Darstellung der Wissenschaftslehre* (J. G. Fichte, *Gesamtausgabe der Bayerischen Akademie der Wissenschaften* (R. Lauth & H. Gliwitzky, Eds., vol. 1.4)). Frommann (original work published 1797–98).

Fine, K. (1994). Essence and modality. *Philosophical Perspectives*, *8*: 1–16.

Grüne, S. (2009). *Blinde Anschauung: Die Rolle von Begriffen in Kants Theorie sinnlicher Synthesis*. Klostermann.

Grüne, S. (2017). Are Kantian intuitions object-dependent? In A. Gomes & A. Stephenson (Eds.), *Kant, and the philosophy of mind: Perception, reason, and the self* (pp. 67–85). Oxford University Press.

Guyer, P. (1987). *Kant and the claims of knowledge*. Cambridge University Press.

[45] This paper was first presented at the Miami Kant Workshop in March 2014. An earlier version, which differs from the one here in the way in which the mental responses are characterized and does not contain the material from section 5, has been available online for some time under the title "Transcendental idealism and the a posteriori contents of experience." Many thanks to the participants at the Miami Workshop and especially to the editors of this volume and to Andrew Stephenson for their very helpful criticism and comments.

Haukioja, J. (2013). Different notions of response-dependence. In M. Hoeltje, B. Schnieder, & A. Steinberg (Eds.), *Varieties of dependence: Ontological dependence, grounding, supervenience, response-dependence* (pp. 167–90). Philosophia Verlag.

Jacobi, F. H. (2004). Ueber den transscendentalen Idealismus. In *Schriften zum transzendentalen Idealismus* (W. Jaeschke & I.-M. Piske, Eds.), Werke—Gesamtausgabe (K. Hammacher & W. Jaeschke, Eds.), vol. 2.1 (pp. 103–12). Felix Meiner Verlag (original work published 1785).

Jauernig, A. (2021). *The World According to Kant. Appearances and Things in Themselves in Critical Idealism*. Oxford University Press.

Johnston, M. (1989). Dispositional theories of value. *Proceedings of the Aristotelian Society, 63*: 139–74.

Johnston, M. (1991). Explanation, response-dependence and judgement-dependence. In P. Menzies (Ed.), *Response-dependent concepts* (pp. 122–83). ANU Working Papers in Philosophy 1. ANU Press.

Johnston, M. (1992). How to speak of the colours. *Philosophical Studies, 68*(3): 221–63.

Johnston, M. (1998). Are manifest qualities response-dependent? *The Monist, 81*(1): 3–43.

Karampatsou, M. (2022). *Der Streit um das Ding an sich: Systematische Analysen zur Rezeption des kantischen Idealismus 1781–1794*. De Gruyter.

Kreines, J. (2016). Things in themselves and metaphysical grounding: On Allais' manifest reality. *European Journal of Philosophy, 24*(1): 253–66.

Langton, R. (1998). *Kantian humility: Our ignorance of things in themselves*. Clarendon Press.

Leslie, S.-J. & Lerner, A. (2016). Generic generalizations. In E. N. Zalta (Ed.), *The Stanford Encyclopedia of Philosophy* (Winter 2016 Edition). https://plato.stanford.edu/archives/win2016/entries/generics/

Longuenesse, B. (1998). *Kant and the capacity to judge: Sensibility and discursivity in the Transcendental Analytic of the Critique of Pure Reason* (C. T. Wolfe, Trans.). Princeton University Press.

McKitrick, J. (2005). Are dispositions causally relevant? *Synthese, 144*(3): 357–71.

McLear, C. (2016). Kant on perceptual content. *Mind, 125*(497): 95–144.

Menzies, P. & Pettit, P. (1993). Found: The missing explanation. *Analysis*, 53(2): 100–109.

Oberst, M. (2015). Two worlds and two aspects. *Kantian Review, 20*(1): 53–75.

Peacocke, C. (1984). Colour concepts and colour experience. *Synthese, 58*: 365–81.

Pettit, P. (1991). Realism and response dependence. *Mind, 100*(4): 587–626.

Pettit, P. (1998). Noumenalism and response-dependence. *The Monist, 81*(1): 112–33.

Prauss, G. (1971). *Erscheinung: Ein Problem der Kritik der reinen Vernunft*. De Gruyter.

Prauss, G. (1974). *Kant und das Problem der Dinge an Sich*. Herbert Grundmann.

Prior, E. W., Pargetter, R., & Jackson, F. (1982). Three theses about dispositions. *American Philosophical Quarterly, 19*(3): 251–7.

Rosefeldt, T. (2007). Dinge an sich und sekundäre Qualitäten. In J. Stolzenberg (Ed.), *Kant in der Gegenwart* (pp. 167–209). De Gruyter.

Rosefeldt, T. (2013). Dinge an sich und der Außenweltskeptizismus: Über ein Missverständnis der frühen Kant-Rezeption. In D. Emundts (Ed.), *Self, world, and art: Metaphysical topics in Kant and Hegel* (pp. 221–60). De Gruyter.

Stang, N. (2015). Who's afraid of double affection? *Philosophers' Imprint, 15*: 1–28.

Stephenson, A. (2015). Kant on the object-dependence of intuition and hallucination. *The Philosophical Quarterly, 65*(260): 486–508.

Stephenson, A. (2016). Relationalism about perception vs. relationalism about perceptuals. *Kantian Review*, *21*(2): 293–302.

Van Cleve, J. (1999). *Problems from Kant*. Oxford University Press.

Velleman, D. (2009). Quality, primary/secondary. In J. Kim, E. Sosa, & G. Rosenkrantz (Eds.), *A companion to metaphysics* (2nd edition, pp. 524–26). Wiley-Blackwell.

Willaschek, M. (1997). Der transzendentale Idealismus und die Idealität von Raum und Zeit: Eine "lückenlose" Interpretation von Kants Beweis in der "Transzendentalen Ästhetik." *Zeitschrift für philosophische Forschung*, *51*: 537–64.

Willaschek, M. (2001a). Affektion und Kontingenz in Kants transzendentalem Idealismus. In Ralf Schumacher (Ed.), *Idealismus als Theorie der Repräsentation?* (pp. 211–31). Mentis.

Willaschek, M. (2001b). Die Mehrdeutigkeit der kantischen Unterscheidung zwischen Dingen an sich und Erscheinungen: Zur Debatte um Zwei-Aspekte- und Zwei-Welten-Interpretation des transzendentalen Idealismus. In V. Gerhard, R. P. Horstmann, & R. Schumacher (Eds.), *Akten des IX. Internationalen Kant-Kongresses* (vol. 2, pp. 679–90). De Gruyter.

2
Schopenhauer's Transcendental Aesthetic

Desmond Hogan

Schopenhauer's magnum opus, *The World as Will and Representation* (1966; hereafter abbreviated as *WWR*), opens with a confident affirmation of philosophical idealism: "'The world is my representation'; this is a truth valid with reference to every living and knowing being, though man alone can bring it into reflective, abstract consciousness. If he really does so, philosophical discernment has dawned on him" (*WWR* 1, p. 3). The work goes on to endorse a variety of idealism according to which space and time have no reality beyond the world of representation; both are "forms of knowledge, not qualities of the thing in itself" (*WWR* 1, p. 134). The *locus classicus* of this doctrine is of course the system of Immanuel Kant, regarded by Schopenhauer as "the most important phenomenon to have appeared in philosophy for two thousand years." He describes Kant's writings as producing an effect "very like that of an operation for cataract on a blind man," a fundamental change of view so profound that "it may be regarded as an intellectual rebirth." Unlike Berkeley or Malebranche, he maintains, Kant alone is competent to conquer the "inborn realism" arising from our "original disposition" (*WWR* 1, pp. xv, xxiii). This epiphany is occasioned especially by the Transcendental Aesthetic of the *Critique of Pure Reason*, a little chapter, "of such merit that it alone would be sufficient to immortalize Kant's name. Its proofs have such a complete power of conviction that I number its propositions among the incontestable truths" (*WWR* 1, p. 437).

This praise is striking, not only because Kant is hardly ever complimented for his mesmerizing prose and matchless clarity. A broad consensus across two centuries holds that the Transcendental Aesthetic's central argument for the idealist theory of space and time is a clear failure. Schopenhauer's positive appraisal is usually taken to indicate that he too simply overlooked the fatal objection to the argument. I wish to argue that Schopenhauer saw exactly why the classical invalidity objection was mistaken—that he praised Kant's argument for transcendental idealism because he understood it. We can use Schopenhauer's insight to arrive at a deeper understanding of one of the pivotal arguments of the Critical philosophy.

1. Misplaced Praise? The Classical Neglected Alternative Objection to Kant's Idealism

I begin with a spare outline of the Transcendental Aesthetic's central argument for transcendental idealism, adequate to bring out the force of the traditional invalidity charge. Kant's investigation of space and time begins with a simple question: "What

Desmond Hogan, *Schopenhauer's Transcendental Aesthetic* In: *The Sensible and Intelligible Worlds: New Essays on Kant's Metaphysics and Epistemology.* Edited by: Karl Schafer and Nicholas F. Stang, Oxford University Press. © Desmond Hogan 2022. DOI: 10.1093/oso/9780199688265.003.0003

are space and time?" The proposed space of possibilities includes three options: both are "real existences"; they are properties or relations of things, "but such as would remain even if [the things] were not intuited"; finally, they "belong only to the form of intuition, and therefore to the subjective constitution of our mind, apart from which they could not be ascribed to anything whatsoever" (B37–38).

The investigation attempts to make progress through the analysis of representations of space and time. Kant argues that both representations are a priori and condition all experience; further, both are immediate and singular "intuitions" rather than concepts, or mediate and general representations. He also claims that non-trivial a priori knowledge, exhibited in geometry and in an unspecified "general theory of motion," "flows" from the representations (B40–41, B49). For present purposes we can pass over Kant's defense of the intuitive and a priori character of representations of space and time, and grant for argument's sake his claim that a body of synthetic a priori knowledge flows from them. This knowledge is only possible, he continues, on the assumption that space and time are merely subjective forms of knowledge:

> How can there exist in the mind an outer intuition which precedes the objects themselves, and in which the concept of these objects can be determined a priori? Manifestly, not otherwise than in so far as the intuition has its seat in the subject *only*, as the formal character of the subject, in virtue of which, in being affected by objects, it obtains immediate representation, that is, intuition, of them. (B41)

The discussion that follows confirms Kant has returned to settle on the third of his initial proposals: his remarkable claim is not simply that space and time are a priori forms but that they are merely such forms, that neither has application to things in themselves. This conclusion he justifies in a few further lines:

> Space represents no property at all of any things in themselves nor any relation of them to each other [...]. For neither absolute nor relative determinations can be intuited prior to the existence of the things to which they pertain, thus [neither] can be intuited a priori. (A26/B42)
>
> Time is not something which exists of itself, or which inheres in things as an objective determination [...]. [Were it] a determination or order inhering in things themselves, it could not precede the objects as their condition, and be known and intuited a priori by means of synthetic propositions. (A32–33/B49)

What are we to make of this argument? Putting together Kant's claims, we might attempt to reconstruct the inference as follows:

(1) No (non-analytic) intrinsic or relational properties of things in themselves can be known a priori.

(2) Some spatial and temporal properties of objects of experience can be known a priori.

(TI) No spatial and temporal properties are intrinsic or relational properties of things in themselves.

The first premise is intended to capture Kant's denial of the possibility of non-analytic a priori knowledge of things in themselves. We have seen this is justified with the remark that "neither absolute [i.e. intrinsic] nor relational determinations of things in themselves can be intuited prior to the existence of the things to which they pertain" (*Weder absolute, noch relative Bestimmungen können vor dem Dasein der Dinge, welchen sie zukommen, mithin nicht a priori angeschaut werden*) (A26/B42); or again, "a determination or order inhering in things themselves [...] could not precede the objects as their condition, and be known and intuited a priori by means of synthetic propositions" (A32–33/B49). These somewhat usual formulations have been taken to express the straightforward idea that we can have no non-trivial knowledge of intrinsic or relational properties of mind-independent entities prior to knowing that these entities exist.[1] On the assumption that such existence itself could never be known a priori—i.e., "absolutely independently of all experience"[2]—it follows that we can have no non-trivial a priori knowledge of the constitution of wholly mind-independent entities.

The second premise records imputed a priori knowledge of spatial and temporal properties. Kant's denial of non-trivial a priori knowledge is limited to things in themselves; he holds that we do possess synthetic a priori knowledge of objects of experience, in geometry and in his general theory of motion. This knowledge is held to precede acquaintance with particular *empirical* objects, so that we can have it prior to encountering these or even knowing of their existence (cf. *Prol* §9, 4:282).

An immediate problem with the argument on this reconstruction is that it is invalid, with form, *No As are B, some Cs are B; therefore no Cs are A*. Less obvious is the ambiguity in its middle term. Its first premise was intended to record the claim that we cannot have non-trivial a priori knowledge of properties of things in themselves—i.e., as properties of those things. One may of course know properties of unknowable objects where ascription of these properties to those objects is not part of the knowledge claim.[3] However, the second premise states only that we can have a priori knowledge of properties as applying to objects of experience. Since the middle term shifts in meaning, we cannot conclude from the premises that *at least those Cs that are Bs are not A*—those spatial and temporal properties known a priori do not apply to things in themselves.

More generally, careful readers have struggled to see how any reformulation of Kant's premises regarding a priori knowledge *of objects of experience* and a priori ignorance *of things in themselves* could support his arresting idealist conclusion, now restated as if to underline its radical character: "If we remove our own subject or even only the subjective constitution of the senses in general, then all constitution, all relations of objects in space and time, indeed space and time themselves would *disappear*" (A42/B59). Neither can we evade this difficulty as Graham Bird (2006)

[1] See e.g. Vaihinger (1881–92, vol. 2, pp. 288, 297). Compare *Prol* §9, 4:282.

[2] "[W]e will understand under *a priori cognitions* in what follows not those that occur independently of this or that experience, but rather those that occur *absolutely* independently of all experience" (B2–3).

[3] E.g., I have knowledge of a property possessed by anything granite. A comet outside of my light-cone happens to be granite. I have knowledge of one of its properties, but not that it has that property.

has recently proposed, namely by glossing Kant as asserting only that, "on balance it is *more plausible* to say that [things in themselves] cannot be spatiotemporal than that they can" (p. 491). Kant's explicit conclusion, on the contrary, is that "it is not merely possible or probable, but *indubitably certain,* that space and time [...] are merely subjective conditions of all our intuition" (A48). This is something, he repeatedly insists, "against which not the least ground of uncertainty can be raised"; it is "no mere hypothesis," it is "demonstrated truth" (*Prol*, 4:289; *FM*, 20:267; Bxxiii).

The charge of invalidity just summarized is today associated with the famous nineteenth-century "neglected alternative" controversy between Adolf Trendelenburg and Kuno Fischer. In his original analysis of Kant's argument, Trendelenburg remarked: "Space and time are something subjective. What prevents them from also being something objective? Might they not perhaps be necessary for the mind because they are for things?" (1840, p. 128). The Aesthetic's argument from synthetic a priori knowledge, he insisted, contains nothing whatsoever to exclude this possibility. He later sharpened this to the charge that Kant "hardly considered the possibility" of correspondence between spatiotemporal features of objects of our experience and properties of things as they are wholly independent of the mind (Trendelenburg, 1870, vol. 1, p. 163; cf. Trendelenburg, 1867, pp. 225–30). Vaihinger's painstaking and influential analysis ultimately concurred: Kant's argument "effectively overlooked" the possibility of such agreement, partly due to "his greatest mistake–he never took it seriously" (Vaihinger, 1881–92, vol. 2, pp. 144, 150–51; cf. Smith, 2003, pp. 113–14).

This last claim is absurd. Kant argues for a radical theory of space and time he contrasts with two dominant realist views, a broadly Newtonian substantivalism and a realist version of relationism. He did not "fail to consider" that the realist theories he claims to refute might be right.[4] This point, however, leaves the main charge untouched; his argument looks like an abject failure. Vaihinger complains that its deficiency seems "so obvious, that it must occur to everyone who doesn't allow himself to be corrupted by transcendental-philosophical formulations" (1881–92, vol. 2, p. 311).

It would be hard to overstate the influence of this problem on the course of Kant studies since the nineteenth century. Faced with the invalidity objection, many readers have seen no alternative to reading Kant's central argument for idealism as guilty of a blunder. This verdict is apparently strengthened by the certainty claimed for its conclusion, since this looks flatly incompatible with his own further thesis that things in themselves are not only unknowable a priori, they "cannot be known at all" (A30/B45). Indeed this last tension provides a key motivation for the Vaihinger–Kemp Smith "patchwork" interpretation of the *Critique of Pure Reason* as a whole—on which the work is an inconsistent hotchpotch of properly critical epistemology and "paleontological leftovers" of a youthful dogmatism.

A principle of charity has led other readers to attempt deflationary glosses of Kant's idealism. Faced with the obvious deficiency of the argument on the traditional

[4] Kant canvasses an objection to his own theory due to Lambert and Mendelssohn, whom he regards as the finest German philosophers of his day (A36–37/B53; cf. *Br*, 10:103ff., 113ff., 10:133–34).

reading, some have defended the notion that the Transcendental Aesthetic didn't actually mean to deny the mind-independent reality of space and time.[5]

2. A Mystery Deepens: G. E. Schulze's Anticipation of the Neglected Alternative Objection

Where does Schopenhauer stand on this famous problem? His praise for the Transcendental Aesthetic's "complete power of conviction" rules out attribution of an interpretation of Kant's argument as invalid (*WWR* 1, p. 437). Janaway has sought to shield him from the charge of overlooking the standard invalidity objection by attributing a deflationary reading of Kantian idealism. This proposal is however misguided. As the Marburg neo-Kantians rightly emphasized, Schopenhauer counts historically as the foremost advocate of a plain metaphysical reading of Kant's idealism.[6] He always presents Kant's position as the straightforward metaphysical doctrine that neither space nor time belongs to the ultimate constitution of things:

> The inner meaning of Kant's great doctrine [...] is that space, time and causality belong not to the thing in itself but only to the phenomenon, that they are only the forms of our knowledge, not qualities of the thing in itself. (*WWR* 1, p. 134; cf. p. 434)
>
> The real side [of the world] must be something *toto genere* different from the world as representation, namely that which things are in themselves; and it is this *complete diversity between the ideal and the real* that Kant has demonstrated most thoroughly. (*WWR* 2, p. 193)

Might Schopenhauer then have simply overlooked the classical objection to Kant's argument? Trendelenburg first published his invalidity charge in 1840. As Shapshay has recently reminded us, the controversy with Fischer broke out in earnest only after Schopenhauer's death. Guyer and McDermid suggest that Schopenhauer simply "took for granted" the correctness of the argument's objectionable step from a priority to subjectivity.[7] Indeed there is no doubt that Schopenhauer presents this problematic step as a philosophical triumph. He writes:

[5] The deflationary approach is seen already in Kuno Fischer, mocked by Vaihinger for presenting Kant's doctrine of the empirical reality of space and time as proof he did not endorse the non-spatiotemporality of things in themselves. According to the version offered by the Marburg neo-Kantian Hermann Cohen, Kant's assertion of the non-spatiotemporal nature of things in themselves merely communicates that space and time have a necessary relation to an experience in which thought plays a constitutive role; see Cohen (1871). For more recent variations, see Bird (1962), Prauss (1974), and Allison (1976); also, Allison (1983).

[6] See Janaway (1989), and contrast Cassirer (1912, p. 269). See also Vaihinger (1881–92, vol. 2, p. 504).

[7] See Guyer (1999, p. 106) and McDermid (2003, p. 78); compare Vaihinger (1881–92, vol. 2, p. 327). Janaway (1989, p. 141) speaks of Schopenhauer's 'complacency' about his idealist 'starting point', while Hamlyn (1985, p. 66) describes *WWR* book 1 as affirming transcendental idealism without substantial argument. Schopenhauer does write that, "No truth is more certain, more independent of all others, and less in need of proof than this, namely that everything that exists for knowledge, and hence the whole of this world, is only object in relation to the subject, perception of the perceiver, in a word, representation" (*WWR* 1, p. 3); also, "'The world is my representation' is, like the axioms of Euclid, a proposition which everyone must recognize as true as soon as he understands it, although it is not a proposition that everyone understands as soon as he hears it" (*WWR* 2, p. 3).

> By pointing out the transcendental principles through which we are able to determine a priori, in other words, prior to all experience, something about objects and their possibility, [Kant] proved that, independently of our knowledge, these things cannot exist just as they present themselves to us. (*Fourfold Root* #12, p. 29)

The claim is repeated elsewhere:

> A world that presents itself by virtue of a priori forms is precisely on that account a *mere* phenomenon. Therefore what holds good of the world merely in consequence of those very forms, cannot be applied to the world itself, in other words, to the thing-in-itself that manifests itself in the world. (*Fourfold Root* #52, pp. 232–33)
>
> From the fact that we can of ourselves state and define the laws of relations in space, without needing experience to do so, Plato inferred that all learning is merely a recollecting. Kant, on the contrary, inferred that space is subjectively conditioned, and is *merely* a form of the faculty of knowledge. How far, in this respect, Kant stands above Plato! (*WWR* 2, ch. 4, p. 32)

These passages appear to lend support to the Guyer–McDermid suggestion that the controversial character of Kant's step from a priority to mere subjectivity is simply overlooked. However, attention to Schopenhauer's intellectual development allows us to rule out such a reading. His early studies already presented him with a lucid statement of what is today known as Trendelenburg's objection. As he explains in an 1851 letter to Erdmann (Schopenhauer, 1893, p. 331), it was G. E. Schulze who first "awakened him to philosophy" in lectures delivered at Göttingen in 1808–1809. Schopenhauer reminds Erdmann that this teacher authored the famous *Aenesidemus*, an anti-Kant polemic of historical significance appearing anonymously in 1792. In *Aenesidemus* we find the Aesthetic's argument from synthetic a priori knowledge to transcendental idealism represented as follows:

> There is only one possible way to think and represent how intuitions and concepts preceding the actuality of objects can be referred to these objects, namely if the intuitions and concepts contain *nothing but* the forms of knowledge of an actual object, which precede in my subject all actual influences through which I am affected by objects:
>
> **Therefore**, the intuitions and concepts a priori present in us really contain and are *nothing but* the forms of knowledge of experience, etc. (Schulze, 1792, p. 151)

Schulze goes on to attack this argument along two fronts. First, it seeks illegitimately to "elucidate objective being from subjective thinking." This is a clever attempt to turn against Kant his own epistemological critique of Christian A. Crusius, an older contemporary who claimed to derive transcendent cognition from supposedly reliable "thinkability" constraints basic to our cognitive make-up.[8] Schulze adds to this

[8] *Prol*, 4:319n; B167; *Log*, 9:21; *Br*, 10:131 (cf. Crusius, 1745, §33, §206) (*V-Met/Schön*, 28:468; *V-Lo/Blomberg*, 24:37, 24:82; *Refl* 4446). Schulze was in all likelihood well acquainted with Crusius's thought; his teacher F. V. Reinhard had been a student of Crusius's nephew and disciple C. F. Schmid; see Wundt (1945, p. 296).

first objection that the premise of the reconstructed argument is false, since it overlooks a possible *pre-established harmony* of representational forms and mind-independent reality:

> Through such pre-established harmony, the mind would represent through a priori intuitions and concepts something which does not have *mere* subjective validity [...] but which corresponds with and represents properties of the thing in itself. *The hypothesis of such a pre-established harmony does not contain anything absurd or unthinkable.* (Schulze, 1792, p. 151)

This objection is repeated in Schulze's major two-volume work, *Kritik der theoretischen Philosophie* (1801), which includes extensive commentary on the critical philosophy (pp. 223–26). Schopenhauer knows and cites both works.[9]

His own writings thus present as completely self-evident an inference from a priority to subjectivity carefully scrutinized and explicitly rejected by his own teacher, who he yet presents as one of Kant's most astute critics. The plot thickens when we add Schopenhauer's objection to what he refers to as Kant's deduction of the existence of thing in themselves as the causal ground of representations. The inadmissibility of this derivation, he writes, was "demonstrated in detail by G. E. Schulze in *Aenesidemus*, and soon recognized as the untenable point in [Kant's] system." According to this charge,

> Kant bases the assumption of the thing-in-itself, although concealed under many different turns of expression, on a conclusion according to the law of causality, namely that empirical perception [...] must have an external cause. Now, by his own correct discovery, the law of causality is known to us a priori, and consequently is a function of our intellect, and so is of subjective origin. Moreover, sensation itself [...] is undeniably subjective; and finally, even space [...] is a form of our intellect given a priori, and is consequently subjective. Therefore the whole of empirical perception remains throughout on a subjective foundation [...] and nothing entirely different and independent of it can be brought in as thing-in-itself, or shown to be a necessary assumption. (*WWR* 1, p. 436)

The passage suggests that Schopenhauer views Kant as lacking an acceptable derivation of the very existence of the thing in itself. If this is true, we may wonder how the Aesthetic's argument for its non-spatiotemporal character could deserve the praise he lavishes on it.

3. Shapshay's Solution

In an important paper seeking to illuminate Schopenhauer's view of Trendelenburg's objection, Sandra Shapshay (2011) has recently noted that he does occasionally entertain in more detail the kind of mind–world agreement the Transcendental

[9] See e.g. *WWR* 1, p. 459. On Schopenhauer's relation to Schulze, see Fischer (1901).

Aesthetic's argument is charged with failing to exclude. One passage curtly dismisses a Leibnizian version of such correspondence:

> [Leibniz] assumed a world of objects in themselves just like, and running parallel to, the world of the representation, and yet connected therewith not directly, but only outwardly by means of a *harmonia praeestabilita*. This is clearly the most superfluous thing on earth, for it never enters perception, and the exactly similar world of representation pursues its own course without it. (*Fourfold Root* #19, p. 51)

Leibniz has familiar arguments for his system of pre-established harmony, which he thinks demand that this be regarded as "more than a hypothesis" (*plus qu'une hypothèse*) (G IV 486). We have seen that Schulze's objection also appealed to a possible pre-established harmony of mind and world, though he hardly intended Leibniz's full-fledged version. The Aesthetic's argument for idealism fails, after all, if its premises are consistent with the much weaker proposition that space and time as represented correspond to the order of things wholly independent of the knowing mind. Since Schopenhauer's superfluity charge does nothing to rule out such consistency, it certainly cannot establish Kant's subjectivity thesis as "incontestable truth" (*WWR* 1, p. 437).[10]

The second volume of *The World as Will and Representation* offers more extensive discussion of the rejected correspondence hypothesis. Its first chapter, "On the Fundamental View of Idealism," argues that perfect agreement between what is known a priori of space and time and the objective order would be "absurd enough." For this knowledge allows us to "state beforehand most minutely and accurately the full conformity to law of all the relations in that [subjective] space [and time] which are possible and not yet actual, [without needing] to examine them first" (*WWR* 2, p. 9). The charge here is thus that the envisaged agreement would be, as Shapshay puts it, a "bizarre coincidence" (2011, p. 337). Even conceding this controversial claim, it again falls short of closing the perceived gap in the Aesthetic's argument.

Schopenhauer adds as an additional consideration that the hypothesis of a world of objects without knowing subject, "carries a contradiction within itself" insofar as any attempt to "realize this abstract thought" reveals that we are "imagining the opposite of what we intended, namely nothing but just the process in the intellect of a knowing being who perceives an objective world" (*WWR* 2, p. 5). This is a self-conscious appeal to the Berkeleyan principle that it is inconceivable for a body to "exist otherwise than in a mind perceiving it."[11] While this principle plays an important role in Schopenhauer's own system, it cannot explain his praise for the argument of the Transcendental Aesthetic. For he also writes that Kant failed to do justice to Berkeley on this very point:

[10] Leibniz, *New System of Nature*, G IV 486. As Vaihinger puts it in discussing the Transcendental Aesthetic's exclusion of a harmony of a priori forms and real order: "We want to concede that [such agreement] violates the *lex parsimoniae* in nature, but we may at least demand that the author does not treat as *unassailable premise* something which has at best *some probability*" (1881–92, vol. 2, p. 289).

[11] Berkeley, *Principles of Human Knowledge* §22 (2009, p. 91).

> It is certainly remarkable that [Kant] did not trace that merely relative existence of the phenomenon from the simple, undeniable truth which lay so near to him, namely, 'no object without a subject', in order thus, at the very root, to show that the object, because it always exists only in relation to a subject, is dependent thereon, is conditioned thereby, and is therefore mere phenomenon that does not exist in itself, does not exist unconditionally. Berkeley, to whose merit Kant does not do justice, had already made that important proposition the foundation stone of his philosophy, and had thus created an immortal reputation for himself. (*WWR* 1, p. 434)

Now according to Shapshay's main proposal, Schopenhauer does nevertheless trace Kant's deepest response to the neglected alternative objection to another Berkeley-style principle—namely, the principle that "properties belonging to a representation in virtue of its character as representation cannot 'resemble' or 'be similar to' the properties in the object which excite the representation" (Shapshay, 2011, p. 327). This principle Shapshay imputes to Kant on the basis of *Prolegomena* §13, in which he writes that he can "attach no sense" to the proposal that the "representation of space is fully similar to the object" (*Prol*, 4:290).

I do not think that this proposal can explain Kant's own argument for idealism or Schopenhauer's praise of it. For firstly, it does not seem to me that Kant argues from the imputed principle, or from its Berkeleyan original that "nothing can be like a sensation or idea but another sensation or idea."[12] Indeed *Prolegomena* §13 constitutes part of his response to the Garve-Feder review's charge of Berkeleyanism, directed against the first edition of the *Critique of Pure Reason*. Kant's reply includes the claim that his own idealism was not meant to cast doubt on the existence of a wholly mind-independent realm, which, he adds, "it never even occurred to me to doubt" (4:293).[13] His is rather a "merely formal" idealism that assumes mind-independent existents while "for weighty reasons" extending Locke's doctrine of the mind-dependence of represented features beyond classical secondary qualities to the *primaria*, "extension, place and more generally space along with everything that depends on it" (*Prol*, 4:289). Kant's own reference here to his "weighty reasons" is naturally read as pointing to the summary just a few paragraphs earlier of the Aesthetic's argument from synthetic a priori knowledge (*Prol*, 4:287–88). His subsequent claim that he can "attach no sense" to correspondence between representations of space and time and features of things in themselves then reads as mere recapitulation of the Aesthetic's conclusion. It is not an independent argument from a Berkeley-style likeness principle.

Even if one contests this reading of Kant, it is hard to deny that Schopenhauer accepts it. He explicitly discusses *Prolegomena* §13 as providing vital insight into origins of Kant's idealism. He claims that it reveals this idealism as an extension of Locke's project, itself "merely a youthful prelude" to Kant's own:

[12] Berkeley, *Three Dialogues between Hylas and Philonous* (2009, p. 189). Here I agree with Allen Wood (2005, p. 69) that Kant does not accept as an independent path to idealism Berkeley's denial that we can intelligibly think a sensible thing as it might exist apart from being sensed.

[13] See also Kant's 1792 letter to J. S. Beck, *Br* 11:395; *Refl* 6316.

> Starting from an incomparably higher standpoint, Kant explains all that Locke had admitted as *qualitates primariae*, that is as qualities of the thing in itself, as also belonging merely to its phenomenon in our faculty of perception or apprehension, and this *precisely because* [*zwar gerade deshalb*] the conditions of this faculty, namely space, time and causality, are known by us a priori. (*WWR* 1, p. 418)

This "precisely because" indicates that Schopenhauer does not read *Prolegomena* §13 as closing the perceived gap in the Aesthetic's argument with a Berkeleyan likeness principle, even if he himself endorses the principle. This underlines the more general point that while Schopenhauer expresses great sympathy for many arguments in support of idealism, his praise of Kant's insight is always directed to the Transcendental Aesthetic's argument from synthetic a priori knowledge. Berkeleyan principles play no role in the Aesthetic, and indeed Schopenhauer notes the B edition's declaration that it is "directly opposed to Berkeley's idealism" (*WWR* 1, p. 435).[14] The problem posed by his insistence on the Transcendental Aesthetic's "complete power of conviction" thus remains.

4. "The Meaning of the *Critique of Pure Reason*": Space and Time as Forms of a Restricted PSR

Schopenhauer's failure to provide clear justification for his praise for the Transcendental Aesthetic has left him open to the charge of overlooking a gap supposedly neglected by Kant himself. On the other hand, the neglect charge is difficult to square with his familiarity with Schulze's incisive formulation of the gap objection and explicit rejection of the mind–world harmony hypothesis.

The solution, as I will argue, is to be found in Schopenhauer's belief that we can map one of his own primary justifications for the ideality of space and time onto a basic philosophical idea underlying the *Critique of Pure Reason* as a whole. The conjunction of two thoughts will do the crucial work. The first is an association of space and time with the Principle of Sufficient Reason (PSR):

> What the thing in itself might be, Kant rightly concluded that time, space and causality (which we later recognized as *forms of the principle of sufficient reason*, this principle being the universal expression of the forms of the phenomenon) could not be its properties, but could come to it only after, and in so far as, it had become representation or appearance, not to it itself. (*WWR* 1, p. 120)

[14] Schopenhauer does express "great joy" on finding something like a "no object without subject" principle in the A-Paralogisms' view of empirical objects as a species of our representations: "I found that, although Kant does not use the formula 'no object without subject', he nevertheless, with just as much emphasis as do Berkeley and I, declares the external world lying before us in space and time to be mere representation of the subject that knows it. Thus, for example, he says there without reserve: 'If I take away the thinking subject, the whole material world must cease to exist, as it is nothing but the phenomenon in the sensibility of our subject, and a species of its representations'" (*WWR* 1, p. 435). Given Schopenhauer's reading of *Prolegomena* 13 and his claim that Kant failed to do justice to Berkeley, we must read him as holding that the Paralogisms chapter doctrine of idealism is justified by the Transcendental Aesthetic.

The second premise is Schopenhauer's claim that the PSR does not apply to things in themselves. This is now held to demand a corresponding restriction of space and time to mere forms of the phenomenon. The key point is expressed in an important passage attacking another of his teachers, J. G. Fichte:

> If Fichte had penetrated only to some extent the meaning of the *Critique of Pure Reason*, the book that made him a philosopher, he would have understood that its principle teaching was in spirit as follows. The PSR is not, as all scholastic philosophy asserts, a *veritas aeterna*; in other words, it does not possess an unconditioned validity before, outside, and above the world, but only a relative and conditioned one, valid only in the phenomenon. Therefore the inner nature of the world, the thing-in-itself, can never be found on the guiding line of this principle, but everything to which it leads is always itself also dependent and relative, always only phenomenon, not thing-in-itself. Further, this principle does not concern the subject, but is only the form of objects, which are for this very reason not thing-in-themselves. (*WWR* 1, p. 32)

In what follows I will briefly explore these two strands of Schopenhauer's argument for idealism, before attempting to map them onto Kant's discussion in the Transcendental Aesthetic.

Consider first Schopenhauer's claim that the PSR governs all phenomena through its association with representations of space and time. In its Leibnizian version, the PSR states that there is "no true or existent fact, no true assertion, without there being a sufficient reason why it is thus and not otherwise" (*Monadology* §32, G VI.611; AG 217). Schopenhauer sees in this principle the common expression of four kinds of necessitation or grounding relation falling under a priori laws that govern the realm of representation.

The first of these laws governs the class of what he calls intuitive, perceptive, empirical representations, where it takes the form of the causal principle (*principium rationis sufficientis fiendi*). In Schopenhauer's version, this law requires that, "if a new state of one or several real objects appears, another state must have preceded it upon which the new state follows regularly" (*Fourfold Root* #20, p. 53).

In its second manifestation, the PSR governs true judgments in the form of the *principium rationis sufficientis cognoscendi*. This requires that "if a judgment is to express a piece of knowledge, it must have a sufficient ground or reason (*Grund*) by virtue of this it receives the predicate true. Truth is therefore the reference of a judgment to something different" (*Fourfold Root* #29, p. 156).

The third form concerns the formal (as opposed to material) part of intuitive representations as *principium rationis sufficientis essendi*, the law in accordance with which the parts of space and time determine one another reciprocally with respect to position and succession (*Fourfold Root* #36, p. 194). The usual example here is the determination of the equality of the angles of a triangle by the equality of its sides and vice versa, a relation Schopenhauer regards as a variety of grounding distinct from that of causality.

Applied finally to the subject of willing, the PSR takes the form of the law of motivation. It requires that any decision be "preceded by something from which it ensued, and which we call the ground or reason, or more accurately the motive, of the resultant action" (*Fourfold Root* #43, p. 212).

Schopenhauer claims that these four laws are all expressions of the PSR, and all are known a priori. They are not reducible to each other, or to any other grounding relation. In this sense he rejects the doctrine of a "unity" of metaphysical grounding as it is debated in the current metaphysics literature.[15] He holds in addition that all necessity is rooted in one or a combination of these forms of the PSR. On this view, all necessity is conditioned; absolute or unconditioned necessity he rejects as incoherent:

> For necessity has no true and clear meaning except that of the inevitability of the consequent with the positing of the ground. (*Fourfold Root* #49, p. 225)

On this last point Schopenhauer departs from Kant, who holds that if God exists it must be by an unconditioned necessity we cannot understand in principle precisely because it is unconditioned. Unlike Schopenhauer, Kant does not believe that we can infer the impossibility of unconditioned necessity. On the contrary, he views divine necessity both as an "abyss" for reason and a positive counterexample to Leibniz's unrestricted PSR.[16]

Schopenhauer combines his fourfold analysis of the PSR with a conception of scientific knowledge he traces to Aristotle's *Posterior Analytics*. While empirical observation can reveal that something is the case, science seeks to show why it is so. This demand is seen as fully met only by knowledge exhibiting a sense in which the *explanandum* must be the case. Both Leibniz and Kant share this traditional conception of scientific knowledge.[17] Since the necessity at issue in scientific knowledge can only be known a priori, and since on Schopenhauer's view one or other version of the PSR must underwrite all necessity, he concludes that the PSR stands at the root of all science.

> [Science] signifies a *system* of notions, in other words, a totality of connected, as opposed to a mere aggregate of disconnected, notions. But what else except the principle of sufficient reason unites the links of a system?
>
> (*Fourfold Root* #4, p. 5, cf. #6, p. 11)

The PSR is thus presented as a principle of connection. Schopenhauer's description of space and time as "forms of the PSR" does not envisage any reduction of the PSR in all its varieties to space and time; it rather reflects his position that the necessary connections grasped in mathematics and natural science are rooted in a priori

[15] For a recent defense of such reducibility, see Berker (n.d.).

[16] "[The PSR] taken in the unlimited universality in which it there stands [in Leibniz], is obviously *false* if applied to entities; for according to this principle there could be absolutely nothing unconditioned. To seek, however, to avoid this embarrassing consequence by saying of a supreme being that he has, indeed, a reason for his existence, but that it lies within himself, leads to a contradiction" (*ÜE*, 8:198; A613/B641).

[17] Leibniz, *Monadology* §28 (1989, pp. 80, 406); Christian Wolff (1720, §372). Kant sometimes speaks of purely empirical as well as rational sciences, but holds that only the latter are really deserving of the name—"all genuine natural science requires a pure [a priori] part, on which the apodictic certainty sought by reason can be grounded" (*MAN*, 4:468–69; *Log*, 9:70–71).

insight into space and time (*WWR* 1, p. 66). We have encountered Kant's claim in the Transcendental Aesthetic that "time and space are [...] two sources of knowledge from which bodies of a priori synthetic knowledge can be derived" (A38–39/B55). Schopenhauer develops this doctrine in a chapter of *WWR* book 2 titled "On Knowledge A Priori." It presents twenty-eight axioms or basic truths supposedly known a priori about space, time and matter respectively. These include the PSR of being and becoming, where the former is rooted in insight into the form of space. The latter now has two versions: an abstract principle concerns conditioning of later by earlier states, while a concrete version governs changes in matter. In this way, insight into forms of space and time is thought to ground a priori knowledge of matter, including its "space-occupation, i.e. impenetrability, i.e. effectiveness, then extension, infinite divisibility, persistence, i.e. indestructibility, and finally mobility" (*WWR* 1, p. 11; cf. bk. 2, pp. 48–51).

This brief discussion suffices to explain the basic sense in which Schopenhauer regards space and time as "forms of the PSR" (*WWR* 1, p. 120). While Kant doesn't articulate the PSR in precisely this way, his writings include analogues of Schopenhauer's forms of the principle.[18] The critical epistemology presents all synthetic a priori knowledge as rooted in a priori representations of space and time. Schopenhauer's theory of space and time as forms of the PSR is best read as an attempt at detailed articulation of this central doctrine of the critical epistemology, and of its relation to Kant's claim that the "principle of sufficient reason is the ground of possible experience" (A201/B246).[19]

5. The Real Inner Nature of Things: Thing in Itself as Absolutely Inexplicable

Schopenhauer's conclusion that space and time are *mere* forms of the phenomenon rests on the above theory of space and time combined with a restriction of the PSR. Crucially this restriction is not epistemic: it is not the claim that we cannot know the PSR to hold beyond experience, but the unabashedly metaphysical doctrine that it does not hold unrestrictedly. This finds many expressions, including the following passages:

> The PSR is not, as all scholastic philosophy asserts, a *veritas aeterna*; in other words, it does not possess an unconditioned validity before, outside, and above the world, but only a relative and conditioned one, valid only for the phenomenon. (*WWR* 1, p. 32)

[18] Schopenhauer is officially critical of Kant's "reciprocal action" or *Wechselwirkung*, presented as production of causes by their effects (*WWR* 1, pp. 459–62). However, he admits a reciprocal grounding relation governed by the *PSR essendi*. His notebooks reveal excitement on finding this anticipated in Crusius's notion of "existential ground"—likely also an inspiration for Kant's *Wechselwirkung*. See Schopenhauer (1988, p. 327).

[19] Kant's theory of time-determination claims to derive the PSR understood as the causal principle from an a priori feature of the time-series. "Now if it is a necessary law of our sensibility, thus a formal condition of all perceptions, that the preceding time necessarily determines the following time (in that I cannot arrive at the following time except by passing through the preceding one), then it is also an indispensable law of the empirical representation of the temporal series that the appearances of the past time determine every existence in the following time" (A199/B244).

> The thing in itself is [...] absolutely inexplicable. (*WWR* 1, p. 81)
>
> There can be no principle in consequence of which the world with all its phenomena would first of all exist; therefore it is not possible, as Spinoza wished, to deduce a philosophy that demonstrates *ex firmis principiis*. (*WWR* 1, p. 82)
>
> If I abstract from my character, and then ask why in general I will this and not that, no answer is possible, because only the appearance or phenomenon of the will is subject to the PSR, not the will itself, which in this respect may be called groundless. Here I in part presuppose Kant's doctrine of the empirical and intelligible characters. (*WWR* 1, p. 106)
>
> [In Leibniz's *Radical Origination of All Things*] the origin and excellent nature of the world are demonstrated a priori in the realistic-dogmatic manner [using] the *veritates aeternae*. It is admitted that experience shows the very opposite [...] whereupon experience is told that it doesn't understand anything about it and should hold its tongue when philosophy has spoken *a priori*. (*WWR* 1, p. 421)

It will be helpful to rehearse how Schopenhauer thinks to establish this restriction. He sets out from the idea that insight into the inner nature of things is possible if "we refer the whole world of phenomena to that one in which the thing-in-itself is manifested under the lightest of all veils" (*WWR* 2, p. 197). This he famously finds in the experience of our own body, which is known not only as represented object, but from the first-person perspective of beings rooted in the world they seek to understand:

> [S]omething in the consciousness of everyone distinguishes the representation of his own [the knowing subject's] body from all others that are in other respects quite like it. This is that the body occurs in consciousness in quite another way, *toto genere* different, that is denoted by the word *will*. It is just this double knowledge of our own body which gives us information about that body itself, about its action and movement following on motives, as well as about its suffering through outside impressions, in a word, about what it is, not as representation, but as something over and above this, and hence what it is *in itself*. We do not have such immediate information about the nature, action, and suffering of any other real objects. (*WWR* 1, p. 103)

The body is thus known not merely as representation but from within, through an immediate cognition described as "more real than any other knowledge" (*WWR* 2, p. 196). What is cognized in this way goes far beyond the conceptual and intuitive representations explored in the first book of *WWR*. It encompasses not just deliberate acts, but also the entire range of feeling, desiring, and suffering, to which Schopenhauer now attaches the term "will." In his crucial transition, this "double knowledge" of our own body as will and representation is presented as the key to the in-itself of every phenomenon. We must judge all objects not given to consciousness in this double way according to the analogy of our own body:

> For what other kind of existence or reality could we attribute to the rest of the material world? From what source could we take the elements out of which we construct

> such a world? Besides the will and the representation, there is absolutely nothing known or conceivable for us. If we wish to attribute the greatest known reality to the material world, which immediately exists only in our representation, then we give it that reality which our body has for each of us, for to each of us this is the most real of things. (*WWR* 1, p. 105)

> I have stressed [...] that we are not only merely the knowing subject, but that we ourselves are also among those realities or entities we require to know, that *we ourselves are the thing in itself*. Consequently, a way from within stands open to us to that real inner nature of things to which we cannot penetrate from without. It is, so to speak, a subterranean passage, a secret alliance, which as if by treachery, places us all at once in the fortress that could not be taken by attack from without. Precisely as such, the thing in itself can come into consciousness. (*WWR* 2, p. 195)

This proposal that self-knowledge provides a key to the inner being of every phenomenon evidently involves rejection of full-fledged noumenal ignorance. No longer wholly unknowable, the thing in itself is now "merely not absolutely and completely knowable" (*WWR* 2, p. 197). Schopenhauer insists on both the reliability of his noumenal insight and its empirical provenance—explicitly rejecting Kant's doctrine that metaphysical cognition must be a priori. He nevertheless seeks to retain a connection to Kant's doctrine of noumenal ignorance, oscillating between emphasizing limits and reliability of his transcendent insight. Self-knowledge, he says, does not furnish "exhaustive and adequate knowledge" of the thing in itself, which has however "to a great extent cast off its veils – though it still does not appear completely naked" (*WWR* 2, pp. 196–97).

The metaphysics of ultimate reality to which Schopenhauer is led along this path bears little resemblance to the familiar pluralistic substance metaphysics common in the medieval and modern tradition. It amounts instead to a kind of force monism, comparable to Spinoza's system in rejecting noumenal teleology, but unlike Spinoza rejecting a *causa sui*, causal rationalism at the level of ultimate reality, and any mentalization of *natura naturans*. In Schopenhauer's theory, "absence of all aim, of all limits, belongs to the essential nature of the will in itself, which is an endless striving" (*WWR* 1, p. 164). Ultimate reality is not subject to the PSR; there is no ground by virtue of which it exists, thus no reason for its existence. Plurality is also foreign to the will as thing in itself, which yet grounds phenomenal reality by providing its "inner being," present "whole and undivided in everything in nature, in every living being." We should conclude that, if "*per impossibile*, a single being, even the most insignificant, were entirely annihilated, the whole world would inevitably be destroyed with it" (*WWR* 1, p. 129). Schopenhauer reveres Hume and shares his rejection of the PSR, but he rejects the ontology of events "entirely loose and separate," "conjoined, but never connected," to which this rejection leads Hume himself (*Enquiry*, sect. XII, 2). His vision of thoroughgoing metaphysical irrationality is very different; it is no event atomism but rather a monism of blind force.

On Schopenhauer's theory, space and time make possible particular objectifications of the will's appearance, and so are termed the *principium individuationis*. Philosophers imputing a libertarian free will dimly recognize the groundlessness now extended to the ultimate constitution of all things. The feeling of libertarian freedom is thus mere presentiment of our connection to an ontological domain unconstrained by the PSR. The association of voluntarism and irrationalism reaching back to Plato's *Euthyphro* motivates the use of "will" to refer to the thing in itself by a *denominatio* a posteriori; "we name the genus after its most important species, the direct knowledge of which lies nearest to us, and leads to the indirect knowledge of all the others" (*WWR* 1, p. 111).[20] Schopenhauer rejects the views of Descartes and Spinoza according to which an act of will is an act of thought, and even identified with a judgment. On such intellectualist theories of action as *sub ratione boni*, a person

> would have become what he is only in consequence of his knowledge. He would have come into the world as a moral cipher, would know the things in it, and would then determine to be this or that, to act in this way or that. He could, in consequence of new knowledge, choose a new course of action, and thus become another person. Further, he would then first know a thing to be good, and in consequence will it, instead of first willing it, and in consequence calling it good. (*WWR* 1, p. 292)

A range of empirical and psychological evidence is presented as evidence that the metaphysical systems of Plato, Descartes, Leibniz, and Spinoza have the cart before the horse in failing to recognize the primacy of the will and reason's role as mere handmaid. Locating the core of being in reason was the original sin of philosophy—often motivated by a pathetic desire for metaphysical elevation above the animal.

This brief sketch of Schopenhauer's metaphysics already puts us in a position to understand his confident inference from the supposed a priority to mere subjectivity of space and time. By virtue of its association with forms of space and time, he maintains, the PSR governs the world as it appears. Our insight into the thing in itself is held to reveal the noumenon as groundless, thus not subject to the PSR. The thing in itself must consequently be free of the spatiotemporal form of the phenomenon into which it passes when it appears.

On reflection some complications arise. Does this line of argument really rule out the existence of space and time as extramental realities imposing intelligible connections on their contents? Might it not, for example, be an ungrounded or brute fact that space and time exist? In that case it appears we can consistently conjoin such existence both with Schopenhauer's conception of space and time as "forms of the PSR" imposing intelligible connections, and with his doctrine that "there can be no principle in consequence of which the world with all its phenomena would first of all exist."

Though he doesn't address this issue explicitly, Schopenhauer provides materials for a clear response. The key point is that that his doctrine of will and associated restriction of the PSR involves a more thoroughgoing noumenal irrationality than a brute fact at the basis of existence. This point is connected to his restriction of

[20] "This means that the fourth class of representation laid down in the essay *On the Principle of Sufficient Reason* must become for me the key to the knowledge of the inner nature of the first class" (*WWR* 1, p. 126).

causation to the phenomenon, expressed in the claim that "the will is never a cause" (*WWR* 1, p. 140). Causality is inseparable from the PSR, thus the relation between will and phenomenon is not causality, for it is "not in accordance with the PSR; but that which in itself is will, exists on the other hand as representation" (*WWR* 1, p. 140). This restriction of causality to the phenomenon is not, however, a restriction of metaphysical grounding. For Schopenhauer does treat the will as the world's ontological substratum—it provides the "inner being," "present whole and undivided in everything in nature, in every living being" (*WWR* 1, p. 129). As he writes elsewhere, the will is "*world-creating* as thing in itself, free from the PSR, and thus from all necessity, and hence completely independent, free, and indeed almighty" (*WWR* 1, p. 503).[21] The dynamic character of the will's activity and grounding of phenomenal existence finds expression in descriptions of the "endless striving" of a "hungry will."

Schopenhauer's inference from a priority to subjectivity of space and time is thus not mediated by a premise that all grounding is phenomenal. The key point is rather the type of grounding at issue. Space and time as disclosed by a priori knowledge involve stable law-governed dependence relations, by virtue of which both can underwrite necessity of connection and count as forms of the PSR. Such law-governed forms of dependence are alien to the thoroughgoing dynamism, contingency, and irrationality of noumenal grounding as Schopenhauer conceives this—as a kind of irrationalist mirror of Spinoza's causal rationalism.[22]

6. "The Point Where Kant's Philosophy Leads to Mine": Freedom and the Thing in Itself

The greatest difficulty in mapping Schopenhauer's argument from a priority to subjectivity of space and time onto Kant's Transcendental Aesthetic concerns the premise that things in themselves are not subject to the PSR. We have seen that Schopenhauer attributes this metaphysical restriction to Kant, but it does not appear to figure in the Aesthetic at all, and we are certainly not told where it is to be found there. Schopenhauer's reason for imputing the restriction thesis does, however, gradually become clear. We discover that he effectively attributes to Kant another deduction of the thing in itself besides the supposed false deduction via causal inference attacked by Schulze. The crucial point emerges in his discussion of the famous

[21] The idea of noumenal grounding is implicated also in Schopenhauer's theory of force as the unfathomable in the representation, pointing beyond it to the thing in itself. He rejects reduction of forces to something empirically intelligible; force is "something on which no [scientific] explanation can venture, but which this presupposes" (*WWR* 1, p. 121). Empirical changes related by the PSR do not produce other changes; they provide mere occasions for the operation of forces. In a striking passage, he compares his view to occasionalism, on which a transcendent being is the only true cause: "Malebranche is right; every natural cause is only an occasional cause. It gives only the opportunity, the occasion, for the phenomenon of that one and indivisible will which is the in-itself of all things, and whose graduated objectification is this whole world" (*WWR* 1, p. 138).

[22] Schopenhauer is thus perhaps not entirely consistent in claiming that if "*per impossibile*, a single being, even the most insignificant, were entirely annihilated, the whole world would inevitably be destroyed with it" (*WWR* 1, p. 129). This inevitability would appear to rest on application of modus tollens, which would presuppose necessitation and not mere grounding of phenomena by noumena.

antinomy between freedom and empirical determinism. Its solution in Kant turns on a distinction between an empirical character manifested in deterministic responses to motives, and an intelligible character grounding the former and rooted in a libertarian free noumenal choice. Schopenhauer comments as follows on this part of Kant's doctrine:

> It is very remarkable that Kant is obliged precisely here, in connection with the idea of freedom, to speak in greater detail about the thing-in-itself, hitherto seen only in the background [...] *In general this is the point where Kant's philosophy leads to mine, or mine springs from his as its parent root.* (*WWR* 1, p. 501)

This echoes a revealing remark already noted in the early development of his theory of will in the second book of *WWR*:

> If I abstract from my character, and then ask why in general I will this and not that, no answer is possible, because only the appearance or phenomenon of the will is subject to the PSR, not the will itself, which in this respect may be called groundless. *Here I in part presuppose Kant's doctrine of the empirical and intelligible characters.* (*WWR* 2, p. 106)

Kant's argument at this point does in fact exhibit a close parallel to Schopenhauer's deduction of the groundless will. In a passage of the *Critique of Pure Reason* echoed in the *Groundwork*, it appeals to an immediate self-consciousness held to disclose a noumenal character connected with our possession of freedom:

> The human being, who is otherwise acquainted with the whole of nature solely through sense, knows himself also through pure apperception, and indeed in actions and inner determinations which cannot be accounted at all among impressions of sense; obviously is one part phenomenon, but in another part, namely in regard to certain faculties, he is a merely intelligible object [...] we call these faculties understanding and reason. (A546–47/B574–75; cf. B157)
>
> The rightful title to freedom of the will claimed by common reason is based on the consciousness and the granted presupposition of the independence of reason from merely subjectively determining causes [...] the human being, who this way regards himself as intelligence, thereby puts himself in a different order of things and in a relation to determining grounds of an altogether different kind when he thinks of himself as an intelligence endowed with a will. (*GMS*, 4:457)

Kant repeatedly presents the "transcendental" freedom at issue here as involving what he terms an absolute contingency (*schlechterdings Zufälligkeit*) of free acts, understood as excluding their necessitation by antecedent causes (*Refl* 4034, 4544, 4693, 5251). Freedom in this sense is therefore incompatible with an unrestricted PSR understood as requiring antecedent determining grounds for all acts.[23] Kant's

[23] "Our free actions *have no determining grounds*, and so we can have no insight into these actions either. This is a reason to acknowledge the limitations of the understanding, but not to deny the thing

mature writings claim that we are justified in affirming the reality of absolute freedom on an evolving combination of theoretical and practical grounds.[24]

Kant's own doctrine of the will does therefore support Schopenhauer's ascription of a metaphysical restriction of the PSR. What remains unexplained is how this metaphysical restriction relates to the Aesthetic's argument for transcendental idealism. One proposal is that Schopenhauer sees this argument as resting on an unstated restriction of the PSR that comes to light only much later in the *Critique of Pure Reason*. Such a reading would, however, make it hard to see why he would claim that the proofs of the Aesthetic itself "have such a complete power of conviction that I number its propositions among the incontestable truths" (*WWR* 1, p. 437).

In my own work (Hogan, 2009) I have defended an interpretation of Kant's argument that I believe solves the puzzle. The reading rests on an analysis of a priori unknowability claims in the rationalist tradition, in Kant's writings and in the Transcendental Aesthetic. The key to the proposal is the observation that Kant sometimes expresses the metaphysically unconditioned character of absolutely free acts as a denial of their *a priori knowability*. This is made possible by his use of "*a priori* knowledge" in two related senses. The *KrV* defines such knowledge as knowledge "absolutely independent of all experience" (B2–3). A different meaning is on display in Kant's claims that free acts, *qua* unconditioned features of reality, are not knowable a priori. He writes that "reason comprehends [something] when it cognizes it *a priori, that is, through grounds* [...] Now first beginnings *have no* [determining] *grounds*, thus no comprehension through reason is possible" (*Refl* 4338, 17:510). Kant's denial of the a priori knowability of free acts rests on a conception of a priori knowledge central to the rationalist tradition. Something is known a priori in the sense at issue when it is known "through," in the sense of being inferable from, its cause or metaphysical ground. Knowability a priori in this "through-grounds" sense

itself" (*V-Met-L$_1$/Pölitz*, 28:270; late 1770s); "The possibility of freedom cannot be grasped because one cannot grasp any first beginning [...] For our understanding cognizes existence through experience, but reason comprehends it when it cognizes it *a priori, that is through grounds* [...] Now first beginnings have no [determining] grounds, thus no comprehension through reason is possible" (*Refl* 4338). These claims do not contradict Kant's mature talk of "determination of the will by pure practical reason." For he holds that such determination, when it occurs, is subsequent to the will's free ordering of its incentives. For additional texts, see Hogan (2009).

[24] Kant upholds the theoretical demonstrability of absolute freedom both before and after the appearance of the *KrV*, and that work contains a similar claim (A546–47/B574–75; *V-Met-L$_1$/Pölitz*, 28:268–69; *Refl* 5110, 5203, 5552; *RezSchulz*, 8:13–14). While A558/B586 appears to deny the demonstrability of absolute freedom, it is unclear on examination whether it means only to rule out some proofs (from "mere concepts *a priori*"). A marginal note to A558 claims that freedom is demonstrable on moral grounds: "*Morality* is that which, if it is correct, positively presupposes freedom. If the former is true, then freedom is proved." From the late 1780s, Kant thinks freedom is demonstrable *only* on such grounds—an agent "judges that he can do something because he is aware that he ought to do it and he cognizes freedom within him, which, without the moral law, would have remained unknown to him" (*KpV*, 5:30). He continues, however, to say we have knowledge (both *Wissen* and *Erkenntnis*) of absolute freedom on practical grounds (*KpV*, 5:4, 121; *FM*, 20:310; *KU*, 5:469). The *Groundwork*'s claim that "a free will, and a will under moral laws, are one and the same" (4:447) is sometimes read as affirming the PSR's consistency with human freedom. But this "reciprocity thesis" analytically links a perfectly rational will and ideal moral agency (cf. Schönecker, 1999, pp. 153–74). Kant's concept of freedom includes two aspects Ameriks dubs "legislative autonomy" and "executive autocracy" (*V-Met/Mron*, 29:626; Ameriks, 2003, p. 272; cf. Wood, 1984, pp. 80–83). The second is the crucial libertarian condition on agency Kant presents as incompatible with Leibniz's unrestricted PSR.

presupposes that there *is* a determining ground from which relevant truths can be inferred.[25] Since the claim that something is knowable a priori in this through-grounds sense presupposes that it has a determining ground, a denial of such a priori knowability can express the metaphysical claim that such a ground is *lacking*. Kant's denial of the a priori knowability of free acts is an example—it records his conception of free acts as lacking determining grounds through which they could be known. It is thus necessary to distinguish two propositions expressible by the claim that epistemic agent S cannot have a priori knowledge of some feature of reality *F*:

(a) Non-empirical knowledge of *F* exceeds S's cognitive capabilities.
(b) *F* lacks a determining ground through which it could be known by S.

The key findings here are that a priori unknowability claims of the second kind incorporate the metaphysical claim that the relevant unknowable feature lacks a determining ground, and Kant explicitly speaks of the a priori unknowability of free acts in this *b*-unknowability sense.[26]

Now we have seen that the Aesthetic's argument for transcendental idealism makes essential use of a premise denying the a priori knowability of things in themselves. Kant writes that "if [time] were a determination or order inhering in things themselves, it could not precede the objects as their condition, and be known [...] a priori by means of synthetic propositions" (A32–33/B49; cf. B41). As we have seen, this is taken to express the idea that we can have no non-trivial knowledge of intrinsic or relational properties of mind-independent entities prior to knowing that these entities exist. Note, however, that Kant's unusual formulation does not simply assert that the a priori principles he associates with temporal order "could not be *known* to precede" things in themselves "as their condition." He seems to proceed instead from the metaphysical-sounding claim that the order in question "could not precede" such things as their condition to the exclusion of non-trivial a priori knowledge of the things in question. I have argued elsewhere that Kant's premise affirming the unknowability a priori of things in themselves should be understood as involving his *b*-unknowability claim affirming the absolute contingency of some features of such things. This reading immediately explains his otherwise baffling inference that a priori knowledge of principles of geometry and of a "general theory of motion" associated with spatiotemporal form entails that such form is *not* that of things in themselves. For Kant argues that a priori cognizable laws of motion impose deterministic order,[27] and he repeatedly claims that if space and time did exist independently of the mind, there could be no absolute contingency in the world—rather "actions would depend

[25] Standard examples of a priori knowledge in this sense include knowledge of theorems by inference from underlying axioms and knowledge of states of affairs by inference from the causes determining them to happen. The term *demonstratio* a priori was introduced by Albert von Sachsen to refer to knowledge through the ground of what is known; this meaning is retained in the 1662 *Port Royal Logic* of Antoine Arnauld and Pierre Nicole (Arnauld & Nicole, 1867, Part IV, Ch. 1).

[26] Compare *V-Met-L$_1$/Pölitz*, 28:270, 332–33; *Refl* 4006, 4338, 5185.

[27] "Neither through a miracle, nor through a spiritual being can a motion be brought about in the world, without producing just as much motion in the opposite direction, thus in accordance with the laws of action and reaction…Motions cannot begin by themselves, nor through something which wasn't itself in motion; and freedom and miracles are not to be met with among the phenomena" (*Refl* 5997, from the 1780s; Bxxvii; A536/B564).

completely on the mechanism of nature, and freedom together with its consequence morality would be destroyed" (*Refl* 6343; Bxxvii; A536/B564; *KpV*, 5:95–97).

Examination of Kant's a priori unknowability premise leads along these lines to the attribution of a valid argument for his notorious conclusion that spatiotemporal form is merely subjective. A key component of this interpretation is its claim that the *KrV*'s doctrine of noumenal ignorance incorporates the *b*-unknowability premise defended by Kant on a complex evolving combination of grounds. Because of this, the Aesthetic's inference to the mere subjectivity of space and time comes out as consistent with the noumenal ignorance doctrine. This interpretation can also help explain Kant's many mature claims to the effect that "the origin of the critical philosophy is morality, with respect to the imputability of action" (*HN*, 20:335; *Br*, 12:257).[28]

The reading also offers a satisfying response to a key argument for the "patchwork" interpretation of the *Critique of Pure Reason*. Vaihinger claims to locate pre-Critical "paleontological leftovers" (*palaeontologische Reste*) in the Transcendental Aesthetic's affirmation of "the ideality of space with respect to things when they are *considered in themselves through reason* (*wenn sie durch die Vernunft an sich selbst erwogen werden*)" (A28/B44; cf. B155; cf. A40–41, A45). Vaihinger objects strenuously, "How according to the broader teaching of the *KrV* can 'reason consider things in themselves'?" (1881–92, vol. 2, p. 354).

What Vaihinger and Kemp Smith overlook in complaining about such language is that it closely echoes many Kantian texts of the period claiming knowledge of absolute freedom. Kant commonly claims that absolute freedom is known—and his distinction between intelligible and sensible worlds demanded—by reflection on the deliverances of the faculties of understanding (*Verstand*) and/or reason.[29]

7. Schopenhauer's Insight: A Metaphysical Meaning of A Priori Unknowability

The findings above can solve the mystery of Schopenhauer's praise for what has traditionally been viewed as the invalid argument of the Transcendental Aesthetic. For we now have a way in which we can say that Kant's restriction of the PSR, which Schopenhauer insists is central to his transcendental idealism, is found in that chapter. The metaphysical restriction is expressed in epistemic form as the unknowability of a priori of features of things in themselves. Of course, this requires us to say that

[28] "The system of the *Critique of Pure Reason* turns on two *cardinal points* as a system of nature and of freedom, from which each leads to the necessity of the other [sic]: the ideality of space and time and the reality of the concept of freedom" (*Refl* 6353; cf. *Refl* 6344, 6349). My interpretation agrees with the conclusions of Guyer (1987, pp. 354–69; also 2014, pp. 64–65), Van Cleve (1999, pp. 34–37), and Strawson (1966, p. 60), that a metaphysical contingency premise drives Kant's inference to the mere subjectivity of space and time. What is lacking in these proposals is an account of the root of the contingency premise and an explanation of its compatibility with noumenal ignorance.

[29] Both Vaihinger and Kemp Smith make a similar objection to *Prolegomena* 13's reference to things in themselves, "as the pure understanding (*pure Verstand*) would cognize them." This is an archaic usage (*eine archaistische Wendung*), objects Vaihinger, violating Kant's own critical strictures on knowledge, so that "the entire probative force of the famous argument [from incongruent counterparts] is reduced to null" (1881–92, vol. 2, pp. 528, 522). For a detailed response, see Hogan (2021).

Schopenhauer *realized* what was going in on the Aesthetic's claim of a priori ignorance of things in themselves—that it includes a metaphysical claim in the dress of an ignorance claim. I conclude by showing that this is indeed plausible, and explains why Schopenhauer presents absolute idealist readings of Kant as so misguided. Consider first his claim that real grounds can double as grounds of knowledge:

> Insight into a ground of being may become a ground of knowledge, just as insight into the law of causality and its application to a definite case is the ground of knowledge of the effect. (*Fourfold Root* #36, p. 195)

We have already seen Schopenhauer's claim that, "the will in itself *has no ground*; the PSR in all its forms is merely the form of knowledge" (*WWR* 1, p. 107). Most significant for present purposes is his gloss of this metaphysical property of groundlessness as the epistemic one of *inexplicability* or non-deducibility from a ground:

> The thing in itself is [...] absolutely *inexplicable*. (*WWR* 1, p. 81)
>
> There can be no principle in consequence of which the world [...] would first of all exist; thus it is not possible, as Spinoza wished, to deduce a philosophy that demonstrates *ex firmis principiis*. (*WWR* 1, p. 82)
>
> [In mathematics and pure natural science] knowledge does not encounter the unfathomable (the groundless, i.e., the will), *that which cannot be further deduced.* (*WWR* 1, p. 121)

The will's groundlessness is here identified with impossibility of its further deduction—precisely its *b*-unknowability a priori in the sense explored above. I submit that this explains Schopenhauer's confident inference from the a priori knowability to the mere subjectivity of space and time; his account of the "meaning of the Critique of Pure Reason"; and his claim that the Aesthetic's proofs are "among the incontestable truths" (*WWR* 1, p. 437). Schopenhauer has seen precisely why the traditional neglected alternative objection to Kant's argument is misguided. The objection fails to understand that the central metaphysical presupposition of Kant's mature practical philosophy, a restriction to the PSR expressed in the form of an assertion of a priori ignorance, plays an essential role in his main argument for transcendental idealism.

If this is the correct solution to the problem of Schopenhauer's praise for the Transcendental Aesthetic, we might speculate as to the source of his insight. My reading of Kant's argument along similar lines had its roots in study of his philosophical engagement with German predecessors; on the one hand the intellectualist philosophy of Leibniz and Wolff; on the other its vigorous rejection by Christian August Crusius. Central to Crusius's critique is his acknowledgment that libertarian freedom imposes a hard limit on intelligibility. Because of this, he insists, the bounds of theoretical intelligibility cannot provide the ultimate measure of reality. We may know a free act through experience, but the act simply admits of no full answer to the question, "Why?":

> Should one deny the free actions of spirits, and what depends on them, because they do not admit of an ideal ground a priori in our understanding, and because by their nature they do not admit of such real grounds as could furnish to our understanding adequate ideal grounds a priori?
>
> (Crusius, *Weg zur Gewißheit*, §142; Crusius, 1964, vol. 1, pp. 261–2)

Here again metaphysical groundlessness or absence of a determining ground is glossed in epistemic terms, as lack of an "ideal ground a priori," or unknowability a priori in the sense above. It is notable that Crusius first advances this critique of unrestricted intelligibility in his 1743 dissertation entitled *De usu et limitibus principii rationis determinantis, vulgo sufficientis* (repr. Crusius, 1964, vol. 4.1). This work is the most important German study of the PSR before Schopenhauer's *Fourfold Root* seventy years later—at least if one omits Kant's first *Critique*. I mentioned that Schopenhauer's teacher Schulze likely had knowledge of Crusius, and it is conceivable that Schopenhauer encountered him in his extensive researches for the *Fourfold Root*, though he is not cited. We do possess a remarkable record of Schopenhauer's private reaction some years later upon reading Crusius's metaphysics textbook, the *Entwurf der nothwendigen Vernunft Wahrheiten* (1766). His Berlin notebooks of the early 1820s testify to a close reading, focusing especially on Crusius's summary of the work's motivation in paragraph 454: "In every soul the will is the preeminent power, for the sake of which all others are there as means, and to which all others must be completely or in part subordinated so that they can be directed and used by it." To this, Schopenhauer responds:

> *Pereant qui ante nos nostra dixerunt*. Donatus [...] In Crusius's *Entwurf* 1745 [...] a complete metaphysics, there are two truths which found no listeners and which I had to discover for a second time (1) [concerning Crusius's notion of an "existential ground"] [...] (2) That the primary and essential in humans is by no means the understanding but the will; the understanding is only there for the sake of the will. *Exposited and established* – It really is quite notable that of all philosophers of all time Crusius was the only one who grasped this great truth to a certain extent prior to me. All others talk about Geist, or soul, or ego, as an indivisible, non-dissectible, so that it always seemed objectionable when the pantheists ascribed this spirit to plants or even the inorganic, whose lack of knowledge is obvious. It looks different when we separate out the will. The division of the spirit or ego into two wholly different parts, one primary or essential, the will, and a secondary, the intellect, is a cardinal claim and achievement of my philosophy, and difference with all other philosophies. (Schopenhauer, 1891, pp. 345–46)

It is both characteristic and amusing that a remark starting out acknowledging Crusius's intellectual priority should end by claiming the doctrine of the will's ontological primacy as Schopenhauer's original insight. Note the ambiguity in his tantalizing reference to discovering Crusius's two truths 'for a second time.' Does he refer to stumbling on them again *in Crusius* or to their independent discovery? The first reading raises the possibility of unacknowledged influence on the early Fourfold Root essay. Either way, the echo Schopenhauer finds in his neglected predecessor is palpable. Given the enormous influence of Crusius's voluntarism on Kant's own progression from logicist rationalism to the Critical philosophy, the note provides further evidence for the interpretation advanced above. Schopenhauer's finely tuned ear for epistemic expressions of metaphysical claims, particularly the central metaphysical claims of a rich voluntarist tradition, allowed him to get Kant's Transcendental Aesthetic right.

References

Allison, H. E. (1976). The non-spatiality of things in themselves for Kant. *Journal of the History of Philosophy, 14*(3): 313–21.

Allison, H. E. (1983). *Kant's transcendental idealism: An interpretation and defense.* Yale University Press.

Ameriks, K. (2003). *Interpreting Kant's Critiques.* Clarendon Press.

Arnauld, A. & Nicole, P. (1867). *Logique de Port-Royal.* J. Delalain.

Berkeley, G. (2009). *Philosophical writings* (D. M. Clarke, Ed.). Cambridge University Press.

Berker, S. (2018). The Unity of Grounding. *Mind* 127: 729–77.

Bird, G. (1962). *Kant's theory of knowledge.* Humanities Press.

Bird, G. (2006). The neglected alternative: Trendelenburg, Fischer and Kant. In G. Bird (Ed.), *A companion to Kant* (pp. 486–99). Blackwell.

Cassirer, E. (1912). Hermann Cohen und die Erneuerung der kantischen Philosophie. *Kant-Studien, 17*(1–3): 252–73.

Cohen, H. (1871). *Kants Theorie der Erfahrung.* Dümmler.

Crusius, C. A. (1745). *Entwurf der nothwendigen Vernunft Wahrheiten.* J. F. Gleditschen

Crusius, C. A. (1964). *Die philosophischen Hauptwerke* (G. Tonelli, Ed.). 4 vols. Olms.

Fischer, E. (1901). *Von G. E. Schulze zu A. Schopenhauer: Ein Beitrag zur Geschichte der kantischen Erkenntnistheorie.* H. R. Sauerländer.

Guyer, P. (1987). *Kant and the claims of knowledge.* Cambridge University Press.

Guyer, P. (1999). Schopenhauer, Kant, and the methods of philosophy. In C. Janaway (Ed.), *The Cambridge companion to Schopenhauer* (pp. 93–137). Cambridge University Press.

Guyer, P. (2014). *Kant* (2nd edition). Routledge.

Hamlyn, D. W. (1985). *Schopenhauer.* The arguments of the philosophers. Routledge & Kegan Paul.

Hogan, D. (2009). Noumenal affection. *Philosophical Review, 118*(4): 501–32.

Hogan, D. (2021). Handedness, Idealism, and freedom. *Philosophical Review, 130*(3): 385–449.

Janaway, C. (1989). *Self and world in Schopenhauer's philosophy.* Clarendon Press.

Leibniz, G. W. (1989). *Philosophical essays* (D. Garber & R. Ariew, Eds.). Hackett. [Cited as G followed by volume and page number]

McDermid, D. J. (2003). The world as representation: Schopenhauer's arguments for transcendental idealism. *British Journal for the History of Philosophy, 11*(1): 57–87.

Prauss, G. (1974). *Kant und das Problem der Dinge an sich.* Bouvier.

Schönecker, D. (1999). *Kant: Grundlegung III; Die Deduktion des kategorischen Imperativs.* Alber.

Schopenhauer, A. (1891). *Handschriftlicher Nachlass* (E. Grisebach, Ed.). vol. 4: *Neue Paralipomena.* Philipp Reclam jun.

Schopenhauer, A. (1893). *Schopenhauer-Briefe: Sammlung meist ungedruckter oder schwer zugänglicher Briefe von, an und über Schopenhauer* (L. Schemann, Ed.). Brockhaus.

Schopenhauer, A. (1966). *The world as will and representation* (E. F. J. Payne, Trans.). 2 vols. Dover. [Cited as *WWR* followed by volume and page number]

Schopenhauer, A. (1988). *Manuscript remains*, vol. 3: *Berlin manuscripts (1818–1830)* (A. Hübscher, Ed.; E. F. J. Payne, Trans.). Berg.

Schopenhauer, A. (1999). *On the fourfold root of the principle of sufficient reason* (E. F. J. Payne, Trans.). Open Court.

[Schulze, G. E.] (1792). *Aenesidemus oder über die Fundamente: Der von dem Prof. Reinhold in Jena gelieferten Elementar-Philosophie.*

Schulze, G. E. (1801). *Kritik der theoretischen Philosophie.* Bohn.

Shapshay, S. (2011). Did Schopenhauer neglect the "neglected alternative" objection? *Archiv für Geschichte der Philosophie, 93*(3): 321–48.

Smith, N. K. (2003). *A commentary to Kant's Critique of Pure Reason.* Palgrave Macmillan.

Strawson, P. F. (1966). *The bounds of sense: An essay on Kant's Critique of Pure Reason.* Methuen.

Trendelenburg, F. A. (1840). *Logische Untersuchungen.* 1st ed. 2 vols. G. Bethge.

Trendelenburg, F. A. (1867). *Historische Beiträge zur Philosophie: Vermischte Abhandlungen.* Bethge.

Trendelenburg, F. A. (1870). *Logische Untersuchungen.* 3rd ed. 2 vols. S. Hirzel.

Vaihinger, H. (1881–92). *Commentar zu Kants Kritik der reinen Vernunft.* 2 vols. Spemann.

Van Cleve, J. (1999). *Problems from Kant.* Oxford University Press.

Wolff, C. von (1720) 1729. *Vernünfftige Gedancken von Gott, der Welt und der Seele des Menschen, auch allen Dingen überhaupt.* 4th ed. Halle.

Wood, A. W. (1984). Kant's compatibilism. In A. W. Wood (Ed.), *Self and nature in Kant's philosophy* (pp. 73–101). Cornell University Press.

Wood, A. W. (2005). *Kant.* Blackwell.

Wundt, M. (1945). *Die deutsche Schulphilosophie im Zeitalter der Aufklärung.* Olms.

3
Relation to an Object
The Role of the Categories

Lucy Allais

1. Introduction

The aim of this chapter is to address one part of Kant's argument in the Transcendental Deduction of the categories: why he thinks that the application of the categories is necessary for all thought to have "relation to an object." The chapter develops and defends the account of this part of the argument presented in chapter 11 of my book, *Manifest Reality* (Allais, 2015). As in that account, this chapter does not say a lot about what is arguably the central notion in the Deduction: the transcendental unity of apperception. At the center of the Deduction, as I read it, is the idea that having a unified self-consciousness that one can be aware of as such is something that comes together with having thoughts about an objective world, or, more specifically, a world of objective particulars. As I read it, the latter involves two parts: having a unified self-consciousness is both something that comes together with experiencing the world as *objective* and it is something that comes together with conceptual *thought*.[1] My reading is thus influenced by P. F. Strawson (2018 [1966]), who says that Kant's concern in the Deduction is how the diverse elements in a subject's experience must be united for that subject to be capable of conceptualizing them, and who sees Kant as arguing that this unity requires "just such a unity as is also required for experience to have the character of experience of a unified objective world and hence to be capable of being articulated in objective empirical judgments" (p. 87). That there are connections between the unity of self-consciousness, thought of objectivity, and conceptual thought more generally is a deep, difficult, and fascinating idea, and is key to understanding the Deduction. However, in my view, there is a prior question that needs to be understood before addressing this central concern, which is why the categories are necessary for thought about objects. This part of the argument I take to be an answer to a Humean/empiricist skepticism about a priori concepts. An empiricist could perhaps agree that there is a connection between self-consciousness and thought about objects or thought about an objective world, while not thinking that we need such categories as substance and cause to have thoughts about objects. My interest is in Kant's response to this empiricist skeptic about a priori concepts.

[1] Kant holds that the form of conceptual thought or judgment is the transcendental unity of apperception; he says that "a judgment is nothing other than the way to bring given cognitions to the **objective** unity of apperception" (B142).

Lucy Allais, *Relation to an Object: The Role of the Categories* In: *The Sensible and Intelligible Worlds: New Essays on Kant's Metaphysics and Epistemology.* Edited by: Karl Schafer and Nicholas F. Stang, Oxford University Press. © Lucy Allais 2022.
DOI: 10.1093/oso/9780199688265.003.0004

It might be doubted whether these parts of the Deduction are separable: perhaps the vindication of the categories as needed for thought about objects comes together with vindication of their being needed for transcendental self-consciousness. However, with an argument as unclear as the Deduction it seems to me worth trying to address some smaller parts of the argument in detail before trying to get an account of the whole. And one of the sub-questions we can try to understand to make progress in understanding the Deduction is, again following Strawson, the question of "[h]ow in general must we conceive of objects if we are to make empirical judgements, determinable as true or false, in which we predicate concepts of identified objects of reference? or: What in general must be true of a world of objects of which we make such judgements?" (Strawson, 2018, p. 82). Kant's answer is that we must conceive of objects as falling under the categories; I want to understand his argument for this.

The Deduction is a notoriously difficult, controversial, and frustrating argument. There is no agreement on what conclusion the argument aims to establish, never mind what the premises or argumentative structure are supposed to be. Kant seems to circle round the argument, repeatedly declaring himself to have proved his point and then immediately starting a new section saying he is about to start proving it, leaving the reader unsure about what is supposed to have been proved at what point. A final starting point I take from Strawson is a general description of the Deduction which strikes me as very helpful to keep in mind in grappling with this torturous yet thrilling text: "though the Transcendental Deduction is indeed an argument, it is not only an argument. It is also an explanation, a description, a story" (Strawson, 2018, p. 86). In my view, we are liable to go astray if we attempt to find careful order, assuming that different stages of the argument as presented in the text must build on each other in a neat, structured sequence. While this may sometimes be the case, it may also be that different sections involve circling round a point Kant is struggling to articulate.

An account of the Deduction should have something to say about how it relates to Kant's transcendental idealism. My view is that transcendental idealism comes in at the end of the Deduction, in understanding its conclusion, and not as a premise in the argument. If we were to approach the Deduction with the assumption of some kind of conceptual idealism (a view which holds that the world is dependent on our concepts), then there would not seem to be much for the argument to prove: we would already know that the concepts we unavoidably use in judging apply to the world. (In addition to not leaving much for the argument to prove, this approach would leave this conceptual idealism unargued for, since it would be established neither by the Aesthetic nor by the Deduction.) On the other hand, if we approach the argument assuming the idealism Kant takes himself to have established in the Aesthetic (that spatiotemporal appearances are limited to our mind-dependent forms of intuition), then the question of why we need to use the categories in order to think of spatiotemporal objects seems a question that is independent of idealism. This approach might seem in tension with Kant's appealing at some points in the argument to the claim that we know appearances only (for example, A114). However, it seems to me that the word appearances can mark out that we are concerned with objects that appear to us—objects that affect our senses—without necessarily bringing with it Kant's full account of the ideality of appearances. I return to the question of the relation between the Deduction and idealism at the end. A final point about my assumptions in approaching the text is that I take Kant at his word in saying that between the two editions he has changed the presentation but not the fundamental philosophical points. I thus draw on points made at different places in both editions in trying to give an account of his picture.

2. Clarifying the Aim of the Deduction

On my reading, Kant's aim in the Deduction is to argue that the categories apply to objects of experience (objects presented to us in spatiotemporal intuition) through showing that they are conditions of any concepts being applied to objects of experience. There are two immediately controversial thoughts here, which I will briefly expand on. The first is the idea that the categories are conditions of empirical concept application; Kant does not directly put his point in this way in the Deduction, but I think it is clear that this is his concern. The second is that, in my view, Kant's aim in the Deduction is to show that the categories are conditions of thinking objects and he denies that they are conditions of objects being given in intuition. This means that his strategy for vindicating the categories is not to show that they are conditions of objects being given to us in intuition and thereby to show that they apply to objects given to us in intuition. I will say something about both of these points, taking them in reverse order.

2.1 The Independence of Intuitions and Concepts

I have argued in numerous places (Allais, 2015, 2016, 2017) for what I call non-conceptualism about intuition: the view that Kantian intuitions are representations that do not depend for their being the representations that they are on being brought under concepts. Non-conceptualism about intuition should be distinguished from non-conceptualism about cognition[2] and experience (which I take to be false), and non-conceptualism about perception (which I take to be controversial).[3] I take non-conceptualism about intuition to be a straightforward reading of Kant's fundamental insistence on the heterogeneity of the fundamental necessary ingredients of cognition: intuitions and concepts. I take it that they are each different kinds of representations, and that while they are mutually dependent as elements of cognition, they do not depend on each other to be the kinds of representations that they are, or to make their distinct contributions to cognition. While Kant says concepts without intuitions are empty, he does not say that without intuitions concepts are not concepts. Concepts are general, mediate representations that enable us to think objects; they need to be applied to objects given to us in intuition in order not to be empty, but

[2] Kant very occasionally refers to the ingredients of cognition as cognitions, but it seems clear that his central account of (theoretical) cognition is as something that requires both concepts and intuitions.

[3] See Tolley 2016; 2019.

they do not need to be applied to objects given in intuition in order to be general, mediate representations that enable us to think objects. Similarly, intuitions need to be brought under concepts to feature in cognition, but they do not need to be brought under concepts in order to be intuitions: singular immediate representations whose contribution to cognition is to give us objects.

Kant opens the Deduction with an explicit denial of conceptualism about intuition: he says that "[t]he categories of the understanding [...] do not represent to us the conditions under which objects are given in intuition at all, hence objects can indeed appear to us without necessarily having to be related to functions of the understanding," and that even if appearances were not in accord with the conditions of the unity of the understanding "[a]ppearances would nonetheless offer objects to our intuition, for intuition by no means requires the functions of thinking" (A89–91/B122–23). In responding to this passage conceptualists frequently argue that Kant is presenting a possibility that he is going to go on to rule out,[4] but while it is true that he is going to rule out the possibility that "appearances could be so constituted that the understanding would not find them in accord with the conditions of its unity," conceptualists are forced to have a highly stretched reading of Kant's clear assertion that we would be presented with appearances in intuition even in the case of the possibility he is going to be ruling out.

Despite this denial, the Deduction has been taken by many as providing strong grounds for conceptualism. In my view, there are two main reasons for this. The first is the thought that only if we take Kant to be showing the categories to be conditions of objects being given to us in intuition will he be able to establish his desired conclusion: showing that the categories apply to the spatiotemporal objects presented to us in intuition. The second is the fact that the categories are clearly involved in the syntheses with which Kant is concerned in the Deduction, and these are frequently taken as something that produces intuition. The first argument depends on its being the case that there is no other way to make sense of the argument of the Deduction. If it turns out that the only way to make sense of the argument is as vindicating the application of the categories through showing the categories to be conditions of objects being given in intuition, then this would indeed count against giving overwhelming weight to the numerous places Kant insists on the distinct roles and representational natures of intuitions and concepts. However, it seems to me that this should be an interpretative strategy of last resort, not least given that, as we have just seen, Kant opens the Deduction asserting the opposite. I return to this at the end, in responding to a concern raised by Anil Gomes. However, the conceptualist about intuition is on apparently stronger ground in insisting on the importance of the connection between the categories and the syntheses Kant is concerned with in the Deduction. This connection plays a role in persuading a number of commentators of conceptualism about intuition.[5] As a representative example, Jessica Williams (2012) argues that "if, as Kant writes, synthesis 'stands under the categories', then it does not seem that intuition can have representational content apart from the categories"

[4] E.g., Bowman (2011, pp. 422–23); Gomes (2014, p. 6); Grüne (2011, p. 476); Land (2015, p. 31).

[5] E.g., Bauer (2012, p. 227); Gomes (2014, p. 3); Griffith (2012, p. 196); Land (2011, pp. 215–16); Williams (2012, p. 67); Ginsborg (2008, p. 66); Grüne (2011, p. 476).

(p. 67). In earlier work (Allais, 2009) I tentatively suggested that it could be that some of the kinds of syntheses at issue in the Deduction are not governed by concepts. However, I have since argued that even if (as I now think plausible) all the syntheses in the Deduction are governed by categories, this does not establish conceptualism about intuition, since syntheses is something done to intuition not something that produces intuition. Kant talks about unifying a manifold of intuitions and the manifold in an intuition; this is most straightforwardly read as something that is done *to* intuition. For example, he says of the synthesis of apprehension that it "is aimed directly at the intuition" (A99). But if synthesis is something done to intuition then it does not produce intuition. To say that we have a manifold of intuitions that must be synthesized is not to say that we do not yet have intuitions (that we have merely a mass of unorganized sensation). On the contrary, the most straightforward reading is that we have intuitions but that the appearances given in these intuitions are not ordered or classified, and that we are not in a position to think about them as objects. Thus, we can take seriously the idea that categorially governed synthesis is necessary for experience or cognition of an object without thinking that this provides any support at all for the view that intuitions depend on concepts to be intuitions. The Deduction is concerned with what needs to be done to intuitions to bring them to concept application, but this is not the same as what needs to be in play for intuitions to be intuitions.

A crucial point here, as a number of non-conceptualists about intuition have noted (Allais, 2015, 2017; McLear, 2015), is that when Kant talks about unifying intuition through synthesis we need not take him as concerned with producing the intuitional unity that is needed for intuitions to be intuitions (and that, in my view, is a function of arranging the mass of sensory input through the structuring representations of the a priori forms of intuition).[6] The unity that is involved in representing an object as a unified subject of properties or a unified complex of parts requires synthesis, but it does not follow from this that the intuitional unity which involves something being represented as a whole prior to representing its parts involves synthesis (see Allais, 2015, 2016, 2017). In my view, the Deduction, and the categorially governed syntheses Kant discusses there, is concerned with the former and not the latter kind of unity.

It should be noted that this discussion also enables us to respond to a further conceptualist worry: that failing to take seriously the role of synthesis does not do justice to the extent to which Kant takes synthesis and concept application to transform the deliverances of the senses. This need not be denied by non-conceptualists. Non-conceptualism about intuition is the view that the application of concepts is not needed for intuitions to be intuitions (singular and immediate representations) or for intuitions to make their fundamental contribution to cognition (giving us objects). It is entirely compatible with this that the conceptually governed syntheses radically transform what is presented in intuition. Further, the view is compatible

[6] Kant says that "[e]very intuition contains a manifold in itself, which however would not be represented as such if the mind did not distinguish the time in the succession of impressions on one another" (A99). Note he does not say this synthesis is necessary for intuition to contain a manifold or to be an intuition, but to be represented as such: to be grasped the manifold in an intuition as a manifold.

with thinking that something needs to be done to intuition to make intuitions suitable for being brought under concepts—in my view, this is the role of schematism.

2.2 The Categories as Conditions of Empirical Concept Application

On my reading, Kant's strategy for vindicating the categories (for showing that they have "relation to an object") is to show them to be conditions of the possibility of empirical concept application. Kant does not make his point exactly in these terms (he does not say, specifically, that he is going to show the categories to be conditions of empirical concept application), so why do I think that this is his aim?[7] The ostensible worry with which Kant opens the Deduction concerns whether we are warranted in thinking that a priori concepts apply to objects. Kant says that with respect to a priori concepts, what we want to know is "how these concepts can be related to objects that they do not derive from experience" (A85/B117) and he says that "I call the explanation of the way in which concepts can relate to objects *a priori* their **transcendental deduction**" (A85/B117). So the Deduction is concerned with explaining how a priori concepts can relate to objects. Kant says explicitly that this is a problem to do with concepts, and that objects can be given in intuition independently of the functions of the understanding. He says that the difficulty is "how **subjective conditions of thinking** should have **objective validity**, i.e., yield conditions of the possibility of all cognition of objects; for appearances can certainly be given in intuition without functions of the understanding" (A89–90/B122). Further, he says that his strategy for showing that the categories do have objective validity and relation to an object is to show that they are conditions of the possibility of experience or conditions of the possibility of cognition. As we have seen, some conceptualist readers understand Kant as arguing that the categories are conditions of the possibility of experience or cognition by first arguing that they are conditions of the possibility of objects being given to us in intuition. We have also seen, however, that he opens the Deduction denying this. On the contrary, he says that our question is "whether a priori concepts do not also precede, as conditions under which alone something can be, if *not* intuited, nevertheless *thought* as object in general, for then all empirical cognition of objects is necessarily in accord with such concepts, since without their presupposition nothing is possible as **object of experience**" (A92–93/B124–25, my emphasis). Here it is clear that what he is investigating is whether the categories are conditions of experience or empirical cognition, and it is further clear that his strategy is *not* to show this by showing them to be conditions under which something can be intuited, but rather to show them to be conditions under which something can be thought. Showing the categories to be conditions under which something can be thought simply is, for Kant, showing them to be conditions under which something can be brought under concepts, and since the categories are the only a priori concepts at issue here, showing them to be conditions under which objects can be

[7] Thanks to Tobias Rosefeldt, Eric Watkins, and Marcus Willaschek (in conversation) for pushing me on this point.

thought is showing them to be conditions under which objects can be brought under empirical concepts.

Kant talks about the conditions of an object's being thought. It might be thought that "an object's being thought" could be understood in a broader and more abstract way than empirical concept application. Am I not at least *thinking* an object when I think about something that does not even exist, such as a unicorn, or when I think about something that couldn't be given in empirical intuition, such as God or a soul-substance, and couldn't there be objects of thought that are other than the spatiotemporal substances to which we apply empirical concepts, such as mathematical objects?[8] If we were to use the phrase "conditions of thinking an object" outside of Kant and the context of the Deduction, we would certainly be likely to mean something broader and more abstract than empirical concept application. However, it seems to me that there are strong reasons for thinking that in the Deduction Kant has the more specific concern. Kant says that "[o]nce I have pure concepts of the understanding, I can also think up objects that are perhaps impossible, or that are perhaps possible in themselves but cannot be given in any experience since in the connection of their concepts something may be omitted that yet necessarily belongs to the condition of a possible experience" (A97). This indicates that the fundamental case he is concerned with is that of applying concepts to objects actually given in experience (the more abstract cases of thought are derivative of this). This just is empirical concept application. Kant's view, it seems to me, is that at least for finite receptive cognizers like us, successful empirical concept application is a condition of having thought. Once we have the capacity to successfully apply concepts to objects of experience we can then have other forms of thought, such as thought of non-existent objects or things not given in experience, but this is possible only because the primary case of applying concepts to spatiotemporal objects is successful.

We have already seen that in talking about the aim of the Deduction Kant presents his concern as being whether a priori concepts are conditions under which something can be thought as object in general, and clarifies this by saying "all empirical cognition of objects is necessarily in accord with such concepts, since without their presupposition nothing is possible as **object of experience**" (A92–93/B124–25). His concern is with thinking objects of experience. He says that the principle to which the transcendental deduction must be directed, then, is "that they must be recognized as *a priori* conditions of the possibility of experience" (A94/B126) and that "the categories do not afford us cognition of things by means of intuition except through their possible application to **empirical intuition**, i.e., they serve only for the possibility of **empirical cognition.** This, however, is called **experience**" (B147). He says that "the objective validity of the categories, as *a priori* concepts, rests on the fact that through them alone is experience possible (as far as the form of thinking is concerned). For they then are related necessarily and *a priori* to objects of experience, since only by means of them can any object of experience be thought at all" (A93/B126). So his strategy is to show that the categories are conditions of the possibility of experience, and, in specific that they are conditions of the possibility of one part of

[8] Thanks to Clinton Tolley (in conversation) for pushing me on this point.

experience, the part that involves concepts—thinking. Further, it is also clear in this quotation that his concern is with relating the categories to objects of experience (which I take to be spatiotemporal substances) and finally it is clear in this quotation that he thinks that we would not have any thought about objects of experience without the categories: "only by means of them can any object of experience be thought at all" (A93/B126). Similarly, he says that "it is already a sufficient deduction of them and justification of their objective validity if we can prove that by means of them alone an object can be thought" (A96–97). To say that without the application of the categories to the objects of experience we would not be able to have any thoughts about the objects of experience is to say that we would not be able to apply empirical concepts to them. This means that the aim is to show that the categories are conditions of empirical concept application.

Kant's strategy is to argue that the categories are conditions of the possibility of experience or empirical cognition. They are conditions of one specific part of experience or empirical cognition: the conditions of thought (as opposed to the conditions of intuition). But the kind of thought that a priori conditions are conditions of must be empirical thought; the only a priori concepts at issue at this point are the categories, so other concepts being used to think objects are empirical. (Later, in the Principles, we will find discussion about what it takes to apply mathematical concepts to the spatiotemporal objects of experience.) Thought, for Kant, paradigmatically is concept application. So it is clear that his concern is with the conditions of empirical concept application.

3. What Is Relation to an Object?

Kant's concern in the Deduction is with whether the categories could lack "relation to an object" and his strategy is to argue that they have relation to an object by showing that they are conditions of all thought's having relation to an object. It is clear that we need to know what is meant by relation to an object. I have argued elsewhere (Allais 2015; 2017) that to understand this in context it is crucial to pay attention to the fact that having relation to an object must be something different from being given an object. Some conceptualist interpreters see the Deduction as arguing that the categories are needed for us to be given objects in intuition. If we weren't paying attention to the context and to his technical terms, Kant's saying things such as that the categories are necessary for anything to be an object of experience might be taken to mean that we do not have phenomenological conscious experience (in the ordinary, non-Kantian sense of experience) of something as something distinct from us without the categories. But we know that for Kant, experience is empirical cognition. And we know that he has said that the categories are not conditions of anything being given in intuition. Further, we know that he has said that the distinct role intuitions contribute to cognition is to give us objects, and that this is something concepts could never do (A50/B74, A92/B125, A239/B298). Thus, there are overwhelming reasons not to read "relation to an object" as being given an object or as something like having a perceptual experience, in our sense of experience, of an object. Rather, relation to an object is something Kant talks about specifically in the context of thought or concepts; it is something concepts can have or lack, and his concern in the Deduction is with the specific worry that the categories could lack relation to an object. Crucially, the way concepts have relation to an object is by being applied to something that is given in or could be given in empirical intuition. Kant thinks that concepts that cannot be brought into relation to intuition are not entirely lacking in meaning, but they lack something: relation to an object.

Kant says that the objective reality of the categories rests on their applying to possible intuitions (A289/B345), that the objective reality of the categories requires not just intuitions "but always **outer intuitions**" (B291), and that "without the conditions of sensible intuition, the synthesis of which they contain, the categories have no relation at all to any determinate object, thus they cannot define one, and consequently they do not have in themselves any validity of objective concepts" (A246/B302). Thus, he wants to show that the categories have relation to objects given in outer intuition. Further, he says that without the application of the categories empirical concepts would not amount to experience, and "all relation of cognition to objects would disappear" (A111; see also A121), and he says that the pure concept of the transcendental object = x "is that which in all of our empirical concepts in general can provide relation to an object, i.e., objective reality" (A109). Without the categories no concepts would have relation to an object, no concepts would have objective reality or be brought into relation to objects given in intuition. So the concern in the Deduction is with the a priori conceptual conditions of experience, where this amounts to the a priori conceptual conditions of empirical thought or concept application. Further, the specific worry with respect to a priori concepts is whether they can be brought into relation to objects given in intuition. And Kant's strategy will be to show that they are conditions of any concept's being brought into relation to objects given in intuition. We are not concerned with mere conceptual thought, but conceptual thought that latches onto a world of objects—that is brought into relation to objects given in intuition—and Kant's strategy is to vindicate the categories by showing that without them all thought would lack relation to an object. In this case, we would have mere thought, but would not be able to bring any concepts into relation to objects given in intuition. Thus, our aim is to show that the categories are conditions of the possibility of bringing empirical concepts into relation to objects given to us in outer intuition: referential empirical concept application.

4. Why Would We Lack Relation to an Object with Empirical Concepts Alone?

Once we understand Kant's problem and strategy in this way, the question we need to clarify is why he thinks that in the absence of the categories we would not be able to apply empirical concepts to objects. Kant says that the empirical synthesis of reproduction presupposes that appearances are reproducible and he says that this requires an a priori ground. (A100). But we might wonder why sufficient empirical similarity and regularity would not suffice for the empirical imagination's finding appearances reproducible. Similarly he says that if we merely had unity of synthesis in accordance with empirical concepts we could have a swarm of appearances without experience; "in that case all relation to objects would also disappear, since the appearances would lack connection in accordance with universal and necessary laws, and would thus be intuition without thought, but never cognition" (A111). Again, we might wonder why unity of synthesis in accordance with empirical concepts would not give us experience or empirical cognition of objects—why it would be a mere chaotic swarm. Note that Kant here makes the strong claim that in the case of merely having a swarm of appearances "all relation to objects would disappear"; I take him to mean here that empirical concepts would not be able to relate to objects, since he says we would still have intuition without thought and we would have appearances (not mere sensation). We need to understand what the problem is—why Kant thinks empirical concept application could not get off the ground without the application of a priori concepts—and what the solution is—how the application of a priori concepts is supposed to help. The rest of this chapter concerns my suggestion for understanding this. To give a complete account of the argument of the Deduction we would then want to understand how the way the categories give relation to an object relates to the transcendental unity of apperception; this is a subject for further work and I do not attempt to make sense of it here.

Kant seems to think that in the absence of the application of the categories we would not have a determinate object of thought. He says that the categories are "concepts of an object in general, by means of which its intuition is regarded as **determined** with regard to one of the **logical functions** for judgments" (A95/B128) and holds that this determination is necessary for empirical concept application. We need to clarify the sense in which what is presented in intuition is indeterminate or not determined without the categories. As we have seen, one way of reconstructing an argument here—the conceptualist route—is to argue that Kant's strategy is to show the categories to be conditions of being presented with perceptual particulars. On this reading, when Kant says "relation to an object would disappear" he means that there would be no consciousness of perceptual particulars. So the sense in which intuition is not determined is that it does not even present a distinct, bounded perceptual particular. The idea would be that the swarm of appearances is the blooming, buzzing confusion of unorganized sensation, and it is the categories that are introducing into this chaos the boundaries and principles of perceptual individuation that are needed to for us to have experience (in the non-Kantian sense of simply phenomenal consciousness) of perceptual particulars. But this is very clearly not what he says. On the contrary, in the case of the swarm of appearances we have "intuition without thought, but never cognition" (A111). The swarm is not a swarm of sensations: we still have both intuitions and appearances. What we lack is a determinate object of thought not an appearance given in intuition.

It seems to me that in addition to not fitting the way Kant presents the problem, this conceptualist strategy does not make sense of his solution. Kant says that what we need in order to solve the problem of the merely swarming appearances is a representation of necessary unity. Representing objects as falling under concepts that contain necessary unity as part of their content is what the categories individually or together (as the concept of an object in general) provide. Invoking the need for representations of *necessary* unity in order to solve the problem of representing distinct perceptual particulars would be a massive over-kill so seems unmotivated. Kant thinks sensation is ordered in the a priori forms of intuition to produce empirical intuitions, and he thinks that both we and other animals have empirical principles of association—ways in which we group together what is presented to us in intuition. He argues that such association is insufficient for us to have an object of thought. But it is unclear why such association should be thought insufficient to have perceptual particulars, and if this is Kant's strategy, his arguments are weak and proceed by an extreme and implausible dichotomy. His arguments oppose a synthesis that connects things with *necessity* to a combination that is entirely arbitrary, haphazard, and random. But these are not the only alternatives. As Graham Bird (2006) says, Kant speaks of conceptual unity variously as a way of avoiding haphazardness, arbitrariness, or merely accidental connections, but "what is left out between the haphazard and the necessary is a stable regularity" (p. 343). Kant insists that the kind of unity we would get through stable regularity, or what he calls the empirical affinity of the manifold, is not enough for our concepts to have "relation to an object." He says that an object "is regarded as that which is opposed to our cognitions being determined at pleasure or arbitrarily rather than being determined *a priori*, since insofar as they are to relate to an object our cognitions must also necessarily agree with each other in relation to it, i.e., they must have that unity that constitutes the concept of an object" (A104). But, as Bird points out, his argument for this seems to be that without a necessary unity we have merely arbitrary or haphazard connections. Why should the only options be, on the one hand, that our cognitions are determined "*at pleasure or arbitrarily*," and, on the other, that they are determined a priori and with necessity? It is hard to see why empirical principles of association, together with the spatiotemporal form of intuition, could not give us perceptual particulars, or why such particulars should be regarded as arbitrary, haphazard, or accidental.

In my view, we can make sense of this opposition between necessary unity and chaos if we pay attention to the requirements of conceptual thought rather than the requirements of being presented with distinct perceptual particulars. Two crucial features of conceptual thought, as Kant understands it, are its generality and its spontaneity. I understand the spontaneity of thought in terms of his claim that combination is never given: there are indefinitely many ways we could potentially synthesize (organize, order, group, classify) the manifold of what is given in intuition.[9] As I understand the generality of thought, the idea is that having a concept, or applying a concept to an object in a judgment, requires having the capacity to combine it with other concepts in different thoughts, and these thoughts involve being able to think of the same object's having other properties and other objects' having this property. One of the basic kinds of judgment Kant is concerned with is basic subject-predicate judgments in which we attribute properties to objects. Properties are essentially general; a property is something which more than one object can have. The generality of

[9] Kant says that combination involves synthesis, but it is not clear that he asserts the reverse—that all synthesis is what he calls combination. It seems to me that his term combination is technical: he says that combination is something specific: the representation of the synthetic unity of the manifold (B130–31). This suggests that it is something specifically to do with the way the manifold is unified when it is represented conceptually, rather than taking combination in a looser, ordinary sense to refer to any kind of ordering or associating. When he speaks of combination not being given, Kant says that this applies both to the combination of intuitions and the combination of concepts (B129)—not, notice, to the binding or ordering of sensation that is needed to for us to have empirical intuitions (singular and immediate representations that give us objects).

properties goes together with the generality of concepts: where I am able to attribute a property to an object by applying a concept to that object, I must also be able to think of that object as having other properties, and I must also be able to think of that property as potentially belonging to other things. Kant says that "if I think of **red** in general, I thereby represent to myself a feature that (as a mark) can be encountered in anything, or that can be combined with other representations [...] A representation that is to be thought of as common to **several** must be regarded as belonging to those that in addition to it also have something **different** in themselves; consequently they must antecedently be conceived in synthetic unity with each other" (B133–34n). My being in a position to think "this thing is red" requires that I am also in a position to think that other things are red (in other words, to categorize this thing with the other things that fall under the concept), and that I am also in a position to think of this thing as having other properties (to represent its redness as combined with, for example, its roundness, both properties of one object). Applying the concept "red" to an object (attributing this property to an object) thus involves at least two different ways in which we must unify representations, and grasp their unity: I represent this thing as combined or unified together with other things which fall under the common property, and I represent the properties of this thing as combined or unified properties of one thing. It is this way of representing objects that, Kant thinks, cannot get started without a priori concepts.

My suggested way of understanding Kant's problem is that it arises out of the fact that the requirements of the generality of thought seem to be in tension with the spontaneity of thought. The generality of thought means that to start investigating something's properties (working out what empirical concepts it falls under) there must be something that I think of as a unified subject of properties to which other properties belong (and where I also represent these properties as things that could potentially belong to other objects). This representation of a unified object requires synthesizing and combining the manifold of intuition and the manifold in an intuition in such a way that this manifold is represented as belonging to one object. But combination is not given, and the manifold in an intuition can be combined in indefinitely many ways. Grouping properties as belonging to one object involves synthesis or combination; this can be done in indefinitely many ways (combination is not given), but the generality of thought requires combination to have taken place (there to be one object to which is represented as a unified subject of properties). Representing an empirical object involves unifying (synthesizing) a bunch of empirical properties; but there are different ways I could have done this (the spontaneity of thought) and what counts as the unified subject of properties is not given. But I can't start learning what empirical properties an object has in order to discover if a particular way of unifying properties corresponds to an object, because I can't start investigating an object's properties without something that I am thinking of as the unified subject of thought. The spontaneity of thought appears to make impossible what the generality of thought needs to get concept application off the ground.

Let us return to the question of the sense in which appearances are indeterminate or not determined in the absence of the application of the categories.[10] Recall that the conceptualist thought that this sense was that we lack distinct perceptual particu-

[10] Thanks to Stefanie Grüne (in conversation) for pushing me on this point.

lars. In my view, although we have perceptual particulars given in intuition, this is not enough to determine a unified object of thought. Consider a dog perceiving a desk with a desk lamp clamped on to it. In my view, Kant's account allows that non-concept having animals can perceive perceptual particulars, and this requires (at least) that the dog has somehow (presumably using biologically determined principles of association) bound together the sensory input so as to perceive something outside of it with respect to which it can perceive the spatiotemporal boundaries. That it can perceive the boundaries of the object enables it to move around it, and would enable it to attend to, follow and track a smaller object, such as a ball. For the dog, is the desk lamp part of the object that is the desk? I claim that this is not determinate for the dog. The dog neither is nor is not representing the lamp as part of the desk; the dog is not representing the desk as an object that has parts. For it to be the case that something is or is not represented as a part of the object, it needs to be determinate what counts as the object—what is being represented as an object. It is not determinate what is being thought of as an object until it is determinate what is being regarded as a subject of properties. The dog isn't thinking of anything as a subject of properties; in this sense, nothing is an object for it. Suppose the table is replaced overnight by an identical one; suppose its surface is replaced. There is no sense in asking the question of whether the dog would think of it as the same table; it can attend to and track the boundaries of something presented to it in perception, but it has no thoughts about the kinds of changes the table can survive while being the same table. The table features for the dog as an appearance in intuition but not an object of empirical cognition or experience.

The conceptualist who thinks that the role of the categories is to determine distinct perceptual particulars both overestimates what is needed for this (why necessity, rather than regularity) and underestimates how much still needs to be done to transform a distinct perceptual particular into an object of thought. The specific features of thought, for Kant, are generality and spontaneity. My suggestion has been that it is paying attention to these that makes sense of Kant's problem: why distinct perceptual particulars plus merely empirical concepts could not constitute cognition of a world of objects. The generality of thought requires not just that there is something represented perceptually as distinct and bounded, but that there is something that is regarded as a subject of properties. Regarding something as a subject of properties is a function of combining and synthesizing. But the spontaneity of thought says that there are indefinitely many ways things could be combined in being regarded as a subject of properties. It could be the brownness or the hardness of the table that is a subject of properties, or the table plus the desk lamp, or indefinitely many other possible combinations. In this situation, we have genuine chaos in which concept application cannot get off the ground, even though we have bounded perceptual particulars. We have a swarm of appearances, but no experience or empirical cognition.

Given the nature of the problem, there is no empirical concept that can solve it; to attribute an empirical concept to anything would require having solved the problem. Kant says that the categories are "concepts of an object in general, by means of which its intuition is regarded as **determined** with regard to one of the **logical functions** for judgments" (A95/B128); this is what we needed: we need (at least) it to be determined what is counting as a subject of properties. Kant holds that representing something as an object requires representing it as a unified subject of properties. It might be tempting to think that the way we do this is by representing all the properties of the thing given in experience and then somehow representing, in addition, the empirical object to which all the properties below. But any representation of the empirical object will be a further empirical representation of which we can ask—what unifies it with the object? If we simply have a bunch of associated properties there is nothing we are representing as an object. Any empirical property of the object we can represent as belonging to it is simply a further feature with respect to which we can ask what unifies it with the object. We therefore need some way of determining which properties hang together. Kant's thought is that the representation of a unified object cannot be some further empirical property and also cannot involve representing empirical properties as attaching to a non-empirical thing in itself; rather it is a matter of representing the properties as being united in the particular way that is involved in belonging to one thing, which Kant takes to be a unity that involves necessity. He notes that we represent properties as bound up with each other with necessity even though this does not mean that the particular combination of properties is necessary and not contingent. He says: "I do not mean to say that these representations **necessarily** belong **to one another** in the empirical intuition, but rather that they belong to one another **in virtue of the necessary unity** of the apperception in the synthesis of intuitions" (B142). We can make sense of this by putting the point in a less abstract way than Kant puts it in the Deduction (and in a way in which we are only fully in a position to do after the Principles): although the particular properties an object has are contingently united in that object, that they belong to one object means that they have causal implications for each other, and in this sense are represented as a unity that contains necessity—a causally unified object. Kant holds that unless we regard the objects given in intuition as causally unified subjects of causal powers, we will not be in a position to think of anything as an object.

Kant says that "an **object**, however, is that in the concept of which the manifold of a given intuition is **united**" (B137). In thinking of properties as belonging to an object we think of them as unified in a particular way, as having "that unity that constitutes the concept of an object" (A105). Kant holds that this is a matter of representing a unity that involves necessity.

Representing something as an object is not a matter of representing a bunch of properties and then representing some further thing to which the properties belong; rather, it is representing the properties as unified in a certain way. This principle of unity can't be a further empirical property and is rather merely the a priori representation of a unity that involves necessity. Synthesizing our empirical representations with the categories therefore enables us to represent empirical concepts as belonging to an object, so enables empirical concepts to have relation to an object. Kant says: the pure concept of the transcendental object = x "concerns nothing but that unity which must be encountered in a manifold of cognition insofar as it stands in relation to an object" (A109). As I understand this, it is by synthesizing according to the pure concept of the transcendental object = x, the a priori concept of an object in general, that we are able to have determinate objects of thought for empirical concept application, and therefore to have cognition that has relation to an object.

5. Application or Instantiation?

Anil Gomes (2017) has objected to my argument that it does not enable Kant to establish what he wants the Deduction to establish: not simply that we cannot help using certain concepts but that these concepts actually apply to objects. He says that my account of the argument, if it worked, would show merely that we must apply the categories (a claim about the way we must think) not that objects actually instantiate the categories (a claim about the objects of experience). My suggestion has been to attribute to Kant the thought that unless we think of objects as falling under the categories we cannot think of them as falling under any concepts. But this might be thought to show merely something about how we unavoidably think, and not something about objects. In my view, this worry can be avoided if we understand Kant's starting point as being that we have experience or empirical cognition. If empirical cognition would be possible only of a world of causally unified substances, and if we have empirical cognition, then we can know the world to be a world of causally unified substances. It is important that the proof is not merely starting with a feature of our phenomenal consciousness, or a feature of the way we think, but with the claim that we do actually have empirical cognition of objects. As I read the Deduction, Kant's target is not a Cartesian skeptic about the outside world (a concern he addresses in the Refutation of Idealism), but rather a Humean-type skeptic about a priori concepts. The latter skeptic grants that we have empirical cognition, but denies the legitimate application of a priori concepts. Kant's argument, as I read it, shows the skeptic who grants that we have empirical cognition that we could have this only of a world of causally unified substances.

Gomes objects that my version of the argument does not show that *correctly* applying the categories is a condition of empirical concept application, but only that thinking that the categories apply is a condition of empirical concept application. There is an extent to which I think this is correct. The argument does not show that any particular application of the categories is correct, and we can be wrong about whether what we take to be a substance in fact is an object. It could be that what we at first took to be one object is in fact a desk lamp clamped onto a desk (two objects). However, we can discover this only if the world consists of causally unified substances, whose principles of causal unity we must discover (and could be wrong about), and this means that the world of experience consists of objects that instantiate the categories.

6. Could There Be Objects Given in Intuition That We Cannot Cognize?

Stephanie Grüne (2016) has objected that on my reading the argument shows only that the categories apply to those objects given in intuition that we can cognize, but not that we can cognize all the objects given in intuition. She takes this to show that my account cannot reach Kant's desired conclusion: that all the objects of experience instantiate the categories. My reading of the argument is supposed to show that the application of the categories is a condition of empirical cognition; if this argument can be made to work, it would show, of any object that we can cognize, that it falls under the categories. Grüne is right that this conditional conclusion is less than the claim that all spatiotemporal objects fall under the categories, which is what Kant wanted to establish. She takes this to show that what we need is a (moderate) conceptualism which argues that synthesis governed by the categories is needed to constitute intuition, which would show that all objects given in intuition fall under the categories.

As I understand the presentation of Kant's argument, getting from the conditional claim to the unconditional claim is the job of section 26 of the B Deduction. Kant starts this section saying that up to now we have explained the possibility of the categories as a priori cognitions of objects of an intuition in general, and we are now going to explain the possibility of cognizing a priori through categories whatever objects may come before our senses. He says that this will show why everything that comes before our senses stands under the understanding's laws. The argument he gives for this says, roughly, that we need to synthesize and unify the representations of space and time in order to cognize them, and that it follows from this that anything given in space and time (therefore all objects of experience) falls under the categories. While the general strategy is clear, what is less clear is the reason for saying that we have to synthesize our representations of space and time under the categories. Kant simply asserts that our representations of space and time must be synthesized and unified and that unity can be nothing other than that provided by the categories, and then says that consequently all synthesis stands under the categories. To understand this argument, we need to know why it is clear that this unity can be nothing other than that provided by the categories. I do not have anything to say about this here; perhaps the key to understanding this move is the central idea of the Deduction about which I have not yet said much—the transcendental unity of apperception.

7. The Transcendental Unity of Apperception

My reading of the argument sees Kant as holding that we need to synthesize and unify the properties of objects under the categories in order to have a determinate object of thought for empirical concept application. Representing a bunch of properties as belonging to a causally unified subject of properties is what it is to regard something as an object. Kant talks about consciousness of a unity and a unity in consciousness, both of which could refer to consciousness of the representation of an object as unified.[11] However, he also says that the transcendental condition for representing objects as unified in this way is the possibility of grasping them as representations for a unified self-consciousness: a self that is aware of itself as thinking about

[11] For example, when he says "[n]ow, however, all unification of representations requires unity of consciousness in the synthesis of them. Consequently the unity of consciousness is that which alone constitutes the relation of representations to an object, thus their objective validity" (B137), this could refer to consciousness of a unified object rather than the possibility of self-conscious awareness of a unified subject.

these objects.[12] He says that without the possibility of the self-consciousness that involves being aware of representations as representations for a unified subject, intuitions would not become objects of thought for me. This is the line of thought that would need to be understood to have a complete account of the argument of the Deduction.

8. Transcendental Idealism

In conclusion, I return to the question of the relationship between the Deduction and transcendental idealism. I take this to be complicated. Kant takes himself to have proven in the Aesthetic that spatiotemporal appearances are mere representations and do not present us with things as they are in themselves. One way of understanding the Deduction is as adding to this that our cognition is limited to such spatiotemporal appearances, because it is only with respect to spatiotemporal appearances that we can succeed in seeing in using a priori concepts in a way that succeeds in relation to an object. On this reading, the Deduction doesn't introduce further idealism (further, conceptual mind-structuring in addition to the mind-structuring that happens through the role of our a priori forms of intuition). However, the Deduction can be read as introducing more strongly idealist considerations. It could be thought that in saying that our concepts determine what counts as an object in general Kant is introducing a strong kind of conceptual idealism. Further grounds for this are given by the various claims Kant makes at the end of the Deduction in both editions, about the mind introducing the lawfulness of nature.

As mentioned at the beginning, I take it that if the Deduction is supposed to bring in a strong conceptual idealism this should follow from its conclusion rather than being a premise of the argument. If we started with the assumption that our concepts determine what counts as an object (a conceptual idealist premise), then proving that the spatiotemporal objects that we can cognize fall under such concepts would not require any work. Thus, in thinking about the sense in which the argument expresses idealism, it is important that it should not involve assuming conceptual idealism (though it could assume the idealism with respect to spatiotemporal appearances that Kant takes to follow from space and time being merely the a priori forms of our intuition).

I have suggested we understand Kant as saying that if we only had empirical concepts, the spontaneity of thought (indefinitely many ways in which things could be synthesized or combined) would mean that we would not have determinate objects of thought, and no concept application could get off the ground. As I understand the argument, synthesizing properties using the non-empirical concept of an object in general is what enables us to produce determinate objects of thought from what

[12] He says that "[a] transcendental ground must therefore be found for the unity of the consciousness in the synthesis of the manifold of all our intuitions, hence also of the concepts of objects in general, consequently of all objects experience, without which it would be impossible to think of any object for our intuitions; for the latter is nothing more than the something for which the concept expresses such a necessity of synthesis" (A106); this "original and transcendental condition is nothing other than the **transcendental apperception**" (A107).

would otherwise be the chaotic swarm of appearances. This might be thought to mean that the way we see the world as divided into objects is not a function of the world. However, here it is crucial that the categories do not have empirical content so they do not impose specific determinate content on the object. The categories are not determining which particular objects there are by determining what principles of unity particular objects have; this is an empirical matter. Rather, what the transcendental concept of an object imposes is simply the idea of necessary unity: a unified subject of properties, where these properties have necessary relations for each other.

Rather than thinking that this means that it is up to us what counts as an object, Kant seems to think the reverse: it is only by thinking of objects in this way that we succeed in thinking of objects as constraining our cognition, rather than simply having a collection of subjective associations. It is only by using these concepts that we can think of a world of objects in such a way that it can give us resistance. In thinking of cognition as relating to an object we think of the object as being responsible for how our cognitions of it are determined: the object "is regarded as that which is opposed to our cognitions being determined at pleasure or arbitrarily [...] since insofar as they are relate to an object our cognitions must also necessarily agree with each other in relation to it, i.e., they must have that unity that constitutes the concept of an object" (A104–105). Kant thinks that in representing something as objective we represent it as constraining our representations of it; but we know that the spontaneity of combination means that combination is not given. As I understand him, Kant takes this to create a problem with how we could manage to represent objects as that which is opposed to our cognitions being determined at pleasure or arbitrarily. The solution is representing properties as unified by the transcendental concept of an object in general, which represents properties as having necessary connections with each other, and this enables us to represent the object as something constraining our cognition. Thinking of properties as unified in the transcendental concept of an object in general is how we are able to think of the properties as determined by the object.

As I understand this argument, it addresses a problem which would be a problem also for a realist: a realist empiricist who takes us to be presented with empirical particulars, but who accepts Kant's account of the spontaneity and generality of conceptual thought would have a problem with explaining how empirical concept application can get off the ground. Thinking that there are objects which, independently of us, are spatiotemporal causal unities is not enough to explain what it takes for us to have successful concept application in which we think of objects as such. It might be thought that the following claims would not apply for a realist:

> [i]t is clear, however, that since we have to do only with the manifold of our representations, that that *X* which corresponds to them (the object), because it should be something distinct from all of our representations, is nothing for us, the unity that the objects makes necessary can be nothing other than the formal unity of the consciousness in the synthesis of the manifold of the representations. Hence we say that we cognize the object if we have effected synthetic unity in the manifold of intuition. (A105)

However, in my view this problem would apply for finite receptive subjects who know things through being affected by them and having sensible representations of them, and don't have access to a thing as it is in itself apart from its sensible appearing. For a realist trying to account for our cognition, it will also be the case that the materials we have to build up our representation of the world are our sensible representations, and we do not have some further representation distinct from our representations of the object that constrains our representations.

It should be noted that seeing the Deduction as not introducing further idealism need not involve watering down transcendental idealism; it is compatible with as strong as you like a reading of the idealism introduced in the Aesthetic. However, the way Kant presents his conclusion at the end of the Deduction in both editions might be thought to indicate some further conceptual idealism. He says that the fact that the laws of appearances in nature must agree with the understanding and its a priori form ("its faculty of combining the manifold in general") is not strange, given that the laws exist only relative to the subject in which the appearances inhere (B164) and that "as exaggerated and contradictory as it may sound to say that the understanding is itself the source of the laws of nature, and thus of the formal unity of nature, such an assertion is nevertheless correct and appropriate to the object, namely experience" (A127). However, I think this can be read as expressing a kind of anti-realism about the necessity introduced by the categories; this necessity is something that we have proved of the spatiotemporal objects of cognition and not a world that exists independently of its cognizability by us. "If the objects with which our cognition has to do were things in themselves, then we would not be able to have any *a priori* concepts of them" (A128), but it is not so strange that the necessity we need to cognize objects is found in the objects of our empirical cognition.

References

Allais, L. (2009). Kant, non-conceptual content, and the representation of space. *Journal of the History of Philosophy*, *47*(3): 383¬–423.

Allais, L. (2015). *Manifest reality: Kant's idealism and his realism*. Oxford University Press.

Allais, L. (2016). Non-conceptualism in Kant: A survey of the recent debate. In D. Schulting (Ed.), *Kantian nonconceptualism* (pp. 1–26). Palgrave Macmillan.

Allais, L. (2017). Synthesis and binding. In A. Stephenson and A. Gomes (Eds.), *Kant and the philosophy of mind: Perception, reason and the self* (pp. 25–45). Oxford University Press.

Bauer, N. (2012). A peculiar intuition: Kant's conceptualist account of perception. *Inquiry*, *55*(3): 215–37.

Bird, G. (2006). *The revolutionary Kant*. Open Court.

Bowman, B. (2011). A conceptualist reply to Hanna's Kantian nonconceptualism. *International Journal of Philosophical Studies*, *19*(3): 417–46.

Ginsborg, H. (2008). Was Kant a nonconceptualist? *Philosophical Studies*, *137*(1): 65–77.

Gomes, A. (2014). Kant on perception: Naïve realism, nonconceptualism and the B-Deduction. *Philosophical Quarterly*, *64*(254): 1–19.

Gomes, A. (2017). Nonconceptualism, Hume's problem, and the Deduction. *Philosophical Studies*, *174*(7): 1687–98.

Griffith, A. (2012). Perception and the categories: A conceptualist reading of Kant's *Critique of pure reason*. *European Journal of Philosophy*, *20*(2): 193–222.

Grüne, S. (2011). Is there a gap in Kant's B Deduction? *International Journal of Philosophical Studies*, *19*(3): 465–90.

Grüne, S. (2016). Allais on intuitions and the objective reality of the categories. *European Journal of Philosophy*, *24*(1): 241–52.

Land, T. (2011). Kantian conceptualism. In G. Abel and J. Conant (Eds.), *Rethinking epistemology* (pp. 197–239). Berlin: de Gruyter, 2011.

Land, T. (2015). Nonconceptualist readings of Kant and the transcendental deduction. *Kantian Review*, *20*(1): 25–51.

McLear, C. (2015). Two kinds of unity in the *Critique of pure reason*. *Journal of the History of Philosophy*, *53*(1): 79–110.

Strawson, P. F. (2018). *The bounds of sense*. Routledge (first published 1966).

Tolley, C. (2016). Between 'perception' and understanding, from Leibniz to Kant. *Estudos Kantianos* 4.2: 71–98.

Tolley, C. (2019). *The meaning of 'perception' in Kant and his historical context*. Natur Und Freiheit: Akten Des XII. Internationalen Kant-Kongresses, De Gruyter (pp. 3243–51).

Williams, J. (2012). How conceptually guided are Kantian intuitions? *History of Philosophy Quarterly*, *29*(1): 58–78.

4

Kant on Concepts, Intuitions and Sensible Synthesis

Stefanie Grüne

In both versions of the Transcendental Deduction in the *Critique of Pure Reason* Kant writes that one function of the understanding is to synthesize sensible representations. In order to distinguish synthesis of sensible representation from synthesis of concepts in a judgment, I will call the first kind of synthesis *sensible synthesis* (cf. B130). For a long time it was usually assumed that sensible synthesis is a synthesis of sensations, that is representations that do not represent an object but refer solely to the subject (A320/B376), and that this synthesis of sensations results in and is a necessary condition for the formation of intuitions (see Ginsborg, 1997; Haag, 2007; Longuenesse, 1998; McDowell, 1994; Sellars, 1968; Strawson, 1982), where the term "intuition" is understood in the sense of Kant's definition from the beginning of the Transcendental Dialectic, namely as "conscious singular representation that relates immediately to its object" (A320/B 376–77). Since furthermore, it is generally agreed that the synthesis of the understanding involves deploying concepts,[1] interpreters like Hannah Ginsborg (1997) and the early John McDowell (1994) have claimed that from Kant's account of sensible synthesis in the Transcendental Deduction it follows that intuitions have conceptual content. In recent years the claim that sensible synthesis is a necessary condition for the production of intuitions has been challenged. Lucy Allais (2015), Robert Hanna (2001, 2005), Colin McLear (2016), and Clinton Tolley (2013, 2020) all argue for the claim that a concept-involving synthesis is not a necessary condition for having an *intuition* of an object, but for having a *cognition* of an object. Since for them the formation of an intuition does not presuppose that sensible synthesis takes place and therefore does not presuppose any deployment of concepts, they all characterize intuitions as having non-conceptual content. In this chapter I will argue for the claim that neither of these two positions is completely right and neither is completely wrong. As I see it, Kant occupies a middle position between the two positions I have just characterized. On the one hand, interpreters like Ginsborg and McDowell are right to insist that for Kant a concept-involving synthesis is indeed a presupposition for the production of intuitions. On the other

[1] As I use the term "deployment", concepts can be deployed without being applied in a judgment. According to my interpretation of Kant's theory of concepts, concepts can be deployed in two ways: either in judgments or in sensible synthesis. I reserve the term "application" for the deployment in a judgment.

Stefanie Grüne, *Kant on Concepts, Intuitions and Sensible Synthesis* In: *The Sensible and Intelligible Worlds: New Essays on Kant's Metaphysics and Epistemology.* Edited by: Karl Schafer and Nicholas F. Stang, Oxford University Press.© Stefanie Grüne 2022.
DOI: 10.1093/oso/9780199688265.003.0005

hand, Allais, Hanna, McLear, and Tolley are right to point out that intuitions have non-conceptual content.[2] At least, they are right if they interpret the term "concept" as we understand it today. This is because Kant distinguishes between different kinds of concepts, namely between obscure, clear, indistinct and distinct concepts. According to him, for a subject to synthesize sensible representations she only has to possess obscure concepts but does not have to possess clear or distinct ones. Yet, if one takes as a basis contemporary conceptions of concepts, then Kantian obscure concepts do not count as concepts at all. If one furthermore assumes that Kant uses the term "empirical intuition" more or less in the same way as we use the term "perception,"[3] then according to my interpretation we get the following result: Even though Kant claims that sensible synthesis requires possession of concepts, his position on the content of intuitions is much closer to the position of those contemporary philosophers who ascribe non-conceptual content to perceptions than to the position of those who believe that perceptions have conceptual content.

Before I argue for this interpretation, however, I need to make a qualification. In the contemporary debate about non-conceptual content, the thesis of non-conceptualism is construed in different ways. The basic distinction is that between state and content non-conceptualism.[4] *State non-conceptualism* says that a mental state has non-conceptual content if and only if it is possible to be in the state without possessing or applying any of the concepts that characterize the content of the state.[5] According to a state non-conceptualist, it is possible to perceive a tomato without possessing the concept of a tomato, of a vegetable, of redness, of a substance that is causally interacting with other substances, or of any other concept that characterizes the perception's content. State non-conceptualism is not a thesis about the *kind* or *structure* of the content of a mental state. Rather, it is a thesis about the conditions under which a subject can be in a mental state with objective representational content. *Content non-conceptualism*, by contrast, says that a mental state has non-conceptual content if and only if that mental state has a different kind of content than do beliefs and thoughts, where the content of beliefs and thoughts is usually understood as consisting of concepts.[6] In this chapter I only argue that Kant is a state non-conceptualist. In order not to confuse state and content non-conceptualism, from now on I will only talk about intuitions being non-conceptual *states*. I will not say anything concerning the question of whether these states have non-conceptual *content*.

[2] As will turn out in a moment, the position I ascribe to Kant should more precisely be characterized as the claim that for Kant intuitions are non-conceptual states.

[3] As I will point out below, Kant uses the term "intuition" in two different senses. The claim that what Kant understands by "empirical intuition" is roughly the same as what we today understand by "perception" is true only if the term "intuition" is understood in the more demanding of the two senses. That Kant's use of "empirical intuition" at least includes a use that corresponds to our use of "perception" is accepted by most Kant scholars regardless of whether they conceive of Kantian intuitions as conceptual or non-conceptual states. For an exception, see Tolley (2018, 2020).

[4] See Byrne (2004) and Speaks (2005). Speaks does not distinguish between state and content non-conceptualism, but rather between relative and absolute non-conceptualism. Nevertheless, these distinctions amount to roughly the same thing.

[5] Cf. Byrne (2004) and Speaks (2005).

[6] For an exception see Stalnaker (1998).

The basic idea of this chapter is that

(1) there is a fundamental exegetical difficulty concerning the interpretation of Kant's characterization of the relation between intuitions and concepts, and that
(2) one can solve this difficulty by assuming that (a) the formation of intuitions requires a concept-involving synthesis, and that (b) the concepts that play a role in sensible synthesis are obscure concepts.

In the first part of the chapter I will present the exegetical difficulty, which consists in the fact that Kant defends two claims with regard to the relation between intuitions and concepts that appear, at least at first glance, to be inconsistent with one another. Very roughly, these two claims are: (i) Human beings can form concepts only if they already possess intuitions. (ii) Intuitions arise only if human beings already possess concepts. In the second part, I will discuss three different ways in which Kant scholars have tried to save Kant from the charge of inconsistency. In the third part, I will present my own solution to the exegetical difficulty. I will argue that it is possible to show that claims (i) and (ii) are consistent, if one assumes that in the first claim Kant talks about clear concepts, whereas in the second claim he talks about obscure ones.

1. The Relation of Intuitions and Concepts

What then are the two apparently inconsistent claims regarding the relation of intuitions and concepts? The first claim follows from Kant's theory of concept-formation in the *Jäsche Logic*. According to Kant, concepts are formed through the acts of comparison, reflection, and abstraction (see *Log*, 9:93–94). This theory entails that in order to be able to form concepts, one must be able to compare objects with one another. However, in order to be able to compare objects with one another, one must perceive them or rather have intuitions of them. It thus follows from Kant's theory of concept-formation that intuitions are more basic representations than concepts. In other words: Kant appears to be assuming a *genetic primacy of intuitions vis-à-vis concepts* in the sense that one must already have intuitions in order to be able to form concepts. This not only follows from the theory of concept-formation in the *Jäsche Logic* but also is asserted by Kant in other works. In the A Deduction of the *Critique of Pure Reason*, for instance, he writes:

> Sensibility gives us forms (of intuition), but the understanding gives us rules. It is always busy poring through the appearances with the aim of finding some sort of rule in them. [...] The understanding is thus [...] a faculty for making rules through the comparison of appearances. (A126)

Since appearances are objects of intuition (see A20/B34) according to this passage, rules or rather concepts are formed by comparing objects of intuitions.[7]

[7] Similarly, in the *Prolegomena*, Kant claims that "sensible intuition [...] is made general through comparison" (4: 304). Since for Kant concepts are general representations, making an intuition general through comparison is nothing else than forming a concept by comparing intuitions or rather objects of intuitions.

On the other hand, from what Kant says about the generation of intuitions in the Transcendental Deduction in the *Critique of Pure Reason* it follows that we must already have concepts in order to be able to form intuitions: For Kant, the causal influence of an object on our senses does not directly bring about the presence of an intuition, but only the presence of sensations. In order for intuitions to arise, sensations must first be processed or synthesized in a certain manner. Furthermore, the synthesis of sensations leads to the formation of an intuition only if concepts function as rules for sensible synthesis.[8] This, at least, is the standard interpretation of Kant's theory of the formation of intuitions and in the second part of this chapter, I will argue that it is the correct one.[9] Given the correctness of the standard interpretation, Kant is asserting a *genetic primacy of concepts vis-à-vis intuitions* in the A Deduction: Intuitions can arise only if we already have concepts.

The two seemingly inconsistent claims regarding the relation of intuitions and concepts thus are:

(1) *The thesis of the genetic primacy of intuitions vis-à-vis concepts:* The understanding can form concepts only if sensibility already has supplied intuitions.
(2) *The thesis of the genetic primacy of concepts vis-à-vis intuitions:* Intuitions are generated only if one already possesses concepts that function as rules for synthesizing sensations into intuitions.

These claims do not seem like they could both be true. For, taken together, on the hand they say that the generation of intuitions presupposes that one already possesses concepts; on the other hand they say that the presence of intuitions is itself a condition on our being able to form concepts at all.

2. Three Conceptions of Sensible Synthesis

Kant's theory of sensible synthesis has been interpreted in three fundamentally different ways and these three different interpretations involve three distinct attitudes concerning the exegetical difficulty I have just outlined. In this part of the chapter, I will sketch these three positions, the proponents of which I refer to as judgmentalists, non-conceptualists, and conceptualists.

Judgmentalists assume that, for Kant, concepts can only be used in judging.[10] They either believe, as Ginsborg (1997, 2006a, 2006b), Robert Pippin (1982, pp. 116,

[8] I use the term "concepts as rules for sensible synthesis" because Kant himself describes concepts insofar as they are deployed in the synthesis of sensible representations as rules (see, e.g., A106). In characterizing concepts as rules for sensible synthesis I neither want to imply that in synthesizing sensations we *follow* a rule nor do I want to imply that sensible synthesis is an act of which we are always conscious.

[9] See pp. 98–100.

[10] I am using the concept of a judgment in a thoroughly Kantian sense and not in a Fregean one. Kant distinguishes between problematic, assertoric, and apodictic judgments. One forms a problematic judgment when one does not combine it with the assertion that it is true. Frege would not regard the forming of a problematic judgment as the forming of a judgment at all, but rather as the grasping of a thought. According to Frege (1918–19), the forming of a judgment presupposes the recognition of truth. The Kantian concept of judging is thus broader than the Fregean one and encompasses both what Frege regards as judging as well as what he regards as the grasping of a thought. Corresponding to this, interpreters like

125–26, 130, 133) and Peter Strawson (1982, pp. 86–89) do, that the concept-involving synthesis of sensible representations is a specific kind of judging, or they assume, as Wolfgang Carl (1992, pp. 150–66) does, that this synthesis involves making a judgment.[11] Since synthesizing sensations either consists in making a judgment or involves making a judgment, and since the components of judgments, for Kant, are concepts, no sensible synthesis can take place without the application of concepts.

How do judgmentalists manage the exegetical difficulty presented earlier? For Ginsborg and Pippin, closer examination reveals that Kant does not at all characterize the relation of intuitions and concepts in a contradictory manner. According to them, Kant is asserting a genetic primacy of concepts vis-à-vis intuitions but is not asserting a genetic primacy of intuitions vis-à-vis concepts. This is because they interpret Kant's theory of concept-formation differently from the way I do. Ginsborg and Pippin believe that the function of comparison, abstraction, and reflection is not to form concepts, but to make already formed concepts distinct.

Even though I think that this interpretation of Kant's claims about comparison, abstraction, and reflection is wrong (see Grüne, 2009, pp. 126–31), this is not the main reason why I reject the judgmentalist position. Mainly, I reject that position because according to Kant sensible synthesis does not involve forming judgments. This is clear from different statements that Kant makes. The first to be mentioned here is a passage from one of Beck's letters to Kant as well as Kant's response to it. On November 11, 1791, Beck writes to Kant:

> The *Critique* calls 'intuition' a representation that relates immediately to an object. But in fact, a representation does not become objective until it is subsumed under the categories. Since intuition similarly acquires its objective character only by means of the application of categories to it, I am in favour of leaving out that definition of 'intuition' that refers to it as a representation relating to objects. I find in intuition nothing more than a manifold accompanied by consciousness (or by the unique 'I think'), and determined by consciousness, a manifold in which there is as such no relation to an object. I would also like to reject the definition of 'concept' as a representation mediately related to an object. For both intuitions and concepts acquire objectivity only through the business (*Geschäft*) of the power of judgment which subsumes them under the pure concept of the understanding.
>
> (*Br*, 11:311; translation modified by author)

The upshot of this letter is that one should not refer to intuitions (as well as concepts, though this is not relevant for the present context) as representations that refer to objects, since intuitions first acquire objective reference "through subsumption under the categories" or rather "through the business of the power of judgment, which subsumes them under the pure concept of the understanding." According to

Ginsborg, who holds that intuiting an object implies making a judgment in the Fregean sense, fall into the first position, as well as interpreters like McDowell (1994, pp. 48–49), who holds that intuiting or perceiving an object only implies grasping a thought.

[11] Other judgmentalists include Paul Abela (2002), Henry Allison (1983), James van Cleve (1999), and the early McDowell (1994).

Beck, an intuition only gets objective reference when one applies a pure concept of the understanding or category to the intuition in a judgment. On the letter from Beck, directly on the margin of the passage cited above, Kant wrote:

> The determination of a concept through intuition for a cognition of the object belongs to the power of judgment but not the reference of the intuition to an object in general [...]. (*Br*, 11:311)

Here Kant explicitly denies that "the reference of the intuition to an object in general" is achieved by means of the power of judgment. He thus explicitly denies that an intuition, understood as a representation with objective reference, would arise as a result of applying concepts to it, or rather its object, in a judgment.

Secondly, there are passages in which Kant defends sensibility against the charge that the representations it supplies—that is, intuitions—are erroneous. For Kant this objection is unjustified, since only judgments can be erroneous, but having an intuition does not entail making a judgment. At the beginning of the Transcendental Dialectic in the *Critique of Pure Reason*, for example, he writes:

> Truth and illusion are not in the object, insofar as it is intuited, but in the judgment about it insofar as it is thought. Thus it is correctly said that the senses do not err; yet not because they always judge correctly, but because they do not judge at all. Hence truth, as much as error, and thus also illusion as leading to the latter, are to be found only in judgments, i.e., only in the relation of the object to our understanding. [...] In a representation of sense (because it contains no judgment at all) there is no error. (A293–94/B350)

And in the *Anthropology*, he writes:

> Semblance (*Schein*) is the ground for an erroneous judgment as a result of subjective causes that are falsely taken for objective; *appearance (Erscheinung), however, is not a judgment, but rather merely empirical intuition.* (7:142; italics mine)[12]

For our purposes, what is important in these two quotations is the following: In the first sentence of the first quotation, Kant distinguishes having an intuition of an object and making a judgment about an object. He would not make this distinction if it were his view that intuiting an object involves making a judgment. Accordingly, in the last sentence of the first quotation he explicitly states that representations of the senses, that is, intuitions, do not contain a judgment.[13] By the same token, he would not say of appearances in the second quotation that they are not a judgment but

[12] See also *Prol*, 4:290–91; *Anth*, 7:146; *Log*, 9:53–54; and *Refl* 241, 15:92.

[13] Against my interpretation, one might object that it is not clear whether in the first quotation Kant actually means intuitions by representations of the senses. Representations of the senses could also be sensations. In this case, the quotation could not be used in order to show that having an intuition for Kant does not involve making a judgment. However, if one proceeds from the plausible assumption that Kant is making the same assertion in the first and last sentence of the quotation, then it turns out that a representation of the senses is a representation of the object insofar as it is intuited, and thus an intuition.

rather mere intuitions if it were his view that having an intuition involves making a judgment.[14]

Lastly, I will cite passages in which Kant distinguishes between aesthetic and logical distinctness and claims that intuitions could be aesthetically distinct without being logically distinct. In *On a Discovery Whereby Any New Critique of Pure Reason Is to Be Made Superfluous by an Older One* which was directed against Johann Augustus Eberhard, Kant writes:

> For there is also a distinctness in the intuition, and hence also in the representation of the individual, not merely of things in general [...], which may be called aesthetic and is quite different from logical distinctness through concepts (supposing an Australian aborigine, for example, were to see a house for the first time, and was near enough to distinguish all its parts, though *without having the least concept of it*) [...]. (8:217; italics mine)

Kant makes a similar assertion in a footnote from the eighth chapter of the First Introduction to the *Critique of Judgment*:

> For even the greatest lack of distinctness of a mode of representation by concepts (e.g. that of right) still retains the specific difference of the latter in regard to its origin in the understanding, and the greatest distinctness of intuition does not in the least bring the latter nearer to the former, because the latter mode of representation has its seat in sensibility. Logical distinctness is also totally different from aesthetic distinctness, and the latter can obtain even though we *do not represent the object to ourselves by means of concepts at all*, that is, even though the representation, as intuition, is sensible. (20:227; italics mine)[15]

For Kant, an intuition is *aesthetically* distinct if and only if the subject of the intuition can spatially or temporally distinguish parts of the intuited object from one another. My intuition of a house is of a very low degree of aesthetic distinctness when I observe the house from a great distance and can only spatially distinguish the roof of the house from its walls. When I move closer to the house so that I can also distinguish its windows and doors, the intuition is aesthetically distinct to a higher degree. A representation of an object x is *logically* distinct if I apply a concept to x or form a judgment about x. The more judgments I form about x, the more logically distinct my representation of x becomes. Interestingly, according to the two quotations, it is possible to have an aesthetically distinct representation of an object without possessing any concept of this object, and hence without forming any judgment about it.[16]

[14] For a different interpretation of these passages see McLear (2016). I argue against this interpretation in Grüne (2014).

[15] See also *Refl* 220, 15:84; and *Log*, 9:33.

[16] I take it that when, in the passages quoted above, Kant claims that having an aesthetically distinct intuition does not require possessing any concepts, he uses the term "concept" in the sense of "clear concept."

Kant thus repeatedly claims that intuiting an object does not involve forming a judgment. Hence, the synthesis of representations that results in the presence of an intuition does not include forming a judgment.

I now come to the second interpretation of Kant's theory of sensible synthesis, namely, non-conceptualism. Non-conceptualists assume that the formation of an intuition does not presuppose any involvement of concepts. According to Allais, McLear, and Tolley this is because sensible synthesis, which—as they agree—is concept-involving, is not necessary to produce intuitions; rather it is necessary for empirical cognition.[17] A different non-conceptualist position is defended by Hanna, who believes that at least certain elements of sensible synthesis, namely synthesis of apprehension and synthesis of reproduction, have to take place in order for intuitions to be produced. Still, he is a non-conceptualist, because he does not take the synthesis of recognition, which according to him is the only element of sensible synthesis that implies the use of concepts, to be a condition for the production of an intuition. Since Hanna does not ascribe apprehension and reproduction to the understanding, the non-conceptualists I have mentioned all agree that the understanding does not play any role in the formation of intuitions.

Just like judgmentalists, non-conceptualists do not think that Kant describes the relation of intuitions and concepts in a contradictory manner. According to them, Kant defends the thesis of the genetic primacy of intuitions vis-à-vis concepts. But since, on their view, deploying concepts is not necessary for having intuitions, they dispute the claim that Kant defends the thesis of the genetic primacy of concepts vis-à-vis intuitions.

Apart from agreeing that for Kant neither concepts nor the understanding play any role in the formation of intuitions, non-conceptualists defend rather different positions. Especially they disagree with respect to their interpretation of Kant's conception of synthesis. Thus, in order to give a thorough critique of non-conceptualism one would have to examine the different positions one by one. For reasons of space I cannot do this here.[18] Instead, I will only make two very general objections against non-conceptualism. The first is that the claim that the generation of intuitions does not presuppose a synthesis of the understanding does not fit very well with textual evidence. The second is that at least so far, non-conceptualists have not been able to explain what exactly is Kant's strategy for proving what he wants to prove in the transcendental deduction.

Before I present these objections, let me make a clarificatory remark. One reason why the debate between conceptualists (and judgmentalists) on the one hand and non-conceptualists on the other hand is rather complicated is that in the *Critique of Pure Reason* Kant uses the term "intuition" in two different ways. Sometimes he uses

[17] To be precise, Tolley's (2020) position is a little bit more complicated than this. As he sees it, only the third element or kind of sensible synthesis, namely synthesis of recognition, which, according to Tolley, results in the generation of cognitions, involves concepts. Synthesis of apprehension, which in Tolley's view, leads to the generation of perceptions, and synthesis of reproduction, which, according to him, leads to the generation of acquaintance, do not involve concepts.

[18] For a specific objection to Hanna's position, which also concerns parts of Allais' position in Allais (2009), see Grüne (2009). For a specific objection against the position Allais defends in Allais (2015), see Grüne (2016).

"intuition" as a term for a manifold of unsynthesized sensations.[19] As I see it, intuitions in the sense of manifolds of unsynthesized sensations are representations that are neither conscious nor intentional. Thus, even though I agree with non-conceptualists that Kant accepts intuitions that are not the product of sensible synthesis, we disagree insofar as for non-conceptualists such intuitions are conscious representations of perceptual particulars,[20] whereas as I see it, intuitions in the sense of manifolds of unsynthesized sensations are neither conscious nor intentional mental states. In other words, the dispute between conceptualists and non-conceptualists is not about the question of whether for Kant there *are* intuitions that do not presuppose sensible synthesis, but about the question of whether intuitions in the sense of Kant's definition of "intuition" at the beginning of the Transcendental Dialectic (A320/B376–77), namely, intuitions as conscious singular representations that relate immediately to objects and thus are intentional states, presuppose sensible synthesis. In this chapter, I use the term "intuition" in the sense of Kant's definition at the beginning of the Transcendental Dialectic.

I now come to my first objection to non-conceptualism. Contrary to what non-conceptualists claim, at least in the A Deduction[21] there is ample evidence that the formation of an intuition indeed presupposes sensible synthesis.[22] At the end of the section on the synthesis of apprehension, for example, Kant points out that besides an empirical synthesis of apprehension there also has to be an a priori one. He writes:

> Now this synthesis of apprehension must also be exercised *a priori* [...]. For without it we would have *a priori* neither the representations of space nor of time, since these can be generated only through the synthesis of the manifold that sensibility in its original receptivity provides. (A99–100)

According to this passage, without a synthesis of apprehension we would not have representations of space and time, because these representations can only be *produced* (*erzeugt*) if a manifold of representations yielded by sensibility is synthesized. Since representations of space and time are either intuitions or concepts of space and time, and since concepts are not generated by "the synthesis of the manifold that sensibility [...] provides," by "representations of space and time" Kant here means

[19] See for example the following sentence from the beginning of the A Deduction: "Now in order for **unity** of intuition to come from this manifold [...], it is necessary first to run through and then to take together this manifold, which action I call the **synthesis of apprehension**, since it is aimed directly at the intuition." Since according to this passage, synthesis of apprehension is *aimed at* intuition, by "intuition" Kant here cannot mean the product of synthesis.

[20] One exception on the side of the non-conceptualists is Tolley, for whom intuitions are unconscious representations. See Tolley (2018, 2020).

[21] I believe that in the B Deduction Kant did not change his mind about the function of sensible synthesis. For reasons of space I will not argue for this claim.

[22] In claiming that sensible synthesis results in the formation of intuitions, I do not want to deny that it results in the formation of cognitions. As I see it, Kant has at least two notions of cognition. According to the narrow notion of cognition, a cognition requires an intuition and a concept. According to the wide notion of cognition, every conscious objective representation is a cognition. Thus, every intuition regardless of whether it is combined with a concept or not is a cognition in the wide sense. Cf. Grüne (2009, pp. 27–30).

"intuitions of space and time." Similarly, in the section on synthesis of reproduction he writes:

> Now it is obvious that if I draw a line in thought, or think of the time from one noon to the next [...] I must necessarily first grasp one of these manifold representations after another in my thoughts. But if I were always to loose the preceding representations (the first parts of the line, the preceding parts of time [...]) from my thoughts and not reproduce them when I proceed to the following ones, then no whole representation [...], not even the purest and most fundamental representations of space and time, could ever arise. (A102)

In this passage Kant claims that in order for the most fundamental representation (*erste Grundvorstellung*) of space and time to *arise* (*entspringen*), representations of the parts of the represented spatial or temporal regions not only have to be apprehended but also have to be reproduced. Since in the Transcendental Aesthetic Kant has made huge efforts to prove that the most fundamental representation of space and time is not a concept, but an intuition, in the quoted passage Kant claims that apprehension and reproduction both have to take place for intuitions to be produced.[23]

Furthermore, in the following passage from the A Deduction Kant writes:

> [W]e say that we cognize the object if we have effected synthetic unity in the manifold of intuition. But this is impossible if the intuition could not have been produced through a function of synthesis in accordance with a rule. (A105)

In the second sentence of this passage, Kant one more time claims what non-conceptualists deny, namely that synthesis (in accordance with a rule) is a necessary condition for the production of intuitions. To give a final example, the section on the synthesis of recognition begins as follows:

> Without consciousness that that which we think[24] is the very same as what we thought a moment before, all reproduction in the series of representations would be in vain. (A103)

According to this passage, reproduction without recognition would be in vain. This means that for whatever reproduction is a necessary condition, recognition is also necessary. Since—as we already know—reproduction is a necessary condition for the

[23] Since at the beginning of the passage from A102 Kant talks about what has to be the case in order for a *thought* of a line or a time to be generated, one might assume that in the passage Kant does not deal with conditions for having *intuitions* of space and time, but deals with conditions for having *thoughts* about space and time. Yet, since according to the last sentence Kant is concerned with conditions for the generation of the *most fundamental* representations of space and time, which are intuitions and not concepts, this assumption cannot be right. I take it that in A102 Kant uses the terms "thought" and "think" in the sense of "representation" and "represent."

[24] I take it that as in the quotation from A102 Kant here uses the term "think" in the sense of "represent." See the preceding footnote.

production of intuitions, it turns out that the same is true of recognition.[25] Furthermore, since, as nobody doubts, synthesis of recognition involves the deployment of concepts the section on the synthesis of recognition shows that one cannot have an intuition without possessing certain concepts.[26]

My second objection to non-conceptualism is that non-conceptualists, at least so far, have not managed to explain how the argument of the transcendental deduction is supposed to work. In §13 Kant points out that a transcendental deduction is "the explanation of the way in which concepts can relate to objects *a priori*" (A85/B117). Accordingly, the transcendental deduction of the categories is supposed to prove that the categories can relate to objects a priori. There are several passages which show that the objects of which the transcendental deduction has to prove that the categories relate to them, are objects of *intuition*. At the beginning of §24 of the B Deduction, for example, Kant writes:

> The pure concepts of the understanding are related through the mere understanding to objects of intuition in general, without it being determined whether this intuition is our own or some other but still sensible one [...]. But since in us a certain form of sensible intuition *a priori* is fundamental, which rests on the receptivity of the capacity for representation (sensibility), the understanding, as spontaneity, can determine the manifold of given representations in accord with the synthetic unity of apperception, and thus think *a priori* synthetic unity of the apperception of the manifold of **sensible intuition**, as the condition under which all objects of our (human) intuition must necessarily stand, through which then the categories, as mere forms of thought, acquire objective reality, i.e. application to objects that can be given to us in intuition. (B150)

From this passage we learn that the categories apply, first, to all *objects of intuition in general* (through the mere understanding), and secondly, to all *objects of our human intuition*. What is important to me in this context is not the fact that in the quotation Kant distinguishes between two steps or parts of the Transcendental Deduction, but the fact that according to Kant in both steps what is shown is that the categories apply to objects of *intuition* (be it objects of intuition in general or objects of our intuition). Furthermore, in this passage Kant characterizes the objective reality of a concept, not—as in other passages—generally as "relation to an object" (A109), but specifically as applicability to "objects that can be given to us in intuition." Thus, from §24 we learn that the goal of the deduction, which on a very abstract level, can be described as proving that the categories have relation to an object, consists in proving that the categories have relation (or are applicable) to objects of (our sensible) intuition (cf. B159–60). My claim that in the deduction Kant wants to prove that the categories are applicable to objects of intuition is also confirmed by those passages in which Kant claims that the categories prescribe laws to appearances (see, e.g., B163). Since for Kant an appearance is the "undetermined object of an empirical intuition"

[25] Thus, Hanna, who claims that apprehension and reproduction jointly are sufficient for the production of an intuition, cannot be right.

[26] Compare also A116, A120–21.

(A20/B34), saying that the categories ascribe laws to appearances is the same as saying that the categories prescribe laws to objects of intuition, which is nothing else than to say that the categories are applicable to objects of intuition.[27]

Conceptualists and judgmentalists usually assume that Kant's strategy to prove that the categories are applicable to objects of intuition very roughly goes like this: Kant tries to show that the categories have to be deployed in every act of synthesis of sensations into intuitions. Furthermore, he assumes that if a concept is deployed in an act of sensible synthesis that results in the formation of an intuition, then this concept is applicable to the object of the resulting intuition. Given that Kant is successful in convincing the reader of the truth of these two claims, he indeed manages to prove that the categories are applicable to all objects of intuitions.

Clearly, non-conceptualists cannot ascribe this kind of argument to Kant because according to them intuitions are not the product of sensible synthesis. Thus, they either have to deny that Kant wants to prove that the categories are applicable to all objects of intuitions, which—as I have just argued—is a claim that comes at a high exegetical cost. Or they have to claim that Kant's strategy to prove the objective reality of the categories is not the one that is usually ascribed to him, but that he pursues a different one, one that does not involve showing that the categories have to be deployed in sensible synthesis. Yet, as I see it, so far, no conceptualist has managed to give a convincing alternative interpretation of how Kant tries to prove that the categories are applicable to objects of intuitions.[28]

Finally, I would like to discuss an interpretation of Kant's theory of sensible synthesis that I refer to as "conceptualism": Conceptualists like Johannes Haag (2007), Thomas Land (2011), Béatrice Longuenesse (1998), Wilfrid Sellars (1968), and Robert Paul Wolff (1963) agree with judgmentalists that the presence of intuitions presupposes the possession of concepts; they agree with the non-conceptualists that intuiting an object does not imply forming a judgment. According to them, sensible synthesis is an activity that is distinct from any form of judging, but nevertheless involves the deployment of concepts. Conceptualists thus assume that concepts can be used in two fundamentally different ways: first, as components of judgments; secondly, in sensible synthesis, where sensible synthesis is not a form of judging.

[27] In saying that the goal of the Transcendental Deduction consists in proving that the categories are applicable to objects of intuitions, I do not want to deny that this goal can also be described as the goal of proving that the categories are applicable to objects of experience. Since experience for Kant is empirical cognition and since Kant uses the term "cognition" in a narrow and a wide sense (see note 22), he uses the term "experience" in a narrow and a wide sense as well. According to the wide concept of experience, every objective, conscious, empirical representation is an experience. Thus, in proving that categories apply to objects of intuitions one proves that they are applicable to objects of experience, where "experience" is understood in the wide sense.

[28] Whereas most non-conceptualists do not address the objection I have just made, in *Manifest Reality* (2015), Allais explicitly claims that Kant wants to prove that the categories are applicable to all objects of intuition, but that he does not argue for this claim by showing that the categories are rules for sensible synthesis. She writes: "[I]t might be argued that Kant's aim in the Deduction is inconsistent with my non-conceptualist reading of intuition, since he wants to show that everything given in intuition must fall under the categories. However, demonstrating the latter is straightforwardly not the same as showing that everything given in intuition must fall under the categories in order to be presented to us in intuition. Similarly, the idea that we need to justify our entitlement to apply the categories to objects does not imply this can be justified only by showing that the categories are conditions of being given objects in intuition" (p. 174). In Grüne (2016), I argue that Allais is not successful in ascribing an alternative strategy to Kant.

In contrast to non-conceptualists and judgmentalists, conceptualists ascribe to Kant both the thesis of the genetic primacy of intuitions vis-à-vis concepts and the thesis of the genetic primacy of concepts vis-à-vis intuitions. They thus have the problem of explaining how Kant can defend both claims without thereby occupying an incoherent position. Conceptualists solve this difficulty by means of the assumption that the term "concept" is used in different ways in the two seemingly contradictory theses. Here, conceptualists have different options. One is to make use of Kant's distinction between empirical and a priori concepts, more specifically, the categories.[29] According to this strategy, for having an intuition it is sufficient that the categories function as rules for sensible synthesis. Kant would thus be asserting the claim of the genetic primacy of concepts vis-à-vis intuitions only in regard to the categories, not in regard to empirical concepts. It is assumed, moreover, that having intuitions is only a presupposition for forming empirical concepts—not for possessing the categories. Kant would thus be asserting the claim of the genetic primacy of intuitions vis-à-vis concepts only in regard to empirical concepts. As a result, the two claims about the relation of intuitions and concepts are interpreted in the following way:

(1) *The thesis of the genetic primacy of intuitions vis-à-vis concepts:* The understanding can form empirical concepts only if sensibility already has supplied intuitions.
(2) *The thesis of the genetic primacy of concepts vis-à-vis intuitions:* Intuitions are generated only if one already possesses categories that function as rules for synthesizing sensations into intuitions.

As I see it, the assumption that the possession of the categories (as clear concepts)[30] does not presuppose having intuitions is false. Kant repeatedly emphasizes that all concepts, not just empirical concepts, are made according to their form.[31] Hence, even the categories must be formed in some manner. Unfortunately, Kant says very little about how this happens. In the *Jäsche Logic* (9:94) he writes that the categories are formed by the act of reflection. One of the very few passages in which Kant illustrates what he might mean by saying that the categories are formed by reflection is a passage from *De mundi sensibilis*, where Kant characterizes the categories or pure concepts of the understanding "as abstracted from the laws inherent to the mind (by attending to its actions on the occasion of an experience) and therefore as acquired concepts" (2:395).[32] It is unclear what exactly the "actions on the occasion of an experience" are supposed to be. Such acts could either be acts of forming judgments or they could be acts of sensible synthesis. In the first case we would acquire the pure concepts of the understanding by reflecting on or paying attention to the laws according to which we form judgments. According to the second model we would

[29] This way of solving the exegetical difficulty is often suggested to me in discussion. See also Wolff (1963).

[30] For the distinction between clear and obscure concepts, see the third section of this chapter.

[31] See *Log*, 9:93–94, *KrV*, A56/B80, *Refl* 2851, 16:546, *Refl* 2855, 16:547, *Refl* 2856, 16:548, and *Refl* 2859, 16:549.

[32] In *MSI*, Kant does not yet speak of categories, but instead of concepts of the understanding.

acquire them by paying attention to the laws according to which sensations are synthesized.

Neither model, however, is consistent with the claim that the possession of the categories (as clear concepts) does not presuppose the presence of intuitions. We can pay attention to the way in which we form judgments only if we actually form judgments. As long as we have not acquired the pure concepts of the understanding, such judgments can only be composed of empirical concepts, but the possession of empirical concepts presupposes the presence of intuitions. Accordingly, on the first model the acquisition of categories presupposes having intuitions. The same holds for the second model. One can pay attention to the activity of sensible synthesis only if this takes place, that is, only if intuitions are formed. Therefore, according to both models, the formation of the categories (as clear concepts) presupposes having intuitions. Thus, the first conceptualist strategy to solve the exegetical difficulty is not successful.

3. My Solution for the Exegetical Difficulty

Like other conceptualists, I assume that Kant's seemingly contradictory characterization of the relation of intuitions and concepts can be proven to be a coherent position by demonstrating that he uses the term "concept" in different ways. However, I distinguish myself from other conceptualists by assuming that the relevant distinction is the distinction between obscure and clear concepts.

According to Kant, all concepts are either obscure or clear, and all clear concepts are either confused or distinct. He explains what it means to possess a concept in an obscure, clear, or distinct way by citing certain capacities that are sufficient for possessing a concept in such a way. Having the capacity to infer from the application of a concept *F* to the application of its component concepts is sufficient for possessing a *distinct* concept *F*.[33] One possesses the distinct concept of a tree, say, if one can infer from the fact that an object falls under the concept of a tree to the fact that it falls under the concept of having a trunk, of having branches and of having leaves. Having the capacity to classify *F*s as such is sufficient for possessing a *clear* concept *F*, where one classifies an *F* if and only if one responds differentially to *F*s and is aware of the fact that the *F* in question agrees with all other *F*s in being *F* (see Grüne, 2009, pp. 84–97).

While I think it is relatively uncontroversial that Kant conceives of distinct and clear concepts in the manner just described, it is fundamentally less clear what exactly he understands by obscure concepts. Kant himself characterizes obscure concepts in a purely negative fashion—namely, as concepts of which the subject is not conscious.[34] I will argue that possessing an *obscure* concept *F* consists in having the capacity to combine sensations[35] with one another in a certain way, where "combining sensations" is understood in the sense of "taking or grasping the sensations'

[33] See, e.g., *Log*, 9:34; *V-Lo/Bus*, 24:617; *Refl* 2385, 16:338–39.

[34] See, e.g., *Refl* 1705, 16:88; *V-Lo/Dohna*, 24:702; *V-Lo/Busolt*, 24:635.

[35] By "sensation" I here mean unsynthesized sensible representations the content of which is spatiotemporally structured.

contents as a unity." Here it is important to note that by "taking or grasping the content of sensations as a unity" I do not mean classifying the sensations as forming a unity or judging that the sensations form a unity. Rather, this capacity is primitive in the sense that its actualization does not presuppose that one judges or makes an inference. For example, one possesses the obscure concept of a tree, if one has the capacity to take the content of various sensations of brownness and greenness as a unity in such a way that intuitions of a stump, branches, and leaves as belonging together are formed, and thus the intuition of a tree is generated. As I have said, taking the contents of the sensations of brownness and greenness as a forming a unity does not consist in classifying them as forming a unity. Instead taking these contents as forming a unity is what is responsible for the fact that the specific intuition of a tree and not another intuition is generated: If one was affected by a tree and one's sensibility delivered sensations of brownness and greenness, but one did not possess the obscure concept of a tree, then one would not have the capacity to grasp the content of these sensations in the required way and thus no intuition of a tree would be formed. Instead, sensible synthesis would result only in the formation of intuitions of brown and green spatial regions that do not belong together.[36]

For Kant, one possesses an obscure *empirical* concept *F*, if and only if one has the acquired capacity to grasp the contents of those sensations as a unity that correspond to the discursive marks contained in the concept *F*.[37] Such a capacity is not acquired through any conscious activity of the subject, but is formed in the same way as empirical mechanisms of association are formed: If certain sensations regularly have occurred together, the subject of the sensations acquires the capacity to conceive of the content of these sensations as a unity.[38]

One possesses an obscure *category*, if and only if one has the innate capacity to grasp the contents of several sensations as a unity in such a way that the resulting complex representation has categorial content.[39]

The main thesis of this chapter is that concepts as rules for sensible synthesis are obscure concepts. If one accepts this proposal, it turns out that Kant is asserting the claim of the genetic primacy of concepts vis-à-vis intuitions only in regard to obscure

[36] As I see it (Grüne, 2009, pp. 215–18), even though in such a case no *empirical* obscure concept would be deployed, the obscure *category* of quantity would be deployed.

[37] To give an example, let us assume that for Kant, the concept of a lemon contains the discursive marks of sourness and yellowness. Given this assumption, one possesses the obscure concept of a lemon if and only if one has the capacity to grasp the content of a sensation of sourness and the content of a sensation of yellowness as a unity in such a way that the intuition of a lemon is formed. As I see it, Kant's conception of empirical concepts gets complicated by the fact that he seems to have two different conceptions of sensible synthesis in mind: First, synthesis of representations of different *properties*, as in the example of the generation of an intuition of a lemon just given. Second, synthesis of representations of the *mereological parts* of an object, as in the example of the generation of the intuition of a tree given above. As I have described this synthesis, the intuition of a tree is generated by grasping the content of the representations of parts of a tree—leaves, branches, and a stump—as a unity. At A106, where, as I see it, Kant explains how concepts function as rules for sensible synthesis by giving the example of the concept of body, Kant seems to have the first conception in mind. By contrast, when Kant describes how sensible synthesis leads to the generation of the intuition of a line, or of a house (A102, B162), he seems to have the second conception in mind. My characterization of obscure empirical concepts fits better with the first conception of synthesis.

[38] For reasons of space, in this chapter I will not say anything further concerning empirical concepts. See Grüne (2009, pp. 232–46).

[39] I will argue for this claim on pp. 107–113 of this chapter.

concepts. Moreover, according to various logic lectures, Kant takes comparison, abstraction, and reflection to be responsible only for the formation of clear concepts, not for the formation of obscure ones.[40] Kant thus asserts the thesis of the genetic primacy of intuitions vis-à-vis concepts only in regard to clear concepts, but not in regard to obscure concepts. Hence, according to this proposal, Kant characterizes the relation of intuitions and concepts in the following way:

(1) *The thesis of the genetic primacy of intuitions vis-à-vis concepts:* The understanding can form clear concepts only if sensibility already has supplied intuitions.
(2) *The thesis of the genetic primacy of concepts vis-à-vis intuitions:* Intuitions are generated only if one already possesses obscure concepts that function as rules for synthesizing sensations into intuitions.

Before I argue for the claim that concepts as rules for sensible synthesis indeed are obscure concepts understood in the way I have outlined above, let me shortly compare my solution of the exegetical difficulty with another conceptualist solution that I have not mentioned so far. According to conceptualists like Haag, Longuenesse, and Sellars, in order to solve the exegetical difficulty, one has to distinguish between clear concepts and schemata. They assume that whereas the understanding can form clear concepts only if sensibility already has supplied intuitions, intuitions are generated only if one already possesses schemata.[41] How does this interpretation relate to my own one? I myself find it very difficult to understand what exactly a Kantian schema is and hence I am not too sure about how obscure concepts relate to schemata. My impression is that schemata, at least as they are conceived of by Haag, Longuenesse, and Sellars are something different from obscure concepts. According to Haag (2007, p. 199, n. 28, and p. 274) and Sellars (1968, pp. 5–7), one possesses a schema only if one also possesses the corresponding clear concept, whereas for my solution of the exegetical difficulty it is extremely important that one can possess an obscure concept without possessing the corresponding clear concept. According to Longuenesse (1998, pp. 116–17, 244–46, and 253), empirical schemata are the objects as well as the products of the three acts of comparison, reflection, and abstraction and the schemata of the categories are rules for *synthesis speciosa* as well as the product of

[40] *V-Met-L$_1$/Pölitz*, 28:328; *V-Met/Mron*, 29:878; *V-Lo/Busolt*, 24:635.

[41] More precisely, Longuenesse assumes that one needs two kinds of distinction between concepts in order to show that Kant has a consistent position concerning the relation between intuitions and concepts, namely the distinction between empirical concepts and the categories *and* the distinction between schemata and empirical concepts. According to Longuenesse, having an intuition, first, only presupposes that the schemata of the categories function as rules of sensible synthesis, and secondly, is a presupposition only for the formation of the schemata of empirical concepts as well as for the formation of empirical concepts and the categories, but not for the formation of the schemata of the categories. Thus, she interprets the two seemingly inconsistent claims in the following way:

(1) *The thesis of the genetic primacy of intuitions vis-à-vis concepts:*

The understanding can form empirical concepts, categories and schemata of empirical concepts only if sensibility already has supplied intuitions.

(2) *The thesis of the genetic primacy of concepts vis-à-vis intuitions:*

Intuitions arise only if one already possesses the schemata of the categories that function as rules for synthesizing sensations into intuitions.

synthesis speciosa. Obscure concepts by contrast are not generated by the acts of comparison, reflection, and abstraction, and they are not the outcome of *synthesis speciosa*.

These considerations at most suggest that schemata, as conceived of by Haag, Longuenesse, and Sellars, are something different from obscure concepts, but do not exclude that obscure concepts could turn out to be nothing else than schemata, understood in a slightly different manner. In claiming that concepts as rules for sensible synthesis are obscure concepts I thus do not want to deny that they might be schemata.

In the remainder of this chapter I will substantiate my claim that concepts as rules for sensible synthesis are obscure concepts. In doing so I will also provide evidence for the claim that Kant indeed conceives of obscure concepts in the way I have described above.

So far, I have argued that in order to understand Kant as characterizing the relation between intuitions and concepts in a consistent way, one has to assume that for him concepts as rules for sensible synthesis are something else than concepts as the result of the three acts of concept formation. Yet, it is not only the case that this view has to be attributed to Kant in order to protect him from the charge of being inconsistent. Furthermore, in the *Critique of Pure Reason* Kant himself distinguishes between these two kinds of concepts. At the beginning of the section on the synthesis of recognition in the A Deduction for example, Kant writes:

> The word 'concept' could itself already lead us to this remark. For it is this one consciousness that unifies the manifold that has been successively intuited, and then also reproduced, into one representation. This consciousness may often only be weak [...]; but regardless of these differences one consciousness must always be found, even if it lacks conspicuous clarity, and without that concepts, and with them cognition of objects, would be entirely impossible. (A103–104)

For my purposes, what is important in this difficult to understand quotation is that Kant uses the term "concept" several times and the passage only makes sense if by "concept" he understands two different things. In first two sentences, Kant characterizes concepts as "this one consciousness" and takes concepts, so understood, to be responsible for the fact that a manifold of sensible representations is unified in a complex representation. Thus, Kant here talks about concepts as rules for sensible synthesis. According to the second clause of the last sentence, without one consciousness concepts would be impossible. Since, in the first two sentences Kant has identified the one consciousness with concepts, what he says in the second clause of the last sentence amounts to the claim that without concepts (as rules for sensible synthesis) concepts would be impossible. If, in this sentence, Kant understood the two tokens of "concept" in the same way, then he would assert an absolute triviality. Thus, in order to make sense of the last sentence one should assume that for Kant concepts as rules for sensible synthesis are something different from concepts the formation of which would not be possible if we did not have concepts of the first kind. This suggests that the general direction of my attempt to prove the compatibility of the two apparently contradictory theses is correct: The reason why the two claims are not incompatible is that Kant uses the term "concept" in different ways.[42]

Furthermore, there is also textual evidence for my claim that the relevant distinction is the distinction between clear and obscure concepts. In the above-cited passage, Kant writes that during every activity of synthesis a consciousness of unity, thus a concept, must "be met with, even if it lacks conspicuous clarity" (A104). Since concepts that are lacking in clarity are obscure concepts, Kant is here claiming that concepts as consciousness of unity can be obscure concepts. And a couple of paragraphs further down he says:

> All cognition requires a concept, however imperfect or obscure it may be; but as far as its form is concerned the latter is always something general, and something that serves as a rule. (A106)

Here Kant explicitly allows that concepts as rules of sensible synthesis could be obscure concepts.[43] In addition, the following reflection, which was likely made around the time of the genesis of Kant's *Dissertation*, also supports the thesis that rules of synthesis, for Kant, are obscure concepts:

> The clarity of intuitions is to be distinguished from the clarity of concepts. The former occurs before all concepts, or at least before the clear ones. (*Refl* 179, 15:67)

What is important for the present context is the second sentence of the reflection. It implies that there are non-clear, that is obscure concepts, in addition to clear ones, and that Kant does not want to claim of obscure concepts that intuitions take place before them. If one understands "*x* takes place before *y*" as a synonym for "*x* has genetic primacy vis-à-vis *y*," then Kant is thus claiming in Reflection 179 that intuitions have genetic primacy vis-à-vis clear concepts. But he is careful not to rule out the possibility that one must have obscure concepts in order for intuitions to be able to arise. The fact that he is careful not to rule this out suggests that he himself holds this view.

Apart from this general evidence for the claim that Kant conceives of concepts insofar they are deployed in sensible synthesis as obscure concepts, there are also specific considerations which show that Kant conceives of the *categories* on the one hand and of *empirical concepts* on the other hand insofar as they play a role in sensible synthesis as obscure concepts. For reasons of space I will not say anything concerning the evidence for assuming that empirical concepts as rules for sensible synthesis are obscure concepts (see Grüne, 2009, pp. 232–46). Instead, I will focus on the categories as rules for sensible synthesis. I will start with discussing a passage

[42] See also A224/B271. For an interpretation of this passage, see Grüne (2009, p. 207, n. 22).

[43] Even though Kant here *allows* that concepts as rules for sensible synthesis can be obscure concepts, he does not claim that they *have* to be such concepts. For an explanation of why he does not make the stronger claim see Grüne (2009, pp. 203–204).

from *On a Discovery*, which does not in itself show that the categories as rules for sensible synthesis are obscure concepts, but which will help us to get a better understanding of two passages in the *Critique of Pure Reason*:

> The *Critique* admits absolutely no implanted or innate *representations*. One and all, whether they belong to intuition or to concepts of the understanding, it considers them as *acquired*. But there is also an original acquisition [...], and thus of that which previously did not exist at all [...] According to the *Critique*, these are, *in the first place*, the form of things in space and time, *second*, the synthetic unity of the manifolds in concepts; for neither of these does our cognitive faculty get from objects as given therein in-themselves, rather it brings them about, *a priori*, out of itself. There must indeed be a ground for it in the subject, however, which makes it possible that these representations can arise in this and no other manner [...] and this ground at least is *innate*. [...] The ground of the possibility of sensory intuition is [...] the mere *receptivity* peculiar to the mind, when it is affected by something (in sensation), to receive a representation in accordance with its subjective constitution. Only this first formal ground, e.g. of the possibility of an intuition of space, is innate, not the spatial representation itself. For impressions would always be required in order to determine the cognitive faculty to the representation of an object (which is always a specific act) in the first place. Thus arises the formal *intuition* called space, as an originally acquired representation [...] the ground of which (as mere receptivity) is nevertheless innate and whose acquisition long precedes the determinate *concepts* of things that are in accordance with this form; the acquisition of the latter is an *acquisitio derivativa*, in that it already presupposes universal transcendental concepts of the understanding, which are likewise acquired and not innate, though their *acquisitio*, like that of space, is no less *originaria* and presupposes nothing innate save the subjective conditions of the spontaneity of thought. (8:221–23)

From this passage we learn that according to Kant all representations, including the pure intuitions of space and time and the categories are acquired. The contrast between the pure intuitions of space and time and the categories on the one hand, and empirical intuitions and empirical concepts on the other hand can be explained as follows: The reason why our representations have empirical content is that there are objects in the world whose properties correspond to the content of the relevant representations. By contrast, the reason why our representations have a priori content is that there is an *innate ground* of this content in us. That the a priori content of our representations does not depend on external things in the world, but on an innate ground in us, is the reason why Kant characterizes a priori representations as *originally* acquired. Still, we would not have any representations with a priori content, if objects did not affect our senses. This is why he characterizes a priori representations as originally *acquired*.

In the case of the pure intuitions of space and time, the innate ground of their content is characterized as "the mere receptivity peculiar to the mind [...] to receive a representation in accordance with its subjective constitution." The subjective constitution or innate ground of our receptivity consists in the disposition to process representations in such a way that their content has a certain formal structure, namely a spatiotemporal structure. The reason why Kant denies that the pure intuitions of space and time are innate is that in order for this disposition or capacity to be activated and thus for representations with spatiotemporal content to be produced, objects have to affect receptivity so that there *are* any representations (namely sensations) that can be spatiotemporally structured. It is important to note that Kant's characterization of the original acquisition of the pure intuitions of space and time in *On a Discovery* is not complete. The representations that are formed when objects affect our receptivity are not a priori intuitions, but empirical intuitions. They are empirical intuitions the content of which also contains an a priori element, namely spatiotemporal structure. As we learn from the Transcendental Aesthetic in the *Critique of Pure Reason*, in order to form an intuition that contains nothing but spatiotemporal structure, we have to abstract from all empirical aspects of the content of an empirical intuition. In this way, we arrive at a pure intuition of space or time (A20–21/B34–35).

In *On a discovery* Kant is much more explicit about the original acquisition of the pure intuitions of space and time than about the original acquisition of the categories. The only thing we learn about the latter is that the innate ground of the categories consists in "the subjective conditions of the spontaneity of thought." These subjective conditions could either be innate dispositions to synthesize sensations in a certain way or they could be innate dispositions to combine concepts in judgments in a certain way. In the remainder of this chapter, I will firstly argue that in the *Critique of Pure Reason* Kant has the first option in mind. Secondly, I will argue that as in the case of the pure intuitions of space and time, Kant's account of the acquisition of the categories in *On a discovery* is not complete, but only is an account of the first step of a two-step theory of the formation of the categories (as clear concepts). Thirdly, I will explain how the fact that Kant has such a two-step theory of the formation of the categories (as clear concepts) speaks in favor of the view that according to him concepts as rules for sensible synthesis are obscure concepts.

Let me start with the first point. In §13 of the Transcendental Deduction Kant writes:

> Now we already have two sorts of concepts of an entirely different kind, which yet agree with each other in that they both relate to objects completely *a priori*, namely the concepts of space and time, as forms of sensibility; and the categories, as concepts of the understanding. [...] Nevertheless, in the case of these concepts [...] we can search in experience [...] for the occasional causes of their generation, where the impressions of the senses provide the first occasion for opening the entire power of cognition to them and for bringing about experience, which contains two very heterogeneous elements, namely a matter for cognition from the senses and a certain form for ordering it from the inner source of pure intuiting and thinking, which on the occasion the former, are first brought into use and bring forth concepts. (A85–86/B118)

As in the passage from *On a discovery* Kant here claims that the categories (as well as the concepts of space and time) are not innate: What he wants to do in the passage is to look for the occasional cause of their *generation* and he ends by claiming that the categories are *brought forth*. In addition, what Kant says in §13 exactly parallels what he says in *On a discovery* in two further respects. Firstly, Kant's talk of the forms of intuiting and thinking in §13 corresponds to his talk about the subjective constitution or subjective conditions of sensibility and understanding. In both passages the idea seems to be that what is responsible for our having representations with a priori content is the fact that understanding and sensibility have a certain form or subjective constitution. And in both passages Kant points out that in order for representations with a priori content to be produced, sensibility and understanding have to be activated. Secondly, according to both passages in the case of sensibility the disposition to generate a priori content has to be activated by there being impressions. In contrast to *On a discovery*, the passage from §13 does not only contain a characterization of the form or subjective constitution of sensibility, but also contains a characterization of the form or subjective constitution of understanding: According to A85–86/B118, experience contains two elements, namely matter and form. The matter consists of the impressions of the senses. The form has two elements, namely the form of intuiting and the form of thinking. What is important is that the form of intuiting and the form of thinking have the function of ordering *exactly the same entity*, namely matter which consists in impressions of the senses. The form of intuiting *as well as* the form of thinking is brought into use "on the occasion of" matter, that is, it is activated when the senses deliver impressions or sensations. Since the way in which the understanding orders impressions or sensations is by synthesizing them, it turns out that according to §13 the innate form or innate subjective constitution of the understanding is not an innate disposition to combine concepts in judgments in a certain way, but an innate disposition to synthesize sensations in a certain way, namely in such a way that the resulting intuition has categorial content.

Let me now come to the second point, namely my claim that Kant's account of the original acquisition of the categories in *On a discovery* is not a complete theory of the formation of the categories as clear concepts, but only amounts to an account of the first part of a two-step theory of the formation of the categories.

As I have pointed out above, in *On a discovery* Kant does not describe how *pure* intuitions of space and time are generated. He only describes how *empirical* intuitions are generated the content of which does not only comprise empirical elements, but also an a priori element, namely spatiotemporal structure. Thus, as an account of the generation of the pure intuitions of space and time, the account in *On a discovery* is incomplete.

In the case of the categories the account is even doubly incomplete. This can easily be seen if one takes into account that the representations that are formed when our innate capacity to synthesize sensations is activated, are neither a priori representations nor concepts. By contrast they are empirical intuitions. Yet, even though they are empirical intuitions, their content does not only contain an empirical element (the content of the synthesized sensations), but also an a priori element, namely categorial structure (as well as spatiotemporal structure). What is missing in *On a discovery* and in the passage from §13 of the *Critique of Pure Reason* is an account of how we form representations that firstly contain *nothing but* categorial structure and secondly are *general* representations of this structure. In other words, what is missing is an account of how we form the categories as clear concepts. When at the very end of the passage from §13 Kant claims that the forms of the understanding, when brought into use, bring forth concepts, I take it that what he means is that in this way categorial content is generated for the first time. He does not want to deny that in order for this content to be the content of the categories as clear concepts some further acts of reflection and abstraction are required. As I have already pointed out in the second part of this chapter, concerning this topic, Kant does not give much of an explanation, even though he insists on the claim that the categories as well as empirical concepts are made according to their form.[44] Furthermore, from the passage from *De mundi sensibilis* (quoted on page 102), we learn that the categories are "abstracted from the laws inherent to the mind" and that this abstraction takes place by "attending to its actions on the occasion of an experience" (2:395). If the picture I have outlined so far is correct, then it should be clear that in the Critical period Kant would understand this passage from *De mundi sensibilis* in the following way: The action of the mind on the occasion of an experience is the act of sensible synthesis. By attending to this act, we attend to the laws inherent to the mind, that is to the laws according to which sensations are synthesized and which are responsible for the fact that the resulting intuitions exhibit categorial structure. In this way, the categories as clear concepts are formed. To sum up, the explanation of how the categories as clear concepts are formed comprises two steps: First, one has to explain how we come to have representations the content of which has categorial structure in the first place. The explanation is that our understanding is constituted in such a way that when it synthesizes sensations it does this in such a way that the resulting intuition has categorial structure. Secondly, one has to explain how we form general representations, that is, concepts of this categorial structure. Here the answer is that we form the categories as clear concepts by attending to or reflecting on the act of synthesizing sensations.

That Kant indeed defends such a two-step theory of the formation of the categories as clear concepts is suggested by the following passage from the very beginning of the Transcendental Analytic:

> I understand by an analytic of concepts [...] the [...] analysis of the faculty of understanding itself, in order to research the possibility of *a priori* concepts by seeking them only in the understanding as their birthplace [...]. We will therefore pursue the pure concepts into their first seeds and predispositions in the human understanding, where they lie ready, until with the opportunity of experience they are finally developed and exhibited in their clarity by the very same understanding, liberated from the empirical conditions attaching to them. (A65/B90–91)

In this passage, we find the same conception of the formation of the categories as in the other two passages I have quoted. Yet, here, in contrast to the other two passages, not only the first, but also the second step of the formation of the categories as clear concepts is mentioned. The last sentence of the quotation comprises three claims

[44] See page 102 of this chapter.

about the categories: The first is the claim that the categories lie ready (*liegen vorbereitet*) in the human understanding's first seeds and predispositions. From §13 we know that the first seeds or predispositions of the understanding are dispositions to order or synthesize impressions. Secondly, Kant claims that the categories are developed with the opportunity of experience. I take it that Kant's idea here is the following: The activation of the disposition to synthesize impressions results in the formation of representations that have categorial content, even though these representations are not concepts but are experiences, where by "experience" Kant here means "empirical intuition."[45] That the categories are developed thus does not amount to the claim that the categories as clear concepts are formed but amounts to the claim that categorial content as the content of an empirical intuition is generated. Thus, here again we find the first step of the formation of the categories, namely the generation of categorial content as part of the content of an empirical intuition.

That this interpretation is correct is substantiated by Kant's third claim, which is the claim that the categories, liberated from the empirical conditions attaching to them, are exhibited in their clarity by the understanding. The fact that the categories have to be liberated from empirical conditions suggests that at the second stage such conditions are still attached to them. This is just what according to the interpretation I have outlined so far is indeed the case. What is formed at the second stage is an empirical intuition, thus a representation that contains categorial as well as empirical content. To liberate the categories from the empirical conditions attaching to them is to separate the categorial content of an intuition from the empirical content. This, I suggest, is done by reflecting on the act of sensible synthesis and results in the formation of the categories as clear concepts. Thus, according to the last passage quoted above the generation of the categories as clear concepts consists of two steps: First, through the activation of the understanding's disposition to synthesize sensations categorial content is generated. Secondly, by separating this categorial content from empirical content the categories as clear concepts are formed.

To come to my third and last point: How does this account of the original acquisition of the categories hang together with my claim that the categories as rules for sensible synthesis are obscure concepts? As I have suggested above, to possess an obscure category is to possess the innate capacity to synthesize sensations in such a way that the resulting intuition has categorial content. This capacity is primitive in the sense that its actualization neither presupposes that one makes a judgment nor that one makes an inference. An obscure category is deployed in sensible synthesis if and only if such a capacity is actualized. Now, the claim that we possess and actualize the innate capacity to synthesize sensations in such a way that the resulting intuition has categorial content and the claim that this capacity is actualized in sensible synthesis are central elements of Kant's account of the original acquisition of the categories: As we have seen, according to Kant the understanding has an innate constitution or form and in §13 he describes this innate constitution as a disposition to order or

[45] As I have pointed out in note 27, Kant uses the term "experience" in a wide and in a narrow sense. I take I that in this passage, he uses "experience" in the wide sense, where "experience" means the same as "conscious objective empirical representation."

synthesize impressions. Furthermore, Kant's claim that by the activation of this disposition, which results in the formation of an intuition, the categories are brought forth or developed suggests that the disposition in question is a disposition to synthesize impressions in such a way that the resulting intuition has categorial content. Finally, according to Kant's account of the acquisition of the categories, the innate capacity to synthesize sensations is clearly primitive. Its actualization does not presuppose that clear or distinct concepts are already formed. Quite the contrary, according to Kant's account of the generation of the categories the formation of the categories as clear concepts presupposes that the capacity to synthesize sensations has been actualized. As we have seen, categorial content has to be generated by an act of sensible synthesis before clear concepts of such a content can be formed. Thus, Kant's account of the acquisition of the categories implies exactly the view of sensible synthesis I am ascribing to him.[46]

Even though in none of the passages about the acquisition of the categories, Kant characterizes categories insofar as they are deployed in sensible synthesis as obscure concepts, in the passage from the beginning of the Transcendental Analytic, Kant characterizes the capacity to synthesize sensations as a *seed* of the categories, thus as something that even though it is not a full-fledged category itself, is something out of which a full-fledged category can be developed. Characterizing our innate capacity to synthesize sensations as a seed of the categories, at least in my ears, comes very close to characterizing it as an obscure concept.

4. Concluding Remarks

In this chapter I have argued for the claim that concepts as rules for sensible synthesis are obscure concepts. On this interpretation it turns out that intuitions are not conceptual states in any interesting sense. Granted, it is not possible to have an intuition without possessing obscure concepts. But according to the understanding of concepts that is prevalent today, Kant's obscure concepts are not concepts at all. Even though there is disagreement as to how one should conceive of concepts, nobody assumes that we possess a concept if and only if we have the primitive capacity to grasp the contents of sensations as a unity.

Consequently, if one wonders where to place Kant in the contemporary debate I would suggest to understand him as defending the claim that perceptions are non-conceptual states.

[46] Note that in dealing with the three passages I have quoted above, denying that having the innate disposition to synthesize impressions in such a way that the resulting intuition has categorial content amounts to possessing an obscure category is of no use for a non-conceptualist. This is because non-conceptualists do not only deny that *concepts* play any role in the ordering of sensations, but more generally deny that *the understanding* plays any role in the ordering of sensations. Yet, in the passage from §13 Kant explicitly states that the understanding has an innate form or disposition to synthesize sensations and that this disposition is activated when sensibility delivers sensations.

References

Abela, P. (2002). *Kant's empirical realism*. Oxford University Press.

Allais, L. (2009). Kant, non-conceptual content and the representation of space. *Journal of the History of Philosophy*, *47*(3): 383–413.

Allais, L. (2015). *Manifest reality: Kant's realism and his idealism*. Oxford University Press.

Allison, H. E. (1983). *Kant's transcendental idealism: An interpretation and defense*. Yale University Press.

Byrne, A. (2004). Perception and conceptual content. In E. Sosa & M. Steup (Eds.), *Contemporary debates in epistemology* (pp. 231–50). Wiley-Blackwell.

Carl, W. (1992). *Die transzendentale Deduktion der Kategorien in der ersten Auflage der Kritik der reinen Vernunft: Ein Kommentar*. Klostermann.

Frege, G. (1918–19). Der Gedanke: Eine logische Untersuchung. *Beiträge zur Philosophie des deutschen Idealismus*, *2*: 58–77.

Ginsborg, H. (1997). Lawfulness without a law. *Philosophical Topics*, *25*(1): 37–81.

Ginsborg, H. (2006a). Thinking the particular as contained under the universal. In R. Kukla (Ed.), *Aesthetics and cognition in Kant's critical philosophy* (pp. 35–60). Cambridge University Press.

Ginsborg, H. (2006b). Empirical concepts and the content of experience. *European Journal of Philosophy*, *14*(3): 349–72.

Grüne, S. (2009). *Blinde Anschauung: Kant über Begriffe als Regeln sinnlicher Synthesis*. Klostermann.

Grüne, S. (2014). Reply to Colin McLear. Critique, Author-Meets-Critics Session. https://virtualcritique.wordpress.com/2014/08/20/reply-to-colin-mclear/

Grüne, S. (2016). Allais on intuitions and the objective reality of the categories. *European Journal of Philosophy*, *24*(1): 241–52.

Haag, J. (2007). *Erfahrung und Gegenstand: Das Verhältnis von Sinnlichkeit und Verstand*. Klostermann.

Hanna, R. (2001). *Kant and the foundations of analytical philosophy*. Oxford University Press.

Hanna, R. (2005). Kant and nonconceptual content. *European Journal of Philosophy*, *13*(2): 247–90.

Land, T. (2011). Kantian conceptualism. In G. Abel & J. Conant (Eds.), *Rethinking epistemology* (pp. 197–239). De Gruyter.

Longuenesse, B. (1998). *Kant and the capacity to judge*. Princeton University Press.

McDowell, J. (1994). *Mind and world*. Harvard University Press.

McLear, C. (2016). Kant on perceptual content. *Mind*, *125*(497): 95–144.

Pippin, R. (1982), *Kant's theory of form: An essay on the* Critique of pure reason. Yale University Press.

Sellars, W. (1968). *Science and metaphysics: Variations on Kantian themes*. Routledge & Kegan Paul.

Speaks, J. (2005). Is there a problem about nonconceptual content? *The Philosophical Review*, *114*(3): 359–98.

Stalnaker, R. (1998). What might nonconceptual content be? *Philosophical Issues*, *9*: 95–106.

Strawson, P. (1982). Imagination and perception. In R. Walker (Ed.), *Kant on pure reason* (pp. 82–99). Oxford University Press.

Tolley, C. (2013). The non-conceptuality of the content of intuitions: A new approach. *Kantian Review, 18*(1): 107–36.

Tolley, C. (2018). The meaning of "perception" in Kant and his historical context. In V. Waibel & M. Ruffing (Eds.), *Proceedings of the 12th International Kant Congress*. De Gruyter.

Tolley, C. (2020). Kant on the place of cognition in the progression of our representations. *Synthese, 197*(8): 3215–44.

Van Cleve, J. (1999). *Problems from Kant*. Oxford University Press.

Wolff, R. P. (1963). *Kant's theory of mental activity: A commentary on the transcendental analytic of the* Critique of pure reason. Harvard University Press.

5

A Transcendental Argument for the Principle of Possibility

Jessica Leech

1. The Principle of Possibility and a Puzzle

In the *Critique of Pure Reason*, Kant famously offers a "transcendental deduction" of the pure concepts of the understanding (categories), an argument intended to show that the categories are applicable to objects of possible empirical experience, in spite of their a priori origins. Following the Deduction, in the Analytic of Principles, Kant then offers more specific arguments for each of the categories: transcendental arguments to show how each of these concepts, and synthetic a priori principles arising from them, are necessary conditions of the possibility of experience of objects, and hence of the possibility of objects of experience. The categories of quantity and quality are necessary conditions for the possibility of magnitudes. The categories of relation—substance, causation, community—are necessary conditions for the possibility of determinate objective temporal relations. At least in the second edition of the *Critique*, the category of actuality—actual existence of outer objects—is arguably presented as a necessary condition for the possibility of inner experience (in the Refutation of Idealism). But what argument does Kant offer in this vein for the (remaining) modal categories, the concepts of possibility and necessity? Standard accounts of the *Critique* typically skip over the modal categories. But one should expect to find an argument here, just as with every other category. My aim in this chapter is to reconstruct a transcendental argument for the principle of possibility from the resources available to Kant, and to explain how the principle therefore has a crucial role to play in Kant's critical system.

Kant discusses the modal categories, and principles arising from them, in the section of the Analytic of Principles entitled "The Postulates of Empirical Thinking in General." A core claim of the Postulates is that, in contrast to the other categories, which determine what objects must be like in order to be able to feature in experience, the modal categories express a relation to our cognitive facilities, to our capacity for having experience of objects, rather than determining anything about those objects of which we have experience.

> The categories of modality have this peculiarity: as a determination of the object they do not augment the concept to which they are ascribed in the least, but rather express only the relation to the faculty of cognition. If the concept of a thing is

Jessica Leech, *A Transcendental Argument for the Principle of Possibility* In: *The Sensible and Intelligible Worlds: New Essays on Kant's Metaphysics and Epistemology.* Edited by: Karl Schafer and Nicholas F. Stang, Oxford University Press. © Jessica Leech 2022.
DOI: 10.1093/oso/9780199688265.003.0006

> already entirely complete, I can still ask about the object whether it is merely possible, or also actual, or, if it is the latter, whether it is also necessary? No further determinations in the object itself are hereby thought; rather, it is only asked: how is the object itself (together with all its determinations) related to the understanding and its empirical use, to the empirical power of judgment, and to reason (in its application to experience)? (A219/B266)

The postulates themselves accordingly express relations between the concept of a thing and conditions of experience: agreement with formal conditions for possibility; connection to material conditions for actuality; and determination in accordance with general conditions for necessity.

> 1. Whatever agrees with the formal conditions of experience (in accordance with intuition and concepts) is **possible.**
>
> 2. That which is connected with the material conditions of experience (of sensation) is **actual.**
>
> 3. That whose connection with the actual is determined in accordance with general conditions of experience is (exists) **necessarily.** (A218/B265–66)

There is a question concerning what the transcendental argument should be in the case of each of the three principles, but in this chapter I will focus on the principle of possibility (1).

The principle of possibility is the synthetic a priori principle arising from the category of possibility. It concerns *real possibility*, the possibility of things, not *logical possibility*, the possibility of thoughts or concepts. Kant writes of real and logical possibility:

> To **cognize** an object, it is required that I be able to prove its possibility (whether by the testimony of experience from its actuality or *a priori* through reason). But I can **think** whatever I like, as long as I do not contradict myself, i.e., as long as my concept is a possible thought, even if I cannot give any assurance whether or not there is a corresponding object somewhere within the sum total of all possibilities. But in order to ascribe objective validity to such a concept (real possibility, for the first sort of possibility was merely logical) something more is required. (Bxxvi)

The Elucidation of the modal categories is put in terms of "the object," i.e., whether the object is merely possible, actual, or necessary, by virtue of whether the concept of that thing bears suitable relations to our cognitive capacities (A219/B266), and not in terms of whether a concept is thinkable. Hence we can be assured that the modal category is, and the principle of possibility concerns, a concept of real, not logical, possibility.

The passage just quoted might already suggest a potential argument: To cognize an object, one must be able to prove its real possibility, but then surely proving the real possibility of something requires one to possess and apply the concept of real possibility, in which case any cognition of objects at all requires the possession and application of the concept of real possibility. This argument may appear to be more straightforward than that which I offer below, but there are a number of reasons to press on and not stop here. First, the argument doesn't explain much, insofar as it is taken for granted that cognition of objects requires a proof of possibility. Why should that be? The account offered below goes some way to providing an explanation of this. Moreover, this does not appear to be the argument presented in the text of the Postulates. The argument just sketched concerns the concept of real possibility in general, but the Postulates are concerned with the *principle of possibility*, given in terms of formal conditions of experience. This ignores another important side to real possibility, namely, the *material* condition of possibility. Objects of experience not only must be compatible with the forms of experience but also must be given to us. I explore this additional condition in detail elsewhere (Leech, 2017) but—anticipating the argument below—it is worth emphasizing one point: this can help us to explain why in his discussion of the principle of possibility, as outlined below, Kant focuses only on the possibility of a priori concepts. Such concepts do not derive their matter or content from experience, hence, they are exempt from the material condition of possibility. If Kant intended the principle of possibility to primarily assure us of the real possibility of the categories, then this explains why he only needed to consider formal, not material, conditions. And it also explains why he does not offer the more general argument canvassed here.

The search for a transcendental argument for the principle of possibility is accompanied by another kind of puzzle. This principle, along with the other postulates, makes explicit reference to conditions of experience, i.e. it makes reference not only to experience, but to the conditions under which experience is possible for us. Given Kant's view that something can only be an object of experience insofar as it conforms to conditions of experience, it makes sense that the real possibility of a thing should be understood as agreement of (the concept of) that thing with conditions on experience. If it didn't thus agree, then it could not be an object of experience, i.e., there could be no such thing in the empirical world. Indeed, in the passage quoted from Bxxvi, Kant is a hair's breadth away from explicitly equating real possibility with objective validity. What is puzzling is the claim that the concept of this should be a category; that not only this agreement, but the *concept* of this agreement, should be required for possible experience. A category is a concept the possession and deployment of which is a necessary condition of the very possibility of experience. We should then ask why the very possibility of experience presupposes our grasp of a concept so sophisticated as to make reference to the conditions under which experience is possible for us. Why should we be required to conceptually reflect upon our cognitive capacities (formal conditions of experience) and the relation between these capacities and the concepts of things (agreement) to make experience possible? In sketching an argument for the principle, I hope to also provide a solution to this puzzle, i.e., to shed light on why, according to Kant, we require such a sophisticated concept as a prerequisite to experience.[1]

[1] I have in mind here a fairly weak notion of experience: empirical cognition, understood roughly as concepts applied to empirical intuition. If one had a much stronger notion of experience, for example, as required by the "qualified phenomenalist" in Stang (2016), this prerequisite would be less puzzling, but one would have more work to do to defend the stronger notion.

Kant sets the modal categories apart from the others. I will expand on this more in due course, but it should already be noted that, as a consequence, Kant takes them to require a different kind of justification to the other categories and their principles. This means that any transcendental argument may likely be of a different kind to those appearing earlier. But it does not mean that there should be *no* argument. For, even a different kind of justification is still justification.

There is a bad solution to the puzzle, which should be dismissed from the outset. Kant's project in the *Critique of Pure Reason* is to examine our ability to form objective representations, to learn what it is possible for beings like us to represent and ultimately, in addition, to know. It is of crucial importance to the project that we be able to justify our concepts as having content and being applicable to the world. The concept of possibility allows us to assess whether our concepts—including the categories—could be instantiated in reality, and thereby underwrites the Critical project. Without it, we could never be sure if our concepts were capable of contributing to objective representations of the world at all. One might put the point: without a concept of possibility with the kind of content evinced by the principle of possibility, Kant's transcendental philosophy would not be possible at all. It is this concept that allows us to think about the legitimacy of our concepts. This boils down to something like the following transcendental argument: (1) We can do transcendental philosophy; (2) a necessary condition of the very possibility of transcendental philosophy is a concept of real possibility; (3) therefore, we have a concept of real possibility. But (1) is hardly a convincing starting point. Even the most committed Kantian must admit that transcendental philosophy isn't an ineliminable condition of the very possibility of empirical experience at all (although it may be considered a welcome by-product of such conditions). So whilst modal concepts may *allow* us to reflect upon our cognitive abilities, e.g. to think about the possibility of experience, it isn't at all clear why we should *need* to do that. We need to find a better reason to explain why modal concepts are built into our capacity for cognition at a fundamental level.

There are two slightly different questions in the vicinity, which it will help to distinguish: (1) What is the role of the modal categories in Kant's account of experience? (2) Does Kant give a transcendental argument for the modal concepts? The first question is largely philosophical, the second largely interpretative. My focus in this chapter will be on the former: I will present an argument that would be available to Kant, which makes sense of the role of modality in Kant's system. Given that there are good philosophical reasons for including this in our understanding of Kant's philosophy, it seems to me likely that Kant had something like this in mind, in answer to question (2). But I will not go so far here as to fully defend that claim.

2. The Argument

Here is the key passage, in which the main inspiration for an argument can be found.

> [T]he principles of modality are also nothing further than definitions of the concepts of possibility, actuality, and necessity in their empirical use, and thus at the

same time restrictions of all categories to merely empirical use, without any permission and allowance for their transcendental use. For if they are not to have a merely logical significance (*Denn, wenn diese nicht eine bloß logische Bedeutung haben*) and analytically express the form of thinking, but are to refer to things and their possibility, actuality, and necessity, then they must pertain to possible experience and its synthetic unity, in which alone objects of cognition are given.

(A219/B266–67, translation amended)

From this, along with the considerations I offer below, we can construct the following argument.

1. The categories are restricted to an empirical use: to application to objects of experience. (Otherwise they would have a merely logical significance.)
2. If the categories are to be restricted to an empirical use, then they must pertain only to possible experience and its synthetic unity (in which alone objects of cognition are given).[2]
3. If the categories are to pertain only to possible experience and its synthetic unity, then the application of the categories must agree with the formal conditions of experience.
4. Therefore, if the categories are to be restricted to an empirical use, then the application of the categories must agree with the formal conditions of experience.
5. That a concept agrees with the formal conditions of experience just is an instance of the principle of possibility.
6. Therefore, the principle of possibility is a transcendental condition of the restriction of the categories to an empirical use.

This argument seems, at least prima facie, to take the form of a valid transcendental argument (or at least as valid as any transcendental argument can be). Premise 1 states an assumed actual truth about the meaning or significance of the categories. Premises 2–4 present a chain of transcendental conditions of premise 1. Premise 5 notes that the ultimate transcendental condition of this chain is equivalent to the principle of possibility. Hence the conclusion in 6 that the principle of possibility is a transcendental condition of the assumed fact in premise 1, that the categories have a restricted use.

Initially, Kant presents the principles of modality as "nothing more than definitions." Does this mean that one should not expect there to be an argument for them? On the contrary, it remains the case that the modal concepts are categories and, as such, their status as categories needs to be explained. Categories in general are

[2] One might worry that in using "possible" in a premise the argument suffers from some kind of vicious circularity. However, given the very basic role that I shall argue the concept of possibility has, it might seem impossible to give an argument that didn't draw on modal concepts at all. One might thereby take the argument to expose or elucidate the role of the concept of possibility, without providing a certain kind of justification of its use. Again, I will ultimately argue that the modal categories call for a kind of justification that reflects their fundamental role. See also Keefe (2002) for a general account of why circularity may not always be vicious.

supposed to contribute to the conditions of possible experience, so even if a definition of some categories is provided, this does not yet explain their more particular transcendental role. One should still expect to find some kind of argument to explain this role.

Premise 1 is particularly important, as it starts off the whole argument. I understand this starting point as distinguishing between schematized categories that apply to objects of experience—categories that have an empirical use—on the one hand, and logical forms of judgment and unschematized categories, neither of which are objectively valid, on the other. First, in the Metaphysical Deduction (A79/B104–105) Kant gives an account of the categories as arising from the logical functions of judgment applied to conditions of sensibility, i.e., the conditions under which objects can be given to us in experience. The logical functions of judgment, laid out in the Table of Judgments (A70/B95), comprise conditions on thinking, i.e., on the well-formedness of a thought or judgment. The different forms of judgment—the different forms that the content of a judgment can take—are the result of the different functions of unity of the understanding—the different ways that the understanding is able to unify representations together into a judgment (A69/B93–94). These are merely conditions on thinking, the activity of the understanding alone. But when these functions of unity of the understanding are applied outside of the understanding, to intuitions, the result is the categories.

> The same function that gives unity to the different representations **in a judgment** also gives unity to the mere synthesis of different representations **in an intuition**, which, expressed generally, is called the pure concept of understanding. (A79/B104–105)
>
> But now the **categories** are nothing other than these very functions for judging, insofar as the manifold of a given intuition is determined with regard to them. (B143)

When combined with the formal conditions of our becoming aware of objects, the logical forms of judgment transform into pure concepts of the understanding, forms that objects of experience must take. Taken on their own, the functions of judgment merely "express the form of thinking." Second, Kant distinguishes between unschematized and schematized categories. The schematized categories are restricted to apply to objects given in sensible intuition; the unschematized categories lack this constraint. Kant argues that the unschematized categories have a merely logical significance, and do not apply to objects. Hence, they are not objectively valid:

> Now if we leave aside a restricting condition, it may seem as if we amplify the previously limited concept; thus the categories in their pure significance, without any conditions of sensibility, should hold for things in general, **as they are**, instead of their schemata merely representing them **how they appear**, and they would therefore have a significance independent of all schemata and extending far beyond them. In fact, even after abstraction from all sensible condition, significance, but only a logical significance of the mere unity of representations, is left to the pure concepts of the understanding, but no object and thus no significance is given to them that could yield a concept of the object. [...] Without schemata, therefore, the

> categories are only functions of the understanding for concepts, but do not represent any object. This significance comes to them from sensibility, which realizes the understanding at the same time as it restricts it. (A147/B186–87)

So again, without a restriction to empirical use the categories would "have a merely logical significance." They would be unschematized categories, or perhaps even mere logical functions of judgment.

The crucial point of premise 1, then, is to emphasize the importance of the categories bearing an appropriate relation to possible experience. Without this they would lack objective validity and would not be able to play the role that Kant describes for them in the deduction or, indeed, in the principles. Instead, we would have only logical forms of judgment or unschematized categories. A restriction to "empirical use" is imperative for there to be objectively valid categories, which apply to objects of experience, at all.[3]

Following premise 1, premises 2–4 elaborate on what the necessary conditions are for the categories to have their full meaning, as opposed to a merely logical meaning. These conditions are the categories being in agreement with the formal conditions of experience. If they are to pertain only to possible experience, then they must be compatible with the conditions under which experience is possible, i.e., the forms of intuition and the other categories. In other words, they must agree with these formal conditions of experience. The final step is then definitional. This condition is just what Kant has defined the principle of possibility to be. Hence the principle of possibility is the ultimate condition of the possibility of the categories having full meaning, not merely logical significance.

My focus in this chapter is to show that such an argument makes good sense of the role that the principle of possibility has to play in Kant's theoretical philosophy. First, I offer textual evidence to support the claim that such an argument coheres with Kant's writings. Second, I offer a philosophical account of how I take this argument to fit in with Kant's critical system.

3. Kant's Applications of the Principle of Possibility

First, I want to consider evidence to show that my proposed argument coheres with Kant's text. In what immediately follows the key passage quoted above (A219/B266–67), Kant effectively applies the principle of possibility to every kind of a priori representation:

> We shall now make obvious the extensive utility and influence of this postulate of possibility. (A221/B268)

[3] There are a number of difficult issues raised by the notion of unschematized categories—such as how to understand the deduction of the objective validity of the categories as coming *before* the Schematism, and the role that unschematized categories might play in thinking of noumena—that I do not have space to do justice to here.

He not only makes the general claim that the principle of possibility is required to explain the meaning of the categories, as restricted to an empirical use; he also proceeds to demonstrate this use of the principle.

To start, he covers the three categories of relation: substance, causation, and community:

> [Substance] If I represent to myself a thing that persists, so that everything that changes merely belongs to its states, I can never cognize from such a concept alone that such a thing is possible. (A221/B268)
>
> [Causation] Or, if I represent something to myself that is so constituted that if it is posited something else always and inevitably succeeds it, this may well be able to be so thought without contradiction; but whether such a property (as causality) will be encountered in any possible thing cannot thereby be judged. (A221/B2689)
>
> [Community] Finally, I can represent various things (substances) to myself that are so constituted that the state of one is followed by a consequence in the state of the other, and conversely; but whether such a relation can pertain to any things cannot be derived from these concepts, which contain a merely arbitrary synthesis. (A221/B269)

Kant then presents us with an application of the principle of possibility to concepts of magnitudes, covering the remaining non-modal categories, those of quantity and quality:

> And thus the possibility of continuous magnitudes, indeed even of magnitudes in general, since the concepts of them are all synthetic, is never clear from the concepts themselves, but only from them as formal conditions of the determination of objects of experience in general. (A224/B271–72)

This is followed by an application to the concept of a triangle—an example of a mathematical concept, another kind of a priori concept:

> It may look, to be sure, as if the possibility of a triangle could be cognized from its concept in itself (it is certainly independent of experience); for in fact we can give it an object entirely a priori, i.e., construct it. But since this is only the form of an object, it would still always remain only a product of the imagination, the possibility of whose object would still remain doubtful, as requiring something more, namely that such a figure be thought solely under those conditions on which all objects of experience rest. (A223–24/B271)

Even though we can construct the concept of a triangle in pure intuition, Kant presses the point that we still need an assurance that such a figure could be instantiated in empirical experience. Without this, it would "remain only a product of the imagination." Hence another application of the principle of possibility is required. We need to be assured that the concept of a triangle can be "thought solely under those conditions on which all objects of experience rest." It must be in agreement with formal conditions of experience. In the case of the triangle, the crucial element of these conditions is space as an a priori form of intuition. It is because space is itself a formal necessary condition of the possibility of experience, that the triangle, as constructed through our pure intuition of space, is guaranteed to agree with formal conditions of experience:

> [S]pace is a formal a priori condition of outer experiences [...] it is this alone that connects with this concept [*triangle*] the representation of the possibility of such a thing. (A224/B272)

Note that the claim is that it can be thought "solely" under those conditions. Why is it not enough that it can be thought under these conditions, never mind whether it can be thought under others? I return to this point below.

We can already note how strange it is that Kant should now query the objective reality of these concepts. Not only has the Transcendental Deduction already purportedly shown the objective validity in general of the categories, but the categories have already been subject to further argumentation. In the Analogies of Experience, Kant has argued that the categories of relation are necessary conditions of objective temporal relations. The concepts discussed here in the Postulates, as well as earlier in the Analogies, are clearly already tied to temporal relations: they are concepts explicitly concerning *simultaneity*, *persistence*, and *succession*. They are already implicated in conditions of experience. Similarly, Kant's arguments of the Axioms of Intuition and the Anticipations of Perception (earlier in the Principles) are already supposed to have shown that mathematics is applicable to experience, in showing that the magnitudes studied in mathematics are necessary features of experience. However, the fact that Kant has offered an application of his principle of possibility to the concepts of magnitude and the concept of a triangle suggests that he does not, after all, take the work to be already complete. This compounds the puzzle introduced above. Kant is supposed already in the Transcendental Deduction to have shown us that the categories are objectively valid. Given that he offers further arguments in the Analytic of Principles—the Analogies, Axioms, and Anticipations—it is doubly puzzling that, even after these two rounds of argument, he still takes the work to be incomplete.[4]

Kant claims that it is only in relation to the formal conditions of experience that we can cognize the objective reality of these categories:

> Thus only from the fact that these concepts express a priori the relations of the perceptions in every experience does one cognize their objective reality, i.e., their transcendental truth, and, to be sure, independently of experience, but yet not independently of all relation to the form of an experience in general and the synthetic unity in which alone objects can be empirically cognized. (A212/B269)

[4] One might take an alternative view: the work is not incomplete, and here Kant is merely making explicit was what already established earlier. Even so, there would still be an explicit explanation of the role of the concept of possibility to be given, and to that extent, at least, the explicit account thus far would be incomplete.

But this doesn't help us much yet. To explain what work is left for the principle of possibility to do, I need to turn to a more detailed discussion of the role the principle could play in Kant's theoretical philosophy.

4. Making Concepts

The application Kant makes of the principle of possibility, in determining a proper restriction of the categories to objects of possible experience, suggests that he takes it to play an important role in his account of concepts. I will argue that there is a role to be played by the principle in Kant's account of the formation and acquisition of concepts.

According to Kant, concepts are characteristically general. They relate to an object "by means of a feature which several things may have in common" (A320/B337). Moreover, the generality of a concept is "made," not given:

> All concepts, as to matter, are either given (*conceptus dati*) or made (*conceptus factitii*). The former are given either a priori or a posteriori. [...] The form of a concept, as that of a discursive representation, is always made. (*Log*, 9:94)

Concepts that have a "made" matter are constructed concepts (factitious concepts), typically mathematical concepts (see Dunlop, 2012). Concepts with a given matter divide into those with a matter given in experience (empirical concepts) and those with a matter given independently of experience (pure concepts). We can think of the generality of a concept as the concept having a sphere or extension—a domain of things to which it applies. In explaining how the generality of a concept is made, then, one challenge is to explain how a concept comes to have a sphere or extension. Proposals for this explanation vary (see, e.g., Longuenesse, 1998; Newton, 2015). To endorse a particular approach here would take us too far from present purposes. Besides, my explanation of the principle of possibility should be available regardless of the account one chooses here.

Another challenge is to explain how a concept comes to have an appropriately *limited* extension. Through some cognitive capacity, our concepts are assured generality—an extension. Through the transcendental deduction, we are assured that the extension of our pure concepts covers objects of possible experience. But the worry remains that the extension of these pure concepts may overrun the bounds of possible experience:

> [If] I leave out all intuition, then there still remains the form of thinking, i.e., the way of determining an object for the manifold of a possible intuition. Hence to this extent the categories extend further than sensible intuition, since they think objects in general without seeing to the particular manner (of sensibility) in which they might be given. (A254/B309)

The categories allow us to think of objects in a quite general manner, and to that extent they can determine, i.e., represent in some way, objects corresponding to possible intuition. However, even in the absence of a restriction to application *only* to objects of possible sensible intuition, there is still that general form of thought. But in that case, this general form doesn't represent a genuine further kind of object that could be presented in a different way; it determines no object at all:

> They do not thereby determine a greater sphere of objects, since one cannot assume that such objects can be given without presupposing that another kind of intuition than the sensible kind is possible, which, we are by no means justified in doing. (A254/B309)[5]

As noted earlier, the categories—with their full, schematized meaning—are restricted to the empirical world, the world of possible experience. By contrast, the unschematized categories only have a merely logical significance. In particular, they no longer give rise to the principles. For example, the pure category of substance—"a something that can be thought as a subject (without being a predicate of something else)" (B186)—doesn't give rise to a principle of the permanence of substance unless time as a pure form of sensibility is introduced.

In short, the categories—full-blooded, schematized categories—have a sphere of application, an extension, which is restricted to objects of possible experience. Something must explain this limitation. We have seen that concepts have both matter and form. The form, *generality*, is made. In the case of an empirical concept, the matter is derived from empirical experience of the relevant kind, e.g. experience of various trees for acquiring the concept *tree*. The matter of the concept serves to limit the extension of the concept, e.g. to objects of possible experience, given that the matter comes from actual experience of objects. But what is to serve as the matter of a pure concept, a category? The logical functions of judgment provide the basis for the content of the categories, but, as we have just seen, these alone are not sufficient to limit the sphere of the categories to the empirical world: they "extend further than sensible intuition," as they are forms of thinking, and do not take into account conditions of intuition.

An additional element is therefore required to ensure that the sphere of these concepts is restricted to possible objects of experience. One might think that this addition is the manifold of intuition, or rather, the pure form of intuition (the categories are pure concepts, and so must have pure beginnings). After all, it is through application to intuition that the functions of judgment become categories. However, this merely shifts the problem to the pure forms of intuition: how can we be assured that they provide the right constraints on the sphere of a category? Recall: Kant also felt he needed to apply the principle of possibility to the concept of a triangle, even though we can construct a triangle in pure intuition.

The most plausible candidate for this additional element is thus the principle of possibility. When a concept is formed, it must be formed in agreement with the formal conditions of experience, i.e., the conditions under which we can have intuitions and concepts. In the case of an empirical concept this condition is satisfied by the

[5] See also A286/B342.

fact that any concept acquired from actual experience is a fortiori in agreement with possible experience. In the case of a pure concept, not derived from experience, agreement with these conditions requires an additional principle: the principle of possibility. Given the fundamental role that such a principle plays, prior even to schematized categories, such a principle must be a priori. Another way to put the point is as follows: we need concepts. In particular, according to Kant, we need the categories as a condition of the possibility of experience. One way to think of a concept is as a rule for picking out a set of possible things, e.g. the extension of the concept *tree* is the set of all possible trees. Hence the principle of possibility expresses a constraint in forming concepts, that one must adhere to the formal conditions of experience to ensure that the extension of the concept is indeed of *possible* things. Of course, I might fail to use the concept correctly and attempt to apply it to non-sensible objects. But the representation itself does not apply to such things, given the way its extension has been made. Indeed, this might help to explain why such a misapplication would be a mistake.

This account of the role of the principle of possibility helps us to make better sense of one of Kant's remarks noted earlier, that the possibility of the concept of a triangle having an object required "that such a figure be thought solely under those conditions on which all objects of experience rest" (A224/B271). We can now understand why he restricts us to thinking the figure *solely* under conditions of experience. It is to restrict the sphere of the a priori concept to objects of possible experience, to ensure that the concept has the right kind of meaning. However, returning to this example also raises the question: the concept of a triangle is not one of the categories, so how should we explain Kant's application of the principle here? The proposal is that Kant sees a need to explain the limitation of the extension of a priori concepts to the bounds of possible experience. Whilst our fundamental presentation of space is as a pure form of *intuition*, and not a concept, it seems right that we do then form geometrical *concepts*, such as the concept of a triangle. The pedigree of a concept such as *triangle* is thus pure all the way down. And so we need to give an account of the limitation of its sphere. Again, the answer offered is that it must agree with conditions of possible experience. Insofar as it is generated from the pure intuition of space, and our intuition of space is a necessary condition of the possibility of outer experience of objects, the concept of a triangle is assured agreement with the conditions of the possibility of experience. Hence the principle of possibility is fulfilled.

If this account of concept-formation in Kant's system is correct, then we can see how the transcendental argument outlined above might be generated. The very possibility of categories with proper schematized content depends upon an application of the principle of possibility in the exercise of our capacity for concept-formation. Moreover, this account provides the key to the solution of the puzzle I posed above. Why on earth do we need such a sophisticated concept as a prerequisite of the very possibility of experience? Because the (schematized) categories are conditions of the very possibility of experience. And the principle of possibility is implicated in those categories having the right kind of content to do their job. Our following this principle ensures that the categories do not have a merely logical significance, but are properly restricted to their empirical use.

5. Making Modal Concepts

If this account of the genesis of pure concepts is correct, and if the modal categories are pure concepts, then the account should also apply to the modal categories. How should we understand the application of the principle of possibility to the concept of possibility itself? Kant offers an answer to this question when he explains why the principles of modality are called "postulates."

The character of the modal categories is very different to that of the others. Recall, the modal categories do not determine a property of an object, but concern only the relation between the concept of an object and our cognitive capacities. Kant takes this to imply that the modal categories are, in an important sense, not objective, but rather *subjectively synthetic*:

> The principles of modality are not, however, objective-synthetic, since the predicates of possibility, actuality, and necessity do not in the least augment the concept of which they are asserted in such a way as to add something to the representation of the object. But since they are nevertheless always synthetic, they are so only subjectively, i.e., they add to the concept of a thing (the real), about which they do not otherwise say anything, the cognitive power whence it arises and has its seat. (A233–34/B286)

To count as objective, the categories of modality would have to say something about what the objects to which they apply are like. Instead of this, they only say something about the relation between the representation of the object and our cognitive faculties.

The modal categories are thus importantly different to other categories. As a consequence, we don't require the same kind of justification of content and applicability as for the others. The first nine categories purport to predicate properties and relations of objects of experience, and so we need to be assured that they properly apply to such objects. The principle of possibility plays a key role in ensuring this. But the modal categories do not predicate properties of objects, and so do not need to be held to the same standard. What then is the appropriate alternative standard? Kant likens the status of the principles of modality to that of postulates in mathematics:

> Now in mathematics a postulate is the practical proposition that contains nothing except the synthesis through which we first give ourselves an object and generate its concept, e.g., to describe a circle with a given line from a given point on a place; and a proposition of this sort cannot be proved, since the procedure that it demands is precisely that through which we first generate the concept of such a figure. Accordingly we can postulate the principles of modality with the very same right, since they do not augment* their concept of things in general, but rather only indicate the way in which in general it is combined with the cognitive power. (A234–35/B287)

We can't prove the proposition which tells us how to draw a circle, because it is only on the basis of this that we can start to prove anything about circles. Likewise, we cannot prove the principle of possibility, because it is only on the basis of this principle that we can prove anything about concepts, in particular the concept of possibility, at all. Such propositions or principles cannot be proved or justified in the usual way, but this is not in virtue of their merely appearing to us to be "self-evident" or "certain" (A233/B285–86).[6] It is because they constitute a prerequisite for proofs or justifications of the usual kind.

Just as the definition of a circle provides a rule for drawing a circle in the first place, and hence is not something that can be proved about circles, so the principle of possibility provides us with a rule for forming a general concept which is objectively valid, and hence is not a concept that is open to the same kind of justification as other concepts. Kant writes in a letter to Marcus Herz in 1789 that:

> the possibility is *given* in the definition of a circle, since the circle is actually constructed by means of the definition, that is, it is exhibited in intuition [...] The proposition "to inscribe a circle" is a practical corollary of the definition (or so-called postulate), which could not be demanded at all if the possibility – yes, the very sort of possibility of the figure – were not already given in the definition.
>
> (*Br*, 11:53)

The postulate which defines a circle itself ensures the possibility of the circle: no further justification is required. This is because the definition itself involves a construction of a circle in pure intuition.[7] The concept of possibility is not a constructed mathematical concept, but it shares the feature of ensuring its own possibility as somehow given. The possession of any concept requires that the form of that concept be made. In the case of pure concepts, the making of that form requires a principle of constraint, the principle of possibility. So one might say: Whereas the definition of a mathematical concept involves the construction of its own object, thereby ensuring its own possibility, the possession of a pure concept involves the construction of its general form within the bounds of possible experience, thereby ensuring its possibility, and also the possibility of the concept implicated in that construction, namely the concept of possibility itself.

Finally, one might wonder, if the modal categories do not require justification in the same way as the others, then why is Kant's Transcendental Deduction—intended to justify or prove the applicability of the categories to objects of experience—extended to the modal categories at all? Why doesn't Kant restrict its scope? In response to this question, we should recall the aims of the Deduction as compared to those of the Principles. The Deduction offers us a quite general argument for why pure concepts of the understanding must be applicable to objects of experience.

[6] This is because often things that are taken to be "self-evident" or "certain" turn out to be wrong. As Kant writes: "since there is no lack of audacious pretensions that common belief does not refuse [...] our understanding would therefore be open to every delusion" (A233/B285–86), if we took these as fundamental grounds for knowledge.

[7] One might worry that the same couldn't be said for all geometrical figures. Although one can plausibly construct something as simple as a circle in pure intuition, others could be coherently *conceptually* defined but not plausibly constructed in this way, e.g. a regular pentecontaheptagon. Even if this is so, it does not affect the analogy between the definition of a circle and the modal categories. It is just that the analogy must be restricted and not extended to all geometrical figures.

Throughout the Principles Kant offers particular arguments for how and why each category does, and must, apply to possible experience. These latter arguments hardly render the initial, general argument obsolete. One might say: the Deduction shows us *that* these concepts are conditions on the possibility of experience, the Principles tells us in more detail *how* these concepts are conditions on the possibility of experience. The category of possibility, like any pure concept, is shown to be applicable to objects of experience. When we consider the details of the particular contribution that this concept makes, it emerges that the reasons for thinking that it is a condition of experience are different in form to those of the other categories, but for all this, it is no less a condition on the possibility of experience. A kind of justification is offered in the Postulates, it is just a very different kind of justification to that of the other categories.

6. Conclusion

If the Postulates are to follow the pattern set by previous sections of the Principles, we should expect to find transcendental arguments which purport to show that the principles of modality are necessary conditions for the possibility of experience. I have sketched what I take to be a plausible candidate for a transcendental argument for the principle of possibility. This argument rests on Kant's account of the nature of concepts in general, and the nature of pure concepts in particular. In short, the principle of possibility is required as part of the account of concept-formation. Insofar as the generality of concepts is made, not given, an additional principle is required to ensure that pure concepts—in themselves unbound by empirical constraints—are not *too* general, and are appropriately restricted to empirical application. This is the role of the principle of possibility. Such an argument helps us to understand passages in which Kant appears to apply the principle to pure concepts to precisely this end. If this account is correct, then it would seem that the modal categories play a much more central role in Kant's theoretical philosophy than has previously been recognized. They are not a mere oddity to be overlooked in favor of the more exciting Refutation of Idealism that is buried in their midst. Rather, the principle of possibility plays a fundamental role in ensuring that the core elements of Kant's philosophy—pure concepts of the understanding—have the right kind of content. In other worlds, the principle of possibility ensures that there are categories *at all*.[8]

References

Dunlop, K. (2012). Kant and Strawson on the content of geometrical concepts. *Noûs*, *46*(1): 86–126.

Keefe, R. (2002). When does circularity matter? *Proceedings of the Aristotelian Society*, *102*(1): 275–92.

[8] Thanks go to audiences in Cambridge and Miami for invaluable feedback and discussion on earlier versions of the paper. Thank you also to the editors, Karl Schafer and Nick Stang, for interesting and insightful comments that led to significant changes in the paper.

Leech, J. (2017). Kant's material condition of real possibility. In M. Sinclair (Ed.), *The actual and the possible: Modality and metaphysics in modern philosophy* (pp. 94–116). Oxford University Press.

Longuenesse, B. (1998). *Kant and the capacity to judge* (C. T. Wolff, Trans.). Princeton University Press.

Newton, A. (2015). Kant on the logical origin of concepts. *European Journal of Philosophy*, *23*(3): 456–84.

Stang, N. F. (2016). Kant's transcendental idealism. In E. N. Zalta (Ed.), *The Stanford encyclopedia of philosophy* (Spring 2016 Edition). https://plato.stanford.edu/archives/spr2016/entries/kant-transcendental-idealism/

6

Kant on the Epistemology of the Obvious

Timothy Rosenkoetter

1. The Question

Kant defines mathematical cognition as "[a priori] cognition from the construction of concepts."[1] This is in the first place an epistemic claim, namely, a *source claim* about the provenance of epistemic warrant within mathematics. Once combined with Kant's definition of construction, it locates ultimate epistemic warrant in intuitions that have been exhibited a priori. Yet the definition of mathematical cognition is more than just an epistemic claim. It is also a semantic claim about how mathematical concepts get their meaning and an alethic claim about what makes mathematical propositions true.[2]

Famously, Kant claims that his definition of mathematical cognition is sufficient to distinguish it from all other types of cognition.[3] So mathematical cognition is unique in its possession of a property that is, among other things, epistemic. Kant's interpreters have generally focused on some combination of the source, semantic, and alethic claims. This chapter takes up an epistemic question that has yet to be treated in any systematic way.

Guiding Question: aside from the source claim, are there any epistemic properties that are sufficient to distinguish mathematical cognition from all other types of cognition?

Just by way of illustration, if we were to find that mathematical cognition admits of a greater degree of certainty than all other cognitions, this would qualify mathematical cognition as unique in a purely epistemic respect, in addition to its uniqueness as a priori cognition from the construction of concepts (the source claim).

A nominal answer to the Guiding Question is easy. Kant tells us in a wide cross-section of texts that mathematical cognition is distinguished from all other types by

[1] This definition calls the cognition "rational" (*KrV*, A713/B741), but that is just another term for a priori (cf. A837/B865, *KpV* 5:12). To construct a concept is "to exhibit (*darstellen*) *a priori* the intuition that corresponds to it" (A713/B741). (All references with A- and/or B-pagination are to *KrV*. My starting point is the Cambridge translations, which I have altered in some instances without noting.)

[2] For the semantic claim, see A239–40/B299; for the alethic claim, see B15 and A736–37/B764–65, where we are told that one can judge the truth of mathematical cognitions without the "direct" support of "something completely contingent, namely *possible experience*."

[3] Cf. A712–38/B740–66, hereafter "the Discipline."

Timothy Rosenkoetter, *Kant on the Epistemology of the Obvious* In: *The Sensible and Intelligible Worlds: New Essays on Kant's Metaphysics and Epistemology.* Edited by: Karl Schafer and Nicholas F. Stang, Oxford University Press.
DOI: 10.1093/oso/9780199688265.003.0007

the fact that it is "evident," while they are not.[4] The hard question is what exactly that property (which I will call *evidence*$_K$ to avoid confusion) amounts to. As we will see in section 3, the relevant texts do not suggest a single, determinate claim; and there is little indication that the claim, however it might be precisified, is significant for understanding Kant. This chapter will argue that Kant is appealing to an epistemic property that his published works do not expound:

(1) A cognition *C* is evident$_K$ iff (i) the proposition *p* that is cognized in *C* is obvious (*offenbar*)[5] and (ii) *C* is grounded upon a priori intuition.

We already knew that all mathematical cognition fulfills (1.ii). That is just the familiar source claim. So what this proposed definition adds, once combined with Kant's claim that all mathematical cognition is evident$_K$, is the assertion that all mathematical cognition is of obvious propositions.[6] It turns out that Kant has a well-developed and philosophically rich theory of the obvious, which has received, so far as I am aware, no attention from commentators. So in order to pursue the Guiding Question it will be necessary to provide a basic reconstruction of that theory, and indeed to defend the claim that Kant *has* such a theory. Thus, alongside the concern with mathematics that provides its outer frame, this chapter will present Kant's theory of the obvious. To become acquainted with this theory is to recognize its far-reaching significance for Kant's philosophy as a whole.

This chapter will use texts scattered widely within Kant's corpus to reconstruct a theory whose key idea is this:

(2) A proposition is obvious if and only if certainty regarding its truth value is accessible to any epistemically considerable subject.

Certainty regarding many propositions is *accessible* to a subject, even though the subject lacks that certainty at the present moment. Seeing how Kant understands this accessibility relation will be the key to fleshing out the basic idea contained in (2). First, though, here's how I propose to use the term *epistemically considerable*, which I am likewise introducing in order to make the structure of Kant's theory perspicuous.

This concept denotes a status in the epistemic realm that is roughly analogous to dignity in the moral realm. For S to be epistemically considerable is for S to be such that there is reason to treat her *as a subject*, rather than as an instrument or mere

[4] A160/B199–200; A734/B762; A423–25/B451; *Prol* 4:327; *V-Lo/Pölitz* 24:544; *V-Lo/Philippi* 24:441–42, 24:481; *V-Lo/Blomberg* 24:150; *V-Met/Mron* 29:751; and *Refl* 2714; cf. A733/B761; *WDO* 8:133. In Kant's idiosyncratic use of this term a cognition is either "evident" or it is not. There is no question of *how* "evident" it is.

[5] "Obvious" captures Kant's meaning in contemporary English better than "manifest." Something can be manifest without being "plain as day." Though "evident" would be a good translation, this would make it difficult to remain impartial about whether Kant's uses of *offenbar* are closely related to his uses of *Evidenz*, as (1) claims.

[6] I use "proposition" merely to designate the content of a cognition and do not wish to suggest that Kant is committed to an ontology that includes abstract objects.

thing, in epistemic matters.[7] Kant has no single term that reliably denotes epistemic considerability all by itself. The closest term is "common human understanding."[8] Note, first, that this is a capacity-concept. S's possession of common human understanding is consistent with temporary interruptions in her ability to use the capacity well, or indeed to use the capacity to any given level of adequacy. Second, Kant often uses this term specifically to designate a minimum: "the least that can be expected from anyone who lays claim to the name of a human being."[9] Third, and consequently, Kant conceives of common human understanding as a capacity that all of us share.[10]

We need to distinguish two respects in which common human understanding can be "the *least* that can be expected." In many contexts Kant uses "common human understanding" in contrast to "learned," "scientific," or "cultivated" understanding to single out those who have not acquired facility with explicitly stated, abstract rules.[11] When I wish to reference this concept, I will use the term *uncultivated understanding*. Though it is not always easy to see, Kant also uses the term "common human understanding," as I will, to single out the capacity that is shared by all of us, regardless of our level of *mental acuity*. I introduce the latter term as a catch-all to designate cognitive abilities that (i) cannot be imparted simply by learning rules, and that (ii) vary in degree from subject to subject. These include, most importantly, the ability to subsume intuitions under concepts (the power of judgment) and the ability to employ ideas to unify a manifold of cognitions in a system.[12] Though one can see how Kant could have easily fallen into the habit of using a single term to designate both uncultivated understanding and this baseline capacity, it is important to distinguish them. After all, there is no reason why subjects with heightened mental acuity cannot be uncultivated, and high levels of cultivation might be possible (it is an empirical question how high) among those with nothing more than the minimum level of mental acuity.

With this distinction on the table, we can state quite generally why common human understanding (as I will use the term) is central to what follows. Namely, Kant believes that certainty regarding many propositions, including many philosophical propositions, is inaccessible except to those with heightened mental acuity.

[7] Cf. *GMS*, 4:435. Section 4 will offer a fuller picture of what is entailed by recognizing another as enjoying this status.

[8] *KU* §40 contains the most informative and sustained discussion of common human understanding. "Understanding" should be taken in the wide sense, which comprises understanding in the narrow sense, the power of judgment, and reason (A131). Kant might emphasize one or another of the three, depending on the context.

[9] *KU*, 5:293. Here Kant notes that the term combines both senses of "common" (*gemein*): merely healthy ("vulgar") and "communal" (cf. *Refl* 430; Hinske, 1980, pp. 35ff.).

[10] It figures centrally in Kant's famous riposte to Eberhard: "... *what is philosophically correct* neither can nor should be learned from Leibniz; rather the touchstone, which lies equally to hand for one man as for another, is common (*gemeinschaftliche*) human reason, and there are no *classical authors* in philosophy" (*ÜE*, 8:218).

[11] E.g., Bxxxii.

[12] A third, though for our purposes less important, capacity that falls under mental acuity is the ability to analyze a concept without the benefit of an explicit rule. My use of a single term as a catch-all for these abilities should not be taken to suggest that there is regular covariance in their levels of realization. Nor do I mean to suggest that all three have a common source or explanation. What they share are features (i) and (ii). They play a particular functional role in Kant's theory of the obvious.

Certainty in other propositions is accessible to anyone with the minimum level of mental acuity, i.e., to any epistemically considerable subject, and it is these propositions that are obvious.[13]

There is one further idea concerning accessibility that it makes sense to preview at this point. There are two interestingly different ways that certainty regarding a proposition might be accessible to an epistemically considerable subject who currently lacks it. First, S might possess all of the "tools" that she would need to be certain of *q*, and simply not be using them correctly. This can occur if S is hallucinating, affected by prejudice, or simply reasoning carelessly. Second, S might lack some of the tools required for certainty. For instance, if S lacks the concepts <cup> and <table>, then she cannot cognize, much less be certain, that a cup is on the table next to her. There is logical space for a distinct type of instruction corresponding to each of these cases. Most straightforwardly, instruction can provide tools that the subject currently lacks. I will call this *rule-based instruction*, since it consists largely in helping the subject acquire concepts, which are themselves rules. I introduce the term *diagnostic instruction* to designate the contrasting case in which someone assists a subject—including cases in which a subject assists herself—in regaining the proper use of her common human understanding. Much of what belongs within this latter class might not strike us as "instruction" in ordinary parlance, given that it includes requests to slow down, think matters through again, and reconsider each chain in one's reasoning. Each of these is, however, a way of trying to improve a subject's momentary epistemic position.

These are the rudiments of Kant's theory of the obvious. Once more of the theory is on the table we will see that though nothing but mathematics is grounded upon a priori intuition, (1)'s other conjunct—obviousness—is far from unique to mathematics. Kant thinks that at least the causal principle, the Formula of Universal Law (FUL), and explicitly analytic propositions ("tautologies") are obvious (section 5). Some empirical facts also enjoy this status.[14] What separates mathematics, according to Kant, is that *all* mathematical propositions are obvious. Kant does not make a parallel claim for any other substantive science, and he denies it in particular of philosophy (section 5). Epistemically, then, mathematics is distinguished not just by its source in a priori intuition but also as the *science of the obvious*. This, in short, is my answer to the Guiding Question.

2. Epistemic Anomaly and an Alternative

Let's suppose that mathematics, and mathematics alone, is a science of the obvious. It then makes sense to ask how, if at all, this fact is related to the source claim, since that more familiar claim concerns the other epistemic property that makes mathematics

[13] For purposes of judging accessibility a subject's level of mental acuity is to be held fixed. Even if it is possible for a subject to increase her level of mental acuity, a proposition is not accessible to that subject if certainty regarding it would require such an increase. Because whether a proposition is obvious depends on its accessibility to *all* epistemically considerable subjects—possible as well as actual—obvious propositions need to be accessible to subjects who possess only the minimum.

[14] *Refl* 2265 provides "The snow is black" as an example. Kant writes very little about the empirically obvious, so it is unclear what the principle of distinction is.

unique. It would be surprising if there were no relation at all. And, indeed, we find Kant suggesting that the evidence$_K$ of mathematics (and so, on my proposal, its obviousness) can be traced to the fact that mathematics draws its epistemic warrant from a priori intuition.[15] But why exactly does a priori intuition confer this epistemic advantage? One response is that a priori intuition is simply sui generis in its epistemic properties in comparison to any other cognitive medium. It is an *epistemic anomaly*, as I will term it. After all, most of what is revealed in empirical intuition is not obvious, so intuition alone cannot explain the contrast. Nor can the contrast be explained simply by the cognition's apriority, since Kant believes that many a priori discursive cognitions (and most of philosophy) are, notwithstanding their certainty, non-obvious. So perhaps nothing informative can be said about *why* all cognition grounded upon a priori intuition has the remarkable property of being obvious.

It must be conceded that some of what Kant writes about construction makes a priori intuition look like an epistemic anomaly.[16] However, this chapter assembles materials for a case against that very natural presumption. We will see that there are specific, identifiable reasons why Kant attributes obviousness to some propositions but not to others. Insight into the structure of Kant's general theory of the obvious will reveal a possible rationale for the obviousness of mathematics. Though a final verdict on the matter will have to wait upon a more exhaustive treatment of mathematics, we will see that this alternative actually makes sense of Kant's commitment, rather than treating it as a brute assumption regarding the epistemic properties of a priori intuition. Moreover, this explanatory alternative fits Kant's tendency to compare epistemic uptake within construction to privileged cases of ordinary sense perception (section 3). Here's a first, quick roadmap to help orient the reader for the more complete presentation that follows.

For Kant there are two possible reasons for classifying a proposition as obvious. The first reason depends on his assumption that there is "an obscurely thought *metaphysics* that is inherent in *every* human being because of his rational predisposition."[17] More precisely, there are two such branches of metaphysics. Likewise, Kant apparently assumes that all epistemically considerable subjects with space and time as their forms of sensibility have some foothold in mathematics. To be sure, the typical subject is uncultivated and lacks scientific understanding of these three disciplines. Yet each and every one of us has a basic grasp of what it is for there to be objective ontic, deontic, and mathematical truths, and takes there to *be* at least some truths of each kind. Moreover, and crucially, all of this is required for epistemic considerability. Kant's next pivotal assumption is that the logical and explanatory structures of these realms are such that a small set of propositions must be presupposed in order

[15] E.g., A734/B762.

[16] One example is from the Architectonic of Pure Reason's comparison of instruction in philosophy and mathematics. Kant tells us that in mathematics reason is "used *in concreto* though nevertheless *a priori*, founded, that is, in *pure and therefore error-free intuition*, and excludes all deception and error" (A837/B865, final italics added). This might be taken to indicate that it is a brute fact that the peculiar constitution of pure intuition makes error impossible.

[17] *MS*, 6:376, second italics added; cf. Bxxxi. As we will see, it is crucial for their status as obvious that *all* epistemically considerable subjects possess the two branches of metaphysics (as Kant reconstructs them), though some of these subjects might at times be unaware of, or even deny, this fact.

to so much as have that grasp, regardless of whether the understanding of these realms is uncultivated or scientific. Subjects must hold-for-true these *absolutely fundamental* propositions (as I will term them) in order to count as epistemically considerable.[18] This is why Kant takes the causal principle and FUL to be obvious (section 5).[19] I propose that axioms and postulates bear the same relation to the body of mathematics, and so are likewise obvious. All of this is critical for making sense of Kant's larger theory of the obvious, as we will see, yet it cannot explain Kant's answer to the Guiding Question. The reason is that all of mathematics is obvious, not merely its axioms and postulates.

Why, then, is mathematics obvious across the board? Answering this question will require that we consider the second reason why something can be obvious, which is exemplified by select empirical cognitions. For now, though, it is best simply to note that all cognitions grounded upon a priori intuition possess a property that is likewise found in select cognitions grounded upon empirical intuition—though only in extraordinary cases, such as when one judges under favorable conditions that a cup is on the table. What explains these similarities and differences? Here is my conjecture, which draws on nearly every strand of the general theory that this paper reconstructs:

(3) Mathematics is the science of the obvious because for any true mathematical proposition q, q is either absolutely fundamental or any epistemically considerable subject, given the proper preparation, can become certain of q using diagram-based reasoning.

A diagram, as I will use the term, is always empirical, whether it is drawn on paper or merely imagined "before the mind's eye." The key point is that Kant believes that if the results of diagram-based reasoning are to count as a priori, this reasoning must be arranged so that there are no "close calls." The apriority-conferring rules of Euclidean diagrammatic reasoning, as Kant interprets them, are such that no measuring or "eyeballing" is permitted.[20] This exacting standard, which much of our actual reasoning with diagrams in fact fails to meet, brings with it an important epistemic payoff. While an attempt to adjudicate a close call by appeal to a diagram is precisely the sort of epistemic act that should be expected to vary in accuracy with the judging subject's level of mental acuity, the diagrammatic reasoning that is definitive of mathematics is such that any epistemically considerable subject, given the proper preparation, has the capacity to attain certainty regarding the diagram's relevant properties. As we will see, this is relevantly similar to the fact that any

[18] Absolute fundamentality is in the first place a proof-theoretic concept. A proposition is absolutely fundamental when a proper science subject to asymmetric grounding relations is dependent on that proposition. For instance, without holding-for-true (*Fürwahrhalten*) the causal principle we cannot so much as comprehend what the metaphysics of nature, and ultimately physics as a whole, is about (section 5). Kant could have maintained this proof-theoretic commitment even if he had never developed a theory of the obvious.

[19] I am simplifying matters for expositional purposes. Strictly speaking, this point holds of the principles of the first and third Analogies of Experience as well. A similar point holds in the practical case (section 5).

[20] For this point in particular I am drawing on the groundbreaking work of Shabel (2003), who has shown that a breach of these rules converts the process into "mechanical construction," which Kant considers a posteriori (pp. 96ff.).

epistemically considerable subject, given the proper preparation (which includes possessing sight and various empirical concepts such as <cup>), can be certain that a cup is on the table.

Importantly, this is not to say that any epistemically considerable subject will be in position to *acquire* the necessary preparation. Indeed, from the perspective of epistemic considerability it is entirely accidental whether any subject possesses sight and the concept <cup>, or has hit upon Euclid's procedure for bisecting a line segment without resorting to eyeballing and approximation. Kant's claims for the obviousness of mathematics are thus logically independent of any position he might take regarding the ease or difficulty of mathematical *discovery*.[21] Correlatively, much of what Kant classifies as obvious in his technical sense is anything but "obvious" in a more colloquial sense of the term.

As will already be clear from the foregoing précis, this chapter touches on a wide array of areas within Kant's philosophy. One reason for this is that any treatment of the obvious that focused solely on mathematics or solely on morality (to name the two most tempting candidates) might elicit the worry that too much weight has been placed on just a handful of passages. This piecemeal approach would fail to convey the strong available evidence that Kant is applying a single theory across a variety of domains. So rather than picking just one domain and developing that application of the theory as far as it can be taken, this chapter will focus on presenting the philosophical rationale for Kant's general theory of the obvious, together with enough about each application to put readers in position to appreciate the textual evidence within that domain.

3. What Is "Evidence"?

What is this property that all of mathematics shares, alone among the substantive sciences? A first answer can be found in the course of the Discipline's catalogue of tools available to mathematics but not philosophy, namely, definitions, axioms, and demonstrations. The subsection on demonstrations explains that while some philosophy is fully certain, this certainty is merely discursive: "…from *a priori* concepts (in discursive cognition)…intuitive certainty, i.e., evidence, can never arise, however apodictically certain the judgment may otherwise be" (A734/B762). This might be taken to suggest that evidence$_K$ is simply a species of certainty, namely, certainty that is grounded upon intuition.[22] Before we declare our question regarding the nature of evidence$_K$ thereby answered, though, we do well to ask why Kant bothers to

[21] Kant often gives the impression that he believes, incredibly, that it is in general easy to discover hitherto hidden mathematical truths (cf. Koriako, 1999). This chapter will not attempt to isolate his precise position on this matter. Importantly, though, even if his considered views regarding mathematical discovery are false, this will not directly affect the logically independent theory reconstructed below.

[22] Or perhaps: upon a priori intuition. The fact that this sub-section is about demonstrations, all of which are a priori, tends to obscure that the quoted passage is consistent with there being *empirical* evidence$_K$, i.e., in cases in which certainty is based upon empirical intuition. For other passages suggesting that there can be empirical "evidence," cf. *TG*, 2:347; *V-Lo/Pölitz*, 24:544; and *MSI*, 2:403.

distinguish intuitive and discursive certainty in the first place. Why is it an advantage for mathematics that it wields demonstrations rather than discursively certain proofs?[23]

There are strong indications that the answer to this question somehow involves the greater reliability of mathematical cognition *as a class* in comparison to philosophical cognition.[24] If so, though there is no absolute barrier to attaining certainty in philosophy, the evidence$_K$ available in mathematics has the effect of making mathematical practice much more reliable on the whole. The Discipline's characterization of evidence$_K$ might then be extensionally accurate and yet fail to single out the precise property that actually explains this superior reliability. To isolate the property we do well to consult an early treatment of evidence$_K$ in the *Prize Essay*, where Kant takes the trouble to explain the mechanism behind this difference. At this point in the text the reader has already been told that mathematics and philosophy can both achieve certainty in individual cases:

> ...mathematics in its inferences and proofs regards its general cognition under signs *in concreto*, whereas philosophy always regards its general cognition alongside signs *in abstracto*. And this constitutes a substantial difference in the way in which the two inquiries attain certainty. For since the signs of mathematics[25] are sensible means of cognition, it follows that one can know (*wissen*) that no concept has been overlooked, and that each particular comparison has occurred in accordance with easy rules, etc. And these things can be known with the same degree of assurance as when one sees something with the eyes. And in this the attention is greatly facilitated by the fact that it does not have to think things in their general representation; it has rather to think the signs as they occur in their singular cognition, which here is sensible. By contrast, the only help which words, as the signs of philosophical cognition, afford is that of reminding one of the general concepts which they signify, and whose meaning one must at all times have immediately before the eyes. The pure understanding must be maintained in a state of constant exertion, and how easily a mark of an abstracted concept escapes without one's noticing, for there is nothing sensible which *makes obvious* its having been overlooked. And when that happens, different things are taken to be the same thing, and the result is cognitive error.[26]

What is most important for our purposes is how Kant invokes ordinary visual experience to explain the additional epistemic advantage that mathematics enjoys. Contrary to what one might initially assume, this is not inherently problematic, since

[23] Kant believes that actual cases of discursive certainty are available, some within his very own philosophy (cf. Axv).

[24] For one thing, this portion of the Discipline is fixated on just this contrast (cf. esp. A736/B763). Philosophy is portrayed as a delicate undertaking that requires that we continually review our progress, searching for previously unnoticed mistakes, while mathematical practice is presented as nearly free from error.

[25] The final sentences of §1 (2:292, not quoted) make clear that Kant intends these signs to include not only algebraic symbols but also diagrams.

[26] *UD*, 2:291–92, my translation, final italics added. The Cambridge translation of this passage is unreliable. Most importantly, Walford and Meerbote render both *Evidenz* and *Gewißheit* as "certainty" (without noting this in the otherwise frequent translational footnotes). This is disastrous, since one of Kant's main points is that not all certain cognitions are "evident."

elsewhere Kant acknowledges that there are actual cases of "empirical certainty."[27] Insofar as we might nonetheless feel pressure to discount the passage's appeal to perceptual experience—and insist that there is simply nothing to be said about the epistemic superiority of mathematics, and consequently that a priori intuition is an epistemic anomaly—it is owing, I suggest, to our underdeveloped conceptual resources for distinguishing two epistemically divergent experiences of "see[ing] something with the eyes" (*UD*, 2:291). After all, Kant can hardly be appealing to cases in which one tries to see whether a tower in the distance is round or rectangular (cf. *Anth*, 7:146). My hypothesis is that the concept we need to make the distinction is none other than the one that Kant goes on to use at the end of the passage ("obvious"), though without pausing to explain what it means.

Most of the rest of the chapter will be spent reconstructing Kant's background theory. Before we begin, though, it is important to notice a first hint contained in Kant's contrast of the uninterrupted presence of a perceived object with the difficulty that philosophers face when they attempt to keep the meaning of a word before the mind's eye, an emphasis that is retained in the *Critique*'s treatment of demonstration: in mathematical cognition "the universal *in concreto* (in singular intuition)" is present throughout the course of demonstrations, which always "*proceed* through the intuition of the object."[28] The same point is illustrated by the Discipline's well-known recounting of Euclid's Theorem I.32, whose demonstration *begins* with the construction of a triangle. Throughout its course, the mathematician is "*always* guided by intuition."[29] The uninterrupted presence of a sensible sign makes it easy for the subject to keep her eye on the object of inquiry, eliminating the errors of mistaken identity that plague philosophy.[30] This calls for a narrowing of our stock example of obvious perceptual experience. However safe it would in fact be to depend on it, we should not presume that it is obvious that this cup is the same one that was on the table last time I looked. What is obvious is simply that there is a cup on the table during the course of my uninterrupted gaze.

It is natural to wonder at what point in the series of intermediate cases between this one and straining to see the tower does a perceptual truth cease to be obvious for subjects with certain visual capabilities. It is tempting to expect that the answer will appeal to quasi-physical features of the perceptual experience, such as how large the intentional object is represented as being, thereby following the model provided by the (partial) criterion of uninterrupted presence. It is clear, though, that Kant does not in general aspire to offer quasi-physical criteria of obviousness. The next section will argue that Kant instead opts for a criterion that is irreducibly normative in the

[27] *Log*, 9:71; cf. *V-Lo/Pölitz*, 24:544; *V-Lo/Philippi*, 24:441; and *V-Lo/Dohna*, 24:734–35.

[28] A734–35/B762–63, italics added. For additional contrasts of mathematics and philosophy with respect to presence, cf. A423–25/B451; and *SF*, 7:113. One reason that the Discipline is less illuminating is that its treatment of demonstration simply takes for granted that geometry illustrates Kant's point—whose precise content remains unclear as a result—and instead devotes space to extending the point to characteristic construction: "Even the way algebraists proceed with their equations...secures all inferences against mistakes by placing each of them before one's eyes" (A734/B762).

[29] A716–17/B744–45, italics added. The secondary literature contains many explications of the proof that Kant is summarizing, among them Friedman (2012, p. 233); cf. Euclid (1956, p. 316).

[30] For paradigm cases, see the fallacies of equivocation that Kant diagnoses in his criticism of the paralogisms of pure reason (B410–11).

following sense. A perceptual truth is obvious relative to a community of perceivers if and only if members of that community have non-instrumental reasons of a particular type to engage in diagnostic instruction when a fellow member of the community errs.

4. Diagnostic Instruction

Obviousness receives its most explicit and direct treatment in several extraordinary passages, which survive in transcriptions of Kant's logic lectures and in associated *Reflexionen*.[31] There can be no doubt that their location is explained by the fact that at these points Kant is lecturing on Meier's conception of the obvious. Since Kant's alternative builds upon an implicit critique of Meier, we do well to begin with the latter.

For Meier, an obvious cognition is one whose truth or falsity "is discovered merely by considering it," without requiring "a more far-ranging inquiry" (*Auszug* §113). His example of a non-obvious ("hidden") truth is that matter cannot think. While this is entirely certain, it can be discovered only through inquiry. As Meier recognizes no fundamental distinction between concepts and intuitions, at the most basic level all inquiry is properly modeled as conceptual analysis: "a cognition is obviously false if the parts from which it is immediately composed contradict one another."[32] His examples are concepts such as <four-angled triangle>, whose explicit marks are already sufficient to reveal the concept as contradictory.

Wit (*Witz*) and astuteness (*Scharfsinnigkeit*) are the Meierian capacities that enable us to recognize sameness and difference of concepts, respectively, and thereby truth and falsehood. All human beings possess these basic capacities—without them judgment would be impossible—but each of us has them to a greater or lesser degree. This is Meier's theory of mental acuity.[33] Whether the truth or falsity of any particular cognition is immediately clear, or can be discovered only after further inquiry, depends on the level of mental acuity that is brought to bear on the problem. For someone with sufficient acuity it would be immediately certain that matter cannot think. Thus, already the mere fact that Meier treats obviousness as a property that any particular cognition either possesses or lacks indicates that he is presupposing some fixed level of mental acuity as the benchmark for determining what is obvious.[34] We will see that Kant adopts a different approach. We will also see that Kant departs from the act-oriented nature of Meier's theory. An *act* is "absurd" (*ungereimt*), for

[31] What I call the "Core Passage" (*V-Lo/Wiener*, 24:832–33) will be subjected to scrutiny below. See also: *V-Lo/Blomberg*, 24:105; *V-Lo/Philippi*, 24:405–406; *V-Lo/Pölitz*, 24:531–32 (1780s); *V-Lo/Dohna*, 24:724–25 (early 1790s); *V-Lo/Busolt*, 24:633 (early 1790s); and *Refl* 2260–74, esp. 2266 (likely 1769–75).

[32] *Vernunftlehre* §142. This longer work, Meier's source for *Auszug*, contains a richer account of obviousness than *Auszug* §113. Kant lectured from the full *Vernunftlehre* at the beginning of his teaching career.

[33] It is a competitor to Kant's because wit and astuteness (i) cannot be imparted simply by learning rules, and (ii) vary from subject to subject. While Kant's theory is at least tripartite (cf. ft. 12), Meier's theory is functionally monist, as there is no indication that Meier takes levels of wit and astuteness to vary independently of one another. Accordingly, I will treat them as a single capacity.

[34] It is possible that what really matters to Meier is a structural point: certainty regarding obvious truths is available without conceptual analysis. He might further doubt that there is any regular relation between what a given level of mental acuity can accomplish and that structural distinction. That said, the main text provides a plausible reading of Meier's brief comments, and I suspect that it is roughly this reading that informs Kant's innovations.

Meier, if it fails at a task that the threshold level is sufficient to accomplish. But what it would take for a capacity or the subject that possesses it to qualify as absurd remains unaddressed.[35] Nor does Meier make further theoretical use of the notion of a capacity, such as would be found in the insistence that a person, some of whose epistemic acts are absurd, ought nevertheless to be treated in certain ways in light of her possession of wit and astuteness.

Against this background, Kant's signal innovation is to define obviousness by recourse to an ungraded capacity that all of us share. It is a *capacity*; *all of us* have it; and it is treated by the theory as *ungraded*. Each of these is essential, and they are interrelated. The lynchpin of Kant's theory is the claim that every epistemically considerable subject possesses an affirmative ability to accomplish certain kinds of tasks. Though Meier held that all of us have wit and astuteness, they play a different functional role within his account. A subject's possession of those capacities is in each case the underlying explanation for whatever she can accomplish, yet there is no presumption that there is a single set of tasks that we can all accomplish. Of course, Kant also allows for varying levels of mental acuity. Yet those variations are irrelevant to his theory, since the obvious is defined by recourse to what anyone who has common human understanding can accomplish.

At this point we need to introduce a concept that resembles the obvious, save that the new concept is relativized to particular *communities*, which are in turn individuated by the concepts all of their members possess, as well as the sets of facts to which all have immediate epistemic access. Though every community possesses non-optional concepts such as the categories—otherwise their members would not qualify as epistemically considerable (section 5)—two communities might be distinguished by whether they possess the optional concept <cup>. This makes a difference for our purposes because someone who lacks that concept can hardly be certain that a cup is on the table. Similarly, two communities might be individuated by whether their members are in the same room with this cup, possess the power of sight, and the like. Let's call the set of propositions, certainty in which is accessible to all members of a particular community using only common human understanding and without learning new concepts or altering what is in immediate epistemic reach, that community's *common ground*.[36] This concept is context-sensitive (where context is a function of community), whereas obviousness is not. For instance, it might be obvious that a cup is on the table, but that proposition will not belong to the common ground of any community that lacks <cup> or finds itself on a different continent. We should expect that the common ground of a community will generally change

[35] Meier is happy to speak of *humans* as "absurd" (*ungereimt*)—or, equivalently, as "dumb" and "stupid" (*abgeschmackt*) (*Vernunftlehre* §142). However, no theory is provided that would allow us to infer from facts about acts to facts about subjects. Is there, for instance, a purely statistical threshold in the former that warrants the latter?

[36] Contrary to various contemporary notions such as Stalnaker's (2002) "common ground" and various theorists' "common knowledge" (cf. Vanderschraaf & Sillari, 2014), there is no requirement that S be aware that others be aware that S be aware that…ad infinitum. A second difference is that not all propositions that an entire community holds-for-true are included; only those of which everyone has (i) the capacity (ii) to be certain (iii) without using more than common human understanding. While Stalnaker and others are interested primarily in explaining what actually occurs in human communication, Kant's interest in common ground is more centrally tied, as we will see below, to his views about the attitudes that we *ought* to take toward ourselves.

over time. S and her interlocutor might acquire <cup>, which they previously lacked. Later, they might walk into a new room and see a cup on a table.[37] Below, I will ask how our common ground changes as we make our way through Euclid's *Elements*.

Kant needs the concept of a common ground because the normative difference that obviousness makes for individual epistemic agents is in the first place relative to the communities in which they find themselves. How I ought to react when my interlocutor denies that a cup is on the table depends on whether she possesses the concept. If she lacks it, there may be no reason to teach her the concept (or there may be a reason, but a reason of a different strength or type), even if the cognition is obvious. As we are about to see, matters are different when the cup's being on the table belongs to our common ground.

Insofar as we limit our view to non-optional concepts such as the categories, there is no extensional rift between the obvious and common ground. Yet Kant's full theory also allows for obvious truths that use optional concepts—so I am arguing. In order to lay out this theory stepwise, let's assume in this section and the next that we are considering a single community. That is, all parties under consideration possess the same concepts and have immediate epistemic access to the same facts, including empirical facts. Kant is in effect allowing himself the same simplifying assumption in his most comprehensive thematic treatment of the obvious, which is from the 1780s:

> *Core Passage*, first half:
>
> [*a*] An incorrectness and a falsehood is obvious if it is clear to common human understanding. If the incorrectness is not clear to every understanding, then it is hidden [*versteckt*], [*b*] but it can be made obvious, and all refutations [*Widerlegungen*] aim at this. In the case of refutations, it is a duty first to show whence this or that incorrectness of human cognition has come, i.e., I must discover the source of the error, i.e., the illusion, and afterward I can prove to him the falsehood [...] [*c*] I must also not call someone absurd (*ungereimt*) immediately. For he would certainly not have accepted this or that cognition if he had not been led by this or that hidden illusion to hold it to be true. Such a man, who immediately calls someone else absurd, insults the other very much and fails to appreciate the interest of universal humanity.[38]

Let's suppose that it belongs to our common ground that a cup is on the table, while whether that cup has a crack does not.[39] In cases of disagreement regarding the latter, it makes sense to engage in inquiry that is directed to the cup. Should your

[37] A fully determinate theory would need to address many technical questions concerning the individuation of communities (etc.) that this chapter can safely ignore, since they are matters that could be handled in a variety of ways, rather than barriers to the theory's viability. As will become clear in section 6, I do not claim that Kant worked out the details that would be required for his theory to yield determinate verdicts in particular empirical cases.

[38] *V-Lo/Wiener*, 24:832–33. This passage, like others listed in note 31, departs from the letter of my interpretation some respects. For instance, Kant uses "obvious" in both absolute ([*a*]) and context-sensitive senses ([*b*], where in this case context is simply a function of the health of the subject), whereas I have introduced common ground as a separate, context-sensitive concept. In general, my goal throughout this chapter is to identify a rigorous model that coheres with the great majority of what we find in the available texts.

[39] To review, even if each of us in fact believes that the cup is cracked and has considerable evidence supporting this belief, that is not by itself enough for it to be in our common ground.

interlocutor sincerely deny the former, however, Kant recommends a shift from *object-directed inquiry* such as that to what I am calling *diagnostic instruction*. Kant's idea is that rather than talking with the errant subject S about cups or tables, in these extraordinary cases we should seek to identify the source of the error within S, thereby allowing S at least to correct for the pernicious effects of an ongoing illusion, if not to go ahead and remove the source of that illusion entirely. Given the simplifying assumption that we belong to a single community, this is not a case of teaching S what a cup is. Neither is diagnostic instruction an exercise in raising S's underlying level of mental acuity. If successful, it merely restores S's various capacities, including the power of judgment, to their unimpeded functioning—or at least to a level sufficient for certainty regarding this particular truth. Two points require clarification.

First, any intervention with a subject will be at best accidentally effective unless it is based upon what we can call *subject-directed inquiry*.[40] By itself this is already a reason to use the term "diagnostic instruction" liberally so as to encompass any subject-directed inquiry that directly informs an episode of diagnostic intervention. However, I will be arguing that if we aim to cut at the joints that Kant deems significant, we should simply classify subject-directed inquiry and diagnostic instruction together, regardless of whether the former eventuates in actual intervention in the cognitive life of a subject. Ultimately, my full argument (section 4) will appeal to Kant's insistence on a sharp distinction between "critique" and the object-directed inquiry that he calls "doctrine."[41] Yet we can already see the outlines of a substantive case without considering Kant's views on the critique-doctrine distinction. The key point is that subject-directed inquiry can be undertaken without any specific plans for intervention, with the general aim of furthering the project of diagnostic intervention. And any line that we might draw between this "pure research" and actual interventions would be largely conventional, and in any case not among Kant's concerns.[42]

Second, the Core Passage seems to simply assume the existence of a sharp distinction between subject-directed and object-directed inquiry. We can see why this would have made sense to Kant by considering cases in which there is an "unnoticed influence of sensibility on understanding, through which it happens that the subjective grounds of the judgment join with the objective ones, and make the latter deviate from their destination" (A294/B350–51). There is no reason to assume that the sensible interference itself always represents a cognitive grasp of the object that competes with understanding's grasp, as would be present, by contrast, were a subject to weigh two competing hypotheses regarding an object's properties. Whether the object of the judgment is a cup or an elephant might be irrelevant to the correct

[40] Such inquiry is described in more or less detail in the many passages in Kant's works and lectures that treat the causes of error (e.g., A294–95/B350–51; *Log*, 9:53; and *V-Lo/Wiener*, 24:833). I take these passages to support the present interpretation. Various questions might be raised about how those passages relate to the obvious, including whether error regarding the obvious is the paradigm case that informs Kant's explanation of error. I must leave these questions for future work.

[41] *KpV*, 5:176; cf. A841/B869.

[42] Here are two supporting points that could be developed, space permitting. First, diagnostic intervention can be performed on oneself, so whether I am communicating with someone else is not an accurate gauge of whether intervention is occurring. Second, it is plausible to hold that intervention occurs only when there is a sufficient uptake on the part of the patient (possibly oneself), but that can be difficult to determine.

diagnosis of the error. Granted, this is a pure case.[43] Other actions that Kant would classify as diagnostic instruction might seem on their face to combine attention to the subject with object-directed inquiry, and this might pose a challenge to his theory. In any case, it is important when reconstructing Kant's theory to bear in mind that he does not treat the distinction between object-directed inquiry and diagnostic instruction as gradual or scalar.

Let's return to the Core Passage, whose next step is to declare, in an apparent strengthening of [*b*], that object-directed reasoning is an *inappropriate* reaction to error regarding the common ground. In doing so Kant uses "proof" ([*d*]) in a strict sense that limits it exclusively to object-directed reasoning:[44]

> *Core Passage*, second half:
>
> [*d*] That which contains an obvious falsehood is an absurdity. But one cannot prove (*beweisen*) an obvious incorrectness to anyone. For through some misunderstanding or other it is not obvious to him. [*e*] The expression 'absurd', 'stupid' (*abgeschmackt*), has to do first of all with the error itself[;] secondly, it has relation to the person who has the error. For I thereby declare the person to be unworthy of being accepted in the class of universal human understanding. [*f*] If I have declared my refutation of the judge whom I hold to be stupid, then I cannot have the purpose of instructing (*belehren*) him. For by denying him common human understanding, I have declared him unworthy of instruction, and I would act stupidly myself. [*g*] My refutation would have to be directed to others, then. But others who have healthy human understanding will see the absurdity by themselves.

For the moment let's ignore the strong claim that it is *always* inappropriate, or perhaps even impossible, to establish the certainty of a truth in the common ground using object-directed reasoning.[45] As we will see in coming sections, there are reasons to think that this is an oversimplification, as would not be surprising in a lecture for beginning students. The crucial point for understanding Kant's theory is his reason for thinking that diagnostic instruction is always, at least in principle, an *option* when there is such an error. The reason is that for purposes of this theory Kant treats common human understanding as a capacity—an affirmative ability—to be certain of *the very propositions that make up the common ground.* To recognize others as epistemically considerable is to attribute precisely this ability to them. Accordingly, so long as their common human understanding remains "healthy," they "will see the absurdity by themselves" [*g*]. So even if it turns out to be possible (or, stronger, both possible and normatively acceptable) to use object-directed reasoning to establish

[43] Rash assertions on the basis of insufficient evidence are another pure case worth considering. I need not draw on any knowledge of objects to realize that I have an intense desire to come across as an expert on everything, regardless of my level of expertise. The role of rash assertion in error is an important topic for further research, in part because it is central to Meier's account of error.

[44] This contrasts with [*b*]'s apparently laxer use of the term, which seems to encompass subject-directed reasoning as well.

[45] This is how I understand the literal content of [*d*]. As we will see in section 5, it *is* impossible to provide an *object-directed* proof of an obvious truth that is also absolutely fundamental. Yet there is no hint from the text that Kant intends to limit the Core Passage to this subclass of the obvious.

some truths belonging to the common ground—we will consider this below—it is always in principle possible to achieve the same effect by helping the errant subject regain the unimpeded use of her capacity. That is why diagnostic instruction is always in theory an option when one is confronted with the absurd assertion of a fellow community member, even though it is doubtless fruitless or impractical in individual cases.

The next two sections will raise some finer points regarding the choice between subject- and object-directed reasoning. Prior to moving on, we need to consider common ground's normative significance. First, it is not at all clear whether the Core Passage is setting forth moral reasons or some other kind of reason. I will return to this point shortly. For now, we can observe that the *form* of these reasons is in any case familiar from Kant's moral philosophy. Most importantly for our purposes, they seem to govern our attitudes toward bearers of common human understanding, and thus our attitudes toward a *status*, epistemic considerability, in a way that parallels morality's connection to the status of personhood and being a rational agent.[46] Though these status-oriented reasons may of course ground further reasons to produce or prevent states of affairs, they are not in the first place reasons to reduce the number of absurd beliefs in existence, to mention one salient alternative. It is worth emphasizing this point because it can be quite tempting to think that epistemic reasons, however deontological they might appear within a limited horizon, must ultimately be justified by their production of true beliefs or avoidance of error. I take Kant to disagree. The reasons associated with the obvious are in the first place reasons to treat people in a way that recognizes their status as epistemically considerable, and thereby as *one of us*.[47]

Looking more closely at the form of these reasons, it would appear that there is a *perfect duty* not to adopt certain attitudes toward epistemically considerable subjects ([*c*]), while we can hypothesize that there is an *imperfect duty* to assist those whom we take to be in error regarding the common ground.[48] Much more would need to be said in order for Kant to have a fully specified theory of these duties. For instance, one component of a complete theory would be directions for handling cases in which a member of our community is repeatedly making assertions that by our lights are absurd, while attempts at diagnostic instruction yield no encouraging results. For how long are we required to retain the diagnostic instruction of such a person as an end before we are permitted to simply give up? Matters would already be complicated enough if each candidate were either epistemically considerable or not for her entire biological existence. However, our actual situation is one in which persons who have been epistemically considerable for a long time cease at some point to enjoy that status, and the point of transition is not always biological death. Yet another source of complication is introduced by the fact that it may not be my interlocutor who has lapsed into absurdity. It may be *me* who needs diagnostic

[46] Cf. *GMS*, 4:428–29 and 4:437.

[47] A further conjecture, whose examination must be saved for future work, is that the reasons we have to treat our fellow subjects as capable of certainty regarding the obvious are second-personal (cf. Darwall, 2006). If this is correct, then intriguing questions arise as to how these reasons are related to epistemic reasons that are not second-personal.

[48] [*b*], and to a lesser extent [*f*] and [*g*], hint at the latter.

instruction.[49] One worthwhile interpretative project is the reconstruction, to whatever degree Kant's texts permit, of the content of all of the reasons and duties related to the obvious. This is not my project in the present chapter.

Nor will this chapter take a position on whether the apparently epistemic reasons treated in the Core Passage are ultimately reducible to moral reasons. The principal argument for reducibility is that Kant believes there is, in the final analysis, only one categorical imperative. Since the reasons just sketched are not merely instrumental, the denial of reducibility would commit Kant to recognizing a second, specifically epistemic categorical imperative.[50] A second indication that the superficially epistemic reasons sketched above are in fact just a species of moral reason can be found in §39 of the Doctrine of Virtue, which under the general heading of "duties of virtue toward other human beings arising from the *respect* due them"—and, in particular, within a discussion of the immorality of contempt—makes some of the same points as the Core Passage.[51] It would thus appear that Kant favors what we can call *Simple Reduction*: duties concerning the obvious are simply one of the many classes of reasons that are "based upon" (*gründet auf*) a moral duty of respect.[52]

Matters are not as straightforward as they might initially appear, however. Taken by itself, §39 is consistent with there being two distinct reasons not to be contemptuous of another epistemic agent: first, a reason that is grounded in the status of epistemic considerability, though not further grounded; and second, a moral reason of respect that applies to all morally considerable individuals in the full gamut of the roles they inhabit (e.g., friend, promisee, etc.), including the role "user of theoretical reason."[53] On this hypothesis, Kant is describing the first type of reason in the Core Passage, while §39 concerns the second type. What we learn from looking at both passages together is that there are two reasons not to be contemptuous of someone's status as an epistemic agent, whereas there is only one reason (a moral reason) not to treat the corpse of an executed criminal in shameful ways, a duty likewise

[49] It is here that Kant's theory might come into conversation with the contemporary literature on disagreement (cf. Christensen, 2009). We might, for instance, accept Kant's basic theory and then go on to insist that whenever one has grounds to perform diagnostic instruction on another and there is no ancillary evidence that this person lacks epistemic health, one ought to flip a coin first and begin diagnostic instruction on oneself if it comes up "heads." I am unaware of passages in which Kant considers some of the many different possible policies.

[50] *GMS*, 4:460. I am supposing that the various epistemic reasons could themselves be reduced to one reason, in much the same way that superficially distinct moral reasons such as the reasons not to lie and to improve oneself are reducible to a single reason.

[51] In particular, the passage says that we have "a duty not to censure [a human being's] errors by calling them absurdities...." It also rehearses the argument of [*f*]. Finally, it provides a description of an imperfect duty to search for the grain of truth that might be contained in that person's errant judgment, as well as to uncover the underlying source of the illusion (*MS*, 6:463).

[52] *MS*, 6:463. For a project in the neighborhood, though not one that concerns obvious truths in particular, see Cohen's attempt (2014) to justify various maxims for epistemic agents by recourse to FUL/FLN.

[53] Upon closer inspection, §39 and the Core Passage are not as similar as they might seem. Most importantly, despite Kant's use of the technical term "absurd," there is no basis for assuming that §39's sideways glance at "the logical use of...reason" is focused specifically on the obvious (*MS*, 6:463–64). Kant's point instead seems to be that we have moral reasons to adopt a constructive and supportive stance whenever a person errs, even if the truth is not obvious and her judgment is wrong only in the details, while correct on the core issue. It would be immoral to *call* such a person "absurd," even though such an error is not in general an absurdity in the strict sense. There is much more to be said about the similarities and differences between these passages, but this will need to be pursued elsewhere.

discussed in §39. If successful, this maneuver would leave the opponent of reducibility with only the (admittedly formidable) argument from monism concerning categorical imperatives to diffuse. The issues that arise at this point are too involved to tackle in this chapter. Here I note only that though there is a striking similarity between the functional roles that precipitate the statuses of moral and epistemic considerability, they are prima facie distinct. This makes it worth exploring proposals that differ from Simple Reduction. For instance, the status of epistemic considerability might somehow be built into the status of moral considerability from the start, such that a full grasp of moral reasons reveals them to be epistemic reasons as well.[54]

5. Invariance in the Common Ground

This section is about what follows from the fact that Kant takes some propositions to belong to all common grounds, regardless of how much rule-based instruction subjects have received, or where those subjects are located, and with which sensory powers. Section 1 of this chapter asserted that the causal principle and FUL, as the absolutely fundamental principles of physics and ethics, fit this bill.[55] Kant apparently assumes, similarly, that the axioms and postulates of geometry belong to the common grounds of all subjects with space and time as their forms of sensibility.[56] This section will provide the background theory enabling us to understand these claims, as well as adduce some textual support. This will have the side benefit of countering a natural worry: "If obviousness is as important to Kant as this chapter contends, isn't it suspicious that he includes no thematic treatment of it in his published works? What reason is there to think that Kant ascribes any real importance to obviousness, given that his only explications of the concept come within a teaching context?" We are about to see published works other than the *Prize Essay* making use of the theory that he explains only in lectures and notes.

Famously, one way in which Kant motivates his philosophical turn toward the subject is by pointing to particular synthetic a priori propositions and asking what could ground their truth, a procedure that he calls "analytic method."[57] It would be ineffective to choose controversial or seldom held propositions as starting points for this method. In general, the more widely the chosen propositions are held-for-true, the better they apparently serve the goals of analytic method. Yet how widespread does the holding-for-true need to be? Is 99 percent sufficient? 99.9 percent?

[54] I hope to pursue this in future work. For one version of what such a project might look like, cf. Merritt (2018).

[55] Recall that "absolutely fundamental" is a proof-theoretic concept that has application in sciences whose structure makes justification and intelligibility asymmetric.

[56] Though I know of no passage in which Kant makes this claim explicitly, he clearly assumes that a subject who lacked (e.g.) the real definition of or the postulate for describing a circle would be unable to prove (or even grasp) the geometrical theorems and problems that they ground (cf. *MSI*, 2:402; A732–33/B760–61). Presumably, there are analogous points to be made about arithmetic, though since Kant's views on the latter are difficult and controversial, I will bracket the case of arithmetic in this chapter.

[57] For a contrast of the two methods, cf. *Prol*, 4:274. Though the first *Critique* as a whole follows the synthetic method, it appeals to the motivating puzzle of analytic method in contexts that are not directly pursuing synthetic method (e.g., A9/B13).

Obviousness provides a non-arbitrary answer. For though some readers will in fact demur on this or that occasion (in part due to sensible interference), or more stably (perhaps because they are in the grip of a philosophical theory that denies the truth of the causal principle), the motivating puzzle of synthetic a priori truths has universal traction under ideal conditions so long as all epistemically considerable subjects, when healthy, are certain of their truth. At base this is important not because the resulting claims are thereby more likely to be adopted by one's audience (an instrumental reason). Instead, we have a categorical reason to treat other subjects as capable of certainty regarding these truths: it is part and parcel of treating them as epistemically considerable. In short, *obvious* synthetic a priori truths are particularly well-suited—perhaps even uniquely well-suited—for the role of starting point in analytic method.[58]

So does Kant in fact regard the starting points of analytic method not merely as certain but also as obvious? An affirmative answer for the theoretical case is strongly suggested by a section added to the second-edition *Critique* (and therefore after publication of the *Prolegomena*), which bears the revealing title "We are in possession of certain *a priori* cognitions, and even common understanding is never without them" (B3). That section first offers "all propositions of mathematics" as examples "from the sciences" and then continues: "If one would have [an example] from the *commonest* use of the understanding, the proposition that every alteration must have a cause will do; indeed in the latter the very concept of a cause so *obviously* contains the concept of a necessity of connection with an effect" that the concept would be "entirely lost" if one accepted Hume's account of its empirical origins.[59] I propose that this passage's contrast of mathematical truths as belonging to science, over against the causal principle as presupposed in the "commonest use of the understanding," is alluding to the fact that certainty regarding the causal principle does not require any optional training.[60] Only a small subset of mathematical truths, namely, axioms, are similarly accessible to wholly uncultivated understanding. Though the rest of mathematics is obvious as well (so this chapter is arguing), it requires optional, rule-based instruction. Kant is able, plausibly, to maintain that the causal principle belongs to all common grounds only because he allows the wholly uncultivated subject's presumption that *something* must have broken the windowpane or caused the household article to disappear—a disposition that he regards as simply universal—to count as certain belief in the causal principle.[61] In a pattern that we will see repeated for other obvious propositions, scientific cognition of the content *in abstracto* is not required. The ability to *use* it when deciding on particular cases ("*in concreto*") suffices.[62]

[58] This conjecture cries out for focused, thorough treatment. I cannot pause to do that here while still pursuing the chapter's overall goals. I trust that it is sufficiently plausible, at least in its weaker version, to make its inclusion in this section, as one piece of evidence among many, appropriate.

[59] B4–5, all italics added. The wording of this difficult passage can give the impression that nothing more than a particular analysis of the concept <cause> is obvious, but this makes no sense of the larger context. I suggest that Kant means to say that the causal principle itself is obvious and then to add that Hume's mistaken analysis of the concept corresponding to the word "cause" makes it impossible even to *state* that principle correctly.

[60] Cf. *V-Met/Mron*, 29:788.

[61] Kant's examples, cf. *Prol*, 4:370.

[62] Mathematical axioms likewise provide examples of this thesis. Even those with no mathematical training assume that three points determine a plane (cf. A732) and that a straight line is shortest path between two points (*Prol*, 4:301) as they go about their daily lives. Similar points could be made regarding the postulates.

The parallel textual case within practical philosophy is strong. There are, *first*, a handful of passages in which Kant uses the word "obvious" to describe basic moral truths.[63] *Second*, there are passages in which Kant says that the truth of this or that moral proposition is clear (i.e., certain) to "common" understanding or reason.[64] In these passages Kant evidently has at least *uncultivated* reason in mind: people who have never even tried to formulate general truths about morality are nonetheless reliably able to use moral criteria in individual cases. However, this does not by itself settle whether Kant wishes to assert, in addition, that even those who possess nothing more than a baseline level of mental acuity share this ability. Strong support for an affirmative answer comes when Kant uses one of Meier's two terms for mental acuity, explaining that we do not "need any wide-ranging astuteness (*Scharfsinnigkeit*) to see what I have to do for my willing to be morally good" (*GMS*, 4:403). Moreover, in other passages we find Kant using a superlative construction ("most common") that would be positively misleading if an uncultivated person needed heightened mental acuity in order to reliably classify individual acts as permissible or impermissible. In sum, it appears that the overall message of this second type of passage is that moral know-how is present in us even when we are *both* uncultivated and lack heightened mental acuity.[65]

A *third* type of evidence for the obviousness of at least some basic moral truths is parasitic on the general case that obvious truths are particularly well-suited—or perhaps even uniquely appropriate—as starting points in analytic method. The question of precisely which truths about value and morality are starting points for analytic method in Section I of the *Groundwork* is an intricate one, yet there can be no doubt that at least one proposition concerning morality or value belongs to that set.[66]

A *fourth* source of evidence can be gained by looking at how Kant reacts to the plain fact that some subjects—subjects who show every sign of generally excellent epistemic health—do in fact reject Kant's candidates for basic moral propositions. In short, Kant offers textbook examples of diagnostic instruction. In some passages Kant makes use of the same vector-metaphor that is pervasive in his many passages on the cause of error.[67] In another discussion Kant predicts that we would react to someone who takes the moral law to be egoistic by assuming that he had "lost his

[63] *KpV*, 5:36; 5:44 (one time each for the impermissibility of lying and suicide). It should be noted that Kant uses *offenbar* sparingly in his writing.

[64] Cf. *GMS*, 4:393; 4:402; *KpV*, 5:35, 5:36, and 5:43 ("the most common attention").

[65] An instructive case is the support that Kant provides for his assertion that "what is to be done in accordance with the principle of the autonomy of choice is seen quite easily and without hesitation by the most common understanding." Kant likely intends this initial use of "common" to include lack of cultivation, and perhaps it could be maintained that he means only this, rather than including lack of heightened acuity. Yet this can hardly be his meaning several lines hence when he writes: "what *duty* is, presents itself (*sich darbietet*) to everyone," since some (at least possible) persons possess only the minimum mental acuity.

[66] If Kant's procedure in Section I of the *Groundwork* were our only guide, there might be a case for limiting the roster of obvious propositions to its famous opening claim (4:393), since he is arguing from it to both the "second" (4:399) and "third proposition" (4:400), as well as to FUL (4:402). As we will see shortly, though, other considerations suggest that Kant ascribes obviousness to propositions at various levels of fundamentality within subject-directed inquiry.

[67] He offers, namely, that philosophers' judgments have been "deflect[ed]...from the straight course" by "a host of alien and irrelevant considerations" (*GMS*, 4:404; cf. A294/B350). One of these will be the direct sensible interference of the desire to promote one's own pet theory (cf. *KpV*, 5:35).

understanding" (*KpV*, 5:36). This discussion does not, to be sure, describe the measures that one might take to help this interlocutor recover his health. It nonetheless provides considerable support for the obviousness of basic moral truths by conveying the potential stakes of disagreement. If the egoist has in fact lost his capacity to credit FUL as true, then he will no longer have the capacity that makes us what we are.[68]

Just as important as Kant's positive responses in these passages is what he does not recommend: object-directed proof. Kant does not, for instance, counter the imagined egoist with a proof that the content of morality is impartial. This should remind us of the Core Passage's claim that "one cannot prove an obvious incorrectness to anyone" [*d*]. Within the context of that entirely general discussion, [*d*]'s unqualified claim was an overreach, since *some* obvious propositions (e.g., Theorem I.32) can be established using object-directed reasoning, as we will see in section 6. Yet for the special case of absolutely fundamental propositions, which "are not themselves grounded in higher and more general cognitions" (i.e., cognitions *of objects*), this is precisely Kant's view. In this special case only "a proof from the subjective sources of the possibility of a cognition of an object as such (*überhaupt*)" is possible.[69] Let's see why.

The impossibility of such proof is based upon the asymmetric structure of proper sciences. Because the textual evidence is more abundant in the theoretical case, I will focus on Kant's contention that the causal principle is that "through which alone appearances can first constitute one *nature*."[70] His point is that absent commitment to the causal principle our thought would not actually be about *objects*. We would have unwittingly replaced nature with the simulacrum that he calls "dreams taken objectively."[71] Because the casual principle must be presupposed in order to conceive of objects in the first place, any proof of the causal principle that begins from premises ascribing this or that property to objects is bound to be circular. We can see the same basic commitment at work in the *Prolegomena*'s claim that the subsumption of intuitions under <cause> and <effect> in accordance with the causal principle is required if a subject is to undertake objectively valid judgment ("judgments of experience"), as opposed to mere "judgments of perception." So long as Kant is assuming that one must understand objective validity in order to be epistemically considerable—a claim that seems natural, since the former just is validity *for all subjects*—then all common grounds will include holding-for-true of the causal principle, at least in the form of an uncultivated disposition to assume that each individual

[68] Kant's thought experiment actually features two different cases, one in which the interlocutor himself acts according to egoistic principles that he takes to be "a true human duty," and another in which the interlocutor recommends a third person as a steward on the basis of the latter's principled egoism (*KpV*, 5:35–36). In the former case, Kant offers as one possibility that we might "shrink back from him with disgust" (*KpV*, 5:35). All of this deserves a more thorough analysis than can be provided here. However, the main text's summary is at least part of what we can take from this rich discussion.

[69] The quotes in this and the previous sentence are taken from Kant's treatment of the principles of pure understanding (A149/B188). In the practical case, I will suggest, basic moral principles admit of proof from the subjective sources of the possibility of *objectively valid propositions concerning goodness*.

[70] A542/B570; cf. *Prol*, 4:294.

[71] This is the term ("*somnio objective sumpto*," *Prol*, 4:376) that Kant takes over from Wolff for manifolds that one misguidedly attempts to treat as objective, without also taking them to be governed by the causal principle (cf. A201–202/B247; A451/B279; Rosenkoetter, 2009). It is not to be confused with the psychological concept of a dream state, but instead belongs to "transcendental philosophy" (*Prol*, 4:376).

alteration has a cause.[72] And, again, any purported proof of the causal principle whose premises simply presuppose that there are truths about objects will be question-begging.

The larger goals of this chapter make it impossible to subject the doctrine just described to the substantive scrutiny it deserves. For our purposes, what is important is that even if Kant proved unable to defend the claim that commitment to the causal principle is a necessary condition on all objectively valid thought about objects, there is abundant evidence that this is in fact his view. It turns out that there is also a wealth of evidence suggesting that Kant believes, in parallel, that commitment to FUL is a condition on objectively valid practical thought. More specifically, holding-for-true FUL—whether in scientific form or merely by virtue of reliably using it in particular cases—is the very condition for conceiving of goodness as an objective property.[73] Only so does a subject realize that anything that is good-for-me in a situation is good-*for-all-agents* in that situation. A subject who lacked the concept of this objective property would have to get by with the concept <agreeable>, which makes no claim to objective validity. Her world would count in practical respects as nothing more than a "dream taken objectively," rather than what all of us actually possess: a single, common world that includes possible instances of objective goodness.[74]

We have just surveyed textual evidence indicating that the absolutely fundamental propositions of physics, ethics, and mathematics are obvious. This has had the ancillary effect of supporting the chapter's overarching claim that Kant is applying a single theory of the obvious across several domains. In closing this section, it makes sense to briefly sketch a hypothesis which, while certainly not required for the defense of my larger interpretation, has the potential to further substantiate its claims, as well as to unify what otherwise might appear to be loose ends. The hypothesis, in slogan form, is that *critique is diagnostic instruction*, namely, the limit case of diagnostic instruction, in which the instruction is relevant to all subjects.

It is important to note up front that I am using the term "critique" in a relatively narrow sense, as Kant sometimes does, specifically as the contrast-concept to "doctrine." While critique "strictly speaking has no domain with regard to objects" because it is *subject*-directed inquiry, doctrines are precisely individuated by the sets

[72] From this starting point we can construct a broadly similar case for the obviousness of explicitly analytic truths ("tautologies"), a position I take Kant to be referencing when he explains that contradictions and identities are "either *obvious* or *hidden*" (*V-Met/L*$_2$, 28:544; cf. *ÜE*, 8:231; and A244/B302.) Given that one and the same concept appears in both the subject and the predicate of "all humans are humans," nothing more is required to be certain of its truth than an understanding of universal affirmative judgment as such. Yet subjects who have not mastered that form of judgment will be unable to take their place in the universal community of subjects proposing objectively valid judgments. The same point would hold for other logical connectives such as <not> and <if…then>.

[73] This allows for cases in which the agent is uniformly weak-willed, as we find with Kant's "most hardened scoundrel," who acts immorally but holds-for-true FUL, at least intermittently. Kant's wording also illustrates his view that understanding *in concreto* is sufficient ("when one sets before him *examples* of honesty of purpose…"; *GMS*, 4:454, italics added).

[74] Though these claims regarding FUL's keystone role in Kant's project are to my knowledge new in the literature and as such would benefit from further explication and defense, the larger goals of this chapter dictate that I offer them here as hypotheses to be fully tested on another occasion.

of objects (or objective properties) to which they are directed.[75] In this sense of "critique," the metaphysics of nature and morals both fall outside of critique. Their identity conditions are supplied by the distinction between being and goodness that has been worked out in theoretical and practical critique.[76] We see Kant acknowledging the difference between critique and doctrine in various ways, as when he explains, in a passage quoted above, that the principles of pure understanding cannot be given object-directed proofs.[77]

Now, rather than having a circumscribed applicability that depends on contingent factors, such as whether a subject possesses the capacity for sight or a brain chemistry that allows her to refocus her attention when she becomes distracted, the diagnostic instruction that makes up critique is supposed to apply to all finite subjects.[78] Critique illustrates the general argument from the previous section, according to which there is no important distinction, from Kant's point of view, between the "pure research" of diagnostic instruction and the difference it makes in the cognitive lives of actual subjects. Theoretical critique draws on that basic research in order to so much as identify assertions that would qualify as errors, such as the denial of the causal principle.[79] This point alone might make it seem as if critique must eventually find uptake in living, breathing errant subjects if it is to count as diagnostic instruction. I would suggest, in contrast, that even if history had never, in the fullness of time, given us a David Hume, critique would still have counted as diagnostic instruction, in part because our underlying reason to undertake the latter is the reason that we have to view ourselves, and each other, as epistemically considerable. The reason that we have to help the causal skeptic regain his health is ultimately explained by our reason to recognize him as exemplifying a status that all of us share.

It is worth mentioning two final questions that the current interpretation prompts, and which deserve to be considered in future work. First, if, as I have argued, critique inter alia provides justification "from subjective sources" for obvious propositions such as the causal principle (A149/B188), we should ask, "How much of what is asserted within critique is obvious?" A plausible case can be made that *all* of the principles of pure understanding are obvious; and Kant predicates obviousness of two truths involving pure apperception (cf. A353–54). Yet we can also be confident

[75] *KU*, 5:176. Kant distinguishes between this relatively narrow sense of "critique" and a wide sense at A841/B869. The former is *relatively* narrow because there is a more restrictive sense, according to which neither the *Prolegomena*, nor *GMS*, 4:412–21 belongs to critique. Though 4:412–21 evidently does not qualify as a "critique of pure practical reason" in Kant's most restrictive sense (4:446, cf. 4:392), it is nonetheless an a priori examination of our capacities, and it investigates whether a corresponding doctrine—metaphysics of morals (comprising at least 4:427–45)—is possible, precisely the criterion cited by *KpV*, 5:176.

[76] That *being* and *goodness*, in particular, define the two domains of metaphysics is controversial—or would be controversial if it were more widely recognized as a pivotal interpretative question. The major competitor for the second role is freedom (cf. *GMS*, 4:387–88; *KpV*, 5:171; and 5:176). Which of these is correct is irrelevant to my present point.

[77] A149/B188. On the practical side, this distinction has the potential to clear up much of the obscurity surrounding the transition to a metaphysics of morals that Kant announces in *Groundwork* II (4:426–27).

[78] I ignore the complication that some portions of theoretical critique hold only for beings with space and time as their forms of sensibility. The frame is universal, and it contains substantive claims.

[79] Kant makes this point vividly when explaining that Hume's skeptical errors "arose" (more plausibly, found fertile soil within which to grow and take hold) from his failure to "systematically survey" all of the functions of judgment (A767/B795).

that far from everything that is adduced within critique is obvious.[80] This plausibly includes certain results, such as transcendental idealism, as well various techniques or forms of argument. Heightened mental acuity might, for instance, be required in order to grasp the success of the Transcendental Deduction of the categories; and it is surely required, in Kant's view, in order to grasp the completeness of the system of the categories.[81] Previously, it was possible to rank various claims within critique as more or less difficult, obscure, or controversial. Insight into Kant's theory of the obvious enables us to ask a more determinate, and possibly illuminating, question.

Second, the present hypothesis regarding critique has the potential to interact fruitfully with the far-reaching question that was raised at the close of the previous section, "What kind of reason is associated with the obvious? Is it a reason that is, in the final analysis, purely moral? Purely epistemic? Or a reason that in some way unifies the two?" Now if our reason to undertake critique is at bottom our reason to carry out diagnostic instruction, as I have just speculated, we can look to Kant's position on the former to help answer the far-reaching question. Though this matter will need to be taken up in a setting in which it can be given focused attention, it is implausible, I submit, that the reason to undertake critique is either narrowly epistemic or narrowly moral. This gives us compelling grounds to pursue an alternative that unifies the two.

6. Rule-Based Instruction and Mathematics

We are finally ready to lift the simplifying assumption that all subjects belong to a single community, and thus share a single common ground. Once we abandon this artificial assumption, disagreement over a proposition, *q*, that you or I take to be obvious no longer automatically gives us a reason to pursue diagnostic instruction. If S denies *q*, there is in general a legitimate question as to whether *q* belongs to the common ground we share with S. Moreover, this question cannot be resolved simply by consulting S's pedagogical history.

There is no reliable list of the concepts that S has learned, and in any case it is an empirical question how quickly S forgets any concepts that once belonged on that list. Similar considerations apply to the factors such as vision that determine which facts are within a subject's immediate epistemic access. For these reasons, once we are considering obvious truths that are not absolutely fundamental, reasons to engage in diagnostic instruction are always subject to potentially defeating conditions. Even if I am at first tempted to wonder whether S has been led astray by prejudice or "lost his understanding" (*KpV*, 5:36), in many contexts the most natural explanation will simply be that we do not belong to the same community, as will be the case if S lacks some of the concepts in *q*.

A second consequence of removing the simplifying assumption of the previous sections is that the extent of the obvious is no longer tethered to what subjects are currently able to accomplish under conditions of good cognitive health. This is

[80] This is why the status of mathematics as the science of the obvious is singular. For a particularly rich contrast, cf. *V-Anth/Collins*, 25:164.

[81] Cf. A834/B862; *SF*, 7:113.

because for any given community, there is an indeterminately large pool of new concepts that its members might learn. Though many truths involving these concepts will not admit of certainty, or will do so only to those with heightened mental acuity, we should expect that the acquisition of concepts will tend to expand a community's common ground. Though my stock example has primed us to think about empirical concepts such as <cup> and <on top of> in this regard, there is no reason why various derivative pure and a priori concepts should not figure in some of these obvious truths. That said, learning new concepts can only take us so far. There is no reason to suppose that truths incorporating a certain class of concepts—whether it be empirical concepts concerning some particular subject matter or the derivative concepts of "transcendental philosophy"—will prove to be obvious across the board.[82]

With Kant's full model on the table, and in the brief space that remains, let's return to the conjecture from section 2 that draws upon all parts of his theory:

(3) Mathematics is the science of the obvious because for any true mathematical proposition *q*, *q* is either absolutely fundamental or any epistemically considerable subject, given the proper preparation, can become certain of *q* using diagram-based reasoning.

Though a full treatment of (3) would have more to say regarding the absolute fundamentality of axioms and postulates, it is easy enough to see the shape of that claim. Therefore, the remainder will concentrate on the second disjunct, with an eye to elucidating why it would have made sense to Kant.

Let's begin with a general observation regarding the rationale for positing obvious perceptual truths—a rationale that differs from the absolutely fundamental, in part because there is no fixed set of perceptual truths of which all subjects must be certain in order to qualify as epistemically considerable. I suggest that we think of obvious perceptual truths as a corollary of our possession of two heterogeneous cognitive capacities, thinking and intuiting, as well as the power of judgment, which enables us to use them cooperatively. That we have these capacities makes it possible for there to be sets of concepts and intuitions such that anyone enjoying health will be certain that the intuitions are correctly subsumed under the matching concepts, so long as she happens to possess these representations.[83] This explains why Kant would have reserved a special term, "evidence," for "the clarity of certain cognition, insofar as it is likened to sensory cognition" (*MSI*, 2:403). Just seeing that a cup is on the table or that the two line segments intersect *is* functionally different from the ways of

[82] On the assumption that there are possible sensory powers that would render any given empirical fact certain for subjects who possess them, this claim is not true of perceptually accessible facts. We can fix this by making obviousness context-sensitive, though to a vastly lesser degree than common ground. On this solution, there are some sensory powers that are too unlike our own to be worth considering. We could retain a concept, <obvious*>, which is not at all context-sensitive, but it is of little use if *all* perceptually accessible facts are obvious*.

[83] This is not a *necessary* corollary of the concept-intuition model. It would have been open to Kant to hold that for any given subsumption, no matter how easy, there are possible, epistemically considerable beings who are unable to perform the subsumption (or at least be certain of it). That Kant does not take this logically possible course can be seen inter alia from his use of obvious perceptual judgments in explaining the singular epistemic advantage of mathematics (*UD*, 2:291).

achieving certainty that are available within philosophy; and the rationale for their obviousness is different.

Among the many partially overlapping communities of epistemic subjects, it is communities that include some degree of scientific mathematical sophistication that concern us here, for it is only in these communities that it is appropriate to expect certainty regarding theorems and problems (i.e., beyond the absolutely fundamental). There are two distinct ways in which rule-based instruction generates such communities. Most straightforwardly, the instruction that one receives when making one's way through the demonstration of a theorem precipitates one of these communities. This can be compared, very roughly, to how learning certain empirical concepts puts one in position to "just see" that a cup is on the table. In mathematical cases the point at which this typically occurs will require that the subject have grasped and retained a number of previous steps in the demonstration, such that she is then ready to "just see," for instance, that a newly drawn line segment intersects two *parallel* lines. That those lines are parallel belongs to our common ground only if both of us have undergone the preparation provided by earlier steps in this demonstration. Whether this has occurred is, of course, a decidedly contingent affair.

In order for us to even be candidates for belonging to the community that is ready for the *n*th step of this or that demonstration, we must already have received a different type of rule-based instruction, one that makes us members of the larger community that can engage in diagrammatic reasoning of the sort that Kant deems a priori. Members of this wider community will understand, though likely not by means of explicitly stated rules, that only certain kinds of information can be gleaned from diagrams.[84] We might start by comparing this to someone who possesses <cup> and makes it a policy never to look at cups from afar or when the lighting is imperfect. The analogy is misleading, though, in that the content of <cup> has nothing to do with obviousness. In contrast, the rules of a priori, diagrammatic construction direct their users non-accidentally toward exclusive attention to the obvious.[85] In this way, the difficulties inherent in proving a given mathematical fact are transferred to those who are attempting to devise a demonstration that meets Kant's standards for apriority. It may or may not be possible to hit upon a demonstration, but once one is discovered, any epistemically considerable subject has the capacity to follow it step by step. Should S demur at some point in the proof, we find ourselves in the situation described at the beginning of this section. Namely, diagnostic instruction will then be warranted, subject to various defeating conditions that include S's not

[84] There has been a flowering of recent work that aims to make explicit the rules that are constitutive of the sort of diagrammatic reasoning that Kant would deem a priori; see Manders (2008a, 2008b), Mumma (2008, 2010, 2012), and Shabel (2003).

[85] It is unclear precisely which *concepts* pupils learn when they are taught Euclidean mathematical practice; and it might be that not all of the required techniques and sensitivities can be plausibly reconstructed as the learning of concepts. Yet this is not an objection to classifying the learning of that practice in the category that I am calling "rule-based instruction." The essential point is that in Kant's view acquiring the ability to follow a priori mathematical proofs does not entail an increase in mental acuity above the baseline level; it is a pedagogical practice that is in fact successful; and it is not an instance of diagnostic instruction.

actually having understood the earlier steps in the proof. In Kant's words, "when a mathematician demonstrates, he compels approval (*Beifall*) in everyone who understands him."[86,87]

References

Christensen, D. (2009). Disagreement as evidence: The epistemology of controversy. *Philosophy Compass, 4*(5): 756–67.

Cohen, A. (2014). Kant on the ethics of belief. *Proceedings of the Aristotelian Society, 114*(3): 317–34.

Darwall, S. (2006). *The second-person standpoint: Morality, respect, and accountability.* Harvard University Press.

Euclid (1956). *Elements* (T. Heath, Trans.). Dover.

Friedman, M. (2012). Kant on geometry and spatial intuition. *Synthese, 186*: 231–55.

Hinske, N. (1980). *Kant als Herausforderung an die Gegenwart.* Alber.

Koriako, D. (1999). *Kants Philosophie der Mathematik.* Meiner.

Manders, K. (2008a). Diagram-based geometric practice. In P. Mancosu (Ed.), *The philosophy of mathematical practice* (pp. 65–79). Oxford University Press.

Manders, K. (2008b). The Euclidean diagram. In P. Mancosu (Ed.), *The philosophy of mathematical practice* (pp. 80–133). Oxford University Press (original work published 1995).

Meier, G. F. (1752). *Auszug aus der Vernunftlehre.* Gebauer. [Cited as *Auszug* followed by paragraph number]

Meier, G. F. (1997). *Vernunftlehre* (Günter Schenk, Ed.). Hallescher (original work published 1752). [Cited as *Vernuntflehre* followed by paragraph number]

Merritt, M. (2018). *Kant on reflection and virtue.* Cambridge University Press.

Mumma, J. (2008). Ensuring generality in Euclid's diagrammatic arguments. In G. Stapleton, J. Howse, & J. Lee (Eds.), *Diagrammatic representation and inference: 5th international conference, Diagrams 2008, Herrsching, Germany, September 19–21, 2008; Proceedings* (pp. 222–35). Springer.

Mumma, J. (2010). Proofs, pictures, and Euclid. *Synthese, 175*: 255–87.

Mumma, J. (2012). Constructive geometrical reasoning and diagrams. *Synthese, 186*: 103–19.

Rosenkoetter, T. (2009). Truth criteria and the very idea of a transcendental logic. *Archiv für Geschichte der Philosophie, 91*: 193–236.

Shabel, L. (2003). *Mathematics in Kant's critical philosophy.* Routledge.

Stalnaker, R. (2002). Common ground. *Linguistics and Philosophy, 25*: 701–21.

Vanderschraaf, P. & Sillari, G. (2014). Common knowledge. In E. N. Zalta (Ed.), *The Stanford Encyclopedia of Philosophy* (Spring 2014 Edition). https://plato.stanford.edu/archives/spr2014/entries/common-knowledge/

[86] *V-Lo/Dohna*, 24:736.

[87] I am extremely grateful to Thomas Land, Karl Schafer, Nick Stang, Jens Timmermann, and Kenneth Walden for helpful comments at various stages of this project.

7
How Does Kant Conceive of Self-Consciousness?

Dina Emundts

Kant's theory of pure apperception, or transcendental self-consciousness,[1] is a central element of his philosophy and has a long and complex history of interpretation. In the Deduction, Kant wants to explain what self-consciousness is and what function it has. The Paralogisms explain, in contrast, previous misunderstandings and misuses of the concept. As far as its function is concerned, it is clear that, for Kant, self-consciousness is a condition for the possibility of knowledge. In current debates, this is reflected in the claim that one must be conscious of the fact that one is judging if one is to make inferences and act in the manner that knowledge requires.

This, however, is not specific enough for what Kant is getting at. Self-consciousness is not merely a condition for knowledge. It is also a condition of our cognizing *objects*. This has to be emphasized because, for Kant, objects are not simply given but rather somehow made by us. Self-consciousness is accorded a special function also, or perhaps precisely, with respect to this construction of objects.[2]

We can already see, based on my short-hand attempt to adumbrate the object function of self-consciousness, that it is difficult to specify the *function* of self-consciousness. But there is still more uncertainty regarding the question of what, to begin with, self-consciousness even is. In this chapter, I will focus on this latter question and largely ignore the *function* of self-consciousness that is at the center of Kant's own account. I will attempt to bring more clarity into the spectrum of interpretations concerning Kant's concept of self-consciousness. Is it something that exists or is it a conceptual construction? If there is an existing Self, what can we say about it? If it is a conceptual construct, what kind of construct is it?

In the first section I will sketch out three interpretations of Kant's concept of self-consciousness. In the sketch, I will simply introduce the interpretations without

[1] Kant doesn't use the term "transcendental consciousness," but he does use expressions like "apperception," "the I," or just "self-consciousness." He also speaks of the transcendental unity of apperception (B139) or of self-consciousness (B132). As a contrasting term to the concept of the empirical, he uses the term "pure." Thus he talks of "pure self-consciousness" (B144). Kant chooses the term "transcendental" when he wants to say that the possibility of knowledge can be deduced from a given principle (see B132), as is the case with the principle of self-consciousness, or the unity of self-consciousness. For this reason I at times employ the somewhat abbreviated term "transcendental consciousness." All translations of the *Critique of Pure Reason* are taken from the Guyer-Wood translation.

[2] I am of the opinion that this point is often overlooked in current debates on Kant. I argue for this in another article (Emundts, 2013). In that article I focus on the question of the relationship between self-perception and self-consciousness and what, for Kant, the function of self-consciousness is.

Dina Emundts, *How Does Kant Conceive of Self-Consciousness?* In: *The Sensible and Intelligible Worlds: New Essays on Kant's Metaphysics and Epistemology.* Edited by: Karl Schafer and Nicholas F. Stang, Oxford University Press. © Dina Emundts 2022.
DOI: 10.1093/oso/9780199688265.003.0008

further elaboration. In the second section I take up the interpretation I find most attractive. I point out its advantages, answer possible objections to it, and begin to compare it with the other interpretations. The third section spells out this interpretation in more detail. This is again accomplished partly by reflecting on the distinctions between this interpretation and the other interpretations introduced in the first section. In the fourth section I will discuss two variants of this interpretation and thereby develop a thesis concerning the question of how we know things about self-consciousness.

1. Three Different Interpretations

Is transcendental self-consciousness something different from the cognition of objects, and, if so, what is it in itself? The three interpretations of self-consciousness that I will mention can be differentiated with respect to how they answer this question.

First Interpretation of Self-Consciousness (1.Int.Self): One reading of Kant claims that self-consciousness is not really different from the cognition of objects. On this interpretation, we obtain the representation of a cognizable object by synthesizing a manifold according to certain rules and self-consciousness is nothing other than the object given by these rules. According to this reading, I just talk of self-consciousness because it is *my* representation of an object. However, the term "self-consciousness" appears here to be out of place. There is nothing that can be distinguished from the act of cognizing the object that we can mean with "self-consciousness." Assuming, then, that self-consciousness is something different from the cognition of objects, in what way is it different? This is the question to which the other interpretations I want to mention try to find an answer.

Second Interpretation of Self-Consciousness (2.Int.Self): Is the Self an idea or a thing of thought (*Gedankending* = mental construct, literally "thought-thing"), and do we *think* the Self as a kind of correlate to objects? One could say here that the Self is different from the objects cognized because it is distinguished in thought as being something else. I call this interpretation the "thing-of-thought" interpretation.[3]

Third Interpretation of Self-Consciousness (3.Int.Self): Perhaps we can and must go further, claiming that there must be something real that corresponds to the thought of self-consciousness. This interpretation still maintains (like the other two) that self-consciousness is always also consciousness of something. But it does not reduce self-consciousness to this function, but rather takes self-consciousness to be something that exists on its own. In order not to contradict Kant's statements regarding the thing in itself, one must add here that we can make this claim even if we don't know how the thing that corresponds to our thought is to be determined, i.e., as an intellectual subject, as an empirical Self, or as something else. According to this

[3] Though I don't follow it in every detail, I take Rosefeldt's interpretation (2002, 2006) here as orientation.

interpretation, the Self is not a mere thought-thing but something that (truly) exists. However, there might be different possible variants of this reading. The interpretation I want to discuss does not assume that there are several existing selves, but assumes rather that there is only one existing Self and that this existing Self is persisting. This is assumed because the synthesis of the manifold is meant to be the synthesis performed by one single Self and not by several Selves. Furthermore, the interpretation assumes, for reasons I'll leave open at the moment, that it can (somehow) be known by the Self that there is a persisting Self. I call this interpretation the persisting-Self interpretation (*sich durchhaltend* = literally "holding itself through"). One could also call it the persisting-consciousness interpretation, for "Self" is supposed to be the expression for a persisting consciousness. In what follows I will spell out this interpretation in more detail. In order to do this, I will mainly be concerned with the difference between the last two interpretations—the Self as a thing of thought (2.Int.Self) and the Self as something that we must assume exists (3.Int.Self). The difference is significant, even though it is rarely thematized. According to the suggestion of the second interpretation (2.Int.Self), the Self is a conceptual construct. With regards to this suggestion, rather than saying that there exists a Self, one could also say, and this would in a way be more appropriate, that one has the abilities to relate in a certain manner to earlier impressions. The particular abilities that are relevant to judgment and cognition can be tied to the idea of a thinking subject. The suggestion of the third interpretation (3.Int.Self) says that there is an existing Self (or something that can be called such) that persists and carries out the various syntheses, and that we can know that this is the case.

This last formulation, namely, that it can be known that there exists a persisting Self, requires a few remarks that are interesting for our discussion here of the various interpretations of Kant's theory of self-consciousness: (a) A difficulty resides in the formulation that we can *know* a persisting Self. This formulation is problematic in the technical sense that, for Kant, theoretical knowledge assumes that something is sensuously given. (b) There appears to be a problem with this formulation when we compare it to the text of the first *Critique*, for Kant does not say that we "know" or "cognize" the Self or self-consciousness. He speaks of "thinking" (*Denken*) (B134–35) and "presupposing" (*voraussetzen*) (A111; B133; B137), and it sounds more as if we have to assume or to suppose such a Self or self-consciousness. For this reason, in a Kantian sense it would be more appropriate to say the following: "We *must assume* that such a Self exists." I use "know" and "knowledge" here in a broader sense than Kant does. For Kant—at least in the theoretical context—it would be more appropriate to say "assume." (c) In addition, this formulation is unclear about when (or where) this knowledge takes place: during every act of synthesis, simultaneously with the cognition of objects, or in a (special) transcendental-philosophical act of deliberation? I want to address, in light of these difficulties, a possible interesting distinction within the third interpretation. The distinction concerns the question of the source of our warrant for assuming that there is a persisting Self.

According to the third interpretation (3.Int.Self) there exists a persisting Self that is conscious of itself. The question that must be made explicit and on the basis of which two different variants within this interpretation emerge is the following: from where does the knowledge come[4] that there exists a persisting Self? One could answer: (3.Int.Self.b) our consciousness is distinguished by the fact that it is (self-) reflexive. Therefore our consciousness is *self*-consciousness. Self-consciousness is an act of relating to oneself, an act in which one is, or becomes, conscious of something, and one can also become conscious of the fact that there exists a persisting Self (consciousness). When one is conscious of this fact, one knows that there exists a persisting Self, even when knowing this can be said to constitute a particular instance of knowledge. Thus, according to this reading, "being conscious" is a (special) kind of knowledge.

In contrast, when I described the earlier interpretation that assumes a persisting Self, I did not regard consciousness as a source of the knowledge that the Self is persisting. Rather, in that interpretation (3.Int.Self.a), it was a philosophical, transcendental, or conceptual reflection that led me to assume that there exists a persisting Self or persisting consciousness. What speaks for this reading (3.Int.Self.a) is that Kant does not speak of knowledge, but seems rather to assume or to deduce (from reflections about conditions) that there is a Self. In the second edition, Kant characterizes the unity of consciousness that is a condition for and the highest principle of knowledge as an analytic proposition, whereas he appears to consider it to be a synthetic proposition in the first edition. This revision is of course in itself worth considering (I will ignore it here),[5] but to begin with, both assertions regarding this principle speak in favor of seeing it as an instance of philosophical knowledge (as in 3.Int.Self.a) and not as something that we are immediately conscious of (as according to 3.Int.Self.b). I will discuss this at greater length in the fourth section.

I have now laid out three different possibilities for how to interpret Kant's basic statement on his understanding of self-consciousness, and I made a further distinction between two variants within the third interpretation concerning the source of knowledge. As far as Kant's text is concerned, each of these interpretations can draw on various passages for support, and there are other passages that fit less well.[6]

[4] According to the thing-of-thought interpretation, one doesn't have to, or isn't permitted to, speak of knowledge, but with respect to the persisting-Self thesis, it is unclear whether we can speak of knowledge. I will come back to this in the fourth section.

[5] More precisely, I will come back to this issue only in notes 47 and 52.

[6] The first reading (1.Int.Self) claims that self-consciousness is in fact nothing other than the cognition of objects. In the act of objectively determining objects (*Gegenstände*), we relate to ourselves, and this is the only way in which we can relate to ourselves. One can refer to B133 to support this reading, understanding "synthesis" here to refer to the synthesis of representations: "Therefore it is only because I can combine a manifold of given representations in *one consciousness* that it is possible for me to represent the *identity of the consciousness in these representations* itself, i.e., the *analytical* unity of apperception is only possible under the presupposition of some *synthetic* one." For the (2.Int.Self) thing-of-thought reading, one can draw on all the passages from the Paralogisms in which Kant says that the Self is only an empty representation (see below). For the persisting-Self reading according to which the transcendental philosopher assumes that there is a persisting self (3.Int.Self.a), one can refer, for example, to A107: "That which should *necessarily* be represented as numerically identical cannot be thought of as such through empirical data. There must be a condition that precedes all experience and makes the latter itself possible, which should make such a transcendental presupposition valid." For the persisting-Self reading that assumes consciousness to be the source of this knowledge (3.Int.Self.b), one can, for example, cite A116: "We are conscious *a priori* of the thoroughgoing identity of ourselves with regard to all representations that can ever belong to our cognition." Passages are, of course, interpreted differently based on the reading that is

As far as the issue of self-consciousness is concerned, all of the interpretations likewise appear to me to at least be defensible. In the literature on Kant it is often not even clear which of these interpretations is being advocated.[7] The reason for this is probably that for Kant and many of his interpreters it is less a matter of working out a concept or theory of the Self than it is of analyzing the *functions* of the Self. A further reason is probably that Kant (and his interpreters) did not conceive of these options as being so mutually exclusive as I have made it seem. It is a philosophical question interesting in its own right to consider if, when, and in what way they really exclude one another. There can be two reasons why these interpretations would not be mutually exclusive. One reason can be that they are somehow combinable.[8] In what follows, I will sometimes evaluate such a possibility. The second reason is that upon further explication these interpretations appear to lose their original distinctness.[9] I will illustrate and discuss this at several places in what follows. This last point concerning the fuzzy boundaries between interpretations is one reason why in this first section I have only sketched the three interpretations and have not yet given a more elaborate account of them: I think that we should develop the interpretations step by step in comparison to one another because then it is easier to see where they overlap and where they can be distinguished sharply.

Although I think that all of the three interpretations are defensible, I want to defend the third interpretation (3.Int.Self.a). In the next section I will give some hints as to why I find it attractive, and I will thereby clarify the main thesis of this interpretation. Then I will spell out the main theses of the third interpretation in even more detail in the subsequent two sections.

being advanced. Thus, in the first reading (1.Int.Self), the "consciousness as synthesis" is taken to mean a consciousness of the synthesized, manifold *representations*, whereas in the persisting-Self reading (3.Int. Self) it is understood (at least in some passages) to mean a consciousness of the *synthesis* (as an action) of representations (on the whole, the text seems to me to speak for the latter option). One could also say that one can find support for any of these interpretations from writings other than the first *Critique*. The practical philosophy could, for example, maybe support the persisting-Self reading. But I cannot discuss this here.

[7] Rosefeldt (especially 2006) clearly advances the thing-of-thought position. Variants of that reading are also advocated by Guyer (1987, p. 135), Carl (1998) (with qualifications), and Keller (1998, p. 67). With some interpretations it is difficult for me to say if they belong to the very first reading (namely, (1.Int. Self) that self-consciousness is nothing other than the cognition of objects) or to (2) the thing-of-thought reading. This is the case, for example, with Falk Wunderlich (2005). The hypothesis of a persisting-Self (or a persisting action) is clearly supported by Henrich (1966, 1976) and Horstmann (1993). Ginsborg (2013) deliberately leaves the question open. For Longuenesse (2012) I would say that she defends a particular variant of the first reading of the persisting Self (3.Int.Self.a). In another essay, she argues that the unity of consciousness is a (mere) idea that does *not* guarantee its reality (Longuenesse, 2007, p. 154). That sounds like a thing-of-thought reading (2.Int.Self), but one must consider that Kant employs the term "I," or Self, in other ways that are not addressed in the article (for example in A682/B711). I include Kitcher (2011) as a defender of (3.Int.Self) the persisting Self interpretation (p. 175), but also in her text there are passages that are not straightforward (pp. 194–96).

[8] The first interpretation (1.Int.Self) is, for example, only exclusive if one maintains that self-consciousness is *nothing other* than consciousness of an object. One could also, for example, claim that consciousness of an object is always also (at least implicitly) consciousness of the Self. This can be also said with regard to the third interpretation (3.Int.Self).

[9] For example, one could argue that only the practical philosophy lends support to something like the persisting-Self reading and that this cannot be reached from a theoretical standpoint.

2. Some Motivations for the Third Interpretation of Self-Consciousness

I see one advantage of the persisting-Self interpretation in the fact that it does more justice to the term "self-consciousness." As I hope will become clearer in the following sections, I think that, at least in a particular variant of the persisting-Self hypothesis, one can say that the Self is *conscious* of itself in the sense of relating mentally to itself, whereas in the other interpretations self-consciousness is more of a designation for the fact that I have certain abilities. Moreover, the persisting-Self reading is capable of allowing for and distinguishing between many different relationships that we have to ourselves, and in this sense, it constitutes a richer theory of self-consciousness. It also could be that it is more compatible with Kant's practical philosophy. However, this is only a conjecture, and I'm not going to show this here. Even when I am of the opinion that the persisting-Self reading is correct, I do not claim to have shown this with my remarks here. But the following considerations also do not require me to do so, for the question I am asking can be formulated this way: If one wants to defend this interpretation, what does that imply for the concept of consciousness, what problems arise and what strategies might we use to deal with them?

Besides the aforementioned advantages, one might also have some general objections against such an understanding of self-consciousness. I would like to address some of them not only because I think one can answer these objections but also because I think that the objections and our response to them help to bring out the assumptions that the persisting-Self interpretation does imply.

One disadvantage of readings that take self-consciousness to be consciousness of a persisting Self is that they are confronted with certain familiar theoretical complications concerning the relationship between the empirical and pure Self. This is so because according to this interpretation we have to take the persisting Self that is the subject of the transcendental synthesis as something that exists, but at the same time (as I will develop further in subsequent sections) we don't want to simply identify this Self with the empirical Self. It is not clear that we need two kinds of subjects—the transcendental and the empirical Self—but we need at least to distinguish between the empirical and the pure Self in our philosophical theory, and at least in this sense we have a duplication of the Self. Although that is a disadvantage in the sense that it makes Kant more unwieldy and less compatible with contemporary philosophical positions, it is in my eyes not a disadvantage in every respect.

With respect to the textual evidence, the duplication of the Self is in my eyes convincing. For Kant does in fact take the duplication of the Self and the ambiguities regarding the relationship between transcendental self-consciousness and empirical self-consciousness more seriously[10] than one would if one were to "simply" say, as in the second interpretation, that transcendental consciousness is the name for abilities that we have as empirical subjects.[11]

[10] Compare *Anth*, 7:134, and concerning this, Klemme (1996, p. 375).

[11] I have kept the account of the thing-of-thought reading here somewhat vague because one would have to more precisely say how, according to this reading, the thinking subject relates to the empirical subject. It seems to me that one would say: "The term 'Self' always refers to the empirical person, but this

As far as the evaluation of the doubling problem itself is concerned, the situation is complicated. For one, a potential problem with identifying two selves can be formulated in the following way: there are cases in which I, with the designation "I" or "myself," no doubt refer to myself as an object, but because we can distinguish between the transcendental and the empirical Self, I have to somehow identify when I am referring to my empirical Self as opposed to my transcendental Self. But how do I know that this is "my" empirical Self? This seems to be a problem and one can even go so far as to claim that this question appears to be absurd, and for this reason it wouldn't bode well for the endeavor if it had to be answered within a theory of self-consciousness.[12] However, it is not at all clear if, within the framework of the interpretation of the persisting Self, this question has been posed correctly. It seems to me that Kant proceeds from a determination of the relationship between the transcendental and the empirical Self that does not require that these two selves can be identified with one other as is presupposed in the previous consideration.[13] Thus, the duplication of the Self might be a problem, but one doesn't have to problematically suppose a kind of act in which the pure Self is identified with the empirical Self.

Second, there could be a reference problem. In order to be meaningful, doesn't the expression "I," or "Self," always have to refer to us as a person in the empirical world, and isn't the third interpretation claiming that there this is an employment of this expression where this is not the case? In discussions of Kant's notion of self-consciousness, the question of reference has been discussed a lot in the past years. In the case of an interpretation that supposes the existence of a persisting, transcendental Self, it could be that, according to the opinion of many interpreters, the referent of the expression "I," or "Self" is undetermined in the case of its transcendental application. That is to say that it is unclear what the expression is referring to, but it is clear that it is referring to something (Longuenesse, 2012). Thus one must not assume that Kant contends with his persisting-Self hypothesis that we can use expressions to (unambiguously) refer to things in themselves, or that we could use our predicates to determine these things in themselves, or that we would ultimately commit a Cartesian fallacy and infer the existence of a thinking substance. Hence, the question of reference does not appear to create serious problems (Longuenesse, 2012).

At this point I want, as I mentioned before, to give an example for how it can be difficult to clearly distinguish the different interpretations of self-consciousness from one another. Note that I don't want to claim that these interpretations really are undistinguishable. Rather I want to show how it comes about that they sometimes sound similar and therefore are often not distinguished carefully.

Instead of talking about a persisting Self, one can, as mentioned earlier, call it a persisting consciousness. For the term "Self" is not intended to signify an entity that is somehow substance-like, but rather something that persists (*sich durchhält* =

person has abilities that I can fixate with the term 'pure Self.' With this locution, there is no object to which it refers. It expresses, rather the kind of connection that I must be capable of achieving."

[12] However, Ginsborg (2013) has recently discussed this and showed that one can in fact, with some effort, provide an answer to this question.

[13] Longuenesse has something like this in mind (2001, p. 393). Ginsborg (2013, p. 126) thinks that an identification would be necessary here (and therefore also necessary in the case of Longuenesse's proposal), but I don't see why this has to be the case.

persists, sustains itself, perseveres) and that consciously, and with a consciousness of itself, combines representations. For Kant it's not a question of the identity of an object, but rather the identity of a consciousness.[14] When this is emphasized, then the distinction to the thing-of-thought interpretation becomes less clear and both readings can sound similar. For the thing-of-thought interpretation takes the unity of consciousness of course also for granted. The supposition which the thing-of-thought interpretation above all opposes is that there is a thing or an object (intelligible or empirical) that exists (and persists). But this appears to be at least in part in agreement with the contrasting position of the persisting Self. For based on what I have just explained, the persisting-Self interpretation claims that the reference is undetermined, and one can understand this to mean that it is not even clear if we are dealing here with some kind of thing, substance or entity, or if, for example, we are dealing instead with an action.[15] Thus, following both interpretations (2.Int.Self and 3.Int. Self) it might be a point to emphasize that there is no existing object that we can refer to. And then it seems as if, by emphasizing the fact that we can replace our talk of a persisting Self with the notion of a persisting consciousness, we end up in a situation where we cannot distinguish the persisting-Self hypothesis from the thing-of-thought hypothesis. Is this impression correct? The impression that there is no longer a distinction between the two readings is incorrect. But before I explain why, I want to hold on to one thesis from the discussion so far: the persisting-Self interpretation is not at all concerned with the identity of an object or an entity; rather, it could have in mind an identical consciousness (perhaps a stream of consciousness) that realizes itself in various entities.

There are two reasons why we don't lose the sharp distinction between the two interpretations (2.Int.Self and 3.Int.Self). Firstly, even if the persisting-Self interpretation claims that the reference is undetermined, it holds on to the thesis that our theory of self-consciousness implies that there is a real Self that is not merely a conceptual construction. Thus, the ontological difference between these interpretations persists. In distinguishing the thing-of-thought reading from the persisting-Self reading, we can still discuss the option of two different ontological commitments.

Secondly, this ontological difference is related to two different possible understandings of the process of synthesizing the manifold into the representation of an object. This difference has not yet been mentioned but we can take it into account now by reflecting on the action of synthesis that came into view in the previous paragraphs.

(2.Int.Self) According to the thing-of-thought interpretation, self-consciousness is something that is posterior to the basal processes of synthesis, for before we grasp this thought, we must have already synthesized.[16]

[14] This is made apparent in the (controversial) example of the elastic ball A363–64.

[15] Rosefeldt (2006) conceives of his interpretation as an answer to a dilemma to which he claims Horstmann (1993) is also reacting (or could be so understood), but not in the best manner possible. In contrast, I would say that, although both want to say that there is no determined object we can relate to, they deeply disagree about what we can say about the action. Whereas for Rosefeldt it is only a thing of thought, Horstmann understands the act as a metaphysical dynamic Self.

[16] One might object here that according to the thing-of-thought interpretation the self-consciousness is not meant to be "posterior" because it is only a thought and not a process in time. However, even then,

(3.Int.Self) In contrast, the persisting-Self interpretation can go in another direction in order to explain the act of synthesis. The actions of synthesis are (self-) conscious (I will explain in the next section in what way), and the unity of consciousness exists without the requirement that we must explicitly relate to it.[17] Consciousness and its reference to itself really do exist (and indeed before we grasp the thought of consciousness). Consciousness is, in this sense, *real.*

Thus, we don't lose the distinction between both interpretations although both can indeed emphasize that there is no determined object to which we can refer. When the persisting-Self interpretation (3.Int.Self) wants to stress that what is at issue is not an identical *object* (*Gegenstand*), it sounds quite compatible with the thing-of-thought interpretation. However, when the thing-of-thought reading emphasizes its claim that the unity of the Self is a sheer construct of our making, it clearly differentiates itself from the persisting-Self reading. This is thus an example of why and how it happens that in the discussion the interpretations are not always sharply distinguished from each other.

At this point it seems to me that it in fact makes sense to introduce a deciding specification or modification to the persisting-Self interpretation: one must distinguish between consciousness and the carrier (or the possessor) of consciousness. The relation to consciousness does not stay undetermined. When we employ the expression "I" or "Self" in a transcendental sense and say that there exists an identical Self, we could equally say: there exists an identical consciousness. That is not undetermined, but rather refers to a synthesis-process of a uniform synthesis. But what *is* undetermined and what we are not capable of determining is the kind of entity that the bearer of consciousness is, and one can also formulate this by saying that it is unclear *whose* consciousness it is: the consciousness of an empirical Self, or of a thing in itself, or if it comes from various entities, or from something that is not an entity at all.[18] Of course we know that it is *our* consciousness, but we do not know who or what we are intrinsically (*an sich*), and by means of our consciousness and our knowledge concerning our consciousness, we do not obtain any more information that would answer this question. This specification seems useful to me for several reasons. For example, it allows us to better come to terms with passages in which Kant emphasizes that the Self is only a form and that the expression "I" "does not distinguish a particular object"[19] (see below). Furthermore, without this specification, the shift that Kant often makes (and that I, too, have made) between talking about a Self and talking about a consciousness is not possible. I will mention additional reasons in the further course of my discussion.

this interpretation seems to reject the notion that processes before the thought of the Self are self-conscious and instead only argue that everything which is part of the process of synthesis can potentially be brought under the concept of self-consciousness.

[17] It has sometimes been asked why Kant's successors can speak of self-consciousness as something that exists without there being an individual who becomes conscious of him- or herself. Here we can see how this manner of speaking can arise: what is meant are real processes that have a certain structure.

[18] Our responses to these questions might be different from a practical perspective, but I cannot discuss this here.

[19] Later, I will examine A346/B404 more closely. Compare also, for example, A341–42/B399–400. Kant says here that the Self *only* serves to present all thinking as belonging to consciousness.

The language concerning a persisting Self is thus ambiguous: it can (a) be taken to mean a Self that has consciousness. This is how it often seems to be understood in the debate when one says that the reference is undetermined. The term "I" or "Self" can (b) also be the expression for a particular form of consciousness, regardless of how this consciousness is instantiated, "materialized," or "realized." One is not entitled to claim that the persisting-Self interpretation considers the Self that persists to be an identical object.

I have also already addressed the question of why, in the remaining discussion, I focus primarily on the persisting-Self interpretation and not on the others. I do not want to further discuss all relevant passages in Kant's text that bear on the various interpretations because, as I said, I think that one can find textual support for all interpretations. But I do want to make something explicit that concerns possible objections on a textual basis against the persisting-Self interpretation (3.Int.Self): at least based on the modification I have made, the persisting-Self interpretation can respond to the objection that it does not fit Kant's claim that the Self designates an *empty* representation (A346/B404) and to Kant's statements that the Self is *logically* simple, that it has a *logical* identity, etc. (e.g., B407, B363). These passages are found in the Paralogisms, and that means that they are intended to bring out the possibility of false inferences. For this reason, one can explain in the way that I have already outlined the claim that this Self only represents a transcendental subject. Namely, what we are saying about the Self does not require us to claim that there is knowledge of an object. In this sense, the representation is an "empty" representation. It would make sense for the persisting-Self interpretation, which wants to stress that there is no known object we can refer to, to put forward this "emptiness" against theories of the Self, such as Descartes's, which go on to determine the Self as a substance. Thus, one could explain these statements in the Paralogisms as consistent with the persisting-Self interpretation (3.Int.Self) if one reads these passages as saying that there is no determined object and not as saying that "empty" means "without any content" as the less metaphysical readings (like 1.Int.Self and 2.Int.Self) would suggest.

In connection with the passage that characterizes the Self as an empty representation (and one can also find other passages that say something similar), Kant says that consciousness is not a representation "distinguishing a particular object, but rather a form of representation in general, insofar as it is to be called a cognition; for of it alone can I say that through it I think anything" (A346/B404). That sounds as if one should view self-consciousness as something that cannot at all be distinguished from the cognition of objects. With this, it seems as if consciousness should be understood according to the very first interpretation (1.Int.Self) I presented.[20] But note that this can also be interpreted in accordance with the persisting-Self interpretation along the lines of what has just been explicated: to say that self-consciousness is only the "form" of representation is then to mean the following: we know that the representations are in some sense conscious—that is their form—but we know nothing about the thing that has this consciousness (the "carrier"). We know that it is our

[20] Compare with the beginning of section 1.

consciousness, but in this context (i.e., aside from inner experience) we know nothing objective about ourselves.[21]

Before this passage, Kant mentions that we are dealing here with a circle, according to which we must make use of the representation of the Self in order to make any kind of judgment about it. This remark fits well with my interpretation, for it pertains exactly to the impossibility of saying something *objective* about ourselves concerning our consciousness in the act of thinking: we can't do that because we would need to consider ourselves as objects, whereas in fact the task here is to thematize the process of determination that brings about objectivity.[22] Mind you, we can relate to ourselves in a determining fashion as persisting, empirical Selves, but this kind of self-relation is not applicable to the actions that achieve objectivity in the first place, and it is these actions that Kant is here concerned with.[23]

The context is also similar in the case of the passages that characterize the Self's qualities as "logical" (e.g., B407, B363). Once more Kant is concerned with making it clear that when talking about our consciousness, we cannot attain any knowledge of the thing in itself (B406–407).[24] Kant then says on B407: "That the I of apperception, consequently in every thought, is a *single thing* that cannot be resolved into a plurality of subjects, and hence a logically simple subject, lies already in the concept of thinking." "Logically" can mean here that Kant is talking not about a *material*, simple subject, but rather a subject that is simple "in thought," and thus a persisting consciousness. Thus, this passage, as well, does not contradict the persisting-Self hypothesis. But be that as it may, all I can argue for is that the persisting-Self interpretation can deal with these passages, but it is not without alternatives. I have already said that for every mentioned interpretation there are passages that fit well and those that fit less well.

In the following section, I will further elaborate the persisting-Self interpretation and examine what can be meant here by the term "self-consciousness." At various points in the next section, I will bring up the thing-of-thought interpretation as a point of comparison. In my account, I will also defer until the final, fourth section the critical discussion concerning our knowledge of the identity of consciousness. Implicitly I will assume that we must accept through transcendental-philosophical reflection the existence of such a consciousness—this is the first version of the

[21] Among other things, Kant's Idealism is central here: the determination of the world also encompasses the determination of myself as an empirical Self. What I am before the world is determined I cannot say.

[22] Let it be noted that one cannot then actually say (as I did above), that the carrier could also be the empirical Self, for this Self is a product of determinacy. However, one can say that the carrier must determine itself to be an empirical Self.

[23] Wolff (2006) says at one point that the term "Self," if it refers to anything at all, refers to us as human beings. I think one can say that when one considers that, for Kant, reference presupposes determinacy. I think, differently from Wolff, that this means that the Self determines itself to be an empirical Self. With this determination, the term refers to the empirical Self. This is related to the idea of a doctrine of self-positing, which I am not going to present here (and which Kant only deals with—if at all—in the *Opus postumum*).

[24] "I do not cognize any object merely by the fact that I think, but rather I can cognize any object only by determining a given intuition with regard to the unity of consciousness, in which all thinking consists. Thus I cognize if I am conscious to myself of the intuition of myself as determined in regard to the function of thought" (B406).

persisting-Self reading (3.Int.Self.a)—but this won't be discussed until the last section. I will then address this issue in the fourth section and with this I will also answer the question if and how the two persisting-Self readings (3.Int.Self.a and 3.Int.Self.b) can be combined. I have already indicated why the compatibility of these readings is a possibility: if, in a transcendental reflection, I infer that there exists a persisting Self, this at least does not contradict the supposition of a self-conscious Self.[25]

3. The Various Ways of Relating to a Persisting Self

In order to clarify what the persisting-Self interpretation does imply, it is worthwhile to compare it with one of the alternative interpretations, especially with the thing-of-thought interpretation. So far the main difference between these interpretations is the existence claim of the persisting-Self interpretation. As I presented it, it claims that a persisting Self exists and we can somehow know this. Furthermore, as I spelled out in the last section, the persisting-Self interpretation also allows for the possibility of describing the act of synthesis as a self-conscious act, something which the thing-of-thought interpretation doesn't allow. This has to do with the fact that for the thing-of-thought interpretation, the thought of self-consciousness is something that is posterior to basic processes of synthesis and that self-consciousness only consists of this thought of self-consciousness. In what follows I will spell this out. I begin with a sketch of the two alternative interpretations (2.Int.Self and 3.Int.Self). Then I will introduce two meanings of self-consciousness and discuss how the two interpretations can account for these meanings. In this context, I will also discuss the role of judgments, for according to the thing-of-thought interpretation judgments are crucial for the thought of self-consciousness. Additionally, I will briefly discuss an objection against the persisting-Self interpretation, namely the objection that a circularity problem arises.

Let us first assume that the Self is purely a thing of thought (2.Int.Self). In this case, pure self-consciousness stands for the fact that I can relate in a particular way to my earlier states and representations. This is done through judgments. This manner of self-relation is one in which I can relate to these representations as *my* representations and thereby also relate to myself as the one who has, for example, connected these representations. Both of these aspects—to relate to representations as mine and to relate to myself as the one who has them—express a self-relation, and thus the term "self-consciousness" obtains its legitimacy. As I have already indicated above, and don't want to explain further here, it is a condition for cognition that I am able to relate in this manner to representations and to myself. That is why one can say that self-consciousness is a condition for cognition (and this likewise says something about how cognition is achieved, namely in accordance with certain rules). One could now ask who, in fact, is making these connections between representations, if it is the case that the Self is purely a mental construct? According to the

[25] In Emundts (2013) I took a different starting point and then argued that self-consciousness must be a kind of consciousness. I am now complementing this thought, but I am also modifying it with my claims in the fourth section.

thing-of-thought interpretation, however, this is a misguided question: of course a person who is engaged in a dialog can answer the question by saying "I, myself" and refer to him- or herself as a person with an empirical body. But the point that the expressions "original apperception" and "pure self-consciousness" are making is precisely that they do not signify an entity or any other sort of thing that exists. Rather, what they signify is a specific manner of connecting representations (namely, the manner in which I attribute these representations to myself as my representations) and therefore the question of reference is here misguided.[26] It's the same story with the question of if and how the Self can be *conscious* of itself. According to this reading, this question is also misguided, for the question takes self-consciousness to mean that something becomes conscious of itself. Meanwhile, all that this interpretation (2.Int.Self) maintains is that I become conscious, for example, of the representations as my own, without being forced to assume that there is a Self to whom the representations become conscious (once again, of course, this is an empirical Self, but the transcendental "I" does not signify here an empirical Self, but rather no entity at all). What I want to show with these considerations is that it cannot be taken as an objection to the thing-of-thought interpretation that it cannot answer these questions because this interpretation says that these questions are based on misunderstandings about what self-consciousness means.

Let us now instead assume that we recognize (for example in the act of transcendental reflection) that there exists a persisting Self. How do things then look with respect to one's consciousness of oneself? Such an assumption opens up an entire range of possibilities for how one relates to oneself in a way that we could then call "self-conscious." In order to illustrate this, I would like to show with more exactitude how one can carry out this interpretation.

Unlike as in the thing-of-thought interpretation, when we talk about self-consciousness we are not yet also dealing here with a judging subject who establishes things about him- or herself on the basis of his or her abilities. Instead, the persisting-Self interpretation can take the self-conscious Self as an existing Self on the level of intuition, as a Self that carries out syntheses, that is, assembles a manifold into unities.[27]

Now, one could say that Kant's theory of self-consciousness includes somehow the claim that the syntheses must be conscious and also self-conscious processes (in order for cognition to be possible). One can therefore also call this activity (*Tätigkeit*) an "action" (*Handlung*). If this is true, how then can the thing-of-thought interpretation (2.Int.Self) take this into account? For the thing-of-thought interpretation this is not the real process of a real conscious Self, but is rather an action of the empirical Self, and the sum of abilities that lead to objective judgments is distinguished in thought as being something different from the object that is called self-consciousness.

[26] I'm going to forgo here a discussion of the extent to which the questions of reference clearly differentiate the various readings. In general, one can perhaps say that according to the thing-of-thought reading, the question of reference does not make any sense, and/or it needs to be clear that the reference is always to the empirical Self. With respect to the hypothesis of the persisting-Self, the question is, in contrast, meaningful.

[27] A well-fitting description for such a process at the intuitive level is offered by Rolf-Peter Horstmann (2017, part 1).

To say that the syntheses are self-conscious thus means, according to the thing-of-thought interpretation (2.Int.Self), that they are part of the action of the (empirical) subject that leads to cognition. Thus, one sees that the concept of self-consciousness is different in the two interpretations discussed here. This cannot, however, be taken as an objection to the one or the other. Maybe one can say that in the persisting-Self interpretation the concepts of the Self and self-consciousness are richer or thicker, and that the thing-of-thought interpretation has a less metaphysical take on these concepts. But this statement does not in any way contradict what the interpretations themselves are claiming and thus does not constitute an objection to them.

If we abstract for a moment from the different interpretations and think about the concept of self-consciousness on its own, one can say that being "self-conscious" can mean two different things:

First Understanding of Self-Consciousness (1.Underst.sc): First, self-consciousness can mean that all of the connections must take place in *one single* consciousness. In order for this to be the case, the synthetic connections have to be carried out consciously and from the *same* consciousness. "Conscious" signifies here that something is represented mentally and "consciousness" means something that mentally represents.[28] As Kant often emphasizes, the representation of this consciousness can be indistinct and weak. The unity of consciousness can be seen as something that the transcendental philosopher proposes. The philosopher can justify this proposal in the following way: if we did not suppose this unity, then we could not at all explain how these representations could be said to belong to me (B132) and how we could combine [*verbinden*] these representations (A116). However, the notion of a representation implies[29] that it can be joined with others.[30] It is justified to call this unity of consciousness *self*-consciousness because it is responsible for the fact that these representations are all *my* representations. Thus Kant says, for example, "It is therefore absolutely necessary that in my cognition all consciousness belong to one consciousness (of myself)"(A117).

One can summarize what I said concerning this first meaning of self-consciousness by saying that, with respect to my representations, the unity of my consciousness is a requirement of these representations being my representations. How do the two interpretation we are comparing (2.Int.Self and 3.Int.Self) spell this out? How does this comport with the interpretation (2.Int.Self) that self-consciousness (as well as the Self that is conscious) is purely a thing of thought? That suggestion is in agreement with what I have just outlined, if one once again takes the unity of consciousness to be a mere conceptual construction. In the sense of this interpretation (2.Int. Self) we can say: There is no consciousness into which the representations

[28] As should have become clear above: we do not know what is representing, i.e., the nature of the thing that is mentally representing.

[29] This could already belong to the concept of a "representation" and that would then explain why Kant regards the unity of consciousness in the B edition to be an analytical proposition.

[30] For this reason, Wolfgang Carl (1998, pp. 192–93) correctly says that this consciousness is only to be regarded as a condition for knowledge if the notion of knowledge is to be explained with the aid of the notion of representation.

(somehow) enter or in which they (somehow) come to be, but the coming together of the representations is what makes a unity, and we can distinguish this unity from the object as the unity of consciousness. In contrast, according to the persisting-Self interpretation, there really is a consciousness that combines representations and allows for their connections on the basis of its unity, and this consciousness is not merely a thought.

Admittedly, one can also respond to what I have pursued by saying that the unity of consciousness is a *thought*, for according to what I have said, the transcendental philosopher must *suppose* that there exists such a unity—but we don't experience it or see it. If the persistent-Self interpretation says this about the transcendental philosopher, it is one variant of the third interpretation (3.Int.Self) in which the source of the assumption is not experience but rather philosophical reflection (3.Int.Self.a). This establishes a proximity to the thing-of-thought hypothesis, but it doesn't eliminate the difference between the two interpretations (2.Int.Self and 3.Int.Self), for according to the persisting-Self interpretation one supposes the *existence* of consciousness. In this context, when we want to talk about knowledge, we only do so in the sense that we know *that* a unity must exist, and not in the sense that we can know this unity (I will come back to this point in the fourth section).

So far we have dealt with self-consciousness as referring to the unity of consciousness. One can also identify another, different meaning of self-consciousness.[31] With respect to what I have said concerning synthesis on the level of intuition according to the persisting-Self interpretation this second meaning is of some importance.

Second Understanding of Self-Consciousness (2.Underst.sc): Kant talks not just about the unity of consciousness, but also about the consciousness of identity and the consciousness of synthesis.[32] Perhaps one can interpret this in the first sense (1.Underst.sc) I have just laid out as the unity of consciousness or conscious synthesis. I suppose that this is what the thing-of-thought interpretation (2.Int.Self) would do. However, one can also take what Kant says literally in the sense that I relate myself to my consciousness or to my own synthesis, and I am conscious of this synthesis. This is the most obvious way to understand many passages in the text about the consciousness of the synthesis (e.g., B133), but what can it mean?

As I have already said: it is possible to read this not in the sense of an immediate self-representation if one attributes to Kant the strategy of intentionally meaning something peculiar with the term "self-consciousness." Then one can namely say: the relation to ourselves is precisely not possible through the act of directly representing ourselves; it is, rather, only possible by means of combining representations into an object according to certain rules. The unity of consciousness *represents* itself in this combination (because otherwise this unity in an object would not at all be possible), but apart from this, the unity (of our consciousness) provides us with nothing that

[31] Cramer, for example, clearly emphasizes that both of these meanings are possible (1993, p. 137).

[32] Kant speaks of the former more in the A edition (A116), the latter more in the B edition (B133). I don't care to comment on this change here, for we will see later, I think, that the consciousness of identity means something similar to the consciousness of synthesis.

could allow us to otherwise relate to ourselves. This can be seen as part of the first interpretation I presented (1.Int.Self), according to which self-consciousness is nothing other than the consciousness of objects. It also can fit within the thing-of-thought interpretation (2.Int.Self) according to which we distinguish self-consciousness from the object because under this name we want to take into account the abilities that lead us to this kind of objectivity. As one can see here, these interpretations (1.Int. Self and 2.IntSelf) have in common the fact that they do not take self-consciousness to be something that exists, nor do they understand it to mean that something really is conscious of something. It is also apparent here that these interpretations must regard as misleading those passages that mention the consciousness of synthesis.[33] All the same, I understand that I have not refuted these readings. I proceed from the assumption that Kant has a more classical understanding of consciousness according to which consciousness is something *in which* representations are and according to which consciousness means that something is conscious to something or somebody.[34] This is what brings forth the persisting-Self interpretation (3.Int.Self).

According to this interpretation, our consciousness distinguishes itself for its ability not only to represent but at the same time to also represent itself. Following Kant, the self- representation only works in a particular way. Normally representations [*Vorstellungen*] are actual mental representations, however, the "representation" of oneself does not constitute an actual mental representation, for it lacks the requisite formedness or determinacy. It is more about *having* something *present* in a very specific way. Kant has a hard time getting a conceptual grasp on this kind of presence, and although this presence might be something peculiar, that doesn't make it nonsensical.[35] I will come back later in this section to the question of why this self-relation is at all necessary. To start with, let us hold on to the suggestion here that self-consciousness means that I am conscious of myself as someone to whom something is conscious.

We must keep in mind, though, what I laid out above concerning a modification to the persisting-Self interpretation: to say that the Self represents *itself* is not to say that it represents a *Self*, but rather that it represents *consciousness*, i.e., the "having" of representations in consciousness and the act or acts[36] of consciously combining representations. This modification makes it easier to grasp the fact that what is supposed to take place here is a peculiar form of "representing." There is not actually any object, but rather a conscious activity involving representations that is supposed to be conscious, i.e., present for us. One might object that it is not possible to be conscious of the activity without at least implicitly representing the subject who is active. However, the point here is that we can leave this subject undetermined while being conscious of having representations. Thus "self-consciousness" signifies that what is conscious

[33] As I already mentioned above, in the sense of interpretation 1.Int.Self and 2.Int.Self the suggestion could also be that with the term "synthesis," what is meant is the synthesized representations.

[34] The appraisal of the connection to tradition plays an important role in this issue. Compare for this Klemme (1996). As examples of the classical understanding we can take Descartes's conscience and Leibniz's apperception; for Descartes, see Simmons (2012).

[35] For an elaboration of this claim, see Emundts (2013).

[36] There is, of course, an additional problem that I am going to ignore for now concerning the singular-plural of "act."

is the "having," or possession, of the consciousness of representations in consciousness and the conscious combination of representations.

Aside from the question of why this is so, it seems to me to be a sensible and possible supposition concerning the nature of our consciousness. It seems right to me that our consciousness is constituted in such a way that it not only represents representations, but also that this fact is itself somehow present to the subject who has representations. The subject is conscious of something, but it is also conscious of being conscious. The fact that this presence does not take the form of representations does not mean that it is not possible.

One might object here that this kind of thinking about consciousness leads to a circularity problem. But it seems to me that a circularity *problem* per se does not arise for Kant (Henrich, 1966, 1982).

If one said not only that we represent representations but also that this fact is represented by us as a representation and, additionally, that this has to be the case, then one would have the problem that all representation presupposes a representation. A circle would arise if we were of the opinion that the consciousness that we are conscious of is a representation like all the others. Then we would always have to presuppose a conscious representation if we wanted to say that all object representation needs to be conscious. That wouldn't work because when dealing with objects and representations we would once again have to presuppose the same self-relation that we set as a condition. But according to what I have said, the consciousness of representing is not a normal representation and thus what holds for representations generally does not have to hold for the consciousness of representing.

At times, Kant alludes to a circularity problem (A345/B404). However, we don't have to address this issue when considering the supposition that there is consciousness—regardless of how I as a carrier of consciousness might be constituted—and that this consciousness is conscious not only of representations but also of the fact that it has, or combines, all of these representations. A circularity *problem* would only arise for Kant if one supposed that consciousness always involves an objectification. Or if one supposed that one cannot at all become conscious of an act without becoming conscious of how the person or thing that is carrying out this act is constituted. Or if one supposed that for *particular reasons* this act required that one also became conscious of how the person or thing carrying out this act must necessarily be constituted (for example because one wants to say something about the agent). So far, though, it is not apparent why we ought to make any of these suppositions.

Thus far I have pointed out two meanings of self-consciousness. These are first (1.Under.sc) the *unity of consciousness* and second (2.Under.sc) the *consciousness of the identity of consciousness or of the synthesis*. The thing-of-thought interpretation reduces both to the first meaning whereas the persisting-Self interpretation has resources enough for both meanings. And here we can also differentiate further meanings. Whenever we make a judgment, we combine representations in such a way that we are entitled to relate both to the representations as ours and to ourselves as those who are doing the judging. I already mentioned this in my discussion of the thing-of-thought interpretation, but it is also valid according to the persisting-Self interpretation. The difference here to the thing-of-thought interpretation consists first of all in the relationship to that which has occurred up until the act of judgment.

According to the persisting-Self interpretation, the Self is not an idea or a thing of thought, but rather there exists a unified, persisting Self or consciousness that, among other things, consciously carries out its syntheses. In spite of this difference, the persisting-Self interpretation can attribute a special role to judgments just as well as the thing-of-thought interpretation can. The persisting-Self interpretation can maintain that only in our acts of judgment are we first in the position to relate to ourselves in a certain way: Only once I objectively combine my representations can I *explicitly* relate to myself as the subject who combined the representations.[37] Self-ascription is only first possible here. Concerning this meaning of self-consciousness one can indeed say (even for the persisting-Self interpretation) that the cognition of objects is a requirement of self-consciousness.[38]

Granted, as is well known, it is not so simple to offer a precise account of this self-consciousness which occurs in judgment. Among other things, one must consider that in most cases of judgment one relates to oneself as a spatial-temporal entity. When the Self becomes aware of itself by making an objective judgment and thereby becoming capable of relating to itself by relating to representations that are spatial-temporally ordered, the Self must have also situated itself in time and space. Mathematical examples offer an interesting exception here, though it is not as if that these are Kant's primary examples for self-consciousness.[39] Thus it is not the case that the self-relation that occurs in objective judgments is itself simply a relation to the pure Self. For Kant, objective judgments should, in their analysis, be considered cases of transcendental (and not *only* empirical) self-consciousness, for the reason that the possibility of judgment shows that the representations that are combined in judgment were combined in a single, identical consciousness.[40] Moreover, we would not be in a position to make these judgments if we weren't self-conscious in such a sense that cannot be reduced to empirical self-consciousness. What is this self-consciousness that is not reducible to empirical self-consciousness? Here we can again look for different answers in the different interpretations—especially the thing-of-thought interpretation (2.Int.Self) and the persisting-Self interpretation (3.Int.Self).

One can reply to this question by describing self-consciousness as the term for the abilities that we necessity require in order to make objective judgments. We must be able to relate to our representations, to the combinations, and to ourselves as those who have made those combinations. These are our capacities and they (in sum) can be called pure apperception. When we introduce the terms "Self" or "self-consciousness"

[37] In Kant's Deduction, the deliberations on the extent to which self-consciousness conditions the cognition of objects tend to merge with the deliberations on the extent to which the cognition of objects conditions self-consciousness, compare B133. This, by itself, could speak for the hypothesis that self-consciousness is nothing other than the cognition of objects (as was claimed in the very first interpretation 1.Int.Self presented).

[38] Mind you, consciousness is always dependent on a content, for the synthesizing and the consciousness of synthesis are not possible without there being something that one is synthesizing.

[39] Such mathematical examples are used to some extent in Descartes, and also in contemporary discussions as an example for the fact that we have experiences in which nothing corporeal plays a role. Compare here Galen Strawson (2009, p. 23).

[40] This explains, as I said, the main point concerning the theory of self-consciousness given in the very first interpretation 1.Int.Self.

in this sense, we are dealing with a thing of thought or an idea.[41] The Self is here a correlate to the object and is conceptually opposed to the object, because the connection to an object is made possible by *subjective* abilities, even if the subject requires objects in order to become conscious of itself.[42] This is the answer offered by the thing-of-thought interpretation (2.Int.Self).

However, one can also reply to the question of what non-empirical self-consciousness is by saying that the self-consciousness that cannot be reduced to empirical self-consciousness is the persisting consciousness that I have so far been describing. We can do in judging that which we do only because our consciousness is a unity and because we are conscious of the syntheses. It is by virtue of our transcendental self-consciousness, and that means by virtue of the fact that we consciously have representations and combine them and are conscious of this, that we are capable of empirical self-consciousness, i.e. of a relation to ourselves as spatial-temporal beings. If one says this, then one is arguing for the persisting-Self or persisting self-consciousness interpretation. One also provides here an answer to the question (that I left open above) as to why we must suppose that there exists a consciousness of identity and of synthesis (and not just a unity of consciousness). Kant considers our consciousness of the activity of having representations and combining them to be a condition both of our ability to have explicit cognition of the combining of representations that occurs in judgments and, as well, a condition of our ability to relate to ourselves as the ones who are doing the combining. When we judge we occasionally do both of these things, and it is a condition of cognition that we are *able* to do it. One can now capture one difference from the thing-of-thought reading in the following way: the thing-of-thought reading takes as its starting point precisely those *capabilities* that—if we follow the persisting-Self reading—Kant wanted to show are premised on the notion of self-consciousness as something *originary* (*ursprünglich* = original, primal, originary).

In light of this account of the persisting-Self interpretation, I now want to turn to the question of the source of our knowledge about the identity of consciousness. This discussion provides the foundation for answering the question of how the two persisting-Self readings that have been presented fit together.

4. The Consciousness of Synthesis

While following the persisting-Self interpretation in the last section, I said that Kant argues for the necessity of the unity of consciousness and that he argues that we must be conscious of the act of synthesis. Kant also claims that we must be conscious a priori of the identity of ourselves in all possible representations. I think we must take

[41] I don't want to say here that the thing-of-thought interpretation requires this understanding of the Self and self-consciousness, but rather exactly the reverse: if one does understand these terms in this way, then one (probably) ends up with a variant of the thing-of-thought reading.

[42] The following passage appears to support this reading: "The abiding and unchanging 'I' (pure apperception) forms the correlate of all our representations in so far as it is to be at all possible that we should become conscious of them" (A123–24). I think, however, that this passage is amenable to all of the readings.

"identity" here not only as numerical identity (A107 and B133): it is one numerical consciousness that has the different representations. One can, for example, formulate what he says in the A Deduction (A116) in the following terms: I am a priori conscious of the fact that, in all of the representations I could possibly have, I am the same being. In spelling out the persisting-Self interpretation I have not thus far discussed how we know about self-consciousness. In the first section I made two suggestions concerning this question (3.Int.Self.a and 3.Int.Self.b). In the last section I pursued more the first suggestion, which takes the source of our knowledge of self-consciousness to be transcendental reflection. For example one can say here: A reason for the claim that all of the representations must be found in one single consciousness is that otherwise they would not be my representations, they could not be joined together, and representations represent something only when they are joined together (A116). This is a philosophical reason. The proposition that there is a unity of consciousness is even perhaps an analytical proposition, as Kant says in the B edition. In contrast, the assertions to the effect that I must be conscious of the act of synthesis and that I must be conscious of my identity sound as if they are describing our thought process and weren't just claims of a philosophical nature. But how is that supposed to work? Do the suggestions (3.Int.Self.a and 3.Int.Self.b) exclude each other or do they fit together?

I claimed above that there is no circularity *problem* at hand. I want to come back to this once more. For the claim regarding identity, however, one might indeed be confronted with circularity. So far I have said that we can relate to ourselves without having to claim that we make consciousness into a representation and in this sense into an object. But this seems not to be true here. Identity namely appears to be a quality that is attributed to an entity. The circularity problem points out that we can only make this identity claim if we regard the consciousness to which we relate as a self-standing entity. Provided that I hereby relate to something that really exists, this seems, however, to imply that I am in fact confronted with the circularity problem. It sounds as if one then had to say: In order to relate to an object, I always also have to relate to myself, and yet relating to myself also means relating to myself as an entity, and an entity can be seen as an object. Successful object-relation thus presupposes successful object-relation. Thus, the identity claim seems to lead to a problem. For this reason I'm going to mainly focus in the discussion that follows on the identity claim.[43]

Kant says that we are conscious of the identity (A116). "Conscious" could mean here that one somehow also knows that one is the same. How is it that we can know of this identity? Does this knowledge come solely from being conscious of oneself, or are there other sources for this knowledge? There are three possibilities here: (a) We know this by means of a transcendental reflection. (b) We know this immediately by virtue of being conscious of ourselves. (c) We know this when we are making objective judgments and thereby ascribing properties and abilities to ourselves. The first two possibilities (a and b) amount to the variants of the persisting-Self interpretation

[43] One should consider here that Kant, in the second edition, foregrounds the thought of the consciousness of synthesis (B133). One could also view this change as a *reaction* to this problem; however, this does not seem to me to be the case.

that I introduced in the first section (3.Int.Self.a and 3.Int.Self.b). The third (c) matches what the thing-of-thought interpretation (2.Int.Self) could say about knowing of our identity.

The second possibility and interpretation (3.Int.Self.b) is strongly argued for by Dieter Henrich.[44] It can be added here that one can only argue for the identity of consciousness when one "runs through" (*durchlaufen*) multiple representations. Henrich claims that one must run through these representations in accordance with certain rules, for only then can a subject become conscious of the transitions. According to Henrich's reading, one can prove, taking self-consciousness as a starting point, that representations must be subject to rules (and this is a decisive step in the Deduction). I am not concerned, however, with whether the proof is successful as a deduction (or as part of the deduction), but rather with Henrich's claims about self-consciousness. In my eyes there are primarily two points that speak against such a reading of self-consciousness.[45] First, it does not fit with the passages in the text that I discussed above, in which Kant speaks as if we must *suppose* such an identity. If we had a "Cartesian certainty" (Henrich, 1976, p. 86) about the identity of consciousness, such a manner of speaking would be odd.

Second, this proposal runs the risk of violating the borders that Kant draws regarding the possibility of knowledge. This is also the reason why Henrich (1966) himself claims that there is a circularity *problem*. As I said above, a circularity problem only exists if one supposes that one must, in the act of relating consciously to oneself, also be conscious of how one must be constituted or which qualities one has as someone or something that carries out this act. If by virtue of self-consciousness we acquire knowledge about the Self's qualities, then a circularity problem is indeed present. Henrich is of the opinion that this knowledge does exist. His reason for supposing this consists in the fact that we must have a priori certainty about the identity of the Self if we are to conclude based on this identity that we a priori have rules at our disposal and synthesize according to these rules. In my eyes, the fact that such a circularity *problem* occurs provides us with a reason not to accept Henrich's proposal.

Above I characterized the consciousness of synthesis by saying that when we are conscious of something, this something is "present to us." By this expression I wanted to account for the special non-representational way in which we are conscious of ourselves. If we do this (and Henrich would probably not do this), then the proposal that one can, by means of such a consciousness, know and say something about the identity also seems very questionable.[46] Kant talks about an identity "with regard to all representations that can ever belong to our cognition" (A116). It seems impossible to claim something about *possible* representations by virtue of a consciousness of oneself as I have characterized it. In this passage Kant says more specifically that we are conscious of our identity "as a necessary condition of the possibility of all

[44] Henrich (1976, p. 86; see also 1988); for the question of numerical identity, see Henrich (1976, pp. 51–56). Allison (1983, p. 138) also takes consciousness as a source of knowledge.

[45] This is, admittedly, a very general rejection of Henrich's subtle interpretation, but his interpretation has also already been discussed a lot. I'm using it here more as a way to advance my discussion.

[46] Horstmann argues that this cannot be the basis for one regarding oneself as identical, compare Horstmann (2016, p. 265). In a different context, Galen Strawson says something similar (2009, pp. 103–104).

representations." This, too, sounds like a transcendental-philosophical consideration. I would thus suggest that we achieve knowledge of our identity in all possible representations through the act of judgment or through transcendental reflection (as in 3.Int.Self.a), but not by means of an originary, conscious relationship to ourselves (as in 3.Int.Self.b). This does not have to mean, however, that there is not consciousness of synthesis or also of an identity in a weaker sense that is already present in the synthesis itself. Independently of the text passage quoted above, one can also take the claim about identity to mean, in a weaker sense, that what is at stake is that I am conscious that I have passed from one representation to another and have combined them. If one understands the claim about identity in this way, then it corresponds to the claim about the consciousness of synthesis.[47] If one supposes such an originary consciousness, then, indeed, one should *only* talk about consciousness and not knowledge.

Thus far I have argued against the claim that we obtain the knowledge of identity by virtue of being self-conscious, and I have argued that we can, nevertheless, maintain that there is consciousness of synthesis and of our identity. The question then is: Why should Kant claim that such a consciousness exists, if he doesn't suppose it to be a source of knowledge about ourselves? Among those who suppose that there is such a consciousness, there exists (as far as I can see) agreement over the fact that Kant does not at length say why he thinks this to be the case, and thus one must resort to speculation. I think that Kant really does think that this consciousness, i.e., consciousness in the sense that the Self is mentally present to itself, is a condition for knowledge.[48] In A108 Kant says, for example, the following (I've rearranged the sentence): the mind must have before its eyes the identity of its act, so that it can think its identity a priori in the manifoldness of its representations. This could amount to the following: in order for us to establish unities, we must *consciously* bring forth unities and that means that we must have a consciousness of the synthesis (and also a consciousness of the fact that we stay the same in the act of synthesizing).

One could also assume that the unity on the level of intuition must already be produced according to rules, and one could view the reflections concerning consciousness to have their function in that regard. Then Henrich would be right in saying that Kant is concerned with the transitions from one representation to another. These transitions in the syntheses, which are ultimately supposed to lead to cognitions, must occur according to rules (in order that the deduction can be at all successful), even if it is not yet clear at all what these rules are. For Kant's point in his Deduction must be that we, in our intuitions, already bring about a synthetic unity which we can successfully relate to with our judgments.[49] Now, Kant might suppose

[47] The B edition thus seems to me to offer a clarification on this point. However, one could also interpret this change much more broadly in the context of my interpretation, saying that in the B edition, Kant eliminates in his formulations the suspicion of a relation to objects (compare Horstmann, 1993), as well as that he handles with more care the question of when knowledge is available.

[48] That this reasoning can be found in the A edition fits with Horstmann's (2017) insight concerning the neglect in the B edition of the synthesis of intuitions. Horstmann sees the reason for this in the attempt to escape the problems that arise when one proposes the existence of a productive imagination.

[49] Compare here, among other passages, B134: "Synthetic unity of the manifold of intuitions, as generated *a priori*, is thus the ground of the identity of apperception itself, which precedes *a priori* all *my* determinate thought." Kant refers to such considerations at the beginning of the Analogies of Experience: "All

that it would not be possible to follow rules if we weren't even conscious of the transitions and thereby of the synthesis (or the act of synthesis). He might also consider consciousness to be necessary on the grounds that, in cognitions, we combine representations in a way that corresponds to the way in which the manifold is combined, and therefore consciousness must accompany both cognition and the manifold. He might also suppose that we must, in a very general sense, be conscious of the representations as combined by us in order that we can combine them according to our rules into knowledge. These all seem to me to be good explanations for why such consciousness is supposed to exist.

I have thus far not discussed the question of whether consciousness of the identity of consciousness (in the demanding sense of the identity in view of all possible representations) comes about in judgment (c) or in the act of transcendental-philosophical reflection (a). I think that this depends again on what one exactly wants to say about the identity. In judgments, we certainly make use of the identity of our Self and (according to Kant) one must also in principle be conscious of one's identity as he or she who judges. I would even go so far as to say that this includes knowledge about our identity.[50] However, the further-reaching supposition concerning my identity as an identity in all possible representations seems to me not to be well-founded here and not even thematized. Although it seems evident that objective judgments are a condition for my ability to explicitly relate to myself as an identical person, the fact that the Self or the consciousness of all syntheses, including the synthesis of unified structures in time and space, is identical is not something that is contained in these judgments. It is not explicit in judgments and, again, only a transcendental reflection can plausibly show that judgments need self-identity. I therefore suppose that this knowledge is obtained in a transcendental reflection (b). One could object here and argue that the identity is the unification in the object—and this is precisely because it is not possible to conceive of an identity independent of objects. As far as I see, one is then once again back to the very first interpretation (1.Int.Self), which says that self-consciousness is nothing other than the cognition of objects.

Thus, in my view, we cannot answer the question of how we *know* that we are the same person by appealing to the consciousness of ourselves. Nevertheless, Kant uses the term "consciousness" in all of these cases and does not clearly distinguish between knowledge and consciousness. That contributes to the confusion. The knowledge of my identity in all possible representations implies more than the consciousness of my synthesis. In the latter case, "conscious" means that something is present to me, or that I am aware of it, even if this presence or awareness is indistinct. Kant can claim, and wants to claim, that there is such a consciousness and that seems to me to be a sensible possibility—regardless of whether or not we can in this way really argue for the validity of the categories.

In what follows I want to discuss two possible objections to my proposal according to which we can combine the two readings of the persisting-Self interpretation by

this manifold must, as regards its time-relations, be united in the original apperception. This is demanded by the *a priori* transcendental unity of apperception, to which everything that is to belong to my knowledge (that is, to my unified knowledge), and so can be an object for me, has to conform" (A177/B220).

[50] This is one of the points that is often in the foreground of the contemporary discussion on self-consciousness (also in connection with Kant); compare Burge (1996) and Boyle (2009).

distinguishing between transcendental reflection as the source of knowledge of our identity (that matches 3.Self.Int.a) and the fact that we can be conscious of ourselves in the sense that we and our acts are present to ourselves (that picks up some points of 3.Int.Self.b). One could reject my suggestion here on the grounds that in the Deduction, Kant is always talking about a consciousness a priori, whereas a consciousness of myself as a mode of having something present appears to be a (very specific) kind of perception, which contradicts a characterization of consciousness a priori. In response, I would like to first make the observation that Kant at times even equates the "I think" of apperception with the empirical "I think" (A346/B404).[51] According to my interpretation we can do this because consciousness really is a mode of having something present. Consciousness is also recognized (by the transcendental philosopher) to be a necessary condition of knowledge. It is important here that the Self does not itself thereby become an empirical representation—for "Self" here is signifying not an object, but the identity and self-relation of consciousness. In reference to the question of apriority, I would say that the transcendental philosopher's knowledge is a priori. It is misleading to say that consciousness is a priori, because that can sound as if it were a consciousness without *any* form of perception. What is crucial to the concept of consciousness as it is handled in the Deduction is that consciousness occurs before the determination of spatial-temporal relationships and thus *before* every experience. If one, in an unspecific manner, designated as a priori that which is prior to every experience, then one can call consciousness a priori.[52]

One could furthermore pose in response to my suggestion the critical question of how we in turn are supposed to know about this peculiarity of consciousness if this peculiarity resides in an *indistinct* presence. It seems quite natural for me to say that this is also a supposition on the part of the transcendental philosopher and that we don't otherwise have any knowledge about it. Though one can also imagine that there is or could be a kind of remembering reference backwards that occurs in judgment. Of course the argument that we know this because of the transcendental philosopher is relevant for the interpretation of the proof of the validity of the categories. We cannot (or no longer) say, for example, that Kant is arguing that no originary self-consciousness is without a rule-governed synthesis—and that this therefore requires us to presuppose the rule-governed synthesis—for in that case originary self-consciousness would have to be an undeniable fact that exists independently of our reflections and that could not then be discovered by the transcendental philosopher as a condition of knowledge. But what I said above about the functions of consciousness did not attribute such a role to consciousness. Even when Kant, for example, wants to argue in his Deduction that, in the manifold of intuition, we must have brought about a synthesis in conformity with rules, he doesn't have to make recourse to the consciousness of synthesis or identity. Rather, he can base his argument on his considerations regarding unity or regarding the notion of representations.[53] On the other hand, and as an example, he would want to suppose, as I explained above, that

[51] The relationship between the empirical and the a priori "I think" is more complicated in B428.

[52] I understand the famous and controversial footnote B422 along these lines; compare Emundts (2013).

[53] One can perhaps read B138 in this way.

there is consciousness, because one cannot suppose rule-governed synthesis without consciousness.

It is clear that Kant does not conceive of the knowledge of the transcendental philosopher in such a way that the philosopher, when he does his job, determines an undetermined, internal perception. In that case we would be dealing with empirical knowledge whose object we would nevertheless not be allowed to determine (because otherwise we would be confronted with Kant's circle). One can say nothing about an object on the basis of our consciousness of what we consciously do, and for this reason consciousness offers us no knowledge and no possibility for the expansion of knowledge. Wanting to determine as an intelligible object the empirical intuition "I think" is, in contrast, one of the mistakes that Kant accuses the rational psychologists of.[54] However, transcendental-philosophical knowledge is also generally not to be regarded as empirical knowledge, but rather as a form of knowledge that is related to the necessary conditions of our knowledge.[55]

The interpretation that I have presented here can be summarized in the following way: I share with the thing-of-thought interpretation the emphasis on the identity of *consciousness* (instead of the identity of the Self as an object), but in contrast to this interpretation, I want to hold on to the hypothesis of a persisting Self. As transcendental philosophers, we know that there must be a persisting Self. To this claim also belongs the claim that there exists a consciousness of the Self's identity and of the Self's syntheses in all of its representations. Kant has sufficient resources to suppose such a consciousness of oneself. It is a feature of our consciousness that it is transparent in the sense that it makes present that which one consciously does such that the doing is conscious—without this feature, knowledge would not be possible.

This interpretation proposes a connection between the two persisting-Self readings (3.Int.Self.a and 3.Int.Self.b) presented above, in which, on the one hand, the role of the transcendental philosopher is emphasized, while on the other, consciousness in the act of synthesis ought to be recognized as indispensable for knowledge. In spite of this admission that consciousness plays a decisive role, I have argued against the thesis that it is *by means* of this consciousness that we come to central insights in the Deduction about the identity of the Self. It is a strong supposition to claim that we come by means of this consciousness to central insights about the identity of the Self, and in my eyes, we cannot suppose this. The two readings can only be combined if one relinquishes this strong supposition.[56]

[54] Kant also assumes in the Paralogisms that the "I think" is an empirical perception. The rationalists' mistake consists in the fact that they want to determine this inner perception as if it were an object.

[55] As long as one can argue for the analyticity of the statements about consciousness, there is no suspicion that we are dealing with empirical knowledge. It seems to me that one also cannot in this way understand the somewhat unclear passage in the A edition, according to which the antecedent unity of consciousness is a synthetic principle. That passage is, however, more unclear.

[56] I would like to thank Marcus Lampert who provided a translation of the first draft of my talk and helped me with his comments. I also would like to thank Rolf-Peter Horstmann for his helpful comments on different versions of this paper. Special thanks are due to Karl Schaefer and Nick Stang for their comments on the paper that led me to clarify and even change some points.

References

Allison, H. (1983). *Kant's transcendental idealism.* Yale University Press.

Boyle, M. (2009). Two kinds of self-knowledge. *Philosophy and Phenomenological Research, 78*: 133–64.

Burge, T. (1996). Our entitlement to self-knowledge. *Proceedings of the Aristotelian Society, 96*: 91–116.

Carl, W. (1998). Ich und Spontaneität. In M. Stamm (Ed.), *Philosophie in synthetischer Absicht/Synthesis in mind* (pp. 105–22). Klett-Cotta.

Cramer, K. (1993). Einheit des Bewusstseins und Bewusstsein der Einheit: Ein Problemaufriß in der Perspektive Kants. In H.-D. Klein (Ed.), *Systeme im Denken der Gegenwart* (pp. 123–51). Bouvier.

Emundts, D. (2013). Kant über Selbstbewusstsein. In D. Emundts (Ed.), *Self, world, and art: Metaphysical topics in Kant and Hegel* (pp. 51–78). De Gruyter.

Ginsborg, H. (2013). The appearance of spontaneity. In D. Emundts (Ed.), *Self, world, and art: Metaphysical topics in Kant and Hegel* (pp. 119–44). De Gruyter.

Guyer, P. (1987). *Kant and the claims of knowledge.* Cambridge University Press.

Henrich, D. (1966). Fichtes ursprüngliche Einsicht. In D. Henrich and H. Wagner (Eds.), *Subjektivität und Metaphysik: Festschrift für Wolfgang Cramer* (pp. 188–232). Klostermann.

Henrich, D. (1976). *Identität und Objektivität: Eine Untersuchung über Kants Transzendentale Deduktion.* Carl Winter Universitätsverlag.

Henrich, D. (1982). Fichte's original insight. *Contemporary German Philosophy, 1*: 15–52.

Henrich, D. (1988). Die Identität des Subjekts in der transzendentalen Deduktion. In H. Oberer and G. Seel (Eds.), *Kant: Analysen, Probleme, Kritik* (pp. 39–70). Königshausen & Neumann.

Horstmann, R.-P. (1993). Kants Paralogismen. *Kant-Studien, 83*: 408–25.

Horstmann, R.-P. (2016). Kant, the German Idealists, the I, and the self: A "systematic reconstruction." *Internationales Jahrbuch des deutschen Idealismus, 11*: 245–71.

Horstmann, R.-P. (2017). Kant on the power of imagination and object constitution. Unpublished manuscript.

Keller, P. (1998). *Kant and the demands of self-consciousness.* Cambridge University Press.

Kitcher, P. (2011). *Kant's thinker.* Oxford University Press.

Klemme, H. (1996). *Kants Philosophie des Subjekts: Systematische und entwicklungsgeschichtliche Untersuchungen zum Verhältnis von Selbstbewußtsein und Selbsterkenntnis.* Meiner.

Longuenesse, B. (2001). *Kant and the capacity to judge: Sensibility and discursivity in the Transcendental Analytic of the* Critique of pure reason. Princeton University Press.

Longuenesse, B. (2007). Kant on the identity of persons. *Proceedings of the Aristotelian Society, 107*(2): 149–67.

Longuenesse, B. (2012). Two uses of "I" as subject? In S. Prosser and F. Recanati (Eds.), *Immunity to error through misidentification: New essays* (pp. 81–104). Cambridge University Press.

Rosefeldt, T. (2000). *Das logische Ich: Kant über den Gehalt des Begriffes von sich selbst.* Philo.

Rosefeldt, T. (2006). Kants Ich als Gegenstand. *Deutsche Zeitschrift für Philosophie*, *54*(2): 277–93.

Simmons, A. (2012). Cartesian consciousness reconsidered. *Philosophers' Imprint*, *12*(2): 1–21.

Strawson, G. (2009). *Selves: An essay in revisionary metaphysics*. Oxford University Press.

Wolff, M. (2006). Empirischer und transzendentaler Dualismus: Zu Rolf-Peter Horstmanns Interpretation von Kants Paralogismen. *Deutsche Zeitschrift für Philosophie*, *54*(2): 265–75.

Wunderlich, F. (2005). *Kant und die Bewusstseinstheorien des 18 Jahrhunderts*. De Gruyter.

8

The Labyrinth of the Continuum

Leibniz, the Wolffians, and Kant on Matter and Monads

Anja Jauernig

1. Introduction

According to a formerly popular story about Kant's philosophical development, he began his philosophical career as a Leibniz-Wolffian of sorts, gradually moved away from Leibniz-Wolffianism throughout his pre-Critical period in response to his study of leading thinkers of the British Enlightenment, especially Newton, Locke, and Hume, and finally settled on a wholesale rejection of the Leibniz-Wolffian philosophy in the *Critique of Pure Reason* and other Critical texts.[1,2] In recent years, several aspects of this lore about Kant's philosophical development have come to be criticized, and, being one of the critics, I agree that it is untenable, or, at least, seriously misleading.[3] The philosophy with which Kant "grew up" and from which he, by and by, emancipated himself is primarily Wolffian, not Leibnizian. Although there are undeniable affinities between Leibniz's philosophical doctrines and the philosophical doctrines of Wolff and his followers, there are also important differences between them that must not be overlooked.[4] The indicated popular story also overstates the influence of British Enlightenment luminaries on Kant's philosophical maturation process. While it is certainly true that the writings of some of these thinkers played some role in the development of Kant's Critical philosophy, the main engine of this development were "home-grown" questions and problems, so to speak, that arose within the framework of the Wolffian philosophy, questions that the Wolffians themselves—and, in many cases, Leibniz himself—had already identified as worthwhile topics of examination, such as the questions of how different substances compose a world, how to conceive of the individuation conditions of

[1] Parts of this material were presented at a conference in honor of Gerold Prauss at the University of Bonn in October of 2016, at the Philosophy Colloquium at Indiana University at Bloomington in February of 2017, and at the 7th Annual New York City Workshop in Early Modern Philosophy at Fordham University in May of 2017. I am grateful to the audience members for helpful comments and discussion.

[2] Versions of this story, or parts of this story, are developed, for example, by Paulsen (1875, pp. 125–45), Adickes (1924–25), Kreimendahl (1990), Friedman (1992, esp. pp. 1–52), and Schönfeld (2000).

[3] See Watkins (2005), Jauernig (2008, 2011), and Stang (2016).

[4] Even Wolff himself repeatedly complains about the label "Leibniz-Wolffian Philosophy"; see Wolff (1841, pp. 140–41). Some of the differences between Leibniz's and Wolff's philosophy are discussed by Arnsperger (1897), École (1964), Beck (1969, pp. 256–75), Corr (1974, 1975), Poser (1975), École (1990, esp. pp. 139–220), and Look (2013). It is also worth emphasizing that there is a considerable spread of different Wolffian positions as well; many Wolffians do not follow Wolff blindly.

Anja Jauernig, *The Labyrinth of the Continuum: Leibniz, the Wolffians, and Kant on Matter and Monads* In: *The Sensible and Intelligible Worlds: New Essays on Kant's Metaphysics and Epistemology.* Edited by: Karl Schafer and Nicholas F. Stang, Oxford University Press. © Anja Jauernig 2022. DOI: 10.1093/oso/9780199688265.003.0009 substances, how to reconcile human freedom with the determinism of nature, how to account for the applicability of mathematics to the physical world, and, more generally, how to think about the relation between natural science and metaphysics. The teachings of the empiricist philosophers from the British Isles played a supporting role in Kant's philosophical journey by contributing to the general pool of ideas from which he drew inspiration and guidance as he worked out his answers to the indicated questions, but it was those Wolffian questions that supplied the driving force behind his inquiries.[5] Last but not least, the sketched popular story seriously misrepresents the relation between the Critical Kant and Leibniz. There are several passages in various later writings, from 1786 onward, in which Kant speaks of Leibniz in rather laudatory terms, and insists that, on a proper understanding of his own and Leibniz's philosophy, they turn out to be quite close with respect to many central issues.[6] In his polemical essay against the self-declared Leibnizian Eberhard, who, in Kant's assessment, misunderstood Leibniz as badly as the *Critique of Pure Reason*, he goes as far as to describe the latter work as the "true apology of Leibniz" (*ÜE*, 8:250). On first glance, these pro-Leibnizian comments are rather surprising, since they stand in marked contrast to Kant's more well-known harshly critical remarks about the Leibnizian philosophy in the *Critique of Pure Reason*, which, I suppose, is why commentators have tended to not pay much heed to the pro-Leibnizian bits. But, as I see it, these comments are worth our attention and being taken seriously; they are neither meant ironically nor can they be dismissed as mere rhetorical posing or heralds of old age dementia. Kant means what he says; and, what is more, he is largely correct. Leibniz's and his own philosophy are indeed strikingly close, in particular, as far as their ontological views are concerned. Of course, this is not to say that Kant's Critical philosophy is a mere rehash of Leibniz, as Eberhard complains—which it clearly is not—or that Kant does not see himself as going beyond Leibniz in several important ways—which he clearly does, in particular with respect to many epistemological issues. But it is to say that Kant eventually came to realize that many of his earlier objections to the ill-named "Leibniz-Wolffian" philosophy do not in fact apply to Leibniz himself but to (some of) the Wolffians, and that his own Critical philosophy, not Wolffianism, is the true successor to Leibniz's philosophy.

Providing a more detailed exposition and defense of this alternative reading of Kant's philosophical development and his relation to both the Wolffians and Leibniz is a massive undertaking that goes well beyond the scope of this chapter.[7] My

[5] Hume stands out in that his analysis of the origin of our concept of causation played into, and reinforced, the question of how synthetic a priori judgments are possible, a question that centrally occupied Kant during his so-called "silent decade" just before the publication of the *Critique of Pure Reason* and functioned as an "engine" for the development of the final missing elements of the Critical philosophy. But, by that point, Kant's journey to his Critical philosophy was already more than half-completed, and, despite Kant's own famous declaration that Hume "awoke" him from his "dogmatic slumber" (*Prol*, 4:260), it can be argued that this particular facet of Kant's awakening was as much self-induced, so to speak, and would have happened regardless, even if he had never come across Hume. The relevant part of the awakening was likely to happen in any case as a result of Kant's struggle with the problem of how to reconcile the Leibniz-Wolffian classification of all true judgments as (what Kant calls) analytic with the obvious fact that the concepts of particular causes do not contain the concepts of their effects.

[6] Cf. *MAN*, 4:507–508; *ÜE*, 8:203, 248–50; Draft notes for *ÜE*, 20:363–64; letter to Herz, May 26, 1789 (*Br*, 9:52).

[7] Some further discussion can be found in Jauernig (2008, 2011).

comparatively modest project for now is to illustrate my reading by comparing the views of Leibniz, the Wolffians, and Kant with respect to one particular question that greatly exercised all of them.[8] This question, which played an especially important role in Kant's philosophical development on his way to transcendental idealism, is the question of the composition of the material continuum. More specifically, the question is how we should conceive of the nature of matter, in particular, of the compositional structure of matter, *given* that space, in which matter exists and which matter fills, is continuous. It is important to stress that we are talking here about the *material* continuum.[9] One could also legitimately wonder about, and all of the mentioned philosophers also did wonder about, the composition of space itself, a problem that is also sometimes referred to as "the problem of the composition of the continuum." The question of the compositional structure of space will be touched on in our discussion as well, but our primary focus will be on the question of the compositional structure of matter. In the seventeenth and eighteenth centuries it was a fairly common figure of speech to refer to the latter question, against the background of the continuity of space, as (leading into) the "labyrinth of the continuum"—hence the title of my chapter. This expression seems to have originated with Libert Froidmont who entitled his 1631 book "Labyrinth, or a book about the composition of the continuum," but it appears to have received its wide currency through Leibniz who, as we will see, uses it at several places.[10] The special version of the question of the composition of the material continuum that Leibniz, the Wolffians, and Kant are foremost concerned with, and that will be at the center of attention of this chapter, is how one can reconcile the continuity of space with a monadological theory of matter, according to which matter is ultimately composed of simple elements. For ease of communication, I will henceforth refer to this special version of the problem of the composition of the material continuum as the "space-matter problem."

So, the primary purpose of this chapter is to illustrate my reading of Kant's philosophical development, and of his relation to the Wolffians and Leibniz, by showing that the problem of the composition of the material continuum, and, more specifically, the space-matter problem, is a problem that Kant inherits from Leibniz and the Wolffians, in whose thinking it already plays an important role, that Leibniz's mature solution to the problem differs markedly from the Wolffian solution, and that Kant's early, pre-Critical solution is largely Wolffian, while his later Critical solution is largely Leibnizian, as he himself notes with gleeful satisfaction. In the course of our discussion, it will also become clear that the space-matter problem represents one of the "home-grown" key problems mentioned above that fueled Kant's philosophical

[8] For the purposes of this chapter, I am also setting aside the question of which of Leibniz's writings Kant could have known and which writings of which Wolffians exactly he is responding to; my main concern right now is, not to trace lines of actual influence, but to offer a comparison of the content of the philosophical views advocated by these thinkers.

[9] Or, more precisely, we are talking about what prima facie seems to be a material continuum. One way of answering the question of the composition of the material continuum would be to say that the structure of matter is not really continuous but merely appears that way—in which case the name "material continuum" would have to be judged as slightly misleading.

[10] Leibniz explicitly refers to Froidmont (by his Latinized name) in the *New Essays*, LA VI.6, 225: "Fromondus, who wrote an entire book about the composition of the continuum, was right to entitle it *Labyrinth*. But that comes from a false idea that one has about the nature of bodies as well as of space."

development and, eventually, led him to the discovery of transcendental idealism. This chapter also has a secondary, more general purpose, namely, to function as an advertisement for a particular approach to studying Kant, namely, by paying close attention to his philosophical development and the historical context, in particular the Leibnizian and Wolffian context, in which he came up with the various doctrines and arguments that make up his Critical philosophy. To my mind, this developmental-historical approach, which is still not as widespread in contemporary Kant scholarship as it should be, is an essential key to unlocking the intended meaning of many of Kant's central Critical views, case in point: his conception of the relation between space, matter, and things in themselves. As a final disclaimer, let me add that the question of the nature and composition of matter is a major topic in Leibniz, Wolff, and Kant research; it would take a multi-volume treatise to adequately address all of the relevant details. For the purposes of this chapter, some simplification will thus be inevitable; my focus will be quite selective and trained exclusively on those aspects of the conception of matter of these philosophers that directly pertain to the space-matter problem, with the aspiration of bringing into relief the main historical trajectories of the key argumentative moves employed in this debate, all with the objective of arriving at a better understanding of Kant's critical views on the topic.

2. Leibniz and the Space-Matter Problem

The particular version of the problem of the composition of the material continuum that we are primarily concerned with in this chapter consists in the seeming incompatibility of the following two claims that (allegedly) can both be justified:

Space-matter problem:

(S) Space, or more generally extension, is essentially continuous.

(M) Material objects or bodies, which are extended, or fill space, are composed of actual simple parts.

(S) is demonstrated, or assumed, in geometry; (M) is demonstrated in metaphysics, or, at least, in certain metaphysical theories. The space-matter problem obviously does not arise for everybody. While (S) is pretty much universally accepted in the seventeenth and eighteenth centuries, at least by most scientifically minded participants in the debate about the composition of matter, (M) does not enjoy universal acclaim. Without going into any of the messy details, Leibniz's main support for (M) rests on the "ens est unum" principle, as we may call it, according to which "what is not truly *one* being is not truly one *being* either," or "one and being are reciprocal things" (letter to Arnauld, April 1687, G II, 97). That is, all fundamentally real entities are true unities, and, consequently, all other real entities must "inherit" their reality from the true unities out of which they are composed.[11] For our modest present

[11] See "Notes on Comments by Fardella," LA VI.4B, 1668: "...if there are many created beings, it is necessary that there be some created being that is truly one. For a plurality of beings can neither be understood nor can it exist unless first a being that is one is understood to which the multitude must necessarily

purposes, there is no need to enter into a discussion about whether (M) can, in fact, be successfully justified along the indicated, or related, metaphysical lines.[12] We will take it as a given that all of the philosophers of present interest endorse both (S) and (M), or, more cautiously put, in the case of Leibniz and Kant, that they endorse (S) and are favorably inclined toward (M), at least initially, and eventually commit themselves to a closely related thesis in the spirit of (M). Accordingly, we will grant both (S) and (M) for the sake of the discussion, and focus on how Leibniz, the Wolffians (as well as the anti-Wolffians), and Kant diagnose, and propose to resolve, the seeming conflict between them.[13]

There are different ways in which the conflict between (S) and (M) can be spelled out, and our protagonists choose interestingly different options. Explaining Leibniz's choice requires taking a look at his conception of continuity that is relevant in this context, which shares much with Aristotle's. A quantity is continuous if, and only if, (i), it is infinitely divisible, and (ii), it consists of possible parts such that the whole is prior to the parts.[14] In his diagnosis of the space-matter problem, Leibniz focuses on the second feature characterizing continuous quantities. (S) is seemingly incompatible with (M), because (S) implies that bodies, qua extended and, hence, continuous, are composed of possible parts to which they are prior, while (M) implies that bodies are wholes whose parts are actual and prior to them. (Textual evidence will be provided shortly.) It is also worth noting explicitly that the inference to the continuity of bodies from the continuity of space, which provides the crucial bridge from "space-talk" to "body-talk" and first makes (S) relevant to (M), can be unpacked in different ways. For example, one could understand (S) as implying a claim about extension in general, namely, that it is essentially continuous, and derive the desired conclusion based on the fact that whatever is true of extension in general is also true of anything that is extended. Or one could read (S) as primarily a claim about space, namely, that it and all of its parts are essentially continuous, and derive the desired conclusion based on the additional assumption that anything that fills a part of space necessarily has the same compositional structure as that part of space, and the understanding that bodies are extended in that they fill a space. The reason why I mention these two particular ways of unpacking the indicated crucial inference is that the first was popular in the context of the so-called *Monadenstreit*, which we will be discussing in section 3, and that the second seems to have been integral to Kant's preferred way of conceptualizing the space-matter problem, as we will see in sections 4 and 5. In the following more precise reconstruction of the space-matter problem as addressed by Leibniz, I will use the first way of cashing out the inference to the continuity of bodies from the continuity of space; in a later reconstruction, I will be using the second way.

be referred. Hence, unless there are certain indivisible substances, bodies would not be real things but apparent things or phenomena such as the rainbow, since all foundation for their composition would have been taken away." Also see "First Draft for the New System," G IV, 473–74.

[12] Wolff bases his main demonstration for the existence of simples explicitly on the principle of sufficient reason, see *Deutsche Metaphysik*, §§76–77.

[13] For a helpful discussion of the different arguments for the existence of simple parts proposed by Leibniz, Wolff, Baumgarten, and the pre-Critical Kant, see Watkins (2006).

[14] See G IV, 394; letter to Electress Sophie, October 31, 1705, G VII, 562–63; letter to Des Bosses, July 31, 1709, G II, 379.

It should be easy enough for the reader to translate all subsequent remarks concerning possible solutions of the problem into formulations appropriate to the other way of presenting the problem:

1. (S) Space and all parts of space are essentially continuous. (From geometry.)
2. What is true of space is true of extension in general. (Widespread assumption.)
3. Extension in general is essentially continuous. (From 1 and 2.)
4. Anything that is extended is continuous. (From 3.)
5. Anything that is extended is such that the whole is prior to its parts. (From 4, and the definition of continuity.)
6. All bodies are extended. (Uncontroversial conception of body.)
7. All bodies are prior to their parts. (From 5 and 6).
8. (M) All bodies are composed of actual simple parts. (From Leibniz's metaphysics.)
9. All bodies are posterior to their parts. (From 8.)
10. All bodies are both prior and posterior to their parts. (From 7 and 9.)

This argument presents a problem because (10) is a contradiction, and contradictions are necessarily false. So, either there is something wrong with the argument, or at least one of the premises is false.

In preparation for unveiling Leibniz's solution to the space-matter problem, one additional aspect of his conception of continuity must be highlighted, an aspect with respect to which he goes beyond Aristotle, namely, that feature (ii), according to which a continuous quantity is composed of possible parts that are posterior to the whole, on his view renders all continuous quantities *ideal*. The parts of a real whole are actual, and, hence, determinate, and prior to the whole, which is generated, among other things, through the successive addition of the parts. The parts of an ideal whole are possible, and, hence, indeterminate, and posterior to the whole, and are generated through the successive division of the whole. It would require an entire further essay to explicate in detail what "ideal" means for Leibniz, which he uses in various different senses. But for our present purposes, it is a defensible simplification of treating it as short for "phenomenal" or "mind-dependent," with the understanding that the relevant minds are finite minds.[15]

> But a continuous quantity is something ideal that pertains to possible things and to actual things insofar as they are possible. The continuum certainly involves indeterminate parts, but in actual things nothing is indefinite, indeed, in them every division that can be made has been made. Actual things are composed like numbers out of unities, ideal things like numbers out of fractions; there actually are parts in a real whole, not in an ideal whole. (Letter to de Volder, January 19, 1706, G II, 282)[16]

[15] Admittedly, it would also require an entire further essay to explicate what exactly "mind-dependent" is supposed to mean in this context. But given present space constraints, I can do no more than ask the reader to supply her own favorite explication. Another noteworthy sense in which Leibniz uses "ideal" is in the sense of "illusory" or "imaginary," e.g., when he distinguishes between ideal and real phenomena.

[16] See also *Primary Truth*, LA VI.4B, 1648; letter to de Volder, June 30, 1704, G II, 268; letter to de Volder, October 11, 1705, G II, 278–279; letter to Des Bosses, July 31, 1709, G II, 379; letter to Des Bosses, January 24, 1713, G II, 475.

The distinction between ideal and real entities, and the characterization of continuous quantities as ideal, puts Leibniz in a position to solve the space-matter problem. As we will see presently, Leibniz in fact has two solutions to the space-matter problem; one appropriate to his earlier theory of matter, which includes (M) as a central element, and one appropriate to his later theory, which no longer includes (M) itself but a related principle in the spirit of (M). Both of these solutions turn on the distinction between ideal and real entities, and on relegating truly continuous quantities to the ideal realm, and restricting the scope of the "ens est unum" principle to the real realm.

> We confuse ideal things with real substances, as long as we look for actual parts in the order of possible things, and for indeterminate parts in the aggregate of actual things, and entangle ourselves in the labyrinth of the continuum and inexplicable contradictions. (Letter to de Volder, January 19, 1706, G II, 282)
>
> The source of our embarrassment with respect to the composition of the continuum comes from the fact that we conceive of matter and space as substances, whereas material things in themselves are merely well regulated phenomena, and space is precisely nothing but an order of co-existence just as time is an order of existence but one that is not simultaneous. Parts insofar as they are not marked in extension by actual phenomena consist only in possibility, and there are no parts in a line except in the way in which fractions are in a unity. But in supposing all possible parts as actually existing in the whole (which is what one would have to say if this whole were a substantial thing composed of all its parts) we disappear into an inextricable labyrinth. (Supplement to a letter to Remond, G III, 612)[17]

In Leibniz's initial solution to the space-matter problem, the indicated strategy for how to escape the labyrinth of the continuum is implemented through a distinction between two different kinds of extension. (S), as a claim about mathematical space, i.e., about the space that is investigated in geometry, has implications for the nature of what we may call "mathematical extension." Mathematical extension is truly continuous and pertains to ideal entities. But (M) is a claim about real entities, entities that are characterized by a different kind of extension, call it "physical extension." Due to the confused nature of our perceptions, bodies are perceived as mathematically extended but in truth they are only physically extended.[18] More precisely, bodies are infinitely divisible and fill a space—which is why they can be characterized as physically *extended*—but, as real entities, they are composed of actual prior parts, which means that they are not truly continuous and hence do not count as mathematically extended. With respect to our argument above, once all occurrences of "space," "extension," and "extended" in lines (1)–(5) have been replaced by "*mathematical* space," "*mathematical* extension," and "*mathematically* extended," respectively, and premise (6) has been changed to (6′), all bodies are *physically* extended, it no

[17] Also see letter to Des Bosses, July 31, 1709, G II, 379; "Remarks on M. Foucher's Objections," G IV, 491–92; letter to Arnauld, October 9, 1687, G II, 119.

[18] Cf. "On the Method of Distinguishing Real from Imaginary Phenomena," G VII, 322: "With respect to bodies I can demonstrate that not only light, heat, color, and similar qualities are apparent but also motion, figure, and extension." Also see letter to de Volder, June 23, 1699, G II, 183; letter to Arnauld, October 9, 1687, G II, 119.

longer follows that all bodies are prior to their parts, freeing us from the contradiction in line 10.

In order to flesh out this sketch of Leibniz's initial solution to the space-matter problem, more needs to be said about how he conceives of the actual simple parts out of which bodies are composed. Leibniz identifies three basic options for what the actual simple parts might be: (a), mathematical points, (b), material atoms, or (c), substances that have a true unity.

> Thus we must necessarily arrive at either mathematical points out of which some authors compose extension, or the atoms of Epicurus and Mr. Cordemoy (which are things that you reject with me), or else we must admit that we cannot find any reality in bodies; or, finally, we must recognize some substances that have a true unity. (Letter to Arnauld, April 30, 1687, G, II, 96)

Leibniz fairly quickly dismisses the first two options. The envisioned simple parts of matter cannot be mathematical points because, on his view, the parts of a whole must be homogeneous with the whole, which means that an extended whole cannot be composed of non-extended parts.[19] (Mathematical points are neither mathematically extended nor physically extended.) Even in the case of the mathematical continuum, Leibniz considers points not as parts but as mere limits.[20] Apart from that, it also seems unintelligible how, by piling one non-extended element onto the other, as it were, one could possibly ever arrive at something extended—even if the relevant kind of extension is only physical extension, and even if the piling on were to go on ad infinitum. Moving on to the second option, the simple parts of matter cannot be material atoms either, Leibniz holds, because every non-substantial thing that is extended is divisible. Material atoms are only contingently one, but not true unities. This process of elimination leaves only Leibniz's substantial true unities as viable contenders to take on the role of the simple parts of matter—at least if we grant that Leibniz's proposed three options are exhaustive.

> Now a multitude can derive its reality only from the true unities which have a different origin and are something completely different from mathematical points, which are nothing but the extremities of extension and its modifications, and of which, it is agreed, the continuum cannot be composed. Therefore, to find these real unities I was forced to have recourse to a formal atom, because a material being cannot be at the same time material and perfectly indivisible, or endowed with a true unity. It was thus necessary to restore and, as it were, rehabilitate the substantial forms which are in such disrepute today. (*New System*, G IV, 478–79)

It is important to emphasize that the substances endowed with a true unity that Leibniz has in mind in this passage are, not monads or simple souls, but corporeal substances or animals. (Remember, the substances in question are supposed to be

[19] Cf. "Metaphysical Foundations of Mathematics," GM VII, 21: "What is in something and is homogeneous to it is called a *part*, and that, in which it is, is called a *whole*, or a part is a homogeneous ingredient."

[20] See letter to Des Bosses, February 14, 1706; *Theodicée*, §384, G VI, 343.

parts of matter; and since matter is extended, its parts must be extended as well.) A corporeal substance consists of a physically extended organic body and a soul that acts as a unifying principle, similar to how substantial forms act as unifying principles on the traditional Aristotelian hylomorphic conception of substance. More precisely, according to Leibniz's notorious "Russian doll" or "bugs within bugs" conception of the parts of matter, bodies are aggregates of corporeal substances, which consist in a soul or (what he later calls a) "master-monad" and an organic body, such that each one of these organic bodies is itself an aggregate of other corporeal substances, which consist in a master-monad and an organic body, and so on ad infinitum.[21] This "nesting" of the actual simple parts of bodies in a hierarchy allows for bodies to be infinitely divisible, in the sense of being composed of infinitely many parts, and still have a merely finite extension, even though each one of their simple parts is physically extended itself, and thus takes up some amount of space. Note in passing that this feature of Leibniz's theory of matter also frees him from the version of the space-matter problem that the Wolffians and the early Kant are concerned with. As we will see, they diagnose the conflict between (S) and (M) as turning on the infinite divisibility of bodies seemingly implied by (S) and their merely finite divisibility seemingly implied by (M). Given his account of the infinite divisibility of bodies despite their composition of simple parts, Leibniz can reject the latter inference and thus escape the problem.

Clever as this initial Leibnizian solution to the space-matter problem is, the requisite account of the composition of matter also raises some worries, of which I will mention here only two. First, one might object that the sketched account of matter is incompatible with the infinite divisibility of bodies after all—which, however, one might think is required for them to count as physically extended.[22] The account may be compatible with the claim that bodies are composed of infinitely many parts, but, the objector says, this is not what their infinite divisibility amounts to. For a body to be infinitely divisible it is required that each one of its parts is itself divisible, or, similarly, that its division into parts does not come to an end. A body that is composed of actual simple parts thus cannot possibly be infinitely divisible; its simple parts are, by definition, not further divisible, and its division into parts necessarily terminates eventually, namely, in precisely these simple parts.[23] (If it is

[21] Cf. "Remarks on M. Foucher's Objections," G IV, 492: "It is true that the number of simple substances that enter into a mass however small it may be is infinite; for besides the soul that makes a real unity of the animal, the body of the sheep (for example) is actually subdivided, which is to say it is in turn an assemblage of invisible animals or plants, also composite except for that which makes their real unity; and even though this goes on ad infinitum it is obvious that in the end all depends on these unities, the rest or the results are only well founded phenomena." Also see letter to Arnauld, October 9, 1687, G II, 118–20; letter to de Volder, June 23, 1699, G II, 184; G IV, 395–96. Leibniz retains the account of animals as compounds of a soul and an organic body in his later philosophy, even though, as we will see, he abandons the view that they are true unities. Cf. *Monadology*, §63, G VI, 618.

[22] Given that, for Leibniz, "extension" conceptually contains "continuity" (see letter to de Volder, March 24/April 3, 1699, G II, 169), one might hold that in order for *x* to count as physically extended, *x* has to be at least infinitely divisible.

[23] This sort of worry is also expressed by Heinrich Gottlob von Justi in his prize-winning essay against monadological conceptions of matter in response to the prize question from 1746–47 of the Prussian Academy, to be discussed in the next section. Cf. Justi (1748, p. 51): "Mr. Leibniz took being infinitely divisible and being composed of infinitely many parts to be the same, which can happen easily if one pays only

not granted that bodies are genuinely infinitely divisible on Leibniz's account, his initial solution to the space-matter problem will also no longer be deemed an acceptable way out of the Wolffian-Kantian version of the problem that is focused on the infinite divisibility of bodies seemingly implied by (S).) Second, doubts can be raised about the claim that corporeal substances are true unities. After all, they include distinct components, a soul and an organic body, and it remains unclear why and how the compound of these heterogeneous components should count as a truly unified being.

It is not implausible to think that these kinds of worries, and especially the second one, were among the factors that eventually led Leibniz to modify his account of the composition of matter. To make a (very) long story (very) short, in his later years, he came around to the view that corporeal substances are not true unities after all,[24] and that bodies are mere phenomena in the sense that, (i) what corresponds to them at the level of fundamental reality (if anything) are aggregates of monads whose unity is mental or ideal in that it is mediated by monadic perceptions, and, even more importantly, (ii), bodies are nothing but the intentional objects of the harmonious perceptions of all monads:

> In fact, considering the matter accurately it must be said that there is nothing in things except simple substances and in them perception and appetite; matter and motion, however, are not so much substances or things than phenomena of perceivers, whose reality is located in the harmony of the perceiver with himself (at different times) and with other perceivers. (Letter to De Volder, June 30, 1704, G II, 270)
>
> This [the return to metaphysics, AJ]...at last made me understand, after many corrections and advancements in my notions, that monads or simple substances are the only true unities and that material things are only phenomena, but well founded and well connected. (Letter to Remond, January 10, 1714, G III, 606)[25]

Souls or monads are the only true unities and hence the only fundamentally real entities, whereas bodies are ideal. This does not mean that for the mature Leibniz bodies are illusory or imaginary, however. They are well-founded or real phenomena, and as such exist at the phenomenal level of reality, where in order for a body to be

scant attention...As identical and similar these concepts look to be on first glance, as exactly opposed are they actually to one another. For that the division proceeds without end and that there are actually final parts are obviously contradictory claims." Also see Euler, *Letters*, #127, p. 230: "For infinite divisibility means nothing other than the possibility to always further continue with the division without ever reaching an end or being forced to stop. He who claims infinite divisibility thus denies the existence of the final parts of a body, and indeed it is an obvious contradiction to assume final parts and still claim infinite divisibility."

[24] A corporeal substance would be a true unity only if its components—or, more precisely, if its master-monad and the monads involved in its organic body—were unified by an additional "substantial chain," a kind of metaphysical glue that binds the distinct elements together and turns them into one substance. But these substantial chains are metaphysically highly suspect. Hence, there are no corporeal substances. See letter to Des Bosses, February 5, 1712, G II, 435–36; letter to Des Bosses, May 26, 1712, G II, 444.

[25] Also see "Elucidation of the difficulties...," G IV, 523; letter to Bourguet, March 22, 1714, G III, 567, bracketed note; letter to Des Bosses, June 16, 1712, G II, 451–52.

well-founded it must, among other things, be grounded in monads by being represented in their harmonious perceptions.[26]

This modified conception of the relation between bodies and true unities also gives Leibniz a new solution to the space-matter problem that no longer relies on the somewhat questionable distinction between two kinds of extension but still centrally utilizes the important distinction between ideal and real entities. Leibniz does not have to worry anymore about the conflict between (S) and (M), because he no longer endorses (M). As just noted, instead of being committed to (M), the thesis that all bodies are *composed of* simple parts, he is now committed to the thesis that all bodies are *grounded in* actual simple entities, namely, monads. Monads are real entities; they are true unities, and are neither extended nor in space.[27] Bodies are ideal entities; they neither are, nor are composed of, true unities. Accordingly, bodies can not only be said to be in space but also be classified as extended in the very same sense as space is extended. That is, they can be classified as genuinely continuous, in the sense of being both genuinely infinitely divisible, i.e., divisible without end, or divisible into parts each one of which is itself divisible, and such that they are prior to their parts. (This also means that Leibniz's new solution constitutes a successful reply to the aforementioned Wolffian-Kantian version of the space-matter problem as well.) Similarly, space does not exist at the fundamental level of reality, neither as a substance nor as a complex of relations between substances. Rather, space is a scheme of order of coexisting phenomena, a scheme that God relies on in His "construction" of representations of the phenomenal components of possible worlds as providing, together with time, an "arena" or "outlay" in which to arrange all bodies, and that is (partly) realized in the actual world at the phenomenal level of reality through the spatial relations between bodies represented in the harmonious perceptions of all monads, with which God equipped them at the time of creation.[28] With an eye to our later discussion, it is important to stress in this context that even though Leibniz holds that, in the actual world, it so happens that to each body there corresponds a certain aggregate of monads—namely, those monads that perceive the body, or a part of the body, most distinctly[29]—and even though he also believes that our perceptions are always confused to a certain degree, it would be a misunderstanding to take him to be committed to the claim that our perceptions of bodies amount to confused

[26] See letter to Remond, January 10, 1714, G III, 606; letter to de Volder, June 30, 1704, G II, 268. Being grounded in monads is not the only condition for a phenomenon to be well-founded. Other conditions are being in conformity with other phenomena, with necessary truths, including the theorems of mathematics, and with the laws of nature. See letter to Electress Sophie, G VII, 564; Supplement to a letter to Remond, July, 1714, G III, 623.

[27] See letter to Des Bosses, June 16, 1712, G II, 450–51: "On this way of explanation space is the order of coexisting phenomena as time is [the order of] successive ones; and there is no spatial or absolute nearness or distance between monads, and to say that they are crowded together in a point or disseminated in space is to use certain fictions of our mind when we willingly want to imagine what can only be understood." Also see letter to Des Bosses, May 26, 1712, G II, 444.

[28] See "On the Radical Origination of Things," G VII, 303–304; "Principles of Nature and Grace," §10, G VI, 603; *Theodicy*, §8, G VI, 107; *Theodicy*, §119, G VI, 169; *New Essays*, LA VI.6, 149. For further explanation of Leibniz's account of space understood along these lines, see Jauernig (2008).

[29] For Leibniz, every monad perceives the entire phenomenal world, and every monad "has" a body, namely, the body that it perceives most distinctly. See *Monadology*, §62, G VI, 617; letter to Volder, June 20, 1703, G II, 253; *New Essays*, LA VI.6, 306.

perceptions of aggregates of monads, or that bodies are aggregates of monads as confusedly perceived by us.[30] For the mature Leibniz, despite their grounding in monads, bodies are numerically distinct from aggregates of monads, and only the former are objects of our perceptions—which would hold even if, *per impossibile*, we could resolve all of the confusion of our perceptions.[31]

Before leaving Leibniz behind (for now), I would like to draw attention to one other, fairly well-known worry regarding his theory of matter that arises, in slightly different versions, for both the earlier and the later version. The worry is fueled by his denial of the existence, or even the possibility, of infinite real wholes, i.e., of wholes that are composed of infinitely many actual prior parts.[32] As noted before, a real whole is composed of actual prior parts. The number of parts of a real whole is thus determinate; the parts of a real whole can be counted. But an infinite multitude, by definition, is composed of more elements than can be counted; the number of its parts is not determinate. An infinite real whole would thus be a multitude whose number of elements is determinate, and whose elements can be counted—since it is a real whole—and whose number of elements is indeterminate, and whose elements cannot be counted—since it is infinite. The concept of an infinite real whole is thus contradictory. Or, put slightly differently, for an infinite real whole to be possible there would have to be a determinate infinite number, which, however, is impossible (according to pre-Cantorian mathematics).[33] The worry about Leibniz's theory of matter that arises from his rejection of the possibility of infinite real wholes is that in describing bodies as composed of infinitely many corporeal substances understood as true unities (as on the earlier version), and in describing bodies as grounded in

[30] That is, if it were the case that Kant had Leibniz in mind when he complained about exactly this kind of view at B60–62/A43–44, he would have gotten him wrong. But since Kant there speaks more generally of the "Leibniz-Wolffian philosophy" it is quite possible that he was primarily thinking of the Wolffians who, indeed, seem to have held the view in question. My assessment that Leibniz should not be understood as holding that bodies are numerically identical to aggregates of monads puts me at variance with Robert Adams's (1994) influential interpretation, according to which the two characterizations of bodies that one can find in Leibniz's mature writings, namely, (i), as intentional objects, and (ii), as aggregates of substances, are not in conflict but materially equivalent (pp. 218–261). I do not agree that the two characterizations can be reconciled. For I take it that Leibniz is clearly committed to the view that the same intentional objects can exist in possible worlds that differ with respect to which, and how many, monads exist. (See the references in the following note.) Accordingly, we must conclude, I think, that Leibniz's use of the term "body" is ambiguous. Bodies in the strict sense are intentional objects. But since, at least in the actual world, to each body in the strict sense there corresponds an aggregate of monads, we might also refer to these aggregates as "bodies" but only in a different, loose sense.

[31] To be sure, we "mirror" all other monads due to the pre-established harmony obtaining between all of our perceptions, but we do not perceive them, not even "non-transparently." I could perceive the exact same bodies as I am perceiving now even if God and I were alone in the universe. (See *Discourse on Metaphysics*, §14, LA VI.4B, 1551; letter to Arnauld, July 14, 1686, G II, 57.) That Leibniz does not subscribe to the view that we confusedly perceive aggregates of monads is also supported by his repeated explicit assertion that monads are not spatially related in any way.

[32] See *New Essays*, LA VI.6, 151: "There is never an infinite whole in the world, although there are always wholes greater than others ad infinitum." See *New Essays*, LA VI.6, 158: "But one would be mistaken if one wanted to imagine an absolute space that is an infinite whole composed of parts; there is nothing like it, it is a notion that implies a contradiction."

[33] Any determinate number can be reached by successively adding 1, starting with 0. But we can never reach infinity by successive addition. Hence, all determinate numbers are finite. Cf. letter to Samuel Masson, G VI, 629: "And notwithstanding my infinitesimal calculus, I do not admit any infinite number, although I admit that the multitude of things goes beyond every finite number, or rather every number."

infinitely many monads (as on the later version), he appears to be committing himself to the existence of infinite real wholes. My purpose in raising this worry is not to enter into a discussion about how Leibniz could respond to it.[34] I bring it up primarily because our other protagonists also reject the possibility of infinite real wholes for the same kind of reasons as the ones just rehearsed, are attuned to the relevance of the impossibility of infinite real wholes for the question of the composition of matter, and are aware that Leibniz's theory appears to be in trouble in this respect.[35]

3. The *Monadenstreit*: The Wolffians and the Space-Matter Problem

In the middle of the eighteenth century, the Prussian Academy of Sciences of Frederick the Great in Berlin was a stronghold of anti-Wolffianism in Germany.[36] The anti-Wolffian leanings of the Academy and its president Pierre Louis Moreau de Maupertuis are reflected in the prize essay contests in the philosophical division that the Academy sponsored during that time. Several of the prize questions invited the contestants to analyze the merits of a central Wolffian doctrine, and many of the winners were drawn from anti-Wolffian ranks. A particularly hotly debated prize question was the one from 1746–47, which was concerned with the theory of monads. The set task was to clearly present and explain the theory of monads, and to examine whether it can be refuted, or whether it can be proved.[37] Even before a winner was announced, a heated controversy broke out between the supporters and opponents of Wolff. Leonhard Euler, who, about a decade later, would take over the presidency of the Academy from Maupertuis whose anti-Wolffian sentiments he shared,

[34] Leibniz's own response strategy seems to be to distinguish between the actual infinite, which he explicitly admits (see letter to Foucher, 1692?, G I, 416), and infinite real wholes, which he rejects, and to base this distinction on the ground that the actual infinite is not a *whole*. See letter to Des Bosses, March 11, 1706: "Arguments against the actual infinite suppose that through its admission an infinite number will be given, and all infinities will be equal. But it is to be noted that an infinite aggregate is neither one whole, or possessed of magnitude, nor is it consistent with number." The reason why an actual infinite is not a whole appears to be that it is not one, i.e., that the parts are not unified or connected in some way. This response is fine as far as it goes but I do not think it successfully addresses the worry articulated in the main text. Whether we call multitudes that are made up of actual prior parts "real *wholes*" or something else, the problem remains that the number of their constituents is determinate and thus countable, which, given the indicated conception of infinite quantities prevalent in seventeenth- and eighteenth-century German philosophy and mathematics, means that there can be no multitudes that are composed of infinitely many parts. (Also, the organic bodies of corporeal substances as understood on the earlier theory are unified and, thus, seem to be wholes even in the stricter sense.) For more discussion of Leibniz's views about infinite multitudes and related worries, see Carlin (1997), Brown (1998), and Arthur (1999).

[35] That Leibniz did not pay sufficient attention to the problem of infinite real wholes is also emphasized with particular vehemence by the anti-monadist faction in the *Monadenstreit* to be discussed in the next section. See Euler (1746, p. 7): "The opinion of Mr. Leibniz seems to flatly contradict his theory of monads…For if one assumes that bodies are composed of simple things, one must admit that their number is determinate. As soon as one assumes a number to be infinitely large, however, it cannot possibly be determinate: in that infinitely large is nothing but that which surpasses with respect to magnitude anything that can be conceived." Also see Euler (1746, p. 17).

[36] For more information on the Academy under Frederick and its warring factions, cf. Calinger (1968a; 1968b).

[37] See Berlin-Brandenburgische Akademie (2003, p. 4).

anonymously published a widely circulated attack essay against the theory of monads, his "Thoughts on the Elements of Bodies," which was answered by a counter-attack treatise by Samuel Formey, the longtime secretary of the Academy, which he apparently penned with assistance by Wolff himself.[38] After that, many others entered the fray, and the *Monadenstreit* (Controversy about monads) was, not only the talk of the town, but the talk of the country. Here is Euler's engaging description of these exciting times:

> When in social gatherings the conversation turns to matters of philosophy it usually concerns points that have caused great controversies among the philosophers. Such a point is the divisibility of bodies about which the scholars are quite divided in their opinions. One party claims that the divisibility goes to infinity, without ever reaching such small particles that are not capable of being divided any further. The other party says on the contrary that the divisibility has limits and that one must eventually reach such small particles that are without all magnitude and thus also cannot be divided any further. They call these final particles from which all bodies are supposed to be composed *simple beings* or *monads*. There was a time when the arguments concerning monads were so lively and so universal that one talked about them very heatedly, and in all sorts of company, even in the guard house. At court there was almost no lady who had not declared herself for or against the monads. In short, everywhere the conversation eventually fell on monads, and one could not talk about anything except them. (Euler, *Letters*, #125, pp. 218–19)

One of the main problems at the center of the celebrated *Monadenstreit* is our old friend, the space-matter problem. As illustrated by the passage from Euler just quoted, the anti-Wolffians cash out the conflict between (S) and (M) by focusing on the *infinite divisibility* of continuous quantities. In doing so, they notably deviate from Leibniz's diagnosis of the problem, which was focused on the priority of all continuous quantities compared to their parts. According to the diagnosis of the anti-Wolffians, (S) is seemingly incompatible with (M), because (S) implies that bodies, qua extended, are infinitely divisible, while (M) implies that bodies are not infinitely divisible. So, we can spell out the space-matter problem as it figures in the *Monadenstreit* more precisely as follows:

1. (S) Space and all parts of space are essentially continuous, and, hence, essentially infinitely divisible. (From geometry.)
2. 1.5A. What is true of space is true of extension in general. (Widespread assumption.)[39]
3. 2A. Extension in general is essentially infinitely divisible. (From 1 and 1.5A.)
4. 3A. Anything extended is infinitely divisible. (From 2A.)
5. All bodies are extended. (Uncontroversial conception of body.)
6. All bodies are infinitely divisible. (From 3A and 4.)

[38] Cf. Harnack (1900, vol. 1, pp. 402–403). See Formey (1747).

[39] The reason for numbering this premise "1.5A" is to ensure that corresponding lines of the argument in the two reconstructions provided here (A) and below (B) have the same numbering.

7. (M) All bodies are composed of simple parts. (From Wolffian metaphysics.)
8. No body is infinitely divisible. (From 6.)
9. All bodies are infinitely divisible and no body is infinitely divisible. (From 5 and 7.)

As remarked in the previous section, there are different ways in which the inference to the infinite divisibility of bodies from the infinite divisibility of space can be unpacked. The reconstruction (A) just presented closely tracks how the anti-Wolffians seem to have conceived of it.[40] Looking ahead to our discussion of Kant later on, it will be helpful to record an alternative reconstruction (B) as well that more closely aligns with how Kant, and, arguably, many Wolffians, seems to have conceptualized the challenge:

1. (S) Space and all parts of space are essentially continuous, and, hence, essentially infinitely divisible. (From geometry.)

2B. Anything that fills a part of space necessarily has the same compositional structure as that part of space. (Widespread assumption.)

3B. Anything that fills a part of space is essentially infinitely divisible. (From 1 and 2B.)

4. All bodies are extended, and, hence, fill a space. (Uncontroversial conception of body and bodily extension.)
5. All bodies are infinitely divisible. (From 3B and 4.)
6. (M) All bodies are composed of simple parts. (From Wolffian metaphysics.)
7. No body is infinitely divisible. (From 6.)
8. All bodies are infinitely divisible and no body is infinitely divisible. (From 5 and 7.)

The anti-Wolffians regard this argument, in either variant, as a *reductio ad absurdum* of the Wolffian theory of monads; that is, on their view, there is no question that (M) in line 6 is the culprit that ultimately leads to the contradiction in 8 and, accordingly, must be discarded if the contradiction is to be avoided. The challenge for the Wolffians is to come up with a different story about what is wrong with this argument.

It would lead us too far afield to examine in detail the various Wolffian contributions to the *Monadenstreit*.[41] Instead, I will confine myself to a few general observations about certain aspects of Wolff's and Baumgarten's theories of matter that directly

[40] Cf. Euler, *Letters*, #125, pp. 220–21: "The whole dispute boils down to the question whether bodies are infinitely divisible or not.... As already remarked, both sides admit that much..., that the extension that one considers in geometry is divisible to infinity; since for every magnitude, as small as it may be, one can think its half, and of this half again its half, and so on without end.... But at the same time it is also the most certain principle of our cognition that everything that belongs to the genus also belongs to the individuals that are comprised under the genus. Thus if all bodies are extended, all properties that pertain to extension in general necessarily must also pertain to every body. But all bodies are extended and extension is infinitely divisible; therefore, every body will be divisible to infinity as well."

[41] Most noteworthy among them is Gottfried Ploucquet's outstanding submission for the prize contest of the Academy who argued in favor of the theory of monads. Ploucquet's piece only received the *accessit*, a sort of honorable mention. Ploucquet's essay is also a very important piece in the puzzle with respect to the question of specific lines of actual influence extending from the Wolffians to Kant.

pertain to the space-matter problem as captured in the above arguments.[42] Like the early Leibniz, Wolff and Baumgarten subscribe to (M), according to which all bodies are composed of simple parts.[43] But, in contrast to the early Leibniz, they regard these simple elements as *non-extended.*[44] This is one of the main features that both of their simple elements share with Leibniz's monads.[45] Wolff and Baumgarten also both acquiesce in (7), and hold that bodies are composed of only finitely many elements, again in contrast to the earlier Leibniz who held that, despite their composition out of simple parts, bodies are infinitely divisible.[46] Their endorsement of (7) has the advantage that, unlike Leibniz, Wolff and Baumgarten need not worry about being stuck with a view that implies the existence of problematic infinite real wholes. But it also has the downside that, given the non-extended nature of their simple elements, it makes it very hard to see how bodies could possibly be extended on their view. It is already difficult to fathom how infinitely many non-extended elements could be put together in such a way as to yield an extended body; but how an extended body could result from the aggregation of only finitely many non-extended elements raises the bar of intelligibility by yet another notch.[47]

One important part of Wolff's story about how this is supposed to work is his relationalism about space. Since distinct elements that exist at the same time are outside one another and thus related to one another, and since space is nothing but this kind of order of distinct elements that are outside one another, an aggregate of such elements necessarily fills a space and, thus, is extended.[48] Another part of the story that was frequently commented upon in the *Monadenstreit* (and later on by Kant) is that Wolff classifies extension and continuity as phenomena that he likens to secondary qualities.[49] It is not entirely clear (to me), though, at which point in the Wolffian account of the genesis of extension our confused perception is supposed to intervene. One possibility is that Wolff is really talking about two kinds of space and two kinds of extension, call them "physical" and "mathematical" space or extension respectively. Bodies are in physical space and are physically extended in the sense that they consist in multitudes of non-extended simple elements in spatial relations, but they are not mathematically extended, since mathematical extension requires

[42] Why those two? One cannot talk about Wolffianism without talking about Wolff, and Baumgarten, arguably, was of particular importance for Kant.

[43] See Wolff, *Deutsche Metaphysik*, §§76–77, 582–83. See Baumgarten, *Metaphysica*, §235, §245, §394, §400. In contrast to Leibniz's view, the simple parts of bodies on Wolff's and Baumgarten's view are not homogeneous with the bodies composed by them, though.

[44] See *Deutsche Metaphysik*, §§81, 583; see Wolff, *Cosmologia*, §184. See *Metaphysica*, §§242, 280, 396.

[45] Baumgarten's simple elements, which he calls "monads," also share with Leibniz's monads that they are souls endowed with the power of representation. (See *Metaphysica*, §400.) By contrast, Wolff, who avoids using the term "monads" for his simple elements (and just calls them "simple elements"), remains explicitly agnostic about whether they are souls or not.

[46] See *Deutsche Metaphysik*, §61; *Metaphysica*, §287. See Euler (1746, p. 6): "Mr. von Leibniz seems to admit the infinite divisibility of bodies in that he claims that actually infinitely many monads are required to make up the smallest body. Mr. von Wolff is here of a completely different opinion in that he claims that the division of bodies does not proceed infinitely far, and that the number of simple things out of which even the largest body is composed is finite and determinate."

[47] See Euler (1746, p. 18): "Thus it runs even more counter to all of our well grounded concepts how a finite number of infinitely small things could make up a finite magnitude. For how could, for example, the thousandth part of a cubic foot of matter be infinitely small, and thus have no magnitude whatsoever?"

[48] See *Deutsche Metaphysik*, §§45–46, 52–53, 602–606; *Cosmologia*, §§219–22.

[49] See *Cosmologia*, §§224–25. Cf. *Deutsche Metaphysik*, §§83–85.

true continuity.[50] However, bodies appear mathematically extended to us due to the confused nature of our perceptions. Another, less likely, possibility is that for Wolff bodies as they are in themselves, i.e., as aggregates of non-extended simple elements in spatial relations, are not extended. Bodies as they are in themselves are internally spatially dispersed, as one might say, but internal spatial dispersion is not a kind of extension, since extension requires true continuity. Only bodies as they appear to us, i.e., only aggregates of non-extended simple elements in spatial relations as confusedly perceived by us, are extended.

Although Baumgarten also describes our perceptions as essentially confused to various degrees, perceptual confusion does not seem to play a role in his account of the extension of bodies. He characterizes his monads as impenetrable, physical points,[51] and seems happy to rely only on his relationalist conception of space and the fact that coexisting distinct beings must be outside one another,[52] as well as on the "heaping together" of monads,[53] to account for the extension of the body that is the resulting composite.[54] For both Wolff and Baumgarten bodies thus are *numerically identical to* spatial aggregates of non-extended simple elements, in marked contrast to Leibniz's mature view, for whom bodies are intentional objects of the harmonious perceptions of all monads, on account of which they can be said to be *grounded in* monads and to *correspond to* aggregates of simple elements, without, however, being numerically identical to them.

Wolff's and Baumgarten's explanations of the extension of bodies raise a number of questions, chief among them whether they indeed have successfully accounted for the *filling* of space by bodies, which is essential to bodily extension. Instead of pursuing those questions, however, which would take us too far afield, we will wrap up this section by briefly examining how Wolff and Baumgarten could respond to the space-matter problem on the basis of their prior commitments. On the first sketched reading that sees Wolff as committed to a distinction between physical space and the physical extension that bodies actually have, and mathematical space and the mathematical extension that bodies appear to have, he can offer a solution of the same kind as Leibniz's initial solution discussed above. Once all occurrences of "space," "extension," and "extended" in lines (1)–(3) have been replaced by "*mathematical* space," "*mathematical* extension," and "*mathematically* extended," respectively, and

[50] This sort of distinction between two kinds of extension is not only advocated by card carrying Wolffians at that time. For example, Crusius who is a vehement critic of many aspects of Wolff's philosophy (and who also greatly influenced Kant), similarly explicitly distinguishes the kind of extension investigated in mathematics, which he considers as an abstraction, and the kind of extension that pertains to real bodies, the latter of which, he agrees with the Wolffians, are composed of simple parts. Cf. Crusius (1745, §§114–20, pp. 183–98).

[51] See *Metaphysica*, §§398–99.

[52] See *Metaphysica*, §§239–42.

[53] See *Metaphysica*, §396, §399. As transpires in later sections of the *Deutsche Metaphysik*, Wolff is also thinking about the simple elements as "heaped together," e.g., when he says that in order for there to result extension and continuity it is not required that the elements are "glued or stitched together" but merely that "they have such an order amongst themselves that between them no others can be posited in a different order" (*Deutsche Metaphysik*, §604).

[54] To be sure, Baumgarten also characterizes bodies as "phenomena substantiata" but this only means that they do not have the status of a substance but must be counted as a determination, or an accident, of substances. If there is any mind-dependence in their phenomenal status involved at all it is the same kind of weak mind-dependence that characterizes aggregates on Leibniz's view, namely, that their unity is "super-added" by our minds; but the confusion of our perceptions does not play a part in the phenomenal status of bodies for Baumgarten (as far as I can tell). Cf. *Metaphysica*, §§193, 201, 234, 295.

premise (4) has been substituted by (4′), all bodies are *physically* extended, and, hence, fill a part of *physical* space, it no longer follows, on either variant of the argument, that all bodies are infinitely divisible. On the second sketched reading, Wolff could reply by insisting on a more precise reformulation of premise (4) to say that bodies as they appear to us are extended, and of premise (6) to say that bodies as they are in themselves are composed of simple elements. After this reformulation, the argument, again, is no longer valid, on either variant.[55] In principle, the same kind of replies are open to Baumgarten as well, even though, as noted, they cannot be as easily tied to his actual text. But, interestingly, there is also another avenue of escape available to him that is worth mentioning. Baumgarten appears to go in for the bold and generally not very popular view that mathematical objects, such as certain lines or planes or volumes, are composed of only finitely many points. For example, he defines a line as an "uninterrupted series of points between points that are distant from one another" (*Metaphysica*, §286), and says that a line's "extension is determined by the number of points out of which it is composed" (*Metaphysica*, §287).[56] Given this view, Baumgarten has a more straightforward response to the space-matter problem up his sleeve. The infinite divisibility of space implies neither that anything that is extended is infinitely divisible, nor that anything that fills a space is infinitely divisible, and both of these two theses are false. It could still be that space as a whole is infinitely divisible, namely, if it is infinitely extended; but every finitely extended part of space is only finitely divisible. This Baumgartenian solution has the advantage that it remains available even if it were to turn out that there is only one space, or that no distinction between mathematical extension and physical extension can be maintained. The obvious and fairly serious drawback of the solution, of course, is that it goes against well-established and commonly accepted results of geometry. Given this drawback, and given that the second of the indicated Wolffian solutions depends on the rather implausible claim that bodies are not extended but merely appear to us to be so, I think it is fair to say that the first of the indicated Wolffian solutions, which is centered on the distinction between two kinds of space, and two kinds of extension, is the Wolffians' best bet. This is also the solution that Kant takes them to have advocated.[57]

4. Kant and the Space-Matter Problem in the Pre-Critical Philosophy

During the heyday of the *Monadenstreit* Kant was puttering around as a private tutor in the countryside, and, as far as his own studies are concerned, mainly occupied

[55] Euler seems to regard the latter response as the only option open to the Wolffians. See Euler, *Letters*, #125, p. 221: "The partisans of monads in order to defend their opinion are forced to say that bodies are not extended, and that they have only an apparent extension, or a quasi-extension.... But if bodies are not extended, I would like to know from where we got our concept of extension?"

[56] Also see *Metaphysica*, §§289, 292. Given the strangeness of this view, one might be tempted to say that Baumgarten must be talking about *physical* objects here, but, in §292, he explicitly calls the described three-dimensional object a "mathematical body."

[57] Cf. *MonPh*, 1:478–80; *NG*, 2:167–68; B468–69/A440–41.

himself with questions in physics. His first philosophical publications fall in the years 1755 and 1756 after his return to Königsberg. The second of these publications, the so-called *Physical Monadology*, which was occasioned by Kant's initially unsuccessful application for the professorship for logic and metaphysics at the local university, contains his somewhat belated contribution to the *Monadenstreit*. In the preface, Kant describes the space-matter problem as one of the central obstacles that stands in the way of a successful and fruitful collaborative combination of metaphysics and natural science:

> But how could metaphysics be brought together with geometry in this business [concerning the question of the composition of matter], since it seems easier to combine gryphons with horses than transcendental philosophy with geometry? For while the former categorically denies that space is infinitely divisible, the latter asserts it with its usual certainty. (*MonPh*, 1:476)

As this passage makes clear, Kant is operating with the same basic diagnosis of the conflict between theses (S) and (M) as the participants in the *Monadenstreit* just discussed, namely, as turning on the question of infinite divisibility. This is no accident; most likely, the space-matter problem was pushed to the forefront of Kant's attention through some of the writings occasioned by the 1746–47 prize contest.[58] In contrast to our previous reconstructions of the problem, which culminate in the derivation of a contradictory proposition regarding the composition of matter, Kant presents the problem in the quoted passage as culminating in a contradictory proposition regarding the composition of space. The matter-space problem, as one may refer to the problem in the variant presented by Kant, can be spelled out as follows:

1. All bodies are composed of simple parts. (From the theory of monads, prop. II in *MonPh*, 1:477.)
2. No body is infinitely divisible. (From 1; prop. IV, *MonPh*, 1:479.)
3. All bodies are extended, and, hence, fill a space. (Uncontroversial conception of body and bodily extension.)
4. Anything that fills a part of space necessarily has the same compositional structure as that part of space. (Widespread assumption.)
5. Not all parts of space are infinitely divisible. (From 2, 3, and 4.)
6. Space and all parts of space are essentially continuous, and, hence, infinitely divisible. (From geometry.)
7. All parts of space and not all parts of space are infinitely divisible. (From 5 and 6.)

It should be no surprise that, as this explicit reconstruction makes clear, the matter-space problem is a mere presentational variant of the space-matter problem as discussed in the *Monadenstreit*. They rest on the exact same premises, and they rely on the same basic inferential relations. The crux of the space-matter argument is the

[58] Although I suspect that Kant's study of Crusius played an equally important part in shaping his approach to the topic. See note 50.

inference to the infinite divisibility of matter from the infinite divisibility of space; the crux of the matter-space argument is the contra-positive inference to the finite divisibility of space from the finite divisibility of matter. And, indeed, in the elucidation to proposition V, which is one of the centerpieces of his solution to the matter-space problem, Kant himself also briefly describes the problem in the form of the space-matter variant.[59]

As noted in the annotations to the above reconstruction, like the Wolffians, Kant endorses the thesis that bodies are composed of simple parts, and, based on it, the thesis that bodies are not infinitely divisible. He also agrees with the claim that all bodies are extended, and, hence, fill a space, and accepts the geometrical result that space and all parts of space are infinitely divisible. His response to the problem, like the Wolffian response, targets the indicated crucial inference to the infinite divisibility of matter/the finite divisibility of mathematical space from the infinite divisibility of mathematical space/the finite divisibility of matter, but in a way that is illuminatingly different from the Wolffian response considered in the previous section. The crucial inference is underwritten by the assumption that the local compositional structure of mathematical space, i.e., the compositional structure of all finitely extended parts of mathematical space, and the compositional structure of all bodies are necessarily the same. This assumption comprises two separate claims that are worth distinguishing explicitly. The first claim is that the compositional structure of matter and the local compositional structure of *physical* space are necessarily the same. Somebody favoring an absolutist view of space might explicate the necessary correlation between these structures by saying that a body automatically "inherits" the compositional structure of the part of physical space that it fills—such a person would naturally gravitate to the space-matter presentation of our problem. Somebody favoring relationalism about space might explicate the correlation by saying that physical space automatically "inherits" the compositional structure of bodies—such a person would naturally gravitate to the matter-space presentation of our problem. The second claim embodied in the indicated assumption is that mathematical space and physical space are identical, or, at least, necessarily have the same compositional structure. Now, given that the assumption that underwrites the crucial inference of the space-matter (and matter-space) argument comprises these two claims, there are two natural ways of blocking the inference, namely, by rejecting either one of these claims. As we have seen, the Wolffians' best response blocks the inference by rejecting the *second* claim. On their view, while matter and physical space indeed necessarily have the same compositional structure, physical space and mathematical space are structurally different with respect to their composition. Accordingly, the extension of bodies is structurally different from the extension of the parts of mathematical space, and the kind of divisibility that characterizes the parts of mathematical space has no implications for the kind of divisibility that characterizes bodies, and vice versa. Kant makes a point of undercutting this maneuver by offering a special proof for the proposition that "the space *that is occupied by bodies* is infinitely divisible…so that those who avail themselves of a general distinction with respect to the difference

[59] See *MonPh*, 1:480.

between mathematical and natural space cannot escape that proof [i.e., the standard proof of the infinite divisibility of mathematical space, AJ] through this kind of move" (*MonPh*, 1:478–79, my emphasis). Accordingly, Kant himself blocks the crucial inference by rejecting the *first* claim comprised in the assumption that the local compositional structure of mathematical space and the compositional structure of matter are necessarily the same. According to Kant, while physical space and mathematical space are the same space, or, at least, necessarily have the same compositional structure, matter and physical space do not have the same compositional structure. Accordingly, the extension of bodies is structurally different from the extension of the parts of space, be it physical or mathematical space, and the kind of divisibility that characterizes the parts of mathematical space has no implications for the kind of divisibility that characterizes bodies, and vice versa. In brief, Kant's solution to the space-matter problem (and the matter-space problem) is to reject the widespread assumption that anything that fills a part of space necessarily has the same compositional structure as that part of space.

The heart of this novel Kantian solution is a smart new account of how matter fills space—which, non-coincidentally, also addresses the difficulties raised by the Wolffian account of the extension of bodies noted in the previous section. According to Kant's physical monadology, bodies fill space, not through the heaping together of their distinct non-extended simple elements, but rather through the activity of the forces of repulsion of their simple parts, which, for each part, extends over a certain spherical volume of space. That is, on Kant's account, not only bodies themselves but also each and every one of their simple parts *fills a space*. But whereas the sphere of the activity of the repulsive forces of such a physical monad by means of which it fills a space can be infinitely divided—just like any other volume of space can be infinitely divided—the monad itself remains indivisible.

> Proposition V. Theorem. Every simple element of a body or every monad not only is in space but fills space despite its simplicity....
>
> Proposition VI. Theorem. A monad defines the small space of its presence not through a plurality of its substantial parts, but through the sphere of its activity, through which it hinders the outer monads that are next to it to approach it still further. (*MonPh*, 1:480)

This clever account of the extension of bodies in terms of the filling of space by their simple parts puts Kant in the position to block the threatening contradiction of the troublesome matter-space (or space-matter) argument without having to introduce a distinction between the compositional structure of physical and of mathematical space. This represents a significant advantage over the best Wolffian solution, at least in the eyes of Kant (and especially the Critical Kant), in that anybody who is committed to this kind of distinction will have a particularly hard time to account for the objective validity of geometry, i.e., for the necessary truth of geometry with respect to the physical world.[60] One common element between Kant and the Wolffians is

[60] This complaint enters center stage in Kant's critical philosophy. Cf. B56–58/A39–41; *ÜE*, 8:202–203.

that he agrees with them that bodies are not infinitely divisible, and thus shares their enviable position of not having to worry about inadvertently being committed to objectionable infinite real wholes. But, in contrast to the Wolffian simple elements, Kant's monads, as beings that fill a space, are *extended*—which is part of why he calls them "physical" monads (another reason being that they are endowed with forces that act on other monads).[61] This represents another advantage of his account over the Wolffian one in that it allows Kant to provide a much more satisfying, straightforward explanation for how an extended body could arise from the aggregation of only finitely many monads. Despite the non-negligible advantages of Kant's pre-Critical treatment of the space-matter problem compared to the Wolffian treatment, the *Physical Monadology* is still a rather Wolffian affair, though. The Wolffians and the pre-Critical Kant agree that bodies are literally made up of simple elements, and, thus, that they are numerically identical to aggregates of these simple elements; he also agrees with them that bodies are not infinitely divisible, and that the compositional structure of matter and the local compositional structure of mathematical space are different; moreover, neither the feature of continuous quantities that the whole is prior to its parts nor the distinction between ideal and real entities plays a role in either one of their theories. For Kant's part, all of this will change in his Critical philosophy.

5. Kant and the Space-Matter Problem in the Critical Philosophy

Although much time has passed since Kant first tackled the space-matter problem with his theory of physical monads from 1756, this problem still plays an important role in his Critical philosophy. The problem resurfaced in the wake of some significant changes in Kant's theory of matter, and, arguably, was one of the central factors that led Kant to the development of his transcendental idealism and, in particular, the discovery of its central thesis that empirical objects, such as tables and cats, are appearances and not things in themselves.[62] In the intervening years, Kant moved from his pre-Critical "Wolffesque" conception of the relation between matter, space, and monads, to a "Leibnizesque" theory, which has as its centerpiece the all-important Critical distinction between the transcendentally ideal and the transcendentally real.

Kant's Critical theory of matter, which finds its most elaborate expression in the *Metaphysical Foundations of Natural Science* (1786), shares with his pre-Critical theory from the *Physical Monadology* the innovative thesis that bodies fill space through the repulsive forces of their parts:

[61] In characterizing Kant's physical monads as extended I am disagreeing with Eric Watkins (2006), who writes that by means of its sphere of activity "a monad can be present throughout an extended region of space, despite the fact that it is itself an unextended point in space" (p. 300). To me, this sounds more like a description of Kant's critical theory of matter, to be discussed in the following section.

[62] Of course, this is not to say that trying to come to grips with the space-matter problem was the only factor that led Kant to the discovery of transcendental idealism. Transcendental idealism recommended itself as the solution to a range of problems, mostly of Leibniz-Wolffian provenience, that Kant had been working on during his pre-Critical phase, as noted in section 1.

> Proposition II. Matter fills space through repulsive forces of all of its parts, i.e., through an expansive force proper to it that has a determinate degree, beyond which smaller or larger ones *in infinitum* can be thought. (*MAN*, 4:499)

It is also still a central feature of Kant's Critical view that physical space and mathematical space are the same space, or, at least, have the same compositional structure.[63] The most important change compared to his earlier account of the nature of matter is that Kant now holds that matter is infinitely divisible. And, particularly interesting for our purposes, he does subscribe to this thesis *on the grounds that* space is infinitely divisible:

> Proposition IV. Matter is infinitely divisible, namely, in parts each one of which is again matter.
>
> Proof: [...] Thus, as far as the mathematical divisibility of space goes that is filled by matter, as far also goes the possible physical division of the substance that fills it. But the mathematical divisibility goes in infinitum, therefore, the physical [divisibility] too, that is, all matter is divisible in infinitum, namely, into parts each one of which itself is material substance again. (*MAN*, 4:503–504)[64]

In stark contrast to his view in the *Physical Monadology*, Kant thus now explicitly endorses the inference to the infinite divisibility of matter from the infinite divisibility of space. But, of course, he did not forget his earlier account of matter in the interim. Kant is well aware that the infinite divisibility of matter does not *directly* follow from the infinite divisibility of space—not even if one assumes, as Kant does, that physical space and mathematical space are structurally identical with respect to their composition. In order to justify this inference, it must first be established that in every part of space that is filled by a body there is a corresponding part of matter or material substance, and not just the activity of material substance, contrary to the main thesis of Kant's physical monadology:

> Through the proof of the infinite divisibility of space the infinite divisibility of matter is a long way from being proved, if it has not previously been demonstrated that in every part of space there is material substance, i.e., parts that are in themselves movable. (*MAN*, 4:504)

[63] Among other things, this is made clear by Kant's appeal to "demonstrations in geometry" (*MAN*, 4:504) in the proof of proposition IV (according to which matter is infinitely divisible) in order to substantiate the crucial premise that space is infinitely divisible. If mathematical space and physical space were not the same space, the inference would not be valid. The same point is underlined by Kant's criticism of the Wolffians on account of their distinction between mathematical and physical space; see note 60. And, of course, his critical account of space as nothing but a form of our sensibility entails that whatever counts as a kind of space for us has the same structure as the space that is represented in our pure intuition of space (which is mathematical space).

[64] Also see in this sense B553/A525: "Its [the body's] divisibility is grounded in the divisibility of space, which constitutes the possibility of the body as an extended whole. The latter is thus infinitely divisible without, however, for that reason consisting of infinitely many parts." Also see B468/A440, B555/A527; *ÜE*, 8:202.

That is, what needs to be demonstrated is the additional premise of the space-matter argument that anything that fills a part of space necessarily has the same compositional structure as that part of space, which is precisely the premise that the pre-Critical Kant targeted for rejection. The envisioned demonstration represents the crucial first step in Kant's proof of the infinite divisibility of matter (prop. IV), which I did not reproduce in the quotation above, both because it is quite opaque, and because it is not directly relevant for our present concerns. All that we need for now is that Kant takes himself to be in possession of an argument that licenses the inference from the premise that space is infinitely divisible to the conclusion that matter, as that which fills space, is infinitely divisible as well.

The indicated changes in his theory of matter compared to his earlier account seem to expose Kant to two familiar problems that he had successfully avoided in his pre-Critical theory and that, as we have seen, constitute the Scylla and Charybdis for all aspiring theorists of matter, as it were: the problem of being committed to the existence of infinite real wholes, which are generally acknowledged to be impossible, and the space-matter problem. Kant's critical solution to both of these problems is to "go transcendental idealist," that is (among other things), to introduce a distinction between transcendentally ideal and transcendentally real entities, and to place bodies on the ideal side of this divide. Things in themselves are mind-independent, and hence transcendentally real; they are not in space, and are not extended. Bodies, which exist in space and are extended, are appearances, i.e., they are fully mind-dependent, and hence transcendentally ideal.[65] Importantly, just as in the case of Leibniz, the characterization of bodies as ideal for Kant does not mean that they are illusory or imaginary. Bodies are not mere appearances, such as dreams or hallucinations. In contrast to mere appearances, they are well-founded, or "empirically real" in Kant's technical terminology, and exist at the phenomenal level of reality,[66] where part of what is required for a body to be empirically real is that it is *grounded* in things in themselves in the sense that its qualitative features are given to us through our sensibility in response to affections by things in themselves.[67] To be sure, when Kant was writing the *Metaphysical Foundations* in 1786, transcendental idealism was already in place, and all he had to do there is lay out for his readers how it allows us to avoid both the whirlpool and the hungry monster, to stay with our learned metaphor. But, arguably, Kant had convinced himself of the necessary correspondence of

[65] Kant argues for these claims in the Transcendental Aesthetic of the *Critique of Pure Reason*. The longer and more detailed version of this stenographic (and controversial) account of Kant's transcendental distinction between appearances and things in themselves can be found in Jauernig (2021).

[66] See B43/A27, B52–53/A35–36.

[67] See *ÜE*, 8:215: "After…asking 'Who (what) gives sensibility its matter, i.e., the sensations?' he [Eberhard] believes himself to have spoken against the Critique in saying: 'We can choose what we want – we end up with things in themselves.' Now, that is exactly the constant assertion of the Critique; only that it locates this ground of the matter of sensible representation not itself in things, as objects of the senses, but in something supersensible, which is the underlying ground of the former and of which we can have no cognition." Being grounded in things in themselves is not the only condition for an appearance to be empirically real on Kant's account. Other conditions include being in conformity with the conditions for objectivity that depend on the nature of our cognitive faculties and are expressed in various necessary truths, including the theorems of mathematics, and the most general laws of natural science. Again, for details and support, see Jauernig (2021).

the compositional structure of matter and the compositional structure of space well before he wrote the *Critique of Pure Reason*. Once that had happened, he saw himself again confronted with the space-matter problem, and newly confronted with the problem of infinite real wholes. The challenge posed by the space-matter problem compounded by the problem of infinite real wholes is, basically, the challenge posed by the second antinomy, i.e., the seemingly provable contradiction between the thesis that every composite thing is composed of simple parts, understood as entailing the claim that every composite thing is composed of a finite number of parts, and the antithesis that no composite thing in the world is composed of simple parts, understood as entailing the claim that every composite thing is composed of an infinite number of parts.[68] And Kant explicitly credits the antinomies of pure reason as having "first awoken him from his dogmatic slumber."[69] The relevant awakening is the first in his overall critical rising, whose initial phase was completed in the "light giving" year 1769,[70] and culminated in the *Inaugural Dissertation* of 1770, in the all-important distinction between the phenomenal realm of bodies and the intelligible realm of things in themselves, and in a half-way Copernican turn, so to speak, expressed in the view that the objects of our senses depend on our sensible representations. The second awakening, helped along by Hume,[71] happened sometime in the following "silent decade," and culminated in the completion of the Copernican turn with the recognition that the objects of our senses depend both on our sensible representations and our concepts. So, even though transcendental idealism was already firmly established when Kant wrote the *Metaphysical Foundations*, his account there of how it provides an answer to both the problem of infinite wholes and the space-matter problem at the same time can reasonably be read as a report about one of the routes that led him to its discovery in the first place.

How, then, does transcendental idealism help us to dodge both Scylla and Charybdis? Let us start with a closer look at the problem of infinite real wholes. Kant is well aware of the worry that his commitment to the infinite divisibility of matter seems to bring with it a problematic commitment to the existence of infinite real wholes. Picking up the well-worn "labyrinth" trope, he concedes that the philosopher here enters

> a labyrinth out of which it is difficult for him to escape.... For if matter is infinitely divisible then (the dogmatic metaphysician concludes) *it consists of an infinite multitude of parts*; for a whole must surely already previously contain all parts in it into which it can be divided. (*MAN*, 4:506)

This is also why and how the antithesis of the second antinomy commits the dogmatic metaphysician to the claim that composite things are composed of infinitely many parts. But this is a problem, Kant acknowledges, citing the usual reasons,

[68] See B462–63/A434–35, B515–16/A487–88.

[69] See letter to Garve, September 12, 1798, *Br*, 12:257–58.

[70] See *Refl* 5037, 18:69.

[71] See note 5.

> since one cannot admit that matter, indeed, not even space, *consists of infinitely many parts* (since it is a contradiction to think an infinite multitude as completed whose concept already carries with it that it can never be represented as completed).
>
> (*MAN*, 4:506)[72]

Kant meets this worry by appealing to the distinction between the transcendentally ideal and the transcendentally real. The worry about infinite real wholes rests on the assumption that bodies are composed of actual parts that are prior to the whole. Given this assumption, it follows that the number of the parts of bodies is determinate, which, on the further assumption that bodies are infinitely divisible, would indeed mean that they are composed of an infinite number of parts. But, says Kant, the principle that the parts are prior to the whole at best only holds for transcendentally real entities, or things in themselves. The parts of transcendentally ideal entities, by contrast, are merely possible and posterior to the wholes of which they are parts.[73] So, if we no longer regard bodies and the space in which they exist as transcendentally real but as transcendentally ideal, the worry evaporates. In that case, bodies are not composed of actual parts that are prior to them, and thus are no real wholes to begin with, which, of course, also means that they are no infinite real wholes either:

> ...for a whole must already previously contain all the parts in it into which it can be divided. This last proposition is indubitably certain of every whole as a thing in itself...Here the philosopher ends up in a bind between the horns of a dangerous dilemma. For to deny the former proposition, that space is infinitely divisible, is an empty undertaking, for mathematics does not permit that any of its content is negated through mere sophistical ratiocination. But it is the same thing to regard matter as thing in itself, and with it space as a property of things in themselves, and still reject this proposition. Thus, he sees himself forced to let go of this last claim, as common and as agreeable to common understanding it may be. (*MAN*, 4:506)[74]

That is, if one regards matter and space as belonging to the mind-independent realm of things in themselves, the only way in which one could avoid being committed to

[72] Also see B460/A432. Interestingly, this is *not* the argument that Kant uses in the *reductio* proof of the thesis of the antinomy. I can guess why, but the explanation would take up too much space. Hint: I suspect the reason may be that Kant does not agree that infinite real wholes are impossible; their notion is contradictory for a finite understanding such as ours but an infinite intellect may be able to conceive of them. See *MSI*, 2:387–89.

[73] See B552/A524. There are some complications in this vicinity, raised by Kant's text, that I cannot address here, due to space constraints. But I want to at least acknowledge them as raising questions for future research. These complications concern, (1), Kant's characterization, in the *Critique of Judgment*, of organisms as seemingly defying the kind of mechanical explanation in terms of the law-governed motion of their actual prior parts that we successfully apply to "dead" bodies (see *KU*, 5:373–74, 407–408), and (2), Kant's characterization, in the chapter on the axioms of intuition in the first *Critique*, of extensive magnitudes, and, hence, of all appearances, as magnitudes "in which the representation of the parts makes possible the representation of the whole" (B203/A162). Both of these characterizations might be taken to suggest that there is a sense, or several senses, in which appearances or transcendentally ideal entities can (or must) be regarded as wholes that are composed of actual prior parts after all. Kant himself hints at a response with respect to (1) at B554/A526.

[74] Also see *Refl* 6330, 18:651.

the existence of infinite real wholes is by denying that space is infinitely divisible. But this is not a viable option, since it is in conflict with the teachings of geometry. So, if one wants to both hold on to the view that space is infinitely divisible and not be committed to the existence of infinite real wholes, the only option is to become a transcendental idealist, and regard bodies, not as things in themselves, but appearances, and space, not as a form of things in themselves, but as a form of appearances, or a form of one of our cognitive faculties.

Adopting transcendental idealism also has the advantage that it puts Kant in a position of being able to *explain* how matter could be infinitely divisible without being composed of an infinite number of parts. Since appearances depend for their existence and all of their genuine properties on our representations, their parts are brought into existence only through our representing them, and thus are merely possible (unless we represent them) and posterior to the whole. Bodies are infinitely divisible in the sense that we can bring about more and more parts by dividing them further and further in our representations. But the number of their parts is necessarily indeterminate since, due to our finitude and the discursive character of our understanding, this division in thought is, of necessity, a continual "work in progress," so to speak:

> What exists only in that it is given in representation, of that no more is given than how much can be found in the representation, i.e., as far as the progress of representations reaches. Thus, of appearances, whose division proceeds in infinitum, one can only say that there are as many parts of the appearance as we may give, i.e., as much as we may ever divide [it]. For the parts, as belonging to the existence of an appearance, exist only in thought, namely, in the division itself. Now the division does go to infinity but it is never given as infinite; thus it does not follow that the divisible contains in it an infinite multitude of parts *in itself* and outside of our representation on account of the fact that its division goes to infinity. [...] The division thus also does not prove a real infinite multitude in the object (which would be an explicit contradiction). (MAN 4:506–507)

This account of how and why, on a transcendental idealist understanding of bodies, the number of their parts is indeterminate, is also the key to Kant's solution to the second antinomy. From the point of view of transcendental idealism, since the number of the parts of bodies is indeterminate, the thesis that bodies are composed of a finite number of parts, and the antithesis that bodies are composed of an infinite number of parts, are both false, and hence not truly contradictory.[75] But, from the point of view of transcendental realism, according to which bodies are things in themselves, since the number of the parts of bodies is determinate, the thesis and the antithesis are indeed contradictory. And since both of these theses can be proved in the framework of transcendental realism (Kant thinks), this result amounts to a refutation of transcendental realism.[76]

[75] See B533–35/A504–507, B551–55/A523–27. A helpful illumination of Kant's proofs of the thesis and antithesis of the second antinomy by appeal to his Wolffian background is offered by Radner (1998).

[76] See B534–35/A506–507.

Turning to the space-matter problem, one might think that, setting the problem of infinite real wholes aside, there is a more straightforward way of escaping it on its own, namely, by simply rejecting the monadist premise, according to which bodies are composed of simple parts. The Critical Kant, in fact, rejects this premise but still remains sympathetic to the standard Leibniz-Wolffian kind of demonstration for the existence of simple elements out of which all real entities are composed.[77] Transcendental idealism allows Kant to both deny the monadist premise and accommodate his sympathy for the underlying argument. Bodies, as appearances or transcendentally ideal entities, are not composed of simple parts; but it still may well be—and, if we rely on pure reason alone, we are inevitably driven to think—that things in themselves are composed of simple parts. So, given that bodies are *grounded* in things in themselves it still may well be that bodies are grounded in simple elements, which is how pure reason inevitably conceives of them (see B468–69/A440–41). Note, though, that, despite Kant's endorsement of the claim that bodies are grounded in things in themselves, it would be as serious a mistake to ascribe to him the view that bodies are things in themselves as they appear to us, or that bodies are numerically identical to aggregates of things in themselves, as it would have been to ascribe this kind of view to Leibniz. For Kant (just like for Leibniz), bodies and things in themselves are numerically distinct entities, and only the former are objects of our perceptions.

Kant's Critical treatment and solution of the space-matter problem is a long way from his *Physical Monadology* but it is *strikingly* similar to Leibniz's treatment and mature solution. Leibniz's escape from the labyrinth of the material continuum also preserves the necessary structural identity of physical and mathematical space with respect to their composition, and also crucially depends on the distinction between ideal and real entities, and on taking space to be a scheme of order of bodies, and extension, which is characterized by the priority of the whole compared to the parts, to be a property of bodies, which are ideal and exist at the merely phenomenal level of reality, and relegating all simple, non-spatial, non-extended elements to the level of fundamental reality, such that the simple elements can be understood as grounding bodies instead of literally composing them. And, sure enough, Kant concludes his discussion of proposition IV in the *Metaphysical Foundations* by commenting on precisely these striking similarities between his and Leibniz's views on the topic at hand. The following quotation is rather long but it is worth being cited in full because it can serve as perfect summary of what we have learned on our journey in this chapter:

> A great man who perhaps contributes more than anyone else to the reputation of mathematics in Germany has several times rejected the impudent metaphysical claims to overturn theorems of geometry concerning the infinite divisibility of

[77] See B469/A441: "Thus it may always hold of a whole of substances, which is thought merely through the pure understanding, that before all of its composition we need to have the simple; but this still does not hold of a totum substantiale phaenomenon, which, as empirical intuition in space, carries the necessary property with it that no part of it is simple, because no part of space is simple.... But if they [bodies] were things in themselves, the proof of the monadists would indeed be valid." See *V-Met-K$_2$/Heinze*, 28:731: "Since matter fills space and thus does not consist of simple parts, the material world is no *monadatum*; for space is always divisible, so everything in it is divisible. – The world, considered as noumenon, does indeed consist of simple parts." Also see *ÜE*, 8:201, 209–210.

> space through the well-founded reminder *that space belongs only to the appearance of outer things*; alas, he was not understood. One took this claim as if he wanted to say that space appears to us, and otherwise it is a thing or a relation of things in themselves, and the mathematician considers it only how it appears. But instead they should have understood by it that space is not at all a property that pertains to a thing apart from our senses in itself but only the subjective form of our sensibility under which objects of outer senses appear to us, objects that we do not know how they are in themselves; this appearance we call matter. In this misinterpretation one thought of space still as a property that pertains to things also outside of our power of representation but that the mathematician conceives of only according to common concepts, i.e., confusedly (for that is how one usually explains appearance). Thus one ascribed the mathematical theorem of the infinite divisibility of matter, which presupposes the highest distinctness in the concept of space, to a confused representation of space, which the geometer presupposed, where it remained open to the metaphysician to compose space out of points and matter out of simple parts and in that way (according to his opinion) bring distinctness into this concept. The ground of this error lies in a badly understood *monadology*, which does not at all belong to the explanation of the natural phenomena, but is an in itself correct *Platonic* concept, developed by Leibniz, of the world insofar as it is merely an object of the understanding, not considered at all as an object of the senses but as a thing in itself, an object that, however, still grounds the appearances of the senses. Now of course *the composite of things in themselves* must consist of the simple; for the parts here must be given prior to all composition. But *the composite in the appearance* does not consist of the simple since in the appearance, which can never be given other than as composite (extended), the parts can be given only through division and thus not prior to the composite. For this reason Leibniz's opinion was, as far as I can see, not to explicate space through the order of simple beings next to each other, but rather to place these beings by the side of space, as it were, as corresponding to it but as belonging to a merely intelligible (for us unknowable) world, and to claim nothing but what has been shown elsewhere, namely, that space and, with it, matter of which it is the form does not contain the world of things in themselves but only their appearance and is itself only the form of our outer sensible intuition. (*MAN*, 4:507)[78]

This is one of the prima facie surprising pro-Leibnizian passages mentioned at the beginning of this chapter that commentators tend to ignore or play down since they

[78] Also see *ÜE*, 8:248: "Is it to be believed that Leibniz, such a great mathematician!, wanted to compose bodies out of monads (and with it also space out of simple parts)? He did not mean the world of bodies but its substrate that is unknowable to us, the intelligible world that merely lies in the idea of reason, and in which we, of course, must conceive of everything that we think there as composite substance as consisting of simple substances." Also see *ÜE*, 8:203: "The simple in the succession of time as well as in space is thus as absolutely impossible, and if Leibniz has sometimes expressed himself in a way so that one could interpret his doctrine of simple beings such as if he wanted to understand matter as composed of them, it is more appropriate, as long as it is compatible with his expressions, to understand him in such a way as if by the simple he did not mean a part of matter but the ground of the appearance that we call matter, a ground that lies entirely beyond all sensible things and is completely unknown to us (which may as well be a simple being, if matter, which constitutes the appearance, is composite), or, if it is not compatible with his expression, to deviate from Leibniz's dictum."

do not seem to fit well with the harshly critical attitude towards the Leibnizian philosophy (seemingly) expressed in the *Critique of Pure Reason*.[79] I have not said anything in this chapter about how to explain this apparent attitudinal mismatch—which is a long story.[80] But I hope to have shown that Kant's assessment of the similarities between his and Leibniz's views on the composition of matter, and the relation between matter, space, and monads/things in themselves, is, in essence, correct. It is the Wolffians who subscribe to the kind of view that Kant calls a "badly understood monadology," according to which bodies are literally composed of simple elements and numerically identical to aggregates of monads, physical space is constituted by the spatial relations between these simple elements, and both appear continuous and infinitely divisible to us due to the confused nature of our perceptions. This is not what Leibniz was going for with his monadology. What he had in mind is, more or less, the same kind of ontological picture of the relation of matter, space, and monads/things in themselves, as the one that forms the core of Kant's transcendental idealism. Of course, I do not mean to suggest that Kant agrees with Leibniz's treatment of the space-matter problem *tout court*, nor, more generally, that the Critical philosophy boils down to a version of Leibniz's philosophy.[81] But Kant is well aware that there is much common ground between his transcendental idealism and Leibniz's metaphysics, and that he, and not Wolff, is the true heir to their famous predecessor, despite the fact that he presents the shared view in a critical rather than a dogmatic key.

[79] This discrepancy, and Kant's characterization of the Leibnizian position in the *Critique* along the lines of what, in the quoted long passage, he calls a "badly understood Monadology," is one of the main reason why Burkhard Gerlach (1998) directly dismisses the suggestion that the "great man" could be Leibniz (p. 20). He proposes instead that Kant is talking about Ploucquet. There is no need for us to decide this question here but I should like to stress that, although I agree that Ploucquet is a plausible candidate for having been the intended referent, Leibniz fits Kant's description of the great man as well. As becomes clear from how the passage proceeds (and from how Kant describes Leibniz's account elsewhere, see previous footnote), Kant clearly holds that Leibniz himself did not badly misunderstand his own monadology but was envisioning exactly the kind of view about the relation between space, bodies, and monads, that Kant applauds as being the right way to think about it, and as having anticipated his own view.

[80] To put my cards on the table, I suspect that Kant closely read Leibniz's own writings, and became aware of the differences between Wolffianism and Leibnizianism, and the uncanny similarities between his own and Leibniz's views, only in the mid-1780s. How so (and why did he not make any changes in the amphiboly chapter in the second edition of the *Critique of Pure Reason*)? That is the long story.

[81] For example, a specific difference is that, since Kant does not follow Leibniz in holding that there are infinitely many things in themselves but remains agnostic about their number, he does not have to worry about problematic infinite real wholes at either the ideal or the real level of reality. Further differences emerge in how Leibniz and Kant account for the role of space as a scheme of order of the phenomenal world. In the long passage from the *Metaphysical Foundations* just quoted, Kant gets a bit carried away when he imputes the view to Leibniz that space is nothing but the form of our outer intuition. That view is proper to Kant and, arguably, one of his major innovations—although on Leibniz's account there is a sense in which space can be described as a form of God's intuition (see Jauernig, 2008). Kant's account of what it means for bodies to be grounded in things in themselves also differs in significant ways from Leibniz's account of what it means for bodies to be grounded in monads. For Kant, the grounding depends on genuine interactions between things in themselves, namely, affections of our sensibility by things in themselves; for Leibniz, the grounding is a merely representational affair, so to speak. More generally, Kant's main progress beyond Leibniz's philosophy undoubtedly consists in his more sophisticated theory of the epistemic status of our conceptions of the supersensible realm. In contrast to Leibniz, Kant holds that we cannot have substantive theoretical knowledge about supersensible matters. But he still thinks that we can have practical cognitions of the supersensible, and he also believes that the nature of our higher cognitive faculties inevitably leads us to conceive of the supersensible realm in roughly the ways in which Leibniz describes it. I take it that both of these factors are part of what Kant has in mind when he calls the *Critique of Pure Reason* the "true apology" of Leibniz.

References

Adams, R. M. (1994). *Leibniz: Determinist, theist, idealist.* Oxford University Press.

Adickes, E. (1924–25). *Kant als Naturforscher.* 2 vols. De Gruyter.

Arnsperger, W. (1897). *Christian Wolff's Verhältnis zu Leibniz.* Emil Felber.

Arthur, R. T. W. (1999). Infinite number and the world soul: In defence of Carlin and Leibniz. *The Leibniz Review, 9*: 105–16.

Baumgarten, A. G. (1757). *Metaphysica* (4th ed.). Hemmerde. [Cited as *Metaphysica* followed by paragraph number]

Beck, L. W. (1969). *Early German philosophy: Kant and his predecessors.* Belknap Press.

Berlin-Brandenburgische Akademie der Wissenschaften (2003). *Die Preisfragen der Berliner Akademie 1744–1938.* Akademiebibliothek.

Brown, G. (1998). Who's afraid of infinite numbers? Leibniz and the world soul. *Leibniz Society Review, 8*: 113–25.

Calinger, R. S. (1968a). The Newtonian-Wolffian confrontation in the St. Petersburg Academy of Sciences (1725–1746). *Journal of World History, 11*: 417–35.

Calinger, R. S. (1968b). Frederick the Great and the Berlin Academy of Sciences (1740–1766). *Annals of Science, 24*(3): 239–49.

Carlin, L. (1997). Infinite accumulations and pantheistic implications: Leibniz and the anima mundi. *Leibniz Society Review, 7*: 1–24.

Corr, C. A. (1974). Did Wolff follow Leibniz? In G. Funke (Ed.), *Akten des 4. Internationalen Kant-Kongresses Mainz 1974* (pp. 11–21). De Gruyter.

Corr, C. A. (1975). Christian Wolff and Leibniz. *Journal of the History of Ideas, 36*(2): 241–62.

Crusius, C. A. (1745). *Entwurf der nothwendigen Vernunft-Wahrheiten, wiefern sie den zufälligen entgegen gesetzt werden.* Johann Friedrich Gleditsch. (Reprinted in 2006 in C. A. Crusius, *Die philosophischen Hauptwerke* [G. Tonelli, Ed.] Olms.)

École, J. (1964). Cosmologie wolffienne et dynamique leibnizienne: Essai sur le rapports de Wolff avec Leibniz. *Les études philosophiques, 19*: 3–9.

École, J. (1990). *La métaphysique de Christian Wolff.* Olms.

Euler, L. (1746). *Gedancken von den Elementen der Cörper, in welchen das Lehr-Gebäude von den einfachen Dingen und Monaden geprüfet, und das wahre Wesen der Cörper entdecket wird.* Haude und Spener. (Reprinted in 1942 in *Opera Omnia*, Geneva, ser. 3, vol. 2, pp. 347–66.)

Euler, L. (1768–72). *Lettres à une princesse d'Allemagne sur divers sujets de physique et de philosophie.* Steidel. (Reprinted in 1942 in *Opera omnia*, Geneva, ser. 3, vols. 11–12.) [Cited as "Letters" followed by letter number, and page number in the original pagination]

Formey, S. J. H. (1747). *Recherches sur les éléments de la matière.* n.p.

Friedman, M. (1992). *Kant and the exact sciences.* Harvard University Press.

Froidmont, L. (1631). *Labyrinthus sive de compositione continui liber unus.* Ex officina Plantiniana Balthasaris Moreti.

Gerlach, B. (1998). Wer war der "grossse Mann," der die Raumtheories des transzendentalen Idealismus vorbereitet hat? *Kant-Studien, 89*: 1–34.

Harnack, A. (1900). *Geschichte der Königlich Preußischen Akademie der Wissenschaften zu Berlin.* 3 vols. Reichsdruckerei.

Jauernig, A. (2008). Kant's critique of the Leibnizian philosophy: Contra the Leibnizians, but pro Leibniz. In D. Garber & B. Longuenesse (Eds.), *Kant and the early moderns* (pp. 41–63, 214–23). Princeton University Press.

Jauernig, A. (2011). Kant, the Leibnizians, and Leibniz. In B. Look (Ed.), *The Continuum companion to Leibniz* (pp. 289–309). Thoemmes Continuum.

Jauernig, A. (2021). *The world according to Kant: Things in themselves and appearances in Kant's critical idealism*, Oxford University Press.

Jauernig, A. (forthcoming). *Thought and cognition according to Kant: Our cognitive access to things in themselves and appearances in Kant's critical philosophy*. Oxford University Press.

Justi, H. G. von (1748). Untersuchung der Lehre von den Monaden und den einfachen Dingen, worinnen der Ungrund derselben gezeigt wird. In *Abhandlung, welche den von der Königlich Preußichen Akademie auf das Lehr-Gebäude von den Mondaden gesetzen Preiß erhalten hat, nebst einigen anderen auf diese Frage eingereichten Schriften* (no. 1, pp. 1–43). Haude und Spener.

Kreimendahl, L. (1990). *Kant—Der Durchbruch von 1769*. Dinter.

Leibniz, G. W. (1849–63). *Leibnizens mathematische Schriften* (C. I. Gerhardt, Ed.). 7 vols. Schmidt. Reprinted in 1962, Olms. [Cited as "GM" followed by volume and page number]

Leibniz, G. W. (1875–90). *Die philosophischen Schriften von Gottfried Wilhelm Leibniz* (C. I Gerhardt, Ed.). 7 vols. Weidmannsche Buchhandlung. Reprinted 1965, Olms. [Cited as "G" followed by volume and page number]

Leibniz, G. W. (1923–). *Sämtliche Schriften und Briefe*. Berlin Academy. [Cited as "LA" followed by series, volume, and page number]

Look, B. (2013). Simplicity of substance in Leibniz, Wolff and Baumgarten. *Studia Leibnitiana*, *45*(2): 191–208.

Paulsen, F. (1875). *Versuch einer Entwicklungsgeschichte der Kantischen Erkenntnistheorie*. Fues's Verlag.

Ploucquet, G. (1748). Primaria monadologiae capita.... In *Abhandlung, welche den von der Königlich Preußichen Akademie auf das Lehr-Gebäude von den Mondaden gesetzen Preiß erhalten hat, nebst einigen anderen auf diese Frage eingereichten Schriften* (no. 11, pp. 272–375). Haude und Spener.

Poser, H. (1975). Zum Begriff der Monade bei Leibniz und Wolff. In *Akten des II. Internationalen Leibniz-Kongresses: Hannover. 17.–22. Juli 1972* (vol. 2, pp. 383–95). F. Steiner.

Radner, M. (1998). Unlocking the second antinomy: Kant and Wolff. *Journal of the History of Philosophy*, *36*(3): 413–41.

Schönfeld, M. (2000). *The philosophy of the young Kant: The precritical project*. Oxford University Press.

Stang, N. (2016). *Kant's modal metaphysics*. Oxford University Press.

Watkins, E. (2005). *Kant and the metaphysics of causality*. Cambridge University Press.

Watkins, E. (2006). On the necessity and nature of simples: Leibniz, Wolff, Baumgarten, and the pre-critical Kant. *Oxford Studies in Early Modern Philosophy*, *3*: 261–314.

Wolff, C. (1729). *Vernünfftige Gedancken von Gott, der Welt und der Seele des Menschen, auch allen Dingen überhaupt*, vols. I.2.1 and I.2.2 in *Gesammelte Werke*. [Cited as *Deutsche Metaphysik* followed by paragraph number]

Wolff, C. (1731). *Cosmologia generalis, method scientifica petractata....* Libraria Regeneriana. [Cited as *Cosmologia* followed by paragraph number]

Wolff, C. (1841). *Wolffs eigene Lebensbeschreibung* (H. Wuttke, Ed.). Weidtmannsche Buchhandlung.

Wolff, C. (1965–). *Gesammelte Werke* (J. École, H. W. Arndt, C. A. Corr, J. E. Hoffmann, M. Thomann, Eds.). Olms.

9

Kant's Appearances as Object-Dependent Senses

Clinton Tolley

1. Introduction: Revisiting the Dual Nature of Appearances

In this chapter I will develop what is, to my knowledge, a novel interpretation of Kant's account of appearances—and with it, a central component of Kant's transcendental idealism. I will argue that, for Kant, the relation between (a) an act of (empirical) intuiting,[1] (b) an appearance, and (c) the "something = X" that lies beyond the appearance should be understood on the model of Frege's conception of the relation between (a) a mental act (e.g., of thinking), (b) a "sense" (*Sinn*) (e.g., a "thought" [*Gedanke*]) that is "grasped" [*erfaßt*] in such an act, and (c) the "reference" (*Bedeutung*) that is represented by way of such a sense. The intended analogy is shown in Table 9.1. More specifically, I will argue that appearances should be understood on the model of what has come to be known as an "object-dependent" sense, or a sense that can only be grasped if its referent is both existent and present to the mind's sensory capacities upon such grasping.[2]

[1] Unless I explicitly say otherwise, throughout I mean to be talking about specifically *empirical* intuition, rather than pure intuition (B34–35) or the intuition of the imagination (*Anth* §28, 7:167). The latter restriction—to intuitions "of sense," rather than "of the imagination"—is important because of the explicit *in*dependence from the existence and presence of their objects that Kant accords to intuitions of imagination; cf. Stephenson (2015). Throughout I will refer to Kant's works besides the first *Critique* by the standard convention of providing the *Akademie Ausgabe* (Kant 1902–) volume number and pagination. For the first *Critique* I will cite by B edition pagination alone, save for cases where passages only appear in the A edition. Where available, I have consulted, and usually followed, the translations in Kant (1991–), though I have silently modified them throughout.

[2] The two people that I am aware of who partially anticipate my interpretive strategy are Wilfrid Sellars and Peter Rohs. In his 1966 Locke Lectures, Sellars (1968) makes the suggestive claim that "the core of the Kantian notion of an appearance is that of an idea or content" (p. 39), in a context in which Sellars both explains the notion of "content" at issue as what "exists 'in' a representing" (p. 36), and even later links such content to Frege's notion of sense (p. 65). More recently, Rohs has claimed that, for Kant, "intuitions are not purely qualitative feelings, nor are they mere sense-impressions; rather, they are directed immediately to objects only as the having (*Haben*) of a singular sense" (Rohs, 2001, p. 224; cf. pp. 217–18). Unfortunately, neither Sellars nor Rohs provides textual evidence for their interpretive suggestions, nor do they show how this analysis of appearances would be compatible with Kant's other commitments concerning appearances, nor do they (finally) stake out how such an account of appearances would differ from other leading interpretations on offer. In addition to Sellars and Rohs, Michael Dummett has used this analogy in the opposite direction, to help explain Frege's notion of sense by appeal to Kant's conception of intuition and appearances (see Dummett, 2001, p. 13; 1997, pp. 242–43). It is worth noting as well, finally, that, shortly after Kant, Bolzano argued even more explicitly for an account of the content of intuitions that parallels quite closely the Fregean approach that I spell out in section 2 below; see Bolzano (1837, §§72–77).

Clinton Tolley, *Kant's Appearances as Object-Dependent Senses* In: *The Sensible and Intelligible Worlds: New Essays on Kant's Metaphysics and Epistemology.* Edited by: Karl Schafer and Nicholas F. Stang, Oxford University Press. © Clinton Tolley 2022. DOI:10.1093/oso/9780199688265.003.0010

Table 9.1. The intended analogy

	(a) mental act	(b) content	(c) object
Kant	intuiting	appearance	"something = X" (thing in itself)
Frege	grasping (e.g., Thinking)	sense (e.g., a Thought)	reference

One of the key motivations for the Fregean interpretation of appearances is that it allows us to make better sense of a certain duality in Kant's discussion of appearances. On the one hand, as many of his readers have noticed, Kant frequently talks about appearances as if they were *objects* in their own right; for example, he calls them "the undetermined objects of empirical intuitions" (B34). Yet, on the other hand, at crucial moments Kant also describes appearances as *representations* of still further objects (e.g., A372 and *Prol*, 4:289 and 293). What is more, Kant sometimes deploys both descriptions in the very same paragraph (e.g., A108–109 and *Prol*, 4:288). If an interpretation of appearances is to do justice to this persistent duality in Kant's account, then it will need to find something that is both (i) graspable by the mind, and so serves as an *immediate* object of consciousness in this sense, but that also (ii) possesses a dimension of intentionality sufficient to relate the mind to some further object and so can serve as a *representation* of something else. This is in addition to accommodating two equally basic commitments that Kant has about appearances: that appearances are (iii) transcendentally *ideal* (B66 and A369), and (iv) *dependent* in some sense on what Kant calls "affection" (B33–34).

As I will argue below, a chief virtue of viewing appearances as Fregean object-dependent senses is that this promises to allow us to keep track of all four of these features of appearances. Most strikingly, object-dependent senses provide us with a model for understanding how the aforementioned duality in appearances can come together in one item, since a Fregean sense is itself at once (i*) that which is "grasped" by a mental act, and so, serves as its immediate object, but is also (ii*) a way for some further object (reference) to be presented or "given" (an *Art des Gegebenseins*, in Frege's words). This mirrors quite closely the fact that, for Kant, an appearance is both (i) that which is "intuited" by an act of empirical intuition (its immediate object), but also (ii) a way of being intentionally related to some further object (namely, a thing that has a way of being "in itself"). This is in addition to the further usefulness of this model, and further distinctiveness of the resulting interpretation, when it is applied to the questions of (iii) the ideality of appearances and (iv) their dependence on affection. Though it has not always found a sympathetic audience, Frege's characterization of senses as (iii*) essentially abstract, even in cases of perception, opens the door for a new way to understand Kant's thesis of (iii) the ideality of appearances. And recent discussion of (iv*) the nature of the object-dependence involved in perceptual senses, along with the connection between this dependence and the causal dependence of the act of grasping such a sense upon the very same object it represents, can also help shed light on the persistently vexing question of how appearances are supposed to be (iv) dependent in some sense upon real things while still themselves remaining ideal.

As I will also show below, the most prominent recent accounts of appearances are alike in failing to accommodate one or another of these aspects of appearances, despite their divergences on many other fronts. The five interpretations I will focus on below are what I will call the *simple phenomenalist* interpretation, put forward early in the last century by Hermann Cohen, Norman Kemp Smith, and H. A. Pritchard; what I will call the *sophisticated phenomenalist* interpretation, put forward by Richard Aquila and James Van Cleve; what I will call the *real relationalist* interpretation, put forward by Rae Langton; what I will call the *direct realist* form of *representational relationalism*, put forward by Lucy Allais; and the *epistemic* or *methodological* approach to appearances presented by Henry Allison. Seeing the contrast between these views and the Fregean interpretation will help point up what is unique, and (I hope) attractive, about the approach developed here. I also hope it will open up new points of entry for future research into the nature and prospects of transcendental idealism more broadly.

I will develop this interpretation in the following manner. In section 2, I will present the interpretive model that I want to bring to bear on Kant's discussion of appearances, by outlining the relevant elements of the general Fregean account of cognitive content. I will focus in particular on the aspect of content that Frege calls "sense" (*Sinn*), as well as on the particular species of sense that has come to be called "object-dependent," such as that which is said to figure in perceptual experience. In the main part of the chapter (section 3), I will then turn to Kant's texts, to show that we can find Kant ascribing to appearances four features (our (i)–(iv) above) that closely parallel features we will have identified in section 2 as characteristic of object-dependent senses (our (i*)–(iv*) above). In section 4 I will use this parallelism to highlight the respects in which the Fregean interpretation stands in sharp contrast with the other influential interpretations of appearances mentioned above. I will also show how the Fregean account would address the traditional questions of whether Kant is committed to either a "one world" or "two world" view, whether he thinks appearances and "things in themselves" are identical or distinct, and if the latter, in what respect (if at all) they still depend on such things; and finally, what Kant might mean by according to appearances an "empirical reality" despite their ideality. In section 5 I will conclude by summarizing the results.

Before I get started, though, let me begin with a concession up front. As I will be restricting myself to drawing attention to key points of contrast with existing interpretations of Kant's doctrine of appearances, rather than showing how the Fregean interpretation can make sense of each and every of the many passages offered as evidence of the alternative views, much more work would need to be done to *refute* the other interpretations. My main goal here, therefore, is simply to introduce the Fregean interpretation—as its very *possibility* has been overlooked—and then show how it can be developed into a serious and substantive interpretive option, in order to secure a place for the Fregean interpretation at the table—with the hope of further demonstrating its promise (and especially its advantages over the alternatives) in future work.

2. The Fregean Account of Cognitive Content

Let me start, then, by giving a sketch of the Fregean account of cognitive content that I intend to deploy as a model for understanding Kant's account of appearances. We can get our bearings by looking to Frege himself—though eventually we will have to look to his successors, as Frege himself did not give much more than the hints of a treatment of the kind of content that is involved in intuition. (This is also why the resulting model will be Fregean, rather than simply Frege's.)

In his mature writings, Frege famously distinguishes between (a) the mental activity or state that belongs to an individual's mind when, e.g., that individual thinks a thought or understands a linguistic expression as meaningful, (b) the objective content that is "grasped" in such mental acts, and (c) the object, property, or state of affairs ("truth-value") that is "given" or "presented" to the mind by grasping this content (cf. Frege, 1984, pp. 163–64). When viewed in relation to a linguistic expression, Frege calls (b) the "sense" (*Sinn*) of the expression, and calls (c) its "reference" (*Bedeutung*) (cf. Frege, 1984, p. 161). Though Frege had initially worked with a simpler picture that distinguished mental acts only from what he called "content" (*Inhalt*) in general, Frege's investigation of informative judgments of identity led him to recognize the need for a further distinction in relation to the content itself (cf. Kremer, 2010, pp. 220, 236–40). If the only thing that could function as the content of an expression were the item to which it related us (e.g., an object *x* or a property *F*), rather than the particular "mode of being given" (*Art des Gegebenseins*) this item that was associated with the expression, then Frege thinks we would not be able to give an account of how statements like "The morning star is identical to the evening star" could be informative in cases where we are already familiar with relevant item (here: the planet) when it is presented in one of these ways but not the other, and so are also not aware of the identity of the item across the different modes of its being presented (cf. Frege, 1984, pp. 157–58). To keep track of this further difference, Frege introduces the term "sense" to pick out the particular manner of being given an item, and the term "reference" to pick out the item itself.[3]

Once Frege distinguishes between the simple identity and difference of the objects of our discourse, on the one hand, and the identity and difference in the ways of being given or presented with these objects, on the other, he then goes on to draw several further consequences of this distinction. First, Frege argues that objects (and references more generally) form no proper "part" of what is contained "in" the senses through which they are given or presented to us. Frege makes this point at various places, perhaps most famously in his correspondence with Russell, concerning the particular species of sense that Frege associates with assertoric sentences—namely, what Frege calls a "thought" (*Gedanke*):

> Mont Blanc with its snowfields is not itself a component part (*Bestandteil*) of the thought that Mont Blanc is more than 4000 meters high. [...] The sense of the word 'moon' is a component part of the thought that the moon is smaller than the earth.

[3] For further references and discussion, see Kremer (2010, pp. 253–58).

> The moon itself (i.e., the reference [*Bedeutung*] of the word 'moon') is not part of the sense of the word 'moon'; for then it would be a component part of that thought.
> (Frege, 1980, p. 245; cf. 1984, p. 164)

Secondly, Frege also takes a sense to be distinct from any component "part" (*Teil*) or "property" (*Eigentum*) of an individual's mind or consciousness (Frege, 1984, p. 160; cf. p. 366). Rather, a sense is something that can be grasped by many different individual mental acts, and so can be "common property" to many different minds (Frege, 1984, p. 160; cf. pp. 362–63, 368). In fact, Frege thinks that a sense is what it is independently of actually being grasped by any mind whatsoever, because a sense is ultimately not itself something "actual" (*wirklich*) at all (cf. Frege, 1984, p. 370). Yet despite its non-actual standing, Frege still takes the sense, or the way of being given an object, to be what is directly "grasped" (*erfaßt*) in mental acts like thinking and judging, rather than its reference (cf. Frege, 1984, pp. 355–56). In other words, senses, rather than referents, are the "immediate objects" of mental acts such as thinking.[4] This is so, despite the fact that this immediate object is itself a representational *relation* to something else, a means to some *further* object (the reference).

Frege provides the following analogy to help illustrate the relationship he has in mind between a mental act or state of an individual mind, a sense, and a reference:

> Somebody observes the Moon through a telescope. I compare the Moon itself to the reference; it is the object of the observation, which is mediated [*vermittelt*] by the real image [*Bild*] projected by the object glass in the interior of the telescope, and by the retinal image of the observer. The former I compare to the sense, the latter with the idea [*Vorstellung*] or intuition [*Anschauung*]. The optical image in the telescope is indeed one-sided and dependent upon the standpoint of observation; but it is still objective [*objektiv*], inasmuch as it can be used by several observers.
> (Frege, 1984, pp. 160–61)

While the moon is the ultimate object that is given to the mind in an individual act of representing or intuiting through the telescope, what is grasped immediately in this act of intuiting is the way in which the moon is being given in this particular case—namely, through the telescope. The moon itself does not form any component part of what is grasped. Rather, what is grasped through the telescope is only a one-sided and standpoint-dependent view ("image") of the moon. Even so, this view is itself "objective" in the sense that the same one-sided and standpoint-dependent view can be grasped in several different mental states by mental acts of different individual minds ("observers")—namely, whoever looks through the telescope. Frege takes this to imply that the view in question is not identical with any real part of any one individual's mental state or act, but is rather something there to be taken up by anyone.

[4] For the description of thoughts in this context as the "objects" of acts of thinking, compare Dummett (1997, pp. 242–43). For one place where Frege himself appears to use "object of my thinking" (*Gegenstand meines Denkens*) to pick out a sense, see Frege (1984, p. 366).

Frege's willingness to countenance senses that are objective and yet standpoint- or perspective-dependent sets the stage for an extension by Frege's later readers (such as John McDowell, and more recently, Jason Stanley and Susanna Schellenberg) who aim to use Frege's distinction between sense and reference to provide an analysis of the content of perceptual experience and of what is expressed by indexical and demonstrative phrases.[5] Starting from the thought that veridical perceptual experience involves a concrete causal relation between a mind and an existent object, it is then argued that this experience *also* involves a sense of a very special sort, one that can be grasped *only* when its reference stands in this causal relation to the mind.[6] The key assumption is that not only can I not be veridically perceptually related to an *object* that is not there, but I also cannot grasp this particular *way of being given* the object if my mind does not, in fact, occupy the relevant causal relation to it.[7] Due to the dependence of the mental act of grasping the sense upon the obtaining of this real relation between the mind and its object (reference), such a sense has itself come to be called "object-dependent."[8]

Nevertheless, to remain broadly Fregean, even cases like this, in which the sense at issue is object-*dependent* in this respect, the sense at issue will nevertheless not be object-*involving* or object-*containing*; it will not have the object in question as a constituent or proper part. For a Fregean, the object (referent) itself is *never* a part or constituent of the sense.[9] As we have already noted, Frege spends a considerable amount of time distinguishing sense (and so, thoughts) from anything real or actual in the sense of being concrete or existing in space and time or being causally efficacious (cf. again Frege, 1984, pp. 159–60, 354, and 364). What is more, in "The Thought," Frege explicitly denies that anything "sensible" (e.g., the mere having of sense-impressions,

[5] Cf. McDowell (1984, 1986, 1991a), Schellenberg (2011), and Stanley (2011, ch. 4).

[6] This kind of extension of the sense/reference analysis to the content of perceptual experience can actually claim to have some roots in Frege's own texts. As we have already seen, many of Frege's own examples involve concrete objects standing in different concrete relations to the mind: the planet Venus and Mont Blanc are surely concrete objects, and the distinction between the sense of "morning star" and that of "evening star" rests on the different times of day at which the planet can be perceived. (See also Frege's discussion of the mountain called both "Aphla" and "Ateb," and the differences in the senses of these terms, in his correspondence with Philip Jourdain; Frege, 1980, pp. 78–80.) Nevertheless, in "The Thought" Frege rejects the idea that this concrete relation is sufficient to account for what is involved in intuition (see below).

[7] As McDowell (1984) puts it, our grasp of these senses "depends essentially on the perceived presence of the objects" (p. 219), such that this sort of "mode of presentation is not capturable in a specification that someone could understand without exploiting the perceived presence of the [object] itself" (1991a, p. 266). McDowell's analysis of Frege here provides an important counterpoint to the still-prominent understanding of Frege as a "descriptivist" about senses, as Saul Kripke and John Searle would have it. For criticisms of such a descriptivist interpretation, compare McDowell (1986, pp. 233–34) and McDowell (1991a, pp. 268–69). In this respect, McDowell's analysis helps to bring out the possibility (already intimated in Frege) of non-discursive senses—which, in turn, keeps room in the Fregean interpretive model for allowing Kant to embrace non-conceptualism about the content of intuitions. I myself favor this further interpretive thesis, though I will not argue for it here; see Tolley (2013).

[8] For this terminology, see McDowell (1986, p. 233).

[9] Recall Frege's letter to Russell cited above; compare McDowell (1991a, pp. 265 and 268). Here, in addition to recalling Frege's own telescope analogy mentioned in a note above, it might also be helpful to think in terms of Searle's (1958) graphic (and so potentially misleading because too concrete) depiction of Frege's conception sense on the model of pipes that lead to bowls. The pipes (senses) are not complexes that contain or include the bowls (references) to which they are directed, but are instead standing routes to the bowls.

the actual effects of causal interaction) is sufficient for vision, holding instead that seeing physical objects requires that something "*non*-sensible" enter into the mix (cf. Frege, 1984, p. 369). Hence, even in cases of being perceptually related to objects, the relevant mode of being presented with an object remains non-"actual" despite the fact that the ultimate reference is something actual or concrete.

For this reason, even the senses apprehended in perceptual experience—as indexical-laden as they may be—remain non-actual, for Frege, and so even these ultimately occupy a realm over and above the realm of the subjective psychologically actual and, more generally, a realm distinct from anything actual, what Frege infamously called "a third realm" (*ein drittes Reich*) (1984, p. 363).[10] Even though the object-dependence of such senses distinguishes them from those senses graspable in purely conceptual reasoning about abstract objects (references) and in merely fictional discourse about non-existents (with the latter in particular having the standing of "object-independent" senses), all of these senses nevertheless belong together in the same realm. For this reason, the phrase "object-dependent" should not be taken to entail a real or causal dependence of the *sense itself* upon some mental act or object. As non-actual, this sense is what it is independently of any actual mental act or actual relation between a mind and an object. What *is* really dependent on such an actual relation, rather, is the (actual) mental *act* of grasping such a sense.

At this point, I hope, we can see more concretely how a broadly Fregean account of the content of intuitions will ascribe the following four features identified at the outset (section 1) to the sense involved in intuition: (i) immediacy, (ii) representationality, (iii) non-actuality, and (iv) object-dependence. The Fregean account takes perceiving ("intuiting") to involve grasping (iv) an object-dependent sense, where this dependence consists in the fact that the grasping of this sense in intuiting is only possible given the existence of its object (reference) and this object's standing in the right concrete (causal) relation to the mind. Yet despite this dependence, the object that is given through such a sense forms no "component part" of (i) what is immediately grasped in such an act; what is so grasped is limited to the sense itself. This follows from the fact that the sense is (iii) something non-actual, a denizen of the "third realm," while its object is something that belongs to the actual (concrete) world. Even so, the non-actual sense (ii) "gives" or "presents" this concrete further object, and does so in a one-sided or standpoint-dependent manner.

We can summarize the core of the broadly Fregean account of the content of intuition as in Table 9.2.

3. Kant's Parallel Account of Appearances

In the previous section I outlined a broadly Fregean account of the content of cognitive acts in general, and of the content of perception in particular (more specifically,

[10] For recent work that joins Frege in construing the representational content of perceptual experience as non-actual and even abstract, see Tye (1995). Burge (2005) identifies the seeming abstractness of even the senses associated with indexicals and demonstratives as one of the most deeply problematic features of Frege's views—though he accepts that Frege does embrace such a commitment (pp. 50–53 and 234–35).

Table 9.2. The Fregean model of object-dependent sense

(actual) (a) mental act	(non-actual) (b) content	(actual) (c) object
e.g., grasping	sense	reference
[contains →]	[represents →]	
[←	—	— causes]

what Frege himself calls "intuition") in terms of what Fregeans call "object-dependent senses." I also highlighted four key features that the Fregean takes to characterize this content: (i) immediacy, (ii) representationality, (iii) non-actuality, and (iv) object-dependence. What I want to show now is that we can find parallels for each of these four key features in Kant's account of appearances. This will provide the core of my positive case that Kant's appearances are best understood as object-dependent senses. I will begin with (ii) representationality, since this is the feature that is both most often neglected in Kant's account of appearances and also the feature that perhaps best motivates the alignment with the Fregean account. What is more, as I will show below, getting this feature in view first will be crucial for coming to a proper understanding of the remaining features.

3.1 The Representationality of Appearances

The representationality of appearances themselves can be seen if we return to the duality in Kant's account of appearances that I noted at the outset (section 1). This duality consists in the fact that Kant often refers to appearances as if they were *objects* of mental acts but then also, and equally often, refers to them as *representations* of further objects. We can see both of these trends manifest, for example, in the following passage from the A Deduction:

> All representations, as representations, have their object, and can be themselves objects of other representations in turn. [i] Appearances are the only *objects* that can be given to us immediately.... [ii] However, these appearances are not things in themselves, but themselves only *representations*, which in turn *have their object*, which therefore cannot be further intuited by us, and that may therefore be called the non-empirical, i.e., transcendental, object = X. (A108–109; my italics)

In the sentence I've marked "[i]," we see Kant speaking of appearances as *objects* that are "given to us immediately." This is something that Kant does with some frequency.[11] In sentence [ii], however, Kant notes that there is more to appearances than simply being the immediate objects of certain mental acts, since appearances themselves are

[11] Kant does this, for example, at the beginning and end of the Aesthetic, describing an appearance as the "undetermined object of an empirical intuition" (B34), and claiming that "we are acquainted with (*kennen*) nothing except our way (*Art*) of perceiving" things, rather than the things themselves (B59); see also B123.

representations that "have" their own further object. This further object that is represented by the appearance is what Kant here identifies with the non-empirical or transcendental "object = X." That appearances represent further things is a feature that Kant also returns to at key points elsewhere. In the B Deduction, for example, Kant describes appearances as "representations *of things* that exist without being cognized [*unerkannt*] as to what they might be in themselves" (B164; my italics). Similarly, in the Second Analogy, Kant distinguishes between appearances "insofar as they *are* (as representations) objects" and appearances "insofar as they *designate* (*bezeichnen*) an object" (B234–35; my italics).[12]

The representationality of appearances themselves is something worth dwelling on, since it is something that has often been overlooked. This is not to say that people have not noticed that Kant *calls* appearances "representations." To the contrary, almost everyone has noted and emphasized this fact. What has been neglected, rather, is the *significance* of this fact. Perhaps the most common understanding of Kant's claim that appearances are representations is that it is Kant's way of signaling, first, that appearances are items that only "exist" or have their being "in" acts of representing, and secondly, that the way that appearances exist in acts of representing is by being what is represented by such acts, where this means that appearances are the intentional objects of such acts.[13] Now, while there is surely something right about the first part of the standard understanding (since Kant himself makes this sort of point explicitly throughout the first *Critique* and elsewhere),[14] it is the second part of the common understanding that gives a misleading characterization of the nature of appearances. This is because it makes an appearance into something that is the final stop, as it were, of the representational relations involved in an intuition. This, however, is to ignore the *further* representational relation that we saw Kant claim above is involved or contained "in" the appearance itself—namely, the manner in which an appearance *itself* is a representation of something else. Far from being *merely* "what is represented" in an intuition, and so functioning as the ultimate intentional object of an intuition, an appearance itself "has" its *own* intentional object (the further "thing," a "something = X"), and so, as it were, passes along the chain of intentionality to one more stop.

In this respect an appearance functions more like an image or picture: something that is, and can be considered as, an object in its own right, but which nevertheless

[12] Compare as well the A edition of the chapter on phenomena and noumena, where Kant infers from the fact that "all our representations are in fact related to some object through the understanding," and the further fact that "appearances are nothing but representations," to the conclusion that "the understanding thus relates them [i.e., appearances] to a something, as the object of sensible intuition"—even while noting that "this something" is "the transcendental object," which "signifies a something = X, of which we know [*wissen*] nothing at all nor can know anything in general" (A250); see also A251–52. Kant describes the relation between an appearance and the thing in itself as that of "correlation" in the Aesthetic: "what we call outer objects are nothing other than mere representations of our sensibility, whose form is space, but whose true correlate (*wahres Correlatum*), i.e., the thing in itself, is not and cannot be cognized through them" (B45).

[13] One such example of this interpretation is Van Cleve (1999), who claims that when Kant says appearances are representations, we should "keep in mind the act-object (or 'ing'-'ed') ambiguity of words like 'representation,'" and so "should construe him as saying that appearances are representeds that have no being apart from the representing of them" (p. 7). I will take up such an interpretation more directly below in section 4.1.

[14] Cf. B164 and B534. I will return to this point below in section 3.4.

involves a representational relation to a further object. In fact, just we saw Frege doing earlier, on a good number of occasions Kant himself actually associates appearances with something that can serve as the basis for an "image or picture" (*Bild*) (cf. B15, B156, B179–82, B496, and A120–21). This comes out especially clearly in his mid-1770s lectures on metaphysics:

> My mind is always busy with forming the image (*Bild*) of the manifold while it goes through it. E.g., when I see a city, the mind then forms an image of the object which it has before it while it runs through the manifold. [...] This illustrative (*abbildende*) capacity is the formative (*bildende*) capacity of intuition. The mind must undertake many observations in order to illustrate an object (*einen Gegenstand abzubilden*) so that it illustrates the object differently from each side. E.g., a city looks differently from the east than from the west. There are thus many appearances of a thing (*Erscheinungen von einer Sache*) according to the various sides and points of view. The mind must make an illustration (*Abbildung*) from all these appearances by taking them all together. (*V-Met-L_1/Pölitz*, 28:235–36)

Here our capacity for forming an image of an object is said to operate by way of "taking together" several appearances of that object, each of which provides a "look" on the object from a certain "side and point of view."[15]

To be sure, Kant doesn't say each appearance is itself already an image (in his sense of the term). Nevertheless, appearances would seem to contribute to the formation of images of objects both compositionally, by serving (or at least providing) as component parts of them, and semantically, by supplying partial (perspectival) views on the object. The last aspect especially reinforces the general point that appearances are not themselves the ultimate intentional objects *of* intuition or the ultimate objects to which we are related representationally through intuition—due to the representationality of these appearances themselves as providing partial perspectives on some further object.

3.2 The Immediacy of Appearances

An appreciation of the representationality of appearances (in this sense) is crucial, in turn, for the appreciation of their immediacy—i.e., our (i) above. Recall that the Fregean analysis of object-dependent senses involves three items standing in various relations to one another (cf. Table 9.2). More specifically, the mental act of intuiting stands in relations to both the sense that it grasps and the reference that is

[15] In the first *Critique*, Kant identifies this capacity for "illustrating" with the "imagination" (*Einbildungskraft*), which he again takes to be a capacity for a certain kind of operation on appearances. Though Kant does not here go into the details of the manner in which each appearance contributes to the image, his characterization of the operation by means of which appearances contribute to images is, in outlines, quite similar to that of the lectures: while "every appearance contains a manifold," the imagination is required "to bring the manifold of intuition into an *image*," which it does by "taking up" this manifold in a certain way (A120). For discussion of the nature of images in Kant's theory of imagination, see Makkreel (1990, pp. 16–17 and 22–23) and Matherne (2015).

represented through this sense, with the sense and reference thereby standing in a kind of relation to one another as well. If we then wished to ask about what sort of immediacy, if any, is involved in an object-dependent sense, it is clear that we would have to be more specific, since there are three relations connected to such a sense, each of which might or might not be an immediate relation. Matters become further complicated by the fact that each of these relations is a distinct kind of relation from the other: the relation between act and sense is the special relation between something real and something non-actual that Frege describes as "grasping"; while the relation between sense and reference (in intuition) is also a relation between something non-actual and something else that is real, it is a representational or intentional relation; in contrast to both of these, the relation between the reference and act (in the object-dependent case) is a real causal relation. This implies, of course, that in each case the significance of calling such a relation "immediate" (or not) will differ as well.

If we focus, first, on the relation between act and sense, we can recall that the Fregean argues that it is a sense and a sense *alone* that is grasped "in" a mental act, and so what is immediately present within consciousness. Let us call this kind of immediacy *phenomenological* immediacy. We also saw, however, that in the case of object-dependent senses, the possibility of such immediate phenomenological presence within the mind through such grasping was something that rested upon the further, real, and perhaps also immediate relation of the mental act to the reference being presented through the sense: let's call this sort of immediacy *causal immediacy*. For the Fregean, even if the phenomenological immediacy of the sense in the act of grasping is made possible only by a causally immediate relation obtaining between this act and the ultimate reference, it would be wrong to infer that the reference itself is also thereby phenomenologically immediately present "within" the mind in the act of grasping. Rather, the sense and *the sense alone* remains the phenomenologically immediate object of the mental act in this sense (cf. section 2).

What I want to show now is that Kant both relies upon this same kind of distinction in types of immediacy and holds the parallel thesis about what is phenomenologically immediate: it is only the appearance, and *not* the further object represented by this appearance, that is contained "in" the mental act of intuiting. This is so, despite the fact that Kant places a clear emphasis on the necessity of a real causally immediate relation obtaining between our sensibility as the capacity for intuiting and the object that will be represented through this act, in order for us to have an appearance of this object "in" mind (see below, section 3.3).

We can see this in Kant's discussion of the "content" (*Inhalt*) of intuitions, and the manner in which he contrasts this content with the ultimate object represented by this content. For Kant, neither the "object in itself," nor anything that "pertains" to it, is "contained" *in* any intuition, whether of inner or outer sense:

> [O]uter sense can also *contain* (*enthalten*) in its representation only the *relation* (*Verhältniß*) of an object to the subject, and *not* that which is internal to the object in itself. It is exactly the same in the case of inner sense. (B67; my italics)
>
> The representation of a body in intuition...*contains* (*enthält*) *nothing at all* that could pertain to an object in itself, but merely the *appearance* of something and the way (*Art*) in which we are affected by it. (B61; my italics)

Rather than containing the object "in itself" or anything that is "internal" to it, intuitions have as their content solely a distinctive representational *relation* between a subject and some object. This is the relation of being appeared to by something, or what Kant here calls "the appearance of the thing and the way in which we are affected by it." In other words, what is immediately "contained in" an intuition is *only* an appearance and *not* the object represented by this appearance.

In fact, once we are on the lookout for this sort of characterization, we can see that Kant actually makes this point quite frequently. In an important footnote to the Aesthetic, Kant again identifies "appearance" with "what is *not* to be encountered *in the object* in itself at all, but is always to be encountered *in its relation* (*Verhältniß*) to the subject and is inseparable from the representation of the object" (B69n–70n; my italics). In the A edition chapter on phenomena and noumena, Kant is even more explicit in his thesis that appearances involve a special kind of relation between an object and its immediate sensible representation:

> [T]he word 'appearance' must...indicate a *relation* (*Beziehung*) to something the *immediate representation of which* is *sensible*, yet something *which is an object that is independent of sensibility*, and so something that is in itself without the constitution of our sensibility (upon which the form of our intuition is grounded).
>
> (A252; my italics)

Kant returns to the characterization of appearances in terms of relations time and again, even on into the *Opus postumum*.[16] In each case, Kant takes the appearance, as what is "contained in" an intuition, and as itself an "immediate representation," to involve only the "relation" of an object to a subject, not anything that is to be encountered "in" the object itself, let alone the object itself.[17]

This provides the proper context for understanding Kant's claim that "appearances are the *only* objects that can be given to us immediately" (A109; my italics). Appearances can be called the immediate objects of intuitions insofar as they serve as the content of intuitions and so serve as what is phenomenologically immediate "in" consciousness in the act of intuiting. This is so, despite the fact that appearances are not the ultimate objects of intuitions, since appearances themselves represent some further object (cf. section 3.1).[18]

[16] Cf. Rosefeldt (2007, §1). In addition to B69, Rosefeldt cites Bxxvii, B306, and *OP*, 22:26 and 43. To these compare *Prol* §13, 4:286, where Kant describes "appearances" as things "whose possibility rests on the relation (*Verhältnis*) of certain things, unknown in themselves, to something else, namely our sensibility."

[17] Kant's belief that an appearance itself is constituted by a relation (i.e., one of appearing and (conversely) being appeared to) would also seem to be behind Kant's description of appearances as "ways" or "modes [Arten]" of representing or perceiving objects, rather than as "things" in their own right (cf., A372, B59; *Prol*, 4:293; and *V-MS/Vigil*, 29:972).

[18] To head off a misunderstanding that might arise at this point, let me emphasize that it is appearances *in general* that Kant claims are immediately given and present to the mind, with no further claim whatsoever being made that any *particular kind* of appearance is more immediately given than another. Perhaps most importantly, let me emphasize that Kant does not hold that the appearances of *mental acts* in *inner* sense are given more immediately than the appearances of *bodies* in *outer* sense. This sort of prioritization of inner sense (or "inner experience") is part of the target of Kant's argument in the Refutation of Idealism (cf. B276).

3.3 The Object-Dependence of Appearances

So far I have argued that, for Kant, an appearance is what is phenomenologically immediately (present and given) "in" an intuition insofar as it serves as its content. What I want to show now is that it is a *different* sense of immediacy that is at issue in Kant's thesis that intuitions depend "immediately" upon things in themselves. This thesis is expressed, for example, in Kant's claim that an intuition is "a representation that would *depend* (*abhängen*) immediately on the presence (*Gegenwart*) of the object," with the context strongly suggesting that Kant has in mind intuitions of sense rather than imagination (*Prol* §9, 4:281; my italics). For if "object" here were taken to signify the relevant appearance, then the "dependence" at issue would be a quite trivial one, since it would only amount to a claim that there could be no intuition without an appearance "present" as its content. Without the appearance it contains, however, an intuition simply would not be the kind of representation that it is. What is more, the fact that Kant countenances intuitions *of the imagination* further suggests that the "presence" in mind cannot be mere phenomenological presence of intuitive content. In imagining there is clearly something we have "in mind"; on Kant's account, in imagining we even "represent an object *in intuition*"—even though, as Kant sees it, the object itself is precisely *not* "present" in the relevant sense (cf. B151).[19]

The "dependence" at issue in *Prolegomena* §9 and elsewhere points instead to the *causal* relation that Kant means to affirm between, on the one hand, an act of intuiting—or, seen from the represented object's point of view, the act of "appearing" (*erscheinen*) (B43, B59, B69; cf. *Prol*, 4:283, 287, etc.)—and, on the other, the object that is external to ourselves and our representations. This is the relation that Kant calls "affection." Kant introduces the concept of affection in the Aesthetic in the course of describing what is responsible for our having sensations. Sensations are said to be the "effect" (*Wirkung*) of an object "affecting" the "capacity for representation" possessed by our mind (B34). The having of sensations, therefore, depends on affection, and so also depends on there being some object affecting our mind. And because empirical intuitions, for Kant, "relate to their object *through* sensation" (B34; my italics), the having of an empirical intuition likewise depends upon affection and there being an affecting object. In fact, it is the affection-dependence of intuition that lies at the heart of what Kant means by calling our intuition "sensible":

> [Our] intuition is called sensible because...it is dependent (*abhängig*) on the existence (*Dasein*) of the object [and] is thus possible only insofar as the representational capacity of the subject is affected through that. (B72)

Now, though some have argued that Kant takes the affecting objects in question to be further appearances,[20] at several points Kant affirms a clear distinction between

[19] For some helpful discussion, see Stephenson (2015). Compare the parallel claim that thinking is a representation that depends immediately on the (phenomenological) presence of *its* content; this claim too must be true, since an act of thinking would not be what it is but for having the kind of content that it does (i.e., a concept or concepts). What an act of thinking of an object through such content does *not* depend immediately on is the presence of this *object* upon our capacity for thinking.

[20] For the classic defense of this so-called "empirical affection," see Adickes (1929), and more recently, see Stang (2015).

"actual" (*wirkliche*) affecting objects, on the one hand, and representations that they bring about or produce so as to allow us to become conscious of their appearance, on the other:

> There are things given to us as objects of our senses existing outside us, yet we know (*wissen*) nothing of them as they may be in themselves, but are *only* acquainted with (*kennen*) their appearances, i.e., with the representations that they produce (*wirken*) in us because they affect our senses. (*Prol*, 4:289; my italics)

A few sentences later, Kant identifies the affecting object as "an object with which we are *not* acquainted (*uns unbekannt*) but which is nevertheless *actual* (*wirklich*)" (4:289; my italics). Appearances, therefore, cannot be identified with these "actual" affecting objects, because we *are* "acquainted" with appearances. Kant instead links appearances to the representations that are involved in the effects or products of this affection. This point is made even more emphatically at the end of the Amphiboly, where Kant claims explicitly that "the cause of appearance" is "*not itself an appearance*," but instead "a transcendental object" (B344; my italics). In these passages and others, the affecting object gets cashed out by Kant in terms of something *other than* further appearances.[21]

All of this implies that we can and should distinguish two senses of immediacy that are at issue, for Kant, in relation to appearances—just as we did above with respect to the Fregean account (section 3.2). While it is right to note that an act of intuiting (and so, an act of "appearing") not only depends on there being a kind of phenomenological or representational existence and presence immediately *"in" consciousness*—namely, the existence and presence of an immediate object (i.e., an appearance)—it is also true that an intuiting or appearing depends as well on the real ("actual") existence and presence immediately *upon sensibility* of the affecting object (i.e., the ultimate intentional object of the intuition that the appearance qua immediate object itself represents). These kinds of immediacy are distinct even though the phenomenological immediacy "in" intuition (in mind) is itself possible only if the latter sort of causally immediate relation obtains. For the real concrete *causally* immediate relation that Kant takes to link an act of intuiting (appearing) with the *object* represented by the appearance is a distinct relation from the non-causal, yet *phenomenologically* immediate relation that Kant takes to obtain between the act of intuiting and the *appearance* itself.

[21] Compare *Prol* §32, where Kant writes that though he "admits" that a thing in itself "underlies" appearances, "the objects of the senses" are still to be viewed as "mere appearances," such that "we are not acquainted with [*kennen*] this thing [in itself underlying appearances] as it may be constituted in itself, but only with its appearance, i.e., with the way [*Art*] in which our senses are affected by this unknown something" (4:315). See also B594, B723–25, *Prol* §36, and *GMS*, 4:451.

For an affirmation of the reality of mental acts over and against appearances, see Van Cleve (1999, pp. 11, 51, 58–59). For a defense of Kant's entitlement to talk about this kind of affection (sometimes called "noumenal" affection), despite its not obtaining between appearances (within the phenomenal world), see Hogan (2009).

3.4 The Ideality of Appearances

This discussion leads quite naturally to see how the Fregean account of object-dependence can help us understand a key part of what Kant means by the ideality of appearances. Recall that Fregean senses are not themselves "real" or "actual" in the same sense as are either the mental acts that grasp them or (in perceptual cases) the concrete objects (references). Most importantly for our purposes, Fregean senses are not caused and do not bring about effects—even in cases where their reference is a concrete causally efficacious object and the act in which they are apprehended is the result (effect, product) of our mind's entering into real causal interaction with this object through sensation. Now, as our above analysis of affection suggests, Kant too accepts, first, that our mental acts of intuiting and sensing (and so the acts of appearing) are real insofar as they are effects of a cause, and also, secondly, that this cause itself is real or "actual." What is more, we have already seen Kant contrast appearances themselves with the "actual" object that functions as the cause of the mental acts in which these appearances are contained. If we could now show that Kant also means to contrast appearances with the "actual" *effects* of the affection-relation—i.e., with the mental acts themselves—then the relevant parallel with Fregean senses would be secured, and we will have been able to fill in a key part of what the Fregean interpretation takes Kant to mean by claiming that appearances are "transcendentally ideal" rather than real. Appearances would be the non-real, non-actual contents that representationally relate real mental acts with those real actual objects responsible for bringing these acts about.

It must be admitted up front that at times Kant seems to describe appearances themselves as if *they* were the results or products of affection (e.g., *Prol*, 4:289), rather than the mental acts in which they are contained—i.e., the intuitions. The first thing to note, however, is that a kind of ambiguity is present in the word "appearance" and its German correlate *Erscheinung*. As many have pointed out, this word can either be used to pick out an act of appearing or that which appears in such an act—much like "representation" (*Vorstellung*) can be used to pick out the act of representing or that which is represented in such an act.[22] Once we bring this ambiguity clearly in mind, it is at least open to us to read the passages in which Kant speaks of appearances as effects of affection as cases in which Kant is using the term "appearance" to pick out the mental act of appearing that arises due to affection, rather than the content of this act.

This reading of some uses of "appearance" is further encouraged by the fact that at *other* places, Kant makes clear that he is using "appearance" to pick out instead something analytically distinct from all such acts (as effects), something that plays the role of the content of these acts. In fact, we have already met with a key piece of evidence for drawing such a distinction, one that comes from the canonical formulation of affection that Kant gives at the outset of the Aesthetic. For here it is specifically *sensation* and not appearance that is called the "effect" of affection (B34). And immediately

[22] For a classic reflection on this point, see Sellars (1968, pp. 33–40); for a more recent discussion, see Van Cleve (1999, p. 7).

thereafter, though Kant explicitly links sensation to the "matter" of appearance, Kant also differentiates sensation from this matter by calling this matter "that *in* the appearance which *corresponds* to sensation" (B34; my italics). Kant makes a similar distinction in the Anticipations, describing "the real," in the empirical sense, as both something "*in* all appearances" and as "the *object* of sensation" (B207; my italics).[23] This again implies that, for Kant, it is not a sensation itself that is "in" an appearance (as a "real" part, as its "matter"); what is "in" the appearance is rather the immediate object of sensation, something that "corresponds" to sensation.[24]

This distinction between sensation and the matter of appearance is confirmed by the further relation Kant portrays as obtaining between the matter and the *form* of appearance, and is especially evident from considerations of space as the form of outer appearance. Kant claims that the matter of appearance is something that is ordered "in" the form of appearance (B34), with space serving as that form within which the matter of outer appearances is ordered. Now, if sensations were identical with the matter of appearances in general and with the matter of outer appearances in particular, then Kant would be forced into a position according to which sensations—and so, mental acts or states themselves—would have to occupy space and have spatial locations. That Kant would reject this position follows from his claims, first, that neither thinking beings nor their thoughts, feelings, or other "inner" states can come before us in outer appearance (A357–58), and, secondly, that space cannot be "intuited as something in us" (B37), which means it cannot be intuited (in pure intuition) as what contains that which is in us (unlike time, which can be intuited "in us" and which can (and does) contain (the appearance of) sensations themselves).[25] If we allow instead for the distinction between sensation and the matter of appearance, by contrast, we need only take Kant to be claiming that it is that which *corresponds* to sensation "in" the appearance which is "in" the space of intuition.

The fact that there is a correspondence, rather than identity, between sensation and the matter of appearance strongly suggests that there should be a similar correspondence, though not identity, between space as the form of an outer appearance and whatever representation it is that has space as its content. And this is, in fact, what we find. For though Kant at times seems to describe space itself as if it were an intuition (cf. B39)—in a manner quite similar to the way he at times slides between the matter of appearance and sensation—at other times Kant shows that he means to draw a distinction between space as the form of outer appearance and the intuition that would "contain" this form (i.e., contain space) and nothing else. It is this latter act that Kant calls a "pure intuition," a representation *in which* space as "the form of all appearances" is "given to the mind" (B42), rather than the space that is given in such an intuiting.[26]

[23] In the A edition Paralogisms Kant describes sensation as "that which designates (*bezeichnet*) a reality in space and time, according to whether it is related to the one or the other sensible intuition" (A373–74).

[24] See also B182 and *Prol* §24 (4:306) and §26 (4:309). Compare as well Aquila (1989, pp. 6–8) and Jankowiak (2014).

[25] For an attempt to interpret sensations as spatial for Kant, by viewing them as states of (parts of) our bodies, despite these (and other) worries, see Falkenstein (1995, ch. 3).

[26] There are further complications here concerning how the Fregean interpretive model I am developing should articulate the relation between the act of pure intuiting, its content (the space immediately

If we now combine the initial distinction between sensation and the matter of appearance which it represents or has corresponding to it, with this distinction between pure intuition and the form of appearance which *it* "contains," we arrive at a picture of an appearance as whole—an appearance as a unity which involves both form and matter—as something that is itself a correlate of the composite act that arises out of the combination of sensation with pure intuition, the act that Kant calls "empirical intuition" (B34). But then, as an appearance is a *correlate* to these acts—more specifically, it is that which is given immediately "in" these acts, as their content (cf. section 3.2)—rather than something that is *identical* to these acts, the appearance itself (as content) cannot be said to be an effect of affection in the same way as these acts themselves are effects. Appearances in this sense are, strictly speaking, not effects of affection *at all*; *only* the mental acts (sensing, intuiting, appearing) are.

Qua contents of intuition, then, appearances are neither the causes nor the effects of affection, despite nevertheless being "contained" in the results of this affection. With this clarification in mind, we are now in a position to see how the Fregean interpretation will provide us with a unique and informative gloss on Kant's well-known claim that appearances are transcendentally "ideal" rather than "real." One of the most common ways Kant unpacks the ideality of appearances is in terms of the fact that appearances exist only "in" representations, i.e., only "in" the representational "relation" that we bear toward some further object, rather than "in themselves":

[A]ppearances exist only *in* representation (*in der Vorstellung*)...(B534)
[A]ppearances do not exist *in themselves* (*an sich*), but only *relative to* [a subject] insofar as it has senses. (B164; my italics)
[A]ppearances in general are nothing (*nichts*) outside our representations, which is just what we mean by their transcendental ideality. (B535)

An appearance itself thus "exists" or is "actual" only in the sense that it is what is contained "in" acts that involve sensations that come about through the real (actual) affection of sensibility by real objects—not because the appearance *itself* is existent in the sense of being "actual" (*wirklich*), i.e., causally efficacious. Predicating actuality of the appearance itself is thus parasitic on its serving as the content of a sensation-involving mental act which is actual—whether this is the initial empirical intuition in which the appearance is first "given," or the act of becoming "conscious" of the appearance in what Kant calls "perception" (*Wahrnehmung*) (cf. B160), or the act of combining such perceptions (and their contents) into an "experience" (*Erfahrung*) (cf. B218). As Kant clarifies in the Dialectic, appearances are thus themselves to be considered "actual" only thanks to the actuality (or real possibility) of very specific mental *acts* in which they would be contained:

given in pure intuition), and the ultimate object that is represented by this content (i.e., by intuitive space). Elsewhere I argue that the further object which is represented by (but not identical to) intuitive space is what Kant calls "physical" and "empirical" space, the space which is filled by corporeal substances and which is not "given" a priori but only a posteriori (cf. *MAN*, 4:481); see Tolley (2016).

> To call an appearance an actual [*wirkliches*] thing prior to perception means either that in the continuation of experience we must encounter such a perception, or it has no meaning at all. [...] [W]hat is in them (appearances) is not something in itself, but mere representations, which if they are not given in us (in perception) are encountered nowhere at all. (B521–22)

Now, it is true that Kant at times unpacks the ideality of appearances simply in terms of appearances existing only "in our mind" (B520), or "in the sensibility of our subject" (A383), "in us" or even as existing only "in me" (cf. A129, A375, A378). This can make it sound as though appearances must be *private* to each individual, and ultimately must be some kind of radically indexical *monadic* property of that individual. If this were Kant's final word, then appearances would contrast sharply with Fregean senses, insofar as Fregean senses would seem to be non-private (since more "objective" than what is merely psychological) and non-monadic (since relational, as a "way of being given" something else (the *Bedeutung*)).

Even so, grounds for ascribing a (relative) publicness to appearances emerges already in the Aesthetic. In §8, for example, though Kant initially puts his thesis of the ideality of appearances in terms of their existence only "in" an individual subject, he then immediately rephrases the thesis in terms of their existence "in" the subjective constitution of human subjects "in general."[27] Immediately thereafter Kant returns to this point, noting that though "our way of perceiving" things "is peculiar to us" and "therefore does not necessarily pertain to every being (*Wesen*)," it *does* nevertheless "pertain to every human being (*Mensch*)" (B59; cf. B62). The relevant context for the existence of appearances is therefore not restricted to what is "in" any one human mind, but rather what could be (potentially) "in" any human mind. And once we recall the texts presented above (in section 3.2), in which Kant clearly spells out the relationality involved in appearances, it is then open to us to see the claims which might seem to characterize appearances as monadic predicates of subjects as instead a kind of shorthand for the more fully expressed point that appearances only have their being or existence "in" a relation that involves us (and is (in some sense) "contained" in us), but nevertheless points beyond us in the manner of a representation relating to its object.

What cannot be emphasized enough, however, is the specificity of which entities Kant is claiming are "transcendentally ideal." First, ideality is predicated of *appearances*, as contained "in" acts of representing, and *not* predicated of the mental *acts* (of sensation, intuition, perception, etc.) in which appearances are contained. Kant nowhere claims that the mental acts of representing objects by way of appearances are also transcendentally ideal. Second, Kant is not claiming that the *causes* of such acts—i.e., the affecting *objects* responsible for bringing about sensations, the further "object = X" which is thereby represented by an appearance (cf. section 3.1 above)—are

[27] Compare: "All our intuition is nothing but the representation of appearance; [...] if we remove *our own* subject or even only the subjective constitution of the senses *in general*, then all constitution, all relations of objects in space and time, indeed space and time themselves would disappear; [...] as appearances they cannot exist in themselves (*an sich selbst*), but only *in us*" (B59; my italics).

transcendentally ideal. As we have seen above, these objects are explicitly distinguished from appearances, and serve as the (real) "ground" of acts of appearing (cf. section 3.3).

To articulate what it could mean for Kant to restrict his thesis of ideality to appearances, rather than be forced to extend it to include either the affecting objects or the acts which their affection brings about (sensing, intuiting), we need to be able to distinguish appearances from both the causes and from the effects of such affection. The Fregean interpretive framework handles this specificity quite nicely, insofar as it sees this particular focus on appearances as Kant simply claiming *solely* that the *contents* of intuitions are transcendental ideal. For the Fregean, too, wishes to emphasize, first, that senses are not identical with any of the real, psychological states in which they are grasped, nor are they made up of such states, nor are they real "component parts" of such states; and emphasize, secondly, that senses are *also* not identical to their references.

This peculiar intermediary standing is what moved Frege to claim that senses form a "third realm." And though many have taken Frege's introduction of a third realm of sense to be ontologically extravagant, we can now better see that the peculiarities of this realm actually share much in common with the peculiarities of the "world" that Kant himself introduces as that which contains all appearances: "the world of sense," "the sensible world," "the world of appearances" (Bxxvii, B63, B312, B409, B447, B839; *Prol* §32 (4:314), §54 (4:354), etc.). For just like the denizens of the Fregean third realm, Kant's appearances are not identical with either the real things that they represent or with the real mental acts in which they are contained, nor are they made up of any real parts of these acts. This is in addition to the parallel that we established above (section 3.1): just like the denizens of the Fregean third realm, the items in Kant's world of appearances occupy a third representational relation slot between (transcendentally real) subjects and (transcendentally real) things.

4. Contrasting the Fregean Interpretation with Several Prominent Alternatives

In the previous section I have developed a novel interpretation of Kant's appearances along the lines of Fregean object-dependent senses. More specifically, I have argued that, like the Fregean account of intuition, Kant's account of empirical intuition also involves a threefold distinction between act, content, and object, with Kant introducing a further distinction between form and matter within both the act and content. We can summarize the resulting picture as in Table 9.3 (cf. Table 9.2).

On this model, the relationship that Kant ultimately takes to obtain between the act of intuiting and the appearance that it involves is something that is a much closer kin to the relationship between what we saw above (in section 2) Frege calling the act of "grasping" (*erfassen*) a sense and the sense itself that is grasped, *rather than* either a relationship which corresponds to that between an act of grasping and the ultimate *object* (Fregean reference) represented by (or "given" through) the sense grasped, or the relation between an act and a real "part" of this act. Just as Fregean senses are (i*) the immediate objects of cognitive acts—what is "grasped" in them—so too are appearances (i) the *immediate* objects of intuitions. Yet just as Fregean senses are (ii*)

Table 9.3. Kant's account of appearances

(real) **(a) mental act**	**(ideal)** **(b) representational "content"** **(*Inhalt*)**	**(real)** **(c) represented object**
empirical intuiting [contains →] as composed of:	appearance [represents →] as composed of:	"something = X" represented by appearance
(1) pure intuiting [contains →]	(1) form (e.g, space)	
(2) sensing [contains →]	(2) matter (the "real")	
[←	—	— causes]

ways of representing further objects (references), so too are appearances (ii) *representations* of something beyond themselves, a transcendental "object = x." And just as the object represented by a Fregean object-dependent sense is not contained in the sense itself as a constituent or component part, despite (iv*) the necessity of the mind standing in a real relation to this object in order to undergo the act of grasping the relevant sense, so too are the objects represented by appearances not contained in the appearance itself as constituents or component parts, even though the intuiting of the appearance is (iv) *dependent* on a real relation of affection obtaining between the mind and this object. Finally, just as a Fregean sense is (iii*) a non-actual object (content), so too is (iii) an appearance a non-actual, *ideal* object (content), with the Fregean account cashing out a key part of Kant's thesis of the ideality of appearances by emphasizing that the only real causal relationship that is involved in the having of an intuition is that between (c) the thing and (a) the act, since (b) the content is not itself something that is in possession of causal powers.

Having now laid out the basics of the Fregean interpretation, and having brought to light some of the important features of Kant's account that it allows us to capture, let me now say how this interpretation differs from some of the more well-known and more sophisticated alternatives currently on offer.

4.1 Upholding the Representationality of Appearances

The first account of appearances that the Fregean account should be contrasted with is what I will call the *simple phenomenalist* account. On this account, appearances are to be *identified with* bundles of sensations that result from affection. Versions of this view were more prominent at the end of the nineteenth century and the early twentieth, with Hermann Cohen, H. A. Pritchard, and Norman Kemp Smith as some of its more distinguished proponents.[28] Now, as we have noted above (section 3.4), there are certainly some passages in which Kant speaks about appearances themselves as if they were simply the effects of affection. Even so, we have also noted that there are further texts that suggest that, strictly speaking, it is only sensation that is the effect of affection, rather than the appearance or its corresponding matter. In fact, Cohen, Pritchard, and Kemp Smith themselves all draw attention to places where Kant contrasts sensation and the matter of appearance, though they each think that this represents an aberration on Kant's part and continue to privilege the other passages.[29] As we have seen, however, rather than dismissing such texts, we can instead take them as providing reason for thinking that it is the passages used to support simple phenomenalism which are in need of a more careful analysis. I have presented one such alternative analysis above, which would let "appearance" in these passages refer to the *act* of appearing, which we have aligned with the act of (empirical) intuiting, rather than to the *content* of this act.[30]

The recognition of the distinction between sensation and appearance has been used recently by Richard Aquila and James Van Cleve to develop what I will call a more *sophisticated* version of *phenomenalism*.[31] Like the Fregean interpretation above, Aquila argues that we should distinguish between intuitions as acts of "sensory apprehension" and what he calls the "intentional correlate" of such acts, with appearances qua objects of intuition being then understood as mere intentional correlates rather than as real parts of the act of intuiting, or as being "made out of sensations" (1989, p. 7; cf. p. 28 and 1979, pp. 301–302 and 308n22). Similarly, Van Cleve (1999) has also argued that we should view appearances as the intentional objects of mental acts, which he takes to make them only "virtual" objects, and so rules them out from having real sensations as their parts (p. 8).

Now, the Fregean interpretation joins readers like Aquila and Van Cleve in distinguishing the acts of sensation and empirical intuition from the appearances that are immediately given through such intuitions—and in also wanting to do so in a way that captures the ideality of appearances in contrast to the reality of mental acts. Nevertheless, the Fregean interpretation ultimately distinguishes itself from the sophisticated phenomenalism of both Aquila and Van Cleve by emphasizing the *further* representationality of these ideal intentional correlates themselves. For both Aquila and Van Cleve, appearances are "merely" the intentional *object* of certain mental acts, and neither recognizes that Kant means to ascribe to appearances a further representational *relation* to things beyond themselves. Though Van Cleve, for example, accepts that appearances are "what is represent*ed*" in certain acts (1999, p. 7), there is no recognition that appearances themselves also represent further objects. And though Aquila recognizes that appearances form the "content" of certain acts, Aquila proposes that we should view this notion through the lens of *Brentano's* account of content, according to which the content of a representation *just is* the

[28] See Cohen (1907, p. 27), Pritchard (1909, pp. 74–75), and Kemp Smith (1918, pp. 83–84).

[29] Cf. Cohen (1885, pp. 150–56 and 433–34), Pritchard (1909, p. 75), and Kemp Smith (1918, p. 84).

[30] For further criticisms of the simple phenomenalist interpretation, see (Allais 2004, pp. 660–65) and McLear (2016, §5.1).

[31] See Aquila (1979, 1989), and Van Cleve (1999). Aquila (2003) also attributes a similar view to Vaihinger (1892). Compare, more recently, the sophisticated phenomenalism developed by Jankowiak (2017).

object toward which the representation is directed, with this object "in-existing" in the representation itself (2003, p. 238).[32] Van Cleve, too, accepts a broadly Brentanian understanding of intentionality, one which works only with an act-object distinction, rather than the threefold act-content-object distinction present in the Fregean picture (1999, p. 10).[33] But then, by taking appearances to be Brentanian contents, and so to be "*mere* intentional objects," these interpretations fail to adequately keep in view the sense in which appearances themselves (as akin to Fregean sense-contents) representationally relate us to some further thing.[34]

4.2 Upholding the Ideality of Appearances

Another way to put the foregoing contrast is that while both the simple and sophisticated phenomenalist accounts view appearances (at best) only as the objects of certain mental acts, the Fregean interpretation holds that an appearance itself is essentially *relational*, in two respects. First, it holds that the appearance is *representationally* relational insofar as it consists in a particular way in which something further is given or represented to the mind (an *Art des Gegebenseins*). Secondly, it holds that the appearance is implicated essentially in a specifically *causal* relationality, insofar as the grasping of the appearance (and its representational relation) is object-dependent in the sense specified above, in that a real causal relation of affection by the object represented is necessary to intuit the appearance that represents this affecting object itself.

In its emphasis on the relation of an appearance to real affecting objects, the Fregean interpretation is closer, therefore, to the more recent "relationalist" approach by Rae Langton. Where the Fregean differs from Langton is in rejecting the idea that an appearance should be *identified* with the *real* relation between the mind of a subject and an affecting object. The distance between the two positions can be seen in the fact that Langton (1998) slides between considering an appearance as a relation, as a relational property (cf. p. 128), and as an "object in a relation" (p. 22). While the Fregean will accept the general point that a representation of an object *includes* or *involves* a kind of relation to that object, the Fregean will reject the idea that, in general, the representation should itself be thought of as a relational *property of* the object that it represents. Just as Fregean senses are not relational properties of

[32] Incidentally, the fact that Aquila does not take care to draw the distinction between his own Brentanian understanding of content as the intentional in-existence of an object and the Fregean understanding of content as sense ultimately vitiates Aquila's (2003) discussion of what Sellars (1968) means by "content." Aquila (2003, p. 238) assumes that Sellars has a Brentanian picture of content in mind, whereas Sellars (1968, pp. 65–66) indicates that he has in mind something much closer to Fregean sense.

[33] Perhaps unlike Brentano, however, Van Cleve (1999, pp. 9–10) argues that we should ultimately analyze the notion of intentional directedness in "adverbial" terms, transforming what seems to be a relation to a virtual object into a monadic predicate of an act or a subject.

[34] Vaihinger also presents a kind of phenomenalist interpretation, though it is less clear of which sort. Though Vaihinger (1892, p. 34), too, notes the importance of the notion of "content" (*Inhalt*) for Kant's account of intuitions, he also seems to think we can only understand this content either in the simple phenomenalist terms of sense-data or in the more sophisticated phenomenalist (Brentanian) terms of the intentional object of such sense-data.

their references, so too are Kantian appearances not relational properties of the objects they represent.

Here it is worth recalling Kant's above alignment of appearances with aspects of images. Though an image (e.g., a picture or photo) bears a special relation to its object, the image itself is not a relational property of its object, nor is the representational relation at issue one that can be said to belong to this object as a property.[35] This is so, even if there are additional, though distinct, relational properties that *are* borne by the object of an image, in virtue of being pictured by this image—e.g., the property of being represented by the image, of being represented to the mind from the points of view and sides that are portrayed by the image, and so on. The key point is simply that none of these further properties are *identical* with either the image itself or with the appearances that contributed their looks to the image's formation.[36]

Now, as we saw above, the distinction the Fregean draws between the real causal relation (and relational properties) and the ideal representational relation is precisely what allows the Fregean room to give conceptual significance to Kant's restricted version of idealism—namely, that appearances, and *appearances only*, are ideal rather than real. As many of her critics have emphasized, Langton, by contrast, has a very difficult time accounting for why her focus on the real relationality of appearances will be sufficient to explain their ideality, in any interesting sense of this term.[37] This is because, on Langton's account, the appearance of an object is just one case *among many* of "objects in a relation" (1998, p. 22; see also pp. 11, 19). Yet as Langton herself acknowledges (and indeed nicely demonstrates), Kant himself accepts that there are not just ideal but also real relations (see Langton, 1998, ch. 5), which implies that simply being an "object in a relation" is not sufficient to render the object ideal.

Langton's more specific strategy for marking what is distinctive about appearances as ideal relations would seem to be to articulate them on the model of Lockean secondary qualities, such that the relations involved in an appearance are ideal because one of the relata is a mind (Langton, 1998, pp. 155–62). This *alone*, however, is unsatisfactory as it would *also* render ideal the affection-relation that we have seen is responsible for sensations, since this relation, too, surely has the mind as one of its relata. But if affection were also merely an ideal relation, then the picture we would be left with is one in which there is *no* real relation or real connection whatsoever between the mind and the things beyond the appearances.[38] Conversely, if we instead

[35] Here it may be useful to return to the graphical illustration of this sort of view by Searle (1958), by reference to pipes and bowls. While it is surely true that pipes (senses) relate us to their bowls (references), it would be wrong to say that any pipe *is* a relational property of its bowl (or that the pipe is *the bowl itself* "in a relation"). Rather, the pipes enable or involve a relation to their bowls.

[36] A further textual point: though (as we have seen) there are a number of passages in which Kant describes appearances as involving *relations to* objects, at least to my knowledge Kant never says explicitly that the appearances themselves are *properties of* them. Furthermore, even if we were to grant that property talk in general *is* a way to capture the ontology of appearances, there would seem to be equal reason for converting the relation involved in an appearance into a relational property *of the subject*, rather than the object (as Langton would have it). Compare Kant's description of colors as "not attaching to the object in itself as properties," but only "to the sense of vision as modifications" (*Prol*, 4:289).

[37] See, e.g., Moore (2001, pp. 118–19). In her Conclusion, Langton herself actually appears to imply that Kant's language of idealism might be best understood as a manner of speaking in which Kant ultimately *misrepresents* his own position (1998, pp. 205–18).

[38] For more discussion of this point, see Ameriks (2001, pp. 156–57).

insist on the reality of affection (as I have done above), then Langton's criterion of mind-relatedness will not be sufficient for singling out what is distinctively ideal about appearances themselves, raising the worry that appearance-relations will simply collapse, on Langton's account, into a subset of the real relations that there are between subjects with minds and things external to them.

4.3 Upholding the Immediacy of Appearances

This points to a further distinction between the real relationalist account of appearances provided by Langton and the Fregean interpretation. Langton says very little about why Kant would be so at pains to continuously tie the ideality of appearances with a specifically *representational* context. Unsurprisingly, Langton also says very little about why Kant would talk about specific kinds of representational entities (appearances themselves) as the sole *immediate* objects of certain mental acts, in sharp contrast to the objects to which appearances ultimately representationally relate us. Put in the terms we have introduced above (section 3.2), while Langton's account is perhaps well-suited to accommodate the *causal* immediacy involved in affection and underwriting sensation and intuition, Langton says very little about the *phenomenological* immediacy of appearances themselves and their function "in" consciousness (in perception) to allow for experience (empirical cognition) of the objects responsible for the affection in the first place.

Along with Tobias Rosefeldt (2007), Colin McLear (2014), and Anil Gomes (2014), Lucy Allais (2004, 2007, 2010, 2011a, 2011b, and, most fully, 2015) has sought to remedy Langton's relationalist account precisely by trying to re-emphasize the representationality of appearances. In this respect, Allais and others draw another step closer to the Fregean interpretation. At least for her part, however, Allais (along with McLear and Gomes) then tries to provide a *direct realist* account of the representational relation involved in appearances, according to which appearances are representational only in the sense of being what is "directly presented" to the mind in intuition. This leaves Allais's account, too, at a crucial remove from the Fregean account spelled out above, due to her distinctly non-Fregean understanding of the immediacy of appearances.[39]

The version of direct realism that Allais means to use to articulate Kant's views on appearances and intuitions is what Allais calls a "relational" view of perceptual experience (Allais 2011b, p. 376; cf. Allais 2011a, p. 93). What Allais has in mind by direct realist relationalism about perception is a view that has its roots in Russell's conception of acquaintance, though Allais herself refers to more recent work by John Campbell and others.[40] According to direct realism, a veridical perception has as its content the ultimate object of the perception (Allais, 2011a, p. 93), with the object

[39] Rosefeldt, to my knowledge, does not make such a strong claim on behalf of the direct realist interpretation, though he appears to be critical of what he calls "indirect realist" interpretations (along with the "mere intentional object" interpretations); see Rosefeldt (2007, §4).

[40] This view has also gone under the name of "austere relationalism," endorsed by Charles Travis and others. In addition to Allais and the others cited above, McDowell (1991b, p. 26) has also aimed to develop a version of Kantianism, if not an interpretation of Kant, that would be compatible with a kind of direct

itself thereby featuring as a "constituent" of the perception (Allais 2011b, pp. 379–80). For Allais, intuitions are veridical perceptions in this sense:

> [I]ntuitions represent objects *immediately* because they *present* the object itself, as opposed to referring to an object through the mediation of further representations.... Immediacy says that an intuition is not simply a representation which is caused by a particular thing, but that it is in fact a *presentation to consciousness of that thing*. (Allais, 2010, p. 59)

The sort of "immediacy" that pertains to an intuition consists, therefore, in the fact that its object is directly "present to consciousness" (Allais, 2011b, p. 383). Indeed, Allais claims that this (along with their mind-dependence) is more or less *all* that is meant by Kant's claim that appearances are representations—namely, that appearances are things which present us with objects directly, where (to repeat) this means that they do so without making use of any other representations (Allais, 2011b, p. 385).

This way of construing an appearance shares a key feature in common with the earlier Brentanian conception of the content of an intuition we met with above (cf. section 4.1): the content of an intuition just is the object of the intuition, where this is exhausted by what is immediately presented "in" the intuition, rather than the content being first and foremost a way of representing some further object. In fact, there would seem to be a direct parallel between Allais's claim that the object forms a real "constituent" of the act and Brentano's claim that the intentional object of an act "in-exists" the act itself (see Brentano, 1874, p. 115).

Despite these parallels, however, Allais is quite concerned to reject the phenomenalism about appearances that such Brentanian ideas have been used to articulate (Allais, 2011b, p. 378). This is because, for Allais, the object being presented in an appearance *is* a real thing, and not a "merely" intentionally in-existing phenomenon. In fact, the appearance is nothing other than *the thing* appearing by way of the appearance, what we saw Kant above call a "something = X." And even if this thing is being presented in a way other than as it is in itself (cf. Allais, 2011b, p. 387), it is still *this thing* that is immediately present in an appearance as its "constituent" and no other. Indeed, it is crucial to Allais's *realism* that she keeps firm hold of the idea that in intuition we are immediately "given" this real object itself: we are given "the things themselves," and not some representational intermediate (cf. Allais 2007, p. 479; 2011b, p. 392).[41]

Now, as we saw in section 2, Fregean accounts of perceptual content would resist this analysis of the immediate objects of our intuition. For the Fregean, the ultimate

realism, such that what is intuited or perceived is nothing short of "how things are" or "aspects of the layout of the world."

[41] Compare the following two remarks: "The view we are considering allows it to be a possibility that the way things visually appear may differ from the way they are in themselves, even though the visual appearing is something which *essentially involves the objects*, and not something which exists merely mentally" (Allais, 2011b, p. 387; my italics); "[A]lthough seeing is relational in the sense that *the object is essentially present to consciousness*, it does not follow from this that the way the object is seen as being is entirely the way it is apart from its being seen, or that seeing is entirely transparent" (Allais, 2011b, p. 387; my italics).

object (referent) *never* forms a "component part" of the sense that is immediately and directly grasped in a cognitive act. All that is grasped "in" the act is a sense, i.e., a representational relation to this further object. And in section 3 we saw Kant saying parallel things about appearances: though he takes appearances to be object-*dependent* contents, he does not take them to be object-*involving* or object-*containing* contents, in the sense that he does not think that appearances "contain" things in themselves or any of their parts or properties as constituents.[42] It is difficult, therefore, to see how Kant could possibly accept that appearances make *their* objects—the "somethings = x," or things in themselves, that they represent—directly or immediately "present to consciousness," in the phenomenological sense, in such a way that these objects *would be* "contained" within the appearance as a component part, and as "present" in the mind as the appearance itself. Rather, to repeat what we found above, what Kant himself says *is* "contained" in an appearance is not its object (or any thing in itself) but rather a special kind of *relation* (*Beziehung, Verhältniß*) to its object; more specifically, it is a representational relation. This ultimate object (the transcendental "object = x") forms no part of the content of the intuition, and so is not itself immediately present *in consciousness* (is not phenomenologically immediate)—even if this object is immediately present *to sensibility* in the real causal relation of affection (cf. section 3.3).[43]

Finally, Allais's direct realist account of appearances will be hard-pressed to make sense of the connection we saw Kant draw between appearances and images. By Allais's own lights, an image of an object is clearly something that stands "intermediate"

[42] Here let me simply note Allais's tendency to identify an appearance with a "property" of the thing that appears—namely, the property of its "appearing" a certain way: "the appearing is something public, a property of the physical object" (2007, p. 472). Following out this tendency would, I think, bring Allais's picture much closer to Langton's than Allais suspects. For the Fregean, even though there is a property of the sort that Allais and Langton wish to emphasize, this property itself should not be *identified* with the appearance, since the appearance (understood as the content of an intuition) is a *representation* of the thing, rather than a property of it. Allais seems to be aware of this distinction, but she instead aligns the "perceptual experience" embodied in an intuition with what represents the thing, rather than the appearance itself (2007, p. 473).

This same tendency can also be seen in Allais's proposal that we should view the mind-dependent though public nature of appearances as more or less on par with the mind-dependent though public nature of secondary qualities (see esp. Allais, 2007). This way of construing the publicness of appearances would again seem to mistake the object of an appearance (or, perhaps, features of this object) for the appearance itself (or, perhaps, what is contained in the appearance itself). Rather than appearances themselves being akin to publicly perceivable secondary *qualities* of things in themselves (or being made up of such qualities), it would seem, at best, that appearances could be akin to publicly available *ways of representing* such qualities. For a more recent analysis of color that incorporates this distinction between the ontological (though still subject-relative) relation that constitutes a *color* (or a color "quality") and the representational relation that is involved "in" a *color-appearance* (i.e., in color "phenomenology"), see Cohen (2009, ch. 6).

[43] The Fregean account would thus reject interpreting intuitions on the model of direct realism's acquaintance for the same reason as it would reject the earlier phenomenalist accounts: regardless of whether what is given "in" an intuition is taken to be a collection or sense-data, or a "merely" intentional (virtual) object, or an "apparent" property of a real thing, or the real thing itself (though in a way different than it is), all of these options fail to make clear that what is immediately present "in" consciousness in intuition is a representation (representational relation) to some further thing and not the thing itself. In the terms we have developed above, the Fregean account insists against both phenomenalisms and Allais's direct realist relationalist approach that an appearance is a content of an intuition and not its ultimate intentional object. For a more recent attempt to defend a direct realist account, according to which the contents of intuitions are "partially constituted" by physical environment, see McLear (2014, §5.2).

between the mind and the imaged object (cf. Allais, 2011b, pp. 386 and 396 n. 25). Yet Kant takes appearances to serve as that out of which images of objects are formed, as we saw above (cf. section 3.1). It is unclear how this could be possible unless appearances themselves were at the same level, representationally speaking, as the resultant images, and so were exactly as "intermediate" as the images themselves. But if this is right, then it is hard to see how we could avoid drawing just the conclusion that Allais wants to resist—namely, that an intuition *does* "refer to its object through the mediation of a further representation" (Allais, 2010, p. 59), since it "refers to" its object by means of the object's appearance.

4.4 A New Approach to Kant's Two Worlds

In distancing itself from both Langton and Allais, the Fregean interpretation also distances itself from the more familiar versions of the "one-world" interpretations of Kant's transcendental idealism. The Fregean interpretation insists that the only "real" things there are in the real world are the things affecting the subject and the affected subject, and that appearances do not belong to this world, neither as parts nor as properties of real things nor as (real) relations between things. For this reason, the Fregean interpretation is committed to a version of the "two-world" interpretation of transcendental idealism. It accepts that there are peculiar kinds of entities that are not identical with either subjects or things in themselves.

For this reason, the Fregean interpretation will also differ from so-called "methodological" one-world theorists like Henry Allison, who consider the distinction between the appearance of something and the thing "in itself" to consist ultimately only in a difference in the kind of standpoint we are taking on the thing in question, or a difference in the way in which we are "considering" that thing (see esp. Allison, 2004). Just as a Fregean sense is distinct from its referent, so too an appearance of something is genuinely distinct from that thing. An appearance is not that same *thing* simply "considered" in a different way, but rather a *way* of representing that thing, *in contrast to* the thing itself.[44]

As I have also tried to emphasize in the preceding, however, the Fregean interpretation leads away from more familiar phenomenalist two-world pictures and toward a decidedly non-traditional two-world interpretation. For one thing, it rejects the simple phenomenalist idea that the world of appearances should be seen as the realm of (typically: psychologically inner) sense-data. It also rejects the sophisticated phenomenalist idea that this world is sufficiently characterized as a realm of merely intentional objects or constructions out of sense-data (virtual objects). While most two-world theorists would accept that some sort of dependence obtains between the world of appearances and that of things in themselves, they cash out this dependence-relation purely in terms of the (second) ideal world of appearances being *caused by* the (first) world of things in themselves. The Fregean interpretation, by contrast, insists that there is ultimately only a real *causal* dependence of acts of intuiting upon

[44] For a nice summary of further difficulties with this sort of approach, see Watkins (2005, pp. 317–23) as well as Van Cleve (1999, pp. 143–62).

these things, whereas it is the *representational* connection that is essential to the link between appearances (qua contents) and things in themselves. Just as Fregean senses are non-actual, so too are Kant's appearances ideal, which makes it impossible for them to depend on affecting objects in a straightforwardly causal manner. On the Fregean interpretation, appearances themselves, qua ideal contents, are dependent upon the things in themselves *only* to provide them (i.e., appearances) with their *intentional* objects (their *Bedeutungen*). (This is in contrast to "appearings" qua acts; cf. sections 3.3–3.4 above.) This is just the non-causal sort of dependence that Fregean senses have toward their references, due to the essential connection they bear to their references, via a relation of intentionality or representationality (cf. section 3.3).

Finally, the analogy with object-dependent senses also points the way toward a distinctive interpretation of what Kant means by ascribing to appearances and their forms (space and time) an "empirical reality" (cf. B44, B52, B54, A370–71). Perhaps the most familiar way of understanding this is that Kant thinks appearances themselves are empirically real because they are *identical with* the substances and causes that we represent in what Kant calls "experience" (*Erfahrung*). Against this, the Fregean interpretation insists that appearances form only part of the *content* of experience, reserving the term "substance" and "cause" for those *objects* that we represent ("determine") *through* appearances (and concepts) in experience. What is empirically real, then, is also limited to these actual substances and causes (the objects of experience), rather than appearances qua what is immediately present "in" our intuitions, since these are ideal.

Kant takes an experience to be composed of intuition and judgment (cf. *Prol* §21a, 4:304). The judgment specifies the concept through which the object whose appearance is contained in an intuition is to be thought, the concept through which the object that "appears" by way of the appearance is to be thought.[45] But then, rather than taking any appearance itself to *be* a substance or cause, experience consists in the cognition of substances and causes *through* appearances—i.e., through intuitions and perceptions.[46] Experience occurs by using the consciousness of appearances that is supplied in perceptions to "determine" what further objects are thereby being represented by these appearances themselves, by judging appearances to representationally relate us to further objects, on the basis of features of the appearances themselves. Tellingly, the Principles (Analogies) which give the rules for constituting experience in particular, as judgments about substances and causes by way of appearances, are principles which Kant says explicitly "do not concern appearances" per se, but rather "*existence*" (*Dasein*) and the relation of "[appearances] to one another with respect to this existence of theirs (*in Ansehung dieses ihres Daseins*)" (B220).

On the Fregean interpretation, appearances can still be what are responsible for a distinctive representational connection to the real substances and causes represented in experience, without being viewed as identical to these objects or belonging to the same realm as them. More specifically, appearances provide the only *object-dependent* part of the content of the experiences that represent these objects. It is only by

[45] Compare: "all experience contains in addition to the intuition of the senses, through which something is given, a concept of an object that is given in intuition, or appears" (B126).

[46] Compare: "Experience is an empirical cognition, i.e., a cognition that determines an object *through* perceptions" (B218; my italics).

including appearances in its content that experience gains the representational link to real substances and causes that suffices for "cognition" (*Erkenntnis*) of these objects, since the remainder of the content of experience—i.e., the pure *concepts* (categories) involved in the constitution of experience—can be present in mental acts (e.g., of thinking) that occur in the *absence* of the objects they represent. But to accord to appearances an 'empirical reality' due to their role or use in cognizing substances in no way converts these appearances into actual substances themselves (just as using the pure concepts to cognize these substances accords to these concepts, too, an empirical reality without converting these concepts into actual substances either).[47]

5. Conclusion

My goal in the foregoing has been in some ways quite modest. I have aimed to introduce the Fregean interpretation of Kant's appearances, by first providing the model it will use to interpret Kant's claims about appearances (section 2), and by then showing that key passages in Kant's texts bear out the applicability of this model (section 3), and, finally, by contrasting this interpretation with some of the most prominent recent alternatives (section 4). To be sure, much more would need to be said to show how the Fregean interpretation could be carried through to accommodate all of the passages that these alternative interpretations take to point in their favor—let alone to show how the Fregean interpretation could accommodate all of the further twists and turns in Kant's account of theoretical cognition as a whole. In the meantime, though, I hope to have made a convincing case that, despite having been overlooked for so long, the Fregean interpretation is actually both textually well-grounded and systematically well-motivated, and so should be taken seriously as a competitor to the other more familiar interpretations on offer.

References

Adickes, E. (1929). *Kant's Lehre von der doppelten Affektion unseres Ich*. Mohr.

Allais, L. (2004). Kant's one world. *British Journal for the History of Philosophy*, *12*(4): 655–84.

Allais, L. (2007). Kant's idealism and the secondary quality analogy. *Journal of the History of Philosophy*, *45*(3): 459–84.

Allais, L. (2010). Kant's argument for transcendental idealism in the Transcendental Aesthetic. *Proceedings of the Aristotelian Society*, *110*(1): 47–75.

Allais, L. (2011a). Transcendental idealism and the Transcendental Deduction. In D. Schulting & J. Verburght (Eds.), *Kant's idealism: New interpretations of a controversial doctrine* (pp. 91–107). Springer.

Allais, L. (2011b). Idealism enough: Response to Roche. *Kantian Review*, *16*(3): 375–98.

[47] In other words, both appearances and concepts are equally "ideal," in the sense that neither are transcendentally real, since both concepts and appearances are ways of representing things, rather than real (actual) things in their own right.

Allais, L. (2015). *Manifest Reality: Kant's Idealism and his Realism*. Oxford University Press.

Allison, H. (2004). *Kant's transcendental idealism* (Revised and enlarged edition). Yale University Press.

Ameriks, K. (2001). Kant and short arguments to humility. Reprinted in Ameriks, 2003.

Ameriks, K. (2003). *Interpreting Kant's Critiques*. Oxford University Press.

Aquila, R. E. (1979). Things in themselves and appearances: Intentionality and reality in Kant. *Archiv für Geschichte der Philosophie*, *61*(3): 293–308.

Aquila, R. E. (1989). *Matter in mind: A study of Kant's Transcendental Deduction*. Indiana University Press.

Aquila, R. E. (2003). Hans Vaihinger and some recent intentionalist readings of Kant. *Journal of the History of Philosophy*, *41*(2): 231–50.

Bolzano, B. (1837). *Wissenschaftslehre*. Seidel.

Brentano, F. (1874). *Psychologie von einem empirischen Standpunkt*. Duncker & Humblot.

Burge, T. (2005). *Truth, thought, reason: Essays on Frege*. Oxford University Press.

Cohen, H. (1885). *Kants Theorie der Erfahrung* (2nd edition). Dimmler.

Cohen, H. (1907). *Kommentar zu Immanuel Kants Kritik der reinen Vernunft*. Dürr.

Cohen, J. (2009). *The red and the real: An essay on color ontology*. Oxford University Press.

Dummett, M. (1997). Comments on Wolfgang Künne's paper. In W. Künne, M. Siebel, & M. Textor (Eds.), *Bolzano and analytic philosophy* (pp. 241–48). Rodopi.

Dummett, M. (2001). Gottlob Frege. In A. P. Martinich & D. Sosa (Eds.), *A companion to analytic philosophy* (pp. 6–20). Blackwell.

Falkenstein, L. (1995). *Kant's intuitionism: A commentary on the Transcendental Aesthetic*. University of Toronto Press.

Frege, G. (1980). *Philosophical and mathematical correspondence* (B. McGuinness, Ed.). University of Chicago Press.

Frege, G. (1984). *Collected papers on mathematics, logic, and philosophy* (B. McGuinness, Ed.). Blackwell.

Gomes, A. (2014). Kant on perception: Naïve realism, non-conceptualism, and the B-deduction. *Philosophical Quarterly*, *64*(254): 1–19.

Hogan, D. (2009). Noumenal affection. *Philosophical Review*, *118*(4): 501–32.

Jankowiak, T. (2014). Sensations as representations in Kant. *British Journal for the History of Philosophy*, *22*(3): 492–513.

Jankowiak, T. (2017). Kantian Phenomenalism Without Berkeleyan Idealism. *Kantian Review* 22 (2):205-231.

Kant, I. (1902–). *Kants gesammelte Schriften* (Königlich Preussische Akademie der Wissenschaften, Ed.). Vols. 1–29. De Gruyter.

Kant, I. (1991–). *The Cambridge edition of the works of Immanuel Kant* (P. Guyer & A. Wood, Eds.). Cambridge University Press.

Kemp Smith, N. (1918). *A commentary to Kant's* Critique of pure reason. Macmillan.

Kremer, M. (2010). Sense and reference. In M. Potter & T. Ricketts (Eds.), *The Cambridge companion to Frege* (pp. 222–92). Cambridge University Press.

Langton, R. (1998). *Kantian humility: Our ignorance of things in themselves*. Oxford University Press.

McDowell, J. (1984). De re senses. Reprinted in McDowell, 1998.

McDowell, J. (1986). Singular thought and the extent of inner space. Reprinted in McDowell, 1998.

McDowell, J. (1991a). Intentionality de re. Reprinted in McDowell, 1998.

McDowell, J. (1991b). *Mind and world.* Harvard University Press.

McDowell, J. (1998). *Meaning, knowledge, and reality.* Harvard University Press.

McLear, C. (2014). Kant on perceptual content. *Mind, 125*(497): 95–144.

McLear, C. (2016). Kant on perceptual content. *Mind, 125*(497): 95–144.

Makkreel, R. (1990). *Imagination and interpretation in Kant: The hermeneutical import of the* Critique of judgment. University of Chicago Press.

Matherne, S. (2015). Images and Kant's theory of perception. *Ergo, 2*(29). https://doi.org/10.3998/ergo.12405314.0002.029

Moore, A. W. (2001). Review of R. Langton, *Kantian humility: Our ignorance of things in themselves. Philosophical Review, 110*(1): 117–20.

Pritchard, H. A. (1909). *Kant's theory of knowledge.* Oxford University Press.

Rohs, P. (2001). Bezieht sich nach Kant die Anschauung unmittelbar auf Gegenstände? In V. Gerhardt, R.-P. Horstmann, & R. Schumacher (Eds.), *Kant und die Berliner Aufklärung: Akten des IX. Internationalen Kant-Kongresses* (vol. 2, pp. 214–28). De Gruyter.

Rosefeldt, T. (2007). Dinge an sich und sekundäre Qualitäten. In J. Stolzenberg (Ed.), *Kant in der Gegenwart* (pp. 167–212). De Gruyter.

Schellenberg, S. (2011). Perceptual content defended. *Noûs, 45*(4): 714–50.

Searle, J. (1958). Russell's objections to Frege's theory of sense and reference. *Analysis, 18*(6): 137–43.

Sellars, W. (1968). *Science and metaphysics: Variations on Kantian themes.* Routledge & Kegan Paul.

Stang, N. (2015). Who's afraid of double affection? *Philosopher's Imprint, 15*(18). http://hdl.handle.net/2027/spo.3521354.0015.018

Stanley, J. (2011). *Know how.* Oxford University Press.

Stephenson, A. (2015). Kant on the object-dependence of intuition and hallucination. *Philosophical Quarterly, 65*(260): 486–508.

Tolley, C. (2013). The non-conceptuality of the content of intuitions: A new approach. *Kantian Review, 18*(1): 107–36.

Tolley, C. (2016). The difference between original, metaphysical, and geometrical representations of space. In D. Schulting (Ed.), *Kantian nonconceptualism* (pp. 257–85). Palgrave Macmillan.

Tye, M. (1995). *Ten problems of consciousness.* MIT Press.

Vaihinger, H. (1892). *Commentar zu Kant's Kritik der reinen Vernunft,* Vol. 2. Union Deutsche Verlagsgesellschaft.

Van Cleve, J. (1999). *Problems from Kant.* Oxford University Press.

Watkins, E. (2005). *Kant and the metaphysics of causality.* Cambridge University Press.

10

Kant's Conception of Cognition and Our Knowledge of Things in Themselves

Karl Schafer

Perhaps the primary concern of Kant's Critical philosophy is the limits of our cognitive faculties.[1] But to understand the nature of this concern, we must first understand what these limits are supposed to be limits of. And, in order to understand this, we need to understand what Kant means by "cognition" or *Erkenntnis*.

Traditionally, *Erkenntnis* was translated into English as "knowledge." And while it is more commonly translated today as "cognition," it is still often thought of in a manner that bears the imprint of past attempts to force Kant's notion of *Erkenntnis* into the framework of contemporary epistemological debates. As I argue below, this has a number of unfortunate consequences for our understanding of Kant. For while *Erkenntnis* is a form of "knowledge" in the everyday sense of this word, what Kant means by *Erkenntnis* is quite different from the sort of "knowledge" that has been the focus of contemporary epistemological discussion. Thus, if we attempt to understand Kant's claims as claims about anything like knowledge in this sense, we will make very little headway in understanding the views that Kant actually wished to defend.[2]

[1] For various reasons, this paper has been forthcoming for many years. In updating it for publication here, I've added *some* discussion of the more recent literature on these topics in footnotes and an appendix, but I choose to leave the main line of argument from the original paper more or less intact, since the paper has already generated a fair amount of discussion. (For an updated version of my views about these issues, see Schafer 2021, forthcoming-b; forthcoming-c, forthcoming-d.) As I note below, the ideas here are deeply indebted to the ideas of many other Kant scholars. Perhaps most notable among these is Houston Smit, whose ideas provided me with the basic structure for thinking about cognition I explore here. Also especially notable are Lucy Allias, Ian Belcher, Andrew Chignell, Steve Engstrom, Don Garrett, Gary Hatfield, Béatrice Longuenesse, Colin Marshall, Colin McLear, Sasha Newton, Tyke Nunez, Tobias Rosefeldt, Kieran Setiya, Nicholas Stang, Clinton Tolley, and Eric Watkins—as well as audiences at Humboldt Universität zu Berlin, University of Miami, University of Wisconsin, Simon Fraser University, University of Pennsylvania, and Harvard University—amongst many others.

[2] Houston Smit stresses this point in the initial sections of his important Smit (2000). For some related discussion, see the excellent Smit (2009). Also compare the Introduction to Hanna (2006), as well as Adams (1997). I learned of Smit's views on this distinction and its potential relevance to the proper interpretation of Kant's transcendental idealism during a very illuminating conversation with him at the 2005 Kant Congress in Brazil. In many ways, the interpretation of Kant I offer below may be thought of as an attempt to build upon Smit's views about these matters—although I am sure he would not agree with everything I say here. (I gather from conversation with Smit that he has also for many years been working on an unpublished paper on the topic of the present paper, which is entitled "Cognition, Understanding, and Determination: A Reply to Jacobi.") As noted above, this paper has been forthcoming for quite some time. In that time, a number of other Kant scholars have also been working on this topic. Particularly notable among this work are Watkins & Willaschek (2017a, 2017b), as well as Tolley (2017). There is a good deal of overlap between my work and these papers, but there are also significant points of disagreement

Karl Schafer, *Kant's Conception of Cognition and Our Knowledge of Things in Themselves* In: *The Sensible and Intelligible Worlds: New Essays on Kant's Metaphysics and Epistemology.* Edited by: Karl Schafer and Nicholas F. Stang, Oxford University Press.
 DOI: 10.1093/oso/9780199688265.003.0011

Nowhere, perhaps, is this clearer than with respect to the vexed issue of what Kant means when he claims that we cannot achieve theoretical cognition of things in themselves. For while Kant insists on this point, it also appears that he believes that we can know many general propositions about things in themselves, even from a theoretical point of view. For example, Kant confidently asserts that things in themselves affect us, that they (at least in part) ground all appearances, and that they are outside of space and time. Thus, if we understand cognition to be knowledge in the contemporary sense, Kant seems to be claiming both that we are totally ignorant concerning things in themselves *and* that we can know a good deal about them.

Nearly every Kant interpreter has his or her preferred solution to this problem. Some argue that Kant did not *really* mean that we cannot cognize things in themselves to anything like the degree it might seem.[3] Others interpret his claims about things in themselves in an "epistemic" or "methodological" fashion that is compatible with total ignorance of them.[4] And not a few simply conclude that his views on these issues are incoherent.[5]

Ultimately, the first of these alternatives comes closest to Kant's intentions.[6] But we can only properly understand why this is the case if we are careful not to assimilate Kant's conception of cognition to anything like a contemporary notion of propositional knowledge. In particular, once we understand how Kant's conception of cognition is different from contemporary notions of propositional knowledge, it will become clear why Kant can maintain both that we can know many general facts about things in themselves, while nonetheless being unable to achieve cognition of them.

In considering these issues, I will proceed as follows. First, in section 1, I will briefly discuss the relationship between Kant's concept of cognition and the contemporary concept of propositional knowledge. Then, in section 2, I will discuss the basic conception of cognition that Kant provides in the first *Critique*. In sections 4–6, I will draw on Kant's discussion of these issues in the *Jäsche Logic* to flesh out this abstract characterization of cognition. Finally, in section 7, I will turn to the connections between this conception of cognition and knowledge more generally, turning last to the issue of how it is possible for us to reconcile Kant's claims about the

as well. In what follows I'll try to say a bit about these, but I'll save detailed engagement with their views for the Appendix. Finally, Sommerlatte (2020) lays out a view of a view of empirical cognition in terms of clear and distinct representation that is quite close to the account I develop below (as applied to the empirical case).

3 For an important recent instance of this line of interpretation, see Ameriks (2003).

4 For a prominent example of this way of reading Kant, see Allison (1983).

5 The most famous example of this response to Kant is, of course, Jacobi.

6 For two very different recent ways of resolving this problem see Langton (1998) and Hogan (2009). Hogan, in particular, agrees with me that to understand Kant's claims about these issues we need to attend closely to the meaning of terms like "cognition" in the post-Leibnizian context in which Kant was operating. But he gives a very different analysis of what is important for Kant about these terms than the one I offer here. For Hogan, "Kant's claims of ignorance incorporate a substantive metaphysical claim about reality in itself," namely, a claim about the undetermined (free) character of things in themselves. There is no space here to give this reading the attention it deserves. But let me simply note that while I'm sympathetic to some of what Hogan says about Kant's views, this way of reading "cognition" seems to me to paint a misleading picture of the argumentative structure of the first *Critique*—and, in particular, of the relationship between the claims Kant makes about the limits of theoretical cognition early in the first *Critique* and the positive claims he makes elsewhere about freedom.

uncognizability of things in themselves with the sort of general knowledge of them that he appears to accept. I will conclude, in an appendix, with a discussion of some of the recent literature on these issues.

1. Cognition and Knowledge

So, what exactly does Kant mean by *Erkenntnis* during the Critical period? In the first instance, cognitions are a subspecies of representations. But what distinguishes these representations from others? As noted above, *Erkenntnis* was traditionally translated as "knowledge." And while translators have come to prefer "cognition" as a translation for this term, many interpretations of what Kant means by *Erkenntnis* still bear the imprint of this tradition.[7] In particular:

(i) Since much of the discussion of knowledge in the second half of the twentieth century has focused on the idea that knowledge is best understood as something like un-Gettiered, justified true belief (or, alternatively, as warranted true belief), the traditional way of translating *Erkenntnis* has encouraged readers of Kant to think that cognitions are primarily distinguished from other representations by the fact that cognitions are better justified or warranted than other representations are.

(ii) Since the recent epistemological discussion has focused on propositional knowledge—on knowledge that P—translating *Erkenntnis* as knowledge encourages one to think that instances of cognition are wholly propositional in nature.

Given the way Kant is often discussed, neither of these assumptions is at all unnatural. But neither gives one an accurate picture of what Kant means by *Erkenntnis*. Taking them in reverse order, the second of them is misleading because when Kant speaks of cognitions, he has in mind—not just judgments—but also concepts and intuitions. And both of the latter two types of representation are primarily representations of objects (or classes or properties of objects) as opposed to propositions. Moreover, while Kant does refer to some judgments as cognitions, he is clear that they count as such because they are cognitions *of objects*.[8] Thus, at the very least, Kant's use of cognition is not limited to representations with propositional content. And while some of the representations that Kant refers to as cognitions do have propositional content, such representations count as cognitions because they provide the subject with cognition of objects—and not because of their propositional content *as such*.

[7] The current preference for "cognition" as a translation of *Erkenntnis* is motivated in the first instance by the desire to reserve "knowledge" as a translation of *Wissen*. As should be clear, I have no complaint with this choice—my only concern is that despite this shift in translation, Kant interpreters sometimes fail to take seriously enough the differences between *Erkenntnis* in Kant's sense and the concept of knowledge that has been the focus of contemporary epistemological debate.

[8] See, for example, Kant's claim that judgments (*qua* cognitions) are "the mediate cognition of an object" (A68/B93).

Of course, it is impossible to make sense of concepts as Kant understands them in isolation from the judgments that can be formed from them. In particular, the role of concepts for Kant is to serve as functions of "unity" among our intuitions. And concepts are capable of playing this role only in virtue of the manner in which they can figure as possible constituents of judgments. Thus, a concept acquires the particular content (object or objects) it has only in virtue of the manner in which it can be embedded in various judgments. So, while a judgment will only *count* as a cognition in virtue of its relationship with concepts that provide one with cognitions of objects, these concepts will only be able to play this role insofar as they are capable of serving as the constituents of possible judgments.

This is what makes it so natural for Kant to speak of both concepts and judgments as forms of cognition. For the sort of cognition involved in intuitions and concepts—i.e., cognition *of* an object or objects—is impossible without the sort of cognition involved in judgments—i.e., cognition *that* these objects possess certain features. But by the same token, judgments only deserve to be regarded as cognitions for Kant insofar as the concepts that figure in them provide us with a mechanism for the cognition of objects.[9] Thus, as will become clearer below, insofar as the traditional translation of *Erkenntnis* as "knowledge" encourages the idea that cognition is always propositional, it can lead to a very misleading conception of Kant's concerns in his discussion of cognition. But while this source of confusion is important, it pales in comparison with the first source of confusion noted above.

Once again, a common thought among readers of Kant is that the distinction between cognitions and other sorts of representations is first and foremost a matter of whether we are justified in taking these representations to be true.[10] That is, it is often assumed that what distinguishes cognitions from other sorts of representations is that we possess a certain sort of warrant for them or that they are justified in some way that other representations are not.

As we will see in more detail below, this paints a misleading picture of the distinction between cognitions and other representations as Kant understands it. For, in fact, a representation counts as a cognition for Kant not primarily because it is better warranted or justified than other representations, but rather because it possesses certain distinctive representational features that mark it off from other sorts of

[9] Ultimately, this means that there is a *sense* in which judgments may be thought of as a species of concepts—in the broad sense of "functions of unity" among one's representations. Compare Kant's definition of judgment in the *Jäsche Logic*, where he writes: "A judgment is the representation of the unity of the consciousness of various representations, or the representation of their relation insofar as they constitute a concept" (9:101).

[10] As noted above, this thought has become less common in the recent literature on these issues. For example, interpreters such as Adams (1997) and Rae Langton have argued that what prevents us from achieving cognition of things in themselves relates to our inability to represent them in sufficiently rich terms. In thinking of cognition in terms of a certain sort of representation, these authors provide an important corrective to the traditional reading of Kant's views concerning cognition. But while I am sympathetic to the general thrust of their interpretations, for reasons that will become clearer, it seems to me that neither Adams nor Langton successfully pinpoint the precise sort of representation that Kant means to pick out in speaking of "cognition." For example, while Adams rightly stresses the importance of intuition in providing cognitions with an object (in Kant's technical sense), he does not do nearly enough to explain *why* intuition is necessary in order for this to come about. For related discussion, see again Watkins & Willaschek (2017a, 2017b) and Tolley (2017).

representations. Thus, when Kant claims that we cannot achieve cognition of things in themselves, this is not a primarily a claim about the limits of our ability to make judgments in a justified or warranted fashion. Rather, it is, first and foremost, a claim about the representational limitations of our faculties—namely, that there is *an* important sense in which we cannot even successfully represent to ourselves the nature of things as they are in themselves. Of course, as will become clear in a moment, these representational features are themselves connected with issues of justification in important ways. In particular, one of the main constraints Kant places on cognition may be understood in terms of our justification for thinking that a certain sort of object is really possible. But this concerns—not our justification for taking the representation in question to be true, as the traditional account would have it—but questions of justification that arise in the context of considering what it would be for a cognition to provide with genuine consciousness of an object.

Of course, to say this is not to say that we cannot understand *Erkenntnis* as a sort of "knowledge" in a broad, intuitive sense of this word. For, in fact, as I will discuss below, it is quite natural to describe what Kant has in mind here as a kind of "knowledge" in the ordinary English sense of this word—namely, knowledge *of* objects. But it does mean that we should not assume that the sort of "knowledge" that Kant means to refer to with *Erkenntnis* is the sort of propositional knowledge that is the focus of contemporary epistemological debate. Nor does it mean that this will be the same as what Kant means to refer to when he speaks knowledge in the sense of *Wissen*.

In order to appreciate this point, it is helpful to consider Kant's explicit discussion of the nature of epistemic justification in The Canon of Pure Reason towards the end of the first *Critique*.[11] For once we do so, it becomes clear that the distinction between cognitions and other representations is not a matter of their epistemic justification in any straightforward sense. There Kant discusses the different forms of "taking to be true" (*Fürwahrhalten*) that can be present when one makes a judgment. These different forms of taking to be true are distinguished from one another in virtue of the different sorts of grounds one can have for accepting a judgment. Crucially, in his discussion of these different sorts of grounds, the distinction between cognitions and other representations plays no explicit role. Rather, Kant's distinction between different sorts of grounds or justification is meant to distinguish between the grounds I can have for taking some judgment to be true. When I take something to be true, I am (of course) making a judgment—a judgment that, much of the time, will count as a cognition. So, for example, according to Kant one can take an empirical judgment to be true because one has objectively sufficient grounds for doing so. In which case, this will count as an instance of *Wissen* or knowledge. But one can also take the same empirical judgment to be true on the basis of grounds that are sufficient only in a subjective sense, as is true in cases of *Glauben* or faith. Nonetheless, in both of these cases, one will be making an empirical judgment that is itself a cognition. Thus, the distinction between empirical judgments that possess objectively sufficient grounds and those that possess merely subjectively sufficient grounds is not identical with the distinction between cognitions and other sorts of representations. Rather, the former

[11] A820/B848–A831/B859.

distinction is a distinction between different sorts of *Fürwahrhalten* involving judgments (which may or may not themselves be cognitions).[12]

Now, to be sure, very often taking a judgment to be true will be based on objectively sufficient grounds in Kant's sense precisely because this judgment is formed from concepts that make us conscious of objects in the sense that (as we will see) is constitutive of cognition in Kant's sense. Thus, a judgment is often based on objectively sufficient grounds *because* it is itself an instance of cognition. But crucially this need not always be the case. For, as we will see, there are instances in which we can assent to judgment on objectively sufficient grounds *even though* the judgment in question does not provide us with cognition of its objects—as is true, for example, with respect to the very abstract claims that Kant himself makes about things in themselves.

Still, those important exceptions aside, it will generally be judgments that reach the level of cognitions which are candidates for the status of *Wissen* or knowledge. For while there are a variety of potential sources of objectively sufficient grounds for assenting to a judgment, by far the most important of these are grounded in that judgment's ability to relate to objects in the manner that is distinctive of cognition. In this way, there is certainly an important connection between Kant's discussion of cognition and his understanding of objective grounds. But this connection is very different from the connection that readers of Kant have often taken for granted. For while these two issues are connected, it is not the case that the primary thing that distinguishes cognitions from other sorts of representations is a matter of their grounds or justification. Rather, being a cognition is normally a contributing—but neither necessary nor sufficient—condition for a judgment to be an object of *Wissen* in Kant's sense.[13]

2. Cognition as Objective Representation

With this in mind, let's return to our original question: what distinguishes cognitions from other representations? As is often true with Kant, answering this question is

[12] For a useful discussion of these passages, see Chignell (2007a, 2007b, 2010)—although he would not agree with everything I say about these matters here.

[13] For example, as I discuss in Schafer (forthcoming-d), our inability to achieve cognition of God is not primarily a matter of the fact that we lack objective grounds for assenting to God's existence (in some sense of "God"). Rather, it is primarily a matter of the fact that we do not possess the sort of concept of God we would need to in order to cognize him. As discussed below, in order to possess such a concept, it would have to both (i) represent God as a determinate object and (ii) represent God in a manner that allowed us to prove his real possibility. Thus, as Kant writes at A827/B855:

> If here too I would call merely theoretically taking something to be true only an hypothesis that I would be justified in assuming, I would thereby make myself liable for more of a concept of the constitution of a world-cause and of another world than I can really boast of; for of that which I even only assume as a hypothesis I must know at least enough of its properties so that I need invent not its concept but only its existence.

Looking ahead for a moment, in passages like this one, the interaction between the two requirements discussed below is particularly important. For while we can come up with a concept of God that represents him in a highly determinate fashion, we cannot do so while preserving our ability to prove that the object of this concept is really possible. This is particularly clear from Kant's discussion of the *ens realissimum*, which I discuss in detail below in the context of Tolley's (2017) objections to my account. (Thanks also to Gary Hatfield for pressing me to say more about this issue.)

complicated by Kant's willingness to be somewhat flexible in his use of philosophical terminology. But while it is clear that Kant sometimes uses "cognition" in different ways, I think we can identify a core notion of cognition that lies at the center of his discussion of these issues.[14]

In considering this issue, it is natural to begin with the taxonomy of different forms of representation that Kant provides in the famous *Stufenleiter* passage of the first *Critique*:

> The genus is representation in general (repraesentatio). Under it stands the representation with consciousness (perceptio). A perception that refers to the subject as a modification of its state is a sensation (sensatio), an objective perception is a cognition (cognitio).[15]

In this passage, cognitions are characterized as possessing two characteristics. First, they are representations "with consciousness"—or "perceptions" in Kant's technical sense. And, second, they are representations that are "objective," as opposed to merely relating to the "subject's state." Or, in other words, they are perceptions that are related both to the subject of the perception and to some object or objects that are at least partially independent of the subject's subjective state.

Beginning with the first of these characteristics, the claim that a cognition is a representation with consciousness might be taken simply to mean that it is a representation that we are conscious of. But this is only part of what Kant has in mind

[14] On this point, Watkins & Willaschek (2017a, 2017b) seem to me to multiply the senses of "cognition" at work in Kant's discussion to an unnecessary degree.

[15] There are many difficulties concerning the proper interpretation of this passage. Most notably, Kant here includes both intuitions and concepts under the heading of "cognitions." And yet elsewhere (e.g., B146) he stresses the claim that (at least from a theoretical perspective) cognition requires the cooperation and connection of both intuitions and concepts. Giving a full account of the compatibility of these passages is no simple matter, but the important point for present purposes is that Kant's insistence in this passage that both intuitions and concepts should count as cognitions in the sense of having the potential to provide us with cognition of an object is perfectly compatible with the claim that intuitions and concepts can only provide us with such cognition insofar as they stand in systematic relations to each other. For example, Kant is quite clear that intuitions are only capable of providing us with cognition of objects insofar as the synthesis involved in intuition has been guided by concepts in their guise as rules for sensible synthesis. And any intuition whose synthesis has been guided by such rules will stand in certain systematic relations with concepts in their guise as discursive, general representations. As such, there need be no conflict between Kant's claim that intuitions are a species of cognition and his claim that theoretical cognition always requires the cooperation of intuitions and concepts. For more on these issues, see the discussion in Longuenesse (1998), and compare the discussion in Schafer (2017). In addition, it has puzzled many readers that Kant here categorizes ideas as a sort of concept and thus, in turn, as a sort of cognition or objective representation. For Kant holds that such ideas—e.g., our ideas of a soul, of God, and of a world whole—lack the sort of relation to an object which is required for a representation to be an objective representation, at least from a theoretical perspective. But to respond to this concern we need only note that Kant is here giving a taxonomy of different varieties of representation in isolation from any of the particular results of the *Critique*. Thus, while it is true that the ideas of pure reason cannot be the basis of any theoretical cognition for creatures like us—they are, at least in principle, the sorts of things that might enable a being to achieve cognition of an object. In particular, while these ideas are such that it is impossible to achieve any cognition through the application of them to the objects of experience, this only generates the result that it is impossible to achieve cognition through them in general if we restrict our attention to beings whose cognitive powers are limited to the objects of experience. And Kant does not believe that every possible being meets this description. Indeed, from a practical perspective, at least some of these ideas may be able to provide us with something very like cognition—at least in the case of our practical consciousness of ourselves as free. For more discussion of this side of Kant's account, see Schafer (forthcoming-a).

here. In particular, when we are dealing with an objective representation—that is, a representation that has a relation to both the subject and some object or objects—this representation will only count as an objective representation with consciousness in Kant's sense if it provides us with consciousness of the object(s) that it is a representation of as objects distinct from our representations of them. Otherwise, the representation would present itself to consciousness merely as a modification of the subject's subjective state—and not as having a relation to an object that is independent of this state. Thus, in order for a representation to count as a cognition for Kant, it must provide its subject with consciousness of its object(s) as objective things in this sense:

> **Consciousness of the Object**: In order to cognize X we must be able to become *conscious* of X as an object, i.e., as something that is independent of the subjective state of mind involved our representations of X.[16]

But what is the nature of the relationship between a cognition and its object? The most fundamental feature of the object of a cognition is the connection between it and the "material truth or falsity" of judgments involving the cognition to which it is related. For example, a judgment whose subject is a singular cognition will be true just in case this judgment attaches to this cognition a predicate that agrees with the cognition's object. And a judgment whose subject is a general concept will be true just in case this judgment attaches to this concept a predicate that agrees with all of the possible objects that fall under the subject concept.[17] Thus, in being related to an object (or objects), a cognition (and its associated judgments) acquires a standard of correctness—of "material truth or falsity"—that extends beyond anything internal to the judgment itself, considered as a state of the subject.

In saying this, it is important to remember that it is *not* the case that only cognitions (in this sense) can be true or false. For instance, it is perfectly possible for a representation to acquire a merely "formal" standard of correctness without thereby qualifying as a cognition in Kant's sense of the term. After all, on Kant's view, a judgment is subject to such "formal standards" simply in virtue of the nature of the concepts involved in it, without consideration of its relationship to any object or objects. Indeed, a representation can even acquire a *material* standard of truth or falsity (in some sense) without counting as a cognition for Kant. For there is a gap between (i) a representation merely *referring* some object in the sense required in order to subject to a material standard of truth or falsity and (ii) it presenting this object *to consciousness* in the manner required for cognition in Kant's sense. For example, as Kant discusses in the *Jäsche Logic*, mere animals possess many representations that do not rise to the level of cognitions.[18] But while these representations do not give the creatures that possess them the sort of consciousness of their objects that is required for cognition, they are used by these creatures to (unconsciously) differentiate between

[16] Here my view and that developed by Tolley are quite close to one another, although we develop this basic thought in different ways.

[17] Here I restrict myself to judgments with the simplest subject-predicate form.

[18] For a helpful discussion of animal cognition in Kant, see McLear (2011).

different things.[19] Thus, although these animal representations will not count as full-fledged cognitions, it does make sense to evaluate their accuracy or inaccuracy in some sense. As such, it is possible for us to think of these sorts of representations as subject to material standards of correctness (in some sense) even when they do not rise to the level of genuine cognition.

As this indicates, what genuine cognition in Kant's sense requires is, not just that a representation has a material standard of correctness, but also that it makes us (at least potentially) conscious of this standard. It is this that separates the view of cognition being developed here from the "semantic" interpretation of Kant's conception of cognition.[20] For what is at issue here is not merely the ability of a cognition to achieve genuine "reference" to an object in the sense familiar from contemporary semantics, but also its ability to make the cognizer *conscious* of the object it refers to and the standards that this object places on our representations of it. This is something that is neither purely epistemic nor purely semantic in character, although it involves elements of both.

As we will see, this additional element in Kant's understanding of cognition is crucial for understanding many of the central features he ascribes to cognition as such. In particular, Kant goes on to argue that in order to provide a standard of material correctness in the sense at issue here, the object of a cognition must have two further features. First, Kant claims, the object in question must be something that could actually exist—or, as Kant puts it, it must be something that is "really possible." And, second, it must be relatively determinate what the object (or objects) of the cognition is and what they are like. Thus, in order for a representation to provide us with objective representation *with consciousness*, it must both possess an object with both of these two features, *and* it must make us (at least implicitly) conscious of this object as something that possesses these features:[21]

Real Possibility: In order to cognize X we must be able to become *conscious* of X as a real possibility.

Determinate Content: We can only cognize X to the degree that we are able to become *conscious* of X's determinate identity.

3. Cognition and Real Possibility

As many commentators have noted, some version of the first constraint appears at many locations throughout Kant's discussion of the nature of cognition. For example:

[19] This is especially true of representations that fall into Kant's third class in this progression: namely those (instances of *Kenntnis*) that allow one to represent something in comparison with other things as to identity and diversity *without* consciousness.

[20] Such as Hanna (2001).

[21] Plainly, the qualifier "implicitly" is crucial to the plausibility of these claims. In Schafer (forthcoming-d), I discuss the sense in which all cognition involves a consciousness of its own standards of correctness in much more detail than I can here.

> To cognize an object, it is required that I be able to prove its possibility (whether by the testimony of experience from its actuality or *a priori* through reason). (Bxxvi)[22]

But why must the object of a cognition be something that is "really possible" in Kant's sense? To understand this, it will be helpful to distinguish three modal statuses that something may have for Kant:[23]

(i) It may be logically impossible.
(ii) It may be logically possible, but really impossible.
(iii) It may be both logically and really possible.

If we consider each of these in turn, we can see why Kant believes that only something that is really possible is capable of playing the role of the object of a cognition (as defined above). For instance, suppose that the putative object of some cognition were logically impossible. In this case, the very concept of the thing in question would involve a logical inconsistency. And such an object could hardly provide the cognitions that are related to it with a non-trivial standard of correctness in the manner the object of a cognition must. So we may safely assume that the object of a cognition must be something that is at least logically possible.

But what of the second possibility? Something is logically possible, but really impossible in Kant's sense, when it is metaphysically impossible for this thing to actually exist, even though the concept of it involves no logical contradiction. The problem with the putative object of a cognition having this status is, once again, that any such object would fail to provide the associated cognition with a non-trivial *material* standard of correctness. After all, since the object in question is incapable of real existence, it cannot provide its concept with a standard of correctness over and above the purely logical or formal standards of correctness that are *already* implicit in the concept in question *considered in isolation from its object*. Thus, any such "object" would simply provide us with another way of articulating these purely logical or formal standards.[24] In this way, the standards generated by a representation's relation to such an "object" would not extend beyond the concept itself in any way. So, such an "object" would not provide its concept with a material (as opposed to formal) standard of correctness in the manner a cognition's object must for Kant.

4. Cognition and Determinate Identity

For these reasons, it is very natural for Kant to claim that a non-trivial standard of material objective correctness can only be provided by an object that is really possible. Thus, in order to cognize something in the sense defined above, we must be able

[22] Compare the discussion at A771/B799. For more on the importance of this constraint in the context of Kant's account of knowledge, see Chignell (2010).

[23] For a detailed discussion of Kant's account of modality, see Stang (2016a).

[24] Alternatively, we might take any such a representation to be "materially false" in virtue of lacking a genuine object. For the purposes of this chapter, I remain agnostic about where Kant falls in terms of this debate.

to become consciousness of it as really possible. This, as we will see below, has important consequences for Kant's understanding of cognition. But before we consider these consequences, I want to discuss the second constraint mentioned above—the idea that it must be determinate what a representation's object is insofar as the representation provides us with cognition of that object. Kant stresses this feature of cognitions again and again. For example, in the B Deduction, he writes:

> Understanding is, generally speaking, the faculty of cognitions. These consist in the *determinate* relation of a given representation to an object. An object, however, is that in the concept of which the manifold of a given intuition is united. (B137; my emphasis)

And a bit further on, we have:

> ...the categories are not restricted in thinking by the conditions of our sensible intuition, but have an unbounded field, and only the cognition of objects that we think, the *determination* of the object, requires intuition. (B166; my emphasis)

Finally, later on in the *Critique*, he writes:

> If we separate [intuitions from concepts], then we have representations that we cannot relate to any *determinate* object. (A258/B314; my emphasis)

But why must the object of a cognition be determinate in some sense? According to Kant, this is a direct consequence of the idea that a cognition's object provides it with a material standard of correctness. For, as Kant puts it: "Material truth must consist in this agreement of a cognition with just that determinate object to which it is related" (*Log*, 9:51).

In particular, an object will only be capable of playing this role if two things are true of it. First, in order to play this role, it must be determinate which object (or class of possible objects) is relevant to the truth or falsity of judgments involving the cognition in question. Or, as Kant puts it:

> If truth consists in the agreement of a cognition with its object, then this object must thereby be distinguished from others; for a cognition is false if it does not agree with the object to which it is related even if it contains something that could well be valid of other objects. (A58/B83)

But in order for an object to provide the cognition associated with it with a material standard of correctness, something more than this is required. For an object will only be able to play this role to the degree that the following is true of it: for a quality, it is determinate whether or not the object in question possesses this quality. Thus, the object of a cognition can only play this role for Kant to the degree that it is determinate in two senses. It must be determinate which thing this object (or class of possible objects) is and it must be determinate what this object (or class of possible objects) is like. Of course, as will become clear, this sort of determinacy is a matter of degree.[25] But a representation will count as a cognition only insofar as it possesses it.[26]

The sort of discriminating consciousness of identity that Kant has in mind here should call to mind a number of similar views within contemporary analytic philosophy. Perhaps most prominent of these is Gareth Evans's defense of what he calls "Russell's Principle":[27]

> **Russell's Principle**: A necessary condition for S to be able to think about an object O (or to make a judgment about) it is that S know which object he is thinking (or attempting to think) about—he must be able to distinguish O from all other objects.

Although it is sometimes taken as a constraint on when it is possible for a subject to refer to a particular object, Evans's discussion makes it clear that the target of his discussion is something subtly different: namely, when it is possible for a subject to think (*de re*) about a particular object.[28] But even when restricted in this way, Evans's claims have seemed to many philosophers to be open to fairly clear counterexamples.[29] For is it really the case that I can only think about a particular object when I can discriminate it from other objects? In this regard, the Kantian constraint we are discussing here is a good deal more plausible—for it is restricted to a particular sort of thought of an object, namely the sort of thought that puts the subject in a position to become conscious of the object of his thought as such. For even if we can think about a particular object (in some sense) without being able to fully discriminate from other things, it does not seem to be possible for us to become conscious of it *as the particular thing it is* under these circumstances. In this way, the Kantian conception of cognition we are discussing might well be regarded as representing the philosophically plausible core within Evans's discussion of singular thought.[30]

[25] Confirmation that cognition is a matter of degree in this sense can be found in many passages. For example consider the following: "What it means that in order to cognize a thing completely one has to cognize everything possible and determine the thing through it, whether affirmatively or negatively. Thoroughgoing determination is consequently a concept that we can never exhibit *in concreto* in its totality" (A573/B601). As this passage indicates, there is a sense in which we never achieve complete cognition of any empirical object for Kant.

[26] As discussed below, the idea that cognition requires the representation of a determinate object has deep roots in the Leibnizian philosophy of mind that was dominant in Germany during Kant's lifetime. But the history of a connection between these two notions is much older than this. In fact, both the idea that cognition requires the representation of a determinate object *and* the idea that this is only possible (in human beings) through the cooperation of an individual's sensible and intellectual faculties is fundamental to a great deal of scholastic philosophy of mind. For instance, compare the following comment of Aquinas in the *Summa contra Gentiles*:

> ...the substance of the human soul is immaterial and consequently, as we saw, is of intellectual nature: all immaterial substances are. But this doesn't yet make it a mind representing this or that thing, which it must be if it is to know determinately this or that thing...So the mind is still potential in regard to determinate representation of the sort of things we can know, namely, the natures of things sensed. Now it is exactly these determinate natures of things that are presented to us in our images....so the images are understandable potentially and determinate representations of things actually...(2.77)

[27] See, in particular, Evans (1982, ch. 4).

[28] Compare his discussion of Kripke in Evans (1982, ch. 3).

[29] See, for example, the discussion in Hawthorne & Manley (2012).

[30] Similarly, there are obvious connections between cognition in this sense and Russellian knowledge by acquaintance, but Kant's target here is considerably more restricted than was Russell's—making Kant's claims easier to defend.

5. The Interaction of These Constraints

As this indicates, for Kant it is only possible to achieve cognition of something insofar as it is possible to satisfy the following two constraints:

> **Real Possibility**: In order to cognize X we must be able to become *conscious* of X as a real possibility.
>
> **Determinate Content**: We can only cognize X to the degree that we are able to become *conscious* of X's determinate identity.

A number of recent Kant interpreters have rightly stressed the importance of the first of these constraints for Kant's claims about the limits of our cognitive faculties.[31] But as important as this first constraint is, it is only possible to satisfactorily explain the limits Kant places on our cognitive faculties if we consider both of these constraints in tandem. For, as I discuss below, it is not impossible, according to Kant, for us to think of things in themselves in a way that makes it possible to prove their real possibility. Rather, what is impossible for us is to think of things in themselves in a way that *both* represents them as having a determinate identity *and* allows us to prove their real possibility.

Thus, while various readers of Kant have stressed one of these two constraints in relative isolation from the other, in order to fully understand Kant's claims about the limits of human cognition, it is crucial to consider how these constraints interact with one another. And, just as importantly, to truly understand Kant's conception of cognition as something more than an ad hoc bundle of such constraints, it is vital to understand how both of these constraints arise naturally out of a single, intuitive conception of what cognition requires. For example, while Chignell quite correctly stresses the importance of a constraint like Real Possibility, for the most part he focuses on this constraint as opposed to constraints like Determinate Content.[32] Thus, for reasons I discuss below, he is poorly placed to explain why cognition of things in themselves is impossible in the manner Kant claims. Moreover, even with respect to Real Possibility, Chignell fails to explain how this constraint is rooted in a more basic conception of cognition.[33]

Similarly, while authors such as Ameriks have stressed the importance of a constraint like Determinate Content for Kant's conception of cognition, they have not focused in the manner that is necessary on the crucial question of how this constraint

[31] See in particular Chignell's important work on these issues.

[32] Chignell does recognize that something like both of these constraints must be active in Kant's discussion. For he stresses that the problem of whether some idea counts as a cognition is tantamount to the problem of "finding *really harmonious positive content*" for this idea. But nonetheless his discussion focuses primarily on the significance of the first of these constraints—while saying rather little about the, to my mind central, role that the second constraint plays in Kant's discussion.

[33] For example, in Chignell (2010), he writes, "It is unclear (to me at least) whether this is Kant's most fundamental answer to the question: there may be more to say about why our faculties do not reliably track real modality or about why proof of real possibility is required for knowledge in the first place" (p. 136). One of my goals here is to offer at least the beginnings of an answer to these questions (although there is much more to be said about both).

interacts with a constraint like Real Possibility.[34] Thus, once again, they have failed to identify the real source of Kant's understanding of the limits of our cognitive capacities. Once again, it is important to stress here that simply combining together the claims of authors such as Ameriks and the claims of authors such as Chignell is not sufficient to generate a compelling picture of Kant's views about these issues. For to do so would give the impression that Kant's claims about the limits of human cognition are the product of a brute and arbitrary combination of different possible constraints on what sort of representation should count as a cognition. Hopefully, I have already said enough here to indicate that, far from this being the case, both of these constraints follow quite naturally from a single, unified, and quite intuitive picture of what cognition requires. Thus, far from being the product of an arbitrary collection of constraints, Kant's understanding of the limits of our cognitive faculties stems from a quite minimal and well-grounded conception of what cognition involves.

As we will see, these constraints on cognition are central to many aspects of the Critical philosophy. For example, intuition is central for Kant's account of theoretical cognition because exhibiting the object of a concept in intuition simultaneously accomplishes two tasks. First, it allows one to establish the real possibility of this object. And, second, it does so in a manner that gives the concept in question the determinacy of content that true cognition of an object requires. While intuition is not the only means for accomplishing these two tasks in tandem, it is the primary means for doing so that we have available to us from a theoretical perspective. As a result, it plays a central role in Kant's account of the possibility of theoretical cognition in the manner that is familiar to any reader of Kant.

More generally, whenever a concept has a possible object in this sense, we may, following Kant, speak of it as having "objective validity." For any concept that has a possible object is, in virtue of this fact, a possible constituent of an objectively valid judgment. Similarly, as noted above, judgments of this sort are the sort of thing that we might (at least in principle) have objectively sufficient grounds to take to be true—thus such judgments are possible candidates for the status of *Wissen* or objectively grounded knowledge. So there is a connection here between (i) a representation having an object in this sense, (ii) it having objective validity, and (iii) the fact that judgments involving it may constitute knowledge (*Wissen*) in Kant's sense.[35] This help to explains why Kant sometimes moves quite freely between the conditions on (say) the possibility of a priori *Erkenntnis* and the conditions on the possibility of a priori *Wissen*. (See, e.g. B2–3.) For what explains such passages is not any equation of *Erkenntnis* and *Wissen*, but instead the idea that (in general) determinate or content fully rich a priori *Wissen* of some subject matter will only be possible to the degree that determinate a priori *Erkenntnis* is.

[34] See again Ameriks (2003).

[35] Once again, there are some exceptions to this—i.e., there are some cases in which we can have objectively sufficient grounds to assent to a judgment that is not a cognition. But these cases mostly involve knowledge that is quite insubstantial—although not necessarily completely trivial.

6. Comparison, Identity and Diversity, and Objective Representation

A cognition, then, is a representation that provides the subject with a consciousness of its object (or objects) as such. In particular, it must represent its object (or objects) so as to make us conscious of the *determinate identity* of this object, while also enabling us to show that this object is really possible.

I've already said a fair amount about what the second of these constraints requires, but the first constraint should remain rather obscure. So, in order to clarify what it requires, I want to turn now to what is, in many ways, Kant's most explicit definition of cognition, which appears in his discussion of the various forms of representation in the *Jäsche Logic*. There, in giving a taxonomy of the different species of representation, Kant begins much as he does in the *Stufenleiter*. In particular, in both these passages he draws a basic distinction between representations with and without consciousness, referring to the former as perceptions. But when he turns to the task of distinguishing cognitions from other perceptions in the *Logic*, he appears to do so in a different fashion than in the *Stufenleiter*. For the definition of cognition that Kant gives in the *Jäsche Logic* makes no explicit reference to the objective character of cognition at all. Instead, the definition Kant provides there contains two main elements. To cognize something is (i) to represent that thing to oneself "in comparison with other things both as to identity and diversity," and (ii) to do so "with consciousness."[36]

Is this, then, a competing conception of what is distinctive about cognitions as a subspecies of conscious representations? Not at all. Rather, Kant is drawing much the same distinction here that he is drawing in the *Stufenleiter* passage—only in somewhat different terms. Thus, we can make use of this definition of cognition to better understand what Kant means by cognition in the first *Critique*—and, in particular, to better understand the Determinate Content criterion on cognition noted above.[37]

In order to do so, though, we need first to understand the definition of cognition that Kant provides in the *Jäsche Logic*. And to do this, we need to understand what it is to represent something to oneself in comparison with other things as to identity and diversity.[38] So suppose I want to compare two everyday objects with one another

[36] *Log*, 9:65. A similar passage appears in the *Vienna Logic*, where Kant writes: "To cognize, *percipere*, is to represent something in comparison with others and to have insight into its identity or diversity from them" (24:846). Compare the discussion in the *Blomberg Logic* (24:135–36). There has been considerable controversy about the degree to which the *Jäsche Logic* represents Kant's own views. In what follows I attempt to explain why it is reasonable to regard what Kant says about cognition there as representative of his views on the subject. But, of course, the more skeptical one is about the status of the *Jäsche Logic*, the less significant such quotes will seem.

[37] Kant also makes the connection between cognition and comparison central to his account of cognition in the lectures on metaphysics: "With respect to the production of representations, the cognitive faculty is (a) the faculty of comparing. To this belongs wit as the faculty whereby we find similarity, and the power of judgment whereby we find difference in things" (*V-Met/Mron*, 29:881).

[38] In the passage under discussion, Kant appears to speak of the comparison of the objects of representations with one another. But in general, when Kant speaks of comparison, what is at issue is the comparison of representations with one another. To some readers, there may seem to be a conflict between these two ways of using "comparison." But, in fact, for Kant there is a close relationship between the two. For Kant, whenever we compare the objects of our representations with one another, we do so via comparing

as to identity and diversity. And suppose I want to do so with consciousness. Then I want to compare these two objects with one another in a manner that makes me conscious of their identity or diversity. As we have already discussed, there are two related notions of identity and diversity that might be at issue here: the numerical identity and diversity of the things being compared and their specific identity and diversity—i.e., whether they share the same qualitative features.

For Leibniz, of course, there was an extremely tight connection between these two forms of identity and diversity—since, on a Leibnizian account of these issues, every instance of numerical diversity must be grounded in a difference in the inner determinations of the things in question. For Kant, the connection between these two forms of identity is somewhat more complicated—since Kant holds that it is possible to distinguish objects in space and time purely on the basis of their spatial-temporal location.[39] Thus, as noted above, the comparison of two things with respect to their numerical identity and diversity can, for Kant, occur in two different ways. First, we may become conscious of numerical identity and diversity through the spatial-temporal relationships between objects in space and time. And, second, we may become conscious of numerical identity and diversity through the predicates or determinations we attribute to the things we are comparing. In the latter case, we will compare two things with respect to their numerical identity and diversity through comparing them with respect to their specific identity and diversity. In former case, on the other hand, no such qualitative comparison may be required. But, of course, this form of comparison will only be available insofar as the objects in question lie within space and time.

Thus, the connection between these two forms of identity and diversity is more complicated for Kant than it is for Leibniz. Still, in the case of non-spatial-temporal things, such as things in themselves, these two forms of identity will line up in much the same fashion for Kant as they do for Leibniz. And when he speaks of our ability to consciously compare things with respect to identity and diversity, Kant appears to have both of these (closely connected) sorts of identity and diversity in mind. Thus, in order to represent my coffee cup C in conscious comparison with the ashtray A, I need to represent C and A in a manner that makes me conscious of their numerical identity and diversity. And this ability must be sufficient to enable me to become conscious of their specific identity and diversity.[40]

Crucially, in both cases, cognition will also require that the objects in question and their relations be something that we are conscious of. Thus, the ability to become conscious that our representations represent one object as opposed to another is the

these representations with one another. So in this sense, the comparison of objects is just a particular instance of the comparison of representations. Or, in other words, one way in which we can compare two representations with one another is to compare them with one another with respect to their objects. See Longuenesse (1998) for a very helpful discussion of the relations between these two forms of comparison.

[39] For Kant's relationship to Leibniz on this issue, see the *V-Met/Mron*, 29:839–40.

[40] Much the same may be said of general cognitions, which represent properties (or classes of possible objects). After all, suppose I want to compare two properties with one another as to their identity and diversity—and that I want to do so with consciousness. Then I must represent these properties in such a way that my representations make me conscious of their identity and diversity. And this will require, at the very least, that my representations put me in a position to be conscious of the possible identity and diversity of the extensions associated with these properties.

distinctive mark of cognition as defined in the *Logic*. Having cognition, in this sense, involves being conscious of *what it is* that you are thinking about—or, in other words, it involves the ability to become conscious of the object—be it particular or general—that your representation represents *as such*.[41]

This, though, may seem an implausibly demanding constraint on when we can be said to cognize something. For surely we can cognize an object even though we are not in a position to compare it with *every* other actual or possible thing with respect to *both* numerical and qualitative identity and diversity? After all, as Kant himself notes, we often to seem to have "confused" or "indistinct" cognitions of an object.[42] And in such cases, it seems that we have some sort of cognition of a thing, even though we are not in a position to compare this thing with every other possible thing. For example, surely it is possible to form a cognition of the Evening Star, even though one is completely ignorant of the fact that it is identical with the Morning Star? And surely it possible for me to form a cognition of the coffee cup in front of me, even though I am not in a position to become conscious of its entire qualitative identity? In such cases, it seems, I have a sort of cognition of a thing, even if it is somewhat confused or indistinct.

What this indicates, of course, is that we should not understand the idea that cognition requires conscious comparison in all-or-nothing terms. Rather, we need to remember that, for Kant, not all cognition is created equal. That is, for Kant—like nearly every early modern philosopher—cognition comes in degrees of clarity and distinctness. And, for Kant, these degrees of clarity and distinctness are determined, at least in part, by our ability to perform the sort of conscious comparison under discussion. For example, as he uses these terms in the *Logic*, the distinctness of a representation is a matter of the "quantitative perfection" of this representation—which, in turn, is a matter of its "objective distinctness." And a representation's level of objective distinctness, as Kant's subsequent discussion makes clear, is determined by the degree to which this representation makes the subject conscious of its object as a distinct thing.[43]

[41] Compare Smit (2000): "To cognize a thing, one must be conscious of a thing in respect of its determinate identity, so as to distinguish it from (some) other things" (p. 243).

[42] See, in particular, the discussion of "confused" and "indistinct" representations at *Log*, 9:35. A representation is "indistinct" for Kant just in case "we are conscious of the whole representation, but not of the manifold contained in it." A representation is confused if it is indistinct as a result of some sort of "disorder" among its parts. As defined here, both distinctness and indistinctness presuppose that we are conscious of the representation in question—that is, they presuppose that the representation is "clear" in the sense of the term that Kant makes use of in this passage (although note that Kant also sometimes refers to distinctness as a "higher degree of clarity").

[43] Here it is crucial to distinguish two ways in which Kant speaks of a representation as distinct or indistinct. First, we can consider whether a representation (considered on its own) is distinct—i.e., we can consider whether all of its component parts or marks are themselves clear (cf. *Log*, 9:58). This sort of distinctness is the product of a full analysis of the concept in question. But, according to Kant, this is not the only sense in which we can consider whether a representation is distinct—nor, in fact, the most important one. For we can also consider whether a representation is distinct in relation to its object—or, in other words, we can consider whether a representation provides the subject with a distinct consciousness of its object. This second form of distinctness requires the first form of distinctness but should not be identified with it. For while the first form of distinctness is the product of analysis alone, this sort of distinctness is always the product of a synthesis that produces a consciousness of the object. Or, as Kant puts it in the *Vienna Logic*, "the act of making objects distinct occurs synthetically, the act of making concepts distinct occurs

This aspect of Kant's conception of cognition is a direct successor to Leibniz's understanding of the same. For example, in his "Mediations on Cognition, Truth, and Ideas," Leibniz defines a clear representation as follows: "a clear notion is like the one an assayer has of gold—that is, a notion connected with listable marks and tests that are sufficient to distinguish the represented thing from all other similar bodies." It is this more demanding sort of distinctness—distinctness as a representation of an object—that Kant appeals to in the *Logic* in distinguishing cognition from lesser forms of conscious representation. In other words, as Kant characterizes it there, we can cognize an object only to the degree that our representations provide us with a clear and distinct consciousness of this object. And this is possible only insofar as we are capable of performing the sort of conscious comparison discussed above.

In this way distinctness is one of the essential perfections of cognitions considered in relation to their objects. That is, the more distinct our cognition of some object is, the more perfect this cognition will be. Or, more helpfully, the more distinct our cognition of something is, the more fully we will cognize this thing. Given this, it is essential to cognition that full or perfect cognition of an object will involve the ability to consciously compare this object with respect to both numerical and qualitative identity and diversity. And, more generally, we can be said to cognize some thing only to the degree that our representation of it allows us to engage in this sort of conscious comparison. Or:

> **Numerical Identity**: One can only cognize X to the degree that one can represent X in a manner that allows one to become conscious of X's numerical identity and diversity.
>
> **Qualitative Identity**: One can only cognize X to the degree that one can represent X in a manner that allows one to become conscious of X's qualitative identity and diversity.

Thought of in this way, these constraints allow that we might have partial or incomplete cognition of something without being able to consciously compare it with every other possible thing. But nonetheless, given these constraints, there is an essential connection between cognition and conscious comparison. For, given them, we can only cognize something to the degree to which we are capable of becoming conscious of its determinate identity.[44]

analytically" (24:845). See also: "The greatest logical perfection as to clarity is distinctness. In Wolffian logics it is always only the analytic mode of distinctness that is considered. There is a far more extensive mode, however, namely the synthetic production of distinctness. Analytic production does not nourish cognition, it only analyzes cognition that is given to me, so I learn to distinguish what was already contained beforehand in that cognition" (*V-Lo/Wiener*, 24:843). Finally, compare the very similar claim at *Log*, 9:64. It is this latter, more comprehensive sort of distinctness that, for Kant, requires that we be able to perform the sort of conscious comparison at issue here. For, as Kant writes in the *Anthropology*—using "clarity" to refer to both the "first degree" of clarity (clarity proper) and the second degree thereof (distinctness): "Consciousness of one's representations, which suffices for the distinction of one object from another, is clarity" (7:137–38).

[44] Although there is a sense in which the resulting notion of cognition is a technical notion, it is important to stress here that it corresponds quite nicely to our ordinary understanding of what it is to know some thing. So, in discussing what it is to cognize an object, Kant is capturing a quite intuitive form of knowledge—even if this sort of knowledge is not the sort of knowledge that is the focus of contemporary epistemological debates.

In this way, although there is an essential connection between conscious comparison and cognition for Kant, this connection does not demand any *particular* degree of consciousness of identity. Rather, cognition comes in degrees, which correspond to the degree to which we are conscious of the determinate identity of thing being cognized. Of course, in some cases, like the case of things in themselves, our consciousness of identity will turn out to be so impoverished that it misleading to speak of us as having *any* cognition of the things in question. But this is ultimately just one case along a progression that runs from full cognition of a thing to a completely indeterminate—and thus contentless—representation.

In this way, Kant's discussion of conscious comparison in the *Logic* shows us how to flesh out the Determinate Content requirement noted above. This requirement was motivated by the idea that a representation can only count as cognition of an object insofar as it makes the subject conscious of its object as such. And this will only be possible insofar as the representation provides the subject with a consciousness of this object's determinate identity—something which, in turn, will only be possible insofar as one is able to consciously compare this object with other things as to identity and diversity. For it is only in virtue of being capable of consciously comparing the object of some representation with those things that are distinct from it that can we become conscious of this object as a determinate thing distinct from other things of a similar sort.[45] Thus, a representation will only satisfy the Determinate Content requirement to the degree that it also satisfies the two Identity requirements we have just noted.

So, even if Kant's two definitions of cognition are not quite equivalent, they are very closely related to one another. In particular, any limitation on cognition qua conscious comparison as to identity and diversity will also count as a limitation on cognition qua objective representation. For we can represent an object in this latter sense only to the degree that we can consciously compare it to other things with respect to identity and diversity. Given this, it is not surprising that Kant often stresses the role that comparison plays as a necessary condition of cognition. For example, he begins the Introduction to the B edition of the *Critique* by stressing that cognition only arises in so far as we compare the representations given to us by the senses:

> There is no doubt whatever that all our cognition begins with experience; for how else should the cognitive faculty be awakened into exercise if not through objects that stimulate our senses and in part produce representations, in part bring the activity of our understanding into motion to *compare these*, to connect or separate them, and thus to work up the raw material of sensible impressions into a cognition of objects that is called experience. (B1, my emphasis)

And Kant makes a similar connection between comparison and cognition explicit at A97 of the *Critique*, where he writes:

[45] As philosophers inspired by Kant, such as Strawson, have often stressed; see Strawson (1959), in particular, his discussion of the connections between being able to identify some particular thing and being able to place this thing within a more general spatial-temporal world.

> If every individual representation were entirely foreign to the other, as it were isolated and separated from it, then there would never arise anything like cognition, which is a whole of compared and connected representations. (A97)[46]

Finally, nowhere is the role of comparison in cognition more clear than in Kant's discussion towards the beginning of the Amphiboly, where he writes:

> Prior to all objective judgments we compare the concepts, with regard to their identity (of many representations under one concept) for the sake of universal judgments, or their difference, for the generation of particular ones, with regard to agreement, for affirmative judgments, or opposition, for negative ones, etc. (A262/B318)

As this last quote in particular makes plain, objective judgment—and so cognition—is only possible for the Kant of the *Critique* insofar as we have compared and connected together many different representations or concepts.[47] Given the Determinate Content constraint on cognition, this should come as no surprise. For given this, cognition of an object will be possible only insofar as we are able to compare this object to other things with respect to their numerical and qualitative identity and diversity. Of course, all three of these passages are concerned, in the first instance, with the sort of pre-consciousness synthesis that makes intuition (or so cognition) possible for Kant. But this synthesis is relevant here only insofar as it lays the groundwork for the sort of conscious comparison that we have been discussing here. Thus, there is a tight connection between the manner in which these two forms of comparison are relevant here.[48]

[46] Both of these quotes stress the role that both comparison *and* connection play in producing cognition. Although this is not my present focus, there is nothing surprising about this given my reading of cognition. After all, given this reading, we can only achieve cognition of an object—and, in particular, of an object as distinct from other things—insofar as we represent this object in relation to these other things. And this, naturally enough, requires that we represent this object using a representation that has been connected to representations of the other objects it is being compared to. So, in Kant's view, no comparison of the objects of representation is possible without these representations being connected together in certain ways.

[47] For further evidence of this sort, see Kant's discussion of whether the "I think" enables us to the achieve cognition of the self in the Paralogisms.

[48] It may at first glance seem as though the role comparison is playing here is subtly different from the role it was playing in the *Jäsche Logic* passage we have been discussing. In particular, in these quotes, it seems as though what is at issue is the comparison of representations—and not the comparison of their objects, which was the focus in the *Jäsche Logic* passage. But while there is a sense in which this is correct, as Kant makes clear immediately following the last quote just noted, the sort of comparison of representations that is at issue here involves the comparison of "the contents of concepts"—i.e., the comparison of "the things themselves" which are the objects of these concepts. Thus, when Kant speaks of the comparison of representations in this context, the sort of comparison he primarily has in mind is the comparison of representations in virtue of their objects. And given this, what is at issue here is ultimately the same sort of comparison as was at issue in the *Jäsche Logic* (insofar as that form of comparison applies to general representations like concepts). At the end of the day, in both cases, the comparison in question is a comparison *both* of representations and of their objects—for it is a comparison of representations in virtue of their objects.

7. Knowledge, Cognition, and Things in Themselves

Thus, despite initial appearances, it is in fact possible to reconcile the descriptions of cognition that Kant provides in the first *Critique* and in the *Jäsche Logic*. And when we do so, we arrive at a conception of cognition according to which a representation counts as a cognition of some thing just in case this thing is the determinate object of this representation—where this requires (at least) that the representation allow us to consciously compare this thing with other possible things with respect to identity and diversity—be this the identity of a particular thing in the case of singular cognitions or the identity of a class of objects in the case of general cognitions.

In addition, remember from our initial discussion of cognition that in order to cognize something we must be able to be conscious of it as really possible. As we will see in a moment, the interaction between these two constraints is crucial for understanding the limits on our cognitive faculties that Kant argues for in the first *Critique*. For, in claiming that we cannot cognize things in themselves, Kant is claiming that we cannot form representations of things in themselves that satisfy both of the requirements just stated.

Before discussing why this is the case, though, I want to return to the differences between the Kantian notion of cognition and the contemporary philosophical concept of knowledge. In particular, it should now be plain that Kant's conception of cognition is quite different from the sort of propositional knowledge that is the focus of contemporary epistemological discussion. For not only is cognition here, at least in the first instance, cognition of a thing or property as opposed to knowledge of a proposition, what is distinctive about having cognition of some thing is not that one's representation of it is particularly well-justified or warranted. Rather, what distinguishes cognition of something from a mere representation of it is that a cognition of something must represent this thing in a manner that makes us conscious of what it is that is the object of our representation. Now this is, to be sure, a species of knowledge in an intuitive sense. For cognition of something constitutes knowledge *of* the thing that is the object of our cognition. When we cognize an object, we will know what it is and how it is different from other things.

In other words, to achieve cognition of some domain of objects in Kant's sense is a matter of *knowing them* in a sense of these terms familiar, I think, from ordinary English. This, of course, will require that we have a good deal of propositional knowledge about them in something like the contemporary sense. And this sort of "knowledge" of objects, of course, often forms the grounds on which our propositional knowledge or *Wissen* is based. But not every instance of propositional knowledge or *Wissen* will count as an instance of cognition in this sense.

This is particularly important with respect to the question, with which we began, of how we can make coherent sense of Kant's claim that we cannot cognize things in themselves, given that Kant plainly does believe that we can know a good deal about the nature of things in themselves in general. Kant interpreters have gone to great lengths to reconcile these two aspects of Kant's theoretical philosophy. But if we conceive of cognition in the manner I have suggested, there is no great difficulty in doing so. In particular, if cognition requires an ability to consciously compare the things cognized with respect to identity and diversity, then it is easy to see why we might, on the one hand, *know* that things in themselves exist, and even that they have certain general properties, without thereby having cognition of them. For this sort of knowledge of general facts concerning things in themselves need not be sufficient to provide us with the ability to consciously compare them with respect to identity and diversity. And, even if did, it might not provide us with the ability to consciously compare them in a manner that also makes us conscious of them as *real possibilities*.

For instance, consider the sorts of facts about things in themselves that Kant accepts. As noted above, the facts in question include the fact that things in themselves affect us, that they are the ground of appearances, and that they lie outside of space and time. At least on their face, these are non-trivial claims about the nature of things in themselves—claims that, at least insofar as they involve existence claims, go beyond mere analytic truths.[49] But while they are by no means trivial, it is also clear that knowledge of these general properties of things in themselves is insufficient to provide us with cognition of them in the sense discussed above.

In particular, knowing these general facts about things in themselves does not put us in a position to know the determinate objects of our representations, when these representations concern things in themselves. For example, given Kant's claims about things in themselves, one way we can represent them is as the grounds underlying the world of appearances. But while doing so may allow me to refer to the things in themselves that ground the appearances I am aware of, it does not allow me to do so in a manner that makes me conscious of the relations of identity and diversity that exist among these things in themselves.

For example, consider two experiences of mine, E and F. I can think about the things in themselves underlying each of these two experiences simply by use of the definite descriptions: "the thing or things in themselves that ground E" and "the thing or things in themselves that ground F." And, given that I have in fact experienced E and F, I may well be in a position to "prove" in the relevant sense that things in themselves answering to these descriptions are actual and so really possible. For I may appeal to the testimony of my experience, plus the connection between the existence of this experience and the existence of the things in themselves in question to do so. But while I can form such representations, these representations—plus all of my general knowledge about things in themselves—do not place me in a position to say anything about whether the thing or things in themselves that ground E are the same as the thing or things in themselves that ground F. So these representations—plus my general knowledge about things in themselves—do not place me in a position to form even a minimally determinate conception of these objects in the sense of interest to Kant.

In particular, these representations will not put me in a position to consciously compare the things in themselves I am thinking about with one another with respect to their numerical identity and diversity. And something very similar is true of my ability to compare the things in themselves I am thinking of in this way with other

[49] That having been said, there may be nothing to these claims that cannot be established on the basis of synthetic knowledge of appearances, plus certain analytic truths about the relations between appearances and things in themselves. I want to remain neutral on this question here.

things in themselves with respect to their qualitative identity and diversity. For while the mode of presentation I am using to think of the things in themselves in question does make certain claims about the sort of things they are, these claims are extremely limited. And beyond these limits, the manner in which I am thinking of them does not put me in a position to determine whether the things I am thinking of are instances of one species (of potential thing in itself) as opposed to another. So while the ability to form these sorts of representations does allow me to form some very general judgments about things in themselves, it does not provide me with an ability to consciously compare them in at least two crucial respects—and so does not amount to an ability to truly cognize things in themselves in the sense of interest to Kant. In other words, these representations of things in themselves provide me with *such* a minimal consciousness of their determinate identity that it would be misleading to speak of me cognizing them in any meaningful sense. In other words, while there are some *very* weak standards of material correctness associated with these representations, they are so weak that it is impossible to speak of us having any genuine cognition of objects in this case. Thus, while we do know some very general truths about things in themselves, these truths are nowhere near substantive enough to provide us with anything like genuine cognitions of these things.

Obviously, this is the product of the impoverished nature of the concepts we are employing to think about things in themselves in this example. So we might try to achieve cognition of things in themselves by "enriching" these concepts in some way—say example, by packaging them with some positive theory of the nature of things in themselves. For example, we might try to accomplish this task by characterizing the nature of things in themselves using the theory of their nature provided by one of Kant's rationalist predecessors. By doing so, we *might* be able to arrive at a set of concepts for thinking of things in themselves that provide us with a basis for consciously comparing them with another as to identity and diversity, at least to a substantial degree. But in arriving at this capacity via this route, we would run afoul of the other restriction on cognition noted above. For once we "enrich" our account of things in themselves in this way, we can no longer rely on the testimony of experience to prove the real possibility of things in themselves so conceived. For the existence of our experiences and the general fact that these experiences must have some ground does not provide us with a basis for claiming that things in themselves meeting this "enriched" description are really possible. So while this maneuver might provide us with the ability to conceive of things in themselves as determinate objects, it would only do so via sacrificing our ability to prove their real possibility. And thus, on balance it would bring us no closer to cognition of them in Kant's sense.

In this way, referring back to our earlier discussion, it is only by considering the interaction between these two requirements on cognitions that it is possible to appreciate why Kant takes intuition to be essential to human cognition, at least of a theoretical sort. For what is distinctive about intuition in the present context is that when we exhibit the object of some concept to ourselves in intuition, we simultaneously accomplish two things. First, we demonstrate that the object of the concept is really (as opposed to merely logically) possible. And second, we provide the concept in question with a determinacy of content that it would otherwise lack. This is what makes intuition so important to human cognition for Kant: intuitions possess the ability to provide our concepts with the determinacy that cognition requires *in such a way* that it is possible to prove the real possibility of the resulting determinate object. Explaining just why this is true is, of course, a complicated issue. But the essential feature of intuition in this regard is the manner in which an intuition makes a *singular* object *immediately* present to the cognizer. For it is precisely the combination of these two canonical features of intuition that allow it to simultaneously present a determinate object to the cognizer in a manner that guarantees its real possibility.[50]

Thus, it is the impossibility of completing both these tasks simultaneously with respect to things in themselves (at least from a theoretical perspective) that makes cognition of them impossible. One of the primary advantages of this way of accounting for the limits of our ability to cognize things in themselves is that it—unlike many other such theories—does not rest on any particular view about what the distinction between things in themselves and appearances amounts to. For the difficulty just described will arise with respect to any conception of things in themselves *so long as it is allowed that the nature of things in themselves extends beyond what we are capable of intuiting*. For so long as this is the case, it will be impossible for us to rely on intuition as a means of simultaneously providing our concepts of things in themselves with determinate content *and* demonstrating the real possibility of the resulting conception of things in themselves. And while there is, of course, a great deal of room for debate about the precise relationship between things in themselves and appearances, this claim—that the nature of things in themselves is not exhausted by how they appear to us—should not be at all controversial. Thus, this way of thinking of the limits of cognition allows us to understand the fundamental limits Kant places on our cognitive faculties without entering into the endless controversies concerning the precise metaphysical status of things in themselves. This, I take it, is one of the primary advantages of the interpretation I have been offering here when compared with other, not-unrelated interpretations in the recent literature.[51]

In any case, I hope I have said enough to indicate that Kant takes the task of cognizing things in themselves to be impossible (in the broadest possible sense) because of the interaction between two fundamental constraints that are built into his conception of cognition: the demand that cognition be cognition of a determinate object and the demand that this object be something we can show to be really possible. If we accept this, then it is clear that, once we properly understand what Kant has in mind when he speaks of "cognition," there need be no great mystery about how Kant can both deny that we can achieve cognition of things in themselves and claim that we can know many general facts about them. For knowing a good deal about the nature of A's in general is not always sufficient to provide one with cognition of any particular A as a determinate and really possible object.

[50] Something similar is true, in a somewhat qualified sense, of the role that the so-called fact of reason plays in practical cognition. But this is a topic that would take us very far afield of the main subject of this chapter. For more discussion, see Kain (2010) and Schafer (forthcoming-a).

[51] For an overview of the contemporary debate about transcendental idealism, see Stang (2016b).

Appendix: Alternative Accounts of Cognition in Kant

In this chapter, I have focused on presenting on my positive views concerning Kant's conception of cognition. In this Appendix, I want to briefly discuss how my view of cognition relates to two other recent accounts. As noted above, all of these accounts agree on a great deal. But nonetheless it will be helpful to say a bit here about the differences between them, and about why I prefer my own account to the others.

The first alternative account I want to discuss is due to Tolley's important work on these issues. Much as I have done here, Tolley emphasizes the manner in which Kant locates "cognition" within a progression of forms of representation. And, in doing so, he similarly emphasizes the idea that cognition in Kant's sense is a matter of a certain sort of representation with consciousness—namely, the sort of representation that makes us conscious of an object as something distinct from our merely subjective state of mind. But, as noted above, Tolley objects to my account of cognition by arguing that my view cannot do justice to one crucial case in which Kant seems to allow that we can, even from a theoretical perspective, achieve a "highly determinate" conception of something supersensible—namely, the conception of God licensed by Kant's discussion of the *ens realissimum*. Here Tolley writes the following:

> What is more, this particular thought [God exists] allows us to think of an object which Kant himself insists is 'determinable or even determined as an individual thing through an idea alone' (B596)—hence, it would seem, determinable without any recourse to intuition. (Tolley, 2017, p. 19)

I have two responses to this objection. First, and more importantly, it seems to me to rest on a conflation of two senses in which we might be said to have a consciousness of something as a determinate object. In the case in question, we do (of course) represent God as wholly determined with regards to all possible predicates—for this is just what representing God as the *ens realissimum* involves. But that conception of God remains highly abstract and indeterminate in the sense relevant to my account of cognition. In particular, in representing God in this way, we do not thereby have any grasp of which particular predicates God possesses. In other words, in conceiving of God in this way, we form a description of God which can only have one thing as its referent (namely, God as the ground of all real possibility), but in doing so, we do not achieve anything like the consciousness of God's determinate nature that cognition requires. Thus, this manner of conceiving of God is very much akin to the conception of things in themselves as "whatever grounds appearances" that we discussed above. In such cases, we know that some thing in itself must satisfy an abstract description of some sort—and, in the case of God, know that there can only be a single individual that can do so—but we do not thereby gain any real consciousness of that thing as a determinate object in the sense relevant to, say, determining which material standards of correctness apply to judgments about it.

Second, in considering this objection, it is important to remember the importance of both of the two constraints on cognition noted above. In particular, while we can come up with a concept of God that represents him in the manner described above, this does not, on its own, mean that we can establish the real possibility of such a being in the manner that cognition would require. So, for example, in Kant's discussion of the *ens realissimum*, Kant acknowledges that such a concept would be sufficient to fully determine a particular individual as its referent—but at the same time insists that we are not necessarily in a position to theoretically know (in the sense of *Wissen*) that such a being is really possible, let alone actual. So, in order to achieve genuine theoretical cognition of God, we would not only need to achieve a real consciousness of God's determinate nature, as opposed to the highly abstract description of this nature that Kant here provides—we would also need to be able to prove (on theoretical grounds) that a thing with this nature is really possible.

Now, as I discuss in detail elsewhere, my views about this second question are rather complicated—since I do believe that theoretical reason provides us with subjectively sufficient grounds for belief in God in some sense. But nonetheless I also maintain that these grounds do not extend to the sort of objectively sufficient grounds which are characteristic of knowledge (*Wissen*). So here we have located a second reason why our conception of the *ens realissimum* does not provide us with theoretical cognition of God in my sense. Indeed, taking these two points together, the discussion of the Transcendental Ideal actually provides us with a particularly elegant illustration of the importance of the interaction of these two constraints for Kant's account of the limits of cognition.

For these reasons, I do not think that Tolley's objection on this point draws blood against my view. But what does Tolley say about the nature of cognition? Unlike me, Tolley does not make very much of either the Determinate Content constraint or the Real Possibility constraint—nor does he attempt to derive these from a more basic notion of "objective representation with consciousness" in the manner I have done here. Instead, Tolley's discussion of cognition focuses on the following conception of cognition:

> More specifically, I have argued that Kant conceives of cognition as a species of representation which involves four features: it is a representation (i) of a real object, which it represents (ii) mediately, by means of representing other representations, and which involves (iii) 'consciousness' [*Bewusstsein*] of the real relation between these other mediating representations and their object, a consciousness enabled by (iv) sensations which arise in the mind due to affection by the object in question.
>
> (Tolley, 2017, p. 28)

As should already be clear, there is much in this characterization of cognition that I agree with. In particular, I agree that cognition always involves a consciousness of at least three elements: (i) a "real object," which it represents, (ii) a representation by means of which this representation occurs, and (iii) some relationship between the two. Moreover, in the theoretical case, the nature of this relationship generally takes much the form that Tolley here describes. In particular, as we have already explained, in theoretical cognition, we generally become conscious of objects as really possible determinate things by conceiving of these objects as standing in "real relations" to our own representations via the dependence of our intuitions on these objects.

The fundamental problem with Tolley's account, to my mind, is that it does not really provide us with a unified account of why these various constraints on cognition follow from Kant's definitions of cognition as "acquaintance with consciousness" or "objective representation with consciousness." For instance, while it does follow from the later definition that cognition must involve some sort of consciousness of a relation between our representations and the objects it represents, in order to understand why this consciousness must involve a consciousness of a "real relations" between the representations and objects of the sort that sensibility provides, we need to consider the manner in which sensibility makes it possible to simultaneous satisfy the two constraints noted above. In this way, it seems to me that my account of cognition takes these matters deeper than Tolley's does.

This issue shows up in a variety of ways, especially when we consider cases other than the standard case of theoretical cognition of empirical objects. For in these cases, Tolley's lack of a deeper explanation of his claims sometimes leads him to the wrong results. For example, consider again the case of the things in themselves which ground the appearances we cognize. On Tolley's account, we can cognize these appearances because we can represent them as standing in real relations to our sensations. But we also know that these appearances themselves stand in a metaphysically real relation of dependence to the things in themselves (whatever they are) which ground them. So, whenever we cognize some appearance, we are also in a position to represent certain things in themselves as standing in a metaphysically real relation to our sensations—since we know that our sensations stand in real relations to certain appearances and that these appearances stand in real relations to certain (indeterminately conceived) things in themselves. Thus, in such cases, Tolley's account implies that we can in fact cognize things in themselves, even from a theoretical point of view. Or, perhaps better, it can only avoid this result by placing what seems like an arbitrary and philosophically unmotivated constraint on Kant's conception of "cognition."

As discussed above, we can avoid this result if we attend to the importance of the Determinate Content constraint in this context. So insofar as it neglects this aspect of Kant's conception of cognition, Tolley's account struggles to properly account for even very basic cases like this one. And, although this lies beyond the scope of this chapter, similar issues with this account also arise when we consider forms of practically grounded cognition—such as our ability to cognize our own nature as free beings from a practical point of view. For in this case, we encounter a form of cognition, which is grounded, not in the receptivity of sensibility, but rather in our own self-activity as practically rational beings. In other words, by treating an appeal to the receptivity of sensibility as part of the definition of Kant's general conception of cognition, Tolley's account seems to me doomed to generate the wrong results when we turn for the more familiar case of empirical forms of theoretical cognition to the forms of cognition that arise in a distinctively practical context.

Once again, I think this is an indication that Tolley has not taken his discussion of "cognition" as deep as it needs to go to cover all of the cases of interest to Kant. And something very similar seems to me to be true of Watkins and Willaschek's insightful recent discussion of these issues. Once again, there is much in their discussion that I am sympathetic to. But I also have a number of issues with it. Some of these I will not dwell on here—such as the manner in which they unnecessarily multiply senses of "cognition." For my fundamental disagreement with their account is in some ways similar to my complaint against Tolley's account—namely, that Watkins and Willaschek take Kant's account of one canonical form of cognition—namely, empirical cognition—and treat this as providing us with a definition of what cognition in general consists in. As a result, Watkins and Willaschek fail to take Kant's account of empirical cognition all the way to its foundations, while also arriving at an overly narrow conception of the scope of cognition in Kant's sense of this term.

More precisely, much as I have been doing here, Watkins and Willaschek take cognition in Kant's sense to be governed by two basic constraints. But they understand these two constraints rather differently than I do here. In particular, they write:

> That is, cognition in this sense must satisfy two conditions: (i) a givenness-condition, according to which an object must be given to the mind and (ii) a thought-condition, according to which the given object must be conceptually determined (cf. A50/B74; A92/B125; B137; B146). Although Kant never explicitly defines givenness as such, in its most general sense it seems to mean that an object is made available to the mind so that one can be aware of the existence of the object and (at least some of) its features. Kant claims that in human beings givenness involves passivity insofar as the object must act on our sensibility to be given to us (cf. A19/B33)....Thus it is only for finite beings like ourselves that objects are given in sensible intuition, which for Kant means that the object is represented not as exhibiting general features, but in its particularity. Similarly, only in finite beings does the thought-condition require the use of general concepts (which represent an object not in its entirety, but only partially, through marks it shares with other objects; cf. A68/B93; A320/B377; 9:58)... (Watkins & Willaschek, 2017a, p. 6)

Now, there is no doubt that Watkins and Willaschek are right to insist that human theoretical cognition requires both the satisfaction of some sort of "givenness-condition" and some sort of "thought-condition." That, of course, is one of the primary lessons of Kant's insistence that human theoretical cognition always requires the cooperation of intuitions and concepts. And it is a result that follows, as we have seen, from the conception of cognition proposed above as well. So the difference between my view and Watkins and Willaschek's view does not relate to whether human theoretical cognition is governed by these two constraints in some form. That is common currency (to a very large extent) between both views, even if we do have some disagreements about how these conditions are best understood. What separates my view from Watkins and Willaschek's is that I believe that these constraints are explained by deeper features of Kant's conception of what cognition is. Thus, what Watkins and Willaschek take to be a primitive assumption at work in Kant's account, I take to be something that Kant explains in terms of a deeper and more general conception of cognition.

One symptom of the issues this raises for Watkins and Willaschek is in the manner in which their conception of cognition forces to read Kant as uses "cognition" in a variety of different senses, even when discussing cognition of a theoretical sort. Of course, it is not implausible that Kant sometimes does this, but it seems to me that Watkins and Willaschek must attribute more such shifts in usage to Kant than is necessary. But more important for present purposes is the relationship of Watkins and

Willaschek's account to Kant's fundamental conception of cognition as something that comes in both a theoretical and a practical form. In particular, as Watkins and Willaschek explicitly acknowledge, their account of cognition is at best only suited to a treatment of what Kant calls "theoretical cognition" or "cognition of what is" and is wholly unsuited to a treatment of "practical cognition" or "cognition of what ought to be."[52] Thus, Watkins and Willaschek's account of cognition is at most suitable to only half of Kant's discussion of "cognition" in this most general sense. Much as was true of Tolley's account, this seems to me a symptom of a failure on Watkins and Willaschek's part to get to the bottom of Kant's conception of cognition. In short, the narrowness of Watkins and Willaschek's conception of cognition (in comparison with Kant's own conception thereof) seems to me to be a sign that Watkins and Willaschek have not really identified the conception of cognition that is most fundamental for Kant's discussion of both theoretical and practical cognition. I believe that the conception of cognition laid out above does better on this score.

This can be seen, I think, even if we set "practical cognition" to the side, as Watkins and Willaschek do, and focus on only cognition in its theoretical forms. For even there, I think we can see that Watkins and Willaschek do not take the matter nearly as deep as Kant himself does in his account of the nature of our form of cognition. For suppose we ask why it is that theoretical cognition must satisfy the two constraints laid out by Watkins and Willaschek. On their account, these constraints define what it is to be an instance of "theoretical cognition" for Kant, so there is rather little we can say in response to this question. But this would have been deeply dissatisfying within the historical context in which Kant was operating. For of course, one of the main opponents of the Kantian account of cognition are broadly Leibnizian accounts of cognition that would deny that theoretical cognition requires that any sort of object be "given" to us via something like affection by objects. Thus, Watkins and Willaschek's reading of "cognition" threatens to make Kant's entire discussion of the nature of cognition *blatantly* question-begging from the start, not just with respect to the contemporary debate about these issues, but also with respect to historical context in which Kant himself was writing.

Of course, Kant has arguments against such alternative views. But, again, these arguments can only be fully understood against the background of a conception of cognition that does not simply take a "givenness-condition" on cognition to be written into Kant's definition of what cognition is. In other words, we can only fully appreciate why Kant thinks we should reject conceptions of cognition that do not require either the "givenness-condition" or the "thought-condition" by going deeper into Kant's own thought about these issues to uncover a more fundamental conception of cognition at work in his thought—a conception of cognition, that is, that does not merely assume that human theoretical cognition is subject to these constraints, but rather explains why it is subject to these constraints in terms even more basic features of the nature of cognition as a cognitive achievement. It is precisely this sort of account of cognition I have tried to develop above. Thus, while I agree with much of what Watkins and Willaschek and Tolley say about the nature of cognition for

[52] For more on "practical cognition" in this sense, see again Kain(2010) and Schafer (2019, forthcoming-a).

Kant, none of them seem to me to capture the most fundamental conception of cognition at work in Kant's thinking about these issues—both as they appear in the theoretical sphere and as they appear in the practical domain.

References

Adams, R. (1997). Things in themselves. *Philosophy and Phenomenological Research, 57*(4): 801–25.

Allais, L. (2015). *Manifest reality: Kant's idealism and his realism*. Oxford University Press.

Allison, H. (1983). *Kant's transcendental idealism*. Yale University Press.

Ameriks, K. (2003). *Interpreting Kant's Critiques*. Oxford University Press.

Chignell, A. (2007a). Kant's concepts of justification. *Noûs, 41*(1): 33–63.

Chignell, A. (2007b). Belief in Kant. *Philosophical Review, 116*(3): 323–60.

Chignell, A. (2010). Real repugnance and our ignorance of things-in-themselves: a Lockean problem in Kant and Hegel. *Internationales Jahrbuch des Deutschen Idealismus, 7*: 135–59.

Evans, G. (1982). *The varieties of reference*. Oxford University Press.

Hanna, R. (2001). *Kant and the foundations of analytic philosophy*. Clarendon Press.

Hanna, R. (2006). *Kant, science, and human nature*. Oxford University Press.

Hawthorne, J. & Manley, D. (2012). *The reference book*. Oxford University Press.

Hogan, D. (2009). How to know unknowable things-in-themselves. *Noûs, 43*(1): 49–63.

Kain, P. (2010). Practical cognition, intuition, and the fact of reason. In B. J. Lipscomb & J. Krueger (Eds.), *Kant's moral metaphysics: God, freedom, and immortality* (pp. 211–30). De Gruyter.

Langton, R. (1998). *Kantian humility: Our ignorance of things in themselves*. Oxford University Press.

Longuenesse, B. (1998). *Kant and the capacity to judge: Sensibility and discursivity in the transcendental analytic of the* Critique of pure reason (C. T. Wolfe, Trans.). Princeton University Press.

McLear, C. (2011). Kant on animal consciousness. *Philosopher's Imprint*, 11(15). http://hdl.handle.net/2027/spo.3521354.0011.015

Schafer, K. (2017). Intuitions and objects in Allais's manifest reality. *Philosophical Studies, 174*(7): 1675–86.

Schafer, K. (2019). Kant: Constitutivism as capacities-first philosophy. *Philosophical Explorations, 22*(2): 177–93.

Schafer, K. (2021). A system of faculties: Additive or transformative. *European Journal of Philosophy*. 29 (4):918-936.

Schafer, K. (forthcoming-a). Practical cognition and knowledge of things-in-themselves. In E. Tiffany and D. Heide (Eds.), *Kantian freedom*. Oxford University Press.

Schafer, K. (forthcoming-b). Transcendental philosophy as capacities-first philosophy. *Philosophy and Phenomenological Research.*

Schafer, K. (forthcoming-c). Kant on method. In A. Stevenson and A. Gomes (Eds.), *The Oxford handbook of Kant*. Oxford University Press.

Schafer, K. (forthcoming-d). *Reason in Kant*. Oxford University Press.

Smit, H. (2000). Kant on marks and the immediacy of intuition. *The Philosophical Review, 109*(2): 235–66.

Smit, H. (2009). Kant on apriority and the spontaneity of cognition. In S. Newlands & L. M. Jorgensen (Eds.), *Metaphysics and the good: Themes from the philosophy of Robert Merrihew Adams* (pp. 188–251). Oxford University Press.

Sommerlatte, C. (2020). Empirical cognition in the Transcendental Deduction: Kant's starting point and his Humean problem. *Kantian Review*, *21*(3): 437–63.

Stang, N. (2016a). *Kant's modal metaphysics*. Oxford University Press.

Stang, N. (2016b). Kant's transcendental idealism. In E. N. Zalta (Ed.), *The Stanford Encyclopedia of Philosophy* (Spring 2021 Edition). https://plato.stanford.edu/archives/spr2021/entries/kant-transcendental-idealism/

Strawson, P. F. (1959). *Individuals*. Routledge.

Tolley, C. (2017). Kant on the place of cognition in the progression of our representations. *Synthese*, *197*(8): 3215–44.

Watkins, E. & Willaschek, M. (2017a). Kant's account of cognition. *Journal of the History of Philosophy*, *55*(1): 83–112.

Watkins, E. & Willaschek, M. (2017b). Kant on cognition and knowledge. *Synthese*, *197*(8): 3195–213.

11
Noumena as Grounds of Phenomena

Ralf M. Bader

1. Introduction

The distinction between noumena and phenomena lies at the core of Kant's transcendental idealism. How exactly this distinction is to be interpreted, however, is much disputed, in particular whether it is a methodological/epistemological distinction or a metaphysical distinction, and, if the latter, whether the contrast is between two types of properties or between two types of objects.[1] Two-worlds accounts of transcendental idealism operate with a robust metaphysical distinction. They consider noumena to be ontologically distinct from phenomena. Things in themselves and things that appear to us form two disjoint classes of objects. Such a robust distinction takes seriously the idea that transcendental idealism is a form of idealism and provides much-needed resources for accomplishing the tasks that Kant envisages, especially when it comes to making room for transcendental freedom and resolving the antinomies more generally.

Though they are distinct, phenomena and noumena are not unconnected. In particular, they are connected by a grounding relation: noumena are the grounds of phenomena (cf. *KpV*, 5:6). Phenomena are derivative entities that owe their existence as well as their determinations to noumena. This is what allows phenomena to inherit their objectivity from noumena and thereby underwrites Kant's empirical realism. Though Kant is committed to a form of idealism, his version of idealism, namely transcendental or formal idealism, is highly distinctive and differs importantly from phenomenalistic approaches that reduce objects to mental states. Though phenomena are mind-dependent, they are not dependent on particular minds or their mental states, but are dependent on the forms of intuition that all of us share. Phenomena are matter-form compounds that depend on noumena for their matter, but depend on us for their form (see *Prol*, 4:375; *Br*, 11:395). Their spatiotemporal form is attributable to the fact that space and time are our forms of intuition. Idealism regarding form is thereby combined with realism concerning matter. It is for this reason that, unlike noumena which are absolutely real and objective in a completely unrestricted sense, phenomena are only real for us (i.e., for beings with our forms of intuition).[2] They are empirically real but transcendentally ideal.

[1] For a helpful overview of this debate, see Stang (2016).

[2] They will not appear to cognitive beings with other forms of intuition (who will have their own appearances that are disjoint from ours). Nor will they appear to an intuitive intellect that does not have any forms of intuition—nothing appears to such a non-receptive intellect.

Ralf M. Bader, *Noumena as Grounds of Phenomena* In: *The Sensible and Intelligible Worlds: New Essays on Kant's Metaphysics and Epistemology.* Edited by: Karl Schafer and Nicholas F. Stang, Oxford University Press.
DOI: 10.1093/oso/9780199688265.003.0012

Not only are the properties of phenomena determined by noumena, the very existence of the phenomenal realm is dependent on noumena. Phenomena are derivative entities. Their matter, which is encapsulated in the manifold of intuition, derives from noumena. This manifold is translated into the spatiotemporal forms of intuition to yield phenomena, i.e., matter-in-form. Since phenomena are constructed out of the translated manifold of intuition, they are not independent existents, but are dependent on noumena. Without noumena there would not be any manifold of intuition, and there would consequently not be anything that could serve as an element in a phenomenal logical complex. Accordingly, not only are the properties of objects within the phenomenal domain supervenient, the domain itself is supervenient.[3] Noumena determine both the existence and the determinations of phenomena—that they exist and how they exist. Given this dependence of phenomena on noumena, we can infer the existence of noumena from the existence of phenomena. For there to be constructions, there must be something out of which they are constructed. There must be things that can feature as the elements of the logical complexes.[4]

This type of determination and dependence can be precisely characterized by means of supervenience relations. Such relations concern the dependent-variation of properties. They hold if two families of properties are functionally connected. More precisely, it is by means of coordinated multiple-domain supervenience relations that we can capture in quasi-formal terms the determination and dependence relations between noumena and phenomena.[5] It will be argued that we are concerned with a multiple-domain, rather than a single-domain, supervenience relation, given that noumena and phenomena are distinct entities that possess different properties and that can be found in different domains (section 2). The fact that noumena and phenomena are connected by the transformation function that is involved in the process of intuition implies that the supervenience relation is mediated and coordinated, such that particular noumenal features are connected to particular phenomenal features by means of this transformation function (section 3). Moreover, the base properties are restricted to transcendental properties, since it is only these properties that play a role in yielding phenomena—the others are not compatible with our forms of intuition and are accordingly filtered out (section 4). Finally, it will be shown that this construal of the relation between noumena and phenomena does not violate noumenal ignorance (section 5), and does not involve a problematic ontologizing of space and time (section 6).

[3] Kim (1993) calls this "existence supervenience": "There is no world in which individuals of D_1 exist but in which individuals of D_2 do not" (p. 114).

[4] This inference to noumena is not an inference from effect to cause (which is at issue when inferring the existence of noumena on the basis of our receptivity, which involves positing noumenal affection as the cause of our representations), but from grounded to ground (cf. Bxxvi–xxvii).

[5] There is an additional hyperintensional aspect involved in the grounding relation that cannot be captured by supervenience. This hyperintensional aspect can, however, be set aside for the purposes of this chapter. In fact, supervenience relations are better suited for our purposes since they allow for greater flexibility and precision.

2. Multiple-Domain Supervenience

Single-domain supervenience concerns the dependent-variation of different families of properties instantiated by the same objects. It holds if objects that are indiscernible in terms of subvening properties are also indiscernible in terms of supervening properties. This understanding of supervenience is not adequate for capturing the grounding relation between noumena and phenomena in the context of a two-world account, given that phenomenal and noumenal properties have different exemplifiers. Since the subvening and supervening properties are instantiated by distinct things that are to be found in different domains, we have to appeal to multiple-domain supervenience relations. Two distinct and disjoint domains are involved in the supervenience relation, whereby indiscernible distributions of properties in the subvening domain give rise to indiscernible distributions in the supervening domain.

In the case of single-domain supervenience relations, A-properties supervene on B-properties iff B-indiscernibility implies A-indiscernibility across the relevant range of possible worlds. Distributions that are B-indiscernible also need to be A-indiscernible, where distributions are understood in terms of assignments of properties to objects. Two distributions are indiscernible with respect to B-properties if there is a B-preserving isomorphism. A one-to-one mapping Γ from distribution D_1 to D_2 is such a property-preserving isomorphism iff any x in D_1 has any B-property F if and only if the object to which x is mapped by Γ in D_2 also has F.[6] Thus, A-properties supervene on B-properties iff all B-preserving isomorphisms are A-preserving.

When dealing with a single domain, every B-preserving mapping also has to be A-preserving. This, however, does not make sense when dealing with a plurality of domains. We then have different mappings for the subvening and supervening domains. As a result, B-preserving isomorphisms cannot be A-preserving. This means that we need to specify the relation between the mappings in the different domains if we are to develop supervenience relations across these domains. We need to connect the domains and thereby connect the mappings.

This can readily be done in the case of transcendental idealism. The phenomenal and noumenal domains are coordinated and connected rather than being independent of each other. In particular, they are connected by means of the forms of intuition. The forms of intuition give rise to a transformation function that connects the two realms and specifies the way in which phenomenal outputs result from noumenal inputs. This function corresponds to the one involved in the processing of the manifold of intuition. The role of this process is captured nicely by Findlay (1981) when he notes that "experience is not a free composition, but rather a translation into the diction of space and time of a text framed in another idiom" (p. 34). The processing functions involved in ordering, processing, and synthesizing the manifold of intuition in accordance with the forms of intuition can be broken down into three component subprocesses, namely (1) imposition, (2) selection, and (3) translation.

[6] If the set of B-properties includes irreducibly plural properties, then the notion of B-indiscernibility must be supplemented by the condition that any plurality of xx's has any plural B-property F iff the image of the plurality under Γ also has F (whereby the image of a plurality is the plurality of the images of the members of the plurality).

Forms of intuition are imposed, the manifold is selected for compatibility with these forms, and the selected manifold is translated into the forms. This ensures that the relation between noumena and phenomena is not direct but mediated by our forms of intuitions. Phenomena are determined by noumena via our forms of intuition.

The forms of intuition thus give rise to a coordination relation R that connects members of the subvening domain to members of the supervening domain. The mappings should, accordingly, not be independent of each other, but should track this connection. This can be achieved by appealing to the coordination relation in order to specify the images of members of the subvening domain in the supervening domain. This allows us to connect the mappings of the members of one domain with the mappings of their images in the other domain. In this way, we are able to track determination and dependency relations across multiple domains.

Multiple-domain supervenience holds iff every property-preserving mapping on the subvening level is such that the images of the mapped objects under the coordination relation R are also indiscernible. This can be stated precisely by means of the notion of an associated mapping.

ASSOCIATED ISOMORPHISM

A one-to-one mapping of members of the supervening domain Γ' from D_S onto D_{S^*} is an associated mapping of a mapping of members of the subvening domain Γ from D_B onto D_{B^*}, if it is the case that if any collection of members $x_1 \ldots x_n$ from D_B is mapped onto $x_1^* \ldots x_n^*$ from D_{B^*} by Γ, then Γ' maps the images of $x_1 \ldots x_n$ under R in D_S, i.e., $y_1 \ldots y_n$, onto the images of $x_1^* \ldots x_n^*$ under R in D_{S^*}, i.e., $y_1^* \ldots y_n^*$.

This allows us to specify strong global multiple-domain supervenience relations, whereby the associated mappings of all B-preserving isomorphisms must be A-preserving isomorphisms if A-properties are to supervene on B-properties.[7]

SG-MDS

for all possible worlds w and w*, every B-preserving mapping of the members of the subvening domains of w and w* is such that all its associated mappings of the members of the supervening domains of w and w* are A-preserving.

[7] This strong version can be distinguished from a weak version, whereby every B-preserving isomorphism must only have some associated A-preserving isomorphism. Since the weak version fails to track interesting dependence and determination relations we can set it aside.

WG-MDS

for all possible worlds w and w*, every B-preserving mapping of the members of the subvening domains of w and w* has an associated A-preserving mapping of the members of the supervening domains of w and w*.

These coordinated versions differ only if the coordination relation fails to be unique, i.e., if $x_1 \ldots x_n$ has a plurality of images under R in the supervening domain. In such cases, a particular mapping of the subvening domain will have a plurality of associated mappings, allowing us to distinguish between a weak version of multiple-domain supervenience that requires only that one of these associated mappings be A-preserving and a strong version that requires all of them to be A-preserving.

Put differently:

> A-properties supervene on B-properties iff for all possible worlds w and w*, every mapping Γ of objects in the subvening domains of w and w* that is such that any x or plurality of xx's has any B-property F if and only if the object or plurality to which x or the xx's are mapped by Γ also has F is also such that any image under R of x or of the xx's has any A-property G if and only if any image under R of the object or plurality to which x or the xx's are mapped by Γ also has G.

3. Domain Coordination

Domains are coordinated when there is some relation between the members of the different domains that establishes a correspondence between objects (or pluralities of objects) in the supervening domain and objects (or pluralities of objects) in the subvening domain. This coordination relation connects the mappings in the different domains that are used for assessing for property-preserving isomorphisms when dealing with multiple-domain supervenience relations. It thereby allows us to make sense of determination and dependence relations between the noumenal and phenomenal realms.

The coordination relation is particularly crucial when dealing with non-holistic forms of determination. If the determination is local, such that particular noumena (or pluralities thereof) determine particular phenomena (or pluralities thereof), then there must be some way of connecting them up and specifying which phenomena correspond to which noumena. However, it is also required if determination should be holistic, as long as it matters not only which properties are instantiated but also which objects are doing the instantiating. Otherwise, all that one can say is that if the subvening domain of noumena is a certain way, then the supervening domain of phenomena is a certain way (where each property distribution is characterized completely independently of the other). This is because one can then only say that there exists an A-preserving mapping of the members of the supervening domain if there exists a B-preserving mapping of the members of the subvening domain. This, however, means that the base is unable to distinguish between any of the permutations of the supervening domain and hence cannot fix which object has which properties, but can only fix that there are some objects instantiating the properties in question.

Incorporating a coordination relation into our supervenience principle allows us to connect the domains in a non-holistic manner. By connecting particular members of the different domains, we can model the fact that particular phenomena are grounded in particular noumena.[8] This is important since the phenomenal sphere is likely not to be determined holistically by the noumenal sphere, but instead result from a more localized form of determination that connects particular objects in the two domains. Even though a holistic determination of the phenomenal sphere as a whole is not ruled out in principle, as far as theoretical reason is concerned, more

[8] As we will see, such a coordination relation is not too restrictive and does not threaten to undermine noumenal ignorance, since the mere condition that it connects members of the domains does not determine whether a one-one, one-many, many-one, many-many, or variably polyadic connection holds.

fine-grained determination relations are necessary when bringing in commitments stemming from the practical side, given that they are required to make sense of the idea that a subject's empirical character is a reflection of its intelligible character (cf. A540/B568).

The role of the coordination relation is particularly clear when considering the multiple-domain supervenience version of individual as opposed to global supervenience:

> Phenomenal properties supervene on noumenal properties relative to coordination relation R just in case for any collections of phenomenal objects $x_1 \ldots x_n$ and $y_1 \ldots y_n$ that have images under R and any possible worlds w and w*, if $R|x_1 \ldots x_n$ in w is indiscernible with respect to noumenal properties from $R|y_1 \ldots y_n$ in w*, then $x_1 \ldots x_n$ in w is indiscernible with respect to phenomenal properties from $y_1 \ldots y_n$ in w*.

The supervenience relation that characterizes the relation between the noumenal and phenomenal realms is a coordinated supervenience relation, where the domains are connected by means of the translation function of the process of intuition. The forms of intuition thus feature in the supervenience relation insofar as they provide the translation function that gives rise to the coordination relation. This function translates the matter provided by noumena into phenomenal properties, into a spatiotemporally ordered manifold, thereby giving rise to the phenomenal "images" of the noumenal entities.[9] The fact that we impose certain frameworks, namely space and time, into which the information contained in the manifold of intuition is translated ensures that noumena and phenomena are coordinated and that the supervenience relation is mediated. The particular translation function associated with these frameworks then determines the precise nature of this mediation, i.e., the way in which the coordination takes place.

The coordination relation, moreover, enables us to individuate the relata of the supervenience relation. On the face of it, our ignorance of noumena would seem to preclude us from giving an adequate account of how noumenal property distributions are individuated. Yet, providing such an account is necessary for making a supervenience claim. This is because supervenience holds if B-indiscernibility implies A-indiscernibility, i.e., if the fact that the base properties are distributed in the same way implies that the supervening properties are also distributed in the same way. Since assessing for indiscernibility requires us to appeal to property-preserving isomorphisms, we need to specify noumenal mappings. Yet, it is not clear what the members of the domain are that should be mapped. These could be noumenal objects, certain aspects of such noumenal objects, or some other individuating characteristic such as noumenal analogues of spatiotemporal locations. There seems to be no way for us to provide an exhaustive list of the possible candidates, nor any

[9] When there is a one-many coordination relation that connects one phenomenal feature to a plurality of noumenal features, there will not be a unique noumenal feature that is the image of x and that can be mapped. Instead, the image of x will be a collection of features and one has to assess the collection for indiscernibility by mapping its members. The same holds, mutatis mutandis, for many-one and many-many relations.

principled way to decide between them. We simply do not know how to individuate noumenal grounds.

This problem can be addressed by appealing to the coordination relation. Rather than providing a direct characterization of the way in which noumenal property distributions are individuated, which seems to be a futile endeavor given noumenal ignorance, we can characterize the individuation indirectly by means of the coordination relation. We can do this by providing an account of the individuation of phenomenal property distributions and then letting the coordination relation pick out the noumenal analogues of these individuating features. An indirect account specifies how to individuate phenomenal properties and then appeals to the images under the coordination relation of these individuating features in order to identify the relevant unit of analysis.[10] Whether the noumenal entities or items that are selected in this way turn out to be objects or aspects of objects or something altogether different can be completely left open.[11] Hence, all we need to do is to give an adequate account of the individuation of distributions of phenomenal properties. The coordination relation will then take care of specifying in an indirect manner the corresponding noumenal individuating features.

How then are phenomenal property distributions to be individuated, and what are the members of the distributions which are mapped when assessing for property-preserving isomorphisms? Two candidates suggest themselves, namely (i) spatiotemporal regions and (ii) phenomenal objects. When the phenomenal realm is considered on its own, it is ontologically amorphous. All there is is a spatiotemporal distribution of intensive magnitudes that can be fully characterized by means of the categories of quantity and quality. All the ontological structure of the phenomenal realm is derived from the noumenal realm. There are, accordingly, no bounded and unified individual objects at the phenomenal level when it is considered in abstraction from its noumenal grounds. We should thus not use a metaphysically substantive notion of objecthood that involves the category of substance in characterizing property distributions.

Instead, we should either use a non-substantive notion of objecthood or appeal to spatiotemporal distributions. These two options turn out to be equivalent since, according to the minimal understanding of objects, phenomenal objects can be understood as filled spatiotemporal regions.[12] An object in this minimal sense is a collection of properties local to a spatiotemporal region. Properties are distributed across regions and objects are then identified with these filled regions.[13] An

[10] There is no need for all of the entities instantiating the properties in the base domain to be of the same kind, i.e., the images under R can be heterogeneous.

[11] Since we are unable to give a transparent specification of R, we only know that there is a correct individuation, without being able to transparently specify what it is. As a result, noumenal ignorance is not undermined.

[12] These minimal objects are contrasted with ontologically substantive phenomenal objects, i.e., with phenomenal substances, which require the properties that are bundled into a minimal object to be bounded and unified as a result of being adequately grounded.

[13] This minimal understanding of an object has close analogues in field theories as well as in supersubstantivalistic theories. Transcendental idealism allows us to reap the benefits of this minimal notion of an object without incurring the costs that this notion brings with it in the context of these other theories. For example, while field theories as well as supersubstantivalistic theories have the problematic consequence

individuation in terms of the minimal notion of objecthood, whereby a phenomenal object is considered as a filled spatiotemporal region, thus coincides with an individuation in terms of spatiotemporal structures of property instantiations. Supervenience, accordingly, holds if we have indiscernible filled spatiotemporal regions, given that the images of those regions are indiscernible.

Finally, the coordination relation plays a crucial role by mediating the grounding relation between noumena and phenomena. Even though facts as to what the world is like for us are determined by facts about noumena together with facts about our forms of intuition, the forms of intuition do not enter into the supervenience base. Instead of entering into the base, the translation function deriving from our forms of intuition mediates the supervenience relation. This means that we do not reduce phenomena to the conjunction of noumena and the forms of intuition, but rather reduce phenomena to noumena via the forms of intuition. Conversely, we generate phenomena out of noumena via forms of intuition, rather than out of the conjunction of noumena and forms of intuition. Matter and form are not on a par but play different roles. The grounds of phenomena are restricted to their matter, whilst their forms do not play a grounding-role. The forms of intuition are not amongst the grounds but mediate the grounds to result in hylomorphic matter-form compounds. In particular, instead of being ingredients in the reductive base, they mediate the relation between noumena and phenomena by specifying the selection, filtering, and translation processes that are applied to the manifold of intuition.

As a result, the existence of phenomena does not presuppose that there are any subjects with our forms of intuition. All that is required for the existence of phenomena is the existence of the relevant kinds of noumena. We need nothing more than noumena to get phenomena. In other words, noumenal properties exhaust the supervenience base. Since the forms of intuition do not enter into the supervenience base, the supervenience claim does not need to be restricted in such a way as to hold only in cases where the forms of intuition are present. This is what ensures that transcendental idealism involves a distinctive form of mind-dependence, whereby phenomena are not dependent on any particular minds or their mental states, but are instead dependent on the forms of intuition. The role that our noumenal selves play is not to function as grounds of the phenomenal realm (except when it comes to grounding the corresponding phenomenal selves), but to fix which transformation functions are applicable. The contribution that we make by supplying the forms of intuition is thus not a contribution at the level of the grounds.

of making all minimal objects modally rigid, we can account for the modal flexibility of minimal objects. This can be achieved without undermining the modal rigidity of spatiotemporal regions and without bringing in any dubious resources such as a counterpart-theoretic account of modality. This is possible because transcendental idealism provides us with two ways of individuating objects, namely (i) in terms of their phenomenal features, and (ii) in terms of their noumenal grounds. Only the former way coincides with the rigid way of individuating spatiotemporal regions. The latter version is independent of spatiotemporal characteristics, thereby providing us with the requisite flexibility.

4. Transcendent and Transcendental Properties

So far, we have indiscriminately referred to the noumenal sphere as constituting the supervenience base of the phenomenal sphere. By appealing to the process of intuition, we can give a more fine-grained account of the base properties as well as of the objects belonging to the subvening domain. This process allows us to distinguish between various kinds of noumenal properties and restrict the set of subvening properties to a proper sub-set of the noumenal properties. In particular, it is the selection function of the process of intuition that is responsible for demarcating those properties which play a role in grounding phenomena and making experience possible and which we can label the transcendental properties from those properties that play no such role and which we can label the transcendent properties.

More precisely, the selection function determines which properties count as transcendent properties. Whether a property is transcendent depends on whether the instantiation of that property can function as a ground of noumenal affection whereby a manifold of intuition is provided that is suitable for being processed by cognitive beings having our forms of intuition. Properties classify as transcendent either if they provide a manifold that is incompatible with the forms of intuition and that is consequently filtered out, or if they are inert and do not give rise to a manifold at all. Such transcendent properties do not enter as input into the translation function and are in that respect irrelevant to the genesis of the phenomenal sphere. They are consequently also irrelevant to the supervenience relation that models the grounding relation between noumena and phenomena. Since they do not affect phenomena, insofar as phenomena do not immediately depend on them and are not determined by them, they do not belong in the supervenience base. We can accordingly restrict the supervenience base such that phenomenal properties supervene only on a sub-set of the properties of the noumenal realm, namely on transcendental rather than transcendent properties.

There may well be relations amongst objects or properties within the noumenal realm that would make some, or maybe even all, transcendental properties dependent on certain transcendent properties. This would, for instance, be the case if everything were to ontologically depend on God. That is, for all we know, it might be the case that there are internal or external necessary connections in the noumenal realm. These connections would ensure that any nomologically or logically possible world (depending on what kind of necessity is involved in the necessary connections) that contains the transcendental properties would also contain those transcendent properties that are connected to these transcendental properties by means of these connections.

This, however, does not affect the supervenience principle, which states that indiscernibility in terms of transcendental properties implies indiscernibility in terms of phenomenal properties. It will still be the case that if the same transcendental properties are instantiated, then the same phenomenal properties will also be instantiated. All it implies is that it might be nomologically or logically impossible to have a possible world that contains an isolated duplicate of the transcendental realm. In other words, it might not be possible to have a duplicate of the transcendental realm without there being transcendent properties of certain kinds (if we have generic dependencies) or without there being particular transcendent properties (if we have rigid dependencies).

In order to get a supervenience principle that takes the restriction of the supervenience base into account, we have to assess for indiscernibility with respect to transcendental properties. The images under R, namely $R|x_1...x_n$ and $R|y_1...y_n$, have to be indiscernible only with respect to transcendental properties in order for indiscernible phenomenal properties to arise, rather than having to be indiscernible with respect to noumenal properties in general. Indiscernibility in terms of transcendental properties suffices for making objects B-indiscernible, given that transcendent properties are excluded from the supervenience base. Accordingly, as long as $R|x_1...x_n$ and $R|y_1...y_n$ are indiscernible in terms of transcendental properties, x and y must be indiscernible with respect to phenomenal properties, even if $R|x_1...x_n$ and $R|y_1...y_n$ differ in transcendent properties.

All the subvening properties are members of the set of transcendental properties. As a result, the coordination relation R connects phenomenal objects and properties to a sub-set of the noumenal realm, namely the transcendental realm. This means that any $R|x_1...x_n$ is an object with transcendental properties. Objects that only have transcendent properties do not feature in the subvening domain, on the basis that they do not (immediately) ground phenomena.

> Phenomenal properties supervene on transcendental properties relative to coordination relation R just in case for any collections of phenomenal objects $x_1...x_n$ and $y_1...y_n$ that have images under R and any possible worlds w and w*, if $R|x_1...x_n$ in w is indiscernible with respect to transcendental properties from $R|y_1...y_n$ in w*, then $x_1...x_n$ in w is indiscernible with respect to phenomenal properties from $y_1...y_n$ in w*.

Alternatively:

> Phenomenal properties supervene on transcendental properties relative to coordination relation R just in case for any possible worlds w and w*, every mapping Γ of transcendental objects from w and w* that preserves transcendental properties is such that all its associated mappings of phenomenal objects from w and w* preserve phenomenal properties.

These supervenience claims reflect the core features of the grounding relation between noumena and phenomena, insofar as they are irreflexive, strong cross-world supervenience claims, that hold with logical necessity for all possible worlds,[14] connecting properties across multiple domains, whereby the domains are coordinated

[14] Since phenomena are not emergent entities that require bridge laws to come into existence, but are logical complexes that have as their elements translated matter provided by noumena, the relation between noumena and phenomena is one of logical supervenience, such that B-indiscernibility implies A-indiscernibility in all possible worlds rather than only in a restricted range of worlds where certain bridge laws obtain.

and whereby we assess the indiscernibility of supervenience bases in terms of transcendental properties.

5. Noumenal Ignorance

Since the phenomenal and noumenal realms are connected to each other and stand in coordinated supervenience relations, it may be wondered why we cannot gain knowledge of noumena on the basis of our knowledge of phenomena. Given that phenomena and noumena correspond to each other and given that there is a metaphysical connection between these two realms, one might think that there is also an epistemological connection that would allow us to identify the noumenal counterparts of phenomena, thereby undermining noumenal ignorance.

To begin with, it is worth noting that our knowledge of phenomena is rather limited. In particular, knowledge of non-structural features is ruled out. We only know phenomenal relations, whilst the underlying non-relational properties, namely the physical intensive magnitudes, are not accessible to us. We can only specify them indirectly in terms of the effects that they can bring about (cf. *Refl* 5590). However, we cannot make an inference from these effects to the underlying categorical properties that ground the relevant causal powers. This is because phenomenal roles might be multiply realizable and because the possible realizers can only be specified in an opaque but not a transparent manner. Though we do know that there must be a role filler, our knowledge is restricted to knowing that the role is filled by something or other. Accordingly, we never know what it is that fills the role. Multiple things could fill this role and there is no way for us to single out the actual role filler. In a sense, our ignorance is ineffable, to borrow Lewis's (2009, pp. 215–216) phrase, since we do not even know what the different options are. That is, we do not even know what the different possible realizers are. Even if there were only one possible candidate for filling the role, we would not know what would be filling the role and would not be able to characterize this unique realizer. This is because we are not acquainted with the realizer and lack the conceptual resources to give a transparent specification of the realizer. Instead, we can only specify it opaquely as whatever it is that fills the role in question.[15]

Moreover, even if we were able to transparently specify the phenomenal role filler, this would not threaten noumenal ignorance since we cannot appeal to the inverse of the translation function. This is because we lack knowledge of the way that the translation function works and are not able to reverse-engineer the process whereby phenomena arise. Since we do not know the input-output relationships, we can only characterize the inputs as whatever it is that gives rise to the phenomena in question. Yet, we cannot specify them in a transparent manner. In addition, the problem of multiple realizability arises again. Supervenience need not be symmetric: though phenomena supervene on noumena, noumena need not supervene on phenomena. Phenomena can be indiscernible even though their images under R are discernible.

[15] The distinction between transparent and opaque specifications is due to Foster (1982, p. 62).

This means that we cannot get from phenomenal outputs to the noumenal inputs that generate them, but only to the range of possible inputs. Accordingly, we cannot construct the base domain on the basis of the supervening facts. Instead, all we can do is use R to pick out the noumenal image of some phenomenal outputs. In that case, one does not try to reverse-engineer the inputs from the outputs, but takes the base domain as being given and picks out the actual ground in this domain. The problem of multiple realizability is then circumvented, since, even though a given output can have multiple possible grounds, it has a unique actual ground and this is the image under R.

Knowledge of the phenomenal realm is thus restricted to structural knowledge. The problem now is that a sufficiently strong connection between noumena and phenomena might underwrite an inference from knowledge of the structure of the phenomenal realm to knowledge of the structure of the noumenal realm. According to Russell, noumenal ignorance is compromised since noumena can be understood as forming "a world having the same structure as the phenomenal world, and allowing us to infer from phenomena the truth of all propositions that can be stated in abstract terms and are known to be true of phenomena" (Russell, 1920, p. 61; cf. Schlick, 1979, p. 104).

Given the transcendental ideality of space and time, it follows that there is no spatiotemporal correspondence between the realms. The non-spatiotemporality of noumena prevents us from getting from the spatiotemporal structure of phenomena to that of noumena. As a result, the noumenal structure that could be inferred from phenomenal structure would only be abstract mathematical structure, rather than concrete spatiotemporal structure. The structure of the phenomenal world, accordingly, could at most allow us to identify the cardinality of the noumenal domain. Unless concrete relations can be identified and suitably connected to known phenomenal relations, any collection of the right cardinality will have the relevant abstract structure, making this kind of knowledge almost trivial.[16]

Yet, even knowledge of the cardinality of the noumenal domain is ruled out. There is no guarantee that the noumenal and phenomenal realms have the same cardinalities. Indeed, given the possibility of transcendent properties and objects any isomorphism claim is almost certain to be false. Transcendent objects do not play any role in grounding experience and thereby ensure that the noumenal realm has additional structure that is not reflected in phenomena. Because of this surplus structure, the structure of phenomena should not be expected to be isomorphic to the structure of noumenal reality, undermining any cardinality claim.

It might be suggested that instead of an isomorphism claim about the relation between phenomena and noumena, we can make an embeddability claim by specifying a sub-set of the noumenal realm, namely the realm consisting of transcendental objects, that stands in an isomorphism relation to the phenomenal realm. We could

[16] This problem for pure versions of structuralism, known as the Newman problem, was first identified by Newman (1928) and Carnap (1928, §§153–55). It can be overcome by transcendental idealists, since the forms of intuition allow one to operate not with abstract mathematical structure but concrete spatiotemporal structure, thereby vindicating structural realism within the phenomenal realm, cf. Bader (2010, ch. 2.2.3).

thereby make cardinality claims about transcendental objects, while lacking knowledge of the noumenal sphere within which the transcendental objects are embedded. This suggestion, however, is also problematic since we do not know how to individuate the members of the domains and since we are ignorant of the translation function that connects the transcendental realm to the phenomenal realm. There are a number of plausible principles of individuation even when it comes to individuating the members of the phenomenal domain. We could appeal to filled spatiotemporal regions, logical complexes, or bounded phenomenal objects. With respect to noumena, things are even less clear. The members of the domain could be analogues of regions, they could be noumenal objects, aspects of such objects, or something altogether different. As we have seen, noumenal ignorance implies that the individuation of noumena is best characterized indirectly via the process of intuition, i.e., via the coordination relation. Since this relation could be a many-one, one-many, many-many, or variably polyadic relation, there is no guarantee that we can identify any isomorphisms and any cardinality claim turns out to be unfounded.

Even though there is a non-arbitrary connection between the phenomenal and noumenal realms, and even though phenomena somehow correspond to and are manifestations of noumena, any isomorphism or embeddability claim is inappropriate. Instead of making such claims, we should argue that the two domains are coordinated, without specifying the precise character of the coordination relation. We only specify this relation functionally insofar as it is equivalent to the translation function that results from our forms of intuition. However, we do not specify the particular input-output relationships. This allows for sufficient flexibility to allow not just for one-one determination or correspondence as would be required for an isomorphism, but also for one-many, many-one, many-many, and variably polyadic relations.

This method only guarantees isomorphisms if we take the units of individuation, which are then mapped by the isomorphisms, as being equivalent to the input and output variables of the translation function. There would then be one output for each input, guaranteeing a one-one relation. This, however, does not say anything about whether these inputs and outputs are simple or complex or whether they can be given more fine-grained individuations. In particular, the individuation principles for the different domains might well turn out to be completely different. This would give rise to disparate units for the two domains, thereby undermining the significance of the isomorphism claim. There is thus no reason to assume that the correct individuation principles imply a one-one function that gives rise to an isomorphism between phenomena and transcendental objects. We are, consequently, ignorant of the cardinality of the transcendental realm as well. By contrast, if one were to adopt a one-world view, then noumenal ignorance could not be preserved. A commitment to an identity claim between noumena and phenomena would imply a one-to-one correspondence ensuring that the cardinality of transcendental objects could be determined on the basis of the cardinality of the phenomenal realm, which would at the same time also determine a lower bound on the cardinality of the noumenal realm.

Thus, even though phenomena are grounded in noumena, the fact that we are dealing with a coordinated supervenience relation that is based on certain translation and filtering processes has the consequence that there is no perfect mirroring relation between the realms and that we are not able to make determinate inferences about the latter on the basis of the former.

6. Ontologizing Space and Time

Phenomena are derivative entities that are grounded in noumena. They are consequently reducible to noumena via the forms of intuition. To this it might be objected that there are irreducible relations at the phenomenal level, that certain phenomenal relations are non-supervenient and that this implies that we cannot consider all aspects of the phenomenal realm as being supervenient. If some phenomenal relations should be irreducible, then this would indeed undermine the claim that the phenomenal sphere supervenes on the noumenal sphere. Yet, although there is a sense in which certain phenomenal relations are indeed irreducible, this turns out to be unproblematic since they are reducible in another sense. More precisely, there are phenomenal relations, such as spatiotemporal relations, which cannot be reduced to the intrinsic properties of their relata. These relations occupy a fundamental position within the ontological inventory of the phenomenal realm. This, however, is unproblematic, given that the fact that something is not reducible to phenomenal properties does not imply that it is not reducible tout court. Though these relations cannot be reduced to any other phenomenal items, they are nonetheless reducible to noumenal features. While they do not supervene on phenomenal properties, they do supervene on noumenal features.[17]

There is nothing that precludes noumenal relations from featuring in the supervenience base of the phenomenal realm. While phenomenal relations might not supervene on noumenal non-relational properties alone, it seems reasonable to claim that they do supervene on a base that includes noumenal relations. Thus, if the "non-supervenient" phenomenal relations are to be grounded, it is not sufficient to ground the intrinsic properties of their relata. Instead, we need to provide a direct ground of these relations. Accordingly, we should claim that phenomenal relations that do not supervene on the intrinsic properties of their relata supervene on noumenal relations. This means that the supervenience principle must include relations in the supervenience base. Unless we want to be extreme Leibnizians and argue that all relational properties are reducible to non-relational properties, we will have to make room for noumenal relations upon which the "non-supervenient" phenomenal relations can supervene.

Relational and non-relational phenomenal properties thus supervene on relational and non-relational noumenal properties. We must take the relational properties of the noumenal grounds into consideration if we are to have a supervenience principle that covers all phenomenal features. Accordingly, the phenomenal sphere is wholly sustained by noumena. It is a logical complex and every aspect of it, including every relational aspect, is reducible to that out of which it is constructed.

[17] How we ought to understand the reducibility of chiral relations and what impact this has on the argument from incongruent counterparts will not be discussed here. An investigation of this intriguing topic will have to wait for another occasion.

The reducibility of phenomenal relations, including the reducibility of spatiotemporal relations, may seem objectionable on the basis that such a reduction of phenomenal relations could be considered to amount to ontologizing space and time in the way done by Leibnizians and that Kantians should be suspicious of such a commitment. To ontologize space and time amounts to treating them as transcendentally real, making them properties of things in themselves. Understood in this way, we can see why Leibnizians ontologize space and time. Even though they argue that monads are atemporal and aspatial, they nonetheless accept the reducibility of spatiotemporal relations. If spatiotemporal relations are reducible to monads, then they are features of monads, even if monads themselves are neither in space nor in time. They are not fundamental features of monads, but are rather derivative features. This means that the reducibility of spatiotemporal relations implies that space and time turn out to be features of monads, that is, of things in themselves.

The Kantian can avoid treating space and time as transcendentally real, while accepting the reducibility of relational properties. This combination of views is possible because of the imposition and translation functions involved in the process of intuition. These functions mediate the supervenience relation. They consequently also mediate the reducibility relation. In both the Leibnizian and the Kantian system there is supervenience and reducibility. Whereas the relation between monads and phenomena in the Leibnizian system is characterized by a non-mediated reducibility relation, in that spatiotemporal relations are immediately reducible to determinations of monads, the supervenience relation in the Kantian system is a coordinated multiple domain supervenience relation, whereby the coordination relation is provided by the process of intuition. This ensures that, even though the Kantian system also includes a commitment to a supervenience relation, the supervenience relation in this system is mediated by the translation function. Rather than understanding phenomena as just being confused perceptions of noumena, they are logical complexes that result from a transformation process that translates the information contained in the manifold of intuition into imposed frameworks, namely the forms of intuition. Accordingly, in order to reduce spatiotemporal relations we need both (i) the supervenience base and (ii) the transformation functions. This means that we are dealing with a mediated reducibility relation.[18]

The difference between the two systems accordingly derives from the forms of intuition. These forms ensure that we have real heterogeneity, rather than merely confused perceptions. The forms of intuition genuinely add something and thereby ensure that we do not end up with direct reducibility to the properties of noumena. We need something in addition to the non-relational properties of noumena to get phenomena. We even need something in addition to the non-relational and relational properties of noumena to get phenomena. What we need is the translation function. It is the translation function that provides the connection between noumena and phenomena, thereby mediating the supervenience and reducibility relations. The forms of intuition ensure, in this way, that the mediated reducibility of spatiotemporal relations does not involve the ontologizing of space and time.

[18] For a detailed account of the resulting metaphysical system, see Bader (2010).

From a Kantian point of view, the kind of reducibility of relational properties to which Leibnizians are committed is particularly problematic, given that Leibnizians hold a relationalist view of space and time. In the context of such a relationalist view, the reduction of spatiotemporal relations amounts to a reduction of space and time themselves. This is something the Kantian cannot accept. Space and time would thereby become relational properties of things in themselves. For the Kantian, however, space and time are forms of intuition. They are not reducible to noumenal relations. Instead, they are our contributions to the phenomenal realm. It is precisely for this reason that the structures of space and time are not contingent but necessary and can be known by us a priori.[19] Whilst the Kantian needs to reject the reducibility of space and time, there is no need to reject the reducibility of spatiotemporal relations. We can reduce spatial relations without reducing space itself. All that needs to be rejected is the relationalist view of space and time. Instead, the Kantian can claim that space and time are mental frameworks. As such, they are independent of any spatiotemporal relations. Things are related within space and time, rather than space and time merely being the systems of spatiotemporal relations.

According to transcendental idealism, spatiotemporal relations are grounded in and supervene on noumenal relations. As a result, we can reduce spatiotemporal relations to noumenal relations. This reduction, however, has to go via the forms of intuition, thereby avoiding worries of ontologizing space and time. To understand how this works, we need to appeal to the coordinated supervenience relation and to the role of the translation function. This allows us to retain our commitment to the view that space and time are nothing but forms of intuition, whilst accepting the reducibility of all phenomenal relations.

7. Conclusion

Phenomena are distinct from noumena, but are nevertheless closely connected to them, in that they are grounded in noumena via the forms of intuition. This grounding relation can be modeled by means of a coordinated multiple-domain supervenience relation, whereby the coordination relation plays a crucial role in preserving noumenal ignorance and avoiding a commitment to ontologizing space and time.[20]

References

Bader, R. M. (2010). The transcendental structure of the world. Unpublished PhD thesis, University of St Andrews.

Carnap, R. (1928). *Der logische Aufbau der Welt*. Felix Meiner.

[19] The structure of space and time is built into the supervenience relation, since the coordination relation is based on the forms of intuition that mediate the relation between noumena and phenomena. As a result, the structural properties of space and time trivially supervene—they supervene on any base, even an empty base, and in that sense are necessary.

[20] Thanks to audiences at Miami and Berlin. Special thanks to Nick Stang and Karl Schafer for very detailed and helpful comments on an earlier draft of this paper.

Findlay, J. N. (1981). *Kant and the transcendental object*. Oxford University Press.
Foster, J. (1982). *The case for idealism*. Routledge & Kegan Paul.
Kant, I. (1900–). *Kants gesammelte Schriften*. Reimer/De Gruyter.
Kim, J. (1993). *Supervenience and mind*. Cambridge University Press.
Lewis, D. (2009). Ramseyan humility. In D. Braddon-Mitchell & R. Nola (Eds.), *Conceptual analysis and philosophical naturalism* (pp. 203–22). MIT Press.
Newman, M. H. A. (1928). Mr. Russell's "causal theory of perception." *Mind*, *37*(146): 137–48.
Russell, B. (1920). *Introduction to mathematical philosophy*. Macmillan.
Schlick, M. (1979). *Philosophical papers* (vol. 2). D. Reidel.
Stang, N. (2016). Kant's transcendental idealism. In E. N. Zalta (Ed.), *Stanford encyclopedia of philosophy* (Spring 2021 Edition). https://plato.stanford.edu/archives/spr2021/entries/kant-transcendental-idealism/

12

Thing and Object

Towards an Ecumenical Reading of Kant's Idealism

Nicholas F. Stang

1. Introduction

The meaning of Kant's transcendental idealism, and of the distinction between appearances and things in themselves, has been controversial ever since the publication of the first edition of the *Critique of Pure Reason* in 1781. It is even controversial how the different interpretations should be characterized. Some parties to the debate abjure the labels given to them by others (the accusation that one has a "Berkeleyan" reading is considered especially inflammatory[1]), and some have argued that the standard ways of dividing up the interpretative terrain are misguided.[2]

In this chapter I will argue that, on one standard way of characterizing the debate, both "sides" are correct, but are about different parts or aspects of Kant's idealism. To invoke a familiar metaphor, they are climbing the same mountain, but from different sides.

One reading takes the distinction between appearances and things in themselves to be a distinction between two domains of objects: those that exist in being experienced (or experienceable) by us, and those that exist *an sich*, independently of such experience. The other reading takes it to be a distinction between two kinds of properties possessed by one and the same domain of objects: the properties that can appear to us in experience, and the properties they have *an sich*. Representatives of the second reading differ over what this distinction is—for instance, whether it is the distinction between relational and intrinsic properties (e.g. Langton, 1998), or between response-dependent and response-independent properties (Rosefeldt, 2013), or between essentially manifestable and non-essentially manifestable properties (Allais, 2015), etc.[3]

[1] Though some have embraced it, e.g., Turbayne (1969). In Stang (2021b) I argue that the "phenomenalist" reading of Kant should be thought of as Leibnizian rather than Berkeleyan. Ameriks (2006) attempts to account for the persistence of the Berkeleyan reading, without endorsing it.

[2] The standard account of the debate remains Karl Ameriks's classic (1982) (cf. Ameriks, 1992), while Beiser (2002) puts this debate in its historical context. Key documents in the contemporary debate include Adams (1997), Allais (2004, 2015), Allison (1983, 2004), Aquila (1979), Bird (1962, 2006), Langton (1998), Marshall (2013), Prauss (1971), Rosefeldt (2013), and Wood et al. (2007). Historically influential accounts that have, unfortunately, attracted less attention recently are Adickes (1924, 1929) and Vaihinger (1881–92). Allais (2015), Schulting (2010), and Stang (2018) contain overviews of the *status controversiae*.

[3] It has become standard to include among Identity readings the "epistemic" reading articulated by Henry Allison, Graham Bird, and Gerold Prauss. However, I am skeptical whether that is the right way of

Nicholas F. Stang, *Thing and Object: Towards an Ecumenical Reading of Kant's Idealism* In: *The Sensible and Intelligible Worlds: New Essays on Kant's Metaphysics and Epistemology*. Edited by: Karl Schafer and Nicholas F. Stang, Oxford University Press.
 DOI: 10.1093/oso/9780199688265.003.0013

These differences among representatives of the second reading will be somewhat immaterial, however, for I am more interested in a more basic difference between the two readings. The first reading denies that the domain of appearances and things in themselves overlap, so it denies that the relation of *identity* can hold between appearances and things in themselves. The second reading holds that the very same objects that have appearance properties also have *an sich* properties. Thus, the second reading holds that appearances (objects with appearance properties) are the very same objects as things in themselves (objects with *an sich* properties): anything with appearance properties must also have *an sich* properties. There may be objects with *an sich* properties that do not appear to us (and thus have no appearance properties),[4] so this reading is not committed to the complete overlap of the two domains of objects, but it is committed to the domain of objects with appearance properties being a subset of the domain of objects with *an sich* properties and, thus, to every appearance (i.e., every object with appearance properties) being *identical* to a thing in itself (i.e., an object with *an sich* properties), namely, itself.[5,6] So the two interpretative claims I want to consider are the following:

Identity. Every appearance is numerically identical to a thing in itself (a thing with *an sich* properties).[7]
Non-Identity. No appearance is numerically identical to a thing in itself (a thing with *an sich* properties).[8]

Upholders of the Non-Identity readings have offered a range of arguments against Identity:[9]

grouping things; see Stang (2018) for some reasons to think the standard categories of interpretation are misguided. Secondly, there is considerable disagreement among "epistemic" readers about Identity. Allison rejects it (1987, p. 168), while Prauss embraces it (1971, p. 22). Bird has a more complex view: Kant is committed only to the conceivability, not to the existence, of things in themselves, so the question of their identity with appearances (to whose existence he is committed) does not arise (Bird 2006, pp. 553–86; cf. Bird, 1962, pp. 18–35).

[4] As Kant admits at B308: "Although beings of understanding certainly correspond to the beings of sense [...] there may even be beings of understanding to which our sensible faculty of intuition has no relation at all" (B308–309), taking "beings of sense" to refer to appearances (objects qua appearing) and "beings of understanding" to refer to things in themselves (objects as they are in themselves).

[5] So formulated, an intermediate position is possible: the appearance and *an sich* domains intersect, but neither is a subset of the other. While this is a position in logical space, it has, to my knowledge, no adherents, and I will temporarily ignore it. (Later, I will argue that it does not significantly alter the dialectic.)

[6] Because there is no totality of objects in space and time (I take this to be the lesson of the mathematical Antinomies), claims about the "domain" of spatiotemporal objects need to be understood as claims involving a universal quantifier: every appearance is identical to some thing in itself.

[7] The Identity claim is explicitly made by Adickes (1924, pp. 20, 27), Allais (2004, p. 657), Langton (1998, p. 13), Prauss (1971, p. 22), and Westphal (1968, p. 120). While Allais (2015) offers a more nuanced approach (see esp. p. 72) she also repeatedly writes as though appearances and things in themselves are the very same objects (e.g. pp. 72–73, 128, 130). See Stang (2016a, pp. 284–86), for a critical discussion of Allais on this issue.

[8] Recent defenders of Non-Identity include Aquila (1979), Marshall (2013), Stang (2014), and Van Cleve (1999). Langton (1998) can also be read as a Non-Identity theorist (as I argue in Stang, 2018, section 5.2).

[9] Informal statements of these arguments can be found in Marshall (2013) and Robinson (1994); a more formal presentation is given in Stang (2014).

Counting. If every appearance is also a thing in itself, then the number of things in themselves must be at least as great as the number of appearances. Thus, in counting appearances we come to know a numerical lower bound on things in themselves, which violates Kant's doctrine of noumenal ignorance.

Modes of existence. Appearances exist in being experienced (or being experienceable), while things in themselves do not. Since no object can enjoy multiple modes of existence, no thing in itself is identical to an appearance.

Modality. Appearances and things in themselves have different *de re* modal properties. Appearances are *de re* necessarily spatial, and would not exist if we did not (or could not) experience them. Things in themselves are not spatial, and hence not *de re* necessarily spatial, and would exist if we could not experience them. Since no object can have distinct *de re* modal properties, appearances and things in themselves are numerically distinct.

Division. Kant resolves the Second Antinomy (between infinite division, on the one hand, and finite division into simple parts, on the other) by claiming that appearances are infinitely divisible (though their complete division is not "given"), but, were they things in themselves, the Antinomy would remain an irresolvable contradiction for reason.[10] Thus, the mereological structure of appearances and things in themselves must be different: appearances are infinitely divisible, while things in themselves are finitely divisible into simples. Since no object can be both infinitely and finitely divisible, appearances and things in themselves are numerically distinct.[11,12]

All of these arguments presuppose, implicitly or explicitly, (i) that appearances and things in themselves are objects of quantification (values of bound variables), (ii) that the relevant relation of "sameness and difference" is numerical identity of objects of quantification, and (iii) that Leibniz's Law governs this relation. I do not have the space here to show this in detail of each such argument, so I will show it in one case; the generalization to other cases (esp. that of Counting) is straightforward. Stang (2014) contains the following version of the modal discernibility argument (reformulated slightly for ease of exposition):

> [Where *a* is any appearance in space and *t* is any thing in itself:]
> (1) It is possible that: *t* exists and there are no cognitive subjects with a spatial form of intuition.
> (2) It is not possible that: *a* exists and there are no cognitive subjects with a spatial form of intuition. (A42/B59, A383)
> (3) $\therefore a \neq t$.

[10] See A525/B553, *Prol*, 4:507.

[11] This argument would need to be spelled out more carefully. In Stang (2014) I argue that, given the infinite divisibility of matter, the Identity thesis entails that there are infinitely many things in themselves (violating our ignorance of them). However, I do not argue directly that the difference mereological in properties entails Non-Identity. See Robinson (1994) and Marshall (2013) for more. In an unpublished paper Tobias Rosefeldt defends the Identity view against this objection.

[12] I am not committing myself to the assumption that one and the same object cannot have distinct modes of existence, *de re* modal properties, or different ways of being divisible; I am expressing this as a premise in an argument against the Identity view. In Stang (2014) I explain how a Non-Identity reading could allow that the mode of existence of an object depends upon whether it is considered as an appearance or as a thing in itself. Ditto for *de re* modal properties.

(4) ∴ No appearance is identical to any thing in itself.

A suppressed premise in this argument is Leibniz's Law:

(LL) For any P, $(x)(y)(x{=}y \supset \mathrm{P}x \leftrightarrow \mathrm{P}y)$[13]

But even with this additional premise, the original argument is valid only if *t* and *a* can be values of (first-order) variables. Otherwise, LL cannot be instantiated and used to show that (1) and (2) are inconsistent with the negation of (3); and if *t* and *a* are not values for bound variables, the universal generalization that licenses (4) would be invalid. But this means that the argument all along assumed that both appearances and things in themselves are objects in the contemporary quantificational sense, familiar to us from Frege and Quine, that is, values of bound first-order variables. A consequence of this presupposition is that identity/sameness of things in themselves and appearances is assumed to be numerical identity, a relation between quantificational objects (namely, the relation every object bears to itself and no other). One could, of course, reject this modal indiscernibility argument by simply rejecting Leibniz's Law altogether; I will not discuss that at the outset, although the solution I will explore involves something equivalent to restricting Leibniz's Law.[14]

In this chapter I attempt to bridge this interpretative divide by exploring Kant's concepts of objects and things. In section 2 I argue that the most general concept of "object" in Kant's philosophy is the concept of the object of the capacity for representation in general. Whenever we talk about objects in Kant, we must first ask ourselves, "objects of what capacity?" In section 3 I make a prima facie textual case for distinguishing Kant's concepts of "object" and of "thing" and I explore the use of "*Ding*" as a technical term by Kant and his rationalist predecessors. I argue that when Kant talks of *Dinge an sich selbst* he means *Ding* as a translation of the Latin *res*, a being possessed with *realitas*, that is, intensively gradable causal force. This reinforces the case for distinguishing these concepts: the semantic-cognitive concept of the object of a representational capacity is, intuitively, distinct from the metaphysical concept of a locus of force.[15] In section 4 I return to the Indiscernibility arguments with which we began and argue that the modern quantificational notion of "object" in those arguments (i.e., the value of a bound variable) has an analogue in Kant's philosophy (what can be assigned as the value of the variable *x* in judgment). We must then ask "object of what capacity?" and I argue that the answer is intuition: for Kant, the "quantificational" concept of an object is the concept of an object of intuition.

With all of these materials in hand I then proceed to answer the original question about Identity. In section 5 I examine what identity and distinctness of (quantificational) objects amounts to, in the sensible case (where both are phenomena), in the non-sensible case (where both are noumena), and in the problematic mixed case

[13] Another implicit premise is that *de re* modal contexts are referentially transparent. A large part of Stang (2014) explores the options for a "one object" reading of transcendental idealism that rejects that premise. Consequently, I do not discuss it further here.

[14] See the Conclusion (section 10).

[15] The same two claims are made in Stone (n.d.), although the arguments for them are somewhat different. Although I developed these ideas independently of Stone, I have learned a great deal from his fascinating paper.

(phenomenal, noumenal). I argue that because there is no intellect that intuits both sensible and non-sensible objects, we can make no sense of the idea that sensible and non-sensible objects are identical (no object can be the object of *both* sensible and non-sensible intuition). Claims of numerical identity *and* of numerical distinctness between sensible and non-sensible objects are incoherent. I express this by saying they are "non-identical" rather than merely not being identical.

In the rest of this chapter I propose a reading of Kant's idealism: appearances and things in themselves are non-identical *objects* but the same *things*. They are loci of force and activity, which are given to us in sensible intuition as objects in space and time, and would be given to an intuitive intellect as objects non-identical to the first. After presenting, in section 6, prima facie textual evidence that this is Kant's view, in section 7 I turn to the hard work of explaining what the sameness of things might amount to. I distinguish two readings of the claim that appearances and things in themselves are the same things: (i) a collective reading, on which it says that the thinghood of appearances is the same as the thinghood of things in themselves, and (ii) a distributive reading, on which it asserts a singular relation of sameness between individual appearances and individual things in themselves. I argue that the collective reading is generally correct, because thing-hood is reality (intensively gradable causal force) and noumenal reality constitutes the common matter from which both things in appearance and things in themselves are constituted. In section 8 I go on to argue that the distributive reading is *also* correct, but only in the case of a finite rational will. I am a locus of causal power (a thing) that is an object to itself (represents itself) in two fundamentally different ways: self-actively in consciousness of my own freedom, and passively in experience of my actions in space and time (section 9). My empirical will and my noumenal will are the same thing but distinct objects. The brief Conclusion in section 10 answers some objections, and, in particular, concerns about whether this interpretation is even consistent.

I want to make absolutely clear going forward that I am not claiming that Kant consistently makes this distinction between "objects" and "things" explicit. I am arguing that his theory involves two distinct conceptual roles, and many of our confusions are dispelled once we carefully distinguish them. It would have been helpful if Kant had marked this distinction lexically, but he often does not. In fact, in several key passages he uses *Ding* and *Sache* to express what I call the object role and *Gegenstand* and *Objekt* to express the thing role. However, because I do not think that Kant himself uses the terms *Gegenstand* or *Objekt* or *Ding* in a particularly consistent fashion, I think we are free to use them to mark, lexically, conceptual distinctions that, I will argue, Kant needs to articulate his transcendental idealism.[16]

[16] I am not the first to argue that Kant's idealism involves a distinction between things and objects; Marshall (2013) argues that appearances and things in themselves are numerically distinct objects because they are distinct "*qua* objects" that take the same things as "bases." Stone (n.d.), from which I have learned a great deal, examines the scholastic background to Kant's notions of object and thing. However, due to limits of space, a detailed *Auseinandersetzung* with Marshall and Stone will have to await another occasion.

2. Objects

In the course of the Critical system Kant deploys many different conceptions of an object, but he also makes clear that these are specifications of a highest, most general concept of an object:

> The highest concept with which one is accustomed to begin a transcendental philosophy is usually the division between the possible and the impossible. But since every division presupposes a concept that is to be divided, a still higher one must be given, and this is the concept of an object (*Gegenstand*) in general (taken problematically, leaving undecided whether it is something or nothing). (A290/B346)

The highest concept of transcendental philosophy is <*object of representation*>, which is confirmed in the metaphysics lectures: "The highest concept under which all other elementary concepts can be ordered is the concept of an object in general, which lies at the ground of representation (*der bey der Vorstellung zum Grunde liegt*)" (*V-Met-*K_3*E/Arnoldt*, 29:960).[17] <*Object*> cannot be defined by giving a more general concept and then defining <*object*> as a species of it through the provision of a differentia, because there is no more general concept; it is the most general concept of transcendental philosophy whatsoever. The most we can do is give informal indications or explications of how this concept is to be used.[18] I take the most general concept of object to be the concept of what a representation is of, or about. Of any representation of anything we can ask "What is it the representation of?," that is, we can ask about its object.[19] This is made especially clear by Kant's definition of the *nihil negativum*, "the object of a concept that contradicts itself" (A291/B348). That even a self-contradictory concept has an object means that the highest concept of an object, <*object of representation*>, is a very weak notion of object indeed. It is little more than a reified way of talking about the "content" (in our contemporary sense, not Kant's technical notion of *Inhalt*) of a representation.[20] "Object" in this perfectly general sense should not be confused with the contemporary "quantificational" notion of an object; indeed, it should not be taken to be "ontologically committal" at all. In contemporary terms, Kant is not ontologically committed to the *nihil negativum* just by describing its concept as an "object."

[17] Cf. *V-Met/Volckmann* (28:410–11), *V-Met/Schön* (28:477–79), *V-Met-*L_2*/Pölitz* (28:542), and *V-Met/Mron* (29:811).

[18] Though we can give more informative definitions of more specific concepts of an object, i.e., "object of experience."

[19] "No object without representation" does not entail "no representation without an object," for Kant appears to allow a class of representations, sensation (or "subjective" sensations in the terminology of the *KU*, 5:206), that have no object. See A320/B376.

[20] A concept is said to have *Inhalt* when it is related to an object that can be given in intuition; this is why concepts of noumena lack *Inhalt*. But our contemporary notion of "content" is much broader; to say that concepts of noumena lack content would be to say that they, and judgments involving them, are meaningless. This confusion between Kant's technical notion of *Inhalt* (as well as *Sinn* and *Gebrauch*) with their contemporary analogues (sense, use) is the source of many of the more "deflationist" (and, I would argue, confused) interpretations of Kant's claims about noumena and things in themselves. See Tolley (2013) for more.

Since the highest concept of transcendental philosophy is <*object of representation*> any more specific concept of objects in that science must be a more specific concept of objects of representation. In particular these will include concepts of objects of specific kinds of representation (e.g. objects of concepts, objects of intuitions), or of specific representational capacities (e.g. objects of understanding, objects of sensibility).

Our mind has certain capacities for representing objects and these capacities operate in distinctive ways, that is, there are multiple distinct ways in which our mind can have objects (in which there can be objects for us). For our purposes, the most important distinction is between our spontaneous capacity for representation, understanding, by which we actively think conceptual representations of objects, and our receptive capacity of representation, sensibility, by which we passively receive intuitive representations of objects. Because "object" is always implicitly "object of representation" and because we have multiple distinct capacities for representation, which operate according to distinct principles, when we talk about objects we must always (at least implicitly) specify which representational capacity they are objects for: objects of intuition, objects of concepts, objects of theoretical cognition (which are both intuited and conceptualized), objects of reason (some of which are not objects of cognition), objects of desire, objects of our representational capacity in general, etc. Objects as such are always objects of some capacity for representation (some capacity for having objects).[21]

This explains a notable syntactic feature of Kant's writings, his frequent use of the genitive expressions *Gegenstand der/einer Anschauung* and *Gegenstand des/eines Begriffs*. This is Kant's way of making explicit the fact that objects are always objects of representational capacities. It also explains his otherwise very puzzling talk about "*the* object" of a concept (*der Gegenstand eines Begriffs*), or, referring to a concept, about "its object" (*ihr Gegenstand*).[22] This is puzzling because concepts, being general representations, do not in general have only one object in their extension; Kant is willing to talk about "the" object of a concept even where the concept has more than one instance, and even where it necessarily has no instances (e.g., from above, the *nihil negativum* or "the object of a concept that contradicts itself"A291/B348). The explanation for this is that "the" object of a concept does not refer to its instances, or to what we would now call its "extension" (the set of its instances), but merely refers to the "content" of that concept. Talk about "the" object of a concept is merely a disguised way of talking about what a concept represents, what it is "about."[23]

[21] This is brought out especially well in Stone (n.d.).

[22] E.g. in the *KrV* alone, see A220/B267, A234/B287, A291/B348, B298, A327/B384, A489/B517, A596/B624n.

[23] This means that Kant uses *Gegenstand/Objekt* as the equivalent of *materia circa quam*, that which a representational act is about. Cf. Baumgarten, *Metaphysica* §344: "If [a being] is conceived of as in the very act of determination, then it is called the MATTER CONCERNING WHICH (an object, a subject of occupation)," to which is added the German gloss "der Gegenstand." Cf. *Ontologia* §949. Kant takes notice of this usage in *V-Met-L$_2$/Pölitz*, 28:575. Thanks to Abe Stone for calling my attention to these passages in Baumgarten and Wolff, and to the notion of *materia circa quam*.

3. Things

There are various passages in the *KrV* that suggest a difference between the conceptual roles of <*object*> and <*thing*>:[24]

> This predicate [space – NS] is attributed to things only insofar as they appear to us, i.e., are objects of sensibility. (A27/B43)
>
> Through [space] alone is it possible for things to be outer objects for us. (A29)
>
> If, therefore, space (and time as well) were not a mere form of your intuition that contains *a priori* conditions under which alone things could be outer objects for you [...] (A48/B66)
>
> [Time] is only of objective validity in regard to appearances, because these are already things that we take as objects of our senses [...] (A34/B51)
>
> In accordance with a natural illusion, we regard as a principle that must hold of all things in general that which properly holds only of those that are given as objects of our senses. (B610)

At the most rudimentary level, <*thing*> and <*object*> are distinct concepts because <*object*> is a relative concept and <*thing*> is not. <*Object*> is the concept of the object *of representation*. In each of these passages, "object" means "object of sensibility *for us*"—hence the frequent use of the genitive expressions *Gegenstand der/einer Anschauung*[25] and *Gegenstand des/eines Begriffs* that I noted earlier.[26] The parallel expression, "the thing of," followed by the genitive, is not found in Kant's corpus, because it is (arguably) meaningless. Things are "for" us only in the sense that they are objects for us, that is, objects of our representations.

Understanding Kant's concept of a thing, and how it differs from his concept of an object, requires understanding the pre-Kantian history of the term *Ding* in philosophical contexts, and its relation to two Latin terms, *ens* and *res*.

Wolff begins the "ontology" section of the so-called German metaphysics with the principle of contradiction (§10), defines the possible as that which contains no contradiction (§12), and then defines *Ding* as that which is possible, that is, that which contains no internal contradictions: "Anything that can be, it may be actual or not, we call a thing (*Ding*)" (*DM* §16). In the later Latin *Ontologia* he defines *ens* in the same way he had earlier defined *Ding*: "That which is capable of existing, and to which existence is therefore not repugnant, is called a thing [*ens*]" (*Ontologia* §134). Baumgarten follows suit, beginning the "Ontology" section of *Metaphysica* with this definition: "Ontology (*metaphysica*, *metaphysica universalis*, *philosophia prima*) is the science of the most general predicates of a thing [*ens*]" (*Metaphysica* §4). He goes

[24] Unless otherwise noted, "thing(s)" translates *Ding*(*e*). When it translates *Sache* I make that explicit. Readers without German should note that "something" sometimes translates *etwas*, which lacks any obvious etymological connection to *Ding* or *Sache*.

[25] E.g. B70, B457, B471.

[26] E.g. B347, B742, *KU*, 5:220.

on to make clear that by *ens* he means any possible being, that is, one that does not contain a contradiction among its determinations (*Metaphysica* §8).[27]

Another Latin term that is sometimes translated as *Ding* in German is *res*. In the *Ontologia* Wolff defines it as follows: "Whatever is, or can be conceived to be, is called thing (*res*), insofar as it is something (*aliquid*); so that it therefore can be defined by this, that it is something. And so to the scholastics, *realitas* and *quidditas* are synonyms" (*Ontologia* §243). Wolff is here referring to a standard scholastic identification of *res* as a locus of *realitas*. For reasons of space I cannot here trace the story of how this scholastic notion of *realitas* makes its way to Wolff and Baumgarten via Leibniz, so I will just cut to the conclusion: Wolff and Baumgarten both think that the essence of an *ens* must include reality, where reality is real determination (e.g. knowledge, light), as opposed to its mere absence (e.g. ignorance, darkness). Reality (*realitas*) comes in degrees (one thing can be more real than another) and the possession of a degree of reality is not grounded in the reality of one's parts (even a simple thing can have a degree of reality).[28] Reality is, to use Baumgarten's term, an "intensive quantity."[29] An *ens* with *realitas* is a *res*, and *realitas* constitutes the *res*-ness of *res*, the thinghood of things (*res*).[30]

We have to be careful about the relation of these two "thing" concepts, however. The question of whether *ens* and *res* are "convertible," or whether *ens* is a broader concept, was highly contentious in scholastic philosophy.[31] Whereas Wolff gives a different definition of *res* (locus of *realitas*) than of *ens* (containing no contradictions), both he and Baumgarten explicitly claim at points that every *ens* has (infinite or finite) reality, and thus is a *res*.[32] However, in other contexts, they are willing to acknowledge a wider sense of *ens* in which not every *ens* is a *res*.[33] This wider sense includes beings like the *ens fictum*, *ens rationis*, or *ens imaginarium*, which, because they exist merely in our representation of them, are not *res* properly speaking.[34] (They are *entia* because they can be thought without contradiction.) But even if *ens* and *res* are necessarily co-extensive, this does not mean they are the same concept: it is a substantive metaphysical thesis, not a mere conceptual identity, that every possible being is a locus of reality. More importantly, I will argue that these concepts are not "convertible" for Kant, because he accepts *entia* that are not *res*.

Kant is of course aware of this Wolffian usage of *Ding* to refer to any possible being whatsoever, for he himself uses it at various points. In the Mrongovius metaphysics lectures, he says "we now begin the science of the properties of all things (*Dinge*) in general, which is called ontology" (29:784) and in the announcement for his lectures for the winter semester 1765–66 he writes: "I shall then proceed to ontology, namely, the science which is concerned with the most general properties of all things (*Dinge*)" (*NEV*, 2:309). But this Wolffian use of *Ding*, on which it is a German equivalent of the

[27] I translate *ens* here as "thing" because Wolff himself identifies *ens* with *Ding*. However, I think it would be more accurate in general to render *ens* as "being" or "entity"; see Stang (2016b, p. 14 n. 8).

[28] *Metaphysica* §§135–36, 141, 248; *DM* §§106, 125, 154.

[29] *Metaphysica* §§165, 248.

[30] For a more complete history see Glezer (2018, chs. 1–3). For some of the scholastic background see Stone (n.d.).

[31] See Courtine (2007a).

[32] *Ontologia* §243, *Metaphysica* §§136, 248.

[33] As many scholastic thinkers did. See Courtine (2007a).

[34] *Ontologia* §141, *Metaphysica* §62.

Latin *ens*, persists into the *KrV* as well, for instance, in Kant's referring to the transcendental idea of God, the idea of a ground of all possibility, as the idea of the ground of "all things *überhaupt*" (B391).[35] God does not merely ground things with *realitas*; he grounds all (real) possibilities whatsoever. Kant's Critical distinction between logical and real possibility means we also need to distinguish between mere logical *Dinge* (objects of logically consistent concepts) and real *Dinge* (objects of really possible concepts), a point to which I will return momentarily.

But in some passages, Kant uses *Ding* in the narrower Wolff/Baumgarten sense of "*res*," locus of *realitas/Realität*. This is clearest in the cases where Kant identifies thinghood with reality itself:

> *Realitas* cannot be translated properly into German. It really means *Dingheit, Sachheit.*[36] (*V-Met/Volckmann*, 28:1146)

> Each thing is reality (*ein jedes Ding ist Realität*). Thinghood, so to speak, consists solely of reality (*beruht blos auf Realität*). The perfection of a thing in general is nothing other than the magnitude of reality. (*V-Met-L$_2$/Pölitz*, 28:560)

> Metaphysical perfection consists in reality. Reality, or thinghood, is, that [*sic*] that something is perfect as a thing (*ist, daß etwas als ein Ding vollkommen sey*). (*V-Met/L$_1$/Pölitz*, 28:211)

Kant agrees with Wolff that *realitas* is what makes a thing (*res*) a thing; *realitas* is thinghood. But Kant transforms the Leibnizian conception of *realitas*, that is, intensive degree of reality, and identifies it specifically with intensive magnitude of causal force.[37] Whereas Leibniz, Baumgarten, and in some moments Wolff as well, deny that real substances can causally interact, Kant was a proponent of real influx from his earliest publications onwards.[38] The forces in substances, their realities, are not merely forces of perception and appetition (as they are for Leibniz); they are real forces of interaction that bind substances into a world. If reality is thinghood, as Kant claims in these passages, then a thing is something that, as such, has an intensive degree of causal force.

There are numerous passages in which Kant clearly means *Ding* in this more concrete, active sense to refer to beings with an intensive degree of force:

> The proposition "the thing (the substance) is a force," instead of the entirely natural one "the substance has a force," contradicts all ontological concepts and has very detrimental consequences for metaphysics. (*ÜE*, 8:225 n.)

[35] Cf. *V-Th/Pölitz*, 28:999. [36] Cf. *V-Met/Dohna*, 28:635, 664.

[37] Admittedly, in the Anticipations of Perception "reality" is originally predicated of the sensory matter of perception (A167/B208). But Kant goes on to attribute *realitas phaenomenon* to the object of sensation, i.e., the forces in objects that cause sensations (cf. A143/B182, A174/B216, A207/B253, A265/B320–21). Kant remarks at one point that not every reality has a degree; I take this to be a reference to God, the *ens realissimum*, whose reality, being infinite, has no degree because it has no limitation (*HN*, 23:29).

[38] See Watkins (2005).

> The unity of a thing alone must have a fundamental force [*Grundkraft*], of which everything can be derived; e.g. because the soul is a simple entity [*Wesen*], it must have an original fundamental force, from which all others derives, even though we cannot derive all of them from the fundamental force. (*V-Met/K*$_1$, 28:1523)[39]

In all of these passages, *Ding* refers to a being that has a force, that is, an intensively determinable degree of causal power. In this usage Kant is treating *Ding* as the German equivalent of *res*. Recall the passage from earlier: "*Realitas* cannot be translated properly into German. It really means *Dingheit, Sachheit*" (*V-Th/Volckmann*, 28:1146). If *realitas* (*Realität*) is thinghood, then to be a thing, something with thinghood, is to be a *res*. Kant is here drawing on the same connection between *realitas* (*res*-ness, effectively) and *res* (that which has *realitas*) as Wolff did.[40]

What relationship does Kant see between thing-as-*ens* (possible being) and thing-as-*res* (locus of force)? It is clear that they are neither extensionally nor intensionally equivalent for Kant. In the Table of Nothings, Kant gives noumena as an example of *ens rationis* and space and time as examples of *ens imaginarium*, the former because they "cannot be counted under the possibilities, though they should not for that reason be taken to be impossible" (A291/B347) and the latter because they are not substances and thus lack causal forces, that is, reality, thinghood. Since noumena are logically, but not really possible, while space and time are not only logically but really possible as well, this means that *ens* here means the more general notion, that which does not contain a contradiction (what is not *nihil negativum*). So for Kant there are *entia*, both logical and real possibilities, that are not *res*, loci of causal force. The more important interpretative point is that Kant will sometimes use *Ding* to mean the more general notion of *ens* (whatever is possible, logically or real) and sometimes in the more demanding sense of *res* (locus of intensive degree of causal force, *realitas/Realität*).

This prompts the question, in the famous phrase *Dinge an sich selbst*, what sense of *Ding* does Kant intend? Insofar as the concept <*things in themselves*> is a logically consistent concept, this is a concept of things in at least the minimal Wolff/Baumgarten sense of that which lacks internally contradictory predicates. But I think it is also clear that Kant means *Ding* in such contexts in a more ontologically robust sense. He means that this is a concept of a kind of real beings, of things endowed with intensive degrees of causal force that appear to us by causally affecting our sensibility.[41] Consider, for instance, that Kant seems to use the expressions "*Sache(n) an sich selbst*" and "*Ding(e) an sich selbst*" interchangeably, for example: "because in both propositions [that the soul is determined and that it is free – NS] I would have taken the soul in just the same meaning, namely as a thing in general (as a thing in itself [*Sache an sich selbst*]), and without prior critique, [...]" (Bxxvii).[42] Recall further Kant's equation of *Sach-heit* with *Ding-heit* and *realitas* (28:1146, above); by

[39] Cf. *V-Met/Herder*, 28:39; *V-Met/Schön*, 514; *V-Met/Mron*, 29:770, 772, 796.

[40] Again, see Courtine (2007b).

[41] See A190/B235, A387, A494/B522; *Prol*, 4:289, 4:314, 4:318; *GMS*, 4:451; and, especially, ÜE, 8:215. The definitive case for attributing "noumenal affection" to Kant remains the classic study Adickes (1924, ch. 3).

[42] Cf. Bxx, Bxxxvii, B42–43, A241, B289, B423 n., A479/B507, A491/B519.

referring to things in themselves as *Sache an sich selbst* Kant is underlining the fact that they are concrete beings with an intensive degree of reality.

That "things in themselves" refers to things as *res* is directly confirmed in Kant's remarks on Jakob's *Examination of Mendelssohn's Morgenstunden*. Responding to the criticism that he has not specified what more there is to things "as they are in themselves" than the sensible properties we cognize, Kant writes:

> But now one will demand that I indicate such properties and effective forces, so that one could distinguish them and through them the things in themselves from mere appearances. My answer is: this has already been done and been done by yourself. Consider only how you bring about the concept of God as highest intelligence. You think in it nothing but true reality, i.e., something that is not only opposed to negations (as one ordinarily believes) but also and primarily to realities in the appearance (*realitas phaenomenon*), such as all realities that have to be given to us through senses and are therefore called *realitas apparens* (although not with an entirely suitable expression). Now diminish all these realities (understanding, will, blessedness, might, etc.) in terms of degree, they will still remain the same in terms of kind (quality), and you will have properties of the things in themselves that you can apply to other things outside of God. (8:154)[43]

To readers who want to know what unknowable properties *Dinge an sich selbst* have, Kant replies that one merely has to think of God, the thing with the maximum reality, and think of limited degrees of his reality. Whereas, for instance, we think of God as having infinite power to act or infinite intellect, we think of things in themselves as having finite limitations of that power and that intellect. Where God has infinite reality, things in themselves have finite realities. There is also intensive degree of reality in appearance, but Kant here describes that as a "property of a thing as object of the senses." In order to make sense of that locution, though, we will need to understand what it is for a thing to be an object of our senses. But first we must get clear on the notion of an object that plays the key role in the Indiscernibility arguments from the Introduction.

4. Objects, Variables, Intuition

Up to this point, I have argued that the Kantian concepts <*object*> and <*thing*> should be carefully distinguished. <*Object*> is a semantic-cognitive concept, the concept of what a representation is "of." <*Thing*> is a metaphysical concept, the concept of a locus of a force that possesses an intensive degree of reality. But this will seem to many readers far afield of my original quarry, the debate between Identity and Non-Identity readings of Kant's transcendental idealism.

To bring this back to the original topic, in this section I examine the concept of object that played the key role in the various Indiscernibility arguments for the

[43] Thanks to Andy Stephenson for pressing me to clarify my reading of this passage.

Non-Identity reading, the so-called "quantificational" concept of an object as the value of a bound variable. In this section, I will argue that there is such a concept in Kant, and it is tightly tied to the concept of the object of an intuition.[44]

Recall Kant's formulations of the logical form of judgment from the Jäsche logic:

> To everything *x*, to which the concept of body (*a*+*b*) belongs, belongs also extension (*b*), is an example of an analytic proposition. To everything *x*, to which the concept of body (*a*+*b*) belongs, belongs also attraction (*c*), is an example of a synthetic proposition. (*Log*, 9:111)[45]

Replacing Kant's style of concept variables (*a*, *b*) with our own (F, G), we can say that the form common to both of Kant's examples of judgment is: to everything *x*, to which the concept F belongs, belongs also the concept G. In terms of Kant's table of logical functions of judgment, both of these judgments are universal in quantity (they are about all *x* to which the concept F belongs), affirmative in quality (they affirm a predicate G rather than deny it), and categorical in relation (they express a relation between two concepts rather than between two or more judgments). The modality of the judgment concerns whether we merely entertain it (problematic), assert it (assertoric), or judge it as the consequence of a rule (apodictic), and will not concern us further here. The logical form of such (universal, affirmative, categorical) judgments cannot be $\forall \mathrm{x}(\mathrm{Fx} \rightarrow \mathrm{Gx})$ for they are categorical judgments, and Kant tells us that categorical judgments do not involve the relation of antecedent to consequent.[46] The most natural alternative is to take the logical form of these judgments in general to be $\forall x_{\mathrm{Fx}} Gx$, where $\forall x_{\mathrm{Fx}}$ abbreviates the restricted quantifier expression "every *x* such that F*x*" that ranges only over objects that fall under the concept F.

This is the logical form of universal affirmative categorical judgments, including judgments about objects we cannot cognize. It expresses a relation between concepts, but one that makes irreducible reference to objects: all of the objects that fall under the subject concept F fall under the predicate concept G.[47] But we can also cognize a given object under a concept. For instance, we cognize an object under the subject concept F and thereby, given our judgment that $\forall x_{\mathrm{Fx}} Gx$, cognize that object under G as well.[48] In Kant's terminology, the former is the "subsumption" of an object under a concept, while the judgment is a "subsumption" of one concept under another.

[44] The section draws on Stang (2021a). Readers interested in the full argument are referred to that paper; here I suppress some of the details for the sake of brevity. In that paper, and elsewhere (esp. Stang, 2016b) I identify the "quantificational" notion of an object of with the notion of an object that can be posited in what Kant calls "absolute positing." In this chapter I focus on the "quantificational" notion of an object that can be the value of the variable of judgment. I think these notions are ultimately identical for Kant, but I will not argue that here.

[45] Cf. *Refl.* 3127 (16:671), which is presumably the *Reflexion* Jäsche drew on when composing this passage from *Logik*. Likewise, see 9:108 in the *Jäsche Logik* and *Refl.* 3096 (16:657–58), a possible source. See also *Refl.* 3062 (16:629) and 4634 (17:616).

[46] *Log*, 9:105. This constitutes a correction of the interpretation offered in some of my earlier work.

[47] Béatrice Longuenesse gives this aspect of Kant's definition of judgment a central place in her interpretation; see esp. Longuenesse (1997, pp. 87, 107).

[48] Cf. Kant's claim that judgment is "mediate" cognition of objects (A68/B93), i.e., cognition of them under the predicate "by means of" subsuming them under the subject.

For the sake of brevity, I will refer to the former as "subsumptions" simpliciter. Subsumptions (in my sense) and judgments are distinct mental acts. Judgment is a relation between concepts, while subsumption relates an object to a concept. We have seen the logical form of judgment, at least in the case of universal affirmative categorical judgment. The logical form of object subsumption is F*a*; it involves thinking of a single object *a* that it falls under the concept F. The object is represented here by the name *a* rather than a variable because we do not subsume objects in general, but individual objects.[49] If we cognize, not just that *a* falls under F but that *all* objects fall under F, then we are judging, that is, judging that $\forall x\mathrm{F}x$. If we cognize that *this F* falls under some further predicate, say G, we are making a singular judgment.[50] But in order for that singular judgment about *a* to be possible, we must have subsumed *a* under F, that is, we must have thought that F*a*. The role of sensibility is to "give" us the object *a*; the role of the understanding is to allow us to think of *a* that it is F. Without concepts we would be given objects but not be able to think them; without intuition, we would be able to think about relations between concepts but not subsume any objects under them.

This means that intuition is the means by which the variable *x* in the logical form of judgment is assigned an object. To go from a general judgment of the form $\forall x_{\mathrm{F}x}\mathrm{G}x$ to the thought G*a* one subsumes *a* under F and thereby under G—but in order to do this one must first intuit *a* itself. This is not an epistemic point about the conditions under which one could know G*a*; it is a semantic point about the relations between the variable of judgment, intuition, and objects. The variable of judgment *x* can be assigned objects as values by intuition, and only by intuition. To judge that $\forall x_{\mathrm{F}x}\mathrm{G}x$ is to judge that any object that falls under F also falls under G, or, equivalently, that any F-object that is assigned to the variable *x* by an intuition also falls under G.

Some readers will object that my talk of intuitions "assigning" objects to the variable of judgment is anachronistic; it imports, they will say, too much of the Fregean function-argument conception of judgment and the Quinean conception of objects as values of bound variables. But Frege did not invent the concept of variables (they were already known to Diophantus of Alexandria), and Kant himself builds an object variable into the very form of judgment.[51] Internal to the idea of an object variable is

[49] Of course we do so in universal judgments, i.e., universal concept subsumptions, but by "subsumption," recall, I mean exclusively object subsumptions, subsumptions of an object under a concept.

[50] The difference between "G*a*" and "This F is G" (where *this F* = *a*) is that the former subsumes an object directly under a concept, while the latter subsumes a single instance of a subject concept under a predicate. Only the latter is a singular judgment, because only it involves two concepts, a subject and a predicate. This is obscured somewhat by the fact that Kant uses the same sentence ("Cajus is mortal") to illustrate singular judgment (*Log*, 9:102), *and* the subsumption of an object under a concept (*V-Lo/Dohna*, 24:703). But they cannot be the same, because singular judgments, being judgments, involve two concepts. The subsumption of an object under a concept, by definition, involves one object and one concept. So the logical form of the object subsumption "Cajus is mortal" is F*a*, while the logical form of the singular judgment is "This *F* (=this Cajus) is mortal." In the former, "Cajus" is a name; in the latter, "Cajus" is a general concept (<*Cajus*>) used singularly.

[51] Unlike Frege, for whom the basic form of judgment is function argument, F*a*. So it would be more accurate to say that, on my interpretation, Kant's theory of *object subsumption* anticipates the Fregean theory of judgment. But a great difference, and thus a great deal of work for Frege to do, remains: first the recognition that the atomic form of judgment is F*a* as well as the generalized theory of relational

the idea of instantiating that variable with a particular object, that is, letting that object be the "value" of that variable (and *mutatis mutandis* for variables for numbers.) So the only thing I have attributed to Kant over and above what is contained in the very concept of an object variable is the idea that intuition is the representational capacity by which we are able to instantiate the concepts contained in judgments and assign objects as the value of the variable x, that is, to go from $\forall x_{Fx} Gx$ to the cognition that a (an object we intuit) is F, and thence to the cognition that a is G. Likewise, it is because objects of intuition are values of the variable of judgment that we can go from the cognition that the object of intuition a is F and the universal judgment $\forall x_{Fx} Gx$ to the singular judgment that *this* F (namely, a) is G. Although I have used some modern terminology ("assigning") and have emphasized the object variable in judgment more than some commentators do, there is nothing problematically anachronistic here.

We can judge not just about objects we can intuit and cognize, but about all objects in general. Given the logical form of judgments, this means the variable of judgment x can take as values objects we cannot intuit. Otherwise we would be unable to even entertain (problematic) judgments about all objects whatsoever. But this means, further, that, built into the very form of judgment itself is the notion of "object" that is relevant to the Indiscernibility arguments from section 1: what can be the value of the variable x in judgment (in contemporary terms, what can be the value of a bound variable). Thus, the notion involved in those arguments and the debate about whether appearances and things in themselves are "the same objects" is a notion of object present in Kant's philosophy. We have also seen that it is not the only such notion (e.g. the notion of an "object of representation in general" from section 2).

But recall that, for Kant, objects are always objects *for some representational capacity*. The concept "object of representation" is the most general concept of transcendental philosophy. So when we say we can judge about objects we cannot intuit, values of the variable x of judgment, we must ask: of which capacity are they objects? By definition they cannot be objects of our intuitions, objects of our sensible capacity. But nor can they solely be objects of our intellectual capacity, understanding. If we possessed only the capacity of understanding, we would only represent concepts, *not* the values of x in judgments and cognitions. Logically, the object of the understanding by itself cannot fill in for the variable x of judgment. If we try to substitute a concept G for the variable x in the judgment $\forall x Fx$, we get nonsense: G(F). The only objects that can substitute for the variable x of judgment are singular instances of concepts (concept instantiators, let us say), rather than concepts themselves. But I have said that objects we intuit, by definition, cannot so substitute in judgments about non-sensible objects. So what substitutes for the variable x of judgment are objects of singular representation, but not objects of our sensible singular representation (intuition): objects of non-sensible singular representation, non-sensible intuition. We cannot intuit such objects; we cannot think *de re* of any one of them that *it* falls under a concept. But we have the concept "non-sensible intuition" and we can entertain thoughts about objects we cannot intuit by thinking of them as objects of

predicates and quantifiers binding their variables. My interpretation does not collapse Kant and Frege to any problematic degree.

such intuition. Because we cannot intuit such objects, we cannot turn these judgments into cognitions. We cannot, so to speak, instantiate them by assigning an object to the variable *x*.[52] We cannot subsume such objects under our concepts of them (though we can subsume our concepts of them under other concepts). But we have the concept of the kind of intellect that could do this, one that possesses non-sensible or "intellectual" intuition. This is how we entertain thoughts about non-sensible objects. This is how we think of objects we cannot intuit as possible values of the variable *x* in our judgments.[53]

We can formulate to ourselves at least two kinds of judgments that are universal in quantity: judgments about *all* sensible objects and judgments about *all* non-sensible objects. Given the logical form of judgment in general, this means we have at least two restricted quantifier expressions: "for all sensible objects" ($\forall x_S$) and "for all non-sensible objects" ($\forall x_{NS}$). Judgments prefaced by the first quantifier are judgments about objects we can cognize *de re* by specifying the variable with respect to an object given in intuition. Judgments prefaced by the second quantifier are judgments of objects we cannot intuit or cognize. But we can think of them as being about *objects* (singular instances of concepts) by thinking of the variable *x* as being able to be instantiated by an object for a non-sensible intellect. A non-sensible intellect could cognize a singular instance of the concepts involved in such judgments. In section 2 I noted that "object" is a very broad notion for Kant. In what follows, unless stated otherwise explicitly, "object" will mean exclusively: what can be the value of *x* in the variable of judgment, that is, a singular instance of a concept.

5. The Identity and Distinctness of Objects

5.1 The Sensible Case

The identity relation that figured in the Indiscernibility arguments in Marshall (2013) and Stang (2014) was numerical identity, a relation between objects. Before we consider whether that relation can obtain between sensible objects (phenomena) and non-sensible objects (noumena), we should first consider how we cognize numerical identity and distinctness in the case of sensible objects.

Kant's most complete discussion of the identity and distinctness of sensible objects occurs in the "Amphiboly" section of the *KrV*. His point there is that, although the principle of the identity of indiscernibles (PII) applies to objects of purely conceptual representation, it does not apply to objects in space and time: there can be objects in space and time that fall under all and only the same general concepts, but which are nonetheless numerically distinct. We cognize the numerical distinctness

[52] We may be able to do this in the course of a demonstration ("Let *x* be a noumenon..."), as long as we later discharge the universal instantiation by another universal generalization ("Therefore, all noumena are such that" etc.), i.e., as long as the conclusion of the demonstration is not an object subsumption or a singular judgment. See Hintikka (1968) for discussion.

[53] Some readers will worry that this threatens to collapse the negative and positive concepts of noumena (respectively, the concepts of what is not the object of sensible intuition, and what is the object of a non-sensible intuition.) I respond to this concern in Stang (2021a).

of spatiotemporal objects by intuiting them in different locations simultaneously: "Thus, in the case of two drops of water one can completely abstract from all inner difference (of quality and quantity), and it is enough that they be intuited in different places at the same time in order for them to be held to be numerically different" (A263–64/B319–20). I want to make three remarks about this.

First, space and time, as forms of intuition, are the necessary conditions for cognizing numerically distinct but qualitatively identical objects. If our representations of space and time were conceptual, Kant thinks, then we would represent the spatiotemporal locations of objects by conceptually representing their intrinsic properties, and this would leave us unable to represent intrinsic duplicates as being in different locations simultaneously. It is because the representations of space and time are irreducible to conceptual representation of objects and their intrinsic states that we can cognize intrinsic duplicates that are simultaneously in distinct locations. And this in turn, as the passage quoted above shows, makes it possible for us to cognize numerically distinct intrinsic duplicates in space and time.[54]

Second, it follows that the numerically distinct intrinsic duplicates we cognize are objects of intuition. Kant's point in the Amphiboly is that we can cognize objects that violate the PII because intuition is irreducible to conceptualization. If we had only a conceptual capacity for representation, all objects of our cognition would be objects of concepts alone, and objects of concepts alone obey the PII. If two objects have all of the same intrinsic properties then they fall under all and only the same concepts; they are one and the same conceptual object, that is, one and the same object of conceptual representation, and so cannot be represented as distinct using concepts alone.[55] This means that the objects we cognize as violating the PII are objects that can take the value of the variable *x* in judgment *and* be intuited by us.

Third, while these PII-violating objects are objects of intuition they are not objects of intuition *alone*. To cognize them as violating the PII we must apply concepts to them; they are objects of intuitions *and* concepts, that is, objects of cognition, and this means that the categories are involved in cognizing their numerical identity and distinctness. The very cognitive situation Kant describes in the Amphiboly—cognizing the numerical distinctness of two water drops by intuiting them in distinct locations "at the same time" (A263–64/B319–20)—requires the capacity to cognize the difference between successive perceptions of simultaneous objects in different locations (which are therefore numerically distinct) and successive perceptions of a succession in one and the same object, that is, its moving (perhaps very quickly) from one location to another. If we could not cognize this difference then we could not cognize two objects as being in distinct locations simultaneously. But this difference (between successive perceptions of simultaneous objects and successive perceptions of successive states in the same object, or, more generally, between subjective and objective succession) is the very difference around which the argument of the Analogies of Experience turns. To bring this back to the Amphiboly, this means that

[54] A264/B320, A272/B328.

[55] This raises the question of why we cannot represent intrinsic duplicates through purely conceptually representable external relations (relations that do not supervene on their intrinsic properties), but that would take us too far afield. See Langton (1998) for more on this issue.

in order to represent spatial objects as simultaneously in different locations, even though our perceptions of them are successive, we must cognize them using the dynamical categories: <*substance-accident*>, <*cause-effect*>, and <*reciprocal action*>.[56]

More generally, the discursive and spatiotemporal nature of our intellects determines the cognitive conditions under which we cognize the identity and distinctness of objects: we passively receive objects of intuition, but in order to cognize them (in particular, to cognize them in respect of identity and difference) we must, through a spontaneous exercise of the faculty of understanding, apply a priori concepts to the passive deliverances of sensibility.

5.2 The Non-Sensible Case

This is how discursive spatiotemporal intellects like ours cognize objects in respect of (numerical) identity and difference. For a non-discursive or "intuitive" intellect, matters are quite different. An intellect with non-sensible or "intellectual" intuition does not passively receive its objects by being affected by them; rather it is active in intuition.[57] Non-sensible intuition generates or creates its own object.[58] Kant says virtually nothing about how an intuitive intellect cognizes sameness and difference among its objects, so my remarks about this will necessarily be somewhat speculative. One possible model would be this: if x and y are objects of non-sensible intuition (positive noumena), an intuitive intellect cognizes them as identical insofar as it cognizes the act that generates x as the very same act that generates y, and as distinct when it cognizes them as distinct acts (even if one is a proper part of the other, or both are proper parts of a single holistic creative act).[59] This, of course, pushes the question of how a non-discursive intellect cognizes the identity and difference of the objects of its cognition back onto the question of how such an intellect cognizes the identity and difference of those very acts of cognition. My aim here is not to defend this model of

[56] It might be objected that in the Amphiboly Kant seems to have the following situation in mind: simultaneously intuiting two objects in different locations in one and the same intuitive manifold. But if our ability to represent simultaneous intrinsic duplicates as distinct were dependent on our happening to intuit them simultaneously, then by the argument of the third Analogy, we would not be experiencing these objects, but only perceiving them, i.e., we would not be cognizing an objectively valid distinction between the (contingent) subjective simultaneity of our intuitions of them and their (necessary) objective simultaneity. Much more could be said here, but in the interests of brevity I will leave it aside.

[57] A note about terminology: "intellectual intuition" refers to a kind of intuition, i.e., non-sensible intuition. "Intuitive intellect" refers to a kind of intellect. Förster (2011) argues that, not only should these concepts be kept distinct, it is in principle possible for them to be extensionally distinct (i.e., intuitive intellect without intellectual intuition). Leech (2014) argues, on the contrary, that any being with one has the other. While I sided with Leech in Stang (2016b), I am now more sympathetic to Förster's view. For the purposes of this chapter, though, I am going to stipulate that they are co-extensive by considering only beings that have both intuitive intellect *and* intellectual intuition.

[58] The term *intellektuelle Anschauung* occurs quite frequently in Kant's writings; the main discussion is in the "Phenomena and noumena" section (A252–56, B307–13; cf. Kant's handwritten marginal notes at A248, 23:36). The term *anschauliche Verstand* occurs less frequently; in the *KrV*, see B135, B138–39, B145, B149, and B159. For a more complete set of references, see Stang (2016b, p. 300 n. 6).

[59] In *KU* §76 Kant seems to claim that an intuitive intellect would cognize the parts in virtue of cognizing the whole. If, therefore, the intuitive intellect's cognition generates or grounds its object, it would follow that it must cognize its acts of cognition as themselves standing in holistic mereological relations (i.e., relations in which the whole is prior to the parts).

non-sensible cognition of identity and difference, but merely to point out that this is a topic about which we can entertain logically consistent thoughts and examine their logical relations, even though none of our thoughts rise to the level of cognition, much less of knowledge. These are logically possible thoughts, even if we cannot know, through theoretical means, whether they correspond to real possibilities, much less what the ground of that real possibility is.

What is more, while these thoughts are "speculative" in Kant's sense (they concern objects beyond the limits of experience) they are not idle speculation, for they are intimately bound up with his conception of God as the ground of the (real) possibility of the highest good. The highest good is the state of affairs in which agents enjoy happiness in proportion to *and because of* the moral goodness of their noumenal wills. Kant explicitly points out that, in order to ground the real possibility of this state, God must be able to cognize the moral goodness of noumenal wills.[60] Although Kant does not state this explicitly, God must also be able to cognize identity and difference *among* noumenal wills. Otherwise, he would not be able to cognize me as worthy of happiness in proportion to the goodness of the noumenal character of *my* will, as opposed to the noumenal character of another's. If God is unable to "distinguish" (i.e., cognize identity and difference among) noumenal wills, then he is unable to make it the case that agents are happy in proportion to and *because of* their moral goodness, as opposed to the moral goodness of others. Even if the model suggested above is wrong (cognition of the identity/distinctness of objects by means of cognition of the identity/distinctness of the acts of creating them), the key point is that the thought $x = y$ can have cognitive content for a non-discursive, that is, intuitive, intellect, when x and y are positive noumena (and must have such content for God).[61]

5.3 The Mixed Case

Kant gives an intricate account of how our discursive spatiotemporal intellect cognizes the numerical identity and distinctness of phenomena; the divine intuitive intellect must cognize numerical identity and distinctness of (positive) noumena, but we can do no more than speculate as to how. However, we lack even the representational resources to speculate, across the sensible-intelligible divide, about numerical identity or distinctness between phenomena and noumena. Where x is a sensible object and y is a non-sensible object we lack the representational resources to think of a kind of intellect that could entertain the content $x = y$.[62] This is because in saying that x is a sensible object and y is a non-sensible object we are implicitly thinking of these variables as bound by quantifiers: the variable x is bound by a quantifier for sensible objects and y is bound by a quantifier for non-sensible objects.[63] To think of

[60] *KpV*, 5:123.

[61] This point is made very well in Schafer (forthcoming).

[62] Consequently we lack the representational resources to entertain the thought that $x = y$ when both variables are bound by unrestricted quantifiers, i.e., to entertain this thought we must implicitly restrict both quantifiers either to sensible objects or to non-sensible objects.

[63] As, for instance, in both the Identity and Non-Identity readings, where $\exists_S$ and $\forall_S$ are quantifiers that range over sensible objects, and $\exists_N$ and $\forall_N$ are quantifiers that range over non-sensible objects:

a variable as bound by a quantifier is to think of it as assignable an object as a value.[64] And we saw in section 6 that it is the role of intuition to assign objects as values to variables. This is why the universal quantifier for all objects $\forall x$ can be glossed as "for all objects of intuition in general"; likewise, the universal quantifier for sensible objects $\forall x_S$ can be glossed "for all objects of sensible intuition," and the universal quantifier for non-sensible $\forall x_N$ objects can be glossed "for all objects of non-sensible intuition."[65] We think of objects as being possible values for the variable x of judgment by thinking of them as possible objects of intuition: intuition in general, or specifically sensible or non-sensible intuition.

But this means that in the identity statement $x = y$, if x is bound by a quantifier for non-sensible objects (or assigned a non-sensible object as a value) and y is bound by a quantifier for sensible objects (or assigned a sensible object as a value), we lack the concept of a kind of intellect that could entertain such a content.[66] This is because we lack the concept of a kind of intellect that could intuit objects assignable as values to both variables. We have the concept of a discursive intellect (i.e., an intellect with sensible intuition), and the concept of a non-discursive, that is, intuitive, intellect (i.e., an intellect with non-sensible intuition). We have no concept of a third kind of intellect that intuits both kinds of objects. The reason for this is simple: a discursive intellect must be receptive (capable of being affected by an object), but an intuitive intellect cannot be receptive. So no one intellect can intuit both sensible and non-sensible objects. Therefore, no one intellect can cognize of a sensible object x and a non-sensible object y either that $x = y$ or $x \neq y$. Where the variables are taken as above, neither $x = y$ nor $x \neq y$ is a content that any intellect can represent or entertain because there is no intellect that can intuit an object or objects that would be values of both variables.[67]

But if we lack the concept of a kind of intellect that can represent this content, then we lack the concept of such content altogether, for talk of "content" is meaningful only if we have at least the concept of a kind of intellect that would represent that content. "Content" after all, is, conceptually, a relative term: a content is a content *of something*, a representation. It makes as little sense to talk of contents, in the complete absence of even a concept of what those contents would be the contents *of*, as it

(Identity) $\forall_S x\left[\exists_N y(x = y)\right]$
(Non-Identity) $\forall_S x\left[\forall_N y(x \neq y)\right]$

[64] The point holds even if we do not think of the variables implicitly as bound. For an unbound variable is a variable that can be bound, i.e., can be assigned an object as a value. The conceptual connection between variables and q-objects remains if the variable is not bound.

[65] This raises the worry that there is no room, conceptually, for "merely negative noumena," i.e., objects that are negative noumena but not positive noumena. See Stang (2021a) for discussion.

[66] But haven't we been entertaining such contents all along, implicitly in the original Non-Identity arguments and explicitly in note 56 above? I think I am committed to saying that in doing so we wrote down apparently well-formed formulas to which no content can be attached. Thanks to Andy Stephenson for pressing me on this.

[67] This entails that God cannot cognize spatiotemporal objects, which might appear to conflict with Kant's doctrine of divine omniscience (cf. *V-Phil-Th/Pölitz*, 28:1012). To anticipate slightly, I will argue that the divine intellect cognizes all things but not all objects, and since objects are metaphysically downstream of things (they are objects for things that have intellects, minds), in doing so he cognizes everything fundamental. See Marshall (2018) for a similar defense of divine omniscience in Kant.

does to speak of matter without even a concept of a form that might en-form that matter. This has no psychologistic implications, however, for it does not require that there *be* such an intellect, much less that it be *our* intellect (much less that contents be private, subjective states of intellects). So it does not entail that all contents are contents of some actual intellect, much less contents of our intellects. It requires merely that coherent talk of content of a certain kind be conceptually dependent upon a coherent concept of a kind of intellect that could represent that content.

Since the thought of a content is conceptually dependent upon the concept of the kind of intellect that could represent such content (i.e., whose representations it could be the content of) we lack the conceptual resources to think of a content without thinking of a kind of intellect that would represent such content. Since we lack the concept of a kind of intellect (a kind of intellect that would intuit both sensible and non-sensible objects), we lack the conceptual resources to think of a kind of content that would be represented by such an intellect, that is, a kind of content that cannot be represented by discursive or non-discursive intellect.[68] Since the thought of identity or distinctness between sensible and non-sensible objects is such a content, we lack the conceptual resources to think of this content.

In the previous two paragraphs I have sketched an argument for a kind of "conceptual" idealism about content: the concept of a content is the concept of the content of some kind of intellect, so to even think about content of some kind we need a concept of the kind of intellect that would entertain such content.[69] But, regardless of what one thinks of this as a piece of philosophy, is there any evidence that Kant would agree? A complete defense of this interpretation of Kant would require more space than I have here, so I will limit myself to arguing, on the basis of very general features of Kant's philosophy, that this is the natural way to read him.

Recall that the highest concept of transcendental philosophy is *<object of representation>*. This means that, of anything in transcendental philosophy, the questions "Of what representation is it the object? And whose representation?" must have answers. I have argued that identity relations between sensible and non-sensible objects cannot be the objects (contents) of any of our representations, nor can they be the objects (contents) of a non-sensible intellect. This means that there is no such object, no such relation. It is not that there are inscrutable relations of identity and distinctness between phenomena and noumena. There are simply no such relations.[70]

Some readers will remain unsatisfied. Why cannot there be unrepresentable facts or propositions? First, somewhat pedantically, a "proposition" (*Satz*) for Kant is an assertoric judgment, and a judgment is an act of conceptual combination by a discursive intellect. So an unrepresentable proposition makes as little sense as an

[68] For now the inconceivability of a third kind of intellect constitutes a kind of simplifying assumption. Below in section 8, I will lift this assumption by arguing, in effect, that our own intellects constitute a kind of "third" intellect.

[69] This argument is given in greater detail in Stang (2017).

[70] I want to emphasize that I am not denying that we can quantify over all objects whatsoever—we do so via the concept of intuition in general, either abstracting from the difference between sensible and intellectual intuition, or disjoining the two concepts.

unjudgeable judgment, for Kant.[71] Likewise, an unknowable fact is a contradictio *in adjecto*, for Kant defines a "fact" as what can be proved, either through experience or pure reason.[72] This leads me to my second point. For Kant to admit unrepresentable facts, relations, etc. would be for him to accept a kind of Platonism about broadly "semantic" entities that goes against the spirit of everything he says about broadly semantic phenomena (concepts, sense, meaning, etc.). Kant's consistent approach to the "semantic," from at least the Critical period onwards, is resolutely representationalist and anti-Platonist: his consistent approach is always to see the "semantic" as anchored in the representational acts of intellects, most importantly, in our intellects. Kant's writings give scant encouragement to the reader who would find in them support for entities of a broadly "semantic" or "logical" nature (i.e., propositions, facts, properties, etc.) that are not contents of the representations of some possible intellect.[73] Thus, from a Kantian point of view, the fact that identity relations between sensible and non-sensible objects cannot be represented by either of the kinds of intellects of which we can form concepts (i.e., sensible, non-sensible) is excellent reason to think that no such identity relation is possible.

There is a long tradition in philosophy of distingushing between, for instance, an object having a color other than red (e.g., a green apple), and an object being of the wrong logical type to have a color at all (e.g., the number 2).[74] In this spirit, I will say that sensible and non-sensible objects are not merely not identical; they are *non-identical*. It is literally *unthinkable* that they are identical.[75] There is no content to the thought that they are identical. In other words, the Non-Identity view is correct about the numerical identity relation between sensible and non-sensible *objects*.[76] It remains to be seen whether the Identity view might be correct, if interpreted as a claim about the relation of being the same *things*.

6. Distinct Objects, Same Things?

But before we turn to that issue, we need to understand why appearances are things in the first place. Given the conceptual separation between objects and things, it is by no means obvious that objects of experience are things (substantial loci of intensively

[71] *Log*, 9:109. This does generate a potential problem: how can we meaningfully talk about noumena instantiating concepts, or some judgments about them being true, if the intuitive intellect that cognizes them cognizes them using neither concepts nor judgments? But I am inclined to think this is a problem for Kant, not for my interpretation. See McLear (forthcoming) for discussion.

[72] *KU*, 5:468. See the entry "Tatsache" in Willaschek et al. (2015).

[73] See the entry "Eigenschaft" in Willaschek et al. (2015).

[74] For instance, *Prior Analytics* I.46.51b10 (quoted in Horn & Wansing, 2020).

[75] Readers will notice, however, that I am using the terms in the opposite of the way they are normally used. Typically, *not being F* refers to lacking the property of being F, while *being not-F* refers to having the negative property not-F. However, I have reversed them (so that *being non-identical* refers to failing to stand in the relation of identity) because the "not-identity" view does not exactly roll off the tongue. Thanks to Banafsheh Beizaei for pointing this out to me, and for pointing me to the sources cited in the previous note.

[76] At one point, Allais seems to endorse exactly this conclusion (2015, p. 72), but elsewhere she claims that the very same objects that have essentially manifestable properties also have *an sich* properties (pp. 72–73, 128, 130); see Stang (2016a) for critical discussion.

gradable causal force, *realitas*).[77] In fact, it will take some quite substantial argument in the Analogies for Kant to prove that objects of experience necessarily must be subsistent (1st Analogy) loci of force (2nd Analogy).[78] Combined with the Anticipations, this also constitutes an argument that objects of experience necessarily possess an intensive magnitude of causal force, *realitas*.[79] In my terminology, this amounts to an argument that objects of experience are necessarily *things*. Accordingly, Kant repeatedly predicates thinghood of objects of experience in the Analogies, for example: "However, the substratum of everything real, i.e., everything that belongs to the existence of things, is substance, of which everything that belongs to existence can be thought only as a determination" (B225, my emphasis).[80] The substances we experience in space, that persist through all time while their accidental determinations change, are *things*.[81]

We are now in a position to understand Kant's controversial distinction between things in themselves and appearances:

> We have sufficiently proved in the Transcendental Aesthetic that everything intuited in space or in time, hence all objects of an experience possible for us, are nothing but appearances, i.e., mere representations, which, as they are represented, as extended beings or series of alterations, have outside our thoughts no existence grounded in itself. This doctrine (*Lehrbegriff*) I call transcendental idealism. The realist, in the transcendental sense, makes these modifications of our sensibility into things subsisting in themselves, and hence makes mere representations into things in themselves. (A490–91/B518–19; cf. A369)

Things, subsistent loci of force, do not, as such, depend upon being objects for us; they have an existence "grounded in itself," which means that their existence does not depend upon how, or whether, they become objects for us (or whether this is even

[77] Consider two Kantian locutions: "things that appear" (to us) (e.g. A268/B324, A277/B333) or "things as they appear" (to us) (e.g. *MSI* §4; *V-Met/Dohna*, 28:653). Prima facie those locutions can be read in two different ways. "Things that appear" can be taken to refer to the things, namely, things in themselves, that appear to us as objects in space and time. Likewise, "things insofar as they appear" can refer to those same thing in themselves insofar as they stand in that relation to us. But we can also read these locutions as referring to appearances *as things*: things that we experience (things that appear) and those very things insofar as we experience them (things as they appear to us). See Oberst (2015).

[78] Cf. B341, A171/B213, *V-Met/L*$_1$ 28:316.

[79] Consider the statement of the Anticipations in the first edition: "In all appearances the sensation, and the real, which corresponds to it in the object (*realitas phaenomenon*), has an intensive magnitude, i.e., a degree" (A165). Cf. A168/B209, A264–65/B320–21. On my reading, the Anticipations prove that sensation has reality (intensive magnitude) and, together with the proofs of the Analogies, this shows that things have reality to the extent that they have the power to cause sensory reality. See, however, Glezer (2018) for a much more detailed account.

[80] A186/B229, B233.

[81] This allows us to understand not only Kant's (implicit or explicit) predication of thinghood of appearances but another Kantian locution as well, *Dinge in der Erscheinung*; see B229, B567, B609, and A400. *Dinge in der Erscheinung* can naturally be read as referring either to things in the "content" of appearance (i.e., objects experienced as things) or things "among" appearances (i.e., objects that are things). But these are equivalent. There are things in the "content" of appearance (i.e., the content of experience) if and only if there are appearances that are things, because, given transcendental idealism, the possibility of the latter (the possibility of objects being things) just is the possibility of the former (the possibility of our experiencing objects as things). See Oberst (2017) for discussion.

possible). Hence, these are "things in themselves." These things can become objects for us in two distinct ways. We can represent them using pure concepts of the understanding (categories) alone, without relating those categories to sensible intuition. (That is what I was doing in the previous three sentences and what Kant is doing at 8:154, quoted above.) In the pure understanding we do not conceive of such things as depending for their existence upon our concepts of them; we conceive of them as existing "in themselves," as independent of their being objects for us.

But these things (in themselves) can also become objects for us by sensibly affecting our sense organs, producing intuitions that we discursively combine to form experience (to simplify Kant's complex story). Kant's radical claim is that the objects of this experience exist only in virtue of being experienced, as he here writes: they "have outside our thoughts no existence grounded in itself." The possibility of such objects is grounded in the possibility of our experiencing them. As we have seen, we necessarily experience objects as things, and hence objects of experience necessarily are things.[82] But the existence of these things, and their very thinghood, depends upon their being objects of experience in a way that the existence and thinghood of things in themselves does not. The reason for this difference derives from the more fundamental difference in thinghood, in the conditions under which these things are possible as things: things in themselves are not essentially objects for us, while appearances of those things are.[83]

Recall the passage from the Introduction that made the Identity reading seem mandatory:

> [...] the same objects can be considered from two different sides, **on the one side** as objects of the senses and the understanding for experience, and **on the other side** as objects that are merely thought at most for isolated reason striving beyond the bounds of experience. (Bxviii–Bxix, note)

But this passage immediately continues:

> If we now find that there is agreement with the principle of pure reason when things (*die Dinge*) are considered from this twofold standpoint, but that an unavoidable conflict of reason with itself arises with a single standpoint, then the experiment decides for the correctness of that distinction. (Bxviii–Bxix, note; my emphasis)

This raises the possibility that appearances and things in themselves are distinct *objects* but the same *things*. Elsewhere in the B Preface (a *locus classicus* for Identity readings) he expresses the very same point again ih terms of things:

[82] It is impossible not to experience them as things, hence impossible for them not to be things.

[83] I thus depart from the interpretation of Abe Stone, from whom I have otherwise learned a great deal. Whereas Stone thinks that the appearance/thing in itself distinction is a distinction between two kinds of objects, I think it is a distinction between two kinds of thing (things that are essentially objects for us, and things that are only contingently so) in virtue of the source of their thinghood (things that are things in virtue of being experienced, things that are things "in themselves"). It is a distinction between two modes of existing, not a distinction between two modes of being an object for a representational capacity. By contrast, phenomena/noumena is a distinction between two kinds of objects: sensible objects and objects that cannot be sensibly intuited. For the appearance/thing in itself distinction see A491/B519; for the phenomena/noumena distinction see B306.

> […] if we are to assume that the distinction between things (*Dinge*) as objects of experience and the very same things as things in themselves (*von eben denselben, als Dingen an sich selbst*), which our critique has made necessary, were not made at all, then the principle of causality, and hence the mechanism of nature in determining causality, would be valid of all things in general as efficient causes.
> (Bxxvii, my emphasis)

In the Fourth Paralogism Kant discusses the possibility that objects of outer and inner sense, which are as such distinct objects, may be the same things:

> In such a way the very same thing that is called a body in one relation would at the same time be a thinking being in another, whose thoughts, of course, we could not intuit, but only their signs in appearance. (A359)
>
> I, represented through inner sense in time, and objects in space outside me, are indeed specifically wholly distinct appearances, but they are not thereby thought of as different things. (A379)

But it is hard to know what to do with this intriguing suggestion unless we understand what it would mean for non-identical objects to be the same *things*. I begin to try to make sense of that notion in the next section.

7. On Being Collectively the Same Things

The claim that appearances and things in themselves are the same things can be read in two different ways, either "distributively" or "collectively," to borrow a Kantian distinction.[84] It can be read *distributively* as saying that every individual appearance is the same thing as some thing in itself. Alternately, it can be read *collectively* as saying that appearances "as a whole" or "taken together" are the same things as things in themselves (or the subset of things in themselves that appear to us). The difference between these two readings could be brought out, somewhat informally, by two different regimentations:

(*Distributive*) $\forall_S x\,(\text{Thing}(x) \rightarrow \exists_N y\,(x \text{ is the same thing as } y))$
(*Collective*) (Appearances) are the same things as (things in themselves)

It might appear that my argument so far has shown that the Distributive reading is incoherent, for my argument against identity relations between sensible and non-sensible objects generalizes to any singular relation of the form $x\text{R}y$, where x is bound by the sensible quantifier and y is bound by the non-sensible quantifier, and the Distributive reading involves just such a relation (y is the same thing as x).[85] In this

[84] A582/B660.

[85] Thanks to Catharine Diehl and Bernhard Thöle for pressing me on this point.

section I am going to temporarily set aside the distributive reading and argue that, on the collective reading, things in themselves and appearances are the same things. In the next section I will argue that, consistent with my larger argument, there is in fact a way to make sense of the distributive reading.

Prima facie the collective reading faces a significant hurdle: it has no recognizable logical form. It cannot assert a relation between two objects, for example, the totality of appearances and the totality of things in themselves, for the central point of Kant's resolution of the Antinomies is that there is no totality of appearances.[86] Here, however, is a way of making sense of it:

(*Collective**) The thinghood of appearances is the same as the thinghood of things in themselves.

Since we know that thinghood (*Dingheit*, *Sachheit*) is reality, for Kant, this is equivalent to saying:

(*Collective***) The reality of appearances is the same as the reality of things in themselves.[87]

But recall that reality, thinghood, for Kant (as well as for Wolff and Baumgarten) is an intensive magnitude: a quality that has a quantity. This means that it functions something like a mass term like "water" or, to use Kant's example, "silver."[88] We can coherently say that the silver that previously was in the mountains is the same silver as the silver that is now in the goblets, without saying that any goblet is identical to any object that existed in the mountains. Likewise, we can say that the reality of appearances is the same as the reality of things in themselves, without making any claim of numerical identity or any singular same-thing relation (as the distributive reading requires). We can say this because the goblets are made up of, or constituted by, the same quantity of silver that was in the mountains. Likewise, we can say that appearances and things in themselves are the same things, are metaphysically "constituted" by the same reality. And in saying this we are not committed to saying that any single appearance is the same thing as any thing in itself. Just as we can say that the goblets are the same thing as the coins, if the goblets were made from the same silver

[86] This raises the question of whether there is a total intensive degree of reality (causal force) in phenomenal substance. I think there is, and that we can determine asymptotically by measuring the total gravitational mass in the universe. The opposite view is defended in Glezer (2018, chs. 8–11), but further discussion would take us too far afield. In *V-Met/Dohna* (28:644) Kant seems to admit that noumenal reality has a degree, but that we cannot cognize it. Thanks to Colin McLear for pressing me on this point.

[87] This does not mean that the degree of reality in phenomena is the same as the degree of reality in noumena, but that it is one and the same reality (thinghood) that in the former can be determinately measured, and in the latter cannot be measured, at least by us. Cf. *V-Met-Dohna*, 28:644. Thanks again to Colin McLear for pressing me to clarify this point.

[88] A170/B211. Although I think Kant's point in that passage agrees quite well with my argument, I won't attempt to interpret that (rather convoluted) text here.

as the coins, so, I will argue, are phenomenal and noumenal things "the same things," for they are constituted by the same thinghood, the same reality.[89,90]

While this may seem excessively "metaphysical" to some readers, it is very much in line with the letter of Kant's text. After schematizing the categories of quality, that is, specifying the temporal determinations that enable our application of these categories to objects (e.g. that reality corresponds to "filled" time and negation to "empty" time), Kant writes:

> Since time is only the form of intuition, thus of objects as appearances, that which corresponds to the sensation in these is the transcendental matter of all objects, as things in themselves (thinghood [*Sachheit*], reality). (A143/B182)

I take this to mean that the schemata given so far allow us to represent sensory states as realities (and as absences of reality, negations), but that the real that "corresponds" to these sensations is the "transcendental matter of all objects," the thinghood of things in themselves. Thinghood (*Sachheit*, sometimes *Dingheit*), as we have seen and as Kant here makes explicit, is reality, intensively gradable causal force. The term "correspondence" here is notable, for it occurs repeatedly in the Anticipations of Perception, where it describes the relation of sensory reality to the phenomenal reality (phenomenal things) that causes it,[91] despite the fact that Kant says explicitly, "I am not yet dealing with causality" (A169/B2111). I interpret this as follows: we must think of our sensations as having "corresponding" things that cause them, but prior to schematizing the categories of cause and effect we think of things in themselves as the "corresponding" cause.[92] This is why the Schematism gives the "transcendental matter of all objects" as what corresponds to sensation. Only after schematizing the category <*cause-effect*> do we have the means to represent spatiotemporal objects as the causes of our sensations, as their "corresponding" objects. In the Anticipations we have not yet proved that it is necessary, or even possible, for spatiotemporal things to cause sensations, but, because these concepts are schematized by this point, we can

[89] A more precise formulation is possible in Kant's technical terminology. We know that, in general, for Kant matter is the determinable, while the form renders the determinable determinate (see A266/B322; cf. Kant's discussion of *materia ex qua* at *V-Met-L*$_2$*/Pölitz*, 28:575). He makes clear, both in published and unpublished texts, that the matter of noumenal things is reality, while their form is limitations of this reality (A266–67/B322, A575/B603; *HN*, 23:37, 473; *Refl* 4113, 17:422; *Refl* 6318, 18:632–33; *V-Met/Mron*, 28:850; *V-Met/Dohna*, 28:634, 644, 663); the matter of phenomenal things is reality, while their form is space and time (A413/B440, A581/B609; *V-Met-L*$_2$*/Volckmann*, 28:411, 421; *L*$_2$*/Pölitz*, 28: 57; *V-Met/Mron*, 29:829; *V-Met-K*$_3$*/Arnoldt*, 29:983, 998; *V-Th/Pölitz*, 28:1021, 1034; *V-Th/Volckmann*, 28:1169; *V-Th/Baumbach*, 28:1252; *Refl* 5875, 18:374). In the main text I argue that noumenal and phenomenal things have the same matter, but have different forms.

[90] Some readers will object that I am illegitimately drawing on Kant's conception of the *ens realissimum* as the "storehouse" of all reality, whereas Kant's point is precisely to diagnose this idea as the product of dialectical illusion. But I have only talked about the reality of noumenal things, not their ground, God. And I am not attributing to Kant any claim to cognize or know the existence of such reality. I am merely claiming that this is how we must *think* about noumenal reality in its relation to phenomenal reality. I defend at length the claim that the Critical Kant retains some commitment to the postulation of God as the ground of all real predicates in Stang (2016b).

[91] In the statement of the Principle itself (A165), and further at B208, A168/B209, A175/B217.

[92] Cf. Kant's descriptions of things in themselves as "correlates" of sensibility (A30/B45, A250, A403) and "corresponding" to our sensibility (A109, A494/B522).

now at least represent spatiotemporal objects as causing our sensations. Phenomenal reality plays the role here that transcendental reality played in the Schematism: the corresponding "object." Then, in the Analogies we prove that phenomenal things are causes, including causes of our sensations.[93] We prove, in other words, that they correspond to our sensations.

But we should not let the cognizable, knowable thinghood (reality) of spatiotemporal things distract us from the merely thinkable thinghood (reality) of things in themselves, for that noumenal thinghood is conceptually prior, as the passage from the Schematism shows: we must think of noumenal thinghood as the "corresponding" object of sensation before we cognize phenomenal things in this role. It is that noumenal reality (the "transcendental material of all objects"), that intensively gradable causal force, that affects us, producing sensory reality, a reality whose corresponding object we first *think* as noumenal and then *cognize* as the thinghood of spatiotemporal substances. But this means that it is one and the same reality that we first think as the reality of noumenal things and then cognize as the reality of phenomenal things. We first think it purely intellectually and then cognize it spatiotemporally. Although the objects we merely think as the loci of this noumenal reality are non-identical to the objects we cognize (as per my earlier argument), it is the same thinghood, the same intensively gradable causal force, that we merely think in things in themselves and cognize in spatiotemporal things. Phenomenal and noumenal things are distinct object but have the same thinghood, the same reality. To use a contemporary metaphor, we "carve up" this reality into spatiotemporal objects, differently than a non-sensible intellect would—different objects, but same thinghood. They are collectively, not distributively, the same things.[94]

8. On Being Distributively the Same Things

In this section I will try to make sense of the idea that (some) appearances are "distributively" the same things as things in themselves; that is, for some appearance *x*, there is a thing in itself *y* such that *x* and *y* are the same thing. To make sense of this, we need to understand more about Kant's ontology of things, forces, and capacities.

[93] The claim that "empirical affection" is proved (or provable) within the Analogies is, I realize unorthodox, but I do not have the space to argue it here.

[94] Kant emphasizes throughout his writings an important difference between noumenal reality and phenomenal reality: the latter can stand in "real conflict" (where one reality "cancels" the other), while the latter cannot. See A264/B320–21. His explanation for this is that our form of intuition allows us to represent different directions in space (A273/B279). However, I do not think this poses an insuperable barrier to my interpretation (on which phenomenal reality is noumenal reality, only represented spatiotemporally), for two reasons. Insofar as Kant's considered view is that there can be no conflicts among noumenal reality, I would read this as meaning that noumenal reality can only conflict in appearance, not as it is "in itself." But I have my doubts as to whether Kant's considered view is that real opposition is impossible in noumena, rather than noumena *when represented through the understanding alone* (rather than conceived through some other faculty, e.g. practical reason) lack real conflict. In both pre-Critical and Critical texts Kant states explicitly that God grounds all (noumenal) realities, but does not instantiate them. My interpretation of this is: he recognizes that there is conflict among (noumenal) realities, and thus God cannot possess all of them. See A579/B607; *BDG*, 2:86; *V-Met/Herder*, 28:132–33, 917; *V-Met-K$_2$/Heinze*, 28:781–82; and, for critical discussion, Stang (2016b).

Things are substances, loci of force and activity. A thing, as such, possesses a capacity, a ground of real possibility. When this capacity is activated it grounds an accident, either in that very thing (immanent causation) or in another thing (transeunt causation). In doing so, it actualizes a passive capacity in the other thing (or itself, in the case of immanent causation), a capacity to be modified, while simultaneously actualizing its own active capacity. This accident is possible in virtue of the active thing's capacity to act (and the passive thing's capacity to be acted upon); this accident becomes actual when that capacity is activated. A thing that is the ground of actual accidents, a substance whose capacity is activated, is said to exercise a *force*. Things are not identical to their forces; a thing is more properly said to *have* or exercise force, that is, when it acts to causally ground accidents. For x and y to be *the same thing*, then, they must have the same force.[95] But things are particulars, not universals. So it is not enough that x and y have the same force *type* (e.g. gravitational force); they must be the same force *token*, the same individual locus of that force.

To make sense of the idea that sensible and non-sensible objects are the same things we need to make sense of the idea that one and the same locus of force can be presented to a discursive and to an intuitive intellect. Discursive intellects represent forces passively, by being affected by them, and combining their passively received representations according to rules. For instance, my sensible faculty is affected by a thing's force and, given the nature of my intuitive forms, this means I have temporally extended intuitive representations of spatially extended objects. In order to cognize a force in a thing I combine these temporally extended representations according to conceptual rules, namely, those specified by the categories of relation.[96]

Kant has much less to say about how an intuitive intellect cognizes force.[97] In various remarks, though, he claims that an intuitive intellect would not cognize its objects passively, by being affected by them, but would cognize them actively: its cognition of its objects would generate or ground those very objects themselves. His most extended remarks on how an intuitive intellect would cognize its objects occur in his discussions of how God (who possesses an intuitive intellect) cognizes his objects in the Pölitz lectures on rational theology.[98] In lecturing on Baumgarten's discussion of divine cognition in *Metaphysica* §§874–75, he makes this remark about God's cognition of actuality:[99]

> We think of *scientia libera* as God's cognition of the actual, insofar as he is simultaneously conscious of his free choice of things; for either all things are actual *by the necessity of God's nature* – which would be the principle of *emanation;* or else they exist

[95] In his metaphysics lectures Kant is adamant that substances have forces, but are not to be identified with those forces. See *V-Met/Herder*, 28:25–26, 129; *V-Met-L_1/Pölitz*, 28:261; *V-Met/Volckmann*, 28:431; *V-Met/Schön*, 28:511; *V-Met/Mron*, 29:770, 833.

[96] See section 3.

[97] This is unsurprising of course, since, not possessing intuitive intellect, we cannot know that intuitive intellect is really possible. No claims about intuitive intellect could constitute cognition, much less knowledge; they are at most analytic truths about the concept of intuitive intellect, a concept introduced to further articulate, by means of contrast, our concept of our own intellects as discursive.

[98] Though see also *V-Th/Volckmann*, 28:1158 and *V-Th/Baumbach*, 28:1266.

[99] Kant's ultimate aim, of course, is to argue that there is no distinction between actuality and possibility in God's cognition (*V-Phil-Th/Pölitz*, 28:1054). Cf. *KU* §76, 5:402.

> *through his will* – which would be the system of *creation*. We think of a *scientia libera* in God to the extent that in his cognition of everything possible, God is at the same time conscious in his free will of those possible things which he has made actual; hence this representation is grounded on the system of creation, according to which God is the author of all things through his will. But so too according to the principle of emanation. For since everything that exists is actual through the necessity of the divine nature, God must be conscious of all things – not, however, as he is conscious of his choice of things, but rather as he is conscious of them insofar as he is conscious of his own nature as a cause of all things. (*V-Th/Pölitz*, 28:1052–53)[100]

We must think of God as the ground of all real possibilities. But God is omniscient, so he must also cognize all real possibilities. Consequently, his cognition of all real possibilities is cognition of himself. This cognition cannot be empirical: empirical knowledge requires passivity, and God is pure activity. So God's cognition of real possibility is purely a priori knowledge of himself as the ground thereof.[101]

The passage continues:

> All God's cognition is grounded on his being an *ens entium*, an independent original being. For if God were not the cause of things, then either he would not cognize them at all, because there would be nothing in his nature which could supply him with knowledge of things external to him, or else things would have to have some influence on him in order to give him a mark of their existence. But then God would have to have sensible cognition of things, consequently he would have to be *passibilis* [capable of being passive], which contradicts his independence as an *ens originarium*. If, therefore, God is able to cognize things apart from sensibility, he cannot cognize them except by being conscious of himself as the cause of everything. And consequently the divine cognition of all things is nothing but the cognition God has of himself as an effective power. (*V-Th/Pölitz*, 28:1052–53)[102]

God does not generate objects and then, in a higher-order act of divine self-reflection, cognize himself as so generating them. Instead, divine cognition grounds the actual existence of the object and is at the very same time self-conscious cognition of itself as so doing. God is passive *neither* in cognition of created beings *nor* in self-cognition: his creation is pure act, and this act of creation is at the same time a cognition of the created object and of itself as so creating the object. Divine intuitive intellectual cognition of objects (which must be non-sensible, i.e., noumena) thus appears to be a case of what is now known as "maker's knowledge": a non-passive or non-sensible cognition of an object as being created by that very cognition itself.[103]

[100] As we know from *KU* §76, Kant's ultimate view will be that there is no difference between actuality and possibility for the intuitive intellect, so the distinction he makes in the course of his theology lectures will ultimately fall away.

[101] Earlier in the same passage: "God cognizes all things by cognizing himself as the ground of all possibility" (28:1052). Cf. *V-Met-L$_1$/Pölitz*, 28:328–29; *V-Met-L$_2$/Pölitz*, 28:606.

[102] Cf. *V-Met-L$_1$/Pölitz*, 28:330–31; *V-Met-K$_2$/Heinze*, 28:803; *V-Met/Mron*, 28:833.

[103] The notion of essentially self-conscious capacities has been the topic of some interesting recent discussions; see Kern (2006) and Boyle (2009).

This gives us a model for thinking of how one and the same thing can be the object of a discursive intellect (i.e., an object of sensible intuition) and the object of an intuitive intellect (i.e., an object of intellectual intuition): the intuitive intellect (i.e., God) self-consciously cognizes a thing with causal force as generated in that very act of cognition, and the discursive intellect is passively affected by that thing, requiring it to combine spatiotemporally dispersed representations into a unified representation of a locus of causal force. In this case, one and the same thing is two distinct objects; equivalently, two distinct objects are one and the same thing. This is highly abstract, and may seem utterly divorced from Kant's actual writings. In the next section I will try to substantiate this model of how distinct objects can be the same thing.

9. Practical and Empirical Cognition of the Will

I am trying to make sense of the idea that appearances and things in themselves are distinct objects but (distributively) the same things, where this means, specifically, that they are the same loci of force. I suggested that the intuitive intellect's self-active cognition of things, and our passive cognition of those things' effects on us, might provide a model for thinking about this. But if we bend the intuitive gaze back towards ourselves, we arrive at, I think, the best Kantian case for one and the same locus of force being given as two distinct objects to two different modes of cognition: our "noumenal causality," represented practically and self-actively in the consciousness of our freedom, on the one hand, and that very same causality cognized theoretically and passively in experience, on the other.[104]

It is well known that Kant rescues our freedom from the threat of determinism by arguing that, considered as a thing in itself, I am free while, considered as an appearance, my actions are bound by deterministic causal laws. At a textual level, it is worth noting that Kant tends to put this point in terms of one and the same *thing* being considered in two different ways or under two different aspects. First, there is this passage from the *GMS*:

> For, that a thing in appearance (belonging to the world of sense) is subject to certain laws from which as a thing or a being in itself it is independent contains not the least contradiction; that he must represent and think of himself in this twofold way, however, rests, as regards the first, on consciousness of himself as an object affected through the senses and as regards the second on consciousness of himself as an intelligence, that is, as independent of sensible impressions in the use of reason (hence as belonging to the world of understanding). (*GMS*, 4:458, my emphasis)

Second, there is the passage from the B Preface I quoted earlier:

> [...] if we are to assume that the distinction between things (*Dinge*) as objects of experience and the very same things as things in themselves (*von eben denselben*,

[104] My discussion throughout this section is indebted to Karl Schafer; see Schafer, "Kant's Conception of Cognition and Our Knowledge of Things in Themselves" (Chapter 10 in this volume) and Schafer (forthcoming).

> *als Dingen an sich selbst*), which our critique has made necessary, were not made at all, then the principle of causality, and hence the mechanism of nature in determining causality, would be valid of all things in general as efficient causes.
>
> (Bxxvii, my emphasis)

However, I do not want to rest too much on passages like this, for two reasons. First, I do not think Kant is consistent enough in his usage of *Ding* and *Gegenstand* for me to base my interpretation on these passages alone. At best, they constitute additional support. Secondly, by themselves, they do not give us any account of what "being the same thing" is. That is what I hope to supply in this section.

What could it mean that I, as a phenomenon governed by deterministic causal laws (object of experience), and I, as a free noumenon (object of practical, i.e., non-sensible, cognition), am one and the same thing? Freedom is a kind of causality, specifically, the capacity to be a self-determining cause, to act autonomously (out of respect for the moral law), rather than heteronomously (from a sensibly given motive). Since it is things (substances) that have capacities to act, it is as a thing (substance) that I have this capacity, that I am free. I am (or must represent myself as) a non-spatiotemporal substance, possessed of the capacity of freedom, that can be an object for itself in two fundamentally different ways: I am conscious of myself as free through pure practical reason, and I cognize myself as a deterministically governed and spatiotemporal thing in (outer and inner) experience. I will explain, first, my practical consciousness of my own freedom and then the more familiar theoretical cognition of myself as a phenomenon. I will argue that, being two fundamentally different modes of representation, they cannot have a common object, though their objects (free noumenon, deterministically governed phenomenon) are one and the same thing.

In the second *Kritik* Kant says that the "fact of reason" (i.e., the consciousness that I am bound by an unconditioned moral law) is the *ratio cognoscendi* of my freedom (the epistemic ground of my cognition of my freedom), while freedom is the *ratio essendi* of the moral law (the ground of the possibility that I am bound by it).[105] This can make it seem that my consciousness of my freedom involves an inference from one claim (i.e., that I am bound by the moral law) to a distinct claim (i.e., that I am free), mediated by a principle to the effect that "ought" implies "can" (if I ought to act autonomously then I am capable of acting autonomously, i.e., I am free).[106] But there are also indications that Kant sees a far more intimate connection between our consciousness of ourselves as bound by the moral law and our consciousness of our own freedom. Consider, for instance, these two passages:

> Thus freedom and unconditional practical law imply one another. Now I do not ask here whether they are in fact different or whether it is not much rather the case that an unconditional law is merely the self-consciousness of a pure practical reason, this [reason] being identical with the positive concept of freedom [...] (*KpV*, 5:29)

[105] *KpV*, 5:4 n. [106] E.g. *RGV*, 6:49–50.

> [This Analytic] shows at the same time, that this fact [of reason] is inseparably bound up with consciousness of freedom, indeed, is identical with it. (*KpV*, 5:42)

In the first passage Kant suggests, without directly stating, that consciousness of the moral law as binding on me is identical to consciousness of myself as free. Later, in the second passage, he comes out and directly states it: the fact of reason, my consciousness of myself as bound by an unconditional moral law, is identical to my consciousness of myself as free.

But if my consciousness of myself as bound by the moral law (consciousness of the fact of reason) is identical, as Kant says, to my consciousness of myself as free, then what becomes of the idea that the moral law is the *ratio cognoscendi* of freedom? How can one thing be a *ratio cognoscendi* of another, if my consciousness of one is identical to my consciousness of the other? The answer, I think, is that my consciousness of myself as bound by the moral law contains within itself, implicitly, consciousness of myself as free. Kant's transcendental investigations in the *KpV* allow me to render explicit what is always already contained in my consciousness of myself as bound by an unconditional moral law: I *can* act autonomously, that is, out of respect for the law. On this model, I do not infer from the fact of reason to my freedom; my consciousness of myself as free is contained, albeit implicitly, in my consciousness of myself as bound by the moral law.[107]

But if we hold on to Kant's claim that freedom is the *ratio essendi* of the moral law, then this means that our consciousness of ourselves as bound by the moral law contains consciousness of the *ratio essendi* of that law. To fill in the gaps in the passage quoted above: "[my consciousness of myself as bound by] an unconditional law is merely the self-consciousness of [...] the positive concept of freedom," the *ratio essendi* of the fact that this law is binding on me. So, my consciousness of the moral law is consciousness of something about myself (freedom) that grounds that law (or grounds its applicability to me). Thus, I do not merely cognize *that* I am bound by the moral law. I cognize *why* I am bound by the moral law, that is, I cognize it from its ground (its *ratio essendi*). What is more, my consciousness of the moral law is, or contains, the ground of the moral law's binding force on me. My consciousness of the moral law is (according to the passages above) identical to my consciousness of my freedom, and my freedom grounds the moral law (grounds its applicability to me). So my consciousness of the moral law is, or contains, consciousness of the grounds of its object: that I am bound by the moral law (i.e., that the moral law takes the form of an "ought" in relation to me).

We attain an even more "active" conception of my practical self-consciousness when we focus on Kant's reference above to the "self-consciousness of a pure practical reason, this [reason] being identical with the positive concept of freedom" (*KpV*, 5:29). The implicit distinction between a merely "negative" and a "positive" concept of freedom is clarified a few pages later when Kant writes:

[107] This is brought out especially well in Schafer (forthcoming).

> Autonomy of the will is the sole principle of all moral laws and of duties pursuant to them: heteronomy of choice, on the other hand, not only does not ground any obligation at all but is instead opposed to the principle of obligation and to the morality of the will. That is to say, the sole principle of morality consists in independence from all matter of the law (namely, from a desired object) and at the same time in the determination of choice through the mere universal law-giving form that a maxim must be capable of. That independence, however, is freedom in the negative sense, whereas this lawgiving of its own (*diese eigne Gesetzgebung*) by pure, and, as such, practical reason is freedom in the positive sense. (*KpV*, 5:33)

The negative conception of freedom is a conception of freedom as the capacity to act independently of the matter of the will (i.e., a particular desired object), which Kant here distinguishes from the positive conception. Kant calls freedom positively conceived "the self-consciousness of pure practical reason" (5:29) and, here, practical reason's own lawgiving. So it is not a mere blind lawgiving, without consciousness of the law; nor it a consciousness of a law given by some other capacity (or some other agent). It is a lawgiving that is essentially conscious of itself as lawgiving. It is lawgiving insofar as it is the ground of the moral law's binding force on it; it is self-conscious insofar as it is consciousness of itself as so doing. But these are two descriptions of one and the same capacity (positive freedom is both law-giving and self-conscious): a capacity that is the ground of something (its boundedness by the moral law) and is self-conscious of itself as so grounding that. Positive freedom is an essentially self-conscious capacity.

But if freedom is an essentially self-conscious capacity then we do not have two distinct capacities: the capacity for freedom, and then a higher-order capacity, the capacity to become conscious of the former capacity (perhaps through inner introspection or inference). There is one unified capacity, (positive, practical) freedom, which is essentially conscious of itself as such. But if this is correct then my consciousness of my freedom is my (positive) freedom itself. Since freedom is the *ratio essendi* of the moral law, it follows that my consciousness of my freedom is the ground of the moral law binding me.

This means that there is a structural similarity between my consciousness of freedom and divine intellectual intuition. Recall that God's cognition of what is actual is self-cognition: God's creative act self-consciously cognizes itself as the ground of its object. But I am not self-consciously aware of the actual exercise of my freedom; merely through practical self-consciousness I am not aware whether I act autonomously (by subordinating my self-love to the moral law), or whether I act heteronomously (by subordinating the law to my self-love). I am only aware of the capacity for autonomous action. Freedom is a capacity, not an act. This means that my practical self-consciousness is structurally similar, not to intellectual intuition of the actual, but of the possible. As Kant writes in the Pölitz lectures on rational theology: "We represent to ourselves that in cognizing his own essence (*simplex intelligentia*) God must also cognize everything possible, since he is the ground of all possibilities. Thus we derive the cognition of all possibilities from his nature and call it *cognitio simplicis intelligentiae*" (*V-Th/Pölitz* 28:1054). But God cannot be passive in self-cognition, any more than he can be passive in cognition of objects other than himself. God's cognition of himself as the ground of all possibilities must be contained in his grounding of all possibilities: his grounding of all possibilities must be essentially self-conscious (self-cognizing). In God, there are not two capacities: the capacity that grounds everything possible, and then a higher-order capacity to cognize the first. There is one single, essentially self-conscious capacity: to be conscious of oneself as the ground all possibility.

My aim is not to raise us up to God's level, much less to bring God down to our earthly one. It is to point out that my consciousness of myself as a noumenal thing possessed of freedom is self-active or non-passive in a way structurally similar to the intuitive intellect: it does not involve a moment of passivity, a moment of inner "intuiting" or "noticing," because what it is consciousness of (freedom) and the consciousness that it itself is, are one and the same.

By contrast, my theoretical cognition of myself, in inner and outer experience, as a relatively subsistent phenomenon, is partly passive. I affect myself in inner sense, and only thereby do I cognize my inner states in temporal order. I am affected in outer sense, and only thereby do I cognize my body in space. My temporally extended inner states, together with my spatially extended body, constitute a relatively subsistent thing in space and time. It does not persist absolutely (alas), so it is not a substance in the strictest sense. Nonetheless, it is not a mere accidental modification. It is something like an empirical "substantiated phenomenon," a relatively stable modification of underlying empirical substance (matter).[108] It constitutes a relatively unified locus of spatiotemporal force. Kant attributes to me as a phenomenon (an object of experience) an "empirical character," which I take to be a law or law-like generalization about the causal powers and forces of this relatively subsistent spatiotemporal thing.[109]

As a noumenal thing with noumenal freedom, I am not a possible object of sensible intuition. As a phenomenal thing, subject to deterministic causality and devoid of freedom, I am not a possible object of practical self-cognition. These are two distinct objects. Despite this, the noumenal thing with the self-conscious power of freedom and the phenomenal thing in space and time are *one and the same thing*: one and the same locus of force and activity presented to itself (to me) in two fundamentally different ways, self-actively in its consciousness of its own freedom and passively in experience of itself as a phenomenon.[110]

One complication should be noted. I originally characterized things as loci of force (grounds of actuality), but forces are always activations of capacities (grounds of possibility). In practical self-consciousness of my own freedom, I am conscious of myself as possessing a *capacity* for self-determination, that is, I am conscious that it is *possible* for me to will autonomously. I am not immediately conscious of the *actual*

[108] My body might be something akin to what Baumgarten calls a *phaenomena substantiata* (substantiated phenomena), a property we treat as a substance by predicating further properties of it. See Baumgarten, *Metaphysica* §193 and Langton (1998, p. 53) for discussion.

[109] A549/B577.

[110] This analysis could be deepened, for I am passively given to myself as a particular kind of object, an organized body. And this carries with it, according to the third *Kritik*, the thought not only of myself as a natural end (*Naturzweck*) but of my species (humanity) in its relation to the final end of nature, the realization of reason. But this would take us too far afield.

content of my will at all (i.e., whether I have subordinated the moral law to self-love, or vice versa). Nonetheless, the capacity of which I am conscious in my consciousness of my own freedom is a capacity to act, indeed, a capacity that is actualized (in what specific way I do not know). Capacities are individuated by the things of which they are the capacities; in practical self-consciousness I am aware of my own capacity to act freely, not yours. So I am aware of myself as a thing, a thing that acts (that has force), but I am aware only of the capacities of that thing.[111,112] But it is one and the same thing (locus of force and capacity) that is represented in practical self-consciousness and experience, because my actual will (i.e., the intelligible character of my will, whether I have subordinated the moral law to self-love or vice versa), the actualization of my capacity for freedom, appears to me as the "empirical character" of the spatiotemporal phenomenon I experience. The empirical character of my (actual) will is a "sensible schema," Kant claims, of the intelligible character of my (actual) will (A553/B581); the empirical character is said to be an "appearance" of the intelligible character (A541/B569). So the capacity (freedom) of which I am in practical self-consciousness is the very same capacity whose actual exercise appears to me as an object of inner and outer experience with a particular empirical character. I am one and the same thing, one and the same locus of capacity and act, but I am an object for myself in two fundamentally different ways. This means that my claim above, in section 5.3 that all conceivable intellects are either sensible or non-sensible (which, in fairness, I flagged as a simplifying assumption), needs to be modified slightly: we both sensibly (passively) intuit outer and inner objects *and* have a non-sensible, purely self-active awareness of our own capacity for freedom. *We* are the third kind of intellect we have been looking for.[113]

10. Conclusion

This chapter has covered a lot of ground, and in conclusion I would like to wrap up a few loose ends.

Leibniz's Law. At the beginning I pointed out that the various discernibility arguments in the literature could be circumvented by simply denying Leibniz's Law:

[111] This raises a problem: if the actualization of my noumenal will (my noumenal character) is the activation of an essentially self-conscious capacity, why is it not, like God's essentially self-conscious capacity for cognizing the actual, essentially self-conscious, i.e., why does it not contain consciousness of itself as grounding the noumenal character it does (either the subordination of the moral law to sensible inclination or vice versa)? I do not have the space to explore that issue here.

[112] Kant, of course, contrasts person and thing (e.g. *KpV*, 5:60), but in such contexts I take him to have a narrower, moral sense of "thing" in mind, i.e., a being that lacks reason. In other contexts, he claims that my substantiality (my thinghood) is evident in self-consciousness (*V-Phil-Th/Pölitz*, 28:1042). Thanks to Colin McLear for pressing me on this point.

[113] I have been working on this paper for a very long time and owe a debt of gratitude to various audiences and readers whose comments I have benefited from over the years. Particular thanks are due to Philip Blum, Catharine Diehl, Tim Button, and Bernhard Thöle, as well as audiences at Cambridge University, the Humboldt colloquium for classical German philosophy, and the Ligerz Workshop on Metaphysics. Extensive and insightful comments by my co-editor Karl Schafer, and by Andrew Stephenson and Colin McLear, on the penultimate draft helped improve this paper immeasurably.

(LL_O) For any P, $(x)(y)(x = y \supset Px \leftrightarrow Py)$

But my proposal has the same effect, for it retains Leibniz's Law as a principle about numerical identity among objects, but denies the corresponding principle about the relation of *being the same thing* (here symbolized as $x =_t y$):

(LL_T) For any P, $(x)(y)(x$ is the same thing as $y \supset Px \leftrightarrow Py)$

Leibniz's Law must be denied for the "same-thing-as" relation because the noumenal self and the phenomenal self are same thing but these are distinct objects with distinct predicates: the former is causally determined while the latter possesses noumenal freedom. In general, properties do not transfer across the relation of being the same thing. One and the same thing can have different properties, depending on what kind of representational capacity that thing is being considered the object of. As an object of experience, the thing I am has certain properties; as an object of practical consciousness of freedom, the thing I am has different ones. I am one and the same thing, but two different objects with two different sets of properties.[114]

Inconsistent? Earlier I argued that where x is a thing in itself and y is an appearance, no intellect can represent the content $x = y$ (where = is the relation of numerical identity between objects) because no intellect has intuitions of both sensible and non-sensible objects. But thinking of a sensible and a non-sensible object that they are the same *thing* also requires intuitions of both objects: one must think of x and of y that they are the same thing, and on my reading this requires an intuition of both x and y. Thus, by parity of reasoning the content "x and y are the same thing" should be unrepresentable by any intellect, and my objection to the Identity view would seem to entail that my own interpretation is literally unthinkable. This is the objection I raised earlier to the coherence of the distributive reading of the claim that appearances and things in themselves are the same things.

It is worth explaining why this same problem does not arise for the collective reading, on which appearances and things in themselves share the same thinghood (reality). Thinghood, reality, is a quantity (the quantity of a quantity, an intensive magnitude) and thus not a single object, that is, not the referent of an intuition and thus not a value for a bound singular variable (I have argued.) Consequently, the way we would represent the collective "same thing" relation (same thinghood) is not through a relation flanked by singular terms bound by (singular) variables. That no singular relation can obtain between sensible and non-sensible objects is no barrier to conceptually representing a generic relation of same thinghood (same reality) among them. So if we want a coherent version of Leibniz's Law, which is nonetheless violated on the collective reading, because appearances and things in themselves share the same thinghood but have different properties, it would be this:

[114] Why not short-circuit the Indiscernibility arguments by simply rejecting Leibniz's Law from the start? Rejecting Leibniz's Law is not enough; one must give a principled explanation of how *one and the same object* can have different properties. My account, however, delivers an elegant account of this difference in predications: it is objects that have properties, and things can be objects in two fundamentally different ways.

(LL_C) For any P, (F)(G)(the Fs are the same things as (i.e., share the same thinghood as) the Gs $\supset$ the Fs are P $\leftrightarrow$ the Gs are P)

In contemporary terms, this involves "mass" or "stuff" quantifiers, but exploring that would take us too far afield.[115]

However, there is precisely one case where we can do more than represent things in themselves in their relation to appearances generically: our practical consciousness of ourselves as free. In that case I represent myself as appearing and myself as I am in myself as *one and the same thing*. Recall that the reason for denying that singular relations (whether of identity or of sameness of thing) between sensible and non-sensible objects were well-formed contents: we lack the concept of an intellect that could so much as entertain these contents, because no intellect is both sensible and non-sensible. But in our case, we have a partial exception to this rule. Our practical consciousness of ourselves as free plays a role very similar to that of intuition: it allows us to represent ourselves, practically at least, *de re* as the very thing we are. My practical consciousness is singular consciousness of myself as free, not consciousness of the freedom of a general class of objects (rational beings, say). This means that in this case, where x is a sensible object (me as object of experience) and y is a non-sensible object (me as noumenon), the content $x = y$ is not unrepresentable or meaningless. We have the concept of an intellect that could represent such a content: ourselves. This means there isn't merely an epistemic difference between the theoretical and the practical case when it comes to identifying and differentiating things in themselves and appearances, but a semantic one. There is a difference in content. Outside of the practical case, there is no further fact of the matter as to which appearances are appearances of the same things in themselves, because there is no conceivable intellect that would represent these facts of the matter. But in the practical case there is a fact of the matter, the very fact of the matter we are conscious of when we are conscious of our freedom as a power of the very thing we passively experience as an object in space and time.

Thus, what appeared initially to be a straightforward inconsistency in my interpretation is revealed, upon further reflection, to constitute evidence in its favor, for it delivers an account of a textual detail that has long been noticed, but never fully explained: almost all of the passages that support the Identity reading are passages about the "identity" (on my reading, sameness of thing) of the empirical self and the noumenal self. Kant's writings are replete with claims to the effect that appearances in general can also be considered as things in themselves, or that objects of experience also have inner properties unknown to us. But all of these claims can be captured on the collective reading of "same things." The self is the one case where Kant repeatedly emphasizes *de re* of a single thing that *it* can be considered both as an object of experience and as a thing in itself. On my interpretation this tracks not merely an epistemic but a semantic difference: in general we lack so much as the concept of an intellect that would think of a sensible object and of a thing in itself

[115] Some of the formal details can be found in Higginbotham (1994).

that they are the same thing. The only case in which we possess such a concept is *ourselves*, the intellects that we, ourselves, are.[116]

References

Adams, R. M. (1997). Things in themselves. *Philosophy and Phenomenological Research, 57*(4): 801–25.

Adickes, E. (1924). *Kant und das Ding an sich*. Pan Verlag.

Adickes, E. (1929). *Kants Lehre von der doppelten Affektion unseres Ichs als Schlüssel zu seiner Erkenntnistheorie*. J. C. B. Mohr.

Allais, L. (2004). Kant's "one world": Interpreting transcendental idealism. *British Journal for the History of Philosophy, 12*(4): 655–84.

Allais, L. (2015). *Manifest reality: Kant's idealism and his realism*. Oxford University Press.

Allison, H. (1983). *Kant's transcendental idealism*. Yale University Press.

Allison, H. (1987). Transcendentalism idealism: The "two aspect" view. In B. den Ouden (Ed.), *New essays on Kant* (pp. 155–78). Peter Lang.

Allison, H. (2004). *Kant's transcendental idealism* (revised and expanded edition). Yale University Press.

Ameriks, K. (1982). Recent work on Kant's theoretical philosophy. *The Philosophical Quarterly, 19*(1): 1–24.

Ameriks, K. (1992). Kantian idealism today. *History of Philosophy Quarterly, 9*(3): 329–42.

Ameriks, K. (2006). Idealism from Kant to Berkeley. In *Kant and the historical turn* (pp. 67–88). Oxford University Press.

Aquila, R. (1979). Things in themselves and appearances: Intentionality and reality in Kant. *Archiv für Geschichte der Philosophie, 61*(3): 293–307.

Baumgarten, A. G. (1757). *Metaphysica* (4th edition). Hemmerde. [Cited as *Metaphysica* followed by paragraph number]

Beiser, F. (2002). *German idealism: The struggle against subjectivism, 1781–1801*. Harvard University Press.

Bird, G. (1962). *Kant's theory of knowledge*. Routledge & Kegan Paul.

Bird, G. (2006). *The revolutionary Kant: A commentary on the* Critique of pure reason. Open Court.

Boyle, M. (2009). Two kinds of self-knowledge. *Philosophy and Phenomenological Research, 78*(1): 133–64.

Courtine, J.-F. (2007a). Res. In J. Ritter, K. Gründer, & G. Gabriel (Eds.), *Historisches Wörterbuch der Philosophie: Völlig neubearbeitete Ausgabe des Wörterbuchs der Philosophischen Begriffe von Rudolf Eisler*, vol. 8 (pp. 892–901). Schwabe.

[116] Robert Merrihew Adams's classic paper (1997) gives an epistemic diagnosis of why Kant is only interested in identity in one case (the self): Kant's philosophy "gives more reasons to believe minds are identical with something noumenal and ultimately real, than to suppose that bodies are. It also gives more reason for believing that some sort of thought characterizes some things as they are in themselves than for believing that material" (p. 824). I have argued, in effect, that the relevant relation is not identity of objects, but sameness of things, and the defect is not epistemic, but semantic.

Courtine, J.-F. (2007b). Realitas. In J. Ritter, K. Gründer, & G. Gabriel (Eds.), *Historisches Wörterbuch der Philosophie: Völlig neubearbeitete Ausgabe des Wörterbuchs der Philosophischen Begriffe von Rudolf Eisler*, vol. 8 (pp. 179–85). Schwabe.

Förster, E. (2011). *Die 25 Jahre der Philosophie*. Klostermann.

Glezer, T. (2018). *Kant on reality, cause, and force*. Cambridge University Press.

Higginbotham, J. (1994). Mass and count quantifiers. *Linguistics and Philosophy*, *17*(5): 447–80.

Horn, L. & Wansing, H. (2020). Negation. In E. N. Zalta (Ed.), *The Stanford encyclopedia of philosophy* (Winter 2020 Edition). https://plato.stanford.edu/archives/spr2020/entries/negation/

Hintikka, J. (1968). On Kant's notion of intuition (*Anschauung*). In T. Penelhum & J. F. Macintosh (Eds.), *The first Critique: Reflections on Kant's* Critique of pure reason (pp. 38–52). Wadsworth.

Kern, A. (2006). *Quellen des Wissens: Zum Begriff vernünftiger Erkenntnisfähigkeiten*. Suhrkamp.

Langton, R. (1998). *Kantian humility: Our ignorance of things in themselves*. Oxford University Press.

Leech, J. (2014). Making modal distinctions: Kant on the possible, the actual, and the intuitive understanding. *Kantian Review*, *19*(3): 339–65.

Longuenesse, B. (1997). *Kant and the capacity to judge: Sensibility and discursivity in the transcendental analytic of the* Critique of pure reason. Princeton University Press.

McLear, C. (forthcoming). Hegel on the subjective nature of Kantian thought.

Marshall, C. (2013). Kant's appearances and things in themselves as qua-objects. *The Philosophical Quarterly*, *63*(252): 520–45.

Marshall, C. (2018). Never mind the intuitive intellect: Applying Kant's categories to noumena. *Kantian Review*, *23*(1): 27–40.

Oberst, M. (2015). Two worlds and two aspects: On Kant's distinction between things in themselves and appearances. *Kantian Review*, *20*(1): 53–75.

Oberst, M. (2017). Kant über Substanzen in der Erscheinung. *Kant-Studien*, *108*(1): 1–18.

Prauss, G. (1971). *Kant und das Problem der Dinge an sich*. Grundman.

Robinson, H. (1994). Two perspectives on Kant's appearances and things-in-themselves. *Journal of the History of Philosophy*, *32*(3): 411–41.

Rosefeldt, T. (2013). Subject-dependence and Trendelenburg's gap. In *Akten des XI. Internationalen Kant-Kongresses*, vol. 2 (pp. 755–64). De Gruyter.

Schafer, K. (forthcoming). Practical cognition and knowledge of things-in-themselves. In E. Tiffany & D. Heide (Eds.), *Kantian freedom*. Oxford University Press.

Schulting, D. (2010). Kant's idealism: The current debate. In D. Schulting & J. Verburgt (Eds.), *Kant's idealism: New interpretations of a controversial doctrine* (pp. 1–25). Springer.

Stang, N. (2014). The non-identity of appearances and things in themselves. *Noûs*, *47*(4): 106–36.

Stang, N. (2016a). Appearances and things in themselves: Actuality and identity. *Kantian Review*, *21*(2): 283–92.

Stang, N. (2016b). *Kant's modal metaphysics*. Oxford University Press.

Stang, N. (2017). Transcendental idealism without tears. In T. Goldschmidt & K. Pearce (Eds.), *Idealism: New essays in metaphysics* (pp. 82–103). Oxford University Press.

Stang, N. (2018). Kant's transcendental idealism. In E. N. Zalta (Ed.), *The Stanford Encyclopedia of Philosophy* (Winter 2018 Edition). https://plato.stanford.edu/archives/win2018/entries/kant-transcendental-idealism/

Stang, N. (2021a). Kant and the concept of an object. *European Journal of Philosophy*, 29 (2): 299–322.

Stang, N. (2021b). Bodies, monads, matter, and things in themselves. In B. Look (Ed.), *Leibniz and Kant* (pp. 142–76). Oxford University Press.

Stone, A. (n.d.). Kant on objects and things. Manuscript. http://www.abocalypse.com/papers/kant_objects_long.pdf

Tolley, C. (2013). The non-conceptuality of the content of intuitions: A new approach. *Kantian Review*, *18*(1): 107–36.

Turbayne, C. (1969). Kant's relation to Berkeley. In L. W. Beck (Ed.), *Kant studies today*. Open Court.

Vaihinger, H. (1881–92). *Commentar zur Kants Kritik der reinen Vernunft*. 2 vols. W. Spemann.

Van Cleve, J. (1999). *Problems from Kant*. Oxford University Press.

Watkins, E. (2005). *Kant and the metaphysics of causality*. Cambridge University Press.

Westphal, M. (1968). In defense of the thing in itself. *Kant-Studien*, *59*(1–4): 118–41.

Willaschek, M., Stolzenburg, J., Mohr, G., & Bacin, S. (2015). *Kant-Lexikon*. 3 vols. De Gruyter.

Wolff, C. (1720). *Vernünfftige Gedancken von Gott, der Welt und der Seele des Menschen, auch allen Dingen überhaupt*. Halle. 7th edition (1751) reprinted as volumes I.2.1 and I.2.2 in Wolff 1965–. [Cited as DM followed by paragraph number]

Wolff, C. (1730). *Philosophia prima sive ontologia methodo scientifica pertractata qua omnis cognitionis humanae principia continentur.* Frankfurt. Reprinted as volume II.3 in Wolff 1965–. [Cited as *Ontologia* followed by paragraph number]

Wolff, C. (1965–). *Gesammelte Werke* (J. École, H. W. Arndt, C. A. Corr, J. E. Hoffmann, & M. Thomann, Eds.). Olms.

Wood, A., Guyer, P., & Allison, H. (2007). Debating Allison on transcendental idealism. *Kantian Review*, *12*(2): 1–39.

13

Kant's One-World Phenomenalism

How the Moral Features Appear

Andrew Chignell

For otherwise there would follow the absurd proposition that there is an appearance without anything that appears.

—Bxxvi

1. The Primacy of the Practical as Interpretive Guide

The interpretative debate about the relationship between the sensible and intelligible worlds in Kant's philosophy is entrenched. Ask two commentators why they are in their respective trenches, and each will wearily produce an array of preferred texts and decisive theoretical considerations, and profess to be unimpressed by the preferred texts and decisive theoretical considerations produced by their opponents. There is rarely any movement across trenches.

My aim here is to break new ground by employing a neglected but very Kantian interpretative tool. In addition to textual and systematic considerations, I think we should take Kant's admonition about the "primacy of the practical" as seriously as we can when reading the entire *oeuvre*. More specifically, we should strive to give primacy to practical concerns not just when describing the relationship between Kant's ethics and other parts of his system, but also when interpreting his main theoretical doctrines. In this spirit, I will propose an account of Kant's signature metaphysical doctrine here that (a) has no supporters—as far as I am aware—in the contemporary literature, and (b) draws its primary motivation (as interpretation) from considerations regarding our *practical* situation and needs as agents.

Given space constraints, I can only focus on one of these considerations in this chapter—namely, the practically crucial idea that people not only *have* mental and moral features but also *appear* to us—in our daily experience—to have such features. Kant speaks for instance in the second *Critique* of the "appearances (*Erscheinungen*) of the fundamental disposition (*Gesinnung*) that the moral law is concerned with (appearance of the character (*Charakter*))" (*KpV*, 5:99). In a lecture from the Critical period, he used straightforwardly perceptual language: "[w]e can perceive virtue in our experience" (*Wir können in der Erfahrung wohl Tugend wahrnehmen*) (*V-Lo/Wiener*, 24:906). The same presumably goes for vice: when I see you casually torturing a cat, you appear to me to be brown-haired, wearing jeans, moving your arms, laughing, and so on, but you also appear to me to be vicious and cruel. Your character

Andrew Chignell, Kant's One-World Phenomenalism: How the Moral Features Appear In: *The Sensible and Intelligible Worlds: New Essays on Kant's Metaphysics and Epistemology.* Edited by: Karl Schafer and Nicholas F. Stang, Oxford University Press.
 DOI: 10.1093/oso/9780199688265.003.0014

shines through in your actions. I can then make a defeasible inference from those appearances to the moral reality. Such appearances and inferences play a central role in our practices of praise, blame, forgiveness, and punishment, as Kant goes on to say in the second *Critique* passage:

> ...[A]ctions (*Handlungen*) can give us acquaintance (*kenntlich machen*) with a natural connection that does not thereby make the vicious constitution of the will necessary, but is rather the consequence (*Folge*) of a freely (*freiwillig*)-adopted evil and unwavering principle, which in turn makes the agent all the more culpable and deserving of punishment. (*KpV*, 5:100)

Vicious actions are the natural consequence of a freely-adopted evil principle; they can also acquaint us with that very fact.

We find further hints of this picture in *Religion*, where Kant speaks of "persons in appearance, i.e., persons as experience acquaints us with them" (*Menschen in der Erscheinung, d. i. wie ihn uns die Erfahrung kennen läßt*) (*RGV*, 6:25n), of "human morality as appearance" (6:39n), and of events in history as "a phenomenon of the mostly hidden inner predispositions of humanity" (*Phänomen der uns großentheils verborgenen inneren Anlagen der Menschheit*) (6:36n). An interpretation of transcendental idealism that gives primacy to the practical will seek to analyze the concepts of *experience*, *acquaintance*, and *phenomenon* in a capacious enough way that they apply to mental and moral features too. Such an interpretation would have a clear practical advantage over those that leave us merely conjecturing from experiences of bodies, gestures, and secondary qualities to moral features that do *not* appear, or even to the non-appearing features of *a distinct set of things*. (Note that I am using "appearance" and "phenomenon" synonymously to mean "object of possible experience." There is another, narrower sense of "appearance" in Kant's writings that refers strictly to the content of intuitions. I'm not using the term in that narrower sense.)[1]

Although practical considerations like these provide the primary motivation for the interpretation proposed here, it will take a while to get back to them (in section 5 below). Before that I will paint the theoretical picture (section 2), distinguish it from some prominent alternatives (section 3), and discuss what kind of mind-dependence it ascribes to the core physical features of objects (section 4). At the end of the chapter (section 6), I'll pose and answer some central questions about the view. Along the way I will cite key passages, but a full textual defense is a project for another day.[2]

[1] Tolley (present volume) makes important use of this way of distinguishing between "appearance" and "phenomenon." He also encouraged me to make this clarification.

[2] Even a book-length treatment of this would not settle the relevant exegetical issues to everyone's satisfaction. That's because Kant's texts simply do not support one self-consistent, coherent position on the relationship between appearances and things in themselves. However, I do think that the key texts from 1783 onwards at least *generally* go in the direction of the hybrid view I present below. For some helpful totting up of the various passages for and against Two-World Phenomenalism, see Collins (1999) and Oberst (2018).

2. Three Levels of Features, One World of Things

In *Prolegomena* (1783) and in the B edition *Critique* (1787), Kant writes and revises in ways that are designed to rebuff the charges of Berkeleyanism that had bedeviled the reception of the A edition of 1781.[3] He also presents his considered account of the ontology of empirical objects. That account, I submit, is that

> *such objects—trees, tables, oceans, and particles—are things (substances) that really (i.e., mind-independently, transcendentally) exist and have various features in- and amongst-themselves. When these things are given to minds like ours in experience, they appear to us to have many features, only a few of which they really (i.e., mind-independently, transcendentally) have.*

To use Kant's own empirical analogy: the universe is like a collection of raindrops that is caught in a "sun-shower" (*Sonnregen*) and appears to us to be a solid, multi-colored arc. Most of the features that the collection appears to us to have (solid, multi-colored, arced, etc.) are *merely* apparent, and not features that the collection genuinely has (A45/B63). Analogously (and quite stunningly), Kant says, *all* of the spatiotemporal-mechanical-dynamical features that things appear to have are merely phenomenal, and not features that they really have.[4]

Another useful metaphor here is that of *projection*: Kant's claim is that when we "look on" (*schau an*) the world, the core physical structure that things appear to us to have is contributed by the various faculties of the projecting mind, though in a manner that is responsive to unknown features of the things themselves.[5] That allows him to accommodate our central commonsense commitment regarding external things—namely, that they exist and have various intrinsic and relational features in and amongst themselves. But it also underwrites his famous Copernican turn, for we can deduce a lot of substantive a priori principles about how those things must appear to us by reflecting on the structure that the mind itself projects.

The view that I take Kant to be proposing is thus *metaphysically realist* about things and their features, but also *broadly phenomenalist* about bodies. Because "Realist Phenomenalism" has such a paradoxical ring, I will use the somewhat less paradoxical name "One-World Phenomenalism." "One-world" and "two-world" talk has become a bit confusing in the literature, but what I mean by "one-world" is simply the view that there is just one set of things—namely, substances with their various features (both intrinsic and relational). However, some of the features these substances really have are *also* features that they appear to us to have. I will call these "*straddling*

[3] By Christian Garve, in the book review first published in 1782 in an edited and abbreviated (by J. G. H Feder) form in the *Göttinger gelehrten Anzeigen*, and later reprised in its original length in the *Allgemeine deutsche Bibliothek*.

[4] Here and throughout I use "real" as short for "transcendentally real." There is another, empirical/intersubjective sense in which the features things merely appear to us to have are "real," and support claims about them that are phenomenally or empirically true. This is not meant to be a kind of Vedic illusionism about the empirical world.

[5] See Ameriks (2003, pp. 154–55) for a seminal version of this "meeting in the middle" account. For more detail regarding how things in themselves can be part of the explanation of the specific a posteriori content of our experience, see Rosefeldt's contribution to the present volume.

features," or "straddlers" for short. Among the straddlers are basic ontological features (e.g. *existing, being a substance, having various grounding abilities*) as well as the key mental and moral features mentioned earlier (e.g. *having a mind, having rational capacities, being free, being radically evil*).[6] The view still counts as a kind of *phenomenalism* about bodies, however, because all of the spatiotemporal-material-causal features are *not* straddlers: they are *merely phenomenal* features that things do *not* really have. That is why Kant remains willing, even amid his anti-Berkeleyan labors, to call bodies "mere representations."

There is a third level: some of the features things appear to *me* or *you* or *me and you and Lampe* to have are a contingent matter of perceptual perspective or equipment, and so not features things appear to *us* to have, much less features things *really* have.

> Ordinarily we distinguish quite well between that which is *essentially attached* to the intuition of appearances and is *valid for every human sense* in general, and that which pertains to them only *contingently* because it is not valid for the relation (*Beziehung*) of sensibility in general but only for a *particular situation or organization* of this or that sense. (A45/B62, my emphasis)

Kant characterizes smells, tastes, and colors as "contingent" features of this sort: they are "linked with the appearance as contingently added effects of the special (*besondere*) organization [of the subject]" (A29/B44; cf. B69–70n). For present purposes, we can also include in this category various misleading seemings: dreams, hallucinations, illusions, color inversions, and so on.

Note that this distinction between the features a thing appears to us to have and the features it appears to some of us to have is *modal* rather than statistical. The former are such that, if the thing appears to well-functioning finite minds[7] at all, then it must appear to us to have those features. The latter, by contrast, are a function of contingent context, perspective, and perceptual equipment. It is possible for the thing to appear to someone else without those specific features.

Kant's ontology thus contains three main levels:

Noumenal: *Features things have.*
  (Straddlers): *Features things both have and appear to us to have.*
Phenomenal: *Features things appear to us to have.*
Perspectival or Illusory: *Features things appear to only some of us to have.*

Three levels of features; one set of things.[8]

[6] I use "feature" throughout rather than "property" or "predicate" because I want to include ontological statuses like *existence* that, for Kant, are not "real" predicates or determinations (*Bestimmungen*). So some of the straddling features are real predicates in Kant's sense; others aren't. Kant himself is willing, at least in some lectures, to say that *existence* and *being a substance* are two of the "realities" that "things in general" have; he calls *existence* a "universal attribute" and even an "ontological predicate" (*V-Phil-Th/Pölitz*, 28:1020).

[7] I refrain from talking about "human" minds since Kant wants to stay neutral on whether to include animal, alien, or angelic minds in the story (see B72). But the modal claims here only govern receptive-discursive finite minds that are saliently like ours; the divine mind is an entirely different story. See Brewer (2018, 2021) for accounts of the doctrine of intellectual intuition in Kant.

[8] My proximate inspiration here is a paper by the first of the two famous Westphals in Kant scholarship, namely, Merold (Westphal, 1968). I'm not sure this is Westphal's view exactly, but it is in the same spirit. There are hints of the view in Adickes (1924), although Adickes is hard to decipher on some of the key

3. How Is This Different from Other Metaphysical Readings?

There is no room here for an extensive comparison between the present account and other recent metaphysical readings of Kant's transcendental idealism, but the main differences should be clear. One-World (realist) Phenomenalism differs from Two-World (idealist) Phenomenalism in rejecting the notion that the objects of our experience are distinct from things in themselves—by being mere collections of (or logical constructions from the content of) mental states, for instance.[9] Rather, One-World Phenomenalism says that there is just one set of things (substances), and that these things appear to us to have many features that they do not really have. In other words, it rejects the assumption that to accommodate all of the texts that phenomenalist readers cite you have to hive bodies off into a separate mentalistic world.

One-World Phenomenalism differs from other recent metaphysical "one-world" or "dual-aspect" readings by rejecting strict property dualisms. A strict property dualism says that the distinction between appearances and things in themselves consists in the difference between "two kinds of properties that belong to one and the same object" (i.e., intrinsic properties vs. relational properties; mind-independent properties vs. essentially manifest properties; response-independent properties vs. response-dependent properties; different kinds of "*qua*-properties"; and so on).[10] One-World Phenomenalism, by contrast, says that the key difference is between *the features things really have* and *the features things appear to us to have*—these are *not* distinct sets of features but rather partially overlapping.[11] In effect, One-World Phenomenalism employs the ancient appearance/reality distinction to plow a viable middle way between the two-worlds trench and the two-kinds-of-properties trench—one that can accommodate the key texts on both sides.

Kant often emphasizes an analogy between his view and a certain early modern account of the primary–secondary quality distinction. Advocates of other one-world

issues. Nick Stang categorizes views like this under the heading of "dual aspect phenomenalism" or "phenomenalist identity theory." I prefer "One-World Phenomenalism" because (a) I think talk of "dual aspects" is inevitably associated with Epistemic One-World readings like that of Prauss (1971, 1974) and (Allison (1987) and (b) it is not clear that a hybrid collection of features that a thing appears to us to have (only some of which the thing really has) should be regarded as *numerically* "identical" with the thing. There is certainly no guarantee of a one-to-one correspondence between the collections of features and the things whose features they appear to us to be. That said, One-World Phenomenalism is an "identity" theory in the sense that there is ultimately only one set of things. See Stang's (2018a) extremely useful taxonomy.

[9] Perhaps the most influential defense of this view in the recent anglophone literature is by Van Cleve (1999). Other two-world phenomenalist interpreters include Stang, Paul Guyer (1987), Timothy Jankowiak (2017), Michael Oberst (2015, 2018), and Mark Pickering (n.d.). Jauernig (2021) appeared after this volume was submitted and so I don't know the details, but I gather her view is also going to be in this camp.

[10] "Strict property dualism" is R. Lanier Anderson's (2021) phrase; intrinsic vs. relational is from Langton (1998); mind-independent vs. essentially manifest is from Allais (2015); response-independent vs. response-dependent is from Rosefeldt (2013); "*qua*-objects" is from Marshall (2013). The quotation is from Rosefeldt's contribution to the present volume (2022).

[11] I'm not suggesting that each of the theorists listed in the previous note is a strict property dualist, although I think some of them must be (how could one and the same property be both mind-dependent and mind-independent?). Some of these theorists might allow that one and the same feature (e.g. *being a substance*) can be ascribed in thought under the unschematized version of the category and ascribed in cognition under the schematized version. This would be very close to treating *substantiality* as what I call a straddling feature. Thanks to Karl Schafer for discussion here.

pictures have made extensive use of this analogy,[12] and so it is worth looking at how One-World Phenomenalism accommodates it. Here is a key passage:

> As little as someone can be called an idealist because he wants to admit colors as properties that *attach not to the object in itself, but only to the sense of vision as modifications*, just as little can my system be called idealist simply because I find that even more, nay, all *of the properties that make up the intuition of a body* belong merely to its appearance: for the *existence of the thing that appears* is not thereby nullified, as with real idealism, but it is only shown that through the senses we cannot cognize it at all as it is in itself. (*Prol*, 4:289, my emphasis)

Kant says here that the "thing that appears" and its "existence" do not consist in being perceived; rather, they are mind-independent, and so he is not a Berkeleyan idealist. When that thing appears to us, however, there are many other features—including (stunningly) all the spatiotemporal features "that make up the intuition" of it as "a body"—that it "merely" appears to us to have but does not really have.

The early modern debate Kant is referencing concerned the status of secondary qualities like *being red* and *being bitter*. One side held that these are *merely* qualities of consciousness that are caused by objects in the world but do not occur outside the mind. (This kind of "eliminativism" is typically associated with Galileo.) The other side held that the primary qualities that *cause* those conscious sensations are, in virtue of doing so, *also* the secondary qualities. On this view there are indeed red, bitter objects in the world, but redness and bitterness are very different qualities than we perceive them to be. (This kind of "reductionism" is typically associated with Locke.)

Note that the two sides agree that primary qualities (extension, shape, texture, motion) are features that objects both have and appear to us to have. They also agree that primary qualities are disposed to cause specific sensations in us. So the "side-on" ontology is similar. The debate is over whether the secondary qualities—the colors, smells, and tastes—are features that objects *merely appear* to us to have (and can thus be eliminated from a scientifically perspicuous description of the world), or whether they are features that they really have (i.e., dispositions to produce specific kinds of sensations in us).

The difference between One-World Phenomenalism and other recent metaphysical "one-world" (or "dual aspect") accounts is analogous. The one-world phenomenalist advocates eliminativism about *all* the spatiotemporal features of bodies: they are "nothing more than the way in which we represent (in appearance) the existence of things," even if they are responsive to unknown features of those things (A186/B229). Other recent one-world accounts, by contrast, seem to *reduce* the phenomenal features to the dispositional features of things in themselves. In Rosefeldt's words:

> To have a response-dependent appearance property just is to have some response-independent property that is characterized by its mental effect. (present volume)

[12] See Rosefeldt (2007), Allais (2007, 2015, ch. 6).

The response-dependent property is still a property *of the thing*, and not a feature it merely appears to us to have:

> *A response-dependent property is a property of an object* that has essentially to do with the kinds of responses, or effects, that object has on certain things, typically human beings. It can be understood as the disposition of the object to elicit these effects. (ibid.; my emphasis)

How should we adjudicate between these two kinds of account? As usual there is no knock-down textual argument, but Kant certainly *sounds* eliminativist in the *Prolegomena* passage above when he draws an analogy between his view (at the transcendental level) and the Galilean view (at the empirical level). Intuited spatiotemporal features, he says, are analogous to colors that "attach *not to the object in itself*, but *only* to the sense of vision as modifications" (*Prol*, 4:289, my emphasis). In the Aesthetic, likewise, he declares that "space represents *no property at all* of any things in themselves *nor any relation* of them to each other" (A26/B42, my emphasis). Analogies and declarations like these make it awkward to say that space is nonetheless a feature of things: i.e., an "essentially manifest" property (à la Allais); a "response-dependent" property (à la Rosefeldt); or a "*qua*-property" (à la Marshall). Analogies and declarations like these make perfect sense if space is not a feature of things at all, but rather a feature that things merely appear to us to have.

One of the main reasons this difference matters is practical: if a response-dependent property just *is* a response-independent property characterized in a specific way, and the former is determined by reciprocal relations with other items in the phenomenal realm, then the latter are clearly at risk of being caught up in deterministic relations. That result is *precisely* what Kant wants to avoid, on practical grounds. One-World Phenomenalism avoids the problem, since it says that all the deterministic features (*materiality*, *extension*, *location*, etc.) are merely phenomenal, and not features that the thing really has. Things may appear to us to be determined, but in reality they are not.[13]

Another reason the difference matters is this: other metaphysical one-world (or "dual aspect") readings imply that there is one complete set of objects in space and time—namely, all the things that have (response-dependent, essentially manifest) spatiotemporal-causal properties. As harmless as that implication seems, it is in tension with Kant's conclusions in the first two Antinomies, according to which the sensible world "does not exist as such a whole, either with infinite or with finite magnitude" (A505/B533). One-World Phenomenalism again has the advantage here: it says that there is just one world of intelligible substances, and that this world *merely appears* to us to be in space and time. So there is no complete set of objects in space and time.[14]

[13] I will discuss the extra complications involved in taking freedom to be a straddling feature at the end of section 5 below.

[14] This is another reason not to think of it as an "identity" theory with one-to-one correspondence relations between things and appearances. Thanks to Nick Stang for discussion of the point in this paragraph.

Two further clarifications: one about truth, the other about cognition. First, as should now be obvious, "appears to us to have" is shorthand for "*appears to all well-functioning, properly-situated finite cognizing minds to have*," where "finite cognizing mind" refers to our essential faculties of intuition and understanding. What appears to us in this way is the basis for intersubjective truth-claims. Kant gestures at this when he analyzes "truth" in the phenomenal world as "correspondence" with facts that are given in "absolutely complete" or "universal" experience.[15] Stang provides a helpful sketch of the latter notion:

> Universal experience is the maximally unified and lawful representation of objects in space and time that is compatible with the *a priori* forms of experience and justified by the totality of subjects' perceptual states, or the conjunction of such representations if there is no unique such representation.
>
> (Stang, 2018a, n.p.; for discussion, see Stang, 2018b)

This is the Kantian gloss on the Leibnizian idea that empirical objectivity consists in lawlike intersubjectivity: representations that "are connected and determinable in these relations (in space and time) according to the laws of the unity of experience, are called **objects**" (A494/B522). Leibniz called them "well-founded phenomena."

So it is phenomenally true that there is a wooden table before us that is five feet long and two feet wide just in case it is noumenally true that there is a substance that appears to us to have those spatiotemporal features together with the material and causal profiles of wood. The truth-makers of phenomenal truths are facts about how things appear to us (including their straddling features).[16] But as we have seen, finite minds also have subjective perspectives and idiosyncratic equipment (colorblindness or scurvy, for instance). These result in "mere semblance" (*bloßen Schein*), i.e., features that things merely appear to *some of us* to have, but not well-founded *Erscheinungen*, i.e., features that things appear to *all of us* to have (see B71 and *FM*, 20:269). So it is not phenomenally true that there is a dagger hanging before me in mid-air, or even that this table is brown.[17]

Second, and relatedly, something's appearing to us to have a feature—even *merely* appearing to do so—involves a complex cognitional process including affection by the thing, the synthesis of intuitional content, the conceptual apprehension of this manifold, and the production of discursive judgments ascribing determinate properties.[18] Mere semblance, by contrast, does not implement this entire process.[19]

[15] For "truth" as correspondence of cognition with its object, see A58/B82. For "possible experience in its absolute completeness" see A495/B524. For "universal experience" see A45/B63 and A110.

[16] Note that this claim about truth-makers is much weaker than the full-blown reductionism about spatiotemporal properties that other one-worlders seem to endorse.

[17] It may still be phenomenally, empirically true that the table seems to me to be brown. But that is a second-order claim about a seeming, not a first-order claim about the table.

[18] For more on Kantian cognition, and Kant's occasional uses of "false cognition," see Chignell (2014), Watkins & Willaschek (2017), Chignell (2017), Tolley (2017), and Schafer (forthcoming).

[19] See Sethi (2020).

Here is the taxonomy of features again, now with further details:

Noumenal: *Features things have; in Kant's terms, they are* ***transcendentally real****.*

> **(Straddlers):** *Features things both have and appear to us to have; these are still transcendentally real.*

Phenomenal: *Features things appear to us to have (in virtue of our shared, essential cognitive faculties). A few of these (the straddlers) are features things also have. The rest are merely phenomenal but still part of "universal experience"; in Kant's terms, these latter (but not the straddlers) are* ***transcendentally ideal****.*

Perspectival or Illusory: *Features things appear to* **some** *of us to have (in virtue of our contingent perspectives, environments, or equipment) but do not appear to us to have (in virtue of our shared, essential cognitive faculties). In Kant's terms, they are* ***empirically ideal****.*

I think this picture is coherent, supported by key texts, and offers resources to accomplish some of Kant's central goals: answering the Humean challenge, repudiating Berkeleyan idealism, refuting Cartesian skepticism, preserving libertarian freedom, and giving primacy to the practical. By retaining a three-level ontology in the one world ("the thing for God, the thing for us, and the thing for me") it also makes Kant's view genuinely novel, and not an exercise in merely "giving fancy names to familiar distinctions."[20] But I can't defend all of that here, obviously. In what remains, my aim is to lay out the view a bit further, advertise one of its key practical attractions, and answer some key questions.

4. Straddling the Phenomenal/Noumenal Divide

4.1 Straddling Features

We pull up our chairs to the table in preparation for a meal. The table appears to us to have a certain size, shape, texture, and so on. It also appears to be made of wood, which is a certain dynamical configuration of matter. According to One-World Phenomenalism, what's happening is that there is something that really has features such as

<u>(Noumenal Level):</u>
existence
being a substance
being in dependence relations with other things
being the ground of thus-and-such perceptions in us

as well as many other intrinsic and relational features that are inaccessible to us. It also appears to us to have various features:

[20] Westphal (1968, p. 119).

<u>(Phenomenal Level):</u>
existence

being a substance
being in dependence relations with other things
being the ground of thus-and-such perceptions in us
being material
being in thus-and-such causal relations
having thus-and-such an extension
having thus-and-such a quantum
having thus-and-such a temporal location
being in thus-and-such spatial relations
etc.

"Thus-and-such" is just a placeholder for specific perceptions, relations, and locations—in the present case, perceptions of a wooden table with a certain position, shape, texture, and so on. As the two lists make clear, some of the features that things appear to us to have are overlapping straddlers (in **bold**): they are also features that they really have in themselves. But most features of phenomena are not straddlers—they are *merely* phenomenal.

Unlike the merely phenomenal features, straddlers can support inferences across the phenomenal–noumenal divide. If the table appears to us to exist, then we can infer that there is something that exists. If the table appears to us to be a substance, then we can infer that there really is a substance, "for otherwise there would follow the absurd proposition that there is an appearance without anything that appears" (Bxxvi). If the table appears to us to be grounding our perceptions of it, then we can infer that there is a ground of our perceptions of the table. In general: when something appears to us, we can infer that it (a substance) exists, and that it is in various dependence and grounding relations, including the relation of grounding precisely those perceptions in us.

It would be worth considering each of the straddlers in turn to work out what the straddling content is, what merely phenomenal content is added when it appears to us, and how all this fits with Kant's talk of pure categories, schematized categories, and the pure principles of the understanding. Here I will set most of that aside for the sake of space. I do want to say a bit more about the straddling feature of *being a substance*, however.

In the chapter on the Analogies of Experience, Kant deduces the principle that (A edition:) substance appears to persist through all state- and property-changes and (B edition:) material substance is an absolute permanent whose "quantum is neither increased nor diminished in nature" (A182/B224). But in addition to such "substances in appearance" (A188/B231) or "substances in space" (A525/B553), Kant says that we can also ascribe the feature of *being a substance*, quite properly, to things in themselves. When we do that, we abstract from the features things merely appear to us to have (i.e., *being material, having thus-and-such an extension*, etc.): "with that which is called substance **in appearance** things are not as they would be with a thing in itself which one thinks through pure concepts of the understanding" (ibid.).

Kant goes on to clarify that the content we univocally ascribe to both sensible and intelligible things under the category of <*substance-attribute*> is that of *being "an absolute subject"*—i.e., an "ultimate subject of existence," one that is not a predicate of something else (ibid.; see also B148). This straddling content is quite thin, of course, and sensible substances will have lots of additional features that they merely appear to us to have. When we perceive the table, something appears to us to be a substance (an absolute subject), and we can infer on this basis that a substance exists and is the ground of these perceptions in us. But the table inevitably also appears to have spatiotemporal-dynamical attributes (*persistence, a certain shape, material-dynamical features*, etc.). The central (and stunning) thesis of Kant's transcendental idealism is that none of these latter attributes straddle; rather, they *merely* appear.

We might wonder, however: do tables and chairs and galaxies really appear to us as absolute subjects? Does this straddling content really shine through? A key passage from *Metaphysical Foundations of Natural Science* indicates that the answer is Yes. There Kant moots the Cartesian idea that the external substance that appears is *matter in general*—the ultimate subject of spatial predication. Loosely speaking, however, we can still call individual configurations of matter "substances" insofar as they are subjects and not "merely predicates" of "other matters":

> The concept of a substance refers to *the ultimate subject of existence*, that is, that which does not itself belong in turn to the existence of another merely as predicate. Now matter is the subject of everything that may be counted in space as belonging to the existence of things. For, aside from matter, no other subject would be thinkable except space itself, which, however, is a concept that contains nothing existent at all, but merely the necessary conditions for the external relations of possible objects of the outer senses. *Thus matter, as the movable in space, is the substance therein*. But all parts of matter must likewise be called substances, and thus themselves matter in turn, insofar as one can say of them that they are themselves subjects, and not merely predicates of other matters.
>
> (*MAN*, 4:503; see also *MAN*, 4:540–41, but cf. B148)[21]

One-World Phenomenalism reads this as the claim that *being a substance* is a straddling feature. When something appears to us in outer sense, it appears to us to have the feature *being a substance* (a feature that it also really has) and the merely phenomenal features associated with *being material*. Put another way: cognition of external substances inevitably involves *schematization* and *materialization*—that is, the ascription of temporal, spatial, and mechanical-dynamical features (e.g. a "quantum" that is conserved through transformations). But when we make an inference across the straddling feature we "abstract" from all that and retain only the content of the "pure concept" (i.e., absolute subjecthood) (A525/B553).

Note that the first three items in the list refer to intrinsic features of a thing, but the fourth—*being the ground of thus-and-such perceptions in us*—can refer *either* to an intrinsic, standing ability to ground specific perceptions in us, or to a relational *manifestation* of that ability in a particular case. Both of these features may be

[21] Thanks to Adwait Parker for highlighting the importance of these passages in *MAN* and to Jessica Leech for discussion. I leave as homework a discussion of other relevant passages about the category of substance and its phenomenal and noumenal instantiations, as well as an engagement with Messina's (2021) important work on this issue.

straddlers, but the latter is also a relation that requires there to be at least one mind in which the power is made manifest. I will call a feature that, by its very concept, entails the existence of a mind an "analytically mind-dependent feature." Other examples include *being a mind*, *being in a world with a mind*, *being seen*, *being free*, *being known*, and various second-order features such as *appearing to a mind to have a feature*. Another and more interesting way for a feature to be mind-dependent is for it to be *merely phenomenal*. I'll now turn to Kant's account of that.

4.2 Merely Phenomenal Features

One of Kant's revolutionary aims is to establish the (stunning) synthetic a priori thesis that spatial extension and temporal "persistence" are merely phenomenal—i.e., "nothing more than the way in which we represent the existence of things (in appearance)" (A186/B229). Here is an account of mere phenomenality that applies to features that are not analytically mind-dependent:[22]

Merely Phenomenal (MP): *For any feature F that is not analytically mind-dependent, any object O, and the set of finite cognizers, ψ, O's being F is merely phenomenal if and only if it is impossible that* **both** *(i) O is F* **and** *(ii) no normal*[23] *member of ψ is able to cognize that O is F.*

For example: the fact that the table is, say, rectangular at time *t* is *merely phenomenal* just in case the table cannot be rectangular-at-*t* unless there is a finite mind that is able to cognize that the table is (or was) rectangular-at-*t*.[24] This is merely a modal connection rather than a real explanation. But the connection is grounded in the fact that part of what it is for an object to have a phenomenal feature is for it to be *able to be cognized to have* that feature. I will not say anything here about what the "ability to cognize" consists in, or how it serves as a partial ground in this way. But obviously Kant has a big story to tell about that.

According to MP, a finite mind need not exist at the time when O has F in order for that fact to be merely phenomenal: we can cognize the dinosaurs' having large teeth via the fossil record, millions of years after they walked the earth. So the

[22] This is not an analysis of mere phenomenality *simpliciter*. It's hard to find a principle that doesn't end up making analytically mind-dependent features like *being a mind* or *appearing to a mind* merely phenomenal—something no Kantian wants to allow. Note too that strictly speaking this is an analysis of a fact. So really it's *O's being F* that is merely phenomenal. However, I speak loosely here and throughout of features being merely phenomenal.

[23] "Normal" here is supposed to make the cognizability of *O's being F* compatible with various contingent and philosophically uninteresting incapacities. We want to allow that even if all the actual cognizers in the world just happen to be deaf, a falling tree still makes a (merely phenomenal) sound. Thanks to Christopher Benzenberg for a question about this issue.

[24] Note that the minds in question are "finite" cognizers with faculties of intuition and discursivity like ours. Any theist is going to say that almost everything is dependent on the infinite mind, but that's not enough to make them merely phenomenal in the MP sense.

connection between having the feature and being cognized by an existing mind to have that feature may be either *Potential* or *Indirect.*

Potential: *O's being F at t* can be merely phenomenal in the MP fashion even if that fact is not cognized or even cognizable by us at *t.* All that is required is that at some time or other an actual finite cognizer exists and was or will be able to cognize that *O* was *F-at-t.* Note, however, that it is not enough for merely possible finite mind to be able to cognize *O's* being *F-at-t.* A non-actual mind is not ontologically substantive enough to be a partial ground of something's having a feature, even in a merely phenomenal way. Put more starkly, if there were no finite cognizers of our sort, there could not be any F-bearing things. The relation invoked in (ii) of MP is thus *actual cognizability.* This is another place where One-World Phenomenalism seems to differ from other recent one-world readings.[25]

Indirect: cognition of a tree falling in a forest (or a dinosaur, or a particle) need not be directly *sense-perceptual*: it can go by way of inference and extrapolation from other observations, testimony, and background knowledge. Kant speaks of expanding our cognition beyond what we perceive by appeal to general and specific natural laws as well as the pure principles of the understanding—together, these are "the laws of empirical advance" (A493/B521). In this way the features of gluons, galaxies, and "magnetic matter" count as actually cognizable and thus as (merely phenomenal) components of the empirical world.

A final, related point: MP says that *if* O is F, then some finite mind exists and is able to cognize its being F. MP does not affirm the absurd converse: i.e., that if some finite mind exists and is in principle able to cognize *O's being F*, then *O* exists and is F. In other words, the fact that an actual mind would be *able* to cognize horses with horns does not entail that unicorns exist. There are other partial grounds of a thing's appearing to us to have a feature, even a merely phenomenal one.

5. Practical Cognition of Persons in Appearance

I noted at the outset that a key advantage of One-World Phenomenalism is that it allows Kant to say that various mental and moral properties are straddlers: they are *both* real features and apparent features of certain things—ourselves included. Here I'll focus on specifically moral features such as *being rational agents*, *being free*, *being*

[25] Allais says that the mind-dependent properties that constitute appearances are "essentially manifest." In the passage that looks like her official gloss on this notion she says: "To capture the idea that a [property, F] is *essentially manifest* we need something stronger: an object is [F] only if there is a way it would appear to subjects who are suitably situated and suitably receptive. Here, the object's being [F] is dependent on its possible appearance to conscious subjects" (2015, p. 123). The subjunctive formulation here suggests that an object can be F even if there are no *actual* finite minds that are able to cognize it as F. Elsewhere Allais says that "[f]or something to be empirically real it is necessary that it could be present in a possible empirical intuition" (p. 144). MP, by contrast, is stronger: it says that O cannot be F unless there *actually* is, at some point, a finite mind that is able to cognize it as F. MP is much weaker, however, than a two-world phenomenalist principle like that defended by Oberst: "all talk about appearances can be reduced to talk about some sort of mental content" (2018, p. 120).

radically evil, being courageous and so on. My suggestion is that these too are straddling features that substances (i.e., agents) both have and appear to us to have.

Kant says in the first *Critique* that our "empirical character" is just a "sensible schema" of our "intelligible character" (A553/B581). In the second *Critique* he says that there is a "natural to our reason, but inexplicable perspective" that "conscience" offers, such that we can be "assured" of a relation by which our "actions as appearances" can be ascribed to "the intelligible substratum in us" (*KpV*, 5:99; compare 5:43–46). One-World Phenomenalism reads this as the claim that something in our experience appears to us to *act*—i.e., it appears to be a rational agent rather than a mere body, whether mechanical or organic. But agency is a function of a rational will—the "intelligible substratum in us." Thus when we observe ourselves (or someone else) *acting*, a substance appears to us to be a rational agent. Just as with the other straddlers, we can then infer on that basis that it really is such an agent: it is a person.

Rational agency is a very general feature, but something similar is true of specific moral maxims and dispositions. Someone appears to us to have a specific moral character, and on this basis we can (defeasibly) infer that he *really has* that specific character. In *Religion*, Kant says that someone's deeds—which we cognize in experience or indirectly via testimony—may be "so constituted that they allow the inference of evil maxims in him" (*RGV*, 6:20). In fact, empirical "anthropological research" gives us "grounds that justify us in attributing one of these two characters [evil or good] to a human being" (*RGV*, 6:25). In one of the most reliable logic transcripts from the critical period ("*Wiener*") Kant reportedly said:

> We cannot encounter a virtue among human beings. But my reason must nonetheless have a concept of virtue, as it must be in its complete perfection. *We can very well perceive* (*wahrnehmen*) *virtue in experience* (*in der Erfahrung*). But much must still be added to it; thus it is an idea. (*V-Lo/Wiener*, 24:906–907, my emphasis)[26]

Certainly we do not encounter a perfected virtue among imperfect human beings, and so that remains a mere idea. But we can nonetheless experience *some* moral qualities in ourselves and others.

These texts (together with those already quoted in section 2) indicate that by 1788, at least, Kant has expanded his official notion of "phenomena" or "objects of experience" to encompass moral features, and not merely the empirical-theoretical features that are the focus of the first *Critique* and *Metaphysical Foundations*. Judgments about moral-agential features are presumably generated in what he sometimes calls "practical cognition," and those that involve straddlers can support defeasible inferences to claims about the features things really have. The parallel to the theoretical case here is very close: in empirical cognition of the table, a substance that grounds

[26] Note that here and elsewhere Kant seems to be saying that we "perceive" these moral features not just in ourselves but also in others ("human beings"). A weaker claim would be that we can perceive them in ourselves but not in others. Although I take texts like these to support the stronger claim, it would be worth considering whether the weaker claim offers philosophical advantages. Thanks to Clinton Tolley for discussion of this difference.

our perceptions appears to us, and this supports the inference that there really is a substance that grounds these perceptions. In practical cognition of someone torturing a cat, a person who is vicious appears to us, and this supports the inference that he really is vicious. That's what it means to say that some noumenal features "*shine through*" (*hervorleuchtet*) in our experience.[27]

In moral cases we are typically dealing with much more specific features than in the empirical case, and so the inferences from the moral features things appear to have to the moral features things really have will not be as reliable. Sometimes what appears will be mere moral semblance, rather than a well-founded moral phenomenon. In the *Groundwork* Kant says that it is absolutely impossible by means of experience to make out *with complete certainty* (*mit völliger Gewissheit*) whether a maxim "rested wholly on moral grounds." The "dear self" is adept at hiding all manner of immoral intentions from others and from itself (*GMS*, 4:407–408).[28] In the *Religion*, however, he allows there is a limited "extent to which one can expect and ask for *evidence* (*Beweisthümer*) *of the inner moral disposition* (*Gesinnung*) *from an external experience*." Such an experience "does not reveal the inner disposition but only allows inference to it, though not with strict certainty" (*RGV*, 6:63, my emphasis). Kant is saying here again that we can defeasibly infer from moral appearances to the features of someone's fundamental maxim and character—*occasionally* if the person is virtuous (as in the case of the "teacher" of the Gospels (*RGV*, 6:66) or a longtime practitioner of the good (6:68)), but much more often if her actions are done from "vice (*peccatum derivativum*) and her ultimate maxim is evil (*peccatum originarium*)" (*RGV*, 6:31; cf. 6:36–37; 6:71; 4:408). Likewise in self-observation: "[someone] can derive no certain and definite concept of his actual disposition (*wirklichen Gesinnung*) through immediate consciousness, but *only* from the conduct he has actually led in life" (*RGV*, 6:77, my emphasis). We appear to ourselves to act courageously, and from that we defeasibly infer that we really are courageous.

A significant advantage of One-World Phenomenalism is that it can make sense of how all this works via the doctrine of straddlers. Some of the intelligible moral features of agents (*being evil*, *being courageous*) shine through, and thus support the relevant inferences from moral appearance to moral reality. In other words, such moral features are phenomenal, but they are not *merely* phenomenal. Of course, as just noted, it's possible for you to appear to some of us to have a moral feature that you do not really have: that's why inferences across straddlers are defeasible in the

[27] In *Perpetual Peace*, Kant says that we have a "guarantee" that we are approaching perpetual peace because through the "mechanical array" generated by "the great artist *nature* (*natura daedala rerum*) purposiveness shines forth visibly (*sichtbarlich hervorleuchtet*)" (*ZeF*, 8:360). This is a nice image that I think the one-world phenomenalist can use to describe how not just purposiveness but also rationality, freedom, and other moral qualities directly appear.

[28] "Indeed even a human being's inner experience of himself does not allow him so to fathom the depths of his heart as to be able to attain, through self-observation, an *entirely* reliable cognition of the basis of the maxims which he professes, and of their purity and stability" (*RGV*, 6:63). For this reason, Kant says we "are acquainted with (*kennen*) ourselves" by "estimating our disposition not directly but only according to our *actions* (*Thaten*)" (*RGV*, 6:75–76, my emphasis). Note, however, that actions are quite different from mere bodily behavior.

moral case. But other things equal, *how you* morally *appear to us* in practical cognition licenses a prima facie conclusion about *how you* morally *really are*.[29]

Note that the inference pattern is typically just one step: from practical cognitions of the moral features people appear to us to have, to a defeasible conclusion about the moral features they really have. Occasionally, however, there will be a *preliminary* inference from mere bodily behavior to the apparent moral features: "I don't have my glasses with me, but tell me: is that person really *laughing* while harming that cat? Or is he *grimacing* while performing a difficult but necessary medical procedure on it? He's laughing? Well, then, it appears he really is vicious!" In such cases, the moral features still appear, but in the indirect way that dinosaurs, distant planets, and magnetic matter appear in empirical cognition. They are features things appear to us to have, but not directly: we infer that they are "given" from testimony or observation of instruments, fossil records, satellite data, etc. In many cases—both theoretical and moral—if we had "finer" faculties, or were closer in space or in time, we might be able perceive the appearances directly. As it is, though, we first infer the moral appearances from physical appearances, and only then make *further* inferences about the features someone really has. Again, however, this two-step process is not the norm: typically it's just a one-step inference across straddlers: from the moral features of appearances to the moral features of things in themselves.

It's not clear how competing views can say something equally attractive here. Two-World Phenomenalism presumably construes human bodies as something like constructed, spatiotemporal avatars of numerically distinct, non-spatiotemporal substances. So with respect to other people, what appears are just the movements and sounds of bodies, from which we then make judgments about the mental and moral features of something *else*—something that does not appear at all. In other words, actions and agents are not given to us in experience, and no character is "made visible"—rather, there is only the opaque and tendentious move from perception of bodies to conjectures about noumena. This is unappealing from a moral-epistemological point of view, and may even lead to a kind of moral skepticism. Interpreters who give primacy to practical concerns should thus prefer One-World Phenomenalism regarding persons at the very least.[30] But once we have the structure in place for persons, it seems impractical if not churlish to refuse to extend it to all the substances that appear to us (which may, after all, be minds or monads of some sort).

Other metaphysical one-world pictures do better in this regard: the things (people) that we observe speaking untruths and violating the bodily integrity of others are the very things that are evil and vicious. Still, all the one-worldisms I'm aware of fail to make room for moral straddlers, and so they aren't able to say that personal, agential, and moral features are genuinely *given* as objects of experience. Rather, we only perceive the "essentially manifest" or "response-dependent" sensible properties—i.e., bodily behavior—and must then try to conjecture about the response-independent properties of which they are the mental effect. But again,

[29] Karl Schafer (forthcoming) discusses the practical need to systematically connect phenomenal and noumenal features.

[30] Compare Adams (1997).

this is both phenomenologically dubious and moral-epistemologically unattractive: typically I simply observe that you appear to be evil; I don't try to infer from your bodily behavior to some *non-appearing* features. In fact, tellingly, Rosefeldt says that I *couldn't* do so:

> Whereas we have access to specific response-dependent properties of objects...we will never be able to specify a single response-independent property and say anything determinate about it. (present volume)

According to One-World Phenomenalism, by contrast, the moral features often shine through in the empirical world: they appear, even if they are not *merely* phenomenal.

There is a special complication here involving the feature of freedom, and so I will conclude this section by considering it. Any plausible reading of the critical philosophy says that incompatibilist, transcendental freedom is a feature that at least some substances—namely, our fundamental selves as agents—really have. In the second *Critique*, for example, Kant says that we can "know" (*wissen*) we are free indirectly via our awareness of the *Faktum* that we are under the demands of the moral law (*KpV*, 5:4). But elsewhere the awareness is more direct: "the human being...recognizes (*erkennt*) himself also through pure apperception, and indeed in actions and inner features" as a "merely intelligible object" and thus as undetermined (A546–47/B574–75). A few pages later, he says that the "causality of reason in the intelligible character **does not arise** or start working at a certain time in producing an effect." Nevertheless,

> this very same cause [i.e., freedom] *in another relation also belongs to the series of appearances.* The human being himself is an appearance. *His power of choice has an empirical character*, which is the (empirical) cause of all of his actions.
> (A551–52/B579–80, my emphasis)

The "causality of reason" is just freedom,[31] so it looks like Kant is saying here that freedom is a feature that the "human being" both has and *appears* to us to have in its empirical character—freedom can shine through in inner and outer experience of actions in the world. Presumably many of the other passages that say that various moral features appear could be taken to imply that freedom (a Kantian precondition for morality) also shines through.

Kant also claims, however, that in other contexts—when we are doing physics or history or empirical psychology, for example—people appear to us to be determined. The compatibilist just leaves it at that: we appear to be free and we appear to be determined because we *are* both free and determined. Kant rejects such compatibilism as incoherent—the mere "freedom of a turnspit"—and instead resolves the antinomy by saying that the deterministic features are *mere* appearances. One-World Phenomenalism reads this as the claim that the deterministic physical features are *merely* phenomenal

[31] Kant wrote here in the margins of his copy of the A edition: "If pure reason has causality, then the will is a pure will, and its causality is called freedom" (*HN*, 23:41).

in the MP way, while freedom is a straddling feature that persons both appear to us to have and really have.

There is a hitch here, however. We saw earlier that it is phenomenally true that *O* is F just in case *O* appears to us to be F. Given what I just said about the feature of freedom, this suggests that it is both phenomenally true that S is free and phenomenally true that S is not free. That's a bad result.

One response to the problem is to say that "appears to us to be" is strictly speaking about the theoretical, scientific image (see Stang's account of "universal experience" above), and so we do not, in fact, appear to ourselves to be free, even though we know we are free. This would be disappointing for friends of One-World Phenomenalism, since then freedom and other moral features would not be straddlers after all. A less concessive approach would relativize phenomenal truth to certain large-scale contexts (the scientific image vs. the manifest image, say). So it can be phenomenally true, relative to the scientific image, that *not-p* and yet still phenomenally true, relative to the manifest image, that *p*. The Kantian way to put this is to say that *not-p* is a *theoretical* phenomenal truth ascertained in empirical cognition, whereas *p* is a *practical* phenomenal truth ascertained in practical cognition. But both are still phenomenal truths—i.e., truths about how things appear to us.

The relativizing approach has some appeal. But another, more radical approach also suggests itself. Since One-World Phenomenalism is already committed to the idea that most phenomenal truths are noumenally false, perhaps a contradiction between two phenomenal truths is less devastating than we usually assume, as long as *at least one of them is noumenally false*. And that is indeed the case here: we appear to ourselves to be free, and we appear to ourselves to be determined—so both of those judgments are phenomenally true. But only the judgment that we are free is noumenally true as well.[32]

6. Questions and Answers

Many questions remain. Here I'll address only a few of the most obvious ones:

1. *What are the implications of this picture for Kant's theory of intuition? How can a thing with a hybrid collection of apparent features—some of which it really has, and some of which it merely appears to us to have—be the object of intuition?*

For Kant, intuiting (literally, "looking on," *anschauen*) is the cognitive process by which the "matter" of sensation becomes susceptible to the "form" of discursive understanding. Intuitions are supposed to be "singular" and bear an "immediate" relation to their objects (A19/B33). One-World Phenomenalism says that when we look-on substances, most of the features they appear to us to have are *not* features that they really have—among these are the spatiotemporal features that are characteristic of

[32] With thanks to Stang, Schafer, Benzenberg, Brennan, and Leech for discussion, I hereby assign myself further consideration of this tricky question (and its connection to the Third Antinomy) as yet more homework.

intuition. Full cognition involves adding conceptual structure to a cluster of such features and ascribing the structured cluster to a thing. So when I cognize the table, I am immediately and singularly related to a thing via a cluster of features that it appears to us to have; when I look on the chair, I am likewise related to a thing via a cluster of features that it appears to us to have. The clusters can be distinguished from one another; they are the content of different intuitions and have different causal profiles.

This does not entail, however, that the things that really have the features that partly constitute these two clusters are *themselves* distinct. For all we know, *one and the same thing* appears to us as both the table and the chair. Indeed, for all we theoretically know, one and the same thing appears to us as *all the matter in the universe*, although on practical grounds we will typically want to count the matter of two distinct human bodies as the appearances of two distinct moral substances. Put more simply: something can appear to us to be distinct from itself, even if it is not distinct from itself. The noumenal ignorance doctrine leaves it open that Leibniz or even Berkeley was right about the ontology of the intelligible world. That is another reason why speaking of the "numerical identity" of appearances and things in themselves is misleading, particularly outside of practical contexts.

2. *Does this view entail that we cognize things in themselves in an objectionable way?*

No. Kant himself is willing to say that we cognize what are in fact things with features in themselves, but by way of clusters of features that they appear to us to have:

> *[T]he things that we intuit are not in themselves what we intuit them to be*, nor are their relations so constituted in themselves as they appear to us...

What we intuit are *the things*, Kant says, but those same things are not in themselves what or how we intuit them to be. The passage continues:

> ...if we remove our own subject or even only the subjective constitution of the senses in general, then all the constitution, all relations of objects in space and time, *indeed space and time themselves would disappear* (*verschwinden würden*), *and as appearances they cannot exist in themselves, but only in us*. What may be the case with objects in themselves and abstracted from all this receptivity of our sensibility remains entirely unknown to us. We are acquainted with nothing except our way of perceiving them, which is peculiar to us, and which therefore does not necessarily pertain to every being, though to be sure it pertains to every human being. We are concerned solely with this. (A42/B59, my emphasis)

Kant says here that we do "perceive them"—i.e., the mind-independent things—although their non-appearing features—"abstracting from all this receptivity our sensibility"—are "entirely unknown to us." Moreover, if there were no cognizing subjects these things would not appear to have the core physical features that they do: rather, space and time would "disappear." This makes sense if the core physical features are merely phenomenal in the MP way, for if there were no finite minds, then such features would not be actually cognizable.

I think that this passage from A42/B59 is a strong one for One-World Phenomenalism. It's also *the* place in the *Critique* (the "General Remark on the Transcendental Aesthetic") where Kant is "explaining as clearly as possible" what transcendental idealism is meant to be.

3. *Can't we still regard the clusters of features—the tables and oceans and particles—as mere mental effects that things have on our minds, as on Two-World Phenomenalism?*

The answer here, again, has to do with the straddlers: some of the key features in the cluster are features of the mind-independent things, and so those clusters cannot be hived off as distinct (mental) objects.

4. *Okay, but why say that the clusters are partly constituted by features of the things, rather than that the clusters and the things have* ***some features-in-common****?*

A good question. Let's consider a flat-footed but useful analogy from within the empirical world. Suppose that our ubiquitous table now has a one Euro coin on it, and we are looking on (intuiting) and cognizing that coin through a slightly deformed pink magnifying glass. The object of this cognition is the coin, not an image of it. The coin has numerous features, some of which it also appears to us to have. The latter include *having the word "EURO" etched on it, displaying a drawing of the venerable continent, lying on its side, lacking motion*, and so on. In addition to these features, however, there are also features that it *merely* appears to us to have: *being oblong* (due to the deformity of the glass), and *being pink*. Obviously there is no requirement to say that the hybrid cluster of features that the object appears to us to have constitutes an object that is distinct from the coin itself. In other words, the "mismatch" in properties does not force the conclusion that there are two distinct objects: the coin (which is circular and silver), and the coin-appearance (which is oblong and pink). To use Kant's own example, just because Saturn appears to us to have handles, we needn't say that there are two things: Unhandled Saturn (the planet in itself) and Handled Saturn (a mere appearance) (B70n). Instead we can say that there is a thing and a cluster of features that it appears to us to have, only some of which it really has. The "mismatch" is accounted for by the appearance/reality distinction.[33]

5. *The example indicates that the fact that we count only one set of things in these empirical cases is a result of the fact that there are a lot of empirical straddlers. What if there were very few?*

[33] For discussion of this "mismatch" problem, I'm indebted to Timothy Jankowiak's recent work, including his presentations at the 2019 Kant Kongress in Oslo and the 2020 APA Eastern Division meeting. Jankowiak, however, takes the "mismatch" problem to be an insurmountable problem for one-world readings.

This too is a good question, and brings us to bedrock in this particular interpretative trench. Let's change the example so that the thing on the table before us is not itself a coin but just a device that projects an image of a Euro coin onto the surface of the pink glass. In that case, there would still be a couple of features shared between the mini-projector and the coin-image—*existing* and *being the ground of thus-and-such perceptions in us*. But the number of these shared features would be very limited, and the "mismatch" would be profound.

As Michelle Montague (2016) points out, when the mismatch is profound in this way, it is natural to say that there are two separate objects: the projector on the table *and* the image it projects on the glass surface.[34] This would mean that the "sharing" of a few features is not a matter of genuine straddling but rather of having some *features-in-common*. The projector is the *ground* of the coin-image, to be sure, and they share some features in common. But they are not the same thing. Likewise, in the transcendental context, given how different things really are from how they appear to us, we might be tempted to think of the cluster of features that appear to us as constituting a *distinct* phenomenal substance—one whose existence and substantiality, too, is merely phenomenal.

This is a good challenge: it shows that the decision whether to distinguish a thing from its appearance often comes down to how robust and numerous the shared features are, and to what sorts of interests we have in thinking of the latter as genuine straddlers rather than just features-in-common. The primacy of the practical again plays a role here, for there is pressure from the ethical point of view to include many of our personal, moral features among the straddlers that genuinely appear. That in turn gives us reason to prefer the One-World Phenomenalism over a two-world account on which those features are merely in-common. To be honest, it's not clear to me what it would mean to say that noumenal agents and their phenomenal avatars *merely* share some features in common. But it's certainly less appealing than to say that some of the features that things have are also features they appear to us to have.

7. Conclusion

My goal in this chapter was to offer grounds for thinking that, by 1783 anyway, Kant had adopted One-World Phenomenalism about the sensible and intelligible world. In other words, by 1783 Kant clearly held that things *exist* and have various features in a mind-independent way, but that (stunningly enough) all of their spatiotemporal-material-dynamical determinations are *merely phenomenal* features. "Mere phenomenality" was characterized in terms of (MP): such features are exemplified only if a finite mind like ours actually exists and is able to cognize them. So something in our manner of cognizing—and here I haven't specified what or how—at once *enables* the appearance of the core physical features of the universe and *ensures* that these features are intersubjective and nomologically stable. That's why Kant thinks we can deduce the categories and various synthetic principles in an a priori way.

[34] See especially chapters 6 and 7.

Finally, I pointed out that a key advantage of this picture is that it allows some mental and moral features to be straddlers—that is, features that some things (persons) really have and also appear to us to have. The straddlers "shine through" in our experience. This is crucially the case with transcendental freedom: although we sometimes appear to ourselves and others to be determined, we also appear to be free. But what we really are is free.[35]

References

Adams, R. M. (1997). Things in themselves. *Philosophy and Phenomenological Research*, *57*(4): 801–25.

Adickes, E. (1924). *Kant und das Ding an sich*. R. Heise.

Allais, L. (2007). Kant's idealism and the secondary quality analogy. *Journal of the History of Philosophy*, *45*(3): 459–84.

Allais, L. (2015). *Manifest reality: Kant's idealism and his realism*. Oxford University Press.

Allison, H. (1987). *Kant's transcendental idealism: An interpretation and defense*. Yale University Press (second revised edition 2002).

Ameriks, K. (2003). *Interpreting Kant's Critiques*. Clarendon Press. Anderson, R. L. (n.d.). Transcendental idealism as formal idealism: An anti-metaphysical reading. In Camilla Serck-Hanssen & Beatrix Himmelmann (Eds.), *The Court of Reason: Proceedings of the 13th International Kant Congress*. De Gruyter, pp. 49–68.

Brewer, K. (2018). Studies in Kant's doctrine of the intuitive intellect. PhD dissertation, Cornell University.

Brewer, K. (2021). Alternate possibilities, divine omniscience and *Critique of Judgement* §76. *Kantian Review, 26*(3): 393–412.

Chignell, A. (2014). Modal motivations for noumenal ignorance: Knowledge, cognition, and coherence. *Kant-Studien, 105*(4): 573–97.

Chignell, A. (2017). Kant on cognition, givenness, and ignorance. *Journal of the History of Philosophy, 55*(1): 131–42.

Collins, A. W. (1999). *Possible experience: Understanding Kant's* Critique of pure reason. University of California Press.

Guyer, P. (1987). *Kant and the claims of knowledge*. Cambridge University Press.

Jankowiak, T. (2017). Kantian phenomenalism without Berkeleyan idealism. *Kantian Review, 22*(2): 205–31.

Jauernig, A. (2021). *The World According to Kant*. Oxford University Press.

Langton, R. (1998). *Kantian humility: Our ignorance of things in themselves*. Oxford University Press.

[35] For helpful discussion of these ideas in earlier drafts, I am grateful to the editors of this volume, and to the participants in workshops at the University of Mainz and the Humboldt University-Berlin for feedback. For written comments and one-on-one conversations, I also thank Uygar Abaci, Karl Ameriks, R. Lanier Anderson, Christopher Benzenberg, Haley Brennan, Alexander Englert, Tal Glazer, Timothy Jankowiak, Anja Jauernig, Brendan Kolb, Jessica Leech, James Messina, Alejandro Naranjo Sandoval, Michael Oberst, Adwait Parker, Mark Pickering, Rory Phillips, Francey Russell, Bernhard Thöle, Clinton Tolley, and Marcus Willaschek.

Marshall, C. (2013). Kant's appearances and things in themselves as qua-objects. *The Philosophical Quarterly*, *63*(252): 520–45.

Messina, J. (2021). The content of Kant's pure category of substance and its use on phenomena and noumena. *Philosophers' Imprint*, *21*(29). URL: <http://hdl.handle.net/2027/spo.3521354.0021.029>

Montague, M. (2016). *The Given: Experience and its content*. Oxford University Press.

Oberst, M. (2015). Two worlds and two aspects: On Kant's distinction between things in themselves and appearances. *Kantian Review*, *20*(1): 53–75.

Oberst, M. (2018). Three objections against phenomenalist interpretations of Kant defeated. *Studi Kantiani*, *31*: 119–36.

Pickering, M. (n.d.). Kant's transcendental idealism as a form of ontological phenomenalism. Draft manuscript.

Prauss, G. (1971). *Erscheinung bei Kant: Ein Problem d. Kritik der reinen Vernunft*. Quellen und Studien zur Philosophie, vol. 1. De Gruyter.

Prauss, G. (1974). *Kant und das Problem der Dinge an sich*. Abhandlungen zur Philosophie, Psychologie und Pädagogik, vol. 90. Bouvier.

Rosefeldt, T. (2007). Dinge an sich und sekundäre Qualitäten. In *Kant in der Gegenwart*, J. Stolzenberg (Ed.). De Gruyter, pp. 167–211

Rosefeldt, T. (2013). Subject-dependence and Trendelenburg's gap. In S. Bacin et al. (Eds.), *Kant und die Philosophie in Weltbürgerlicher Absicht*. De Gruyter, pp. 755–64.

Schafer, K. (forthcoming). Practical cognition and knowledge of things-in-themselves. In E. Tiffany & D. Heide (Eds.), *Kantian freedom*. Oxford University Press.

Sethi, J. (2020). "For me, in my present state": Kant on judgments of perception and mere subjective validity. *Journal of Modern Philosophy*, *2*(1) Article 9: 1–20.

Stang, N. F. (2018a). Kant's transcendental idealism. In E. N. Zalta (Ed.), *The Stanford encyclopedia of philosophy* (Winter 2018 edition). https://plato.stanford.edu/archives/win2018/entries/kant-transcendental-idealism/

Stang, N. F. (2018b). Hermann Cohen and Kant's concept of experience. In C. Damböck (Ed.), *Philosophie und Wissenschaft bei Hermann Cohen/Philosophy and Science in Hermann Cohen* (pp. 13–40). Springer.

Tolley, C. (2017). Kant on the place of cognition in the progression of our representations. *Synthese*, *197*(3): 3215–44.

Van Cleve, J. (1999). *Problems from Kant*. Oxford University Press.

Watkins, E. & Willaschek, M. (2017). Kant's account of cognition. *Journal of the History of Philosophy*, *55*(1): 83–112.

Westphal, M. (1968). In defense of the thing in itself. *Kant-Studien*, *59*(1–4): 118–41.

14

Kant's Enigmatic Transition

Practical Cognition of the Supersensible

Uygar Abaci

In his Royal Academy prize-essay, sketched about a decade after the completion of his Critical trilogy, "What Real Progress Has Metaphysics Made in Germany Since the Time of Leibniz and Wolff?," Kant defines the ultimate purpose of metaphysics as a "progress by reason from the cognition (*Erkenntnis*) of the sensible to that of the supersensible" (*FM*, 20:260).[1] Kant thereby seems to take no issue with the traditional conception of metaphysics as aiming at rational or a priori cognition of supersensible things. His critique is rather that the tradition pursued this progress in the wrong, namely theoretical, domain of reason. In an obviously self-referential tone, Kant suggests that the route that pure reason has to take to achieve this goal should come in three stages: first, a doctrine of science which achieves "a sure advance" by the theoretico-dogmatic use of reason; second, a doctrine of doubt which is a skeptical "halting-point" in reason's progress; and third, a doctrine of wisdom which achieves the actual transition to the ultimate purpose of metaphysics by the practico-dogmatic use of reason (*FM*, 20:273). He insists that via this transition we can attain practical cognition (*Erkennen*) and knowledge (*Wissen*) of the cardinal supersensible objects of traditional metaphysics, freedom, God, immortality, "the supersensible *in* us, *above* us, and *after* us," none of which we can even hope to cognize or know by theoretical reason (*FM* 20:295–300).

The contrast between the theoretical restriction of our cognition to appearances and the practical extension of it with regard to supersensible things is in fact a recurring theme in the Critical corpus. In the *Critique of Pure Reason*, the idea of this transition is presented not only as a problem but also as a hope for better luck in the practical use of reason for what is denied in its theoretical use (Bxxi, A796/B824). The *Critique of Practical Reason* opens with a promise of the solution of the problem of transition, labeling it the "enigma" of the entire Critical philosophy: "how one can *deny* objective *reality* to the supersensible *use of the categories* in speculation and yet *grant* them this *reality* with respect to the objects of pure practical reason" (*KpV*, 5:5).

[1] Quotations from Kant's works are translated from the edition published by the Königlich-Preussischen Akademie der Wissenschaften zu Berlin and then by de Gruyter (Kant, 1900–), cited in the text with an abbreviated title followed by volume and page numbers, with the exception of the *Critique of Pure Reason*, which is cited by the standard (A/B) pagination. Where available and unless otherwise is stated, I will follow the translation of the Cambridge Edition of the Works of Immanuel Kant. In this first quote, I deviate from the Cambridge translation, because the latter is insensitive to *Erkenntnis/Wissen* distinction and captures the former as knowledge.

Uygar Abaci, *Kant's Enigmatic Transition: Practical Cognition of the Supersensible* In: *The Sensible and Intelligible Worlds: New Essays on Kant's Metaphysics and Epistemology*. Edited by: Karl Schafer and Nicholas F. Stang, Oxford University Press.
 DOI: 10.1093/oso/9780199688265.003.0015

Kant states that we know (*wissen*) the objective reality of our transcendental freedom and cognize (*erkennen*) the existence of God and the immortality of the soul, in the practical use of pure reason. The *Critique of the Power of Judgment* reiterates the idea of the practical cognition of the supersensible in its final sections (§§88–91), this time in connection with the postulation of a morally purposive nature, implying again that practical cognition constitutes the summit of Critical philosophy.

The question of whether, despite Kant's statements to the contrary, there is any sense in which we can have theoretical insight into the realm of supersensible objects has attracted significant scholarly attention recently.[2] Excellent work has also been produced on Kant's approach to the supersensible objects as articles of practical postulation and practical (rational) belief.[3] However, Kant's conception of practical cognition, both in general and with regard to the supersensible objects in particular, has not enjoyed the level of interest it deserves.[4] One reason for this may be that Kant's claim that we can have practical cognition of the supersensible is not taken seriously, and his use of the term "cognition" in this context is regarded as too loose to signify anything like the full-fledged cognition we know from his theoretical works. In the following, I will argue that there is a strong sense in which what Kant refers to as the practical cognition of the supersensible is a genuine instance of cognition. In the first section, I will provide a reconstruction of Kant's account of cognition in general. In the second and third sections, I will discuss how theoretical and practical cognition, respectively, both fit this general account and yet differ radically such that while the former is limited to the sensible the latter extends to the supersensible realm of objects.

1. Cognition in General

In the *Critique of Pure Reason*, Kant does not present a systematic account of cognition in general. In fact, he talks surprisingly little about what cognition in general really means independent of our specific mode of theoretical cognition. Still, however, he locates cognition in a taxonomy of representations in his famous *Stufenleiter* passage:

> The genus is representation in general (*repraesentatio*). Under it stands the representation with consciousness (*perceptio*). A perception that refers to the subject as a modification of its state is a sensation (*sensatio*); and objective perception is a cognition (*cognitio*). The latter is either an intuition or a concept (*intuitus vel conceptus*). (A320/B377)

[2] See, for instance, Langton (1998), Allison (2004), and Hogan (2009). On this question, see also Karl Schafer's "Kant's Conception of Cognition and Our Knowledge of Things in Themselves" in this volume. Tolley (2012) offers a notable analysis of Kant's conception of cognition in general.

[3] See Chignell (2007), Wood (1970, 1978), and Willaschek (2010).

[4] Engstrom (2002, 2009) and Kain (2010) have been valuable exceptions. Schafer (2018) will be another major contribution to this flourishing discussion of Kant's theory of practical cognition and its application to the supersensible.

So cognition is a species of representation that is objective and combined with consciousness. It is not easy to make out how exactly Kant construes these two conditions of cognition, "objectivity" and "consciousness," but we can find a useful clue by looking at the two complementary ways in which, he thinks, cognition can be analyzed into its elements. First, cognition can be considered with regard to the matter and form of the representation that constitutes it: "The object as we represent [it] is the *material* [element], while the manner of the representation is called *formal* [element]" (*V-Lo/Blomberg*, 24:40).[5] Second, cognition can be considered with regard to its relations: "All our cognition has a twofold relation, first a relation to the object, second a relation to the subject. In the former respect it is related to the representation, in the latter to consciousness [of the representation]" (*Log*, 9:33).[6] So in every cognition, there is a material content that is represented, and a certain mental state in the subject modified in accordance with this content. The "objectivity" condition is therefore about the material and objective component of cognition, and the "consciousness" condition is about its formal and subjective component.

1.1 The Objectivity Condition

The objectivity condition states that cognition must have an objective content or be the representation of an object. But there is a sense in which every representation is of some objective content. As Kant notes, "one can, to be sure, call everything, and even every representation, insofar as one is conscious of it, an object (*Objekt*)" (A189/B235). This sense of "object" amounts to whatever is contained in the representation regardless of the question of whether this content refers to anything apart from the representation itself.[7] Therefore, if the objectivity condition is to bring any constraint on (conscious) representations, what Kant has in mind must have something to do with the latter question. This is made clearer by the way Kant contrasts cognition with two other classes of representations, sensation and thinking.

Both sensation and cognition are species of perception or conscious representation. Kant sets up the contrast between the two on the basis of what the representation in question relates to: "In general, the relation of representation to the subject is called *sensation*, to the object, *cognition*" (*V-Lo/Wiener*, 24:904).[8] This is in line with the definition of sensation provided in the *Stufenleiter* passage as a conscious representation that refers to the modification of the mental state of the subject, and with that provided in the Transcendental Aesthetic, as the way in which our mind is affected (by things).[9] On all accounts, sensation is a representation considered only in its relation to the mind. That is, it refers only to a mental state, which may or may not have a relation to an object that is independent of the subject's mental state. Kant

[5] Cf. *Log*, 9:33. [6] Cf. *V-Lo/Wiener*, 24:805.

[7] This is akin to the Scholastic notion of "objective reality." In the Dialectic, Kant characterizes object in this broad sense of conceptual content as something given (to my reason) only as "an object in the idea" (*Gegenstand in der* Idee) as opposed to something given as "an object absolutely" (*Gegenstand schlechthin*) (A670/B698).

[8] Cf. *V-Lo/Dohna*, 24:702. [9] See A20/B34.

cites "good feeling, pain" and "pleasure" as examples of the kind of sensation, which is "only a mode of representation" and "lies merely in me – not in the object" (*V-Lo/Wiener*, 24:904).[10] In such merely subjective representations, since the content is entirely dependent on the representation itself, there is no independent criterion of truth applicable to the representation beyond its logical possibility or internal consistency. The role of the relation to an object is then to provide such an independent and material criterion of truth, as Kant defines the latter as the "agreement of cognition with its object."[11] Thus, in cognizing, we are not just consciously representing some content, but we are also conscious that this content refers to an object that is distinct from our representation of it.[12]

It must be noted, however, Kant's Copernicanism consists in reversing the traditional construal of the direction of fit between cognition and object and adopting that "objects must conform to our cognition" (Bxvi). Accordingly, Kant's Critical epistemology maintains that the sensible (i.e., space and time) and intellectual (i.e., categories) form of the object is provided by the subject. We should, therefore, at first approximation, understand the independence of the object from the representation as its existential independence.[13] So only an object that is at least capable of existing independently of the subject's particular mental state can be an object of cognition.

This point is more directly suggested by the modal distinction Kant observes between cognition and thinking. Thinking is representation through concepts. Even though all concepts have some material content, the objectivity of the content is not warranted by the mere fact that it is conceptually represented. Kant writes:

> To cognize an object, it is required that I be able to prove its possibility (whether by the testimony of experience from its actuality or *a priori* through reason). But I can think whatever I like, as long as I do not contradict myself, i.e., as long as my concept is a possible thought, even if I cannot give any assurance whether or not there is a corresponding object somewhere within the sum total of all possibilities. But in order to ascribe objective validity to such a concept (real possibility, for the first sort of possibility was merely logical) something more is required. (Bxxvi)

Two notions of possibility are at work here, logical and real. In Kant's modal terminology, logical possibility refers to the possibility of *thinking* (some content) without logical contradiction and thus is properly predicated of conceptual or propositional representations of things rather than things themselves.[14] Real possibility is a metaphysical notion of possibility and refers to the possibility of the *being* or *existence* of

[10] Cf. *V-Lo/Dohna*, 24:702, and *EEKU*, 20:206.

[11] See, for instance, A58/B83, A821/B849, *V-Lo/Wiener*, 24:823, *V-Lo/Dohna*, 24:718, *Log*, 9:50, *Refl* 2155, 16:254, *Refl* 2162, 16:256.

[12] For an elaborate articulation of this issue, see Smit (2000, pp. 239–42).

[13] Stephen Engstrom also makes this point about the formal dependence of objects on our cognition of them, and yet restricts existential independence to the object of theoretical cognition. See Engstrom (2002, p. 59). As will be seen later, I diverge from Engstrom on the interpretation of "existential independence" with regard to practical cognition.

[14] See Bxxvi, A244/B302, A596/B624. Cf. also *Refl* 4801, 17:732; *Refl* 5184, 18:111; *Refl* 5556, 18:232; *Refl* 5565, 18:235; *Refl* 5569, 18:235–6; *Refl* 5572, 18:237; *Refl* 5722, 18:335; *Refl* 5772, 18:349–50.

things.[15] Kant insists that we cannot infer real possibility from logical possibility, for while the latter reflects merely the formal structure of our thinking, the former reflects the real constitution of things. The logical possibility of a concept proves only that its content satisfies the formal condition of thinking, i.e., freedom from contradiction, but this does not mean that the content of that conceptual representation designates a really possible object or can be instantiated by an object outside the representation. Kant calls a conceptual content's designating a really possible object its "objective reality" (B268, B291), and argues that we need "something more" than its logical possibility to ascribe objective reality to a concept. If we do not have the grounds to ascribe objective reality to logically possible concepts, their contents designate mere "thought-entities" (*entia rationis, Gedankendinge*) (B347; A771/B799). I will revisit the question of what this ground or "something more" would be; it is safe for now to conclude that a conscious representation satisfies the objectivity condition of cognition only if it has a reference to at least a really possible object.

1.2 The Consciousness Condition

The consciousness condition has to do with the formal and subjective aspect of cognition. Kant presents three definitions of consciousness in relation to a representation. First, and most often, he defines consciousness as the "clarity" of the representation, as opposed to its "obscurity."[16] Second, he defines it as representing something "in comparison with others and to have insight into its identity and diversity from them" (*V-Lo/Wiener*, 24:845–46).[17] Third, and only rarely, he defines it as a reflective kind of representation, as a "representation of our representation" (*V-Lo/Dohna*, 24:701) or "a representation that another representation is in me" (*Log*, 9:33). I suggest that there is a sense in which all these definitions collectively explain the consciousness condition of cognition.

By a clear representation Kant means a representation that we can distinguish from other representations. However, clarity applies to the whole of a representation, and signifies that it picks out an object apart from other objects, but does not secure the consciousness of what the object is.[18] For the latter, we first need what Kant calls "distinctness," which is the clarity of the parts (i.e., marks) of a representation.[19] So a representation as whole can be clear but "indistinct" or "confused" if we cannot distinguish its constituent marks from one another. "E.g., if I see a cheese mite, my representation of it is in the beginning confused. But if I take a *microscopium* in hand and become aware in it of a jaw full of teeth, 2 rows of feet, 2 black eyes, then...my cognition becomes distinct" (*V-Lo/Blomberg*, 24:41). However, in addition to having such distinctness, my awareness of what the object under the microscope is further requires a comparative representation as to which of its properties are identical with

[15] See Chignell (2009), Stang (2011), and Abaci (2014, 2016) on the distinction between logical and real modalities in Kant.

[16] See B414–15; *V-Lo/Wiener*, 24:805; *V-Lo/Dohna*, 24:702, 725; *Log*, 9:33–34.

[17] Compare *Log*, 9:58, 64.

[18] See *V-Lo/Wiener*, 24:805.

[19] See *V-Lo/Blomberg*, 24:41–42; *V-Lo/Wiener*, 24:805; *V-Lo/Dohna*, 24:702, 725; *Log*, 9:33–34.

and which of them are diverse from those of other objects. When a biologist specializing on mites and I look at the same object under the microscope, we would surely have the same clear and distinct intuitive content (i.e., shapes and colors), but while I could only identify the object as some tiny bug, the biologist, acquainted with the differences and resemblances between this particular mite and others, would identify it as a cheese mite or *Tyrophagus putrescentiae*. For Kant, the reason for this difference in manner of representing the same content would be that the biologist has the concept of a *Tyrophagus putrescentiae* and I don't.[20]

Kant distinguishes intuitions and concepts on the basis of their logical extensions and the mode of their relations to objects. "[Intuition] is immediately related to the object and is singular; [concept] is mediate, by means of a mark, which can be common to several things" (A320/B377). So through intuition we can represent the object immediately in its singularity, both with respect to its whole and its properties. But the determination of the object in comparison with other objects and their properties requires concepts which, as general representations, can pick out sets of objects and properties. This explains why, as Béatrice Longuenesse observes, Kant somewhat puzzlingly holds that even though intuitions are singular and thus "fully determinate," determination is still a "conceptual operation."[21] This is also why Kant sees consciousness as necessarily involved in discursive activity and defines the former as a "representation of our representation" or "a representation that another representation is in me." If intuitions are the kinds of representations providing us with immediate relations to objects, concepts are representations making it possible for us to determine the objective contents of intuitions. The consciousness condition of cognition should therefore be understood as bringing a determinateness constraint to our objective representations. In order to cognize an object, we have to represent it determinately, both in its singularity, as a distinct individual object with distinct individual properties, and in its identity and diversity in comparison with other objects and their properties.

This might lead to the worry that the consciousness condition is too demanding, perhaps even impossible to satisfy. After all, as Kant himself states, our concepts are, in principle, always further determinable and thus never completely determinate.[22] Yet Kant also recognizes that as much as our concepts have varying degrees of determinacy, we represent objects with varying degrees of consciousness: "there are infinitely many degrees of consciousness down to its vanishing" (B415). He argues, for instance, that animals cannot cognize in the sense under consideration, because they are not capable of forming concepts and lack consciousness, even if they have intuition.[23] Again, in cognizing a house that we both see, I might display a higher consciousness than a "savage" who is not "acquainted with it as a dwelling established for men" (*Log*, 9:33). But in cognizing the cheese mite, I would be less conscious than a

[20] See *Log*, 9:33 for Kant's example. Kant also suggests that the fundamental and insurmountable difference between human and animal cognition is that animals lack concepts and therefore cannot be conscious of their representation.

[21] Longuenesse (2005, p. 215). This certainly seems to lead to a problem of circularity in Kant's account of empirical concept-formation, according to which we form empirical concepts through such discursive acts of comparison, reflection, and abstraction.

[22] See A571/B579.

[23] See *V-Lo/Dohna*, 24:702.

biologist, who in turn might be less conscious than a future researcher who will discover further determinations of the mite.

Therefore, the consciousness requirement of cognition, like the objectivity requirement, serves to provide cognition with a material criterion of truth. While the content of a representation must relate to an (at least really possible) object for there to be any independent and material criterion of truth for the representation in question, this representation must represent the object with sufficient determinacy for the object to play the role of such a criterion. For since the truth of a representation lies in its agreement with its object, such agreement can only be meaningfully tested if the object is determined with respect to its identity (what it is) and diversity (its difference from other objects). This is why Kant insists that while the logical criterion of truth abstracts from the differences between object and thus universally applies to all representations, the material criterion of truth has to be particular to the representation in question as it lies in the difference among objects.[24] So Kant proposes two conditions for cognition: (1) a cognition must have objective reality, that is, its content must refer to at least a really possible object; (2) a cognition must be accompanied by consciousness, that is, the content must be represented determinately. Cognition in general is then a determinate representation of a really possible objective content.[25]

1.3 Cognition vs. Knowledge

Before examining how Kant's conception of cognition in general is realized in theoretical and practical cognition, respectively, it would be helpful to underline a crucial distinction Kant makes between "cognition" (*Erkenntniss*) and "knowledge" (*Wissen*).

Kant maintains that representations can play their role in cognition of objects only as parts of judgments, which are "functions of unity among our representations" or of ordering different representations under a common one (A69/B94). More specifically, he argues, concepts (mediate representations of objects) can relate to intuitions (immediate representations of objects) and help determine their undetermined objective contents only in the context of possible judgments as their predicates. Despite this indispensable role of judging in cognition, propositionality does not figure as a part of Kant's account of cognition. On the other hand, Kant cashes out knowledge in terms of the manner in which one assents to the truth of a proposition. Kant lists three such modes of assent or of holding to be true (*Fürwahrhalten*): opinion (*Meinung*), belief (*Glaube*), and Knowledge (*Wissen*). What differentiates these modes is the kind and sufficiency of the grounds upon which the subject justifies her holding a proposition to be true. Having an opinion is the mode the subject adopts when she is conscious that her grounds for holding a proposition to be true are both objectively and subjectively insufficient. If the grounds are only subjectively sufficient

[24] See *Refl* 2132, 16:247; *Refl* 2155, 16:254; *Refl* 2173, 16:258, *Refl* 2177, 16:259.

[25] For an alternative and more holistic treatment of the objectivity and consciousness conditions, according to which both conditions are reflected in the real possibility constraint, see Schafer's chapter in this volume.

but objectively insufficient, then the mode of holding a proposition to be true is called believing, and if they are both subjectively and objectively sufficient, it is called knowing.[26] What constitutes objectivity and subjectivity of grounds for holding to be true, on the one hand, and their sufficiency, on the other hand, are questions of great weight that go beyond the scope of this chapter.[27] But I only wish to point out, quite broadly, that by "objective grounds," Kant means, primarily, grounds that are rooted in the constitution of the object in question, and by "subjective grounds," grounds that motivate the subject's assent, which may involve objective grounds or other non-epistemic grounds that are rooted in the constitution of the subject.[28]

Cognition and knowledge are then related but significantly different items for Kant. Cognition is a kind of representing objects. When the subject forms a proposition based on a certain instance of cognition, she may still adopt different modes of assent to that proposition depending on the totality of her grounds. So even if, as Kant suggests, "every ground of cognition, even supposing it is insufficient, is nevertheless a ground for holding-to-be-true" (*V-Lo/Blomberg*, 24:143), and every instance of cognition may lead to a mode of assent in the subject, the latter will not always be that of knowing.

2. Theoretical Cognition and Its Limits

A genuine instance of cognition must be a determinate representation of objective content. On Kant's account of human mode of theoretical cognition, producing such a representation is possible only through a combination of intuition and concepts. Intuition is necessary because it is the only way in which we can immediately relate to an objective content; and concepts are necessary because through them alone can we determine the objective content presented through intuition.[29]

There is then a receptive and a discursive component to our theoretical cognition. Kant specifies the human intuition as sensible: "It comes along with our nature that intuition can never be other than sensible, i.e., that it contains only the way in which we are affected by objects" (A51/B75). And since, as he also deduces, the pure forms of our sensible intuition are space and time, our intuitions can represent only spatio-temporal objects. On the other hand, our discursive faculty, the understanding, performs the act of thinking about objects by making judgments about them through concepts. Kant argues that our judgments about objects have certain forms, i.e., "logical functions," and our empirical concepts of objects or of their properties must conform to corresponding forms, i.e., "categories," such that we can use these concepts in judgments about objects. Kant also importantly argues that the categories necessarily apply to all data received through sensible intuition if these data are to

[26] See A822/B851.

[27] For two very insightful discussions of the subject, see Stevenson (2003) and Chignell (2007).

[28] Kant also counts "intersubjective validity" or "communicability" as a feature of objective grounds, but this does not seem to me to be a decisive distinguishing mark between objective and subjective grounds, as the latter can be communicable to other rational subjects. On this particular point, see Chignell (2007, p. 337).

[29] A50/B74.

become objects of cognition.[30] That is, all the undetermined but determinable objective contents of sensible intuitions are made into determinate representations by our empirical concepts, which themselves are formed in accordance with the categories. This account, of course, brings a significant constraint to the scope of our theoretical cognition. We can empirically cognize only those objects that conform to space and time as forms of our sensible intuition and to the categories as forms of our thinking. We can cognize a priori only these necessary formal conditions of empirical cognition, i.e., "experience," and the principles following from them.[31]

Given what has been said so far, Kant's claim that supersensible or noumenal things cannot be theoretically cognized by us means that it is impossible for us to produce determinate representations of these things. The root of the problem is that the supersensible nature of these things does not conform to the sensible form of our intuitions and thus we lack an immediate relation to them. There is, however, a point that needs careful attention here. For the purpose of theoretical cognition, the use of categories is restricted to the objects of sense, and they are "empty" (A51/B75) and lack "sense" or "significance" (A240) without intuitions, through which alone can they relate to objects. But categories, as a priori and thus independent of any sensible conditions, must still keep their logical functions of thinking an object in general even when they are abstracted from all intuitive content:

> If…I leave out all intuition, then there still remains the form of thinking, i.e., the way of determining an object for the manifold of a possible intuition. Hence to this extent categories extend further than sensible intuition, since they think objects in general without seeing to the particular manner (of sensibility) in which they might be given. But they do not thereby determine a greater sphere of objects, since one cannot assume that such objects can be given without presupposing that another kind of intuition than the sensible kind is possible, which, however, we are by no means justified in doing. (A254)

This suggests two things. First of all, we can have no theoretical cognition of the noumena not primarily because we do not have the conceptual means to *think* them, but because we do not have the appropriate kind of intuition (i.e., a non-sensible) to relate them to our categories.[32] Cognition requires that the objective reality of the conceptual representation or the real possibility of the object of that representation be provable. We can only prove the real possibility of an object if we can establish that it "agrees with the formal conditions of experience (in accordance with intuition and concepts)" (A218/B266), that is, receivable through forms of our intuition, i.e., space and time, and thinkable through the forms of our thought, i.e., the categories and the principles of the understanding. In fact, Kant further argues that we can only assert such an agreement if the concept of the object in question is "borrowed from experience." If we overlook this material constraint, we might end up with logically consistent concepts of mere "thought-entities" or "figments of the brain, for the [real]

[30] B138. [31] B166.

[32] Kant suggests that such a non-sensible intuition that can relate to things in themselves is an "intellectual intuition." See A256/B311–12, A279–80/B335–36, 8:216.

possibility of which there would be no indications at all" (A222).[33] Ultimately, therefore, we have "no insight into the [real] possibility of...*noumena*" (A255/B311), since we have no grounds to assert their real possibility.

Secondly, in the absence of intuitive content, the abstract, logical extension of the categories beyond the sensible brings no positive cognition-yielding use with it but only the mere thought of an indeterminate object in general.[34] That is, even if we can conceptually represent noumenal things with our unschematized categories, we are bound to fail to produce determinate conceptual representations of them. Both the idea of a noumenon in general, and the ideas of God, freedom, and immortality are concepts that we form by means of our unschematized categories such as unity, substance, causality, and necessity, but as such these concepts remain too indeterminate to represent their alleged objects in their identity and diversity.

Therefore, in our theoretical attempts to represent the supersensible, we are bound to fail to satisfy both the objectivity and the consciousness or determinateness conditions of cognition. If the theoretical cognition of the supersensible is impossible, so is theoretical knowledge based on it. This picture surely marks a "halting point" in reason's progress toward the ultimate purpose of metaphysics, the cognition of the supersensible, but not a complete dead end. First of all, theoretical reason at least opens up the logical for the ideas of supersensible things like freedom, God, and immortality as well as the idea of a supersensible world in general, while leaving the real possibility of their objects as a problem. Second, there remains the hope that what human reason fails to do in its theoretical use, it can accomplish in its practical use.

Toward the end of the *Critique of Pure Reason*, Kant underscores this hope:

> [T]here must somewhere be a source of positive cognitions that belong in the domain of pure reason...Pure reason has a presentiment of objects of great interest to it. It takes the path of mere speculation in order to come closer to these; but they flee before it. Presumably it may hope for better luck on the only path that still remains to it, namely that of its practical use. (A795–96/B823–24)[35]

3. Practical Cognition

Kant explores the hope of transitioning from theoretical agnosticism regarding the supersensible to its practical cognition most systematically in the *Critique of Practical Reason*, where he repeatedly states that via this transition what was "merely thought indeterminately and *problematically*" in the theoretical domain of reason gets "determined" and "cognized assertorically" in the practical domain or "from a practical perspective" (*KpV*, 5:105).[36] The question of how the latter happens finds its answer in Kant's conception of practical cognition. Unfortunately, Kant does not offer a detailed account of practical cognition but still provides bits of clues out of which we can construct a working framework for it.

[33] Cf. also A770–71/B798–99.
[34] See B312.
[35] Cf. Bxxi, Bxxvi.
[36] Cf. *KpV*, 5:5, 5:7, 5:134.

3.1 Practical Cognition in General

There are at least four tightly related respects in which practical cognition differs from theoretical cognition: (i) the use of reason; (ii) its purpose; (iii) the causality of the representation and its object; and (iv) its objects.

First, Kant makes it clear that practical cognition, just like theoretical cognition, is a "material" kind of rational cognition, i.e., cognition of objects through the use of reason (*GMS*, 4:387). Yet while in its theoretical use reason is merely a cognitive faculty, i.e., a faculty for theoretical cognition, in its practical use reason is both a cognitive faculty, i.e., a faculty for practical cognition, and a desiderative faculty, i.e., a faculty of desire:

> The theoretical use of reason was concerned with objects of the cognitive faculty *only* (*des Erkenntnißvermögens*)...[In its practical use] reason is concerned with the determining grounds of the will, which is a faculty either of producing objects corresponding to representations or of determining itself to effect such objects.
>
> (*KpV*, 5:15, my emphasis)[37]

Reason, in its practical use, not only cognizes an object but determines the will to produce that object. In fact, given that Kant famously asserts that "the will is nothing other than practical reason" (*GMS*, 4:412), these two acts, cognition of an object and determination of the will, can be understood as two aspects of a single act of self-determination of practical reason. The dual nature of practical cognition is also apparent in Kant's characterization of its purpose in contradistinction with the purpose of theoretical cognition. Cognition in general consists in representing objects determinately. The purpose of theoretical cognition is exactly and only to yield a determinate representation of the object. Practical cognition, however, aims both to yield a determinate representation of the object and to actualize the object that is represented:

> Cognition can relate to its object in either of two ways, either *merely* (*bloß*) determining the object and its concept (which must be given from elsewhere), or *else also* (*oder auch*) making the object actual. The former is theoretical, the latter practical cognition of reason. (Bix–x, my emphasis)[38]

This difference in purpose of cognition leads to a difference in the causal relationship between the representation and the object in each type of cognition. In theoretical cognition, the object, as given to us "from elsewhere," is existentially independent of the representation and the causal ground of the latter. On the other hand, since practical cognition is concerned with bringing its object into existence or it is "a cognition insofar as it can become the ground of the existence of objects" (5:46), the very act of representation in practical cognition is the causal ground of its object. This causal order appears natural when practical cognition is considered in relation to its

[37] Cf. *KpV*, 5:20. [38] Cf. *KpV*, 5:57, 5:89–90.

desiderative aspect, since Kant understands the latter to consist in causing objects to become actual by means of representing them. However, it is not quite so easy to see how this is compatible with Kant's account of cognition in general.[39] In particular, one wonders how practical cognition can satisfy the objectivity condition which requires the existential independence of the object from the representation and/or that the representation be objectively real in the sense that it designates an at least really possible object that can exist apart from the representation.

We should first recognize how the nature of the objects of practical cognition differs from that of the objects of theoretical cognition. In the broadest terms, Kant defines theoretical cognition as "that through which I cognize what exists," and practical cognition as "that through which I represent what ought to exist" (A633/B661). So as opposed to the mere representing of what exists in theoretical cognition, practical cognition involves the representation of what I ought to bring into existence through my action, that is, what I ought to do. Practicality or efficacy of practical cognition lies in this action-orientedness of its representation. This is also why the representation of the object is *prior* to, and the causal ground of its existence in practical cognition. Similarly, practical reason can be efficacious of its object, because its object is either the action (where the action itself is the end) or the consequence of the action (where the action is a means to a distinct end), toward which reason determines the will to move.

However, in practical cognition the action is not represented descriptively, not as what one is doing or will do, which would indeed be an object of theoretical cognition. Instead, the action is represented normatively. The cognition that I ought to perform a particular action is the cognition that it is good (either in itself or as a means to another end) to perform that action. In this sense, the ultimate aim of practical cognition is not the action per se, but the valuable "end," "the good," which is to be produced through this action.[40] Kant thus identifies "the good and the evil" as the only objects of practical reason. Kant also suggests that practical judgments (at least in the case of finite rational beings like us) take the form of imperatives prescribing one to perform (or omit) an action.[41] Imperatives are either hypothetical, if they prescribe actions as means to attain other, arbitrarily chosen or contingent ends (i.e., "You ought to do A in order to attain B"), or categorical, if they prescribe actions as necessary ends in themselves (i.e., "You ought to do A").[42] The former express practical rules (of skill or prudence) that we ought to follow, on the condition that we want to attain the end in question. The latter express moral obligations or duties that we ought to follow unconditionally as commands or prohibitions of the moral law.

[39] See *KpV*, 5:9; *MS*, 6:211.

[40] At places where Kant is more attentive to this crucial nuance, he formulates the *Gegenstand* of practical cognition not as the *Handlung* itself, but, more generally, as that which will be made actual through this *Handlung*. See, for instance, *Refl* 2796, 16:517; *Refl* 3316, 16:666. Again, in a 1772 letter to Marcus Herz (*Br*, 10:131), Kant identifies "moral ends" as the kind of objects, which we cause through our representations rather than vice versa as in the case of the objects of theoretical cognition. This formulation is also more suitable for Kant's idea that the ultimate and necessary object of a will determined by the moral law is the highest good, which is not an act per se but an ideal of a world that is to be brought about through free action.

[41] See *Refl* 2798, 16:518; *Refl* 3115, 16:665; *V-Lo/Wiener*, 24:900–901; *Log*, 9:86.

[42] See *MS*, 6:222.

Although practical cognition encompasses both types of imperatives, in the rest of this chapter, I will focus only on the categorical imperatives, since, as will be seen, the practical cognition of the supersensible is connected to the latter.

The object of practical cognition, conceived as an action to be performed, is surely not existentially independent from but causally grounded by the representation itself. As Stephen Engstrom suggests, quite rightly, while in theoretical cognition the object is existentially independent from but formally dependent on our representation of it, in practical cognition the object is both existentially and formally dependent on our representation of it.[43] But how can we then make sense of the objectivity condition in the case of practical cognition? What would objectivity or objective content really mean in practical context?

Since the action that is the object of practical cognition is represented as an imperative expressing an obligation deriving from the moral law, every instance of practical cognition is the cognition of the moral law, which in fact is the universal form of a law, interpreted in accordance with the specific circumstances. Let us remember first that the idea underlying Kant's suggestion of existential independence of the object from the representation as a condition of cognition was to provide an objective, i.e., non-arbitrary, criterion of truth. Now, although my performing the action commanded by the moral law may well be caused by my representation of it, whether there really is an imperative for me to perform that action is independent from whether or I successfully represent that imperative in this particular instance. For it is my general capacity to represent the imperatives of the moral law to myself, but not my consistent success in doing so, which is the condition of the application of the moral law to me. I might fail to derive the specific imperative from the moral law due to, for instance, my incorrect application of the categorical imperative procedure, but this does not mean that the obligation to perform that particular action does not apply to me. Therefore, the objectivity question in the practical context in general, that is, the question of whether there really is objective content that would serve as a non-arbitrary criterion of truth for our practical judgments, should be reframed in terms of the universal application of the moral law to all free rational agents. Then, the "success" or "truth" of our particular practical judgments would be a matter of correctly representing this objective content in specific cases. For only if there is such a moral law binding us to act in certain ways can we have a non-arbitrary standard of meaningfully talking about the "success" of our practical judgments. Setting the question of whether the moral law really applies to us aside for the next section, I want to make a couple of other points about this practical notion of objectivity.

First, Kant's modal approach to the objectivity condition proves useful in the practical context as well. As we saw earlier, Kant cashes out the objectivity condition of cognition in terms of the real possibility of the object of representation. Now, if my suggestion above to understand objectivity of our practical cognition in terms of the application of the moral law to us is correct, then asking if something is a really possible object of practical cognition is asking primarily whether it is representable as an action that our will can be determined to take. Kant states exactly this point:

[43] See Engstrom (2002, p. 59; 2009, pp. 13, 27).

> By a concept of an object of practical reason I understand the representation of an object as an effect possible through freedom. To be an object of practical cognition so understood signifies, therefore, only the relation of the will to the action by which it or its opposite would be made real, and to appraise whether or not something is an object of pure practical reason is only to distinguish the possibility or impossibility of willing the action by which, if we had the ability to do so (and experience must judge about this), a certain object would be made real. (*KpV*, 5:57)

As I emphasized earlier, the proper object of practical cognition is not merely an action per se, but an action represented as an imperative, as something "good" to do. The real possibility of an object of practical cognition is just the real possibility of our will being determined by the representation of this imperative.[44] But it seems as though the real possibility of our executing the commanded action should also be taken into account in practical cognition. There is an important nuance here. Kant argues that when the determining ground of the will is regarded as the representation of the moral law alone, as a specific categorical imperative, then "the moral possibility of the action," i.e., the real possibility of willing it, "must come first" and "precede" the question of "the physical possibility of it by the free use of our powers" (*KpV*, 5:57–58). It is worth noting that while the former falls clearly within the jurisdiction of practical cognition, as the cognition of what ought to happen given the moral law, the latter requires theoretical cognition, as the cognition of what can really happen given the causal laws of nature and my physical power. However, although Kant distinguishes between these two possibilities, and promotes the priority of the former to the latter in our moral/practical reflections, he also famously suggests that the former implies the latter as a basic rule of rational coherence (i.e., "ought implies can").[45] That is, my practical cognition of an action as my duty implies, or must at least be compatible with, my theoretical cognition that I can really execute that action. The tight connection between these two distinct possibilities will prove crucial for Kant's account of the practical cognition of the supersensible.

It should also be underlined that the actual application of the moral law to us, which is what constitutes its objectivity, does not in fact require more than this real possibility of it being the determining ground of the will. For the application of the moral law to us means that we do have actual moral duties, but not that we necessarily fulfill those duties. Duties obligate without metaphysically necessitating. To underline this difference, Kant sometimes calls the kind of necessity expressed by moral obligations "practical necessity."[46] The actual application of a duty or the practical necessity expressed by it implies exactly that it is really possible for it to determine my will. In other words, the objectivity of the moral law consists in its *actual* application to us as "practically *necessary*," which in turn consists in the "moral *possibility*" of the moral law determining our will.

[44] If the imperative in question is a hypothetical one, then the will is determined not only by the representation of the action as imperative but also by the representation of a further end, to which the action in question is a means.

[45] See A543/B576.

[46] See *GMS*, 4:414, 4:434, 4:442, 4:449.

There is one important implication of this account of the objectivity of the moral law for practical cognition in general. Now, the moral law (or any of its specific injunctions) is cognized by us through practical judgments that employ the concepts of the good and evil. Practical cognition is thus certainly discursive. Kant even presents a "table of the categories of freedom with respect to the concepts of the good and evil" as the practical analogue of the table of categories in his account of theoretical cognition. So, like the categories of theoretical cognition are pure concepts through which an object (of theoretical reason) in general is thought, the categories of freedom are pure concepts through which "good and evil," the objects of practical reason in general, are thought. However, in order for concepts to be used in representing objects determinately, a relation to those objects must be established. While the objects of theoretical cognition are given through sensible intuition, the objects of practical cognition are not "given" to, but "produced" by practical reason. Then practical reason must relate to its objects either through a non-sensible or intellectual intuitive power or in an altogether non-intuitive way. The first is not an option. Kant unambiguously insists both that sensible intuition is our only mode of intuition and that we cannot even comprehend the real possibility of intellectual intuition.[47] Therefore, there must be a non-intuitive way in which practical reason relates to objects.

3.2 Practical Cognition of the Supersensible

With this framework of practical cognition at hand, we can now look at Kant's claims that we can have practical cognition of supersensible things such as freedom, God, and immortality. The framework that I proposed above is based on the paradigm case of practical cognition, the primary objects of which are actions as imperatives. Kant also defines a second kind of objects of practical cognition, which are not imperatives themselves but are connected to imperatives in a certain manner. Kant characterizes this connection in terms of "grounding": "Practical cognitions are, namely, either 1. imperatives, and are to this extent opposed to theoretical cognitions; or they contain 2. the grounds for possible imperatives and are to this extent opposed to speculative cognitions" (*Log*, 9:86).[48] So objects of the second kind are not to be categorized under "what ought to exist" but under "what exists (or can exist)" with a special relation to the former. Abstracted from this practical "grounding" relation, they would be considered articles of speculation expressed in formally theoretical propositions. It can be readily seen that if supersensible things are to be objects of practical cognition, they will be objects of the second kind. And given Kant's talk of "grounding," it can also be conjectured that these objects are necessary conditions of the real possibility of either our moral imperatives or of the ends that these imperatives command us to realize. As I will demonstrate, Kant has both in mind: the first type of necessary grounding operates in the case of freedom, and the second, in the cases of God and immortality.

[47] See, for instance, B148–50, B307.

[48] Cf. *V-Lo/Dohna*, 24:751; *V-Lo/Wiener*, 24:901; *Refl* 2798, 16:518.

The relevant conception of freedom here is that of noumenal or transcendental freedom of the will, understood as "absolute causal spontaneity," a capacity of initiating a causal chain in nature without being conditioned by any previous determining cause of nature.[49] This means that if we actually have transcendental freedom, first, our will is determinable by something other than empirical causes; second, our existence has a noumenal aspect that expresses itself in nature through moral actions; and third, the category of causality as contained in the concept of transcendental freedom has a legitimate supersensible application. Then the objective reality of this concept of freedom, if proved, will constitute a bridge between the sensible and the supersensible. Hence, Kant stresses that the concept of freedom "constitutes the keystone of the whole structure of a system of pure reason, even of speculative reason" and provides the other ideas of speculative reason with objective reality (*KpV*, 5:4).

Kant argues that we can cognize, and in fact, even know the actuality of freedom through its connection with the moral law: "Freedom is real, for this idea reveals itself through the moral law. [F]reedom is...the only [speculative idea] the (real) possibility of which we know (*wissen*) a priori...because it is the condition of the moral law, which we do know (*wissen*)" (*KpV*, 5:4). Kant's argument seems to come in three steps: (i) Freedom is the condition of the moral law; (ii) We know that the moral law is actual; (iii) If the moral law is real, then our freedom, as its necessary condition, must also be actual. Obviously, (ii) carries the weight of the argument, but it is also important to understand the true nature of the connection between freedom and the moral law as indicated in (i) and (iii) for our purposes here.

(i) suggests that the actuality of the moral law depends on the actuality of our freedom. As I suggested earlier, the actuality of the moral law should be construed as its actual application to us. Therefore, the claim here is that our freedom is the necessary condition of the actual application of the moral law to us. The actual application of the moral law to us requires that the moral law can be the sole determining ground of our will and this is possible only if our will has the property of being determinable by grounds other than empirical causes. (iii) is based on the idea that the implication between freedom and the moral law is reciprocal. For as much as only a free will is determinable by the moral law, a free will that is independent of the empirical law of causality and must nevertheless be determinable can find a determining ground only in the moral law which is in fact the mere form of a law independent of any empirical matter.

This reciprocal implication at least demonstrates that freedom, as inseparably connected to the moral law, qualifies as a good candidate for the second kind of object of practical cognition. The question, of course, is whether we can cognize either side of the reciprocal implication as actual. The reciprocity suggests that the cognition of one is rather difficult or impossible to distinguish from the cognition of the other. My cognition of the moral law as actually binding me involves or is identical to my cognition of myself as free. But Kant still raises the question of "from what our cognition of the unconditionally practical starts, whether from freedom or from the practical law" (*KpV*, 5:29). We have established earlier that practical cognition is primarily

[49] See A446/B474, A803/B381.

always of the moral law or a specific imperative. Freedom is practically cognized only through its relation to the moral law. So Kant takes the moral law to be the ground of the cognition (*ratio cognoscendi*) of freedom, and claims that "it is…the moral law, of which we become immediately conscious (as soon as we draw up maxims of the will for ourselves), that first offers itself to us, and…leads directly to the concept of freedom" (*KpV*, 5:29).

Kant characterizes this "immediate consciousness" of the fact that we are obligated under the moral law as a "fact of reason" (*Faktum der Vernunft*).[50] Kant's overall idea of the fact of reason is notoriously mysterious. But he makes at least some of the relevant features of this "fact" sufficiently clear. First, it is a fundamental fact in the sense that "one cannot derive it from antecedent *data* of reason" (*KpV*, 5:31, my emphasis) or explicate it "from any *data* of the sensible world of reason and from the whole compass of our theoretical use of reason" (*KpV*, 5:43, my emphasis). Second, it is not a theoretical fact in the sense that it is "not based on any intuition, either pure or empirical" (*KpV*, 5:31). Third, even if it can neither be derived nor deduced from anything else, it is *given* to us at the strongest, i.e., apodictic, level of certainty.[51] So we surely have a *sui generis* kind of fact here. Yet Kant's talk of its immediacy and fundamentality, his reference to its givenness, and his contrasting it with intuition suggest that he has in mind something like a practical analogue of intuition, a mode of immediate relation to objective content. On the other hand, it should still be noted that the fact of reason as our immediate consciousness of the objective reality does not explain our cognition of specific imperatives. The moral law itself is a universal law-giving form and we determine the content of this law by means of a rational procedure, which consists in testing whether our subjective maxims or principles of action conform to it. Depending on the mode of its conformity with the moral law, a maxim could be merely permissible—neither commanded nor forbidden by the moral law—or an actual duty, which in turn could be perfect, if it admits no exception in any circumstances, or imperfect, if it allows exceptions depending on the empirical circumstances.

Thus, once we become conscious of the fact of reason that we are actually bound by the moral law, by making the moral law the universal form of our particular maxims, we gain a determinate cognition of what moral law is. The cognition of the moral law is indistinguishable from that of the actuality of our freedom. So not only do we cognize that we actually are free through our consciousness of the moral law, but we also gain a determinate cognition of what it is like to be free by harmonizing the maxims of our specific actions in accordance with the constraints of the moral law.[52] Thereby "Freedom…is not merely *thought* indeterminately and problematically (speculative reason could already find this feasible) but is even *determined with respect to the law* of its causality and *cognized* assertorically" (*KpV*, 5:105). Moreover, since "the concept of a being that has free will is the concept of a *causa noumenon*," the determinate cognition of freedom provides us with insight into our noumenal selves (*KpV*, 5:55).

[50] See *KpV*, 5:6, 31, 42–43, 47–48, 91–94, 104–108.

[51] See *KpV*, 5:47.

[52] This is why Kant sometimes argues that the reality of freedom can be proved in real actions. See *KpV*, 5:56; *KU*, 5:468, 5:474. On this point, see also Adams (1997, pp. 815–16).

This last point also suggests that with the objective reality of the concept of freedom, the category of causality contained in it gains a supersensible use for practical purposes. This is of paramount importance for the resolution of the "enigma" of critical philosophy. For Kant says that the objective reality of a category in the field of the supersensible, "once introduced, gives all other categories objective reality as well," but he warns, "only insofar as they stand in necessary connection with the determining ground of the pure will (the moral law)" (*KpV*, 5:56). We can draw several conclusions here. (i) Practical cognition of the second kind of objects uses the same stock of categories as theoretical cognition, for "every use of reason with respect to an object requires pure concepts of the understanding (*categories*)" (*KpV*, 5:136). (ii) The transcendent use of categories, which is "no use at all" (A248) in theoretical cognition, turns into an immanent use in practical cognition. (iii) In practical cognition, the condition of the application of the categories to noumena is that the latter stand in a necessary connection with the moral law. The concepts of noumenal objects are not only provided with objective reality but also determined with respect to this very connection.

We can now look at Kant's account of "the postulates of pure practical reason" through which he claims that we also have a practical cognition of God and immortality.[53] Kant defines a practical postulate as "a theoretical proposition, though one not demonstrable as such insofar as it is attached inseparably to an a priori unconditionally valid practical law" (*KpV*, 5:122). Along similar lines, he identifies the postulates as "theoretical in themselves," that is, they are propositions that purport to report what exists or can exist, but "practical *in potentia*," in that they ground possible imperatives for our actions.[54] Thus, only through this "grounding" relation do we gain a "practical point of view" on the postulates and consider them to be items of practical cognition. However, even though both freedom, on the one hand, and God and immortality, on the other hand, fall under the same, secondary category of objects of practical cognition, the nature of the "necessary connection" or the "grounding" relation with the moral law is significantly different in each case. While the actuality of freedom is the necessary condition of the actuality of the moral law, the existence of God and the immortality of the soul are the necessary conditions not of the actuality of the moral law itself, but of the realizability of its ultimate "end" or "object."

In all three *Critiques*, Kant consistently claims that the ultimate end of the moral law is the highest good, which is the ideal of a moral world where virtue (which implies moral desert of happiness) and happiness are proportionately maximized in rational beings.[55] This ideal is the necessary object of any will determined by the moral law such that every free rational being ought to strive toward the realization of it. Now, the idea of the highest good itself appears to be another problematic concept, since such a world is not logically impossible but its real possibility, i.e., whether it

[53] Although Kant does not provide a separate postulate for the actuality of freedom, and his proof of the latter does not rely on the reasoning of the postulates, he does list freedom as a postulate. See, *KpV*, 5:132. For the sake of clarity, God and immortality are sometimes called "religious" or "theological" postulates.

[54] *V-Lo/Wiener*, 24:901; *V-Lo/Dohna*, 24:751; *Log*, 9:86.

[55] See A814/B842; *KpV*, 5:110; *KU*, 5:451.

can be realized in the sensible world, is not theoretically provable either. For reasons I will explicate later on, Kant insists that for finite rational beings like us, it is necessary to presuppose the realizability of a command of the moral law if we recognize the authority of the moral law on us, i.e., its actuality for us. But the realization of the highest good is obviously not a task that we humans can accomplish given our physical and cognitive limitations. The postulates of immortality and God play their roles here. Kant argues that the immortality of the soul is the necessary condition of the real possibility of the first element of the highest good, i.e., the complete conformity with the moral law or holiness, and the existence of God is the necessary condition of the real possibility of the second element, i.e., happiness proportionate to that morality.[56] If we hold that the highest good is really possible or realizable, we also have to hold that the necessary conditions of its real possibility, God and immortality, are actual. Thus, God and immortality are objects of our practical cognition through this very necessary connection to the moral law. We can also further determine these objects by assigning specific properties to them in connection with their practical roles. For instance, God, Kant suggest, must have the properties of omniscience, all-beneficence, and omniscience, if he is to play the role of a just distributor of happiness in accordance with moral desert.[57]

3.3 Practical Knowledge and Practical Belief

Now, while all of the moral law (and its specific imperatives on us), freedom, God and immortality are objects of practical cognition, Kant introduces an epistemic distinction between these different instances of practical cognition, and claims that we can *know* the moral law and freedom through our practical cognitions of them, but our practical cognition of God and immortality can only constitute practical *belief*.

I have noted earlier that Kant makes the distinction between belief and knowledge in terms of the kind and sufficiency of the grounds upon which the subject holds a proposition to be true. Knowledge is based on both objectively and subjectively sufficient grounds, while belief is based only on subjectively sufficient grounds but lacks objectively sufficient grounds. I have also mentioned that Kant construes "objective grounds" broadly as the ones that are rooted in the constitution of the object in question, and "subjective grounds" as those that are rooted in the constitution of the subject. How do all these epistemic standards apply to practical cognition?

The truth or actuality of the moral law consists in its being binding for us. On Kant's account, the fact that the moral law is universally binding is given to all rational beings as a fundamental fact of reason. It is, of course, questionable whether this fact is given to all rational beings, and even if that is granted, why the immediate consciousness of this "fact" should count as objectively sufficient and not just subjectively sufficient evidence for holding its content to be true. But given his emphatic

[56] See, respectively, *KpV*, 5:122, 5:124. The idea of a purposive nature that is physically hospitable to the realization of the highest good is an unsaid postulate in the second *Critique*, but it will take its place as the fundamental presupposition of Kant's "moral teleology" in the third *Critique*. Consider, for instance: "For the objective theoretical reality of the concept of a final end of rational beings in the world it is thus requisite...also that the existence of creation, i.e., the world itself, has a final end" (*KU*, 5:453).

[57] See A814–15/B842–43; *KpV*, 5:138–40; *KU*, 5:444.

references to its immediacy, fundamentality, and apodictic certainty, Kant seems to think that there could be no grounds or evidence for any rational being to hold this fact to be true other than the sheer givenness of this fact itself. In other words, the consciousness of the fact of reason conveys a brute, self-sufficient or self-validating truth. If this is a defensible claim, then we can make better sense of the further claim that we have practical knowledge of freedom. For freedom consists in the real possibility of the determination of the will by the moral law alone, which in turn is the necessary condition of the moral law to bind us. The truth of the latter would therefore imply the truth of the former. So if we do have objectively sufficient grounds for holding that we are actually bound by the moral law to be true, the same grounds will be sufficient for holding that we are actually free to be true as well.

However, the postulates of God and immortality do not enjoy the same objectively sufficient grounds as our cognition of freedom. These two objects postulates need to be postulated because they are the necessary conditions of the real possibility of the highest good, the ultimate end of the moral law. Thus, the grounds for holding the postulates of God and immortality to be true should be traced back to the grounds for holding the real possibility of the highest good to be true. Kant's claim is that "there is *in us* not merely the warrant but also the necessity...to presuppose the possibility of the highest good" (*KpV*, 5:125). I have mentioned earlier that Kant takes it as a basic rational rule that my willing an action as a command of the moral law should implicitly contain my theoretical cognition that I can really execute that action. Yet here the command in question is not to bring about the highest good on my own, which is, obviously, not really possible, but to "strive to promote" or "promote the highest good" (*KpV*, 5:125), which is something really possible for me to do. So why do I have to presuppose the realizability of the final end of the moral law?

The answer turns around the kind of necessity that Kant ascribes to the presupposition in question. Kant characterizes this necessity as a "subjective necessity" or as "a need of pure reason."[58] We are familiar with this kind of modality from the Dialectic of the *Critique of Pure Reason*, where Kant uses it to describe the way pure (theoretical) reason is compelled to make certain presuppositions. These presuppositions do not carry "objective (real) necessity," since they are not necessary due to the constitution of objective reality, which we can legitimately ascribe only to the universal conditions of theoretical cognition themselves or to whatever is determined to exist by those conditions. But they are necessary to hold due to the "natural need" or "urge" of pure reason for completeness in its inferences from the conditioned to its conditions. Now, the idea of an ultimate end of the moral law is a product of the dialectic of pure practical reason, and this time, we are talking about a practical or moral "subjective necessity" or "need" of pure practical reason to presuppose the real possibility of this idea. It is not a practical objective necessity to presuppose the real possibility of the ultimate end of morality. For, first, it is not a duty to make such a

[58] See *KpV*, 5:4–5; 5:125, 5:142. This subjectivity is usually tied to the element of happiness involved in the idea of the highest good. It is argued that such a system of "self-rewarding morality" suggested by the idea of the highest good would appeal only to finite rational beings like us, who, thanks to the empirical aspect of their existence, have the natural goal of happiness (A810/B383). See, for instance, Kain (2010). While this is true, I think it misses the main point that such "subjective necessity" applies to any duty, and not just the highest good.

presupposition, because no epistemic commitment or belief can be a duty.[59] The duty is to "promote" the highest good, and the presupposition of the realizability of the highest good is rather a rational "need connected with this duty" (*KpV*, 5:125). I suggest that the need in question is again about a rational urge for completeness, this time, in our practical commitments. The moral law is itself purely formal and unconditional, and it binds us, as long as we are free, independent of any physical or metaphysical conditions regarding the ends that it commands us to promote. Our unconditional duty here is to will and strive toward the realization of the highest good as far as we can within our power. "The fulfilment of duty consists in the form of earnest will, not in the intermediate causes of success" (*KU*, 5:451). And yet we still need a rational hope for success when we engage with a given project. Even if the hope of success in realizing the highest good is not a necessary condition of our original submission to the moral law and of our moral conduct in the world, such hope is still necessary for rational human agents to keep striving toward that end.[60] Without that hope, practical reason would be committed to a project that is bound to remain incomplete. Thus, whereas pure theoretical reason is in need of assuming the availability of an unconditioned to complete its pursuit of conditions for any given conditioned, practical reason is in need of assuming the achievability of an end that it is committed to pursue for its sense of completeness or integrity. Since the existence of God and immortality are to be postulated because they are the necessary conditions of the realizability of the highest good, these postulations must also be based on the same subjective rational need. They are, therefore, articles of practical belief, based on a need for hope.

4. Conclusion

Practical cognition is therefore a genuine kind of cognition in the fundamental sense of being the conscious and determinate representation of at least really possible objective contents. The paradigm instance of practical cognition differs from theoretical cognition in a number of important ways: it is a product of the practical use of reason; its purpose is not only to cognize but also actualize its objects; it is the causal ground of the actualization of its object; and its primary objects are actions, understood as imperatives following from the moral law.

Yet the most crucial difference is that reason, in its practical use, has a non-intuitive way to relate to objects, making it possible for reason to cognize supersensible things. The practical cognition of supersensible things such as freedom, God, and immortality is derivative of the paradigm instance in that our cognition of the moral law and of the fact that we are actually bound by it provides us with a relation to these objects insofar as they stand in a necessary connection with the moral law, as in the case of freedom, or with its ultimate end, as in the case of God and immortality.

[59] See Willaschek (2010, pp. 180–81).

[60] Why the mere logical possibility of success is not sufficient for that rational hope would be an interesting question in its own right, but it remains rather peripheral to the main concern of this chapter. For a broad discussion of this question see Guyer (2000).

The major philosophical thesis to be drawn from Kant's conception of practical cognition is that our moral commitments inform our metaphysical commitments. This also marks the critical Kant's move toward a moral metaphysics, a "doctrine of wisdom," the claims of which are validated on moral-practical grounds.

References

Abaci, U. (2014). Kant's only possible argument and Chignell's real harmony. *Kantian Review, 19*(1): 1–25.

Abaci, U. (2016). The coextensiveness thesis and Kant's modal agnosticism in the "Postulates." *European Journal of Philosophy, 24*(1): 129–58.

Adams, R. M. (1997). Things in themselves. *Philosophy and Phenomenological Research, 57*(4): 801–25.

Allison, H. E. (2004). *Kant's transcendental idealism: An interpretation and defense*. Yale University Press.

Chignell, A. (2007). Belief in Kant. *Philosophical Review, 116*: 323–60.

Chignell, A. (2009). Kant, modality, and the most being. *Archiv für Geschichte der Philosophie, 91*(2): 157–92.

Engstrom, S. (2002). Kant's distinction between theoretical and practical knowledge. *The Harvard Review of Philosophy, 10*(1): 49–63.

Engstrom, S. (2009). *The form of practical knowledge: A study of the categorical imperative*. Harvard University Press.

Guyer, P. (2000). *Kant on freedom, law and happiness*. Cambridge University Press.

Hogan, D. (2009). How to know unknowable things in themselves. *Noûs, 43*(1): 49–63.

Kain, P. (2010). Practical cognition, intuition, and the fact of reason. In B. Lipscomb & J. Krueger (Eds.), *Kant's moral metaphysics: God, freedom and immortality* (pp. 211–30). De Gruyter.

Langton, R. (1998). *Kantian humility: Our ignorance of things-in-themselves*. Oxford University Press.

Longuenesse, B. (2005). *Kant on the human standpoint*. Cambridge University Press.

Schafer, K. (2018). Practical cognition and knowledge of things-in-themselves. In D. Heide and E. Tiffany (Eds.), *The idea of freedom: New essays on the interpretation and significance of Kant's theory of freedom*. Oxford University Press.

Smit, H. (2000). Kant on marks and the immediacy of intuition. *Philosophical Review, 109*(2): 235–66.

Stang, N. (2011). Did Kant conflate the necessary and the a priori? *Noûs, 45*(3): 443–71.

Stevenson, L. (2003). Opinion, belief or faith, and knowledge. *Kantian Review, 7*: 72–101.

Tolley, C. (2012). Kant on the content of cognition. *European Journal of Philosophy, 20*(4): 200–28.

Willaschek, M. (2010). The primacy of practical reason and the idea of a practical postulate. In A. Reath & J. Timmerman (Eds.), *Kant's* Critique of practical reason*: A critical guide* (pp. 168–96). Cambridge University Press.

Wood, A. W. (1970). *Kant's moral religion*. Cornell University Press.

Wood, A. W. (1978). *Kant's rational theology*. Cornell University Press.

15
Kant's Derivation of the Moral "Ought" from a Metaphysical "Is"

Colin Marshall

Perhaps the most widely accepted claim in contemporary metaethics is that there is some sort of important "gap" between facts or judgments about what merely *is* and facts or judgments about what morally *ought to be* (or facts or judgments about moral goodness, moral reasons, etc.). Most of Kant's readers have taken him to have recognized the gap and to have incorporated it into his metaethical views. My aim in this chapter is to argue that there is a defensible reading of Kant according to which Kant rejected the gap in the strongest possible terms: taking "ought" judgments to follow *analytically* from certain purely "is" judgments (and vice versa). On this reading, a true "ought" judgment simply describes a metaphysical fact, namely, the presence of certain competing motivational forces in a subject. Kant would therefore accept a form of analytic reductionism about at least some moral facts. Though this interpretation is unorthodox, I attempt to show here that it is neither exegetically absurd nor philosophically uncharitable.

My interpretative proposal has two parts. While each part is consistent with extant readings of Kant,[1] the only commentator I know of who explicitly suggested anything like their conjunction is G. E. Moore (discussed below). The two parts are as follows:

Analytic Equivalence: Kant holds that "S ought to F" is analytically equivalent to "If, as it can and would were there no other influences on the will, S's faculty of reason determined S's willing, S would F."

Non-Normative Freedom: Kant's notions of reason, the will, and (thereby) freedom are all non-normative.

The notion of normativity I have in mind is very broad, including all practical prescriptions, evaluations, recommendations, etc. (more on this below). Moreover, in saying that a notion is non-normative, I allow that it can be used in defining

[1] Henry Allison, who puts the reciprocity of freedom and morality at the center of his interpretation of Kant's metaethics, seems to accept Analytic Equivalence (Allison, 1990, p. 203), though that is not entirely clear. Dieter Schönecker has made some proposals that are similar in spirit to mine, but denies that it makes sense, strictly speaking, to talk of analyzing the imperatival "ought" (Schönecker, 2013, p. 232). Karl Schafer (forthcoming) defends a related view in forthcoming work. Some of Christine Korsgaard's descriptions also suggest that she accepts something along the lines of Non-Normative Freedom (2008, p. 3, but cf. 2009, p. xi). Clinton Tolley (2006) has argued that moral laws would not be normative for beings with holy wills, which suggests something like Non-Normative Freedom, though Tolley's notion of normativity is narrower than mine.

Colin Marshall, *Kant's Derivation of the Moral "Ought" from a Metaphysical "Is"* In: *The Sensible and Intelligible Worlds: New Essays on Kant's Metaphysics and Epistemology.* Edited by: Karl Schafer and Nicholas F. Stang, Oxford University Press.
 DOI: 10.1093/oso/9780199688265.003.0016

normative notions. An analogy: the notion of a person is a non-corporate concept, even though the definition of "corporation" involves the notion of a person.

My argument proceeds as follows. In section 1, I offer direct textual grounds for Analytic Equivalence, and, in section 2, I offer some indirect evidence for that claim. In section 3, I defend Non-Normative Freedom, discussing Kant's notions of reason, the will, and freedom in turn. In section 4, I describe the interpretative payoff of accepting the conjunction of interpretative claims. In section 5, I address three potential objections concerning Kant's other philosophical commitments. Finally, in section 6, I address the most important philosophical objection: that any interpretation according to which Kant denied any is-ought gap is unacceptably uncharitable. While not attempting to give a decisive answer to this objection, I argue that, on my interpretation, Kant would be able to go a long ways towards accommodating the main intuitions behind the two best-known statements of the gap: those of Hume and Moore.

Four caveats. (1) While I aim to show that Analytic Equivalence and Non-Normative Freedom are defensible, I do not try to rule out other readings of the relevant passages, or to show that my overall interpretation is better than extant interpretations. A proper comparison of interpretations would take more than a single chapter.

(2) My textual arguments draw from a variety of Kant's writings, relying most heavily on the *Critique of Pure Reason* (hereafter: *KrV*), the *Groundwork for the Metaphysics of Morals* (hereafter: *GMS*), the *Critique of Practical Reason* (hereafter: *KpV*), and the *Critique of the Power of Judgment* (hereafter: *KU*). It is unlikely that Kant's views remained perfectly fixed through the decade during which these works were produced. I assume, however, that Kant's core views remained relatively stable.

(3) My discussion bypasses most of the essential details of Kant's moral theory. I do not attempt to spell out how Kant's universalization test works, how to reconcile the different formulations of the moral law, what the fact of reason involves, or how we should understand Kant's theory of freedom. The claims I make here concern very general themes in Kant's metaethics, and their implications for such details must wait for another occasion.

(4) Finally, since the basic idea is familiar to contemporary readers and there are significant disagreements concerning its details, I do not attempt to explain the nature of the is-ought gap (assuming there even is a single such gap). I also sometimes characterize it as the descriptive-normative gap, though some metaethicists would distinguish those gaps. There are, however, different sorts of "ought." I am primarily concerned with practical "oughts," which concern how we ought to *act*, whether prudentially, instrumentally, or morally. In section 3, I am also concerned with epistemic or theoretical "oughts," which concern how we ought to reason and judge. There are, however, at least two other sorts of "ought" I do not consider: the semantic "ought" and the teleological "ought." Some philosophers believe that any representation with general content must involve some form of semantic normativity. I remain neutral on this issue in what follows, though there are grounds for thinking Kant would have been sympathetic.[2] In addition, Kant often uses strongly teleological

[2] For a relevant discussion, see Ginsborg (2008) (but cf. Tolley, 2006).

language in describing our faculties, especially reason (for instance, see A307/B364, A326–28/B383–84, *GMS* 4:395). How seriously we should take such language, and whether it is normative in some way, is a difficult question.[3] Many of Kant's readers have taken issues of semantic and teleological normativity to be distinct from Kant's main views on practical rationality, however, and I do as well. When I talk of a notion being non-normative below, I mean to deny only that the notion is practically and epistemically normative.

1. Textual Motivation for Analytic Equivalence

Analytic Equivalence states that Kant holds that "S ought to F" is analytically equivalent to "If, as it can and would were there no other influences on the will, S's faculty of reason determined S's willing, S would F." This takes Kant to be offering a definition of "ought." For Kant, "ought" (*Sollen*) is a central normative notion, perhaps the central practical normative notion. In his 1783 review of Johann Schulz's book on morality, Kant says that the "ought" or the imperative "distinguishes the practical law from the law of nature" (*RezSchulz*, 8:13, cf. *GMS*, 4:413). So if Analytic Equivalence is right, it promises to shed light on Kant's central moral notion. In this section, I argue that there is a plausible reading of Kant that supports Analytic Equivalence. In section 2, I then argue that attributing this view to Kant has significant interpretative payoffs.

1.1 The Core Textual Motivation for Analytic Equivalence

The passage that most directly supports Analytic Equivalence is Kant's introduction of "ought" in *KpV*:

> A practical rule is always a product of reason. [...] But for a being in whom reason quite alone is not the determining ground of the will, this rule is an imperative, that is, a rule indicated by an 'ought' (*Sollen*), which...signifies that (*bedeutet, dass*) if (*wenn*) reason completely determined (*gänzlich bestimmte*) the will the action would without fail take place in accordance with this rule. (*KpV*, 5:20)[4]

[3] See Johnson (2005). For discussion of the complications involved in Kant's use of teleology, see Ameriks (2012, chapter 11) and Mensch (2013). As Karl Schafer pointed out to me, an appeal to Kant's teleological views could potentially provide the basis for an objection to Non-Normative Freedom. A proper discussion of this issue would require more space than I have here, but it is worth noting that at *GMS*, 4:396 Kant seems to suggest that the purpose of reason is posterior to its moral properties. If that is correct, then reason's teleological properties do not play a role in defining its moral properties.

[4] On the basis of this passage, one might predict that the *theoretical* "ought" would signify that if reason completely determined our faculty of judgment, some judgment would without fail take place. However, for reasons discussed in section 3, that would seem to imply that we ought to accept transcendental illusions, and that is not Kant's view. Given Non-Normative Freedom, this is less of a puzzle for my reading than for others, but it still calls for explanation.

My focus is on the last part of this passage, where Kant tells us what "ought" *signifies*.[5] In glossing this claim as Analytic Equivalence, I am taking the "signifies" (*bedeutet*) to describe an analytic relation. This requires some defense. A less pressing issue is how to understand the "if" (*wenn*). I discuss each point in turn.[6]

1.2 *Bedeutet dass* as Analytic Equivalence

Unlike Frege, Kant never explicitly discusses what he means by *bedeuten/Bedeutung* (contrasted with *Sinn* or otherwise). Moreover, some of his uses of these terms clearly do not concern the sort of meaning revealed by analysis. For instance, in Section 13 of *KrV*, he says that were appearances sufficiently confused, the concepts of cause and effect would be *ohne Bedeutung* (A90/B123). Presumably, confusion among appearances could not deprive concepts of their meaning in the sense of meaning that is relevant to analyticity. Similarly, at A71/B96, Kant appears to use the term to compare the extensions of predicates. Arguably, a concept's extension should be distinguished from the meaning that analysis concerns.[7]

Nonetheless, many of Kant's uses of these terms plausibly do concern the sort of meaning revealed by analysis. Perhaps his most common use of *bedeuten/Bedeutung* is in discussions of ambiguities (*Zweideutigkeiten*). In *KpV*, he uses it to disambiguate the expression *sub ratione boni* (*KpV*, 5:59n.) and the term "highest" (*KpV*, 5:110). The latter passage runs as follows: "The concept of the highest already contains an ambiguity that, if not attended to, can occasion needless disputes. The highest can mean (*bedeuten*) either the supreme [...] or the complete." Kant is here pointing to a difference in meaning that can be avoided with attention. It is hard to see how this could concern anything other than analyticity.[8]

In addition, the *KpV*, 5:20 passage uses a propositional construction as opposed to an object construction: "signifies that" (*bedeutet dass*). This construction is most easily read in analytic terms (see A493/B521). So while Kant's use of *bedeutet* is not consistent, it is most naturally read in *KpV* 5:20 as concerning analytic relations.

[5] The "ought" here is supposedly involved in both categorical and hypothetical imperatives. My focus will be on the former below, but my proposal naturally extends to the latter.

[6] Another difficult question here is what determining (*bestimmen*) amounts to. While Kant sometimes uses the term for causation (e.g., *MAN*, 4:508, 4:521), he more often uses it to describe something being made more metaphysically determinate/specific (e.g., A186/B229, A571–72/B599–600), or being represented more specifically (e.g., Bx). None of these involve (non-semantic) normativity in any obvious way. The best gloss for the *KpV*, 5:20 passage is probably in terms of metaphysical specificity. For the will to be made more specific, as the capacity to act in accordance with rational representations, would just be for it to act on a specific representation instead of others (e.g., that of universal law instead of mere inclination).

[7] Concerning A71/B96, Guyer and Wood note: "Kant here uses *Bedeutung* [...] to mean the reference or denotation of the concept." They go on to say, however, that "more typically, he uses it to mean something closer to what Frege called *Sinn* or sense, that is, the connotation" (Guyer and Wood, 1998, p. 207).

[8] These terms also appear in the *KrV*'s disambiguations of "object" (Bxxvi), "analogy" (A179/B222), "absolute" (A324–25/B380–81), "noumenon" (B307), "idea" (A312/B369), "thought" (B411–12), and "draw a line" (A511/B539).

1.3 *Wenn* as a Power-Indicating Counterfactual

If the claim of the previous subsection is right, then *KpV*, 5:20 can be read as saying that "S ought to F" just means that if S's reason completely determined S's will, S would F. For this to support Analytic Equivalence, however, the "if" needs to mean "if, as it can and would were there no other influences on the will." This is not the only way to understand the "if" (perhaps one could read it as a simple material conditional), but I think it makes the most sense of how Kant ties "ought" claims to the freedom of beings whose will can also be determined by sensible inclinations (that is, finite agents). In the *KpV* 5:20 passage, and in others I discuss below, that tie is the semantic point that Kant seems most concerned with. Spelled out this way, the claim can be read as a description of a motivational power (reason) that is in conflict with others. This tension would be one common to all humans. No such conflict is found in a perfect will like God's, however, which is why imperatives do not apply to God.

1.4 Related Claim in *GMS*

Though the *KpV* 5:20 passage is the best motivation for attributing Analytic Equivalence to Kant, there are also grounds in *GMS*, where Kant claims:

> this 'ought' is strictly speaking a 'will' that holds for every rational being under the condition that reason in him is practical without hindrance; but for beings like us [...] that necessity of action is called only an 'ought,' and the subjective necessity is distinguished from the objective. (*GMS* 4:449)[9]

It is not obvious how to understand the "is strictly speaking" (*ist eigentlich*) relation that Kant asserts holds between this "ought" and "will." If Analytic Equivalence is correct, though, then we can give a clear sense to this passage. Kant is then saying that there is a relation in the meaning of "ought" and "will," such that "S ought to F" means "If S's reason were practical without hindrance (i.e., completely determined the will), S would F."

2. Indirect Interpretative Motivation for Analytic Equivalence

The previous section argued that Kant's most prominent claim about "ought" in *KpV* directly supports Analytic Equivalence. At least as important as that direct support, though, is how this proposal can make sense of an otherwise puzzling feature of Kant's metaethics: his claim that morality and freedom mutually imply one another.

To get this result, one further assumption is needed: that what is described in the right half of Analytic Equivalence ("if, as it can and would were there no other influences on the will, S's faculty of reason determined S's willing, S would F") captures

[9] See also *MS*, 6:222 on obligation and imperatives.

what Kant means by freedom. This assumption is not trivial, but it is defensible (see sections 3.2 and 3.3 below for some of the relevant passages).

In *KrV*, *GMS*, and in *KpV*, Kant makes a number of statements about freedom and morality implying one another, sometimes mentioning analyticity explicitly. Here are some of his stronger statements:

> practical freedom [...] presupposes that although something has not happened, it nevertheless *ought* to have happened, and its cause in the appearance was thus not so determining that there is not a causality in our power of choice such that [...] it [...] might begin a series of occurrences entirely from itself. (A534/B562)[10]
>
> that this reason has causality, or that we can at least represent something of the sort in it, is clear from the *imperatives* that we propose as rules to our power of execution in everything practical. The *ought* expresses a species of necessity and a connection with grounds which does not occur anywhere else in the whole of nature. (A547/B575)
>
> If, therefore, freedom of the will is presupposed, morality together with its principle follows from it by mere analysis (*GMS*, 4:447)
>
> Morality [...] must be derived solely from the property of freedom (*GMS*, 4:447)
>
> freedom is real, for this idea reveals itself through the moral law (*KpV*, 5:4)
>
> freedom and unconditional practical law reciprocally imply each other [...] the moral law [...] leads directly to the concept of freedom. (*KpV*, 5:29–30)
>
> [consciousness of the moral law] would be analytic if the freedom of the will were presupposed (*KpV*, 5:31)
>
> the moral law...is still something in itself positive – namely, the form of an intellectual causality, that is, of freedom (*KpV*, 5:73)[11]

To be sure, Kant sometimes talks of the analytic in describing things other than analytic semantic relations (e.g., the analytic method of the *Prolegomena* (4:263), and the analytic unity of apperception (B133n.)). In addition, nowhere does he claim that implication relations are always based on analytic relations. Nonetheless, analytic relations are surely *included* in inferential relations (see A303–304/B360), and it is not obvious how to understand his mention of analyticity in the above passages except in terms of analytic semantic relations. The most straightforward way to understand how freedom and morality could reciprocally imply one another is if they are analytically equivalent.[12] While many of Kant's readers have pointed out

[10] I am setting aside the question of whether practical freedom differs from transcendental freedom (see, e.g., A533–34/B561–62).

[11] One of Kant's pre-Critical reflections is also striking: "On freedom: We can consider one of our actions either as something that happens, i.e., as an appearance, or as something that ought to happen, *i.e.*, as an intuition of self-activity for possible effects" (*Refl* 4334, 17:508–509, my emphasis).

[12] Strictly speaking, the moral "ought" does not express only the moral law, since imperatives only hold for imperfectly rational beings, while the moral law holds for imperfectly and perfectly rational beings. But all that is needed is to drop the counterfactual part of the description of freedom so as to remain neutral on whether reason alone determines the will. Analytic Equivalence captures this well enough.

that Kant thinks the claims of morality point to or even "reveal" our freedom to us, few have attempted to explain the exact nature of that epistemic relation.[13]

One might worry that Analytic Equivalence makes freedom and morality *too* close. Kant insists that our consciousness of morality is prior to our consciousness of freedom (e.g., *KpV*, 5:5n.). On my reading, however, these "consciousnesses" are analytically equivalent representations, and it may be hard to see how one could be prior to the other. However, thoughts can differ in ways besides meaning. The concept "ought," on my reading, involves a *unified* grasp of concepts of the will, reason, and determination. The latter concepts are "covertly" (*versteckter Weise* (A6/B10)) contained in the former, and "already thought in it (though confusedly)" (A7/B11). So there is an action required to derive one from the other, namely, a judgment of clarification, and this makes one thought prior to the other.[14]

A related point is that Analytic Equivalence makes sense of how imperatives can be analytic or synthetic, something Kant explicitly claims (e.g., *GMS*, 4:417, 4:420). Dieter Schönecker objects that such claims, strictly speaking, make no sense, because imperatives do not express propositions (Schönecker, 2013, p. 232). Analytic Equivalence implies otherwise, for it entails that Kant took imperatives to indeed express propositions, and so be evaluable for analyticity the same way as other judgments.

3. In Support of Non-Normative Freedom

Non-Normative Freedom states that Kant's notions of reason, the will, and (thereby) freedom are all non-normative. The notion of reason here is of the *faculty* of reason. To modern ears, talk about the faculty of reason might sound like talk about our capacity to respond to reasons.[15] Many philosophers think that reasons cannot be characterized non-normatively, some even holding that it is *the* central normative notion. Yet Non-Normative Freedom says only that the most fundamental characterization of the faculty of reason Kant describes (*Vernunft*) is in non-normative terms. Whether Kant accepts that we also have the capacity to respond to normative reasons (in the contemporary sense) is a separate question.

[13] Irwin holds that, for Kant, the claims of morality reveal our practical freedom to us (Irwin, 2009, pp. 80–82), though Irwin seems to think the relevant notion of freedom is essentially normative. Others (e.g., Tolley, 2006; Allison, 2011; Schönecker, 2013) have claimed that there is an analytic relation between the idea of a *holy* will and the moral law in a non-imperatival form, but have stopped short of claiming that this holds for beings like us and imperatives. Schafer (forthcoming) comes closest to the present proposal.

[14] A further issue here is whether my reading makes freedom too close to be the *ratio essendi* of the moral law (*KpV*, 5:5n.). This is a subtle point, but even in Plato's *Euthyphro*, "in virtue of" relations are claimed to hold between what are, in effect, analytically equivalent facts (e.g., someone is carried in virtue of someone carrying). In addition, contemporary metaphysicians who think disjunctions are grounded in their disjuncts would allow that A-or-A holds in virtue of A holding (see Fine, 2012). A-or-A might or might not be analytically equivalent to A, but that equivalence is similarly trivial and a priori.

[15] For instance: "Reason is the universal capacity to recognize reasons, one which in principle enables us to recognize any reason which applies to us, and to respond to it appropriately" (Raz, 2010, p. 6). Many of Kant's readers assimilate Kant's talk of the faculty of reason to contemporary reasons-talk without argument (e.g., Irwin, 2009, pp. 1–2; Wood, 2009, pp. 16–20). For a more historically sensitive interpretation of the role of normativity in Kant's understanding of mental faculties, see Anderson (2001).

If my overall proposal is correct, then he presumably would see such a normative capacity as built up out of non-normative elements, such the faculty of reason in his sense. But that is not my concern in this section.

In making my textual case for attributing Non-Normative Freedom to Kant, I begin with the most difficult topic: Kant's notion of reason. Since Kant's notions of the will and of freedom are closely tied to that of reason, showing that we can understand his notion of reason as non-normative provides a basis for showing that the same holds for the other notions.

3.1 Reason as Non-Normative

Consider the notion of a capacity for moral knowledge or practical wisdom. This is a normative notion, in my sense, because it is part of the notion that such a capacity is *good to have* or *correct* in some respect. By contrast, I do not count the capacity for thought as normative, even though that is a capacity that can have normative representations. My aim here is to show that there are textual grounds for thinking that Kant's notion of the capacity of reason (*Vernunft*) is non-normative. As before, I allow that other interpretations can accommodate the passages I appeal to. I only claim that the reading I have described is defensible. I also allow that, for Kant, reason has a necessary relation to the normative. I only deny that this relation is built into the notion of reason itself.

A key premise in my discussion here is that theoretical and practical reason are, at root, the same faculty: "there can, in the end, be only one and the same reason, which must be distinguished merely in its application" (*GMS*, 4:391). This means that Kant's discussion of reason in the *KrV* can shed light on his practical works, such as the key passage from *KpV*, 5:20 discussed above. With that in place, I turn to two lines of argument for taking Kant's notion of reason to be non-normative.

The first line of argument rests on the fact that Kant's characterizations of the faculty of reason in the *KrV* are non-normative. These characterizations are not entirely consistent, not least because Kant had wider and narrower senses of "reason" (see A130–31/B169–70, A835/B863). Nonetheless, his clearest definitions of reason in the general sense are focused on the quantitative content of its representations, in particular, their generality. In the Dialectic of the *KrV*, Kant says that the "universal concept of the faculty of reason" is "the faculty of the unity of the rules of understanding under principles" (A302/B359, cf. A299/B356). Later, Kant says that "[r]eason, considered as the faculty of a certain logical form of cognition, is the faculty of inferring, i.e., of judging mediately" (A330/B386), which Kant thinks is part of the "demand of reason" (A332/B389) for the unconditioned totality of conditions (e.g., the idea of the world-whole).[16] What I want to draw from this now is that Kant characterizes reason here essentially as the capacity to form certain representations, representations that are distinguished primarily by their quantitative content (the generality of

[16] Such passages suggest that Kant sees reason as having an aim of some sort, and so perhaps as involving a certain sort of teleological normativity. Yet Kant does not give such teleology any clear place in his core characterizations of reason.

principles, or the unconditioned totality of their series). These characterizations do not say that reason is a *good* capacity to have, or that these representations are *correct*.[17] Assuming that these characterizations are supposed to provide an analysis of the notion of reason, the *KrV* therefore provides grounds for taking Kant's notion of reason to be non-normative.

Kant gives a similar characterization of reason in the first introduction to *KU*, where he describes reason as "the faculty for the determination of the particular through the general (*Allgemeine*) (for the derivation from principles [*Principien*])" (*EEKU*, 20:201; cf. A300/B357),[18] and we can see a similar idea in *KpV*'s claim that "[o]nly rationalism of judgment is suitable for use of moral concepts, since it takes from sensible nature nothing more than what pure reason can also think for itself, that is, conformity with law" (*KpV*, 5:71). The conformity of sensible nature with law is presumably a matter of its conformity with physical laws, and so something non-normative.

It is hard to precisely characterize the quantitative content that is distinctive of reason's representations. It is not hard to see, however, how the above passages can be read as defining a capacity in terms of certain representations without implying anything about the goodness or correctness of that capacity. This capacity could still be a component in good things (like the good will) and can lead to bad things (like the illusions of dogmatic metaphysics, discussed below), but the notion of the capacity itself is not normative.

While Kant's characterizations of reason focus on its distinctive representations, he also claims that it (along with understanding) has a distinctive metaphysical status: being a spontaneous, noumenal faculty. In *KrV* he states that "in regard to certain faculties, [the human being] is a merely intelligible object, because the actions of this object cannot at all be ascribed to the receptivity of sensibility. We call these faculties understanding and reason" (A546–47/B574–75), where Kant has just defined "intelligible" as "that in an object of sense that is not itself appearance" (A538/B566) and made it clear that this is noumenal (A541/B569). Similar claims appear in *GMS* and *KpV* (e.g., *GMS*, 4:452, *KpV*, 5:97–98). Some of Kant's readers have claimed that spontaneity and noumenality are normative notions,[19] but this a fairly radical interpretation. As Kant presents them, spontaneity and noumenality seem to be metaphysical notions that enter into normative notions, but are themselves non-normative. Hence, their connection to the notion of reason does not support seeing the latter as normative.

[17] One could insist that the action of *inferring* (*schliessen*), for Kant, is always correct, so that his characterization of reason as the faculty of inferring would be at least epistemically normative. While some passages suggest as much, Kant also speaks of sophistical inferences (*Schlüsse*), which he says "have sprung from the nature of reason" (A339/B397).

[18] See also *KU*, 5:250 and 5:255 on reason's being distinguished from the imagination in virtue of its ability to represent the absolutely infinite.

[19] E.g., Allison (2012, p. 113), Skorupski (2010, ch. 19). Korsgaard (1996, p. 2019) says that "[t]he trouble with the way Kant phrases the argument in *Groundwork III* is that it can make it sound as if...[he is] deriving a normative sensible 'ought' from a descriptive intelligible 'is'. But he is not, for the laws of the intelligible world are normative through and through." Of course, denying that spontaneity is a normative notion is consistent with saying that there is a norm directing us to be spontaneous; see Merritt (2009).

The second line of argument for this conclusion about Kant's notion of reason comes from the evaluative claims Kant makes about reason in the *KrV*. Strikingly, Kant says that, in the Transcendental Dialectic, his aim is to "determine and evaluate the influence and the *worth* of pure reason" (A319/B376, my emphasis). This would be an odd claim to make if his notion of reason were normative, for then facts about its worth would be built into the very notion of reason. By analogy, we would be more surprised to hear someone ask about the worth of practical wisdom (whose notion is normative) than about the worth of moral belief (whose notion is not).

Moreover, Kant's conclusions about the worth of reason in the *KrV* are, on the whole, negative. There, Kant describes at length how the illusions of dogmatic metaphysics ("sophistries...of pure reason itself" (A339/B397)) arise from the faculty of reason, and claims that certain representations arising from reason end up being "self-contradictory" (A340/B398). Now, if Kant's notion of reason were theoretically or practically normative, we would expect it to be normative in some *positive* way. The notions of practical wisdom and moral knowledge are positive in this sense: they are capacities that are, *by definition*, good, or get things right. By contrast, the notion of moral ignorance would be normative in a negative way: a capacity that, by definition, missed out on moral facts. Yet Kant clearly regards the illusions of dogmatic metaphysics in a primarily negative light. Since he directly attributes these illusions to reason, and does not seem to have a negatively normative notion of reason, there are grounds for taking him to understand reason in a non-normative way.[20]

It may be useful to look more closely at some of the relevant passages. In the A edition Preface, Kant describes human reason as "burdened with questions which it cannot dismiss, since they are given to it as problems by the nature of reason itself" (Avii). In the B edition Preface, Kant states that metaphysics is "a wholly isolated speculative cognition of reason" (Bxiv). The problems of metaphysics are, in fact, the main motivation he gives for undertaking a critique of *pure* reason at all. The Transcendental Dialectic of the *KrV* describes these problems in detail, and it begins by describing how they arise from reason itself (see A310/B366–A340/B398). There, Kant describes how, in contrast to the faculty of understanding, "reason in its attempts to make out something about objects a priori [...] is wholly and entirely dialectical" (A131–32/B170–71). "Dialectical" is a term of condemnation for Kant that is closely connected with illusion (see A61/B85, A131/B170, A293/B349). In fact, the title for the second section of the Dialectic is "On pure reason as the seat of transcendental illusion" (A298/B355). When, near the end of the Dialectic, he comes to the metaphysical proof he most strongly condemns, Kant states: "In this cosmological argument so many sophistical principles come together that speculative reason seems to have summoned up all its dialectical art so as to produce the greatest possible transcendental illusion" (A606/B634). Kant attributes this argument to reason, but he clearly does not think we should accept it or act on it. Such attributions can be plausibly read as involving a notion

[20] I am assuming that it is unlikely that the notion of reason is both positively and negatively normative (as opposed to reason becoming so when other factors are added). For similar points, see Ameriks (2012, p. 196), Chignell (2014, p. 267). Grier (2001, chapters 4 and 8) is in a similar spirit.

of reason that is not positively normative, and so (given that it is unlikely the notion is negatively normative) not normative at all.

To be sure, there are some passages in the Dialectic that do suggest a positive, normative understanding of reason (e.g., since reason is the "highest court of appeals for all rights and claims of our speculation[, it] cannot possibly contain original deceptions and semblances" (A669/B697)), and Kant gives a positive, regulatory role to the ideas of reason. Yet Kant's writing outside *KrV* contains further negative statements, often with reminders of the Dialectic. At the beginning of *KpV*, in fact, Kant reminds us that speculative reason (the topic of *KrV*), "presumptuously oversteps itself" (*KpV*, 5:3), right before discussing the nature of that same faculty (reason) in its practical capacity. There are grounds, then, for thinking that when Kant talks of reason, his notion is not normative, though it undoubtedly plays a role in certain normative contexts.

3.2 The Will as Non-Normative

Non-Normative Freedom also claims that Kant's notion of the will is non-normative. Kant definitionally ties the will to reason,[21] so we should expect the normative status of the two notions to be similar.

In the *GMS*, Kant claims that "the will is nothing other than practical reason" (*GMS*, 4:412). One might suspect that "practical" here is a normative term, but Kant spells it out primarily in causal terms. At the beginning of *GMS* 3, he defines "will" as "a kind of causality of living beings insofar as they are rational (*vernünftig*)" (*GMS*, 4:446).[22] In *KpV*, Kant seems to maintain this view. In light of Kant's way of characterizing reason in general, it is not surprising to see him also describe the will there as "the ability [of rational beings] to determine their causality by the representations of rules" (*KpV*, 5:32).[23] Some of Kant's other descriptions of the will do not directly refer to reason, but, in a similar vein to the above passages, talk of causation and representations. The first description in the *KpV*, for instance, states that "the will [...] is a faculty either of producing objects corresponding to representations or of determining itself to effect such objects (whether the physical power is sufficient or not), that is, of determining its causality" (*KpV*, 5:15). Similarly, in *KU*, Kant says that "[t]he faculty of desire, insofar as it is determinable only through concepts, i.e., to act in accordance with the representation of an end, would be the will" (*KU*, 5:220).

In Kant's definitions of "will," then, the ingredient notion that most obviously calls out for a normative understanding is that of reason. The other notions seem to

[21] The *GMS* and the *KpV* do not (explicitly) make the distinction between *Wille* and *Willkür* that is found in Kant's later works (e.g., *MS*, 6:226). The definitional connection between *Wille* and reason is stronger than that between *Willkür* and reason. The crucial *KpV*, 5:20 passage concerns *Willkür*, however, and that is my focus here.

[22] In *KrV* Kant identifies reason's *producing* actions with "reason in a practical respect" (A550/B578). Similarly, in *KpV*: "pure reason can be practical – that is, can of itself, independently of anything empirical, determine the will" (*KpV*, 5:42).

[23] Similarly: "the understanding [...] has [...] a relation to the faculty of desire, which is therefore called the will and is called the pure will insofar as the pure understanding (which in this case is called reason) is practical through the mere representation of a law" (*KpV*, 5:55).

concern causation and representation, and so do not seem to involve normativity. Yet if reason can be understood as non-normative, then the same would be true of the will.

3.3 Freedom as Non-Normative

The final notion to consider for Non-Normative Freedom is that of freedom. Kant has more than one notion of freedom, but as with his notion of will, it is plausible that whether these notions are normative hinges on whether his notion of reason is.

Some of Kant's descriptions of freedom are negative, focusing on how we are not determined by external causes. Following the definition of the will as causality in rational beings in *GMS* 3, he describes freedom as "that property of such causality that it can be efficient independent of alien causes determining it" (*GMS*, 4:446). Similarly, in *KpV*, he says that "freedom in the strictest, that is, in the transcendental sense" is being "independent of the natural law of appearances in their relations to one another" (*KpV*, 5:29), and that "the concept of a being that has free will is the concept of a *causa noumenon*" (*KpV*, 5:55). Beyond whatever may be included in the concept of a will, nothing obviously normative is involved in such definitions, which is presumably why Kant ties *KpV*'s notion of freedom to that described in the Dialectic of *KrV* (see *KpV*, 5:15). In *KrV*, freedom "in the practical sense" is described as "the independence of the power of choice from necessitation by impulses of sensibility" (A534/B562), while freedom in the "cosmological sense" is just "the faculty of beginning a state from itself" (A533/B561).

Kant's positive descriptions of freedom concern autonomy. While "autonomy" is sometimes used today as a normative notion, Kant's initial explanation of it in *GMS* does not invoke anything obviously normative. In *GMS*, he says that "freedom, although it is not a property of the will in accordance with natural laws...must instead be a causality in accordance with immutable laws but of a special kind [...] what, then, can freedom of the will be other than autonomy, that is, the will's property of being a law to itself?" (*GMS*, 4:446–47). The talk of "being a law" is the most obscure part of this passage, but the earlier clauses make room for understanding it as causality in accordance with a certain type of law, one based in reason. The same is true for Kant's introduction of the notion of autonomy in *KpV*, where autonomy is described as "this lawgiving of its own on the part of pure, and as such, practical reason" (*KpV*, 5:33). The notion of lawgiving can be understood normatively, but Kant's comparison of the lawgiving of reason with the laws of nature at least allows us to understand it non-normatively, on analogy with God's giving physical laws to finite bodies. If so, then reason gives a law by generating a certain structure for our activity.

To be clear: I am not claiming that Kant's theory of the autonomous will becomes less mysterious overall if we see the relevant notions as non-normative. Normativity itself is (arguably) mysterious, and taking some of Kant's notions as intrinsically normative would give us a familiar *categorization* for the mysteriousness of passages like the above. However, making a mystery more familiar is not a decisive advantage for an interpretation. As I discuss in section 4, Non-Normative Freedom offers some significant interpretative payoffs, especially if accepted along with Analytic Equivalence.

4. Indirect Interpretative Motivation for Accepting Non-Normative Freedom and Analytic Equivalence

The conjunction of Analytic Equivalence and Non-Normative Freedom calls for further defense. In this section, I describe the payoff for accepting that conjunction. In the next, I begin considering objections to doing so.

The main payoff of my conjunctive proposal is straightforward: it offers us an especially clear, systematically cohesive picture of Kant's philosophy. On my proposal, there is no conceptual gap in Kant's philosophy between the non-normative and the normative. Kant introduces reason in *KrV* along with the basic concepts of laws and the will, and appears to give them non-normative characterizations. My proposal takes the central normative notion of his practical philosophy to be defined in terms of these (though that does not imply that everything in Kant's practical philosophy is analytic). To the best of my knowledge, no other interpretative approach yields a comparably straightforward way of putting together the differences pieces of Kant's views on reason and morality.

If my proposal is correct, then "ought" claims describe a motivational tension in the human will. This tension can be seen as the practical parallel of what happens in the theoretical case. In a passage partly quoted above, Kant describes the theoretical tension in quite metaphysical terms:

> error is effected only through the unnoticed influence of sensibility on understanding, through which it happens that the subjective grounds of the judgment join with the objective ones, and make the latter deviate from their destination just as a moved body would of itself always stay in a straight line in the same direction, but starts off on a curved line if at the same time another force influences it in another direction. In order to distinguish the proper action of the understanding from the force that meddles in, it will thus be necessary to regard the erroneous judgment of the understanding as a diagonal between two forces that determine the judgment in two different directions, enclosing an angle, so to speak, and to resolve the composite effect into the simple effects of the understanding and of sensibility. (A294–95/B350–51)

Reason would be a force that determines the will towards certain actions, while, for beings like us, sensible inclinations influence the will in a different way. Taking "ought" judgments to describe this ties Kant's philosophy together in a straightforward way.[24] This extends to his notion of autonomy (which is central to his moral philosophy), since the actions of reason, like those of understanding, would be *our*

[24] Cf. Kant's discussion of the feeling of humiliation in *KpV*, 5:78–79. For a helpful discussion of Kant's views on reason as a causal power that fits with my proposal, see Wuerth (2010). For some relevant concerns about understanding Kant's view of the will on analogy with conflicting forces, see Baron (1999, pp. 219–20), Reath (2006, pp. 12–13), and Korsgaard (2008, pp. 100–101). I do not directly address these concerns here, though I hope that what I say below provides some resources for answering them.

own actions, not those of outside influences (see *KrV* B153–58, *GMS*, 4:457). This can be seen as a metaphysical fact, however, not a normative one.[25]

5. Interpretative Objections and Replies

This section addresses three potential objections concerning the relation between my interpretation and Kant's other views. The next section considers the worry that, by denying the is-ought gap, my interpretation uncharitably attributes an implausible view to Kant.

5.1 Analyticity and Obviousness

The first potential objection is as follows: Kant takes some time to spell out the relation between reason, the free will, and the moral "ought." But if this relation were analytic, then he would have thought it was obvious, and so would not have spent so much time describing it.

In reply: Kant does not think that analytic relations are always obvious. He holds that the analysis of philosophical concepts is much more difficult than the analysis of mathematical concepts: "in philosophy [in contrast to mathematics] the definition [...] must conclude rather than begin the work" (A730–31/B758–59). The reason for this is that mathematical concepts are constructed. Since we have deliberately created these concepts, analyzing them is a straightforward matter. Concepts like those involved in morality, however, were not constructed, and this makes their analysis much more difficult. Hence, he reminds us early in *KpV* that the "complete analysis of the concept...is often achieved very late" (5:10n.).

In addition, Kant thought that otherwise insightful philosophers (such as Hume and Leibniz) had mis-classified judgments as analytic vs. synthetic. Kant spends some time arguing that properly mathematical judgments like "7 + 5 = 12" are synthetic (B15–16, *Prol*, 4:268–69). Further, at least part of his diagnosis of the errors of rational psychology is that merely analytic facts about the "I think" are mistaken for synthetic judgments (B409).[26]

Kant therefore does not think all analytic relations were obvious. Not only is philosophical analysis itself difficult, but people sometimes fail to recognize which judgments are analytic. Under such circumstances, it would make sense to spend some time spelling out important analytic relations.

[25] For an interpretation of Kant's view of the self that supports this, see Marshall (2010).

[26] Another significant example is the Metaphysical Deduction of the Categories. Kant thinks that (e.g.) the concept of causation is derived from the hypothetical form of judgment. Whether or not he takes this to be analytic is not clear, but Kant seems to regard it as being as certain as any analytic truth. Nonetheless, despite his brief discussion, he must have thought that the relation between forms of judgment and categories had been entirely missed by all previous philosophers.

5.2 The Gap Kant Draws

The second potential objection runs as follows: against the present interpretative proposal, Kant himself draws a strong is-ought gap on multiple occasions. After all, Kant begins the *Groundwork* by endorsing the classical division of ethics from physics and logic (*GMS*, 4:387).

This worry may be the main reason why the interpretation I have described has not been seriously considered. However, while Kant does insist on two sorts of gap concerning morality, the gaps he describes are the gaps between (a) empirical facts and moral facts and between (b) theoretical and practical reason. Both such gaps are consistent with my proposal.

When describing the distinctiveness of morality, Kant's main insistence is that morality cannot be derived from facts about the empirical world. Here is a representative passage:

> In practical philosophy [...] we have to do not with assuming grounds for what happens but rather with laws for what ought to happen even if it never does [...] Here [...] it is a question of objective practical laws [...] for then everything that has reference to the empirical falls away of itself, since if reason entirely by itself determines conduct...it must necessarily do so a priori.
>
> (*GMS*, 4:427; see also A318–19/B375, A547/B575, A802/B830)

Kant does hold that we cannot figure out what ought to happen on the basis of what happens, but *what happens* (a temporal notion) concerns the empirical world. As noted in section 3.1, Kant does not think reason is an empirical faculty. Here, his main point is that empirical facts cannot settle the question of whether reason can determine conduct. This description, connected with the "ought" earlier in the passage, is just what we should expect if my proposal is correct.

While the main gap Kant insists on is the gap from the empirical, he also posits a gap between theoretical and practical reason. This gap seems to be less deep. In the final section of *GMS*, Kant seems to argue that the spontaneity of theoretical reason in ideas provides grounds for accepting the reality of practical reason (*GMS*, 4:452).[27] Nonetheless, Kant treats theoretical and practical reason at least somewhat separately—hence the division between the first two *Critiques* (see *KpV*, 5:3). Hence, when Kant discusses the distinctive status of practical reason and the moral law, he emphasizes that their reality can be proved neither through experience nor through any exercise of theoretical reason:

> whatever needs to draw the evidence for its reality from experience must be dependent for the grounds of its possibility upon principles of experience, whereas pure but practical reason, by its very concept, cannot possibly be held to be dependent in this way. Moreover the moral law is given [...] as a fact of pure reason [...]

[27] It is unclear whether Kant continues to hold this in the *KpV*. For an influential discussion, see Ameriks (1981). For a nice discussion of the theoretical/practical contrast in Kant, see Schafer (forthcoming).

> though it be granted that no example of exact observance of it can be found in experience. Hence the objective reality of the moral law cannot be proved by any deduction, by any efforts of theoretical reason, speculative or empirically supported. (*KpV*, 5:47, cf. A84–85/B116–17)

Kant seems to treat practical reason and the moral law similarly here. If, as I suggested above, practical reason is a matter of reason's being able to determine the will, then all Kant is saying is that neither experience nor any other exercise of theoretical reason can establish the fact that reason can determine the will. That is consistent with my proposal.

5.3 The Limits of Cognition

I have claimed that "ought" facts analytically imply certain facts about reason, which is noumenal. However, one might object that this violates Kant's strictures on the bounds of cognition. Though Kant thinks we must *assume* or *postulate* noumenal freedom, my proposal, when combined with the plausible assumption that we know some "ought" facts, may seem to imply that we have more noumenal knowledge than Kant would allow.[28]

A full reply to this worry would require spelling out Kant's general theory of cognition. I do not attempt such a full reply here. I instead just note that there are passages where Kant seems to make strong epistemological claims about supersensible freedom, such as:

> there is now disclosed a very satisfying confirmation of the speculative *Critique*'s consistent way of thinking [...] now practical reason of itself, without any collusion with speculative reason, furnishes reality to a supersensible object of the category of causality, namely to freedom (although, as a practical concept, only for practical use), and hence establishes by means of a fact what could there [in the first *Critique*] could only be thought. (*KpV*, 5:6)

Here, Kant claims that the fact established by practical reason is the same fact that was thought in the *KrV*, which is almost certainly meant to be about the thought of freedom Kant describes in the resolution to the Third Antinomy (A532–58/B560–86). The latter is non-normative and, as it is described in the resolution, is clearly supersensible. On the natural reading of the above passage, Kant seems to be saying that the practical lets us *establish* something about supersensible freedom. This is what we should expect if my proposal were correct. To be sure, there is a further question of how to make these sorts of affirmations consistent with (e.g.) his claim that if we remove the categories (including causation) from "conditions of sensibility [...] all

[28] For a worry along these lines, see Skorupski (2010, p. 487).

significance, i.e., relation to the object, disappears" (A241/B300).[29] But all interpretations face that question.

6. The Big Philosophical Objection, and a Tentative Reply

This section turns to the most important potential objection to my proposal, namely, that some form of the is-ought gap must be endorsed by any good metaethicist, so that denying that Kant accepts it is unacceptably uncharitable.

The best way to respond to this objection would be to directly cast doubt on the existence of an is-ought gap. Instead of attempting that, I respond by making a methodological point and then arguing that, on my reading, Kant can accommodate most of the intuitions behind the two most famous statements of the is-ought gap.

The methodological point is this: as Hume presents it, the is-ought gap has been overlooked in "every system of morality" which he has "hitherto met with" (*Treatise* 3.1.1.27). Perhaps Hume is being hyperbolic, but he seems to be taking himself to be offering a novel insight. As far as we know, Kant had limited access to Hume's *Treatise*, and never carefully studied Book 3. So even if Hume is right about the philosophical issues, his insight might well be one that Kant simply never considered. This weakens the appeal to charity, just as facts about the development of logic in the nineteenth century should perhaps limit our appeals to charity in interpreting Kant's logic.

That said, even if Kant does make a mistake concerning the is-ought gap, that mistake is hard to pin down. To see this, I consider the two best-known statements of the is-ought gap: Hume's and G. E. Moore's. Despite an obvious similarity, Hume and Moore's approaches and concerns are different. Without attempting a comparison of their views, I argue that my proposed reading of Kant contains the resources to accommodate many of the intuitions Hume and Moore draw on. If so, then my proposal does not obviously put Kant in a philosophically bad position.

6.1 Hume and Kant on "Is" and "Ought"

Hume's well-known discussion occurs as a paragraph near the beginning of Book 3 of his *Treatise*. It runs as follows:

> In every system of morality, which I have hitherto met with [...] the author proceeds for some time in the ordinary way of reasoning, and establishes the being of a God, or makes observations concerning human affairs; when of a sudden I am surpriz'd to find, that instead of the usual copulations of propositions, *is*, and *is not*, I meet with no proposition that is not connected with an *ought*, or an *ought not*. This change is imperceptible; but is, however, of the last consequence. For as this *ought*, or *ought not*, expresses some new relation or affirmation, 'tis necessary that it shou'd

[29] For some thoughts about how to make sense of the Phenomena and Noumena chapter (from which this latter claim is drawn), see my Marshall (2010, pp. 5–6), which follows the general line described in Findlay (1981) and Adams (1997). See Schafer (in this volume; forthcoming) for helpful discussions.

> be observ'd and explain'd; and at the same time that a reason should be given, for what seems altogether inconceivable, how this new relation can be a deduction from others, which are entirely different from it [...] [I] am perswaded, that this small attention wou'd subvert all the vulgar systems of morality, and let us see, that the distinction of vice and virtue is not founded merely on the relations of objects, nor is perceiv'd by reason. (*Treatise* 3.1.1.27)

It is not obvious how strong a claim Hume is making here.[30] Even so, we can see that nearly everything Hume says here is consistent with Kant, as I read him. The initial characterization Hume gives of his target is an inference from "the being of a God" or "observations concerning human affairs" to an "ought." Kant could agree that those particular inferences were "of the last consequence," and mistaken. Kant denies that we can reach moral conclusions from theological premises, since he thinks that moral cognition is epistemically prior to cognition of God (see *GMS*, 4:408–409). As we saw in section 5.2, Kant also accepts that there is a gap between any empirical facts (such as human affairs) and "ought" facts. It is significant that Hume does not include an "et cetera" in the above passage. Taken at face value, Hume seems to be saying that the "change" that requires explanation occurs only in views that derive "oughts" from one of these two particular sources.

In addition, Hume does not state that "oughts" can never be inferred from cases of "is." Rather, he states that this change is surprising, "of the last consequence," "shou'd be observ'd and explain'd," and that "a reason should be given." To be sure, he also says that this deduction "seems altogether inconceivable." Now, if Hume is only considering the theories he describes, then Kant could agree that such inferences seem inconceivable. But even if Hume's concern is broader, then Kant can still agree that this deduction must be explained. Kant's explanation, on my reading, would appeal to a non-obvious analytic equivalence. So Kant could agree that any shift from "is" to "ought" is surprising and requires explanation, though he could go on to add that, for some shifts, there is such an explanation to be had.

At the end of the paragraph, Hume states that "the distinction of vice and virtue is not founded merely on the relations of objects." If "object" here is in contrast to "subject," then Kant could agree that "oughts" are not founded on relations of objects, since what "ought" facts describe is a feature of the subject's will. But even if we count the subject's will as an object, Kant could agree that "objects" are not *founded* on any facts about the will, so long as "founded" is taken in an epistemological sense, since our awareness of the moral law (as such) is epistemologically prior to our awareness of our own freedom (as such) (see *KpV*, 5:5n., 5:31; and section 2 above).

This leave the last clause, where Hume states that "the distinction of vice and virtue is not [...] perceiv'd by reason." There may be a genuine disagreement here, but it takes some work to pin it down, for Hume and Kant have different notions of reason. Hume defines reason in this section of the *Treatise* as "the discovery of truth or falshood" (*Treatise* 3.1.1.9). If my argument in section 3.1 is correct, however, then this is a different sense of "reason" than Kant's. The capacity for representations with

[30] For one modest reading, see Pigden (2010), whose discussion partly aligns with mine in this section.

universal quantitative contents may or may not be a capacity for discovering truth and falsity. So while reason, in Kant's sense, does have an essential role in "discovering" moral distinctions,[31] that alone does not show that Kant disagrees with Hume's statement.

Nonetheless, on my reading, Kant does hold that the discovery of at least some moral facts would also be the discovery of certain truths about reason and the will, though the latter might be only confusedly grasped. In Hume's sense of "reason," this would perhaps be a matter of moral truths being perceived by reason. Still, this is a very different sort of discovery than one concerning God or human affairs, which fits with Hume's main emphasis in the passage. In locating the basis for our perceptions of moral distinctions in the subject (and not anything in the world of experience), it has some significant points of similarity to Hume's view.[32] So while Hume and Kant probably do differ here, my reading of Kant allows him to agree with much of Hume's best-known description of the is-ought gap.

6.2 Moore and Kant on the Good

Hume did not have Kant's view in mind when he wrote the *Treatise*. G. E. Moore, however, did have Kant in mind when he made his Open Question Argument. The Open Question Argument is meant to support an is-ought gap of some sort, one that is stronger than Hume's in at least one respect (insofar as it is supposed to conflict with naturalism) and perhaps weaker than Hume's in another (insofar as it is more amenable to cognitivism than Hume's). As with Hume, my aim here is not to settle any of major interpretative questions about Moore's argument, but only to show that my interpretation leaves Kant in a position to agree with many of the intuitions Moore invokes.

Before looking at Moore's main argument, I want to highlight a passage from his discussion of Kant in chapter 4 of the *Principia*. There, Moore offers several (not obviously consistent) characterizations of Kant's metaethical view, some of which resemble the interpretation I have proposed:

> The fallacy of supposing moral to be analogous to natural law [...] is contained in one of the most famous doctrines of Kant. Kant identifies what ought to be with the law according to which a Free or Pure Will *must* act. [...] And by this identification he [...] means that what [the Free Will] ought to do *means* nothing but its own law – the law according to which it must act. [...] If that 'This ought to be done' means 'This is willed by a Free Will,' then, if it can be shewn that there is no Free Will which wills anything, it will follow that nothing ought to be done. (*Principia*, §75)

[31] Strictly speaking, for Kant, as I read him, reason itself (in Kant's sense) does not *discover* moral distinctions. Rather, moral distinctions are *about* reason, namely, about what the agent would do if reason determined her will. For Kant, the discovery of these latter facts is probably not achieved by reason alone. It also requires the distinct capacity of reflection; see Marshall (2014).

[32] Hence Hume's claim that the fact of vice "lies in yourself not in the object" (*Treatise* 3.1.1.26).

Moore takes Kant to be making a semantic claim about "ought," as I do. The objectionable implication Moore mentions at the end here is presumably one Kant would accept: if it could be demonstrated that there was no free will (or, more strongly, that free will was not possible), then it would indeed follow for Kant that nothing ought to be done.[33] The important point for my purposes, though, is that Moore's reading of Kant is similar to my own. Given that, testing my reading against his Open Question Argument provides a useful test of whether my reading is uncharitable.

The main lines of the Argument are laid out in chapter 1 of the *Principia* (see esp. §§11 and 13). Moore's presentation is confusing in several respects, and my purposes only require that Kant's view stand up to the most common understanding of the argument. In sum, the argument is typically understood as follows. If someone could ask, without any sign of conceptual confusion, whether some moral property M is instantiated by something with non-moral property N, then M ≠ N. Applied to my interpretation, the objection would run as follows: We can ask, with significance, if we ought to do what reason alone would determine our wills to do. Therefore, "ought" does not mean "what reason alone would determine our wills to do."

A common response to Moore in contemporary philosophy is to say that the identity of M and N is a synthetic fact, not an analytic one. That response is not available to Kant, as I read him. Even so, Kant could respond to this objection on two levels. He could (i) allow that there is a certain first-order openness about moral questions, such that knowing Analytic Equivalence does not itself tell us which actions we ought to perform, and (ii) allow for a certain higher-order openness, such that being improperly reflective can keep us from fully understanding moral terms.

On (i): By itself, Analytic Equivalence states only that "ought" facts are facts about what reason would do if it alone determined the will. By itself, this gives us no knowledge about which particular actions we ought to perform. To know what we ought to do, we have to know how reason *would* in fact determine the will, and neither analysis nor empirical facts tell us that. That further knowledge requires applying the universalizability test, which is not a matter of mere analysis. The same holds for knowing which things are morally good and evil, since Kant defines these in terms of objects of the faculty of desire "in accordance with a principle of reason" (*KpV*, 5:58). So there is a strong sense in which, on my proposal, the questions of what we ought to do are "open": knowing the analysis of "ought" (or of similar notions like "good") does not give us first-order guidance on what to do. By way of contrast: if the correct analysis of "good" were "pleasurable," then we would have much concrete guidance on what to do, since there are straightforward empirical facts about pleasure. But the analysis of "ought" I am attributing to Kant is too open-ended by itself to help with moral decisions, even if complemented by empirical facts.

On (ii): Kant thinks that his ethical views are somehow contained in "the common idea of duty and of moral laws" (*GMS*, 4:389, see also *KpV*, 5:8n.). Nonetheless, he

[33] "the *ought*, if one has the course of nature before one's eyes, has no significance [*Bedeutung*] whatsoever" (A547/B575). Kant, of course, does not think such a demonstration is possible (see Bxxix ff.).

knows that other philosophers take moral terms to refer to other things, such as education, physical feelings, moral feelings, or the will of God (see *GMS*, 4:441–43, *KpV*, 5:39ff.). Despite morality being a priori and even contained in "common rational moral cognition," Kant holds that philosophers can still get morality wrong. Any interpretation must allow for this. If analytic facts were always obvious, then my interpretation might face a special problem here, but as we have seen, Kant does not think this (perhaps in contrast to Moore: see *Principia* §6). In fact, we need some story along these lines in the theoretical case. Kant thinks it is analytic that the concept of causation involves (genuinely) necessary connection (see, e.g., *Prolegomena* 4:257), yet he knows that Hume attempts to derive the concept from subjective association and habit (B5). Kant must hold that, at some point, it seemed like an open question to Hume whether the causation involved genuine necessity, despite this being analytically true. Since Kant is already committed to having that kind of explanation in the case of causation, he could well hold that a similar explanation holds in the moral case.

What might that explanation look like? Here is one possibility. Kant thinks that empiricists like Locke misunderstand the nature of our higher faculties, such as reason (see A271/B327). Now, if part of the *meaning* of "ought" is "reason," then if one does not have a clear conception of reason, one's grasp of the meaning of "ought" will be problematic, such that it might seem like an open question as to how one should use the term. As an analogy: a creature who lacks a clear concept of politeness might think that there is an open question as to how one should use the term "gaffe." It might seem to him or her that, for any particular social interaction, it is an open question whether that could count as a gaffe. This felt openness comes from being semantically ungrounded. Failing to properly understand the faculty of reason, for Kant, would be a serious impediment to philosophical understanding, not least since reason is the core of our proper self (*GMS*, 4:457). Since Kant thinks it is possible for philosophers to misunderstand our faculty of reason, we should expect him to allow for similar openness in the use of any terms whose corresponding concepts analytically involve the notion of reason.

7. Conclusion

My aim in this chapter has been to show that there is significant textual support for thinking that Kant derives an "ought" from an "is," and that this interpretation is not obviously uncharitable. If my argument is successful, then the next question is how it compares to other defensible interpretations. I have not attempted such a comparison here, but I hope to have shown that what might otherwise have seemed like an absurd interpretative approach to Kant's metaethics deserves consideration.[34]

[34] Thanks to Paul Franco, Patrick Frierson, Mike Raven, Marília Espírito Santo, Cass Weller, the members of the 2014 Miami Kant Workshop (especially Timothy Rosenkoetter), and the audience at the University of Victoria. Special thanks to Karl Schafer and Nick Stang for their extensive comments on the final draft.

References

Adams, R. M. (1997). Things in themselves. *Philosophy and Phenomenological Research*, *57*(4): 801–25.

Allison, H. (1990). *Kant's theory of freedom*. Cambridge University Press.

Allison, H. (2011). *Kant's* Groundwork for the metaphysics of morals*: A commentary*. Oxford University Press.

Allison, H. (2012). *Essays on Kant*. Oxford University Press.

Ameriks, K. (1981). Kant's deduction of freedom and morality. *Journal of the History of Philosophy*, *19*(1): 53–79.

Ameriks, K. (2012). *Kant's elliptical path*. Oxford University Press.

Anderson, R. L. (2001). Synthesis, cognitive normativity, and the meaning of Kant's question, "How are synthetic cognitions possible a priori?" *European Journal of Philosophy*, *9*(3): 275–305.

Baron, M. (1999). Sympathy and coldness in Kant's ethics. In *Kantian ethics almost without apology* (pp. 194–226). Cornell University Press.

Chignell, A. (2014). Ogilby, Milton, canary wine, and the red scorpion: Another look at the Deduction of Taste. In D. Emundts (Ed.), *Self, world, and art: Metaphysical topics in Kant and Hegel* (pp. 261–82). De Gruyter.

Findlay, J. N. (1981). *Kant and the transcendental object*. Oxford University Press.

Fine, K. (2012). Guide to ground. In F. Correia & B. Schnieder (Eds.), *Metaphysical grounding* (pp. 37–80). Cambridge University Press.

Ginsborg, H. (2008). Was Kant a nonconceptualist? *Philosophical Studies*, *137*(1): 65–77.

Grier, M. (2001). *Kant's doctrine of transcendental illusion*. Cambridge University Press.

Irwin, T. (2009). *The development of ethics*, vol. 3: *From Kant to Rawls*. Oxford University Press.

Johnson, M. R. (2005). *Aristotle on teleology*. Oxford University Press.

Korsgaard, C. (1996). *Creating the kingdom of ends*. Cambridge University Press.

Korsgaard, C. (2008). Self-constitution in the ethics of Plato and Kant. In *The Constitution of Agency* (pp. 100–26). Oxford University Press

Korsgaard, C. (2009). *Self-constitution*. Oxford University Press

Marshall, C. (2010). Kant's metaphysics of the self. *Philosophers' Imprint*, *10*(8): 1–21. http://hdl.handle.net/2027/spo.3521354.0010.008

Marshall, C. (2014). Did Kant demand explanations for all synthetic a priori claims? *Journal of the History of Philosophy*, *52*(3): 549–76.

Mensch, J. (2013). *Kant's organicism: Epigenesis and the development of critical philosophy*. University of Chicago Press.

Merritt, M. (2009). Reflection, enlightenment, and the significance of spontaneity in Kant. *British Journal for the History of Philosophy*, *17*(5): 981–1010.

Moore, G. E. (1966). *Principia ethica*. Cambridge University Press (original work published 1903).

Pigden, C. (2010). Snare's puzzle/Hume's purpose: Non-cognitivism and what Hume was really up to with no-ought-from-is. In C. Pigden (Ed.), *Hume on is and ought* (pp. 169–91). Palgrave Macmillan.

Raz, J. (2010). Reason, reasons and normativity. *Oxford Studies in Metaethics*, *5*: 5–24.

Reath, A. (2006). Kant's theory of moral sensibility. In *Agency and autonomy in Kant's moral theory* (pp. 8–32). Oxford University Press.

Schafer, K. (forthcoming). Practical cognition and knowledge of things-in-themselves. In E. Tiffany and D. Heide (Eds.), *Kantian freedom*. Oxford University Press.

Schönecker, D. (1999). *Kant: Grundlegung III. Die Deduktion des kategorischen imperativs*. Alber.

Schönecker, D. (2013). A free will and a will under moral laws are the same. In O. Sensen (Ed.), *Kant on moral autonomy* (pp. 225–45). Cambridge University Press.

Skorupski, J. (2010). *The domain of reasons*. Oxford University Press.

Tolley, C. (2006). Kant on the nature of logical laws. *Philosophical Topics, 34*(1–2): 371–407.

Wood, A. (2009). *Kantian ethics*. Cambridge University Press.

Wuerth, J. (2010). Sense and sensibility in Kant's practical agent. *European Journal of Philosophy, 21*(1): 1–36.

Index

Note: Tables are indicated by an italic "*t*", and notes are indicated by "n." following the page number.

For the benefit of digital users, indexed terms that span two pages (e.g., 52–53) may, on occasion, appear on only one of those pages.